Butterworths Education

Kenneth P Poole
Solicitor of the Supreme Court

John E Coleman
Solicitor of the Supreme Court

Peter M Liell
Solicitor of the Supreme Court

Butterworths
London, Edinburgh, Dublin
1997

United Kingdom	Butterworths, a Division of Reed Elsevier (UK) Ltd, Halsbury House, 35 Chancery Lane, LONDON WC2A 1EL and 4 Hill Street, EDINBURGH EH2 3JZ
Australia	Butterworths, SYDNEY, MELBOURNE, BRISBANE, ADELAIDE, PERTH, CANBERRA and HOBART
Canada	Butterworths Canada Ltd, TORONTO and VANCOUVER
Ireland	Butterworth (Ireland) Ltd, DUBLIN
Malaysia	Malayan Law Journal Sdn Bhd, KUALA LUMPUR
New Zealand	Butterworths of New Zealand Ltd, WELLINGTON and AUCKLAND
Singapore	Reed Elsevier (Singapore) Pte Ltd, SINGAPORE
South Africa	Butterworths Publishers (Pty) Ltd, DURBAN
USA	Michie, CHARLOTTESVILLE, Virginia

All rights reserved. No part of this publication may be reproduced in any material form (including photocopying or storing it in any medium by electronic means and whether or not transiently or incidentally to some other use of this publication) without the written permission of the copyright owner except in accordance with the provisions of the Copyright, Designs and Patents Act 1988 or under the terms of a licence issued by the Copyright Licensing Agency Ltd, 90 Tottenham Court Road, London, England W1P 9HE. Applications for the copyright owner's written permission to reproduce any part of this publication should be addressed to the publisher.

Warning: The doing of an unauthorised act in relation to a copyright work may result in both a civil claim for damages and criminal prosecution.

Any Crown copyright material is reproduced with the permission of the Controller of Her Majesty's Stationery Office.

© Reed Elsevier (UK) Ltd 1997

Reprinted 1997

A CIP Catalogue record for this book is available from the British Library.

ISBN 0 406 898952

Typeset by M Rules
Printed and bound in Great Britain by Redwood Books, Trowbridge, Wiltshire

PREFACE
and instructions for use

This book is for consulting, not reading. Nevertheless, please read the preface! Failure to do so may mislead or leave puzzles in the text unresolved. Equally, the second part (Interpretation) of Chapter 1 is a necessary aid to understanding.

Our aim has been to write a plain summary of the law, intended in the first place for the legal profession. We do not presume to offer guidance to those who carry out the functions we describe but we hope that they—teachers, LEAs, governing bodies and others—may also find our unvarnished account helpful. It scarcely needs saying that only by constant reference to statute law, as illuminated by the decisions of the courts, can choices safely be made, policies determined and discretions exercised. The present work cannot substitute for its encyclopaedic parent, *The Law of Education*, in three looseleaf volumes by the same authors and publisher, but may provide a springboard to it.

This publication marks the repeal of the Education Act 1944 and the whole of 17 subsequent Education Acts. Although the repeal of the 1944 Act was long overdue, it is difficult to stifle a nostalgic sigh at the demise of a statute which was a cornerstone of postwar reconstruction and the 'principal Act' for over half a century. In place of the repealed legislation come the consolidating Education Act 1996 and School Inspections Act 1996. These incorporate recommendations of the Law Commission which are not of substance but clarify the law. Despite 583 sections and 40 Schedules in the former of the two Acts and 48 and 8 in the latter, they do not make a clean sweep: all or part of 15 earlier Education Acts remain in force, mostly as amended, notably the Further and Higher Education Act 1992. The current Education Acts and those wholly repealed by the Education Act 1996 are listed at Appendix 1.

The School Inspections Act 1996 came into force on 1 November 1996, as did the Education Act 1996 except for sections 8, 317(6), 348, 528 and related amendments and repeals. Those come into force on days to be appointed by order of the Secretary of State, 1 January 1997 in the case of s 317(6). The Nursery Education and Grant-Maintained Schools Act 1996 was brought into force on 1 September 1996 and later dates up to 1 April 1997. It preceded the consolidation Acts on to the statute book on the same day (24 July) and was promptly amended by them. They have been followed by the Education Act 1997. The new Government has introduced the Education (Schools) Bill to bring to an end the assisted places scheme (with a

Preface

saving for pupils currently assisted) and have promised a raft of wide-ranging measures.

The 1997 Act received the Royal Assent on 21 March, and section 50, mentioned at paragraph 13.25, came into force. This provision apart, at the time of completion of the text it was not known when, or to what extent, the Act would be brought into force. It was, therefore, not integrated into the text, but is included, fully annotated, at Appendix 9. Subsequently, at the time of going to press, the following commencement orders have been made: the Education Act 1997 (Commencement No 1) Order 1997, SI 1997/1153 and the (Commencement No 2 and Transitional Provisions) Order 1997, SI 1997/1468. The main provisions in the Act relate to extension of disciplinary powers; school admissions; baseline assessments and pupils' performance; supervision of school curriculum and external qualifications; inspection of LEAs and school inspections; careers education and guidance; and also expansion of the assisted places scheme to cover primary schools (but it is intended that the scheme be abandoned, as mentioned above). Especially in relation to these topics, it is essential that the reader should consult Appendix 9 to complement all references to the text.

We have concluded that readers will best be served by our following, for the most part, the arrangement of the consolidation and other Acts. At appropriate places in the text and in appendices we have added other material closely allied to the Education Acts, for example on the School Sites Acts. Here and there we have managed to fold procedural provisions and parts of legislation headed (necessarily but unhelpfully) 'supplemental' or 'miscellaneous' into the narrative at appropriate points, or into the notes. The proportion of notes to text may in places seem high, but this results from a deliberate attempt to release the narrative from detail which would interrupt the flow of the exposition and so make it less coherent.

Chapters are divided into named parts, and parts into named sections. After Chapter 1, the introduction, Chapters 2 to 7 largely follow Parts I to VI of the main Act; Chapter 8 is on inspection and special measures; Chapter 9, on independent schools, expounds Part VII of the Act; Chapter 10 is on further and higher education; Chapters 11 and 12 return to the consolidation Act, Parts VIII and IX, and the former mentions the nursery education voucher scheme; Chapter 13 relates to teachers and other staff; Chapter 14 is entitled 'Wrongdoings' and is concerned with unlawful discrimination and the torts which have been committed in and around, or in connection with, educational institutions; and finally Chapter 15 contains Part X, 'Miscellaneous and General', together with some additional material. Such is the extent and importance today of recourse to judicial review that, in a part named 'Complaints and remedies', the book concludes with some introductory words and relevant cases.

Thus within its compass *Butterworths Education Law* aims to provide a complete and self-contained account of the law relating to education in England and Wales, but it cannot find room to reproduce statutory provisions in extenso, or, save exceptionally, for verbatim extracts from the decisions of the courts. Since some of the reports cited may not be in a series readily available to the reader, references are made, in the notes to the text, to Division F of the parent work

Preface

(Divisions B, C and D of which contain statutes and statutory instruments). Thus, for example, *Fitzgerald v Northcote* (1865) 4 F and F 656 is followed by the reference F[53], where a summary of the report on that case will be found.

Similarly Circulars sent to LEAs in England and Wales (or in England alone) by the Department for Education and Employment and its predecessors may not come to hand, so notes refer to Division E, where they are reproduced in full. For example Circular 19/94, 'Arrangements for Education Committees', is followed by the reference E[3077]. Little purpose would be served by specifying under which particular nomenclature (reflecting the Minister's title) the Department was operating at the time of issue. Welsh Office Circulars appear as 'WO' followed by number and year. Circulars issued before 1980, few of which remain current, are not reprinted in the parent work. The Department have also issued Administrative Memorandums (shown as 'AM' followed by number and year).

Reference to provisions in Acts and statutory instruments is to be taken, unless the context otherwise requires, as reference to those provisions as amended. This economy in presentation runs little risk, we believe, of misleading readers, most of whom will no doubt refer to *Halsbury's Statutes* or *Statutory Instruments* when occasion arises.

Schedule 39 to the Education Act 1996 contains transitional provisions and savings. In particular, where the context so requires, reference to provisions in repealed legislation is to be taken to apply to the equivalent superseding provisions in the 1996 Act (and vice versa). The derivation of 1996 Act provisions is at Appendix 2. The destination of repealed provisions can be traced by reference to the table at Appendix 3.

Those LEAs and others affected by the current bout of reorganisation in England are reminded to have regard to the provisions of Local Government Changes for England Regulations, namely the 1994 Regulations, SI 1994/867, the (Property Transfer and Transitional Payments) Regulations 1995, SI 1995/402, the (School Reorganisation and Admissions) Regulations 1995, SI 1995/2368, the (Local Management of Schools) Regulations 1995, SI 1995/3114 and the (Education) (Miscellaneous Provisions) Regulations 1996, SI 1996/710; also the Local Government Changes for England (Education) (Miscellaneous Provisions) Order 1997, SI 1997/679.

The reader is referred to D J Farrington, *The Law of Higher Education*, (Butterworths, 1994), to which Chapter 10 is complementary, and which deals with its subject matter more discursively than is possible in this compendium; and he may need to consult other, specialist, works when he seeks guidance on an educational problem which touches on the law relating, in particular, to child care, employment (notably in connection with dismissal of teachers), health and safety, and improper discrimination on grounds of race or sex. These topics gives rise to much of the litigation in the field of education but fall outside the Education Acts and comparatively little room can be found for treatment of them here.

We are indebted to Ivor Widdison, Administrator of the Council of Local Education Authorities, for his advice on the brief reference made in Chapter 13

Preface

to the non-statutory conditions of service of school teachers. Our thanks also go to Arabella Wood, of the Department for Education and Employment Public Enquiry Unit, for her patience and helpfulness in response to our requests, and above all to our equally patient and helpful publishers.

The book incorporates material available up to 1 April 1997, with a few later additions.

April 1997

KPP
JEC
PML

CONTENTS

Preface	v
Table of statutes	xiii
Table of statutory instruments	xxix
Table of cases	xxxvii

1 Introduction — 1
Historical background — 1
Interpretation — 3

2 Principles and administration — 9
The statutory system of education — 9
Functions of the Secretary of State — 13
Local education authorities — 13
The funding authorities — 18
Allocation of functions — 19
Provision of information — 19

3 Schools maintained by local education authorities — 21
Categories and definitions — 21
Establishment, alteration etc of schools — 22
Funding of voluntary schools — 29
Government of local education authority schools — 32
Financial delegation to governing bodies — 39
Conduct of schools — 43
Discontinuance of schools — 52

4 Grant-maintained schools — 54
Acquisition of grant-maintained status — 54
Property, staff and contracts — 58
New grant-maintained schools — 61
Government and conduct — 63
Funding — 67
Alteration etc — 70
Discontinuance — 73
Groups of schools — 78
General and miscellaneous — 80

5 Special educational needs — 84
Children with special educational needs — 84
Schools providing for special educational needs — 93

Contents

6 The Curriculum	**99**
Secular education	100
Religious education and worship	105
Miscellaneous and supplementary provisions	113
7 School admissions, attendance and charges	**117**
School admissions	117
School attendance	127
Charges	130
8 Inspection and special measures	**134**
School inspections	134
Schools requiring special measures	140
9 Independent schools	**145**
Registration	145
Assisted places at independent schools	149
City colleges	151
10 Further and higher education	**153**
Councils and sectors	153
Further education	154
Higher education	165
Local education authority functions	172
Freedom of speech	174
Students' unions	175
Fees, awards and loans	177
11 Grants and other financial matters	**180**
Grants	180
Payment of school fees and expenses	184
Recoupment	184
12 Ancillary functions	**186**
Ancillary functions of the Secretary of State	186
Ancillary functions of local education authorities and governing bodies	192
Provision of information by governing bodies and school proprietors	199
13 Teachers and other staff	**202**
Training	202
Qualifications, fitness, appraisal	205
Appointment and dismissal	207
Conditions of employment: general legislation	210
Conditions of employment: education provisions	217
14 Wrongdoings	**223**
Unlawful discrimination	223
Litter	226
Tort and breach of statutory duty	226
15 Conclusion	**232**
Educational premises	232

Punishment	235
Educational trusts	236
Religious educational trusts The School Sites Acts	238
Employment of children and young persons	239
Educational records	240
Certificates of birth and registrars' returns	240
Evidence	240
Audit Commission services	241
Complaints and remedies	241
Appendix 1 The Education Acts	245
Appendix 2 Derivation of the provisions of the Education Act 1996 and of the School Inspections Act 1996	247
Appendix 3 Destination table to the Education Act 1996 and the School Inspections Act 1996	297
Appendix 4 Reverter and the School Sites Acts	353
Appendix 5 The Education Assets Board	356
Appendix 6 Core governors for groups of grant-maintained schools	359
Appendix 7 Constitution and procedure of admission appeal committees	360
Appendix 8 Staffing of LEA schools (except aided schools) without delegated budgets	362
Appendix 9 Education Act 1997	365
Appendix 10 Glossary	439
Index	455

TABLE OF STATUTES

References in this Table to *Statutes* are to Halsbury's Statutes of England Fourth Edition, showing the volume and page at which the annotated text of the Act may be found.
References in the right-hand column are to paragraph numbers.

	PARA
Acquisition of Land Act 1981 (9 *Statutes* 366)	2.33; 4.16
Arbitration Act 1996	5.34
Pt I (ss 1–84)	9.11
Building Act 1984 (35 *Statutes* 619)	
s 4 (1)	15.06
(a) (iv)	7.25
Charities Act 1960 (5 *Statutes* 805)	10.23
s 2	15.19
Charities Act 1993 (5 *Statutes* 866)	3.37; 10.66, 10.70, 10.74
s 1	15.19
3	4.01
96	4.01
Sch 2	4.01
para (da)	6.14
Children Act 1972 (6 *Statutes* 201)	
s 1	15.30
Children Act 1989 (6 *Statutes* 387)	5.16, 5.29
s 3 (5)	14.18
18	12.38; 13.68
19 (1) (a)	12.60
27 (4)	5.15
28	5.17
29	12.38
36	7.51
(10)	2.15
63	9.06
(6)	5.49
87	9.09
Sch 2	
para 3	5.17
Sch 3	
Pt III	7.51
para 13	2.15
Children Act 1996	
s 317(6)	3.118
Children and Young Persons Act 1933 (6 *Statutes* 18)	15.32
s 18	15.30
20, 21	15.30
23–27	15.30
28	15.30
(1), (3)	15.31
29, 30	15.30
96, 97	15.30
Children and Young Persons Act 1963 (6 *Statutes* 89)	15.32
s 34–44	15.30
Children and Young Persons Act 1969 (6 *Statutes* 136)	15.32
Chronically Sick and Disabled Persons Act 1970 (15 *Statutes* 241)	
s 8	15.07
Church Schools (Assistance by Church Commissioners) Measure 1958 (14 *Statutes* 1092)	3.34
Compulsory Purchase Act 1965 (9 *Statutes* 214)	
s 11	4.16
Courts and Legal Services Act 1990 (11 *Statutes* 1211)	
s 71	5.33
Criminal Justice Act 1982 (27 *Statutes* 326)	
s 37 (1)	1.25
46	1.25
Criminal Justice Act 1991 (27 *Statutes* 363)	
s 17	1.25
Diocesan Boards of Education Measure 1991	
s 3	3.04, 3.126, 3.128
(4)	4.07
(5)	4.51

Table of statutes

Diocesan Boards of Education Measure
1991 – *contd*
- 5 .... 4.09
- 6(1) 6.36
  - (3) 4.100
- 7 .... 3.04, 3.19
  - (3) 3.31
- 9 .... 13.29
- 10 .... 4.51

Disability Discrimination Act 1995 ... 3.118; 5.07, 5.10; 10.14; 13.62; 14.02
- s 1 .... 13.56
- Pt II (ss 4–18) 13.56, 13.58
- s 4–8 .... 13.56
- Pt III (ss 19–28) 14.11
- s 24 (2) 3.118
- 29 (3) 13.06

Disabled Persons (Services, Consultation and Representation) Act 1986 (40 *Statutes* 348) 5.07
- s 5, 6 .... 5.17

Education Act 1902 .... 1.04; 12.03

Education Act 1918 (Fisher Act) (15 *Statutes* 119) 1.02; 15.19
- s 47 .... 15.19

Education Act 1944 (Butler Act) (15 *Statutes* 120) 1.06, 1.07, 1.08; 2.17, 2.24; 6.33
- s 1, 7 .... 6.01
- 8 .... 12.40
- 15 .... 3.04, 3.31
- 35 .... 2.11
- 68 .... 9.22; 12.05, 12.08
- 81 .... 12.42
- 86 .... 15.26, 15.28
- 100 .... 11.12
- Sch 3 .... 3.04

Education Act 1946 (15 *Statutes* 203)
- s 2 .... 3.04

Education Act 1962 (15 *Statutes* 226)
- s 1 .... 10.106
  - (6) 10.108
- 2 .... 10.108
- 3 .... 10.109
- 4 .... 10.106, 10.108, 10.109
- 9 .... 2.12
- Sch 1 .... 10.106

Education Act 1967 (15 *Statutes* 236)
- s 4 .... 13.03

Education Act 1973 (15 *Statutes* 247)
- s 1 .... 15.19
  - (1) 3.23
  - (4) 15.19
- 2 .... 15.26, 15.28
- 3 .... 10.106
- Sch 1 .... 15.19
- Sch 2 .... 15.19

Education Act 1980 (15 *Statutes* 264): 1.08; 15.24
- s 7 .... 7.20

Education Act 1980 – *contd*
- s 12 .... 1.19
- 15 .... 7.15
- 20 .... 10.111
- Sch 2 .... 7.20

Education Act 1981 (15 *Statutes* 300) .. 1.08; 5.01
- s 8 .... 5.23

Education Act 1986 (15 *Statutes* 333)
- s 1 .... 11.04
- 23 .... 3.109
- 43 .... 10.97
- 49 .... 13.17
- 50 .... 11.05
  - (3) 11.04
- 54 .... 3.04
- 61, 62 .... 10.90

Education (No 2) Act 1986 (15 *Statutes* 335) 1.08

Education Act 1993 (15 *Statutes* 800) .. 1.08; 2.39, 3.91; 4.18, 4.38, 4.41, 4.89; 5.02, 5.19, 5.31
- Pt II (ss 22–155) 4.01
- s 41 .... 4.19
- Pt III (ss 156–191) 5.01
- s 255 (1) 6.36
- 298 .... 1.36

Education Act 1994 (15 *Statutes* 1145) 1.08; 10.104
- Pt I (ss 1–19) 13.01
- s 1(1) 13.06
  - (2), (3) 13.10
  - (4) 13.06
- 2 .... 13.07
- 3 .... 13.08
  - (2) 13.08
- 4 .... 13.04
  - (3), (4) 13.04
- 5 .... 13.04, 13.12
- 6 .... 13.13
- 7 .... 13.14
- 8–11 .... 13.15
- 11A 13.02
- 12 .... 4.88; 13.04
  - (5) 3.10; 4.49
  - (6) 3.80; 4.38
  - (7) 3.80
- 13 .... 11.05
- 14 .... 13.09
- 15 .... 13.11
- 16 .... 13.09
- 17 .... 13.10
- 18 .... 10.61; 13.75
- 20 .... 10.98
- 21 .... 10.103
- 22 .... 10.102
  - (4) (c) 10.97
- 23 .... 13.15
- Sch 1 .... 13.07

Education Act 1996 ...... 1.09, 1.10, 1.31; 2.19, 2.33

Table of statues

	PARA
Education Act 1996 – *contd*	
Pt I Ch I (ss 1–9)	2.01
s 1	2.02
2	10.02
(1)	2.04
(2)	2.05
(3)	2.06
3	2.03
4	2.07
(2)	2.07
5	2.08
(4)	3.27
6(1)	2.08
(2)	2.09
7	2.10; 9.09
8(2)	2.11
(3), (4)	2.12
(5)	3.62
9	2.15
Pt I Ch II (ss 10, 11)	2.17
s 10	2.17; 6.01
11	2.18
Pt I Ch III (ss 12–19)	2.20
s 12	2.21
13	2.24
14 (1)	2.25
(2), (3)	2.27
(4)	2.25
(5)	2.25
(c)	12.36
(6)	2.30
(7)	2.30; 5.42
15	10.87
(5)	5.06
16	3.07
(1)	9.02
17	3.07
(2)	2.25
18	2.26; 12.40
19	2.31; 5.13
Pt I Ch IV (ss 20–26)	2.35
s 20, 21	2.35
22	2.35, 2.36
23	2.36
24	2.36; 12.05, 12.09
25	2.35
26	2.35
Pt I Ch V (s 27)	2.38
s 27	2.25, 2.39; 3.12; 7.61
(1) (b)	6.34; 7.42
Pt I Ch VI (ss 28–30)	2.38, 2.41
s 28	2.40; 12.04
29 (1)	2.42; 10.93
(2)–(6)	2.42
30	2.43
Pt II (ss 31–182)	3.01
Pt II Ch I (ss 31–34)	3.02
s 31	3.03, 3.04
32	3.04
33	3.03
34	3.05

	PARA
Education Act 1996 – *contd*	
Pt II Ch II (ss 35–58)	3.06
s 35	1.18; 2.32; 3.69; 12.11, 12.14
(1)	3.08
35 (b)	3.04
(c), (d)	12.11
(2)	3.08
(b)	3.69
(3)	3.08
(4)	3.08
(5)	3.08
(6)	3.09
(7), (8)	3.11
36	2.32
(1)–(6)	3.12
37	2.32; 3.14
(4)	12.11
(7), (8)	12.11
38	2.32; 3.16
39	2.32; 3.17; 15.06
40	2.32; 3.18
41	3.19, 3.69; 4.04
(2)	12.11
(a), (b)	3.60
42	3.19
43	3.19, 3.42, 3.59
(3)–(5)	12.11
44	3.19; 15.06
(3), (4)	3.19
45 (1), (2)	3.21
(3)–(6)	3.22
(7)	3.21, 3.22
46	3.23, 3.69
47	3.24, 3.69
48	3.04, 3.26, 3.31, 3.43
49	3.27
50	3.04, 3.28, 3.69
(3)	2.30
51	3.04, 3.28, 3.31, 3.69
52	3.29, 3.59, 3.69
53	3.29
54	3.04, 3.30, 3.31
55	3.30
56	3.30
57	3.31, 3.69
58	3.04, 3.31, 3.32, 3.43
(1)	3.69
Pt II Ch III (ss 59–75)	3.33
s 59 (1)–(4)	3.34
(5)	3.24, 3.36
60	3.21, 3.22, 3.30, 3.38
(4)–(7)	3.39
61 (1)	3.38
(4)–(6)	3.39
62	3.21, 3.22
(1)	3.38
(2), (3)	3.38, 3.40
(4)	3.40
63	3.30, 3.41, 3.128
64	3.30, 3.42, 3.128
65	3.21, 3.24, 3.43, 3.128

Table of statutes

Education Act 1996 – contd

Section	PARA
66	3.21, 3.24, 3.43
67	3.21, 3.24, 3.43
68	3.21, 3.24, 3.36, 3.44; 12.09
69	3.21, 3.24, 3.44
70	3.44
71	3.05
72	3.37
73	3.37, 3.100
74	3.35
75	2.34
Pt II Ch IV (ss 76–100)	3.45
s 76	3.47
77	3.47, 3.68
78	3.48
(5)	3.48
79	3.50, 3.67
(1), (2)	8.32
80	3.67
(1)–(6)	3.51
(7)–(9)	3.52
81	3.54, 3.67
82	3.56
(3)	3.61
83	3.57
84	3.59, 3.67
(2), (4)	3.59
85	3.59
(2)–(7)	3.59
86	3.60
(2)	3.61
87	3.61
(3)	3.61
88	3.47, 3.67, 3.70
89	3.67
(4)	3.67
90, 91	3.67
92	3.68
93	3.48, 3.68
94	3.69
95	3.69
96	3.70
97	3.71
98	3.72
99	3.70; 12.09
100	3.67
Pt II Ch V (ss 101–126)	3.73
s 101, 102	3.73
103	3.73, 3.74, 3.76
104	3.74
105	3.73
106	3.75
107	3.76
108	3.76
109	3.76
110	3.77
111	3.78
112	3.78
(4)	3.78
113	3.78
114	3.79

Education Act 1996 – contd

Section	PARA
115, 116	3.80
117	3.82
118	3.83
119	3.84
120	3.73, 3.76
(2)	3.77
121	3.85
122	3.86, 3.118
123	3.86
124	3.118
125	3.80, 3.87, 3.118
126	3.72, 3.73
Pt II Ch VI (ss 127–166)	3.88
s 127	3.89
128	3.90
129	3.89
130	3.91
131	3.93
132	3.94
133	13.27
134 (1), (2)	13.30
(3)	13.30, 13.43
(4)	13.30
(5), (6)	13.31
135	13.27
(8)	3.64
136	4.16; 13.18
137, 138	13.29
139	13.25
140	13.19
141	13.18
142	13.18
143	6.45; 13.33
144	6.47; 13.33
145	6.48; 13.34
146	13.69, 13.71
147	3.95; 4.05
148	3.95
149	3.97
150(1)–(3)	3.99
151	3.99
152	3.99
(1)–(3)	3.99
153	3.99, 3.101
154	3.105
155	3.107
156	3.108
157	3.109
158	3.110
159	3.117
(3), (4)	3.117
160	3.117
161(1), (2)	3.118
(3), (4)	3.119
162	3.120
163	3.120
164	3.122
165	3.123
166	3.72, 3.124; 13.18

Table of statues

	PARA
Education Act 1996 – *contd*	
Pt II Ch VII (ss 167–175)	3.125
s 167	3.69, 3.126; 4.04, 4.09; 12.11
168	3.126
169	3.126; 4.09
170	3.126
171	3.126
172	3.127
173	3.23, 3.43, 3.128; 4.04
174	3.129
175	3.130
(2) (b)	4.04
176	3.92
178	13.18
179	3.15, 3.23, 3.24, 3.126; 15.20
180	3.48; 15.24
181	3.124
Pt III (ss 183–311)	4.01, 4.84; 5.46
Pt III Ch I (s 183)	4.02
s 183	4.04
Pt III Ch II (ss 184–200)	4.02
s 184	4.04
185	4.05
186	4.07
187	4.07, 4.16
188	4.07
189	4.08
(4)	4.08
190	4.08
191	4.08
192	4.08
193	4.09
194	4.09
195	4.10
196	4.10
197	4.05
198	4.11
199	4.09, 4.11
Pt III Ch III (ss 201–210)	4.12
s 201	4.13
(1) (a)	4.14
(8), (10)	4.13
202	4.15
203	4.16
204	4.14, 4.16
(3)	4.16
(7)–(9)	4.16
205	4.16
(9)	4.16
206	4.16
207	4.16
208	4.16
209	4.15, 4.16
210	4.14, 4.58
(1)–(4)	4.14
Pt III Ch IV (ss 211–217)	4.17; 5.37
s 211	2.37; 4.18; 12.11
212	4.18
213	4.19
214	4.20
(5), (6)	4.21

	PARA
Education Act 1996 – *contd*	
215	4.21
216	4.23
Pt III Ch V (ss 218–243)	4.10, 4.24, 4.25; 4.31; 5.37
218	4.25
219	4.28
220	4.29
221	4.29
222	4.31
223	4.31
(5)	4.31
224	4.31
225	4.31
226	4.31
(2)	4.32
227	4.33
228	4.31
(2)	4.32
229	4.31
230	4.33
(2)	4.31
231	4.34
(5)(e)	13.32
(6)	4.45
232	4.35
233	4.36
234–242	4.31
Pt III Ch VI (ss 244–258)	4.02, 4.22, 4.37
s 244	4.38
(1), (3)	4.44
245	4.39
(1)	4.44
246	4.40
(1)	4.44
247	4.40, 4.41, 4.44
248	4.43, 4.44
(6)	4.23
249–254	4.37, 4.44
255	4.45
256	4.46
(6)	4.46
257	4.46
258	4.47
259	4.51
260	4.52
261	4.53
262	4.54; 5.41
263	4.55
264	4.51, 4.57
265	4.58
266	4.49
Pt III Ch VII (ss 267–279)	4.59; 8.38
s 267	4.61
268	4.63; 12.11
269	4.64
270	4.65
271	4.61, 4.67
272	4.68
273	4.69

Table of statutes

Education Act 1996 – *contd*
	PARA
s 274	4.71; 8.43
275	4.71; 8.43
276	4.72; 8.43
277	4.75; 8.43
278	4.76; 8.43
279	4.77; 8.43
Pt III Ch IX (ss 280–290)	4.78, 4.79, 4.84; 5.47, 5.48
s 280	4.79
281–285	4.80
286	4.81
287	4.81
288	4.34, 4.82
289	4.82
290	4.83
291	4.85
292	4.86
293	4.87
294	4.88
295	4.89
296	4.92, 4.99
(1)	4.23, 4.40
297	4.92, 4.93, 4.97, 4.99
(1)	4.93
(2)	4.94
(3)	4.95
(4)	4.96
298	4.92, 4.93, 4.97
299	4.92, 4.93, 4.98
300	4.92, 4.93
(1), (2)	4.99
301(1)	4.93, 4.97
(2)	4.92
(3)	4.93
302	4.100
(1)	4.25
(a)	4.09
(b)	4.35
303	4.101
304	13.69
305(2)	13.70
(3)	13.71
(4)	13.72
306	13.72
307	4.26
308	4.27
310	2.36; 4.102
311(2)	4.29
(4)	7.25
Pt IV (ss 312–349)	5.01, 5.04, 5.39; 12.40
Pt IV Ch I (ss 312–336)	5.03
s 312	5.06
313	5.07
314	5.07
315	5.07
316	5.09
317	5.10
(6)	3.118
318	5.12

Education Act 1996 – *contd*
	PARA
s 319	5.13
320	5.13
321	5.14
322	5.15
323	5.16
(3)(b)	5.16
324	5.17
325	5.21
326	5.23
327	5.24
328	5.25
329	5.16, 5.27
330	5.28
331	5.29
332	5.30
333	5.32
334	5.33
335	5.33
336	5.34
Pt IV Ch II (ss 337–349)	5.35
s 337	5.35
338	5.36
339	3.69; 5.37; 12.11
340	5.37, 5.39
341	5.37, 5.41
342(1), (2)	5.43
(3)–(5)	5.42
(6)	5.42; 6.51
(7), (8)	5.42
343	5.37
344(1)	5.44
(2)	5.45
345	5.46; 8.36
346	5.47
347	9.06
(1)–(4)	5.49
(5)	5.50
348	2.30; 5.51
(2)	12.40
349	5.52
Pt V (ss 350–410)	6.01
Pt V Ch I (ss 350–352)	6.01
s 350	6.01
351	6.01
352	6.02
Pt V Ch II (ss 353–374)	6.03
s 353	6.04
354	6.05
(6)	6.07
355	6.08
(5)	12.16
356	6.10
(2)(a)–(c)	6.10
357	6.13
358	6.14
359	6.15
360	6.17
361	6.17
362	6.18
363	6.19

Table of statues

	PARA
Education Act 1996 – *contd*	
s 364	5.17
365	6.20
366	6.21
(6)	5.16
367	6.22
368	6.07
369	6.05
370	6.23
371	6.24
372	6.28
373	6.29
374	6.30
Pt V Ch III (ss 375–399)	6.31
s 375	6.33
376	6.43
(2)	1.03
377	6.44
378	6.46
379	6.49
380	6.49
381	6.49
(2)	6.49
382	6.49
383	6.50, 6.52
384	6.31
385	6.52
386	6.53
387	6.54
388	6.31
389	6.59
390	6.36
391(1), (2)	6.40
(3)–(5)	6.41
(6)–(10)	6.42
392	6.36
393	6.39
394	6.55
(8)	6.55
395	6.56
396	6.57
397	6.32
398	6.59
399	6.44, 6.46
Pt V Ch IV (ss 400–410)	6.61
s 400	6.63
401	6.64
402	6.65
403	6.66
404(1), (2)	6.27
(3)	6.24, 6.28
405	6.67
406	6.69
407	6.69
408	6.70; 12.57
409	6.72
410	6.01, 6.31
Pt VI Ch I (ss 411–436)	7.01
s 411	12.57; 14.09
(1)–(5)	7.03
(6), (7)	7.07

	PARA
Education Act 1996 – *contd*	
s 412	7.10
413	7.11
414	7.12
415	7.15
416	7.13, 7.15
417–419	7.13, 7.16
420	7.13, 7.17
421	7.18
422	7.19
423	7.20, 7.28
424	7.02
(3)	5.17
425	7.21
426	7.22
427	7.24
428	7.25
(2) (b)	15.06
429	7.21
430	1.28; 4.35; 7.26
431	7.28
432	7.28
433	2.11; 7.32
434	4.07; 7.35
435	7.38
436	7.03, 7.15, 7.22
Pt VI Ch II (ss 437–448)	7.39
s 437	7.40
438	7.42
439	7.42
440	7.42
441	7.44
442	7.45
443	7.46
(4)	7.49
444	7.47
(8)	7.49
(9)	7.47
445	7.49
(3)	15.35
446	7.50
447	7.50
(5)	7.51
448	2.11; 7.32
Pt VI Ch III (ss 449–462)	7.53, 7.54
s 450(1), (2)	7.55
451(1)–(5)	7.55
452	7.56
(6)	7.58
453	7.55
454(1)–(4)	7.55
455	7.58
456	7.58
457	7.59
458	2.30; 7.61
459	7.53, 7.59
460	7.54
461	7.53, 7.55
462	6.65; 7.55
(2)	7.56

Table of statutes

	PARA
Education Act 1996 – *contd*	
Pt VII Ch I (s 463)	9.01
s 463	9.01
Pt VII Ch II (ss 464–478)	9.03
s 464	2.10; 9.04
465	9.04
466	9.05
467(1), (2)	9.06
(3)	9.07
(4)	9.08
468	9.07
469	9.10
(6)	9.10
470(1)	9.10
(2)	9.12
471	9.13
472	9.13
473	9.14
474	9.15
475	9.07, 9.12
476	9.10
(5)	9.12
477	9.12, 9.13
478	9.16
Pt VII Ch III (ss 479–481)	9.17
s 479	9.18
(10)	9.18
480	9.21
481	9.24
Pt VII Ch IV (ss 482, 483)	9.25
s 482	9.27
483	9.28
Pt VII (ss 484–494)	11.03
s 484	11.06
485	9.28; 10.31; 11.07; 12.40; 15.22
486	11.09
487	11.10
488	11.11
489(1)	11.04
(2)	3.80; 11.06
(3), (4)	11.08
490	11.15
491	11.16; 15.16
492	11.18
493	11.19
494	11.20
Pt IX (ss 495–541)	12.01
Pt IX Ch I (ss 495–507)	12.02
s 495	12.03; 15.32
496	2.36; 6.57, 6.72; 10.54; 10.65; 12.05; 13.62; 14.02, 14.07, 14.10; 15.32
497	2.28, 2.36; 6.57, 6.72; 12.09; 13.62; 14.02, 14.07, 14.10; 15.04
498	12.10
499	2.23
500	4.04; 12.11
501	12.14
502	4.04; 12.11, 12.16

	PARA
Education Act 1996 – *contd*	
s 503	12.17
504	12.11, 12.17, 12.18
505	12.11
(5)	4.04
506	12.19
507	10.54; 12.20
Pt IX Ch II (ss 508–532)	12.22
s 508	12.23
509(1), (2)	12.24
(3)	12.28
(4)	12.26
(5), (6)	12.24
510	12.30
(1)	4.89
(3)–(5)	4.89
511	12.30
512	12.32
513	12.34
514	2.30
(1)	12.36, 12.37
(a)	4.89
(2), (3)	12.36
(4)–(7)	12.37
515	12.38; 13.68
516	4.89; 5.12
517	2.26; 7.03; 12.40; 15.16
(1), (3)	9.02
518	2.26; 7.03, 7.09; 9.02; 11.16; 12.42; 15.16
519	12.42
520	12.45
521	12.48
522	12.48
523	12.49
524	12.49
525	12.49
526	12.50
527	12.50
528	10.11, 10.92
529(1)	2.32
(2)	2.32
530	2.33; 3.07
531	2.33
532	2.22
Pt IX Ch III (ss 533–536)	12.22
s 533	12.33
534	12.32
535	12.38; 13.68
536	12.45
Pt IX Ch IV (ss 537–541)	12.56
s 537	12.57
(9)	9.08
538	12.59
539	12.60
540	12.61
541	10.52; 12.62
Pt X (ss 542–583)	15.01
Pt X Ch I (ss 542–547)	15.03
s 542	3.24, 3.34; 14.22; 15.04
543	14.22; 15.04

Table of statues

	PARA
Education Act 1996 – *contd*	
s 544	15.05
545	15.06
546	15.08
547	15.09
Pt X Ch II (ss 548–550)	15.15
548, 549	15.15
550	15.18
Pt X Ch III (ss 551–557)	
s 551	2.13
552	14.06
(3)	4.52
(4)	5.37
553	15.25
554	3.126, 3.128; 15.25
555	15.26
556	15.26
557	15.28
Pt X Ch IV (ss 558–560)	15.29
s 558	15.30
559	15.31
560	15.32
(7)	12.03
Pt X Ch V (ss 561, 562)	15.02
s 561	15.02
562	15.02
(1)	10.19
Pt X Ch VI (ss 563–583)	15.02, 15.33
s 563	15.33
564	15.34
565(1)	7.49
566	15.36
567	4.75, 4.77, 4.97; 15.02
568, 569	1.31; 15.02
570	1.20, 1.28; 15.02
571	2.19; 3.74; 4.08, 4.18; 5.39
572	1.31; 5.39; 15.02
573	3.09; 15.01
(2)	3.34
(4), (5)	4.49
574	15.01
575	4.08; 15.01
576	4.07; 15.01
577	15.01
578	15.01
579	2.21; 10.02; 15.01
(1)	3.34
(4)	10.107; 11.17
(6)	10.31, 10.92
580	15.01
Sch 1	2.20, 2.31; 12.05
para 6 (1)	6.23
(2)	6.01
(3)	6.72
8	6.66, 6.69
9 (1)	7.53
13	5.10, 5.12, 5.17
14	7.40, 7.42
(1)	7.42
(6)	7.47

	PARA
Education Act 1996 – *contd*	
Sch 2	2.35
para 3 (1)	4.18
15	2.35
Sch 3	2.35, 2.36
para 1	4.29, 4.36, 4.100
2	9.29
3	11.15
Sch 4	2.25, 2.30, 2.37, 2.38, 2.39; 3.07
para 1 (2)	7.61; 12.37
7	12.14
9, 10	15.16
13	12.36
(1) (a)	7.61
(c)	12.40
17 (c)	7.25
19	4.52; 5.37
22	4.68
Sch 5	3.01, 3.02, 3.04
para 4 (1)	6.47
Sch 6	3.01, 3.02, 3.17
Sch 7	3.01, 3.45, 3.47, 3.66, 3.69
para 2	3.91
3	3.66, 3.70
4	3.66, 3.67
7	4.31
Sch 8	3.01, 3.45, 3.47
para 2	3.48, 3.50
(2)	3.67
3–6	3.48
7	3.49
8–13	3.62
14, 15	3.63
16	3.31, 3.63
17, 18	3.65
19, 20	3.66
21	3.62
Sch 9	3.01, 3.45, 3.72
para 19	12.43
Sch 10	3.01, 3.45, 3.70
para 5 (2)	3.60
Sch 11	3.01, 3.73
Pt I, II	3.86
Sch 12	3.01, 3.72, 3.73
Sch 13	3.01, 3.88, 13.27
Sch 14	3.01, 3.88, 13.21
para 16, 17	13.26
23–25	13.29
26	13.26, 13.29
27, 28	13.29
Sch 15	3.01, 3.88
Pt I	3.109
para 14	3.110
Pt II	3.114
Sch 16	3.88, 3.117
Sch 17	3.88, 3.118
Sch 18	3.88, 3.121
Sch 19	3.72, 3.88, 3.124; 13.18, 13.20, 13.27

Table of statutes

	PARA
Education Act 1996 – *contd*	
Pt IV	
para 26	3.95
27	3.105
Sch 20	4.01, 4.09
Pt I (paras 1–6)	4.02
para 2 (1) (a)	4.09
Pt II (paras 7–12)	4.19
8	6.49
12	4.21; 5.41
Sch 21	4.01, 4.02, 4.10
para 2	13.32
Sch 22	4.01, 4.24, 4.25, 4.79
para 11	4.31
14	4.25, 4.79
Sch 23	4.01, 4.24, 4.25, 4.79
para 4	6.30
5	7.21
6	7.21
(1)	4.27
7	4.05
Sch 24	4.01, 4.24, 4.31
para 7, 12	4.13, 4.31
Sch 25	4.01, 4.78, 4.81
Sch 26	5.01, 5.03
Sch 27	5.01, 5.03, 5.17, 5.21
para 10	7.44
Sch 28	5.01, 5.35, 5.45, 5.46
para 1, 2	5.47
4	5.47
12	13.32
Sch 29	6.03, 6.14
para 16	8.04
Sch 30	6.17
Sch 31	6.31, 6.33, 6.34
para 4	6.41
Sch 32	7.01, 7.17
Sch 33	3.117; 7.01, 7.20
Sch 34	9.03, 9.11
Sch 35	9.17, 9.20
Sch 36	15.28
Sch 37	
Pt I (paras 1–132)	
para 22	2.23
55	15.09
59	7.25
77	12.03, 12.05, 12.09, 12.10
96	2.23
112, 113	12.05
Sch 39	
para 1 (2)	1.33
24, 25	4.28, 4.29
26	4.28
36	6.14
Sch 40	
para 1	2.11, 2.12
Education Act 1997	1.09; 2.19; 6.14
s 1	9.18
27	6.17
50	13.25

	PARA
Education (Fees and Awards) Act 1983 (15 *Statutes* 321)	
s 1	10.104
2	10.108
Education (Miscellaneous Provisions) Act 1948	
s 2	15.26
Sch 1	
Pt II	15.26
Education Reform Act 1988 (15 *Statutes* 425)	1.08; 6.72; 10.66
s 1	6.01
41	3.76
Pt I Ch IV (ss 52–104)	4.01, 4.28
s 74	4.13
79 (1), (2)	4.37
81 (8) (b)	4.46
86 (2)	6.49
120	10.88
121	10.66
122	10.68
122A	10.68
123	10.68, 10.70
124	10.69
(2)	10.26
124A	10.68, 10.70
(3)	10.70
124B	10.71
124C	10.70
124D	10.70, 10.79
125	10.68, 10.73
126	10.67
127	10.67, 10.68
128	10.68, 10.74
129	10.48, 10.74, 10.103
129A	10.76
129B	10.77
130	10.75
133	10.61; 13.75
137	10.66
138	10.66, 10.67, 10.75
157	10.04
158	2.42; 10.93
159	10.93
197	4.13
198	4.13; 10.67, 10.75
199	4.13
200	4.13
201	4.13; 10.66
202	10.80
203	10.80
204	10.83
205	10.83
206	10.84
207	10.83, 10.84
209	10.106
210	11.11
211	11.15
214	10.85
215	10.85

Table of statues

	PARA
Education Reform Act 1988 – *contd*	
s 216	10.85
218	2.18; 13.16
(1) (e)	10.47; 15.08
(f)	15.33
(2A)	13.09
218(4)	15.33
(7)	10.47; 15.05
(9) (a)	10.105
(b), (c)	13.02
(10)	10.47, 10.105; 13.02; 15.05, 15.08, 15.33
(11)	10.105; 13.02
219	12.03, 12.05, 12.09, 12.10
220	4.102; 15.37
(4)	10.53
221	13.46
226	12.21
Sch 6	10.02
Sch 7	10.70
Sch 7A	10.70
Sch 8	4.13
Sch 9	10.66
Sch 10	4.13
para 2 (1)	4.16
3	10.75
Sch 11	10.80
Education (Schools) Act 1992 (15 *Statutes* 769)	1.08
Education (Scotland) Act 1980	
s 100	9.12, 9.13
Education (Student Loans) Act 1990 (15 *Statutes* 649)	
s 1	10.113
Sch 1	10.113
Sch 2	10.113
Education (Student Loans) Act 1996	1.08
s 1	10.113
Sch 1	10.113
Elementary Education Act 1870	1.02, 1.03; 6.43
Employment and Training Act 1973 (16 *Statutes* 62)	
s 8–10	12.52
10A	12.52
Employment of Children Act 1973 (6 *Statutes* 203)	15.30
s 2	15.31
Employment of Women, Young Persons and Children Act 1920 (16 *Statutes* 13)	
s 1 (2)	15.32
Employment Rights Act 1996 (16 *Statutes* 557)	
s 50–63	13.37
71–85	13.38
86–93	13.41
Pt X (ss 94–134)	10.80
s 94–96	13.42
98	13.44
99	13.45

	PARA
Employment Rights Act 1996 – *contd*	
s 105	13.44
107	13.45
108, 109	13.42
111	13.44
134	13.43
Pt XI (ss 135–181)	10.51; 13.48
136	13.47
139	13.44, 13.46
140	13.49
141	13.49
158	13.49
163	13.49
173	13.46
197	13.42
209	13.49
210	13.39, 13.41
216	13.41
235(1)	13.52
Endowed Schools Acts 1869–1948	3.23; 15.19, 15.25, 15.26, 15.28
Environment and Safety Information Act 1988 (35 *Statutes* 772)	13.39
Environmental Protection Act 1990 (32 *Statutes* 308)	
s 86–98	14.14
Equal Pay Act 1970 (16 *Statutes* 34)	
s 1, 2	13.50
2A	13.50
6	13.50
Factories Act 1961 (19 *Statutes* 646)	
s 86–119	15.30
Family Law Reform Act 1969 (6 *Statutes* 128)	
s 9	1.13
Financial Services Act 1986 (19 *Statutes* 146)	
Sch 11	
para 1–6	4.77
11	4.77
Further and Higher Education Act 1992 (15 *Statutes* 664)	1.08, 1.10; 10.01, 10.78
s 1	10.05
2	10.06, 10.19
3	10.06, 10.19
4	10.09
5	10.11
6 (1)–(4)	10.12
(5), (6)	10.13
7	10.06
8	10.14
9	10.15
15	10.20, 10.48
16	10.21
(2)	10.21
17	10.20, 10.21
18	10.25
19	10.26
(1)	10.26
20	10.27

Table of statutes

Further and Higher Education Act 1992
– contd
	PARA
s 21	10.27
22	10.28
23	10.29
24	10.29
(1), (2)	10.96
25	10.29
26	10.30
26	10.23
27	10.23
28	10.31, 10.48, 10.74, 10.103
29	10.33
30	10.33
31	10.34
32	10.35
33	10.36
34	10.37
35	10.39
36	10.40
37	10.41
38	10.42
39	10.43
40	10.43
41	10.44
42	10.44
43	10.50
44	10.45
45	10.45
46	10.46
47	10.48
(4)	10.48, 10.74
48	10.50
49	10.51
50	10.52; 12.62
51	10.24
52	10.16
53	10.53
54	10.17
55	10.92
56	10.18; 12.05
57	10.54; 12.20
58	10.55
60	10.19
62	10.56
(7A), (7B)	10.57
63	10.56
64	10.56
65	10.58, 10.61, 10.103
66	10.61
68	10.58
69	10.62
70	10.63
72	10.48
74 (2)	10.71
76	10.79
77	10.78
78	10.70, 10.71
79	10.64
80	10.79
81	10.65

Further and Higher Education Act 1992
– contd
	PARA
s 82	10.03
85	10.89
91	10.04
Sch 1	10.05, 10.15, 10.56, 10.63
Sch 2	10.06, 10.87
Sch 3	10.20
Sch 4	10.27
Sch 5	10.40
Sch 7	10.40
Sch 8	
para 62–64	10.75
Sch 9	10.74

Further Education Act 1985 (15 Statutes 326)
s 1–3	10.95

Health and Safety at Work etc Act 1974 (19 Statutes 796)
s 2, 3	13.39
4	13.39; 14.22
7	13.39
18	13.39
27–28	13.39
33	13.39
47	13.40
52	13.39

Industrial Tribunals Act 1996 (16 Statutes 504) 13.49
s 18	13.44, 13.54
Pt II (ss 20–37)	13.44

Interpretation Act 1978 (41 Statutes 985) 9.22
s 17	1.33

Jobseekers Act 1995
s 1	12.32

Land Compensation Act 1973 (9 Statutes 258)
s 52A	4.16

Landlord and Tenant Act 1954 (23 Statutes 142)
Pt II (ss 23–46)	4.93
s 37	4.93

Local Authorities (Goods and Services) Act 1970 (25 Statutes 139) 4.01, 4.89; 5.12

Local Government Act 1966 (25 Statutes 131)
s 11	11.15

Local Government Act 1972 (25 Statutes 166)
s 101	2.22
(5)	2.22
102	2.22
104	2.23
111	2.22
120	2.33
123(2)	2.34; 4.16
134	15.13
139	2.32
250(2)–(5)	12.17, 12.20

Table of statues

	PARA
Local Government Act 1974 (25 Statutes 495)	
s 25	15.40
Local Government Act 1986 (25 Statutes 834)	6.67
s 2A	6.66
Local Government Act 1988 (25 Statutes 870)	
s 4	4.16
Local Government Act 1992 (25 Statutes 1248)	
s 17	3.08, 3.21
Local Government and Housing Act 1989 (25 Statutes 987)	
Pt I (ss 1–21)	2.22
s 13	2.23
Local Government Finance Act 1982 (25 Statutes 656)	
s 29 (1) (d)	3.86
Local Government Finance Act 1988 (25 Statutes 854)	
Pt V (ss 76–88B)	11.01
Local Government Finance Act 1992 (25 Statutes 1130)	
s 43 (2) (a)	4.46
Local Government (Miscellaneous Provisions) Act 1976 (35 Statutes 447)	
s 19	12.23
Local Government (Miscellaneous Provisions) Act 1982 (15 Statutes 317)	
s 40 (2)–(5)	15.09
Local Government, Planning and Land Act 1980 (25 Statutes 566)	
s 7	4.16
Sch 10	
para 6	11.18
London Government Act 1963 (26 Statutes 412)	
s 31	2.25; 3.07
(5)	3.126
Magistrates' Courts Act 1980 (27 Statutes 143)	1.34
s 58 (1)	1.15
96	1.15
127(1)	1.15
Merchant Shipping Act 1995	
s 55 (1)	15.32
National Audit Act 1983 (30 Statutes 149)	
s 6	4.102
National Health Service 1977 (30 Statutes 788)	
s 5	12.45
21 (2)	2.32
28A	11.02
Sch 1	12.45
Nursery Education and Grant-Maintained Schools Act 1996	5.12
s 1–3	11.12
4	11.13
5	11.14

	PARA
Nursery Education and Grant-Maintained Schools Act 1996 – *contd*	
s 6	11.12
Sch 1	11.14
Sch 2	11.12
Occupiers' Liability Act 1957 (31 Statutes 238)	
s 2	14.22
Parliamentary Commissioner Act 1967 (10 Statutes 350)	
s 4	2.18
Sch 2	2.18
Pension Schemes Act 1993	
s 160	13.73
Pensions (Increase) Act 1971 (33 Statutes 414)	
s 5 (2)	13.74
Public Health (control of Disease) Act 1984 (35 Statutes 514)	
s 10	12.47
21, 22	12.47
Public Passenger Vehicles Act 1981 (38 Statutes 391)	
s 46	12.25
Race Relations Act 1976 (6 Statutes 828)	
s 1	13.53; 14.08
(1) (b)	14.08
2	14.08
3, 4	13.53
5	13.53
17, 17A	14.09
18	7.05; 14.09
18A, 18C	14.09
19	14.09, 14.10, 14.11
20, 21	14.11
25	14.11
27	14.09
34, 35	14.09
41 (1)	10.104, 10.108
42	14.09
47	13.55
48	14.02
51	14.02
54	13.54
56	13.55
57	14.10
58 (6)	14.02
Representation of the People Act 1983 (15 Statutes 1226)	
s 23, 36	15.12
95, 96	15.12
Sch 1	
Pt III (paras 18–49)	
para 22	15.12
Sch 5	15.12
Reverter of Sites Act 1987 (37 Statutes 460)	3.126, 3.128; 15.27
s 1	3.39
5	15.27

Table of statutes

	PARA
School Inspections Act 1996	1.09, 3.128; 8.01
Pt I (ss 1–25)	8.01
Pt I Ch I (ss 1–10)	8.02
s 1	8.03
2 (1)–(6)	8.04
(7)	8.05
5 (8)–(10)	8.06
3	8.07
4	8.03
5 (1)–(6)	8.04
(7)	8.05
(8)–(10)	8.06
6	8.07
7	8.09
8	8.10
9	8.11
10	8.04, 8.07, 8.08, 8.12, 8.16, 8.18, 8.19, 8.22, 8.28, 8.40
Pt I Ch II (ss 11–22)	5.48; 8.02
s 11	8.13
(2), (3)	8.13
12	8.14
13	8.16
14	8.18
15	8.19
16	8.13, 8.21
17	8.13, 8.22, 8.32
18	8.13, 8.23, 8.32
19	8.13, 8.24
20–22	8.13, 8.26
23	8.28
24	8.29
25	2.24; 8.29
Pt II (ss 26–41)	8.30
s 26	8.31
27	8.32
28	8.32
29	3.67; 8.33
30	8.34
(2)	5.46
31	8.37
32	8.37
33	5.37; 8.36
34	8.40
35	8.38
36	8.39
37	8.36, 8.42
38	8.43
39	8.44
40	8.41
41	8.36, 8.40, 8.42, 8.43
42	8.13
44	8.43, 8.44
Sch 1	8.03
Sch 2	8.11
Sch 3	8.08
para 1	8.12
2	8.12, 8.29
3–5	8.12

	PARA
School Inspections Act 1996 – contd	
Sch 3 – contd	
para 6–8	8.15
Sch 4	8.28
Sch 5	8.30, 8.37
Sch 8	1.78
para 1 (2)	1.33
School Sites Act 1841 (15 *Statutes* 1172)	1.01, 3.128; 4.94; 15.27
s 14	3.39
School Sites Act 1844 (15 *Statutes* 1180)	1.01, 3.128; 15.27
School Sites Act 1849 (15 *Statutes* 1182)	1.01, 3.128; 15.27
School Sites Act 1851 (15 *Statutes* 1185)	1.01, 3.128; 15.27
School Sites Act 1852 (15 *Statutes* 1186)	1.01, 3.128; 15.27
School Teachers' Pay and Conditions Act 1991 (15 *Statutes* 654)	4.35; 13.60, 13.62
s 1	13.62
2	13.63, 13.65
3	13.64
3A	13.62
Sch 1	13.62
Sex Discrimination Act 1975 (6 *Statutes* 753)	5.37; 13.50
s 1, 2	13.51; 14.04
4	14.05
6	13.51
7	13.52
22	14.05
22A	14.05
23	14.06
23A	14.06
23C	14.06
24	14.05
25	14.06, 14.07
26	14.06
27	4.11; 14.06
28	14.06
Pt V (ss 43–52A)	13.51
s 46	13.52
56A	13.55
57	14.02
60	14.02
63	13.54
65	13.54
66	14.07
67 (6)	14.02
77	13.51
78	15.23
Sch 2	14.06
para 1	4.11
Sex Discrimination Act 1986 (6 *Statutes* 949)	
s 6	13.51
Social Security Administration Act 1992 (40 *Statutes* 786)	
s 105–108	12.32

Table of statues

	PARA
Social Security contributions and Benefits Act 1992 (40 *Statutes* 492)	
s 123–127	12.32
Superannuation Act 1972 (33 *Statutes* 453)	
s 9	13.73, 13.74
24	13.74
Teachers' Pay and Conditions Act 1987	1.05
Technical Instruction Act 1889	1.04
Town and Country Planning Act 1990 (46 *Statutes* 514)	4.54; 5.41
Trade Descriptions Act 1968 (39 *Statutes* 41)	
s 29	10.85
Trade Union and Labour Relations (Consolidation) Act 1992 (16 *Statutes* 180)	13.65
s 152	13.45
168, 170	13.37
188	13.47
189	13.47

	PARA
Trade Union and Labour Relations (Consolidation) Act 1992 – *contd*	
s 193	13.47
194	13.47
282	13.47
Trade Union Reform and Employment Rights Act 1993 (16 *Statutes* 485)	
s 45, 46	12.52
Tribunals and Inquiries Act 1992	5.34
s 1 (1) (a)	9.11
11	9.11
(1)	5.34
Sch 1	
Pt I (paras 1–45)	
para 15 (a)	9.11
Weights and Measures Act 1985 (50 *Statutes* 9)	
s 69 (5)	10.85
Welsh Intermediate Education Act 1889:	1.04
Welsh Language Act 1993	4.01
Young Persons (Employment) Act 1938	15.30

TABLE OF STATUTORY INSTRUMENTS

References in the right-hand column are to paragraph numbers.

	PARA
Certificates of Births, Deaths and Marriages (Requisition) Regulations 1937, SR & O 1937/885	15.34
Charities (Exemption of Voluntary Schools from Registration) Regulations 1960, SI 1960/2366	3.37
Colleges of Education (Compensation) Regulations 1975, SI 1975/1092	13.74
Direct Grant Grammar Schools (Cessation of Grant) Regulations 1975, SI 1975/1198	12.42
Disability Discrimination (Services and Premises) Regulations 1996, SI 1996/1836	14.11
Education (Abolition of Corporal Punishment) (Independent Schools) (Prescribed Categories of Persons) Regulations 1989, SI 1989/1825	15.16
Education (Abolition of Corporal Punishment) (Independent Schools) Regulations 1987, SI 1987/1183	15.16
Education (Acquisition of Grant-maintained Status) (Ballot Information) Regulations 1993, SI 1993/3189	4.08
Education (Acquisition of Grant-maintained Status) (Transitional Functions) Regulations 1993, SI 1993/3072	4.10
Education Act 1996 (Amendment) Order 1996, SI 1996/3210	3.118
Education (Amount to Follow Permanently Excluded Pupil) Regulations 1994, SI 1994/1697	1.20
Education (Annual Consideration of Ballot on Grant-Maintained Status) (England) Order 1993, SI 1993/3115	4.05
Education (Annual Consideration of Ballot on Grant-Maintained Status) (Wales) Order 1994, SI 1994/1861	4.05

	PARA
Education (Application of Financing Schemes to Special Schools) Regulations 1993, SI 1993/3104	3.73, 3.76; 13.18
reg 2	3.80, 3.86
Education (Areas to which Pupils and Students Belong) Regulations 1996, SI 1996/615	10.107; 11.17
Education Assets Board (Transfers under the Education Reform Act 1988) Regulations 1992, SI 1992/1348	10.75
Education (Assisted Places) (Incidental Expenses) Regulations 1995, SI 1995/2017	9.24
Education (Assisted Places) Regulations 1995, SI 1995/2016	9.21
Education (Assisted Places) (Amendment) Regulations 1996, SI 1996/2113	9.21
Education (Ballot Expenditure) Regulations 1995, SI 1995/628	4.06
reg 4	4.06
Education (Bursaries for Teacher Training) Regulations 1994, SI 1994/2016	11.05
Education (Chief Inspector of Schools in England) Order 1994, SI 1994/1633	8.03
Education (Chief Inspector of Schools in Wales) Order 1992, SI 1992/173	8.03
Education (Chief Inspector of Schools in Wales) Order 1997, SI 1997/288	8.03
Education (Designated Institutions in Further Education) Order 1993, SI 1993/435	10.31, 10.33, 10.36
Education (Designated Institutions in Further Education) (No 2) Order 1993, SI 1993/562	10.31

Table of statutory instruments

	PARA
Education (Designated Institutions in Further Education) (Wales) Order 1993, SI 1993/215	10.31, 10.33, 10.36
Education (Designated Institutions) Order 1989, SI 1989/282	10.74
Education (Designated Institutions) Order 1993, SI 1993/404	10.74
Education (Designated Institutions) (Wales) Order 1992, SI 1992/2622	10.74
Education (Disability Statements for Further Education Institutions) Regulations 1996, SI 1996/1664	10.11
Education (Dissolution of the Council for National Academic Awards) Order 1993, SI 1993/924	10.79
Education (Distribution by Schools of Information about Further Education Institutions) (Wales) Regulations 1994, SI 1994/1321	12.62
Education (Exclusion from Schools) (Prescribed Periods) Regulations 1994, SI 1994/2093	3.110
Education (Fees and Awards) Regulations 1994, SI 1994/3042	10.104, 10.108
Pt IV (regs 11–13)	10.112
Education (Financial Delegation for Primary Schools) Regulations 1991, SI 1991/1890	3.76
Education (Financial Delegation for Primary Schools) (Amendment) Regulations 1992, SI 1992/110	3.76
Education (Funding for Teacher Training) Designation Order 1995, SI 1995/1704	13.04
Education (Funding for Teacher Training) Designation Order 1996, SI 1996/1832	13.04
Education (Funding for Teacher Training) Designation Order 1997, SI 1997/515	13.04
Education (Further Education Corporations) (Designated Staff) Order 1993, SI 1993/465	10.30
Education (Further Education Corporations) (Designated Staff) (Wales) Order 1993, SI 1993/612	10.30
Education (Further Education Corporations) Order 1992, SI 1992/2097	10.20
Education (Further Education in Schools) Regulations 1993, SI 1993/1987	3.92
Education (Further Education Institutions Information) (England) Regulations 1995, SI 1995/2065	10.52; 12.62
Education (Further Education Institutions Information) (Wales) Regulations 1993, SI 1993/2169	10.52

	PARA
Education (Government of Further Education Corporations) (Former Further Education Colleges) Regulations 1992, SI 1992/1963	10.27
Education (Government of Further Education Corporations) (Former Sixth Form Colleges) Regulations 1992, SI 1992/1957	10.27
Education (Government of Groups of Grant-maintained Schools) Regulations 1994, SI 1994/2281	4.83
reg 4	5.47
Education (Governors of New Grant-maintained Schools) Regulations 1994, SI 1994/654	
reg 2–5	4.21, 4.31
6, 7	4.31
Education (Grant) (Bishop Perowne High School) Regulations 1995, SI 1995/1688	11.07
Education (Grant) (Henrietta Barnett School) Regulations 1994, SI 1994/156	11.07
Education (Grant) Regulations 1990, SI 1990/1989	10.31; 11.05, 11.07
reg 11	15.20
14	11.09
15	15.20
Education (Grant-maintained and Grant-maintained Special Schools) (Finance) Regulations 1996, SI 1996/889	4.23, 4.37
reg 42	4.46
Education (Grant-maintained and Grant-maintained Special Schools) (Finance) (Wales) Regulations 1997, SI 1997/599	4.37, 4.46
Education (Grant-maintained Schools) (Initial Governing Instruments) Regulations 1993, SI 1993/3102	4.28
Education (Grant-maintained Schools) (Initial Sponsor Governors) Regulations 1993, SI 1993/3188	4.31
Education (Grant-maintained Schools) (Loans) Regulations 1993, SI 1993/3073	4.45
Education (Grant-maintained Special Schools) (Initial Governing Instruments) Regulations 1994, SI 1994/2104	5.45
Education (Grant-maintained Special Schools) Regulations 1994, SI 1994/653	3.14; 4.03; 5.45, 5.46
reg 6 (2)	5.39
12–13A	5.37
16	13.32
24	5.37
26, 27	5.37
38	13.69
40	6.27
41	6.15

Table of statutory instruments

	PARA

Education (Grant-maintained Special Schools) Regulations 1994 – *contd*
  reg 42 .... 3.65; 6.02, 6.67, 6.70; 7.35, 7.53; 10.11; 12.05, 12.09, 12.24, 12.45, 12.57; 13.02, 13.46, 13.62; 15.04, 15.32
    (1) 11.15
  Schedule
    Pt I 3.65; 6.02, 6.67, 6.70; 7.35, 7.53; 10.11; 11.15; 12.05, 12.09, 12.24, 12.45, 12.57; 13.02, 13.46, 13.62; 15.04, 15.32
Education (Grant-maintained Special Schools) (No 2) Regulations 1994, SI 1994/2247 .... 5.45; 13.04
Education (Grants) (City Technology Colleges) Regulations 1987, SI 1987/1138 .... 9.28; 11.07
Education (Grants for Education Support and Training) (England) Regulations 1997, SI 1997/519 .. 11.06
Education (Grants for Education Support and Training: Nursery Education) (England) Regulations 1996, SI 1996/235 .... 11.06
Education (Grants for Education Support and Training) (Wales) Regulations 1997, SI 1997/390 .. 11.06
Education (Grants for Nursery Education) (England) Regulations 1996, SI 1996/353 .... 11.12
Education (Grants) (Higher Education Corporations) Regulations 1992, SI 1992/3237 .... 11.07
Education (Grants) (Music, Ballet and Choir Schools) Regulations 1995, SI 1995/2018 .... 11.07
Education (Grants) (Purcell School) Regulations 1996, SI 1996/757 .. 11.07
Education (Grants) (Travellers and Displaced Persons) Regulations 1993, SI 1993/569 .... 11.11
Education (Grants) (Voluntary Aided Sixth Form Colleges) Regulations 1992, SI 1992/2181 .... 11.07
Education (Groups including Grant-maintained Special Schools) Regulations 1994, SI 1994/779 ...... 4.79, 4.82; 5.47
  reg 3 .... 4.83
    (a) 4.80
Education (Groups of Grant-maintained Schools) (Finance) Regulations 1994, SI 1994/1195 .... 4.82
Education (Groups of Grant-maintained Schools) (Initial Governing Instruments) Regulations 1994, SI 1994/2896 .... 4.80
Education (Groups of Grant-maintained Schools) Regulations 1994, SI 1994/1041 ..... 4.03, 4.79, 4.83; 5.47

	PARA

Education (Groups of Grant-maintained Schools) Regulations 1994 – *contd*
  reg 45 .... 5.37
    (2) 5.39
    (3) 5.41
    (4) 5.42
Education (Higher Education Corporations) (Designated Staff) Order 1989, SI 1989/369 .... 10.67
Education (Higher Education Corporations) Order 1988, SI 1988/1799 .. 10.66
Education (Higher Education Corporations) (No 5) Order 1989, SI 1989/17 .... 10.66
Education (Individual Pupils' Achievements) (Information) Regulations 1993, SI 1993/3182 .... 6.70
Education (Individual Pupils' Achievements) (Information) (Wales) Regulations 1997, SI 1997/573 .. 6.70
Education (Information as to Provision of Education) (England) Regulations 1994, SI 1994/1256 .... 2.43
Education (Initial Government of Grant-maintained Special Schools) Regulations 1994, SI 1994/2003 ... 5.37, 5.45
Education (Inspectors of Schools in England) Order 1992, SI 1992/1713: 8.03
Education (Inspectors of Schools in England) Order 1996, SI 1996/2594: 8.03
Education (Inspectors of Schools in Wales) Order 1992, SI 1992/1740 .. 8.03
Education (Inspectors of Schools in Wales) Order 1995, SI 1995/1628 .. 8.03
Education (Inter-authority Recoupment) Regulations 1994, SI 1994/3251 .... 11.18
Education (Lay members of Appeal Committees) Regulations 1994, SI 1994/1303 .... 4.27
Education (Listed Bodies) Order 1997, SI 1997/54 .... 10.85
Education (Maintained Special Schools becoming Grant-maintained Special Schools) (Ballot Information) Regulations 1994, SI 1994/1232 ... 4.08; 5.46
Education (Mandatory Awards) Regulations 1995, SI 1995/3321 ..... 10.106
  Sch 2
    Pt III 10.106
  Sch 4 .... 10.106
Education (Mandatory Awards) Regulations 1997, SI 1997/431 .... 10.106
Education (Middle Schools) Regulations 1980, SI 1980/918 .... 2.08; 3.27; 4.11
Education (Modification of Enactments Relating to Employment) Order 1989, SI 1989/901 .... 13.18

xxxi

Table of statutory instruments

	PARA
Education (National Curriculum) (Assessment Arrangements for the Core Subjects) (Key Stage 1) (England) Order 1995, SI 1995/2071	6.10
Education (National Curriculum) (Assessment Arrangements for the Core Subjects) (Key Stage 2) (England) Order 1995, SI 1995/2072	6.10
Education (National Curriculum) (Key Stage 3 Assessment Arrangements) (England) Order 1996, SI 1996/2116	6.10
Education (National Curriculum) (Assessment Arrangements for English, Welsh, Mathematics and Science) (Key Stage 1) Order 1995, SI 1995/2207	6.10
Education (National Curriculum) (Assessment Arrangements for English, Welsh, Mathematics and Science) (Key Stage 2) Order 1995, SI 1995/2208	6.10
Education (National Curriculum) (Assessment Arrangements for English, Welsh, Mathematics and Science) (Key Stage 3) Order 1995, SI 1995/2209	6.10
Education (National Curriculum) (Attainment Targets and Programmes of Study in	
Art) (England) Order 1995, SI 1995/58:	6.10
Art) (Wales) Order 1995, SI 1995/71	6.10
English) (No 2) Order 1990, SI 1990/423	6.10
English) Order 1995, SI 1995/51	6.10
Geography) (England) Order 1995, SI 1995/55	6.10
Geography) (Wales) Order 1995, SI 1995/72	6.10
History) (England) Order 1995, SI 1995/54	6.10
History) (Wales) Order 1995, SI 1995/73	6.10
Mathematics) Order 1991, SI 1991/2896	6.10
Mathematics) Order 1995, SI 1995/52	6.10
Modern Foreign Languages) Order 1995, SI 1995/57	6.10
Music) (England) Order 1995, SI 1995/59	6.10
Music) (Wales) Order 1995, SI 1995/70:	6.10
Physical Education) Order 1992, SI 1992/603	6.10
Physical Education) Order 1995, SI 1995/60	6.10
Science) Order 1991, SI 1991/2897	6.10
Science) Order 1995, SI 1995/53	6.10
Technology) Order 1995, SI 1995/56	6.10
Welsh) Order 1990, SI 1990/1082	6.10
Welsh) Order 1995, SI 1995/69	6.10

	PARA
Education (National Curriculum) (Exceptions in Welsh at Key Stage 4) Regulations 1994, SI 1994/1270	6.19
Education (National Curriculum) (Exceptions) Regulations 1996, SI 1996/2083	6.19
Education (National Curriculum) (Exceptions) (Wales) Regulations 1990, SI 1990/2187	6.19
Education (National Curriculum) (Exceptions) (Wales) Regulations 1991, SI 1991/1657	6.19
Education (National Curriculum) (Exceptions) (Wales) Regulations 1995, SI 1995/1574	6.19
Education (National Curriculum) (Exceptions) (Wales) (Revocation) Regulations 1996, SI 1996/2259	6.19
Education (National Curriculum) (Modern Foreign Languages) Order 1991, SI 1991/2567	6.05
Education (National Curriculum) (Temporary Exceptions for Individual Pupils) Regulations 1989, SI 1989/1181	6.20, 6.21, 6.22
Education (Parental Ballots for Acquisition of Grant-maintained Status) (Prescribed Body) Regulations 1992, SI 1992/2598	4.08
Education (Particulars of Independent Schools) Regulations 1982, SI 1982/1730	9.04, 9.05, 9.07
Education (PCFC and UGC Staff) Order 1993, SI 1993/434	10.56
Education (Polytechnics and Colleges Funding Council) (Prescribed Expenditure) Regulations 1991, SI 1991/2307	10.61; 13.75
Education (Pre-Scheme Financial Statements) Regulations 1989, SI 1989/370	3.86
Education (Prescribed Public Examinations) Regulations 1989, SI 1989/377	6.65; 7.55
Education (Provision of Clothing) Regulations 1980, SI 1980/545	12.30, 12.31
Education (Publication of Draft Proposals and Orders) (Further Education Corporations) Regulations 1992, SI 1992/2361	10.24
Education (Publication of Notices) (Special Schools) Regulations 1994, SI 1994/2167 reg	24.31
Education (Publication of Proposals for Reduction in Standard Number) Regulations 1991, SI 1991/411	7.17
Education (Publication of Schemes for Financing Schools) Regulations 1993, SI 1993/3070	3.85

Table of statutory instruments

Education (Publication of School Proposals and Notices) Regulations 1993, SI 1993/3113 ... 3.08, 3.29; 4.11
reg 3 .... 4.51, 4.52, 4.61, 4.63
  4 .... 4.18
  5 .... 12.16
  6 .... 4.31
  7 .... 4.09, 4.51, 4.52
  (2) 12.16
Sch 2 .... 4.09
Education (Pupil Referral Units) (Application of Enactments) Regulations 1994, SI 1994/2103 ... 2.31, 2.42; 3.109, 3.110; 7.12; 12.57
reg 2 ...... 3.95, 3.101, 3.107, 3.123; 6.02, 6.24, 6.27, 6.67; 15.31
  3 .... 7.03, 7.20
Sch 1 .... 6.02
  para 1 .... 15.31
  2 .... 3.107, 3.123
  (1) 3.95, 3.101; 6.24
  3 (2) 6.67
  4 .... 6.27
Sch 2
  para 1 .... 7.03, 7.20
Education (Pupil Registration) Regulations 1995, SI 1995/2089
reg 8 .... 2.14; 7.47
Education (Pupils' Attendance Records) Regulations 1991, SI 1991/1582 .. 2.42; 7.12
Education (Recognised Awards) Order 1988, SI 1988/2035 .... 10.85
Education (Recognised Awards) (Richmond College) (No 2) Order 1996, SI 1996/2564 .... 10.85
Education (Recognised Bodies) Order 1997, SI 1997/1 .... 10.85
Education (Registered Inspectors) (Fees) Regulations 1992, SI 1992/2025 . 8.09
Education (Registered Inspectors of Schools Appeal Tribunal) (Procedure) Regulations 1994, SI 1994/717 .... 8.11
Education (School Attendance Order) Regulations 1995, SI 1995/2090 .. 7.40
Education (School Curriculum and Related Information) Regulations 1989, SI 1989/954 ... 2.42; 6.70; 7.12
Education (School Financial Statements) (Prescribed Particulars etc) Regulations 1994, SI 1994/323 .. 3.86
Education (School Financial Statements) (Prescribed Particulars etc) Regulations 1995, SI 1995/208 .. 3.86
Education (School Government) Regulations 1989, SI 1989/1503 ..... 3.62, 3.63; 13.27
reg 14 .... 4.07
  19 .... 4.07
  23 .... 3.93

Education (School Government) Regulations 1989 – *contd*
reg 24 .... 3.63
  30 .... 3.93, 3.110, 3.114
  31 .... 3.93
Schedule
  para 2 (4) 4.07
Education (School Government) (Amendment) Regulations 1996, SI 1996/2050 .... 3.63
Education (School Hours and Policies) (Information) Regulations 1989, SI 1989/398 ...... 2.42; 7.12, 7.53, 7.59
Education (School Information) (England) Regulations 1996, SI 1996/2585 .... 2.42; 6.70; 7.12; 12.57, 12.60
reg 6 .... 12.24
Sch 1
  para 7 .... 12.24
Education (School Information) (Wales) Regulations 1994, SI 1994/2330 . 2.42; 6.70; 7.12; 12.57, 12.60
reg 7 .... 12.24
Sch 1
  para 8 .... 12.24
Education (School Inspection) (No 2) Regulations 1993, SI 1993/1986 . 8.08
reg 6 .... 8.15
  7 .... 8.19, 8.22, 8.23
  8 .... 8.21
  9–12 .... 8.28
  13 .... 8.29
Education (School Inspection) (Wales) (No 2) Regulations 1993, SI 1993/1982 .... 8.08
reg 6 .... 8.15
  7 .... 8.19, 8.22, 8.23
  8 .... 8.21
  9–12 .... 8.28
  13 .... 8.29
Education (School Performance Information) (England) Regulations 1996, SI 1996/2577 ...... 6.70; 7.12; 12.57
Education (School Performance Information) (Wales) Regulations 1995, SI 1995/1904 .... 6.70; 7.12; 12.57, 12.60
Education (School Premises) Regulations 1996, SI 1996/360 ... 3.24, 3.34; 8.36; 15.04
reg 17 .... 14.22
Education (School Teacher Appraisal) Regulations 1991, SI 1991/1511 . 13.17
Education (School Teachers' Pay and Conditions) (No 2) Order 1996, SI 1996/1816 .... 13.63
Education (School Teachers' Pay and Conditions) Order 1997, SI 1997/755 .... 13.63

xxxiii

Table of statutory instruments

Education (Schools and Further and Higher Education) Regulations 1989, SI 1989/351 ..... 15.05, 15.06
  reg 7 .... 10.47; 15.08
    8 .... 10.47
    11–13 .... 13.02
  Sch 1 .... 10.41
  Sch 2 .... 13.02
Education (Schools and Further Education) Regulations 1981, SI 1981/1086 .... 2.18
  reg 10 .... 2.04, 2.13; 3.95
    (4) 2.08
Education (Schools Conducted by Education Associations) (Initial Articles of Government) Regulations 1994, SI 1994/2849 .... 8.39
Education (Schools Conducted by Education Associations) Regulations 1993, SI 1993/3103 .. 3.14; 4.03; 5.10; 8.36
  reg 2 .... 2.36, 2.39; 5.47; 8.40
    4 .... 7.22
  Sch 1 .... 5.10
    para 2 .... 7.53
    3, 4 .... 8.28
    6 .... 2.36
    7 .... 2.39; 8.40
    9 .... 5.47; 8.40
  Sch 3 .... 7.22
Education (Special Educational Needs) (Approval of Independent Schools) Regulations 1994, SI 1994/651 .. 5.49
  Sch 2
    para 8 (5) 5.25
Education (Special Educational Needs Code of Practice) (Appointed Day) Order 1994, SI 1994/1414 ...... 5.07
Education (Special Educational Needs) (Information) Regulations 1994, SI 1994/1048 .... 2.42; 5.12; 7.12; 12.57, 12.60
  reg 6 .... 5.45
Education (Special Educational Needs) (Prescribed Forms) (Welsh Forms) Regulations 1995, SI 1995/45 ... 5.17
Education (Special Educational Needs) Regulations 1994, SI 1994/1047
  reg 5–10 .... 5.16
    11 .... 5.16
    (7), (8) 5.15
    13 .... 5.17
    15–17 .... 5.25
  Schedule
    Pt B 5.17
Education (Special Schools Conducted by Education Associations) Regulations 1994, SI 1994/1084 ... 4.03; 8.36
  reg 5 .... 5.39
    6 .... 5.37
    7 .... 5.37, 5.42, 5.44; 5.47

Education (Special Schools Conducted by Education Associations) Regulations 1994 – contd
  reg 8 .... 5.10, 5.44; 7.32, 7.35, 7.40; 13.69
    (1) 3.65, 3.108; 6.02; 7.53; 10.11; 11.15; 12.05, 12.09, 12.24, 12.37, 12.45, 12.57, 12.60; 13.02, 13.46, 13.62; 15.04, 15.32
    9 .... 5.44; 6.02, 6.67, 6.70
  Sch 2
    Pt I 3.65, 3.108; 5.10; 7.32, 7.35, 7.40, 7.53; 10.11; 11.15; 12.05, 12.09, 12.24, 12.37, 12.45, 12.57, 12.60; 13.02, 13.46, 13.62, 13.69; 15.04, 15.32
Education (Special Schools) Regulations 1994, SI 1994/652 .... 5.42
  reg 4 .... 5.43
  9–11 .... 5.37
  Schedule
    Pt I (paras 1–5) 5.43
    Pt II (paras 6–20)
      para 10 .... 6.51
      16 .... 13.69
      19 (2) 5.25
Education (Student Loans) Regulations 1996, SI 1996/1812 .... 10.113
Education (Teachers) Regulations 1993, SI 1993/543 .... 13.16
  reg 9 .... 13.24
    10 .... 9.07; 13.16, 13.24
    14–17 .... 13.16
  Sch 2 .... 13.16
  Sch 3 .... 13.16
    para 2 (1A) 13.09
Education (Transfer of Functions Relating to Grant-maintained Schools) Order 1997, SI 1997/294 .... 4.34
Education (Variation of Standard Numbers for Primary Schools) Order 1991, SI 1991/410 .... 7.17
Education (Welsh Medium Teacher Training Incentive Supplement) Regulations 1990, SI 1990/1208 .. 11.05
Employment Protection Code of Practice (Disciplinary Practice and Procedures) Order 1977, SI 1977/867: 13.44
Further and Higher Education Act 1992 (Commencement No 1 and Transitional Provisions) Order 1992, SI 1992/831 .... 10.30
  Sch 3 .... 10.45
Further and Higher Education Act 1992 (Commencement No 1 and Transitional Provisions) (Amendment) Order 1992, SI 1992/2041 ...... 10.30
Further Education (Attribution of Surpluses and Deficits) Regulations 1993, SI 1993/609 .... 10.41

Table of statutory instruments

	PARA
Further Education (Exclusion of Land from Transfer) Order 1993, SI 1993/901	10.29
Further Education (Exclusion of Land from Transfer) (No 2) Order 1993, SI 1993/937	10.29
Further Education (Sponsoring Bodies) Order 1992, SI 1992/2400	10.13
Grants for Welsh Language Education Regulations 1980, SI 1980/1011	11.10
Independent Schools Tribunals Rules 1958, SI 1958/519	9.11
Inspection of Premises, Children and Records (Independent Schools) Regulations 1991, SI 1991/975	9.04
Local Government Changes for England (Education) (Miscellaneous Provisions) Regulations 1996, SI 1996/710	
Pt 2 (regs 3–8)	6.55
reg 8	6.40
Pt 3 (regs 9–16)	5.16
Pt 4 (regs 17, 18)	11.06, 11.11
Pt 5 (reg 19, 20)	11.17
Local Government Changes for England (Local Management of Schools) Regulations 1995, SI 1995/3114	3.73; 13.18
Local Government Changes for England (School Reorganisation and Admissions) Regulations 1995, SI 1995/2368	2.21; 3.08, 3.21
reg 3	5.37
4	7.17
5	7.15, 7.17
Local Government (Compensation for Premature Retirement) Regulations 1982, SI 1982/1009	13.74
Local Government (Compensation for Redundancy and Premature Retirement) Regulations 1984, SI 1984/740	13.74
Local Government Reorganisation (Compensation for Redundancy or Loss of Remuneration) (Education) Regulations 1996, SI 1996/1240	13.74
Local Government Reorganisation (Compensation) Regulations 1986, SI 1986/151	13.74
Local Government Superannuation Regulations 1986, SI 1986/24	13.74
North East London Education Association Order 1995, SI 1995/2037	8.37
Nursery Education Regulations 1996, SI 1996/2086	11.12
Nursery Education (Amendment) Regulations 1996, SI 1996/3117	11.12
Pensions Increase (Compensation to Staff of Teachers' Training Establishments) Regulations 1975, SI 1975/1478	13.74
Public Service Vehicles (Carrying Capacity) Regulations 1984, SI 1984/1406	12.25
Race Relations Code of Practice Order 1983, SI 1983/1081	13.55
Redundancy Payments (Exemption) Order 1980, SI 1980/1052	13.48
Redundancy Payments (Local Government) (Modification) Order 1983, SI 1983/1160	13.48
Redundancy Payments Pensions Regulations 1965, SI 1965/1932	13.49
Redundancy Payments Statutory Compensation Regulations 1965, SI 1965/1988	13.49
Religious Education (Meetings of Local Conferences and Councils) Regulations 1994, SI 1994/1304	6.32
Revenue Support Grant (Specified Bodies) Regulations 1992, SI 1992/89	11.01
Scholarships and Other Benefits Regulations 1977, SI 1977/1443	12.42
Sex Discrimination Code of Practice Order 1985, SI 1985/387	13.55
Special Educational Needs Tribunal Regulations 1995, SI 1995/3113	5.32
State Awards Regulations 1978, SI 1978/1096	10.109
State Awards (State Bursaries for Adult Education) (Wales) Regulations 1979, SI 1979/333	10.109
Teacher Training Agency (Additional Functions) Order 1995, SI 1995/601	13.09
Teachers' (Compensation) (Advanced Further Education) Regulations 1983, SI 1983/856	13.74
Teachers' (Compensation for Redundancy and Premature Retirement) Regulations 1989, SI 1989/298	13.74
Teachers (Compensation for Redundancy and Premature Retirement) Regulations 1997, SI 1997/311	13.75
Teachers' Superannuation (Consolidation) Regulations 1988, SI 1988/1652	13.73, 13.74
Teachers' Superannuation (Provision of Information and Administrative Expenses etc) Regulations 1996, SI 1996/2282	13.73
Teaching as a Career Unit (Transfer of Property, Rights and Liabilities Order 1994, SI 1994/2463	13.10
Transfer of Undertakings (Protection of Employment) Regulations 1981, SI 1981/1794	13.62

TABLE OF CASES

PARA

A

Abbott v Isham (1920) 18 LGR 719, 85 JP 30, 90 LJKB 309, 124 LT 734, 37 TLR 7: 14.22
Affutu-Nartoy v Clarke (1984) Times, 9 February 14.19
Agricultural, Horticultural and Forestry Industry Training Board v Aylesbury Mushrooms Ltd [1972] 1 All ER 280, [1972] 1 WLR 190, 7 ITR 16, 116 Sol Jo 57 .... 1.16
Ahmad v Inner London Education Authority [1978] QB 36, [1978] 1 All ER 574, [1977] 3 WLR 396, 75 LGR 753, [1977] ICR 490, 142 JP 167, 121 Sol Jo 676, CA 13.69
Alton Evans v Leicestershire Local Education Authority (19 August 1996, unreported): 5.34
Associated Provincial Picture Houses Ltd v Wednesbury Corpn [1948] 1 KB 223, [1947] 2 All ER 680, 45 LGR 635, 112 JP 55, [1948] LJR 190, 92 Sol Jo 26, 177 LT 641, 63 TLR 623, CA 12.06
A-G v Ross [1985] 3 All ER 334, [1986] 1 WLR 252, 130 Sol Jo 184, [1985] LS Gaz R 869 .... 10.102

B

B (infants), Re [1962] Ch 201, [1961] 3 WLR 694, 59 LGR 475, 105 Sol Jo 682, sub nom Re Baker (infants) [1961] 3 All ER 276, 125 JP 591, CA 7.50
B v Isle of Wight Council (30 October 1996, unreported) 5.20
Baker v Earl (1960) Times, 6 February 2.10
Baraclough v Bellamy (1928) Times, 18 July 14.25
Barnes (an infant) v Hampshire County Council [1969] 3 All ER 746, [1969] 1 WLR 1563, 67 LGR 605, 133 JP 733, 113 Sol Jo 834, HL 14.19
Beard v Governors of St Joseph's School [1978] ICR 1234, [1979] IRLR 144, 77 LGR 278 .... 13.44
Beaumont v Surrey County Council (1968) 66 LGR 580, 112 Sol Jo 704 .... 14.19
Bell v Graham [1907] 2 KB 112, 5 LGR 738, 71 JP 270, 76 LJKB 690, 21 Cox CC 461, 97 LT 53, 23 TLR 435, DC 7.47
Belling, Re, Enfield London Borough Council v Public Trustee [1967] Ch 425, [1967] 1 All ER 105, [1967] 2 WLR 382, 110 Sol Jo 872 .... 2.24
Bevan v Shears [1911] 2 KB 936, 9 LGR 1066, 75 JP 478, 80 LJKB 1325, 105 LT 795, 27 TLR 516, DC 2.10, 9.09
Birmingham City Council v Birmingham College of Food and Sutton Coldfield College [1996] ELR 1 .... 10.41, 11.02
Biggs v Somerset County Council [1995] ICR 811, [1995] IRLR 452, EAT; affd [1996] 2 All ER 734, [1996] 2 CMLR 292, [1996] ICR 364, [1996] IRLR 203, 140 Sol Jo LB 59, [1996] NLJR 174, [1996] 06 LS Gaz R 27, CA 13.44
Birmingham City Council v Elson (1979) 77 LGR 743, EAT 13.44
Birmingham City Council v Equal Opportunities Commission [1989] AC 1155, sub nom R v Birmingham City Council, ex p Equal Opportunities Commission [1988] 3 WLR 837, 86 LGR 741, [1988] IRLR 430, 132 Sol Jo 993, CA; affd sub nom Birmingham City Council v Equal Opportunities Commission [1989] AC 1155, [1989] 2 WLR 520, 87 LGR 557, [1989] IRLR 173, 133 Sol Jo 322, [1989] 15 LS Gaz R 36, [1989] NLJR 292, sub nom Equal Opportunities Commission v Birmingham City Council [1989] 1 All ER 769, HL 2.28, 14.04, 14.06

Table of cases

	PARA
Black v Kent County Council (1983) 82 LGR 39, CA	14.17
Blanchard v Dunlop [1917] 1 Ch 165, 85 LJ Ch 791, 81 JP 9, 15 LGR 25, 115 LT 467, CA	13.20
Bleis v Ministère de l'Education Nationale: C–4/91 [1991] ECR I–5627, [1994] 1 CMLR 793, ECJ	13.16
Blencowe v Northamptonshire County Council [1907] 1 Ch 504, 5 LGR 551, 71 JP 258, 76 LJ Ch 276, 51 Sol Jo 277, 96 LT 385, 23 TLR 319	12.03
Board of Education v Rice [1911] AC 179, 9 LGR 652, 75 JP 393, 80 LJKB 796, [1911-13] All ER Rep 36, 55 Sol Jo 440, 104 LT 689, 27 TLR 378, HL	12.03, 12.09
Borders Regional Council v Maule [1993] IRLR 199, EAT	13.37
Bostock v Kay (1989) 87 LGR 583, 153 JP 549, CA	3.63
Bowen v Hodgson (1923) 21 LGR 778, 87 JP 186, 93 LJKB 76, 27 Cox CC 551, 68 Sol Jo 187, 130 LT 207, 40 TLR 34, DC	7.47
Bradbury v London Borough of Enfield [1967] 3 All ER 434, [1967] 1 WLR 1311, 66 LGR 115, 132 JP 15, 111 Sol Jo 701, CA	15.04
Bradford City Metropolitan Council v Arora [1991] 2 QB 507, [1991] 3 All ER 545, [1991] 2 WLR 1377, [1991] ICR 226, [1991] IRLR 165, CA	13.51
Bradford Metropolitan Borough Council v A (8 May 1996, unreported)	5.20
Brent and Harrow Health Authority, ex p Harrow London Borough Council (8 October 1996, unreported)	5.15
Bridgen v Lancashire County Council [1987] IRLR 58, CA	13.42
Bridgman v Stockdale [1953] 1 All ER 1166, [1953] 1 WLR 704, 97 Sol Jo 353	14.25
Brown v Knowsley Borough Council [1986] IRLR 102, EAT	13.42, 13.46
Brown v Nelson (1970) 69 LGR 20	14.22
Brunyate v Inner London Education Authority [1989] 2 All ER 417, 87 LGR 725, 133 Sol Jo 749, [1989] 1 Admin LR 65, sub nom Inner London Education Authority v Brunyate [1989] 1 WLR 542, sub nom R v Inner London Education Authority, ex p Brunyate [1989] COD 435, HL	1.17, 3.62
Bullock v Alice Ottley School [1993] ICR 138, [1992] IRLR 564, 91 LGR 32, CA	14.04
Bunt v Kent [1914] 1 KB 207, 12 LGR 34, 78 JP 39, 83 LJKB 343, 23 Cox CC 751, 110 LT 72, 30 TLR 77, DC	7.47
Butt v Cambridgeshire and Isle of Ely County Council (1969) 68 LGR 81, CA	14.19
Butt v Inner London Education Authority (1968) 66 LGR 379, 118 NLJ 254, CA	14.19
Byrd v Secretary of State for Education and Science (1968) 112 Sol Jo 519, DC	9.12

C

C (a minor), Re [1994] ELR 273, CA	7.47
Cahill v West Ham Corpn (1937) 81 Sol Jo 630	14.19
Camden London Borough (Mayor and Burgesses) v Hadin and White [1996] ELR 430:	5.34
Camkin v Bishop [1941] 2 All ER 713, 165 LT 246, CA	14.17
Campbell and Cosans v United Kingdom (1982) 4 EHRR 293	15.15
Carmarthenshire County Council v Lewis [1955] AC 549, [1955] 1 All ER 565, [1955] 2 WLR 517, 53 LGR 230, 119 JP 230, 99 Sol Jo 167, HL	14.19
Champion v Chief Constable of the Gwent Constabulary [1990] 1 All ER 116, [1990] 1 WLR 1, 88 LGR 297, 134 Sol Jo 142, [1990] 2 LS Gaz R 36, HL	13.20
Charters-Ancaster College v Girls Public Day School Trust (1872) [1996] ELR 123	9.01
Cheshire County Council v C [1996] 2 FCR 365, [1995] 2 FLR 862, [1996] Fam Law 72	5.20
Chief Adjudication Officer and Secretary of State for Social Security v Clarke [1995] ELR 259, CA	10.106
Chilvers v LCC (1916) 80 JP 246, 32 TLR 363	14.19
Ching v Surrey County Council [1910] 1 KB 736, 8 LGR 369, 74 JP 187, 79 LJKB 481, 54 Sol Jo 360, 102 LT 414, 26 TLR 355, CA	14.22
Church Education Corpn v McCoig and McCoig (8 December 1995, unreported)	9.01
Clark v Monmouthshire County Council (1954) 52 LGR 246, 118 JP 244, CA	14.19
Cleary v Booth [1893] 1 QB 465, 57 JP 375, 62 LJMC 87, 17 Cox CC 611, 5 R 263, 41 WR 391, 37 Sol Jo 270, 68 LT 349, 9 TLR 260, DC	15.15
Cohen v London Borough of Barking [1976] IRLR 416, 12 ITR 73	13.44
Cole v Birmingham City District Council (1978) 77 LGR 285, [1978] ICR 1004, [1978] IRLR 394, 13 ITR 505	13.48
Coney v Choyce [1975] 1 All ER 979, [1975] 1 WLR 422, 119 Sol Jo 202	3.08

Table of cases

PARA

Conrad v Inner London Education Authority (1967) 65 LGR 543, 111 Sol Jo 684, CA 14.19
Cooke v Birmingham City Council (14 November 1996, unreported), CA 13.74
Corner v Buckinghamshire County Council (1978) 77 LGR 268, [1978] ICR 836, [1978] IRLR 320, 13 ITR 421, EAT 13.37
Costello-Roberts v United Kingdom (1993) 19 EHRR 112, [1994] 1 FCR 65, [1994] ELR 1, ECtHR 15.15
Coult v Szuba [1982] RTR 376, [1982] ICR 380, DC 13.39
Council of Civil Service Unions v Minister for the Civil Service [1985] AC 374, [1984] 3 All ER 935, [1984] 3 WLR 1174, [1985] ICR 14, 128 Sol Jo 837, [1985] LS Gaz R 437, sub nom R v Secretary of State for Foreign and Commonwealth Affairs, ex p Council of Civil Service Unions [1985] IRLR 28, HL 15.42
Crisp v Thomas (1890) 55 JP 261, 63 LT 756, CA 14.19
Crouch v Essex County Council (1966) 64 LGR 240 .... 14.19
Crump v Gilmore (1969) 68 LGR 56, [1970] Crim LR 28, 113 Sol Jo 998 .... 7.47
Cumings v Birkenhead Corpn [1972] Ch 12, [1970] 3 All ER 302, [1970] 3 WLR 871, 69 LGR 47, 134 JP 636, 114 Sol Jo 786; on appeal [1972] Ch 12, [1971] 2 All ER 881, [1971] 2 WLR 1458, 69 LGR 444, 135 JP 422, 115 Sol Jo 365, CA 1.23, 2.16, 2.28, 12.05, 15.43

D

D (a minor), Re [1987] 3 All ER 717, [1987] 1 WLR 1400, 86 LGR 442, [1988] 1 FLR 131, [1988] Fam Law 89, 131 Sol Jo 1485, [1987] LS Gaz R 3415, CA: 5.16, 5.20, 7.50
Darling and Jones v Minister of Education (1962) Times, 7 April 2.16
Debrell, Sevket and Teh v London Borough of Bromley (12 November 1984, unreported): 14.04
Devon County Council v George [1989] AC 573, [1988] 3 WLR 1386, 87 LGR 413, [1989] 1 FLR 146, [1989] Fam Law 149, 153 JP 375, [1989] 4 LS Gaz R 41, sub nom George v Devon County Council [1988] 3 All ER 1002, HL 7.47
Duncan v Bedfordshire County Council (1996) unreported 5.34
Dunton v Dover District Council (1977) 76 LGR 87 .... 14.24

E

E (a minor) v Dorset County Council [1994] 4 All ER 640, [1994] 3 WLR 853, [1995] 1 FCR 1, [1994] ELR 416, CA; varied [1995] 2 AC 633, [1995] 3 All ER 353, [1995] 3 WLR 152, 160 LG Rev 103, [1995] 3 FCR 337, [1995] 2 FLR 276, [1995] Fam Law 537, [1995] ELR 404, 26 BMLR 15, HL 5.14, 14.16
Ellis v Sayers Confectioners Ltd (1963) 61 LGR 299, 107 Sol Jo 252, CA 14.17
Enfield London Borough Council v F and F (1986) 85 LGR 526, [1987] 2 FLR 126, [1987] Fam Law 163, sub nom Enfield London Borough Council v Forsyth and Forsyth 151 JP 113 .... 7.40
Equal Opportunities Commission v Birmingham City Council. See Birmingham City Council v Equal Opportunities Commission
Essex County Council v B [1993] 1 FCR 145, [1993] 1 FLR 866, [1993] Fam Law 457 .... 7.50, 7.51
Essex County Council v Rogers [1987] AC 66, [1986] 3 WLR 689, 151 JP 32, sub nom Rogers v Essex County Council [1986] 3 All ER 321, 85 LGR 15, [1987] 1 FLR 411, [1987] Fam Law 155, 130 Sol Jo 785, [1986] LS Gaz R 3508, [1986] NLJ Rep 1013, HL 7.47

F

F, Re [1990] 2 AC 1, [1989] 2 WLR 1025, [1989] 2 FLR 376, [1989] Fam Law 390, 133 Sol Jo 785, [1989] NLJR 789, sub nom F v West Berkshire Health Authority (Mental Health Act Commission intervening) [1989] 2 All ER 545, 4 BMLR 1, HL 15.15
Fairpo v Humberside Council [1997] 1 All ER 183, [1997] 1 FLR 339, [1997] ELR 12: 5.21
Fay v North Yorkshire County Council (1986) 85 LGR 87, [1986] ICR 133, sub nom North Yorkshire County Council v Fay [1985] IRLR 247, CA 13.44, 13.46
Ford v Warwickshire County Council [1983] 2 AC 71, [1983] 1 All ER 753, [1983] 2 WLR 399, 81 LGR 326, [1983] ICR 273, [1983] IRLR 126, 127 Sol Jo 154, HL 13.41, 13.42
Fowles v Bedfordshire County Council [1996] ELR 51, CA 14.19

Table of cases

PARA

Fox v Burgess [1922] 1 KB 623, 20 LGR 277, 86 JP 66, 91 LJKB 465, 27 Cox CC 162, [1922] All ER Rep 754, 66 Sol Jo 335, 126 LT 525, 38 TLR 289 . . . . 7.47, 12.49
Fryer v Salford Corpn [1937] 1 All ER 617, 35 LGR 257, 101 JP 263, 81 Sol Jo 177, CA 14.22

G

Gardiner v Newport County Borough Council [1974] IRLR 262 . . . . 13.44
Gardner v Bygrave (1889) 53 JP 743, 6 TLR 23, DC 15.15
Gedge v Independent Schools Tribunal (1959) Times, 7 October 9.12
General of the Salvation Army v Dewsbury [1984] ICR 498, [1984] IRLR 222, EAT . . 13.41
George v Devon County Council. See Devon County Council v George
Gibbs v Barking Corpn [1936] 1 All ER 115, CA 14.17
Gilham v Kent County Council (No 2) [1985] ICR 233, sub nom Kent County Council v Gilham [1985] IRLR 18, CA 13.44
Gilham v Kent County Council (No 3) [1986] ICR 52, [1986] IRLR 56, EAT 13.44
Gillmore v LCC [1938] 4 All ER 331, 37 LGR 40, 103 JP 1, 82 Sol Jo 932, 159 LT 615, 55 TLR 95 . . . . 14.19
Gillow v Durham County Council [1913] AC 54, 11 LGR 1, 77 JP 105, 82 LJKB 206, 57 Sol Jo 76, 107 LT 689, 29 TLR 76, HL 6.01
Gloucestershire County Council v Spencer [1985] ICR 223, [1985] IRLR 59, EAT; revsd sub nom Spencer and Griffin v Gloucestershire County Council [1985] IRLR 393, CA 13.49
Gorse v Durham County Council [1971] 2 All ER 666, [1971] 1 WLR 775, 135 JP 389, 115 Sol Jo 303, 69 LGR 452 . . . . 13.20
Goslett v Garment (1897) 13 TLR 391 . . . . 14.25
Griffiths v Smith [1941] AC 170, [1941] 1 All ER 66, 39 LGR 1, 105 JP 63, 110 LJKB 156, 85 Sol Jo 176, 164 LT 386, 57 TLR 185, HL 3.99
Guardian of the Poor of Gateshead Union v Durham County Council [1918] 1 Ch 146, 16 LGR 33, 82 JP 53, 87 LJ Ch 113, 62 Sol Jo 86, 117 LT 796, 34 TLR 65, CA 2.28, 3.104
Gunton v Richmond-upon-Thames London Borough Council [1981] Ch 448, [1980] 3 All ER 577, [1980] 3 WLR 714, 79 LGR 241, [1980] ICR 755, [1980] IRLR 321, 124 Sol Jo 792, CA 13.20

H

HTV Ltd v Price Commission [1976] ICR 170, 120 Sol Jo 298, CA 15.42
Haddow v Inner London Education Authority [1979] ICR 202, EAT 13.44
Hampson v Department of Education and Science [1991] 1 AC 171, [1990] 2 All ER 513, [1990] 3 WLR 42, [1990] ICR 511, [1990] IRLR 302, 134 Sol Jo 1123, [1990] 26 LS Gaz R 39, [1990] NLJR 853, HL 13.16, 14.08
Hampstead Garden Suburb Institute, Re (1995) Times, 13 April 3.128
Hannam v Bradford City Council [1970] 2 All ER 690, [1970] 1 WLR 937, 68 LGR 498, 134 JP 588, 114 Sol Jo 414, CA 13.28
Happe v Lay (1977) 76 LGR 313, 8 Fam Law 54 . . . . 7.47
Hardwick v Daily Express (1972) Times (news item), 22 December 14.25
Hares v Curtin [1913] 2 KB 328, 10 LGR 753, 76 JP 313, 82 LJKB 707, 23 Cox CC 411, 108 LT 974 . . . . 7.47
Haringey London Borough Council v Special Educational Needs Tribunal (10 September 1996, unreported) 5.34
Harries v Crawfurd [1918] 2 Ch 158, 16 LGR 663, 87 LJ Ch 465, 62 Sol Jo 621, 119 LT 200, 34 TLR 448, CA; affd [1919] AC 717, 17 LGR 509, 83 JP 197, 88 LJ Ch 477, 63 Sol Jo 589, 121 LT 398, 35 TLR 543, HL 6.48
Harrison v Stevenson (1981) unreported 2.10
Harvey v Strathclyde Regional Council 1989 SLT 612, HL 1.23, 2.16, 3.126
Henthorn and Taylor v Central Electricity Generating Board [1980] IRLR 361, CA . . . 13.65
Hereford and Worcester County Council v National Association of Schoolmasters and Union of Women Teachers (1988) Times, 26 March, (1988) Independent, 1 March 13.65
Herring v Templeman [1973] 2 All ER 581, 71 LGR 295, 137 JP 514, 117 Sol Jo 223; affd [1973] 3 All ER 569, 72 LGR 162, 117 Sol Jo 793, CA 10.54, 12.05

Table of cases

PARA

Hinchley v Rankin [1961] 1 All ER 692, [1961] 1 WLR 421, 59 LGR 190, 125 JP 293,
   105 Sol Jo 158, DC 2.10, 7.47, 15.36
Holtom v Barnet London Borough Council (1993) Times, 30 September 2.10, 5.14
Hume v Marshall (1877) 42 JP 136, 37 LT 711 .... 14.25
Huth v Clarke (1890) 25 QBD 391, 55 JP 86, 59 LJMC 120, 59 LJQB 559, 38 WR 655,
   [1886–90] All ER Rep 542, 63 LT 348, 6 TLR 373 .... 2.22

I

Inner London Education Authority v Lloyd [1981] IRLR 394, CA 13.44
Ishak v Thowfeek [1968] 1 WLR 1718, 112 Sol Jo 802, PC 1.23
Islwyn Borough Council v Newport Borough Council [1994] ELR 141, CA 3.97

J

Jackson v Helsey Group (Case No 40121/95) 1996 Industrial Tribunal 13.51
Jackson v LCC and Chappell (1912) 10 LGR 348, 76 JP 217, 56 Sol Jo 428, 8 TLR 359,
   CA 14.19
Jacques v Oxfordshire County Council (1967) 66 LGR 440 .... 12.24, 14.19
Jarman v Mid-Glamorgan Education Authority (1985) Times, 11 February 7.47
Jefferey v LCC (1954) 52 LGR 521, 119 JP 45 .... 14.19
Jenkins v Howells [1949] 2 KB 218, [1949] 1 All ER 942, 47 LGR 394, 113 JP 292,
   [1949] LJR 1468, 93 Sol Jo 302, 65 TLR 305, DC 7.47
Jones v Dorset County Council (25 January 1996, unreported) 5.20
Jones v Jones [1916] 2 AC 481, 85 LJKB 1519, [1916-17] All ER Rep 1348, 61 Sol Jo
   8, 115 LT 432, 32 TLR 705, HL 14.25
Jones v Lee and Guilding (1980) 78 LGR 213, [1980] ICR 310, [1980] IRLR 67, 123 Sol
   Jo 785, CA 13.30
Jones v LCC (1932) 30 LGR 455, 96 JP 371, 48 TLR 577, CA 14.19
Joyce v Dorset County Council [1997] ELR 26 .... 5.34
Julius v Lord Bishop of Oxford (1880) 5 App Cas 214, 44 JP 600, 49 LJQB 577, 28 WR
   726, [1874-80] All ER Rep 43, 42 LT 546, HL 1.22

K

Kenny v South Manchester College [1993] ICR 934, [1993] IRLR 265 .... 10.30
Kent County Council v Gilham [1985] ICR 227, sub nom Gilham v Kent County
   Council [1985] IRLR 16, CA 13.41
King v Ford (1816) 1 Stark 421 .... 14.19
Kingsbury v Northamptonshire Education Department [1994] COD 114, CA 14.06
Knight v Dorset County Council (1996) unreported 5.16

L

L, Re [1994] ELR 16, CA 5.21
Langham v Wellingborough School Governors and Fryer (1932) 30 LGR 276, 96 JP 236,
   101 LJKB 513, 147 LT 91, CA 14.19
Lee v Nottinghamshire County Council. See Nottinghamshire County Council v Lee
Lee v Secretary of State fo. Education and Science (1967) 66 LGR 211, 111 Sol Jo 756: 1.16
Leeds City Council v Pomfret [1983] ICR 674 .... 13.74
Legg v Inner London Education Authority [1972] 3 All ER 177, [1972] 1 WLR 1245, 71
   LGR 58, 116 Sol Jo 680 .... 3.08, 3.15
Lewis v Dyfed County Council (1978) 77 LGR 339, 123 Sol Jo 15, CA 13.63
LCC v Hearn (1909) 78 LJKB 414 .... 7.47
LCC v Stansell (1935) 154 LT 241 .... 12.49
London Hospital Medical College v IRC [1976] 2 All ER 113, [1976] 1 WLR 613,
   [1976] TR 29, 120 Sol Jo 250 .... 10.102
Lyes v Middlesex County Council (1962) 61 LGR 443 .... 14.22

M

M (judicial review: education), ex p (1994) Times, 22 March 7.03
M (a minor), Re [1996] ELR 135, CA 5.21

xli

Table of cases

PARA

M'Alister (or Donoghue) v Stevenson [1932] AC 562, 101 LJPC 119, 37 Com Cas 350, 48 TLR 494, 1932 SC (HL) 31, sub nom Donoghue (or McAlister) v Stevenson [1932] All ER Rep 1, 1932 SLT 317, sub nom McAlister (or Donoghue) v Stevenson 76 Sol Jo 396, 147 LT 281 .... 14.16
M'Carogher v Franks (1964) Times, 25 November 14.25
McGoldrick v Brent London Borough [1987] IRLR 67, CA 13.20
MacMahon v Department of Education and Science [1983] Ch 227, [1982] 3 WLR 1129, [1982] 3 CMLR 91, 81 LGR 146, [1983] ICR 67, 126 Sol Jo 657 .... 10.107
Malloch v Aberdeen Corpn [1971] 2 All ER 1278, [1971] 1 WLR 1578, 115 Sol Jo 756, 1971 SC (HL) 85, 1971 SLT 245, HL 13.20
Manchester City Council v Greater Manchester Metropolitan County Council (1980) 78 LGR 560, HL 9.02
Mandla v Dowell Lee [1983] 2 AC 548, [1983] 1 All ER 1062, [1983] 2 WLR 620, [1983] ICR 385, [1983] IRLR 209, 127 Sol Jo 242, HL 14.08
Mansell v Griffin [1908] 1 KB 947, 6 LGR 548, 72 JP 179, 77 LJKB 676, 52 Sol Jo 376, 99 LT 132, 24 TLR 431, CA 15.14, 15.15
Margerison v Hind & Co Ltd [1922] 1 KB 214 .... 15.31
Marshall v Graham [1907] 2 KB 112, 5 LGR 738, 71 JP 270, 76 LJKB 690, 21 Cox CC 461, 97 LT 53, 23 TLR 435, DC 6.52, 7.47
Martin v Middlesbrough Corpn (1965) 63 LGR 385, 109 Sol Jo 576, CA 14.19
Matheson v Northcote College Board of Governors [1975] 2 NZLR 106 .... 14.24
Mays v Essex County Council (1975) Times, 11 October 14.19
Meade v London Borough of Haringey [1979] 2 All ER 1016, [1979] 1 WLR 637, 77 LGR 577, [1979] ICR 494, 123 Sol Jo 216, CA 2.28, 12.09, 15.43
Merton London Borough Council v Gardiner [1981] QB 269, [1981] 2 WLR 232, 79 LGR 374, [1981] ICR 186, [1980] IRLR 302; affd [1981] QB 269, [1981] 2 WLR 232, 79 LGR 374, [1981] ICR 186, sub nom Gardiner v London Borough of Merton [1980] IRLR 472, 125 Sol Jo 97, CA 13.41
Milligan v Securicor Cleaning Ltd [1995] ICR 867, [1995] IRLR 288, EAT 13.42
Milne v Bauchope 1867 SC 1114 .... 14.25
Milne v Wandsworth London Borough Council (1992) 90 LGR 515, [1994] ELR 28, CA 3.12
Moore v Hampshire County Council (1981) 80 LGR 481, CA 14.17
Morris v Carnarvon County Council [1910] 1 KB 840, 8 LGR 485, 74 JP 201, 79 LJKB 670, 54 Sol Jo 443, 102 LT 524, 26 TLR 391, CA 14.22
Myton v Wood (1980) 79 LGR 28, CA 12.24

N

National Association of Teachers in Further and Higher Education v Manchester City Council [1978] ICR 1190, EAT 13.47
National Union of Teachers v Avon County Council (1978) 76 LGR 403, [1978] ICR 626, [1978] IRLR 55, EAT 13.47
National Union of Teachers v St Mary's Church of England (Aided) Junior School (Governing Body) [1995] 3 CMLR 638, [1995] ICR 317, EAT; revsd [1997] ICR 334, [1997] IRLR 242, CA 13.28, 13.44
National Union of Teachers v Solihull Metropolitan Borough Council unreported 13.46
Neale v Hereford and Worcester County Council [1986] ICR 471, sub nom Hereford and Worcester County Council v Neale [1986] IRLR 168, CA 13.44
Nichol v Gateshead Metropolitan Borough Council (1988) 87 LGR 435, CA 1.16, 3.13
Noble v Inner London Education Authority (1983) 82 LGR 291, CA 3.63, 13.20
Norfolk County Council v Bernard [1979] IRLR 220 .... 13.44
North Yorkshire County Council v Fay. See Fay v North Yorkshire County Council
Norwich City Council v Secretary of State for the Environment [1982] 1 All ER 737, 2 HLR 1 .... 12.06
Nothman v Barnet London Borough [1978] 1 All ER 1243, [1978] 1 WLR 220, 76 LGR 617, [1978] ICR 336, [1978] IRLR 489, 13 ITR 125, 121 Sol Jo 813, CA; affd [1979] 1 All ER 142, [1979] 1 WLR 67, 77 LGR 89, [1979] ICR 111, [1979] IRLR 35, 123 Sol Jo 64, HL 13.42
Nottinghamshire County Council v Bowly [1978] IRLR 252 .... 13.44
Nottinghamshire County Council v Lee (1980) 78 LGR 568, [1980] ICR 635, sub nom Lee v Nottinghamshire County Council [1980] IRLR 284, CA 13.46

Table of cases

PARA

Nwabudike (a minor) v Southwark London Borough [1997] ELR 35, 140 Sol Jo LB 128: 14.19

O

O'Neill v Governors of St Thomas More Roman Catholic Voluntary Aided Upper School
 [1997] ICR 33, [1996] IRLR 372, EAT 14.04
Orphanos v Queen Mary College [1985] AC 761, [1985] 2 All ER 233, [1985] 2 WLR
 703, [1986] 2 CMLR 73, [1985] IRLR 349, 129 Sol Jo 284, [1985] LS Gaz R 1787,
 HL 14.08
Osborne v Martin (1927) 25 LGR 532, 91 JP 197, 28 Cox CC 465, 138 LT 268, 44 TLR
 38, DC 2.10

P

P v Harrow London Borough Council [1993] 2 FCR 341, [1993] 1 FLR 723, [1993] Fam
 Law 21, [1992] PIQR P 296 .... 5.07, 5.49
Palmer v Harrow London Borough Council [1992] PIQR P 296 .... 14.20
Pearce v University of Aston in Birmingham [1991] 2 All ER 461, CA 10.84
Pearse v City of Bradford Metropolitan Council [1988] IRLR 379, EAT 13.50, 14.04
Pearson v Kent County Council (1979) 77 LGR 604 .... 13.74
Pendlebury v Christian Schools North West Ltd [1985] ICR 174, EAT 13.44
Pepper (Inspector of Taxes) v Hart [1993] AC 593, [1993] 1 All ER 42, [1992] 3 WLR
 1032, [1992] STC 898, 65 TC 421, [1993] ICR 291, [1993] IRLR 33, [1993]
 NLJR 17, [1993] RVR 127, HL 1.35
Perry v King [1961] CLY 5865, CA 14.19
Pfaffinger v City of Liverpool Community College [1997] ICR 142, [1996] IRLR 508,
 EAT 13.41
Phillips v Brown (20 June 1980, unreported), DC 7.40
Phillips v Derbyshire County Council (9 October 1996, unreported) 5.34
Pickstone v Freemans plc [1989] AC 66, [1988] 2 All ER 803, [1988] 3 WLR 265,
 [1988] ICR 697, [1988] IRLR 357, 132 Sol Jo 994, [1988] NLJR 193, HL 1.35
Pickwell v Lincolnshire County Council (1993) 91 LGR 509, [1993] ICR 87, [1992] 41
 LS Gaz R 36, EAT 13.47
Plunkett v Alker [1954] 1 QB 420, [1954] 1 All ER 396, [1954] 2 WLR 280, 52 LGR
 156, 118 JP 156, 98 Sol Jo 113, DC 12.49
Poplar and Blackwall Free School, Re (1878) 8 Ch D 543, 42 JP 678, 26 WR 827, 39
 LT 88 .... 2.32
Porcelli v Strathclyde Regional Council [1985] ICR 177, [1984] IRLR 467, EAT; affd
 [1986] ICR 564, sub nom Strathclyde Regional Council v Porcelli [1986] IRLR 134,
 Ct of Sess 13.51
Port Louis Corpn v A-G of Mauritius [1965] AC 1111, [1965] 3 WLR 67, 109 Sol
 Jo 413, PC 1.16
Powell v Lee (1908) 6 LGR 840, 72 JP 353, 99 LT 284, 24 TLR 606, DC 13.30
Price v Wilkins (1888) 58 LT 680, 4 TLR 231 .... 15.14

R

R v Appeal Committee of Brighouse School, ex p G and B [1997] ELR 39 .... 7.21
R v Barnet London Borough Council, ex p B [1994] 2 FCR 781, [1994] 1 FLR 592,
 [1994] ELR 357 .... 1.16, 12.38
R v Berkshire County Council, ex p Glenister (20 March 1986, unreported) 3.09
R v Bexley London Borough, ex p Jones [1995] ELR 42, [1994] COD 393 .... 10.108
R v Birmingham City Council, ex p Equal Opportunities Commission (No 2) (1992) 90
 LGR 492, [1992] 2 FCR 746, [1992] 2 FLR 133, [1992] Fam Law 433, [1994] ELR
 37, 136 Sol Jo LB 96; affd (1993) 91 LGR 15, [1993] Fam Law 338, [1994] ELR
 282, CA 2.27, 14.04, 14.06
R v Birmingham City Council, ex p Kaur (1990) Times, 11 July 1.17
R v Birmingham City Council, ex p McKenna (1991) Times, 16 May 3.93, 13.20
R v Birmingham City Council, ex p National Union of Public Employees (1984) Times,
 24 April 2.22, 13.36, 13.44
R v Board of Governors of Stoke Newington School, ex p M [1994] ELR 131 ... 3.117, 15.42
R v Bradford Metropolitan Borough Council, ex p Ali [1994] ELR 299, [1993] 40 LS
 Gaz R 42, 137 Sol Jo LB 232 .... 7.09
R v Bradford Metropolitan District Council, ex p Parkinson (1996) Times, 31 October: 10.87

xliii

Table of cases

	PARA
R v Brent London Borough Council, ex p Assegai (1987) 151 LG Rev 891, DC	3.62
R v Brent London Borough Council, ex p Gunning (1985) 84 LGR 168	1.16
R v Bromley London Borough Council, ex p C [1992] 1 FLR 174, [1992] Fam Law 192, 135 Sol Jo LB 59	7.09
R v Buckinghamshire County Council, ex p Milton Keynes Borough Council (1996) Times, 13 November	3.08
R v Camden London Borough and Hampstead School Governors, ex p H [1996] ELR 360, CA	3.117
R v Carr-Briant [1943] KB 607, [1943] 2 All ER 156, 41 LGR 183, 29 Cr App Rep 76, 107 JP 167, 112 LJKB 581, 169 LT 175, 59 TLR 300, CCA	15.35
R v Cheshire County Council, ex p Cherrih (11 July 1996, unreported)	5.34
R v Cheshire County Council, ex p Halton College (30 July, 1996, unreported)	10.87
R v Cleveland County Council, ex p Commission for Racial Equality (1993) 91 LGR 139, [1993] 1 FCR 597, [1994] ELR 44, CA	7.06, 14.09
R v Comr for Local Administration, ex p Croydon London Borough Council [1989] 1 All ER 1033, sub nom R v Local Ombudsman, ex p London Borough of Croydon [1989] Fam Law 187, [1989] COD 226	7.07, 7.20, 15.40
R v Coventry City Council, ex p Newborn (26 September 1985, unreported)	1.16
R v Croydon London Borough Council, ex p Leney (1986) 85 LGR 466	6.14, 8.37
R v Cumbria County Council, ex p NB [1995] 3 FCR 252, [1996] ELR 65	5.19, 5.21
R v Cumbria County Council, ex p P [1995] ELR 337	5.19
R v Department of Education and Science, ex p Dudley Metropolitan Borough Council (1992) 90 LGR 296, [1992] Fam Law 483, 135 Sol Jo LB 123	4.37, 11.15
R v Department of Education and Science, ex p Kumar (1982) Times, 23 November	15.42
R v Devon County Council, ex p Baker [1995] 1 All ER 73, 91 LGR 479, 11 BMLR 141, CA	1.16, 15.43
R v Dorset County Council, ex p Greenwood [1990] COD 235	7.08
R v Dorset County Council and Further Education Funding Council, ex p Goddard [1995] ELR 109	5.20
R v Dunbar [1958] 1 QB 1, [1957] 2 All ER 737, [1957] 3 WLR 330, 41 Cr App Rep 182, 121 JP 506, 101 Sol Jo 594, CCA	15.35
R v Dyfed County Council, ex p S (minors) [1995] 1 FCR 113, [1995] ELR 98, 138 Sol Jo LB 194, CA	7.47
R v East Sussex County Council, ex p D [1991] COD 374	7.47
R v East Sussex County Council, ex p National Union of Public Employees [1985] IRLR 258, CA	13.42
R v East Sussex County Council, ex p T (1997) Times, 29 April	1.36, 2.31
R v Education Appeal Committee of Leicestershire County Council, ex p Tarmohamed [1997] ELR 48, [1996] COD 286	7.20
R v Educational Services Committee of Bradford City Metropolitan Council, ex p Professional Association of Teachers (1986) Independent, 16 December	15.42
R v Essex County Council, ex p C (1993) 93 LGR 10, CA	7.47
R v Essex County Council, ex p Jacobs [1997] ELR 190	7.08
R v Essex County Council, ex p Ongar Parish Council (6 November 1986, unreported)	1.16
R v Fernhill Manor School, ex p A [1993] 1 FLR 620, [1993] Fam Law 202, [1994] ELR 67, [1992] COD 446	9.01
R v Funding Agency for Schools, ex p Bromley London Borough Council (15 February 1996, unreported)	4.23
R v Further Education Funding Council, ex p Parkinson [1997] 2 FCR 67	10.09
R v Gloucestershire County Council, ex p Barry [1997] 2 All ER 1, [1997] 2 WLR 459, 141 Sol Jo LB 91, [1997] NLJR 453, HL	1.36
R v Gloucestershire County Council, ex p P [1994] ELR 334, [1993] COD 303	5.21
R v Governing Body of Irlam and Cadishead Community High School, ex p Salford City Council [1994] ELR 81	4.08
R v Governors of Astley High School, ex p Northumberland County Council [1994] COD 27	4.08
R v Governors of Bacon's School, ex p Inner London Education Authority [1990] COD 414, DC	3.63
R v Governors of La Sainte Union Convent School, ex p T [1996] ELR 98	7.09
R v Governors of Litherland High School, ex p Corkish (1982) Times, 4 December, CA	13.20

Table of cases

PARA

R v Governors of Pate's Grant Maintained Grammar School etc, ex p T [1994] COD 297 .... 7.21
R v Governors of St Gregory's Roman Catholic Aided High School, ex p Roberts (1995) Times, 27 January 3.109, 3.117
R v Governors of Small Heath School, ex p Birmingham City Council [1990] COD 23, CA 4.08, 12.03
R v Governors of the Bishop Challoner Roman Catholic Comprehensive Girls' School, ex p Choudhury [1992] 2 AC 182, [1992] 3 WLR 99, 90 LGR 445, [1992] 2 FCR 507, [1992] 2 FLR 444, [1993] Fam Law 23, [1992] 27 LS Gaz R 36, sub nom Choudhury v Governors of Bishop Challoner Roman Catholic Comprehensive School [1992] 3 All ER 277, HL 7.09
R v Governors of the Buss Foundation Camden School for Girls, ex p Lukasiewicz [1991] COD 98 .... 7.08
R v Governors of the London Oratory School, ex p Regis [1989] Fam Law 67 .. 3.117, 15.42
R v Greenwich London Borough Council, ex p Governors of John Ball Primary School (1990) 88 LGR 589, [1990] Fam Law 469, CA 7.08, 7.09
R v Gwent County Council, ex p Harris [1995] 1 FCR 551, [1995] 2 FLR 1021, [1995] ELR 27 .... 12.24
R v Gwent County Council, ex p Perry (1985) 129 Sol Jo 737, CA 2.10, 15.42
R v Gwent County Council and Secretary of State for Wales, ex p Bryant [1988] COD 19 .... 1.18, 3.126
R v Gwynned County Council, ex p W (1994) 158 LG Rev 201 .... 6.05
R v HM the Queen in Council, ex p Vijayatunga [1990] 2 QB 444, [1989] 3 WLR 13, 133 Sol Jo 818, [1989] 28 LS Gaz R 40, sub nom R v University of London Visitor, ex p Vijayatunga [1989] 2 All ER 843, CA 10.84
R v Haberdashers' Aske's Hatcham College Trust (Governors), ex p T [1995] ELR 350: 9.27
R v Hackney London Borough, ex p GC [1996] ELR 142, CA 5.20, 5.21, 12.40
R v Hackney London Borough, ex p T [1991] COD 454 .... 7.03, 7.08
R v Hampshire County Council, ex p Martin (1982) Times, 20 November 10.107
R v Hampshire County Council, ex p W [1994] ELR 460 .... 5.27
R v Hampshire Education Authority, ex p J (1985) 84 LGR 547 .... 5.06, 5.51, 12.40
R v Harrow Borough Council, ex p M [1997] ELR 62 .... 5.20
R v Hasmonean High School (Governors), ex p N and E [1994] ELR 343, CA 7.09
R v Headmaster of Fernhill Manor School, ex p Brown (1992) Times, 5 June 15.42
R v Hereford and Worcester County Council, ex p P [1992] 2 FCR 732, [1992] 2 FLR 207, [1992] Fam Law 431 .... 5.20, 12.24
R v Hereford and Worcester County Council, ex p Wimbourne (1983) 82 LGR 251 .. 10.107
R v Hertfordshire County Council, ex p Cheung (1986) Times, 4 April, CA 10.107
R v Hertfordshire County Council, ex p George (27 July 1988, unreported) 1.19
R v Hertfordshire County Council, ex p National Union of Public Employees [1985] IRLR 258, CA 13.44
R v Higher Education Funding Council, ex p Institute of Dental Surgery [1994] 1 All ER 651, [1994] 1 WLR 242 .... 10.61
R v Hillingdon London Borough Council, ex p Governing Body of Queensmead School (1997) Times, 9 January 5.17, 5.19
R v Hopley (1860) 2 F & F 202 .... 15.15
R v Hudson [1966] 1 QB 448, [1965] 1 All ER 721, [1965] 2 WLR 604, 49 Cr App Rep 69, 129 JP 193, [1965] Crim LR 172, 109 Sol Jo 49, CCA 15.35
R v Inner London Education Authority, ex p Ali [1990] COD 317, [1990] 2 Admin LR 822 .... 2.28
R v Inner London Education Authority, ex p F (1988) Times, 16 June: 5.21, 5.51, 12.40, 12.42
R v Inner London Education Authority, ex p Hinde [1985] 1 CMLR 716, 83 LGR 695: 10.107
R v Isle of Wight County Council, ex p AS [1994] 1 FCR 641, [1993] 1 FLR 634, CA : 5.21
R v Islington Borough Council, ex p Rixon [1997] ELR 66 .... 10.87
R v Kent County Council, ex p Parker (26 June 1986, unreported) 1.16
R v Kent County Council, ex p W (1995) 159 LG Rev 629, [1995] 2 FCR 342, [1995] ELR 362 .... 5.19, 5.20
R v Kingston upon Thames Royal London Borough, ex p Emsden (1994) 91 LGR 96, [1994] 1 FCR 212, [1993] 1 FLR 179, [1993] Fam Law 120 .... 7.09
R v Knight, ex p Khan [1989] COD 434 .... 4.07
R v Lambeth London Borough, ex p G [1994] ELR 207 .... 2.16, 7.09, 12.42

Table of cases

	PARA
R v Lambeth London Borough, ex p M (1995) 160 LG Rev 61	5.20
R v Lambeth London Borough, ex p N [1996] ELR 299	1.17, 5.39
R v Lancashire County Council, ex p Foster [1995] 1 FCR 212, [1995] ELR 33	7.09
R v Lancashire County Council, ex p Huddleston [1986] 2 All ER 941, [1986] NLJ Rep 562, CA	10.107
R v Lancashire County Council, ex p M [1989] 2 FLR 279; affd (1989) 87 LGR 567, [1989] 2 FLR 279, [1989] Fam Law 395, 133 Sol Jo 484, [1989] 17 LS Gaz R 37, CA	5.20
R v Lancashire County Council, ex p Maycock (1995) 159 LG Rev 201	7.20
R v Lancashire County Council, ex p West unreported	7.09
R v Leicestershire Education Authority, ex p C [1991] FCR 76, [1991] Fam Law 302, [1991] COD 120, DC	15.42
R v Liverpool City Council, ex p Ferguson (1985) Times, 20 November	2.28, 13.16
R v Liverpool City Council, ex p Professional Association of Teachers (1984) 82 LGR 648	2.22
R v Local Comr for Administration for the North and East Area of England, ex p Bradford Metropolitan City Council [1979] QB 287, [1979] 2 All ER 881, [1979] 2 WLR 1, 77 LGR 305, 122 Sol Jo 573, [1978] JPL 767, CA	15.40
R v Lord President of the Privy Council, ex p Page [1993] AC 682, [1992] 3 WLR 1112, [1993] ICR 114, [1993] 10 LS Gaz R 33, 137 Sol Jo LB 45, sub nom Page v Hull University Visitor [1993] 1 All ER 97, [1993] NLJR 15, HL	10.84
R v Manchester City Council, ex p Fulford (1982) 81 LGR 292	3.91
R v Manchester Metropolitan University, ex p Nolan [1994] ELR 380, DC	10.84
R v Merton London Borough, ex p Wiggins [1996] ELR 332, CA	5.07
R v Mid-Glamorgan County Council, ex p B [1995] ELR 168	5.21
R v Mid-Glamorgan County Council, ex p Greig (1988) Independent, 1 June	2.28, 5.09
R v Neale, ex p S [1995] ELR 198	3.108, 14.09
R v Newham London Borough Council, ex p D [1992] 1 FLR 395, [1992] Fam Law 190	5.16
R v Newham London Borough Council, ex p R [1994] COD 472	5.21
R v Newham London Borough Council, ex p X [1995] ELR 303	3.108
R v Newport (Salop) Justices, ex p Wright [1929] 2 KB 416, 27 LGR 518, 93 JP 179, 98 LJKB 555, 28 Cox CC 658, 73 Sol Jo 384, 141 LT 563, 45 TLR 477, DC	15.15
R v Norfolk County Council, ex p Coulten unreported	1.19
R v Northampton County Council, ex p Gray (1986) Times, 10 June	12.09
R v Northamptonshire County Council, ex p K [1994] ELR 397, CA	2.27, 13.126, 14.06
R v Northamptonshire County Council, ex p Tebbutt (26 June 1986, unreported)	1.18, 3.13
R v Nottinghamshire County Council, ex p Jain [1989] COD 442	10.107
R v Oxfordshire County Council, ex p B [1997] ELR 90, CA	5.20
R v Oxfordshire County Council, ex p P [1996] ELR 153	3.73, 3.75, 5.19
R v Oxfordshire County Council, ex p Roast [1996] ELR 381	5.21
R v Oxfordshire County Council, ex p W [1987] 2 FLR 193	2.19
R v Powys County Council, ex p Smith (1982) 81 LGR 342	12.05, 13.20
R v Redbridge London Borough Council, ex p East Sussex County Council (1992) 158 LGR 101, [1993] COD 256	10.107
R v Rochdale Metropolitan Council, ex p Schemet (1993) 91 LGR 425, [1993] 1 FCR 306, [1993] COD 113	2.16, 7.09, 7.47
R v Rotherham Metropolitan Borough Council, ex p Croft (29 April 1996, unreported)	10.106
R v Royal Borough of Kingston-upon-Thames, ex p Kingwell [1992] 1 FLR 182, [1992] Fam Law 193	7.09
R v Secretary of State for Education, ex p Banham [1992] Fam Law 435	15.41
R v Secretary of State for Education, ex p C [1996] ELR 93	5.06, 5.09
R v Secretary of State for Education, ex p E [1996] ELR 312	5.21
R v Secretary of State for Education, ex p G [1995] ELR 58	7.44
R v Secretary of State for Education, ex p London Borough of Southwark [1994] COD 298	4.09
R v Secretary of State for Education, ex p Prior [1994] ICR 877, [1994] ELR 231	13.32
R v Secretary of State for Education, ex p R and D [1994] ELR 495	6.53
R v Secretary of State for Education, ex p Ruscoe (26 February 1993, unreported)	6.53, 6.72
R v Secretary of State for Education, ex p S [1994] ELR 252; revsd [1995] 2 FCR 225, [1995] ELR 71, CA	5.14
R v Secretary of State for Education, ex p Skitt [1995] ELR 388	3.12

Table of cases

PARA

R v Secretary of State for Education, ex p Standish (1993) Times, 15 November ... 9.07, 13.16
R v Secretary of State for Education, ex p Warwickshire County Council (1996) unreported 4.09
R v Secretary of State for Education and Employment, ex p M [1996] ELR 162; affd [1996] ELR 162, CA 1.18, 12.06
R v Secretary of State for Education and Employment, ex p McCarthy (1996) Times, 24 July 5.49
R v Secretary of State for Education and Employment, ex p Morris (1995) Times, 15 December 8.43
R v Secretary of State for Education and Governing Body of Queen Elizabeth Grammar School, ex p Cumbria County Council [1994] ELR 220, [1994] COD 30 ...... 4.51, 7.21
R v Secretary of State for Education and Science, ex p Avon County Council (1990) 88 LGR 716 .... 2.28
R v Secretary of State for Education and Science, ex p Avon County Council (No 2) (1990) 88 LGR 737n, CA 3.11, 15.42
R v Secretary of State for Education and Science, ex p Birmingham City Council [1992] RVR 218, DC 4.37
R v Secretary of State for Education and Science, ex p Birmingham District Council (1984) 83 LGR 79 .... 3.126
R v Secretary of State for Education and Science, ex p Chance (26 July 1982, unreported) 12.05, 12.09
R v Secretary of State for Education and Science, ex p Davis [1989] 2 FLR 190, [1989] Fam Law 319 .... 5.21
R v Secretary of State for Education and Science, ex p E [1993] 2 FCR 753, [1992] 1 FLR 377, [1992] Fam Law 189, CA 5.20, 5.21
R v Secretary of State for Education and Science, ex p Gray (20 July 1988, unreported): 12.09
R v Secretary of State for Education and Science, ex p Hardy (1988) Times, 28 July, DC: 3.15
R v Secretary of State for Education and Science, ex p Inner London Education Authority (1990) Times, 17 May, CA 3.128
R v Secretary of State for Education and Science, ex p Islam [1994] ELR 111 .... 3.19
R v Secretary of State for Education and Science, ex p Keating (1985) 84 LGR 469 .... 14.04, 14.06
R v Secretary of State for Education and Science, ex p Lashford (1988) 86 LGR 13, [1988] 1 FLR 72, [1988] Fam Law 59, CA 5.16, 5.20, 5.27
R v Secretary of State for Education and Science, ex p London Borough of Lambeth (22 December 1992, unreported) 4.08
R v Secretary of State for Education and Science, ex p Malik [1994] ELR 121, [1992] COD 31 .... 3.126, 14.06
R v Secretary of State for Education and Science, ex p Newham London Borough Council [1991] COD 279 .... 4.09
R v Secretary of State for Education and Science, ex p Royal Institute of British Architects [1991] COD 281 .... 10.106
R v Secretary of State for Education and Science, ex p Talmud Torah Machzikei Hadass School Trust (1985) Times, 12 April 2.10, 9.09
R v Secretary of State for Education and Science, ex p Threapleton [1988] COD 102, (1988) Times, 2 June 3.13
R v Secretary of State for Social Services, ex p Association of Metropolitan Authorities [1986] 1 All ER 164, [1986] 1 WLR 1, 83 LGR 796, 130 Sol Jo 35 .... 1.16
R v Secretary of State for the Environment, ex p Ward [1984] 2 All ER 556, [1984] 1 WLR 834, 82 LGR 628, 48 P & CR 212, 128 Sol Jo 415, [1984] LS Gaz R 2148, [1984] JPL 90 .... 12.09
R v Secretary of State for Wales, ex p Gwent County Council [1995] ELR 87, CA 4.46
R v Secretary of State for Wales, ex p South Glamorgan County Council (1988) Times, 25 June 3.14
R v Secretary of State for Wales, ex p Williams [1997] ELR 100 .... 1.18, 5.37
R v Secretary of State for Wales and Clwyd County Council, ex p Russell (28 June 1983, unreported) 3.12, 15.42
R v Sefton Metropolitan Borough Council, ex p Help the Aged [1997] NLJR 490 .... 1.36
R v Sheffield City Council, ex p Parker [1994] 1 FCR 383, [1993] 2 FLR 907, [1993] Fam Law 677 .... 10.106
R v Sheffield Hallam University (Board of Governors), ex p R [1995] ELR 267 ...... 10.73

xlvii

Table of cases

	PARA
R v Shropshire County Council, ex p Jones (23 August 1996, unreported)	10.108
R v South Glamorgan Appeal Committee, ex p Evans (10 May 1984, unreported)	7.07, 7.20
R v Southwark London Borough, ex p Udu [1996] ELR 390, CA	10.108
R v Special Educational Needs Tribunal, ex p F [1996] ELR 213	5.21
R v Special Educational Needs Tribunal, ex p South Glamorgan County Council [1996] ELR 326, CA	5.34
R v Staffordshire County Council, ex p Ashworth (1996) Times, 18 October	3.108
R v Surrey County Council, ex p G (1994) Times, 24 May	5.27
R v Surrey County Council Education Committee, ex p H (1984) 83 LGR 219, CA	5.09
R v Surrey Quarter Sessions Appeals Committee, ex p Tweedie (1963) 61 LGR 464, 107 Sol Jo 555, DC	2.10
R v Sutton London Borough Council, ex p Hamlet (26 March 1986, unreported)	1.17
R v Tameside Metropolitan Borough Council, ex p Governors of Audenshaw High School (1990) Times, 27 June	1.16, 4.13, 10.66
R v Universities Funding Council, ex p Institute of Dental Surgery [1994] ELR 506, [1994] COD 147	10.03
R v University College London, ex p Riniker [1995] ELR 213	10.97
R v University of Liverpool, ex p Caesar-Gordon [1991] 1 QB 124, [1990] 3 All ER 821, [1990] 3 WLR 667	10.97
R v Walton, etc Justices, ex p Dutton (1911) 9 LGR 1231, 75 JP 558, 27 TLR 569, DC:	2.10
R v Warwickshire County Council, ex p Collymore [1995] ELR 217	10.108
R v Warwickshire County Council, ex p Dill-Russell (1990) 89 LGR 640, CA	3.62
R v Warwickshire County Council, ex p Williams [1995] ELR 326	10.108
R v West Riding of Yorkshire Justices, ex p Broadbent [1910] 2 KB 192, 79 LJKB 731, sub nom R v Morris, etc, West Riding Justices, ex p Broadbent 8 LGR 777, 74 JP 271, 102 LT 814, 26 TLR 419, DC	2.10
R v Westminster Roman Catholic Diocese Trustee, ex p Andrews (1989) Independent, 27 July, CA	3.62
R v Wiltshire County Council, ex p D [1994] 1 FCR 172	5.20
R v Wiltshire County Council, ex p Razazan [1996] ELR 220	7.09
Race Relations Board v Ealing London Borough (No 2) [1978] 1 All ER 497, sub nom Commission for Racial Equality v Ealing London Borough Council [1978] 1 WLR 112, 121 Sol Jo 712, 76 LGR 78, CA	14.09
Ralph v LCC (1947) 111 JP 548, 63 TLR 546, CA	14.17
Rawsthorne v Ottley [1937] 3 All ER 902	14.19
Redbridge London Borough Council v Fishman (1978) 76 LGR 408, [1978] ICR 569, [1978] IRLR 69, EAT	13.44
Reeve v Widderson (1929) Times, 24 April	14.25
Reffell v Surrey County Council [1964] 1 All ER 743, [1964] 1 WLR 358, 62 LGR 186, 128 JP 261, 108 Sol Jo 119	14.22, 14.23, 15.04
Rich v LCC [1953] 2 All ER 376, [1953] 1 WLR 895, 51 LGR 467, 117 JP 353, 97 Sol Jo 472, CA	14.19
Ricketts v Erith Borough Council [1943] 2 All ER 629, 42 LGR 71, 108 JP 22, 113 LJKB 269, 169 LT 396	14.19
Ripper v Rate (1919) Times, 17 January	14.25
Rollo v Minister of Town and Country Planning [1948] 1 All ER 13, 46 LGR 114, 112 JP 104, [1948] LJR 817, 92 Sol Jo 40, 64 TLR 25, CA	1.16
Rootkin v Kent County Council [1981] 2 All ER 227, [1981] 1 WLR 1186, 80 LGR 201, 125 Sol Jo 496, CA	7.47
Royle v Trafford Borough Council [1984] IRLR 184	13.66

S

S (minor), Re [1978] QB 120, [1978] 3 WLR 575, 75 LGR 787, 7 Fam Law 140, 121 Sol Jo 407, sub nom Re DJMS (minor) [1977] 3 All ER 582, 141 JP 660	7.51
S (minors), Re [1995] ELR 98, CA	7.47
S (a minor) v Special Educational Needs Tribunal [1996] 2 All ER 286, [1996] 1 WLR 382, [1996] 2 FCR 292, [1996] 1 FLR 663, [1996] Fam Law 405, [1996] ELR 228, CA	5.21, 5.34

Table of cases

PARA

St Matthias Church of England School (Board of Governors) v Crizzle [1993] ICR 401,
 [1993] IRLR 472, [1993] 15 LS Gaz R 39, EAT 6.01, 6.49, 13.30, 14.08
Sandhu v Department of Education and Science and London Borough of Hillingdon
 [1978] IRLR 208, 13 ITR 314 . . . .   13.44
Scott v Aberdeen Corpn 1975 SLT 167; revsd 1976 SLT 141, Ct of Sess 13.20
Scullard and Knowles v Southern Regional Council for Education and Training [1996]
 IRLR 344, EAT 13.50
Secretary of State for Education and Science v Birchall [1994] IRLR 630, EAT 13.42
Secretary of State for Education and Science v Tameside Metropolitan Borough Council
 [1977] AC 1014, [1976] 3 All ER 665, [1976] 3 WLR 641, 120 Sol Jo 539 CA; on
 appeal [1977] AC 1014, [1976] 3 All ER 665, [1976] 3 WLR 641, 75 LGR 190,
 120 Sol Jo 735, HL 12.06
Secretary of State for Employment v Associated Society of Locomotive Engineers and
 Firemen (No 2) [1972] 2 QB 455, [1972] 2 All ER 949, [1972] 2 WLR 1370,
 [1972] ICR 19, 13 KIR 1, 116 Sol Jo 467, CA 12.06
Shah v Barnet London Borough Council [1983] 2 AC 309, [1983] 1 All ER 226, [1983]
 2 WLR 16, 81 LGR 305, 127 Sol Jo 36, HL 10.106
Shaxted v Ward [1954] 1 All ER 336, 118 JP 168, sub nom Farrier v Ward [1954]
 1 WLR 306, 52 LGR 97, 98 Sol Jo 113, DC 7.47
Shrimpton v Hertfordshire County Council (1911) 9 LGR 397, 75 JP 201, [1911-13] All
 ER Rep 359, 55 Sol Jo 270, 104 LT 145, 27 TLR 251, HL 12.24, 14.17
Sim v Rotherham Metropolitan Borough Council [1987] Ch 216, [1986] 3 All ER 387,
 [1986] 3 WLR 851, 85 LGR 128, [1986] ICR 897, [1986] IRLR 391, 130 Sol Jo
 839, [1986] LS Gaz R 3746 . . . .   13.66
Simmons v Hoover Ltd [1977] QB 284, [1977] 1 All ER 775, [1976] 3 WLR 901,
 [1977] ICR 61, [1976] IRLR 266, 10 ITR 234, 120 Sol Jo 540, EAT 13.45
Sinfield v London Transport Executive [1970] Ch 550, [1970] 2 All ER 264, [1970] 2
 WLR 1062, 68 LGR 512, 114 Sol Jo 285, CA 1.16
Smerkinich v Newport Corpn (1912) 10 LGR 959, 76 JP 454, DC 14.19
Smith v Inner London Education Authority [1978] 1 All ER 411, 142 JP 136, CA 2.29
Smith v Macnally [1912] 1 Ch 816, 10 LGR 434, 76 JP 466, 81 LJ Ch 483, 56 Sol Jo
 997, 106 LT 945, 28 TLR 332 . . . .   6.48
Smith v Martin and Kingston upon Hull Corpn [1911] 2 KB 775, 9 LGR 780, 75 JP 433,
 80 LJKB 1256, [1911-13] All ER Rep 412, 55 Sol Jo 535, 105 LT 281, 27 TLR 468,
 CA 14.16, 14.19
Smoldon v Whitworth (1996) Times, 18 December, CA 14.19
South Glamorgan County Council v L and M [1996] ELR 400 . . . .   5.34
Spencer and Griffin v Gloucestershire County Council. See Gloucestershire County
 Council v Spencer
Spiers v Warrington Corpn [1954] 1 QB 61, [1953] 2 All ER 1052, [1953] 3 WLR 695,
 51 LGR 642, 117 JP 564, 97 Sol Jo 745, DC 7.47
Staffordshire County Council v J and J [1996] ELR 418 . . . .   5.34
Suckling v Essex County Council (1955) Times, 27 January 14.19
Sunderland City Council v P and C [1996] ELR 283 . . . .   5.21, 5.34
Surrey County Council v Ministry of Education [1953] 1 All ER 705, [1953] 1 WLR
 516, 51 LGR 319, 117 JP 194, 97 Sol Jo 191 . . . .   7.47
Sykes v Holmes (1985) 84 LGR 355, [1985] Crim LR 791 . . . .   15.09
Symes v Brown (1913) 11 LGR 1171, 77 JP 345, 23 Cox CC 519, 109 LT 232, 29 TLR
 473, DC 7.47

T

T and M (minors), Re [1995] ELR 1 . . . .   6.59
Taylor v Kent County Council [1969] 2 QB 560, [1969] 2 All ER 1080, [1969] 3 WLR
 156, 67 LGR 483, 113 Sol Jo 425, DC 13.49
Terrington v Lancashire County Council (28 August 1986, unreported) 15.14
Terry v East Sussex County Council [1977] 1 All ER 567, 75 LGR 111, [1976] ICR 536,
 [1976] IRLR 332, 12 ITR 265, EAT 13.44
Three Rivers District Council v Governor of the Bank of England (No 2) [1996] 2 All ER
 363 . . . .   1.35

Table of cases

PARA

Toole v Sherbourne Pouffes Ltd (1971) 70 LGR 52, [1971] RTR 479, CA 14.17
Trevor v Incorporated Froebel Institute (1954) Times, 11 February 14.19

U

University of Liverpool v Humber and Birch [1984] IRLR 54, EAT; affd sub nom Birch
    v University of Liverpool [1985] ICR 470, [1985] IRLR 165, 129 Sol Jo 245, CA: 13.48

V

Van Oppen v Clerk to the Bedford Charity Trustees [1989] 3 All ER 389, [1990] 1 WLR
    235, [1990] 16 LS Gaz R 42, [1989] NLJR 900, CA 14.19

W

Waite v Government Communications Headquarters [1983] ICR 359, [1983] IRLR
    161, CA; affd [1983] 2 AC 714, [1983] 2 All ER 1013, [1983] 3 WLR 389, 81
    LGR 769, [1983] ICR 653, [1983] IRLR 341, 127 Sol Jo 536, [1983] LS Gaz R
    2516, 133 NLJ 745, HL 13.42
Walker v Cummings (1912) 10 LGR 728, 76 JP 375, 23 Cox CC 157, 107 LT 304, 28
    TLR 442, DC 7.47
Wandsworth London Borough Council v National Association of Schoolmasters/Union
    of Women Teachers (1994) 92 LGR 91, [1994] ICR 81, [1993] IRLR 344, [1994]
    ELR 170, [1993] NLJR 655n, CA 13.65
Ward v Hertfordshire County Council [1970] 1 All ER 535, [1970] 1 WLR 356, 68 LGR
    151, 134 JP 261, 114 Sol Jo 87, CA 14.19, 14.23, 15.04
Watkins v Birmingham City Council (1975) 126 NLJ 442, CA 14.19
Watt v Kesteven County Council [1955] 1 QB 408, [1955] 1 All ER 473, [1955] 2 WLR
    499, 53 LGR 254, 119 JP 220, 99 Sol Jo 149, CA 1.23, 2.16, 12.40
Watts v Monmouthshire County Council (1967) 66 LGR 171, 111 Sol Jo 602,
    CA 13.20, 14.19
West Suffolk County Council v Olorenshaw [1918] 2 KB 687, 16 LGR 711, 82 JP 292,
    88 LJKB 384, 120 LT 94, DC 12.03
Whitley v Harrow London Borough Council (1988) Guardian, 29 March 13.20
Wilford v West Riding of Yorkshire County Council [1908] 1 KB 685, 6 LGR 244, 72
    JP 107, 77 LJKB 436, 52 Sol Jo 263, 98 LT 670, 24 TLR 286 .... 12.03
Williams v Eady (1893) 10 TLR 41, CA 14.17
Wilson v Pringle [1987] QB 237, [1986] 2 All ER 440, [1986] 1 WLR 1, 130 Sol Jo 468,
    [1986] LS Gaz R 2160, [1986] NLJ Rep 416, CA 15.15
Wiltshire County Council v National Association of Teachers in Further and Higher
    Education (1980) 78 LGR 445, [1980] ICR 455, [1980] IRLR 198, CA 13.42
Winder v Cambridgeshire County Council (1978) 76 LGR 549, CA 13.20
Winward v Cheshire County Council (1978) 77 LGR 172, 122 Sol Jo 582 .... 2.16
Wiseman v Salford City Council [1981] IRLR 202, EAT 13.44
Wood v Ealing London Borough Council [1967] Ch 364, [1966] 3 All ER 514, [1966]
    3 WLR 1209, 65 LGR 282, 131 JP 22, 110 Sol Jo 944 .... 2.16, 2.29
Wood v York City Council [1978] ICR 840, [1978] IRLR 228, 122 Sol Jo 192, CA ... 13.41
Wray v Essex County Council [1936] 3 All ER 97, 80 Sol Jo 894, 155 LT 494, CA ... 14.19
Wrexham Parochial Educational Foundation, Re, A-G v Denbighshire County Council
    (1910) 8 LGR 526, 74 JP 198 .... 6.46
Wright v Cheshire County Council [1952] 2 All ER 789, 51 LGR 14, 116 JP 555, 96 Sol
    Jo 747, [1952] 2 TLR 641, CA 14.17, 14.19

X

X v Bedfordshire County Council [1995] 2 AC 633, [1995] 3 All ER 353, [1995] 3 WLR
    152, 160 LG Rev 103, [1995] 3 FCR 337, [1995] 2 FLR 276, [1995] Fam Law 537,
    [1995] ELR 404, 26 BMLR 15, [1995] NLJR 993, HL 14.16, 14.21

Y

Y v United Kingdom (Application 14229/88) (1992) 17 EHRR 238, E Ct HR 15.15

l

Chapter 1

INTRODUCTION

HISTORICAL BACKGROUND

1.01 The first government grants to school promoters were made by the Treasury in 1833, towards the building of what would now be called voluntary schools, by two societies which had been formed earlier in the century, representing the established and non-conformist churches. In 1839 the Committee of the Privy Council for Education came into being to administer the distribution of annual grants, as they soon became, for the provision of education for the poor. Grants were paid subject to stipulated conditions being met, which included standards of building. In 1840 inspection of schools began. The School Sites Acts of 1841, 1844, 1849, 1851 and 1852 (which remain on the statute book) facilitated the conveyance of sites of up to one acre for schools and school teachers' houses where the grantor was not the absolute owner of the land; and, as an encouragement to private landowners, it was also provided that if the land ceased to be used for the purpose for which it had been granted it would automatically revert to the grantor.

1.02 In 1856 the Committee of the Privy Council gave way to an Education Department, whose functions grew when the Elementary Education Act 1870 provided for elected school boards to be set up in areas where there were not enough church schools. The boards were empowered to raise a rate. A few years later elementary education became compulsory, but gaps in the legislation meant that it was not until 1918 that fees were finally abolished by the (Fisher) Act of that year.

1.03 Under the the Cowper-Temple clause in the 1870 Act no religious catechism or formulary distinctive of a particular denomination was to be taught in a board school. That requirement remains part of the law on religious education in county schools.[1]

1.04 The Welsh Intermediate Education Act 1889 introduced maintained secondary schools in Wales; in the same year the Technical Instruction Act supported the provision of technical colleges and schools; and in 1899 a Board of Education came nominally into existence, its President in effect the Minister of Education. The Department's powers were enlarged by the Act of 1902, marking in particular the growth of secondary and technical education. The Act

---

1 1996 Act s 376(2).

1.04   Introduction

established county boroughs and counties as local education authorities (LEAs); also teacher training colleges. Board schools were superseded by council schools.

1.05   Between 1902 and 1944 LEAs provided, at minimum, education from the age of 5 to 14. The partnership between the maintained and the voluntary sector continued. New secondary schools supplemented endowed grammar schools, so that by the end of the First World War few towns of any size lacked some provision for secondary education. Technical and trade schools were established in some large urban areas. As the years passed some authorities, under the impetus of the Fisher Act and the Hadow report, *Education of the Adolescent*, 1926, subdivided their provision of schooling into three departments—infants 5 to 7, juniors 7 to 11 and seniors 11 to 14. In the inter-war years of economy and depression free secondary education was exceptional and turned on selection by examination at the age of 11. A feature of the same period was the negotiation of national salary scales for teachers in the Burnham Committees, which survived from 1919 until the coming into effect of the Teachers' Pay and Conditions Act 1987.

1.06   The 1944 Act (the Butler Act, but also a monument to James Chuter Ede, R A Butler's Labour Parliamentary Secretary in the wartime coalition Government) created a Minister of Education in place of the President of a Board (and the Minister was superseded by a Secretary of State in 1964). The Act laid down three stages of education – primary, secondary and further. Free schooling was to be provided for all children up to the age of 15, eventually 16, and transfer from primary to secondary schools was to take place between the ages of 10 years 6 months and 12 years. The powers of LEAs to provide secondary, technical and adult education became duties, and authorities were to prepare development plans for approval by the Minister showing how they proposed to meet the new requirements. These included making provision for nursery education, special schools and boarding accommodation, for altering buildings to bring them up to prescribed standards or replacing them, and adding new schools. The use of development plans for building programmes continued until the early 1960s.

1.07   The 1944 Act was one of few pieces of legislation the existence of which was common knowledge. It embodied optimistic hopes for the future, not all of which have been disappointed. It is easy to forget that the abolition of fees for secondary education at maintained schools and the other developments mentioned above marked in their time important progress in popular education. Although the providers were LEAs, 'State education' has long been the common usage—a form of words which has become more apt with the growth of government intervention over the last decade. The wasting of the 1944 Act has been a symbol of changing perceptions about the purposes of education and the best means of providing it—of the collapse of near consensus which marked at least the earlier half of the post-war period, and was based in part upon shared (or at least widely tolerated) social and constitutional values.

1.08   Upon the foundations of the 1944 Act there was erected over the ensuing 50 years a more and more ramshackle statutory edifice, as the role of LEAs was elaborated (or, more recently, diminished) by one amending Act after another. These included the 1980 Act (which aimed to enhance parental choice of school), the 1981 Act (which made new arrangements for handicapped children) and the 1986 (No 2) Act (new arrangements for school government and conduct). The pressure of some 30 amending Acts eroded the foundations of the 1944 Act, which could scarcely have been expected to survive the addition of a penthouse—the Education Reform Act 1988 (introducing, inter alia, grant-maintained schools and a National Curriculum)—more extensive than the foundations themselves. These crumbled under the added weight of an even heavier burden, the Education Act 1993. That Act, having been preceded by two Acts of 1992, on schools and on further and higher education, was supplemented by the 1994 Act, establishing the Teacher Training Agency, and the Education (Student Loans) Act 1996—straws on the already broken back of 'the principal Act' of 1944.

1.09 Consolidating legislation—the Education Act 1996 and the School Inspections Act 1996—has now improved the accessibility of education law but does not provide a comprehensive code[2]). The pace of change does not slacken—Parliament has added the Education Act 1997, which, inter alia, extended the assisted places scheme (now proposed to be ended) to cover independent schools providing only primary education, and elaborated the law on school discipline. To ensure the Bill's passage before the dissolution, clauses were dropped which had been designed to relax the controls on changes affecting the character or premises of schools and to extend the power of the funding authority to establish grant-maintained schools.

INTERPRETATION

1.10 William of Occam would have blunted his razor in the attempt to pare down the concepts employed in education law. 'Initial', 'new' and 'first' governors all have their proper place in the grant-maintained schools scheme, and terminology has proliferated to the point at which the Further and Higher Education Act 1992 and the 1996 Act contain an index of the expressions used, in addition to the usual interpretation provisions.

1.11 Appendix 10 contains the definitions of many of the terms used in the Education and some other Acts, together with a glossary of other terminology derived from statute and the decisions of the courts.[3] The reader should be alert to the need to keep one finger in the glossary while consulting the text, because there are few passages in the narrative that do not contain words or phrases that are defined in legislation or have not been the subject of judicial consideration. But it is unnecessary, as it would have been clumsy and a blemish on the record, to draw attention expressly to each example by the use of italics or footnoting.

1.12 Additional points of interpretation and usage are listed alphabetically below.

2 Appendix 1 lists the Education Acts (and those repealed in the consolidation). Appendix 2 shows the derivation of the consolidation provisions and Appendix 3 the destination of repealed legislation.
3 On points of construction of words and passages in the statutes and statutory instruments, and particularly in connection with judicial review, reference may often usefully be made to the current editions of HWR Wade, *Administrative Law* and SA de Smith, *Judicial Review of Administrative Action*.

1.13 *Introduction*

Age

1.13 A child, pupil or other person attains a particular age expressed in years at the commencement of the relevant anniversary of the date of his birth.[4]

City Colleges

1.14 The abbreviation 'city colleges' is used in these pages to refer to city technology colleges and city colleges for the technology of the arts.

Civil debt

1.15 A magistrates' court has power to make an order on complaint for the payment of any money which is recoverable summarily as a civil debt. The complaint may not be heard unless it was made within six months from the time when the matter of complaint arose.[5]

Consultation

1.16 Many statutory provisions place upon the Secretary of State or LEAs a duty to consult interested parties.[6] Failure to comply may be held by the courts to render an action or decision ultra vires and void. The requirements of the statute will not be satisfied unless adequate and accurate information is provided as a basis for consultation—or for making objections or representations—and sufficient time is allowed.[7] Moreover consultation should take place at the formative stage—'before the mind of the executive becomes unduly fixed', per Sachs LJ in *Sinfield v London Transport Executive*,[8] and proper regard is to be had to its outcome before the final decision is made: *R v Kent County Council, ex p Parker*.[9] But in the words of O'Connor LJ in *Gateshead Metropolitan Borough Council v Nichol*[10] 'consultation is not and should not be a referendum' and 'the fact that consultation does not result in any change in a proposal is not a ground for asserting that the consultation must have been flawed as to timing, content or consideration.'

1.17 A distinction is to be drawn between circumstances in which there is an

---

4 Family Law Reform Act 1969 s 9.
5 Magistrates' Courts Act 1980 ss 58(1) and 127(1). For restrictions on commital for non-payment see s 96.
6 See, in addition to the cases mentioned in the text, *Rollo v Minister of Town and Country Planning* [1948] 1 All ER 13, CA, F[1] (see Preface for explanation of this abbreviation, used throughout this work); *Port Louis Corpn v A-G of Mauritius* [1965] AC 1111, PC, F[2]; *Agricultural, Horticultural and Forestry Industry Training Board v Aylesbury Mushrooms Ltd* [1972] 1 All ER 280, F[3]; *R v Coventry City Council, ex p Newborn* (26 September 1985, unreported), F[6]; *R v Essex County Council, ex p Ongar Parish Council* (6 November 1986, unreported), F[9]; *R v Tameside Metropolitan Borough Council, ex p Governors of Audenshaw High School* (1990) Times, 27 June, F[11]; *R v Devon County Council, ex p Baker* [1995] 1 All ER 73, CA, F[13]; and *R v Barnet London Borough Council, ex p B* [1994] 1 FLR 592.
7 As to what constitutes reasonable time see *Lee v Department of Education and Science* (1967) 66 LGR 211, F[69]; *R v Brent London Borough Council, ex p Gunning* (1985) 84 LGR 168, F[4]; and *R v Secretary of State for Social Services, ex p Association of Metropolitan Authorities* [1986] 1 WLR 1, F[5].
8 [1970] Ch 550 at 558.
9 McCowan J, 26 June 1986, unreported, F[8].
10 (1988)87 LGR 435.

explicit statutory right to be consulted and those in which there is a legitimate expectation of consultation. Thus the duty of the LEA to consult appropriate persons under s 35 of the 1996 Act (establishment, alteration etc of schools) does not give parents a statutory right to be consulted, but rather, to the extent necessary in the interests of fairness, a legitimate 'expectation that they will be given a fair opportunity constructively to criticise the proposal, and to express their own preferences in relation to it' per Webster J in *R v Sutton London Borough Council, ex p Hamlet*.[11]

1.18 In *R v Northamptonshire County Council, ex p Tebbutt*[12] Woolf LJ explicitly adopted the approach of Webster J in *Hamlet* and also said 'In my view, in considering whether there has been unfairness, one is entitled to take into account the fact that the objections have been made to the Secretary of State and he has given approval notwithstanding those objections. The approval is by no means decisive, but it can be relevant'; and in *R v Gwent County Council, ex p Bryant*[13] it was held that in the case of 'legitimate expectation', failure to consult could be cured in the Secretary of State's later decision-making process. In *R v Secretary of State for Education and Employment, ex p Morris*[14] it was held that there is no obligation to consult where a school was to be closed for failure to provide an acceptable standard of education.

1.19 In *R v Norfolk County Council, ex p Coulten*, unreported,[15] Nolan J said

'I do not accept that the publication of s 12 [of the 1980 Act] proposals necessarily puts an end to the requisite consultation process. If some subsequent event shows that the consultations had been based on a fundamental mistake or misunderstanding, it would be absurd to regard them as having fulfilled their intended purpose and absurd, accordingly, to say that they could not be reopened.'

Directions

1.20 Directions made or given by, may also be varied or revoked by, the Secretary of State, the funding authority or an LEA, subject to the same conditions as applied when the direction was made or given.[16]

Discretion

1.21 Various expressions are associated with the exercise of discretion, for example, 'thinks fit', 'considers necessary', 'is satisfied', 'is of the opinion' (in the following pages sometimes reduced to 'thinks'). The courts have in recent times been unwilling to regard the use of subjective language as conferring an unfettered discretion, and are ready to question whether the Secretary of State

---

11 (26 March 1986, unreported), F[7]; and see also *Brunyate v Inner London Education Authority* [1989] 2 All ER 417, F[101] and *R v Lambeth Borough Council, ex p N* [1996] ELR 299. There is no obligation upon an LEA to arrange for interpreters at a consultative meeting (*R v Birmingham City Council, ex p Kaur* (1990) Times, 11 July, F[12]).
12 (26 June 1986, unreported).
13 [1988] COD 19. See also *R v Secretary of State for Wales, ex p Williams* [1995] ELR 100.
14 [1996] ELR 162.
15 But cf *R v Hertfordshire County Council, ex p George* (27 July 1988, unreported), F[10].
16 1996 Act s 570.

1.21 *Introduction*

or LEA could reasonably have been 'satisfied' (or as the case may be),[17] as well as to question whether the action—or inaction—complained of was taken on proper grounds and in good faith.

1.22 'May' generally confers full discretion on whether to act, but a power becomes a duty if prescribed circumstances come into existence or if failure to exercise a discretion would frustrate a statutory provision.[18]

1.23 An LEA or governing body may be required to 'have regard to', for example, guidance given by the Secretary of State. In *Ishak v Thowfeek*[19] it was held that a duty to have regard was not a duty to comply. Matters to which regard is to be had are to be taken into account, considered and given due weight, but an ultimate discretion remains. See also *Watt v Kesteven County Council*,[20] *Cumings v Birkenhead Corpn*[1] and *Harvey v Strathclyde Regional Council*.[2] 'Take into account' also appears in statute, and is difficult to distinguish from 'have regard to'.

Europe

1.24 The complexity of education law has been aggravated by British membership of the Council of Europe and of the European Union, which introduce legal obligations in connection with the provision of education and the granting of rights to parents. Those obligations supplement, and may override, domestic legislation. They are mentioned, as necessary, in the following pages.

Fines on the standard scale

1.25 A standard scale of fines for summary offences was introduced by the Criminal Justice Act 1982 ss 37(1) and 46. New amounts were fixed by the Criminal Justice Act 1991 s 17 as follows.

Level 1	£200
Level 2	£500
Level 3	£1,000
Level 4	£2,500
Level 5	£5,000

Maintained schools

1.26 'Maintained school' is given different meanings in different parts of the legislation. To avoid ambiguity, in these pages that expression is used only where reference is intended both to schools maintained by LEAs and to grant-maintained (but not grant-maintained special) schools. 'LEA schools' is used to refer to county and voluntary schools and those nursery and and special schools which LEAs maintain; and reference is made likewise to 'LEA further and higher education institutions' where those institutions are maintained by LEAs.

---

17 See para 12.05 ff.
18 See *Julius v Bishop of Oxford* (1880) 5 App Cas 214 at 225.
19 [1968] 1 WLR 1718 at 1725.
20 [1955] 1 QB 408, F[41].
 1 [1972] Ch 12, F[42].
 2 1989 SLT 612, HL, F[48].

Notice

1.27 Not less than, eg, one week's notice means that one clear week must intervene between the day on which the notice is given and that on which the action in question is taken.[3]

Orders

1.28 Many orders are of limited application, and in the following pages it is to be taken that an order is *not* a statutory instrument (SI) unless the contrary is indicated. Orders (including those made by LEAs and funding authorities for schools) not made by SI may be varied or revoked by further orders.[4]

Prescribed

1.29 'Prescribed' means prescribed by regulations made by the Secretary of State.

Regulations

1.30 Regulations are made by the Secretary of State. Only exceptionally (see para 3.29 n 11) are they not SIs.

Service of documents

1.31 Under the 1996 Act an order, notice or other document may be served on a person by delivering it to him, or leaving it at, or sending it by post to, his usual or last known place of residence.[5]

Statutory instruments

1.32 For the most part SIs are subject to the negative procedure in Parliament (ie subject to annulment by a resolution of either House), may make different provision for different cases, circumstances or areas (usually including Wales), and may contain incidental, saving or transitional provisions.[6]

1.33 When SIs have been made under a superseded provision but remain in force because they could have been made under current legislation[7] it has not been thought necessary to call attention to that fact.

Summary conviction

1.34 This is mainly governed by the Magistrates' Courts Act 1980.

---

3 See the cases cited in 45 Halsbury's Laws (4th edn) para 1133 (and para 1111 as to the day of expiry of periods of a month or a specified number of months).
4 1996 Act s 570. Where an order (not an SI) is made subject to consultation or is otherwise subject to conditions, the same conditions apply to the subsequent order. This section also applies to a scheme under s 430 (see para 7.26).
5 1996 Act s 572.
6 1996 Act ss 568 and 569.
7 1996 Act Sch 39 para 1(2), 1996 SI Act Sch 8 para 1(2) and Interpretation Act 1978 s 17.

1.35 *Introduction*

1.35 Finally, attention is drawn to two recent developments in constitutional and administrative law which bear upon education law and administration. First, in *Pepper (Inspector of Taxes) v Hart*[8] the House of Lords held that courts may refer to parliamentary material recorded in *Hansard* when construing a statute, if the statute is ambiguous or obscure or leads to an absurdity and the material consists of clear statements by a Minister or other promoter of a Bill. This was a limited relaxation of the historic rule that courts may not look at the parliamentary history of legislation or *Hansard* for the purpose of construing legislation.

1.36 Secondly, the House of Lords, by a majority of three to two, reversed a decision of the Court of Appeal, and held that a local social services authority were entitled to take account of their own resources in establishing an applicant's need for services that they were under a statutory duty to provide.[9] If this *ratio* is applied generally and not modified in subsequent decisions[10] it could have a profound effect on public service provision by LEAs and other public bodies.

---

8 [1993] AC 593. See also *Pickstone v Freemans plc* [1989] AC 66, *Three Rivers District Council v Governor of the Bank of England (No 2)* [1996] 2 All ER 363, and Practice Direction: Reference to Extracts from *Hansard*, 20 December 1994.
9 *R v Gloucestershire County Council, ex p Barry* [1997] 2 All ER 1, HL, followed in *R v Sefton Metropolitan Borough Council, ex p Help the Aged* [1997] NLJR 490.
10 *Barry* was distiguished in *R v East Sussex County Council, v ex p T* (1997) Times, 29 April, in which it was held that the LEA were not allowed to take their financial resources into account in providing 'suitable education' (under 1993 Act s 298), but that there might be more than one way of providing a suitable education, and in deciding which way an LEA could properly have reference to financial resources.

Chapter 2
PRINCIPLES AND ADMINISTRATION

THE STATUTORY SYSTEM OF EDUCATION

2.01 Chapter I of Part I of the 1996 Act (sections 1 to 9) specifies the stages of the statutory system and contains some basic definitions. It also states the duty of parents to secure the education of children of compulsory school age as defined, and indicates how far parents' wishes are to be respected.

The stages of education and some definitions

2.02 The statutory system of public education consists of three stages, primary, secondary and further.[1]

2.03 'Pupil' means a person for whom education is being provided at school but who is not (a) 19 or over and being provided with further education or (b) being provided with part-time education suitable for persons over compulsory school age. Junior pupils are children under 12; senior pupils are aged 12 or over but under 19.[2]

2.04 Primary education is full-time[3] education suitable to the requirements of junior pupils who are aged under ten years six months and older junior pupils whom it is expedient to educate with them.[4]

2.05 Secondary education is (a) full-time education suitable to the requirements of pupils of compulsory school age (see paras 2.11 and 2.12) who are either senior pupils or junior pupils of ten years six months and over whom it is expedient to educate with them; and (b) full-time education for pupils over compulsory school age but ordinarily under 19, which is suitable for, and provided at, a school (see para 2.07) for younger pupils.[5]

2.06 Further education is full-time and part-time education for persons over compulsory school age (including vocational, social, physical and recreational training) and organised leisure-time occupation (see para 10.02) connected

---

1 1996 Act s 1.
2 1996 Act s 3.
3 The duration of the school day and year are prescribed by the Education (Schools and Further Education) Regulations 1981, SI 1981/1086, reg 10. See para 2.13.
4 1996 Act s 2(1).
5 1996 Act s 2(2).

2.06 Principles and Administration

with that education, but excluding secondary or higher education (see para 10.02); so that full-time education for persons over compulsory school age but under 19 is further, and not secondary, education unless it is secondary education under (b) in the previous paragraph. Education (other than higher education) provided for persons of 19 and over is further education except where a person began, and continues to attend, a course of secondary education before becoming 18.[6]

Educational institutions

2.07 A school is an educational institution outside the further or higher education sectors[7] providing one or more of (a) primary education, (b) secondary education as defined in paragraph (a) in para 2.05, and (c) full-time education for persons over compulsory school age but under 19, in each case whether or not the institution also provides part-time education suitable to the requirements of junior pupils, further education or other secondary education.[8]

2.08 A primary school provides primary education, whether or not it also provides part-time education suitable to the requirements of junior pupils or further education; a secondary school provides secondary education whether or not it also provides further education. Middle schools straddle the primary and secondary age ranges, and are deemed primary if the age range of pupils is wider below than above the age of 11, otherwise secondary.[9] Nursery schools are primary schools mainly used for children aged over two but under five.[10]

2.09 A special school is one organised to make special educational provision for pupils with special educational needs and approved as such by the Secretary of State.[11]

Compulsory education

2.10 During the period of compulsory school age (see paras 2.11 and 2.12 below) parents are to ensure that, by regular attendance at school or otherwise (see para 2.31), a child receives efficient full-time education suitable to his age, ability and aptitude and any special educational needs he may have.[12] To be

6 1996 Act s 2(3) to (7).
7 See para10.04.
8 1996 Act s 4. By sub-s(2) an institution that provides part-time rather than full-time education is to be treated as a school if the part-time education is under s 19(1) (see para 2.31).
9 1996 Act s 5 and the Education (Middle Schools) Regulations 1980, SI 1980/918.
10 1996 Act s 6(1). As to the provision by LEAs of nursery schools and classes see para 3.07; as to the duration of the nursery school day the Education (Schools and Further Education) Regulations 1981, SI 1981/1086 reg 10(4); and as to the 'voucher scheme' para 11.12.
11 1996 Act s 6(2) and see para 5.35 ff.
12 1996 Act s 7. See Circular 11/91 (WO 45/91) 'The Education (Pupils' Attendance Records) Regulations 1991', E[1581]. In *Harrison v Stevenson* (1981) unreported, Worcester Crown Court held that a system of education is 'efficient' if it achieves what it sets out to achieve, and 'suitable' to a child's age, ability and aptitude if, and only if, the education (a) prepares the child for life in a modern civilised society and (b) enables the child to achieve his full potential. 'Efficiency' is now, presumably, to be construed having regard to the National Curriculum. See also *R v Secretary of State for Education and Science, ex p Talmud Torah Machzikei Hadass School Trust* (1985) Times, 12 April, F[85]. As to an unsuccessful application to the European Commission of Human Rights see Application No 10233/83 (Harrison).

regular, attendance must be at the times prescribed for the school—late arrival will not do.[13] Whether education is 'efficient' and 'suitable' is a matter for the LEA who are responsible for enforcement. It is for the Secretary of State to decide whether an independent school is efficient: the fact that it is registered under the 1996 Act s 464[14] is not evidence to that effect. In practice the efficiency and suitability of education has been challenged in the courts mainly where parents have taken advantage of statutory provisions that full-time education may be received otherwise than at school.[15] The advent of the National Curriculum has made the onus on the parent the more difficult to discharge.

2.11 A child is of compulsory school age on attaining the age of five [16] and is to attend school from the beginning of the term which begins next after he attains that age (which includes a term beginning on his birthday). Where a child attains that age during a term there is no obligation on the school to admit him as a registered pupil (see para 7.35) during the currency of the term unless he was prevented from starting at the beginning because he was ill or entry was otherwise impracticable, for limited reasons; and in those circumstances the parent's obligation to secure the child's full-time education is also deferred.[17]

2.12 Compulsory school age ends on the school-leaving date for each year (prescribed by the Secretary of State), for children who become 16 on or before that date, or after it but before the next school year begins.[18] This provision comes into force on a day appointed by a commencement order. In the meantime there remain two school-leaving dates: if a child reaches school-leaving age in the five months September to January inclusive he is to stay at school until the end of the following spring term; if he reaches (or would reach) that age in February to August inclusive he is to stay at school until the Friday before the last Monday in May.[19]

Duration of the school day and year   Leave of absence

2.13 The school day at LEA schools and all special schools is ordinarily to be divided into two sessions separated by a break in the middle of the day. In each

---

As to a child with no fixed abode see para 7.47.
See (a) para 7.39 ff as to the obligations of LEAs where a parent appears to fail to perform his duty, and (b) *Holtom v London Borough of Barnet* (1993) Times, 30 September, as to the circumstances in which parental duties fell upon the local authority, on which see also Circular 13/94 (WO 58/94), 'The education of children being looked after by local authorities'.
13 *Hinchley v Rankin* [1961] 1 WLR 421, F[183]; see also *Spiers v Warrington Corpn*, para 7.47 n 20.
14 Since 1978 the Secretary of State has not recognised any category of independent schools as efficient.
15 See *R v West Riding of Yorkshire Justices, ex p Broadbent* [1910] 2 KB 192; *R v Walton, ex p Dutton* (1911) 75 JP 558; *Bevan v Shears* [1911] 2 KB 936, F[191]; *Osborne v Martin* (1927) 91 JP 197; *Baker v Earl* (1960) Times, 6 February; and *R v Gwent County Council, ex p Perry* (1985) 129 Sol Jo 737, CA, F[192]. It was held in *R v Surrey Quarter Sessions, ex p Tweedie* (1963) 61 LGR 464, that exceptionally it may be permissible for the LEA to inspect the home.
16 1996 Act s 8(2). This provision comes into force on a day appointed by a commencement order. In the meantime, by Sch 40 para 1, 'compulsory school age' in substance follows repealed 1944 Act s 35.
17 1996 Act ss 433 and 448.
18 1996 Act s 8(3) and (4).
19 1996 Act Sch 40 para 1 (following repealed 1962 Act s 9).

2.13 *Principles and Administration*

school (academic) year (usually beginning on 1 September) there are normally to be at least 380 sessions (nursery classes excepted) and sessions are to include recreation time, time occupied by medical or dental examinations or treatment and, at voluntary schools, time taken for inspection of religious education. If a school meets on six days a week there need be only one session on two of those days. The regulations do not specify the number of terms in an academic year.[20]

2.14 Leave of absence from maintained and all special schools is not to be granted to enable a pupil to take paid or unpaid employment except (i) to gain permitted work experience (see para 15.32), (ii) to take part in a licensed performance, or (iii) to take up employment abroad for a licensed purpose (see para 15.30). A pupil may be granted leave to go away on holiday with the parent with whom he normally lives, but only exceptionally for more than ten school days in any school year.[1]

Education in accordance with parental wishes

2.15 In performing their functions the Secretary of State, funding authorities and LEAs are required to

> 'have regard to the general principle that pupils are to be educated in accordance with the wishes of their parents, so far as that is compatible with the provision of efficient instruction and training and the avoidance of unreasonable public expenditure.'[2]

2.16 This general principle is subject to other considerations (*Watt v Kesteven County Council*).[3] In *Wood v Ealing London Borough Council*[4] Goff J held that the requirement merely qualified the powers and duties of LEAs and of the Minister under the Act as a whole; breach of it could not of itself give rise to a right of action; and in *Cumings v Birkenhead Corpn*[5] Denning MR remarked that it was in order for an LEA to have a general policy regarding admission to schools, and 'there are many things to which the education authority may have regard and which may outweigh the wishes of [particular] parents'.[6]

---

20 1996 Act s 551. This section applies to grant-maintained as well as LEA schools, but the current regulations—the Education (Schools and Further Education) Regulations 1981, SI 1981/1086 (see reg 10 on the duration of the school year and day)—do not apply to grant-maintained schools. See also Circular 7/90 (WO 43/90), 'Management of the School Day' E[1213]. For LEA school terms see para 3.95.
1 See the Education (Pupil Registration) Regulations 1995, SI 1995/2089 reg 8, and Departmental Guidance, May 1994 (WO 53/94) 'School Attendance: Policy and Practice on Categorisation of Absence', E[2734].
2 1996 Act s 9. 'Efficient': see n 12 above. As to the disapplication of this section when an education supervision order (see para 7.50 ff) is in force see the Children Act 1989 s 36(10) and Sch 3 Part III para 13.
3 [1955] 1 QB 408, F[41].
4 [1967] Ch 364.
5 [1972] Ch 12, F[42].
6 As to admission to schools see now para 7.01 ff. See also *Darling and Jones v Minister of Education* (1962) Times, 7 April; *Winward v Cheshire County Council* (1978) 77 LGR 172, F[188]; *Harvey v Strathclyde* 1989 SLT 612, HL, F[48]; *R v Rochdale Metropolitan Borough Council, ex p Schemet* [1993] COD 113, F[213]; and *R v Lambeth London Borough, ex p G* [1994] ELR 207, F[49].

FUNCTIONS OF THE SECRETARY OF STATE

2.17 Chapter II of Part I (sections 10 and 11) of the 1996 Act states the general functions of the Secretary of State.[7] He is to promote the education of the people of England and Wales. He no longer has a further duty, as under the 1944 Act, to promote 'the progressive development of institutions . . ., and to secure the effective execution by local authorities, under his control and direction, of the national policy for providing a varied and comprehensive educational service in every area'. Indeed this approach to educational administration has to a large extent been abandoned: in recent times the Secretary of State, by taking and diffusing powers, has less need to secure execution of his policies by LEAs.

2.18 The Secretary of State is required to exercise his powers in relation to bodies in receipt of public funds so as to promote primary, secondary and further education; and to improve standards, encourage diversity and increase opportunities for choice in schools and in the further education sector.[8] His specific functions, which include wide regulation-making powers over schools and further and higher education institutions,[9] are outlined throughout this book.

2.19 Among the concluding sections of the 1996 Act is a requirement upon the Secretary of State to publish, as he thinks fit, guidance about provisions in the 1996 Act.[10] In addition he issues Circulars and other documents which may be advisory or explanatory or serve other purposes, including the giving of decisions and approvals which do not require incorporation in a statutory instrument. In form Circulars are not legislation (cf the remarks of May LJ in *R v Oxfordshire Education Authority, ex p W*[11]), but even when advisory in character they may convey more or less directly that the Secretary of State is prepared to use collateral powers—or indeed to legislate—to achieve his purposes. Failure to follow advice without good cause may be held unreasonable. In some cases a requirement to have regard to guidance is imposed.

LOCAL EDUCATION AUTHORITIES

2.20 Chapter III of Part I of the 1996 Act (sections 12 to 19 and Schedule 1) specifies which local authorities are LEAs; also the general functions of LEAs, including provision of education in its three stages (but in this work their further education functions are mentioned in Chapter 10, on further and higher education generally). Reference is made here to the powers of LEAs to establish, maintain and assist primary and secondary schools and in respect of nursery

---

7 1996 Act s 10. As to the teacher training duties of the Secretary of State see para 13.02.
8 1996 Act s 11. The section does not, as such, extend the Secretary of State's powers and duties. 'Bodies in receipt of public funds' include, as well as LEAs, the funding authorities for England and for Wales, the city colleges and the Further Education Funding Councils.
　　For the power of the Parliamentary Commissioner to investigate the administrative actions of the Department for Education and Employment and the Welsh Office see the Parliamentary Commissioner Act 1967 s 4 and Sch 2.
9 See 1988 Act s 218; also the Education (Schools and Further Education) Regulations 1981, SI 1981/1086 and Circular 7/81 (WO 52/81), 'Education Act 1980, sections 27 and 33(3): Regulations', E[113].
10 1996 Act s 571 (as amended by the 1997 Act).
11 [1987] 2 FLR 193.

2.21 *Principles and Administration*

education, and to other arrangements they may make for provision of education.

The authorities and their committees

2.21 In England LEAs are the councils of counties, metropolitan districts, London boroughs and the City of London, together with those of newly established (district) unitary authorities. Wales is now divided into 22 unitary authorities: the councils of the 11 counties and 11 county boroughs are the LEAs.[12]

2.22 LEAs are no longer obliged to appoint education committees as such, but they may delegate education functions to committees;[13] and joint committees of two or more authorities may be established.[14] LEAs remain obliged to appoint a chief education officer,[15] to whom (or to any other officer, but not a committee chairman[16]) functions may be delegated—by the authority, not by a committee.[17]

2.23 So as to secure that persons who appoint foundation governors (see para 3.48) for voluntary schools in their areas are represented, the Secretary of State may give local authorities directions[18] about the composition of committees (including joint committees and subcommittees) who discharge LEA functions. Persons so appointed have the right to vote.[19] Teachers may be appointed to committees, whether or not they are employees of the authority, but no longer have the right to vote.[20]

General responsibility for education

2.24 LEAs '(so far as their powers enable them to do so) [are to] contribute towards the spiritual, moral, mental and physical development of the

---

12 1996 Act s 12. Until the creation of unitary authorities in parts of England following the recommendations of the Local Government Commission, and the restructuring of local government in Wales, there were 116 LEAs in England and Wales. From 1 April 1997 there are 153, and from 1 April 1998, with the creation of additional unitary authorities, 171. Some subseqent increase in the number of unitary authorities is possible. The 1996 Act, by s 579, also applies to the Isles of Scilly.
    See the Local Government Changes for England (School Reorganisation and Admissions) Regulations 1995, SI 1995/2368.
    For grants to LEAs see Chapter 11.
13 Local Government Act 1972 s 102. Delegation does not prevent the LEA from continuing to exercise the function themselves (*Huth v Clarke* (1890) 25 QBD 391).
14 Local Government Act 1972 s 101(5). There have been joint committees for further education institutions, and a special case is the Welsh Joint Education Committee (now established as a company limited by guarantee under ibid s 111), on which LEAs in Wales are represented and which has a wide range of functions.
15 1996 Act s 532. The post is politically restricted under the Local Government and Housing Act 1989 Pt I.
16 *R v Liverpool City Council, ex p Professional Association of Teachers* (1984) 82 LGR 648.
17 Local Government Act 1972 s 101. See *R v Birmingham City Council, ex p National Union of Public Employees* (1984) Times, 24 April.
18 1996 Act s 499. See Circular 19/94 (WO 22/94), 'Arrangements for Education Committees', E[3077], Annex, E[3081].
19 Local Government and Housing Act 1989 s 13 and 1996 Act Sch 37 para 96.
20 Local Government Act 1972 s 104 and 1996 Act Sch 37 para 22.

community by securing that efficient primary education, secondary education and further education are available to meet the needs of the population of their area'. The duties of LEAs do not arise where duties are imposed upon further and higher education funding councils (see paras 10.05 ff and 10.56 ff respectively).[1] Their functions in respect of primary and secondary education are mentioned below; those in respect of further education at para 10.87 ff.

Functions in respect of primary and secondary education

2.25 Every LEA are to secure that sufficient schools are available for their area to provide (a) primary education and (b) secondary education for senior pupils and junior pupils who are at least 10 years six months old and whom it is expedient to educate with senior pupils of compulsory school age. The duty does not extend to children under five, but LEAs have power (see para 3.07) to establish, maintain and assist schools where education is provided both for under-fives and older pupils (including schools with nursery classes for under-fives).[2]

2.26 To secure provision does not necessarily mean 'provide'. Provision may be secured in the schools of another LEA (who may claim recoupment of the cost: see para 11.17 ff), and LEAs may make arrangements for the provision of primary and secondary education at schools not maintained by them or another LEA. Where they are satisfied that no place is available at a reasonably convenient LEA school at which suitable education can be provided they are to pay fees and if need be the cost of board and lodging.[3]

2.27 The schools available for an area are not to be regarded as sufficient

> 'unless they are sufficient . . . in number, character and equipment to provide for all pupils the opportunity of appropriate education [ie] . . . education which offers such variety of instruction and training as may be desirable in view of (a) the pupils' different ages, abilities and aptitudes, and (b) the different periods for which they may be expected to remain at school, including practical instruction and training appropriate to their different needs.'

1 1996 Act s 13. The equivalent passage in the 1944 Act was described by Government spokesmen in Parliament as declaratory, ie underlying more specific legislative provisions. As to enforcement of the duties of LEAs see para 12.09.
  By 1996 SI Act s 25 if it is not otherwise reasonably practicable to obtain information about an LEA school which is required for the purpose of any of the LEA's functions they may have the school inspected by one of their officers, who has the right of entry to the school premises at all reasonable times.
  An LEA has no locus standi to institute legal proceedings for the construction of a will purporting to create a charitable trust (*Re Belling, Enfield London Borough Council v Public Trustee* [1967] Ch 425).
2 1996 Act s 14(1) and (4), and s 17(2). See also, as to Greater London, London Government Act 1963 s 31. 'Primary' and 'secondary' education are defined in paras 2.04 and 2.05.
  By s 14 (5) LEAs have power to secure the provision of full-time education for persons up to 19, including those from other areas.
  As to obligations towards the children of migrant workers see Circular 5/81 (WO 36/81), 'Directive of the Council of the European Community on the education of children of migrant workers', E[104].
  When powers are transferred to funding authorities under s 27 (see para 2.39), by Sch 4 they assume responsibility under s 14. See also s 501(1)(b) (para 12.14).
3 See 1996 Act ss 18 and 517 (see para 12.40). By s 518 (see para 12.42) LEAs may pay the whole or part of the fees and expenses of pupils attending non-maintained schools. See also para 9.02.

2.27 *Principles and Administration*

In assessing 'sufficiency', all schools (including private schools and grant-maintained schools) are to be taken into account.[4]

2.28 The courts have considered the meaning of 'availability' in various contexts. It was held in
- (a) *Guardians of the Poor of Gateshead Union v Durham County Council*[5] that 'the accommodation in the school cannot be said to have been made "available" for children if they are refused admission unless and until their parents comply with some request to pay money which the statutes do not confer upon the LEA any right to demand';
- (b) *Cumings v Birkenhead Corporation*[6] that 'availability' referred to sufficiency of provision in schools, not to places at a school where a parent wishes to have his child educated; and that, following the view expressed by Denning LJ and Parker LJ in *Watt v Kesteven* (see para 2.16), the duty to make schools available can ordinarily be enforced only by the Secretary of State (now under 1996 Act s 497), but see *Meade v Haringey* below;
- (c) *Meade v London Borough of Haringey*[7] that whether closing a school was a breach of statutory duty turned on the facts of the case (the council had closed schools in consequence of a caretakers' strike); and that [the 1996 Act s 497] does not exclude any other remedy available in the courts when a person has suffered special damage;
- (d) *R v Liverpool City Council, ex p Ferguson*[8] that dismissal of all teachers, in disregard of the council's duty as an LEA, was unlawful;
- (e) *R v Mid-Glamorgan County Council, ex p Greig*[9] that the obligation of the LEA does not extend to providing the *most* suitable education;
- (f) *Equal Opportunities Commission v Birmingham City Council*[10] that availability of places is subject to the avoidance of sex discrimination;
- (g) *R v Inner London Education Authority, ex p Ali*[11] that if statutory standards are not being met the LEA are not necessarily in breach of their duty. The question is whether they have taken the steps the statute requires to remedy the situation;
- (h) *R v Secretary of State for Education and Science, ex p Avon County Council*[12] that an LEA are entitled and required to take into account the provision of all schools (including the fact that some children go to independent schools) to determine what numbers and sorts of schools are to be provided to secure that there are sufficient schools; and there is no general obligation to provide single sex schools.

2.29 'Variety of instruction and training' may be had at maintained 'comprehensive schools', established to provide secondary education for all levels and types of ability.[13]

4 1996 Act s 14(2) and (3). See *R v Birmingham City Council, ex p Equal Opportunities Commission (No 2)* [1992] 2 FLR 133; and *R v Northamptonshire County Council, ex p K* [1994] ELR 397, CA, F[110].
5 [1918] 1 Ch 146.
6 [1972] Ch 12, F[42].
7 [1979] 1 WLR 637, F[75].
8 (1985) Times, 20 November, F[86].
9 (1988) Independent, 1 June.
10 [1989] 1 All ER 769, F[34].
11 [1990] COD 317, DC.
12 (1990) 88 LGR 716, F[99].
13 *Wood v Ealing London Borough Council* [1967] Ch 364; and *Smith v Inner London Education Authority* [1978] 1 All ER 411, F[74].

2.30   LEAs are to have regard to
(a) the need for securing that primary and secondary education are provided in separate schools, except in the case of special and middle schools (as to which see paras 5.35 ff and 2.08 respectively);[14]
(b) the need for securing that special educational provision is made for pupils with special educational needs (see Chapter 5); and
(c) the expediency of securing boarding accommodation where thought desirable by parents and authority, at boarding schools or otherwise.[15]

Other arrangements for the provision of education

2.31   LEAs are to provide suitable full- or part-time education at school or otherwise for children of compulsory school age who would otherwise not receive it for some reason, including ill-health or exclusion from school. (Education is 'suitable' when it is efficient and has reference to age, ability and aptitude, and special educational needs.) A school organised for these children, whether or not already in existence, is called a 'pupil referral unit' if it is not a county or special school. It may include boarding accommodation. Authorities may also make provision otherwise than at school for young persons up to the age of 18, for example in hospital.[16]

Land and other property   Acquisition, holding and disposal

2.32   LEAs may accept, hold and administer property upon trust for educational purposes.[17] An LEA's intention to vest a school (other than a nursery school or a special school) in themselves as trustees is to be treated as their intention to maintain the school as a county school,[18] and any school so vested is to be such a school. In addition to exercising their own powers, express and implied, to provide premises, furniture and equipment, an LEA may, with permission, use those of a local social services authority, on terms to be agreed which may include the services of the latter's staff.[19]

2.33   The Secretary of State may authorise LEAs to purchase compulsorily land required for schools and other institutions which they maintain or have power to assist (see para 3.07), or otherwise for the purposes of their functions under the 1996 Act. The land may be within or outside the LEA's area. An LEA

14   It appears from the 1996 Act s 50(3) (see para 3.28) that complete physical separation is not required to constitute separate schools.
15   1996 Act s 14(6) and (7). As to charges at maintained boarding schools, see s 458 (para 7.61); as to separate boarding accommodation, s 514 (para 12.35 ff) (in the case of funding authorities, Sch 4); and as to special educational provision at non-maintained schools, s 348 (para 5.51).
16   1996 Act s 19 and Sch 1. See the Education (Pupil Referral Units) (Application of Enactments) Regulations 1994, SI 1994/2103, Circulars 11/94 (WO 61/94), 'Education by LEAs of children otherwise than at school', E[2931], and 12/94 (WO 57/94), 'Education of sick children', E[2971]. See also *R v East Sussex County Council, ex p T* (1997) Times, 29 April.
17   1996 Act s 529(1). As to the application of an endowment of an existing school transferred to the LEA see the remarks of Jessel MR in *Re Poplar and Blackwall Free School* (1878) 8 Ch D 543. As to the acceptance, generally, of gifts of property by local authorities, see Local Government Act 1972 s 139.
18   1996 Act s 529(2). Accordingly the requirements of ss 35 (including those as to publication and submission), and 36 to 40 apply (see para 3.08 ff).
19   National Health Service Act 1977 s 21(2).

are not ultimately to bear expenditure on land for a voluntary school that would have fallen on the governing body had that body purchased it – unless the LEA are proposing to exercise their power to give assistances to governing bodies of aided and special agreement schools.[20] LEAs may by agreement acquire land required for maintained or assisted schools and other institutions, including cases in which they will not hold the land.[1] The same requirement as to the burden of expenditure applies as in the case of compulsory purchase, but without the exception.

2.34 The general prohibition on the disposal of local authority land below market value without the consent of the Secretary of State does not apply in the case of disposals to the governors of existing voluntary aided and special agreement schools and to promoters of new voluntary aided schools.[2]

THE FUNDING AUTHORITIES

2.35 Under Chapter IV of Part I of the 1996 (sections 20 to 26, Schedules 2 and 3) Act the Funding Agency for Schools in England remains in existence, and a Schools Funding Council for Wales may be established. Both funding authorities are constituted and financed by the Secretaries of State.[3]

2.36 Funding authorities have funding responsibility only for grant-maintained schools, and initially their main functions are the calculation and distribution of grant to those schools. They are to carry out value-for-money studies.[4] The Secretary of State may, by order, and, if reasonably practicable after consultation, give them directions about all, or a particular category of, grant-maintained schools.[5] He may transfer to them certain of his functions in relation to those schools (see, in particular, paras 4.29 n 14, 4.36 n 7 and 4.100).[6]

2.37 When an order is made transferring responsibility for provision of school places in a particular area to a funding authority (see para 2.30), the law as stated is amended in accordance with Schedule 4 to the 1996 Act; and in those

---

20 1996 Act s 530. 'Authorise': as to authorisation procedure see the Acquisition of Land Act 1981.
1 1996 Act s 531. The substantive authority for acquisition, by lease or purchase, is the Local Government Act 1972 s 120. See Circular 2/60 'Land questions'.
2 1996 Act s 75. The prohibition is under the Local Government Act 1972 s 123(2). As to the *disposal* of land no longer used for a voluntary or grant-maintained school see para 15.26 ff.
3 1996 Act ss 20 to 22, 25, 26 and Sch 2. The Agency are to consist of between 10 and 15 members, the Council of between 8 and 12. The Secretaries of State are to have regard to the desirability of including persons with specified types of experience.
   The Council will begin to exercise their functions on a date specified by order of the Secretary of State. In the meantime he exercises their functions.
   The Secretaries of State may make grants to the funding authorities, subject to terms and conditions. Schedule 2 para 15 relates to the keeping of accounts by the authorities.
4 1996 Act s 23. This requirement is additional to that contained in s 310 (see para 4.102). By the Education (Schools Conducted by Education Associations) Regulations 1993, SI 1993/3103 reg 2 and Sch 1 para 6 it does not apply where a school is conducted by an education association.
5 1996 Act s 24. Sections 496 (acting unreasonably) and 497 (default) apply to funding authorities as they apply to LEAs (see paras 12.05 ff and 12.09).
6 1996 Act s 22 and Sch 3.

circumstances a funding authority may propose the establishment of new grant-maintained schools.[7]

ALLOCATION OF FUNCTIONS

2.38 Chapters V and VI of Part I of the 1996 Act (sections 27 to 30, Schedule 4) make the following provisions.

2.39 When, of the total of all pupils at maintained schools in the area of an LEA, the percentage of pupils registered at grant-maintained schools is
(a) less than ten, responsibility for provision of schools lies with the LEA;
(b) ten or more, the Secretary of State may by order divide responsibility for providing sufficient school places between the funding authority and the LEA;
(c) not less than 75, the order may give responsibility to the funding authority alone.
If the percentage is between 10 and 75, the LEA may request the Secretary of State to make an order giving responsibility to the funding authority alone. An order may relate to primary education, to secondary education or to both.[8]

2.40 The Secretary of State is to decide disputes between an LEA and a funding authority as to which should exercise a function.[9]

PROVISION OF INFORMATION

2.41 Chapter VI of Part I of the 1996 Act (sections 29 and 30) also makes requirements about the provision of information by LEAs and funding authorities. (Other requirements are at para 6.70.)

2.42 LEAs are to make reports and returns to the Secretary of State and give him the information he requires for the purposes of his functions. They are under the same obligation to the funding authority.[10] They are to compile information and conduct or support research, as prescribed, so as to give the Secretary of State and the funding authority prescribed information about primary or secondary education, especially for children with special educational needs.[11]

---

7 See 1996 Act s 211 (para 4.17 ff).
8 1996 Act s 27 and Sch 4. As to orders made under (b) and (c), see Government statements made during the passage of the Bill for the 1993 Act (*Hansard*, HL Committee, 24 April 1993). Where a school is conducted by an education association see SI 1993/3103 reg 2 and Sch 1 para 7.
9 1996 Act s 28.
10 1996 Act s 29(1) and (2). See also the 1988 Act s 158 and para 12.56 ff. The information the funding authority will require includes projected numbers of pupils in each age group requiring places in LEA and grant-maintained schools, and the amount of provision that already exists in county and voluntary schools.
11 1996 Act s 29(3) to (6). See the Education (School Hours and Policies) (Information) Regulations 1989, SI 1989/398; Education (School Curriculum and Related Information) Regulations 1989, SI 1989/954; Education (Special Educational Needs) (Information) Regulations 1994, SI 1994/1048; Education (School Information) (England) Regulations 1996, SI 1996/2585; Education (Pupils' Attendance Records) Regulations 1991, SI 1991/1582; Education (Pupil Referral Units) (Application of Enactments) Regulations 1994, SI 1994/2103; and Education (School Information) (Wales) Regulations 1994, SI 1994/2330.

2.43 Principles and Administration

2.43 Funding authorities have similar obligations to the Secretary of State and reciprocal obligations to LEAs.[12]

2.44 The Secretary of State has made regulations requiring LEAs to publish information about their policies and arrangements regarding primary and secondary education in their areas. The requirement does not apply to nursery schools or to children who will be under five on admission to school.

---

12 1996 Act s 30. The information and advice the Secretary of State will require is likely to include a management plan as defined in 'Non-departmental Public Bodies: A guide for Departments' published by the Office of Public Service and Science, and the statements of accounts and report of the Comptroller and Auditor General (see para 2.35 n 3). See the Education (Information as to Provision of Education) (England) Regulations 1994, SI 1994/1256.

Chapter 3

SCHOOLS MAINTAINED BY LOCAL EDUCATION AUTHORITIES

3.01 This chapter outlines Part II of the 1996 Act (sections 31 to 182, Schedules 5 to 19).

CATEGORIES AND DEFINITIONS

3.02 Some preliminary provisions are in Chapter I (sections 31 to 34, Schedule 5) as follows.

3.03 LEAs maintain county and voluntary schools; also nursery schools, special schools and pupil referral units.[1]

3.04 Primary and secondary schools which are maintained by LEAs, and have been established by them, are county schools; otherwise they are voluntary schools, falling into the categories of controlled, aided or special agreement. A voluntary school is controlled unless there is in force an order of the Secretary of State directing that it be aided or subject to a special agreement.[2] A special agreement was, but may no longer be, made between LEA and school promoters for a grant in consideration of the establishment of, or alteration of premises for, a secondary school.[3] Usage recognises other (non-statutory) terms, such as 'infant' and 'grammar'.

3.05 'Maintenance' of LEA schools means defraying all the expenses, with the exception of certain expenses of aided and special agreement schools which are payable by the governing body (see para 3.34). And in specified circumstances LEAs have the duty of providing new premises for voluntary schools.[4]

---

1   1996 Act ss 31 and 33. As to nursery schools, special schools and pupil referral units see paras 2.08, 2.09 and 2.31.
2   1996 Act ss 31 and 32. Within the category of county schools also fall schools which were not established by LEAs but which (a) were maintained as such before the 1996 Act commenced, (b) are maintained as county schools pursuant to s 35(1)(b) (see para 3.08); and (c) are maintained as county schools pursuant to an order under s 50 (see para 3.28).
    Orders creating aided status may be made under 1996 Act ss 48, 51, 54 or 58 (see paras 3.25, 3.28, 3.30 and 3.32) or have been made under 1944 Act s 15, 1946 Act s 2 or 1986 Act s 54.
    The Diocesan Boards of Education Measure 1991 ss 3 and 7 give boards certain supervisory and reserve functions in relation to Church of England voluntary schools.
3   Agreements were made under 1944 Act s 15 and Sch 3. See now 1996 Act Sch 5.
4   1996 Act s 34. The costs of maintaining a voluntary school include the payment of rates and outgoings such as meeting the cost of damage to adjacent properties by the roots of trees growing on school premises.

3.06 *Schools Maintained by Local Education Authorities*

ESTABLISHMENT, ALTERATION ETC OF SCHOOLS

3.06 The following account of Chapter II of Part II of the 1996 Act (sections 35 to 58, Schedule 6) refers to the establishment, alteration or change of site of county and voluntary schools; also to the status of new voluntary schools as controlled or aided, change of status of voluntary schools, proposals for middle schools and division of a single school into two or more schools.

3.07 LEAs may establish and maintain, and assist non-maintained, primary and secondary schools, inside or outside their areas, except that they may not establish schools intended to provide part-time education for those over compulsory school age, or full-time education for those of 19 and over.[5] They may also establish and maintain nursery schools, and assist those not established by LEAs, including schools which are for both under fives and five-year-olds upwards.[6]

County schools: establishment, alteration or change of site

3.08 Where an LEA intend to
(a) establish a new county school;
(b) start maintaining a school as a county school;
(c) make any significant change in the character, or significant enlargement of the premises of a county school; or
(d) transfer a county school to a new site in the area
they are first to consult appropriate persons (having regard to any guidance published by the Secretary of State), then publish the proposals in the manner he prescribes and submit them to him.[7] The proposals are to state proposed date(s) of implementation and the number of pupils intended to be admitted in

---

By s 71 if an LEA default in their duty to maintain a voluntary school and the governing body act in lieu the Secretary of State may reimburse them, and the sums paid become a debt due to him by the LEA which he may recover by deduction from grant.

5 1996 Act s 16. As to (a) Greater London see the London Government Act 1963 s 31; (b) restriction on the powers of LEAs where responsibility for providing places has been transferred to a funding authority see the 1996 Act Sch 4; (c) acquisition of land see the 1996 Act s 530, para 2.32.

6 1996 Act s 17. As to the nursery school 'voucher scheme' see para 11.12.

7 1996 Act s 35(1) and (5). By s 35(2) the requirement to publish proposals does not apply in relation to the transfer of a county school to a new site temporarily or in other limited specified circumstances. See para 15.20 as to variation of trust deeds.

The LEA's 'intention' is formed when they resolve to publish proposals. No time limit is set for publication or for the period within which a copy is to be submitted to the Secretary of State.

As to (a) public notice inconsistent with proposals see *Legg v Inner London Education Authority* [1972] 3 All ER 177; (b) proposals by a prospectively superseded LEA, see *R v Buckinghamshire County Council, ex p Milton Keynes Borough Council* (1996) Times, 13 November; (c) proposals to remedy excess provisions see para 12.11 ff. Where reorganisations of schools involve establishment of further education corporations provision is made for transfer of ownership of land see para 10.55.

See the Education (Publication of School Proposals and Notices) Regulations 1993, SI 1993/3113. It was held in *Coney v Choyce* [1975] 1 All ER 979, F[71], that the regulations were directory not mandatory—non-compliance in minor respects did not invalidate the Minister's approval of proposals. See the Local Government Changes for England (School Reorganisation and Admissions) Regulations 1995, SI 1995/2368 where the functions of an LEA in England are exercisable by a new authority in consequence of structural or boundary changes effected by an order under the Local Government Act 1992 s 17.

See, generally, Circular 23/94 (WO 13/95), Circular on the Supply of School Places, E[3151], and as to consultation with parents para 1.16 ff.

each relevant age group (see para 7.15). A statement about the manner of making objections is to accompany the proposals.[8]

3.09 A change in the character of a school includes, in particular, one resulting from a change in its age range or sex composition, or from selection for admission by reference to ability or aptitude. 'Significant' implies a substantial change in function or size of the school—determined if need be, if a question arises (as is any question about significant enlargement), by the Secretary of State,[9] who has stated that he would usually regard the following as significant (but the list is not exhaustive):

(a) changes in the age range of a school by a year or more,
(b) selecting more than 15 per cent of a school's intake on the basis of ability in particular subjects or general ability,
(c) the introduction or removal of places in an 'ordinary' school for pupils with statements of special educational needs,
(d) changes from single sex to co-educational or vice versa (but not the admission of a small number of pupils of the opposite sex in a sixth form),
(e) initial provision of boarding places or removal of a significant number, and
(f) change in the religious character of a voluntary or grant-maintained school.

3.10 Embarking on, or discontinuing, the provision of teacher training is not a significant change of character.[10]

3.11 Before an LEA formulate proposals under (c) or (d) above relating to a school eligible for grant-maintained status (see para 4.04) they are to consult the governing body. No proposals are to be published as above where proposals for acquisition of that status have been approved.[11]

3.12 Objections to proposals published by an LEA may be submitted to them, within two months of first publication, (a) by ten or more local government electors for the area, (b) by the governing body of any school affected by the proposals, (c) by any other LEA concerned or (d) by the appropriate further education funding council if the proposals would affect the facilities for full-time education for persons over compulsory school age but under 19. Within one month after the two-month objection period the LEA are to send the

---

8 1996 Act s 35(3). By sub-s (4) pupils intended to be admitted for nursery education are to be disregarded but counted on transfer to a reception class.
9 1996 Act s 573.
    By 1996 Act s 35(6) the LEA are to consult the appropriate further education funding council before publishing proposals for significant change or enlargement which would affect the facilities for full-time education for persons over compulsory school age but under 19.
    If a parent considers that a proposed change or enlargement would be significant he may ask the Secretary of State for a determination. Where the LEA, knowing of the request to the Secretary of State, voted for the change and began to implement it, the High Court prohibited further implementation in advance of the determination (*R v Berkshire County Council, ex p Glenister* (20 March 1986, unreported)).
    As to the basis of the Secretary of State's determination, see Circular 6/96, 'Admissions to Maintained Schools', Annex B, and Circular 23/94, Appendix 2, E[3151].
10 1994 Act s 12(5).
11 1996 Act s 35(7) and (8). See *R v Secretary of State for Education and Science, ex p Avon County Council (No 2)* (1990) 88 LGR 737, CA, F[99].

3.12 Schools Maintained by Local Education Authorities

Secretary of State copies of all objections made (and not subsequently withdrawn) together with the LEA's observations on them.[12]

3.13 The approval of the Secretary of State to proposals is required[13] if (a) it is intended to maintain a voluntary school as a county school, or (b) if he 'calls in' the proposals within two months of submission, or (c) objections have been made within that period and not withdrawn. If he gives his approval he may do so with or without modifications of the proposals, in the former case only after consulting the LEA. He is not to approve proposals under paragraph (a) above unless he has approved an agreement between the LEA and the school's governing body for the transfer to the former of all necessary interests in the school's premises.

3.14 If proposals for acquisition of grant-maintained status (see para 4.04 ff) have been published and not determined or withdrawn before proposals under para 3.08 above have been published (or vice versa) the Secretary of State is to consider both sets of proposals together and determine the grant-maintained status proposals first. If he approves them he is also to approve proposals under paragraphs (c) or (d) in para 3.08 if the governing body of the grant-maintained school consent, but otherwise reject them.[14]

---

12 1996 Act s 36(1),(2) and (4). By sub-s (3) objections may also be submitted by the funding authority where an order under s 27 applies and primary or secondary education in the area is affected. As to 'first publication' see sub-ss (5) and (6).
    Minor authorities are not 'statutory objectors'.
    Two separate objections, each containing fewer than ten local government electors' signatures, cannot be read together so as to constitute a single valid objection, unless (per Stuart-Smith LJ) it is 'demonstrated...on the face of the documents that all ten [electors] are submitting the same objection either by signing it or by signing another document in which they expressly associate themselves with the objections in question' (*Milne v London Borough of Wandsworth* (1992) 90 LGR 515, CA).
    In *R v Secretary of State for Wales and Clwyd County Council, ex p Russell* (28 June 1983, unreported), F[80], it was held that objectors are not entitled to see the LEA's observations on their objections. Exceptionally there may be circumstances in which fairness requires that objectors should be given the opportunity to comment on the content of the LEA's observations, for example if those observations contain relevant new facts which are not public knowledge during the formative stage of proposals.
    See also *R v Secretary of State for Education, ex p Skitt* [1995] ELR 388.
13 In *R v Northamptonshire County Council, ex p Tebbutt* (26 June 1986, unreported) Woolf LJ said: 'In considering the court's role the fact that a proposal requires the approval of the Secretary of State and cannot be implemented until he gives such approval is an important consideration. The function of the Secretary of State does not exclude this court's jurisdiction, but in my view the court should bear in mind that Parliament has expressly bestowed this function upon the Secretary of State and not on the courts, and unlike the courts the Secretary of State can consider not only the same matters that can be considered by this court but also the merits of the application'. Taylor LJ in *Nichol v Gateshead Metropolitan Borough Council* (1988) 87 LGR 435, CA, indicated that a challenge to proposals by way of judicial review should take place at an early opportunity, whereas Woolf LJ in *R v Secretary of State for Education and Science, ex p Threapleton* [1988] COD 102, said that 'normally it was likely to be advantageous to allow the Secretary of State's decision to be given prior to making an application for judicial review' so as to avoid successive applications, challenging the LEA's and then the Secretary of State's, decisions.
14 1996 Act s 37. See *R v Secretary of State for Wales, ex p South Glamorgan County Council* (1988) Times, 25 June.
    Examples of proposals which may be 'called in' by the Secretary of State under paragraph (b) are given in Circular 23/94 para 130, E[3187].
    For application see the Education (Grant-maintained Special Schools) Regulations 1994, SI 1994/653, and, where a school is being conducted by an education association, the Education (Schools Conducted by Education Associations) Regulations 1993, SI 1993/3103.

3.15 The Secretary of State is to convey his decision on proposals formally in writing.[15] He may not substitute his own proposals for those submitted to him.[16] He may, after consultation with the governing body of the school, modify trust deeds so far as necessary on the transfer of a school to a new site.[17]

3.16 If proposals do not require the approval of the Secretary of State the LEA are by resolution to determine whether they are to be implemented, and are to do so not later than four months after submission to the Secretary of State. They are to notify him of their determination.[18]

3.17 Proposals submitted to the Secretary of State for establishment and alteration of county schools are to be accompanied, for his approval, by the particulars he requires of premises.[19]

3.18 LEAs are under obligation to implement proposals (and particulars of premises) approved by the Secretary of State or which they have formally determined to implement. The Secretary of State may modify proposals at the request of the LEA. Compliance with requirements and approval of proposals may not be anticipated by LEAs or others except to the extent the Secretary of State thinks reasonable in the circumstances.[20]

Voluntary schools: establishment, alteration or change of site

3.19 Where (a) it is proposed that an existing or new school should be maintained by an LEA as a voluntary school,[1] or (b) the governing body of a voluntary school intend to make a significant change in its character (see para 3.09) or enlargement of premises, or to transfer it to a new site, the procedures specified are similar to those applying in the case of county schools. The approval of the Secretary of State is required in each case. He is not to approve proposals for a school to provide part-time education for persons over compulsory school age or full-time education for persons of 19 or over (and a

---

15 See *R v Secretary of State for Education and Science, ex p Hardy* (1988) Times, 28 July, F[47].
16 *Legg v Inner London Education Authority* [1972] 3 All ER 177, F[197]. An example of a proper modification (per McNeill J in *Hardy*) is deferment of implementation of proposals for one year.
17 1996 Act s 179.
18 1996 Act s 38. If the LEA fail to make a decision within four months it seems that the proposals lapse.
19 1996 Act s 39. Premises the Secretary of State approves are not subject to building regulations (see para 15.06), but the Department has recommended standards in AM 2/85, 'Construction standards for maintained educational building in England', and AM 1/86, 'Modification of approved procedures for LEA school and further education building projects'.
 As to agreements for transfer of premises on a voluntary school becoming a county school see Sch 6.
20 1996 Act s 40. As to variation of trust deeds see para 15.20.
1 In *R v Secretary of State for Education and Science, ex p Yusuf Islam* [1994] ELR 111, F[106] (proposal for a school to be granted voluntary aided status) an application for judicial review succeeded because of procedural impropriety in the Secretary of State's decision-making process.

3.19 Schools Maintained by Local Education Authorities

'change in character' does not include one resulting from beginning or ceasing to provide such education).[2]

3.20 If proposals for acquisition of grant-maintained status (see para 4.04 ff) have been published and not determined or withdrawn before proposals as above have been published (or vice versa) the Secretary of State is to consider both sets of proposals together and determine the grant-maintained status proposals first. If he approves them he is also to approve proposals as above if they were made to ensure consistency of provision of education in the LEA's area, but otherwise reject them.

3.21 The persons (or those they represent) making proposals and the LEA are to implement proposals under (a) in para 3.19 above; the governing body those under (b). The LEA (or on approval of transfer of a school to a new site in the area of a different LEA, that authority[3]) are to implement approved proposals (i) for transfer of a controlled school to a new site (and any associated proposals for change in character) so far as involving provision of premises or removal or provision of equipment, (ii) in any other case, so far as relating to playing fields or buildings, other than school buildings, which are to form part of the school premises.[4]

3.22 Proposals are to be implemented in accordance with particulars of premises approved by the Secretary of State. The Secretary of State may modify proposals at the request of the LEA in the case of proposals under (a) above, by the governing body those under (b). Compliance with requirements and approval of proposals may not be anticipated by LEAs or others except to the extent the Secretary of State thinks reasonable in the circumstances.[5]

3.23 Where a denominational body seek to establish a new voluntary school or schools in substitution for one or more which are to be closed the Secretary

---

2 1996 Act ss 41 to 44.
  See para 3.59 where proposals approved under s 43 include the naming of a sponsor.
  By s 44(3) and (4) particulars of proposed premises are to be submitted for consultation with the LEA by whom the school is to be maintained before submission to the Secretary of State. Premises he approves are not subject to building regulations (see para 15.06).
  See the Diocesan Boards of Education Measure 1991 s 7 as to the powers of a Board to give directions in respect of Church of England voluntary aided schools.
  As to establishment and enlargement of controlled schools see paras 3.41 and 3.42 respectively, and as to variation of trust deeds, para 15.20.
3 In the case of controlled schools the new LEA are also to provide a new site and buildings as under 1996 Act ss 60 and 62 (see para 3.38).
4 1996 Act s 45(1),(2) and (7).
  Where the functions of an LEA in England are exercisable by a new authority in consequence of structural or boundary changes effected by an order under the Local Government Act 1992, s 17, see the Local Government Changes for England (School Reorganisation and Admissions) Regulations 1995, SI 1995/2368.
  As to the powers of (a) the Secretary of State (i) to make grants or loans to the governing bodies of aided or special agreement schools, see ss 65 to 67 (para 3.43), (ii) to amend trust deeds see para 15.20; (b) LEAs to assist the governing bodies of aided or special agreement schools and promoters of new voluntary schools see ss 68 and 69 (para 3.44).
5 1996 Act s 45(3) to (6). By sub-s (7) where transfer is approved to a site in a different area the duty to maintain falls to the new LEA and in the case of a controlled school ss 60 and 62 (see para 3.38 below) apply.

of State may, where he approves proposals as above, by order authorise the substitution, having first consulted any LEA and governing body (on whom the order may impose conditions) he thinks will be affected.[6]

3.24 The Secretary of State may also, after the same consultation, by order (which may contain conditions and incidental provisions) authorise the transfer of a voluntary school to a new site (a) because it is not reasonably practicable to bring the existing school premises up to the prescribed standards, or (b) where the transfer is dictated by a movement of population, or by action taken or proposed to be taken relating to housing or town and country planning. But he is not to authorise the transfer of an aided or special agreement school unless satisfied that the governing body will be able and willing, with the assistance of his grant, to defray the expenses of providing school buildings on the new site.[7]

Status of new voluntary school

3.25 Where the Secretary of State is
(a) satisfied that the governors of a new voluntary school are able and willing, with the assistance of his grants (see para 3.43) to defray their share of maintenance expenses (see para 3.34) he is, upon their application, by order to direct that the school is to be an aided school;
(b) not satisfied that the governing body will be able to defray those expenses without both grants and a loan (see para 3.43), and he thinks the area will not also be served by a county or controlled school, he is to defer determining the application until after consulting religious representatives and if need be calling a local inquiry.

3.26 If the Secretary of State does not direct that the new school is to be an aided school he is to direct by order that it be a controlled school.[8]

Proposals for a middle school

3.27 A proposal for the establishment of a new county or voluntary school (see paras 3.08 or 3.19) may be for a middle school, providing full-time education for pupils of below 10 years 6 months and above 12. (Middle schools straddle the primary and secondary age ranges, and are deemed primary if the age range of pupils is wider below than above the age of 11, otherwise secondary[9] unless equal, when the Secretary of State determines the status of the school by order.)

Division of a single school into two or more schools

3.28 LEAs (county schools), and governing bodies after consultation with the LEA (controlled and aided schools), may propose to the Secretary of State that

6 1996 Act s 46. Section 173 (see para 3.128) is not to apply. By s 179 (see para 15.20) trust deeds may be modified. (The 1973 Act s 1(1) repealed the Endowed Schools Acts 1869 to 1948.)
7 1996 Act s 47, and see s 59(5). 'Prescribed standards': see s 542 (para 15.04) and the Education (School Premises) Regulations 1996, SI 1996/360. By s 179 trust deeds may be modified.
 As to the powers of (a) the Secretary of State (i) to make grants or loans to the governing bodies of aided or special agreement schools, see ss 65 to 67 (para 3.43), (ii) to vary trust deeds see para 15.20; (b) LEAs to assist (i) the governing bodies of aided or special agreement schools and (ii) promoters of new voluntary schools see ss 68 and 69 (para 3.44).
8 1996 Act s 48. 'Local inquiry': see para 12.20.
9 1996 Act s 49. See s 5(4) and the Education (Middle Schools) Regulations 1980, SI 1980/918.

3.28 *Schools Maintained by Local Education Authorities*

a school organised into separate departments should be divided into separate schools, and the Secretary of State may by order direct accordingly. Governing bodies of aided schools may propose that any or all of the separate schools should be controlled schools. The publication requirements mentioned in paras 3.08 or 3.19 above do not apply.[10]

Change of status from controlled school to aided school

3.29 Where the governing body of a controlled school propose to apply for an order that the school should become an aided school they are first to consult the LEA, then publish their proposals in accordance with regulations and submit a copy of the published proposals to the Secretary of State together with other information he reasonably requires. In an accompanying statement they are to explain the provisions about objections and specify the date on which it is proposed the change should occur. Procedures are laid down (similar to those for the establishment and alteration of voluntary schools) for the submission of objections to the Secretary of State.[11]

3.30 The Secretary of State may by order direct that the school become an aided school if he is satisfied that with the assistance of his grants (see para 3.43) the governing body will be able and willing to defray their share of maintenance expenses (see para 3.34) and pay compensation to the LEA in respect of relevant capital expenditure. The amount of compensation is to be settled by agreement between governing body and LEA, or otherwise as the Secretary of State thinks fit having regard to the current value of the property. The order may change the date of implementation after consultation with the LEA, specify the amount of compensation (if any) payable and make transitional provisions, some of which are specified. The Secretary of State may vary his order in specified circumstances.[12]

Change of status from aided or special agreement school to controlled or aided school

3.31 If governors of an aided or special agreement school need or wish to relinquish their maintenance obligations (see para 3.34) they are to apply to the Secretary of State, who is to revoke his initial order, whereupon the school assumes controlled status unless the LEA exercise their power to give assistance.[13]

---

10 1996 Act s 50 and s 51. 'Department' means a part of the school organised under a separate head teacher. An order may contain incidental provisions and in particular define the premises of the separate schools—from which it appears that complete physical separation is not required.
11 1996 Act ss 52 and 53. See para 3.59 where proposals published under s 52 include the naming of a sponsor. Proposals are to be in accordance with the Education (Publication of Proposals to Change Status of a Controlled School) Regulations 1987 (not an SI), as amended by the Education (Publication of School Proposals and Notices) Regulations 1993, SI 1993/3113. See Circular 2/87 (entitled as the 1987 regulations) E[277].
12 1996 Act ss 54 to 56. 'Relevant capital expenditure' is expenditure incurred under ss 60, 63 or 64 (see paras 3.38 to 3.42) or the provisions those sections supersede.
13 1996 Act s 57. The 'initial order' in the case of (a) aided schools is one made under ss 48, 54 or 58 (or a direction in an order under s 51) or the provisions those sections supersede, (b) special agreement schools is one made under the 1944 Act s 15.
  As to procedure at a governing body's meeting about the making of an application see Sch 8 para 16.

3.32 If the Secretary of State, on application by the governing body of a special agreement school, is satisfied that the grant made under the agreement has been repaid to the LEA maintaining the school, he is by order to revoke the initial order and direct that the school become a controlled school, unless he is satisfied that the governing body are able and willing to defray their specified share of maintenance expenses (see para 3.34) with the aid of his financial assistance, in which case it is to be an aided school.[14]

FUNDING OF VOLUNTARY SCHOOLS

3.33 Chapter III of Part II of the 1996 Act (sections 59 to 75) concerns the obligations of governing bodies of voluntary schools and those of LEAs as regards new sites and buildings. It also sets out the provisions for financial assistance by the Secretary of State and LEAs, together with miscellaneous and supplemental provisions.

Obligations of governing bodies

3.34 The governing bodies of controlled schools do not meet any maintenance expenses. Those of aided and special agreement schools are responsible for
(a) discharging liabilities they or former governors or any trustees have incurred in providing school premises[15] and equipment;
(b) altering[16] school buildings[17] to bring the school premises up to prescribed standards;[18] and
(c) repairs to the school buildings other than (i) those to the interior or (ii) those made necessary by use of school premises for other than school purposes at the instance of the LEA. Thus the cost of internal repairs falls to the LEA, as does that of other maintenance, for example of playing fields and playgrounds.[19]

3.35 An LEA may use their own employees to carry out building etc work at a controlled school where they are liable to pay the expenses, and the trustees and governors are to provide facilities to ensure that the work is properly executed.[20]

See also the powers of a Diocesan Board under the Diocesan Boards of Education Measure 1991, s 7(3) in relation to Church of England aided schools.
14 1996 Act s 58.
15 By 1996 Act s 579(1) school premises include any detached playing fields, but not, ordinarily, a teacher's dwelling house.
16 By 1996 Act s 573(2) an alteration of school premises includes improvements, extensions and additions, but not any significant enlargement.
17 By 1996 Act s 579(1) school buildings are any buildings forming part of the school premises with the exception of a caretaker's dwelling, and of buildings for use in connection with (a) playing fields, (b) medical and dental inspection and treatment (c) provision of refreshments.
18 Standards prescribed under the 1996 Act s 542. See the Education (School Premises) Regulations 1996, SI 1996/360 (para 15.04 ff).
19 1996 Act s 59(1) to (4). 'Other than school purposes': see eg para 3.99. Church of England aided schools may receive financial assistance under the Church Schools (Assistance by Church Commissioners) Measure 1958.
20 1996 Act s 74.

3.36 Where an order is made authorising the transfer of an aided or special agreement school to a new site (see para 3.24) the governing body are responsible for meeting the expenses of providing any school buildings.[1]

3.37 Where income from endowments of voluntary schools is, under a trust deed, to be used for purposes of maintenance, it is to be applied towards meeting the obligations (if any) of the governing body, or as determined by a scheme for administering the endowment.[2] Sums received by the governing body or trustees for use of school premises other than school buildings are to be paid over to the LEA.[3]

Obligations of LEAs as regards new sites and buildings

3.38 Except where others have a duty to provide a school site or buildings under the provisions mentioned above (see para 3.21) LEAs are to provide new or additional sites for voluntary schools, and, for controlled schools, also buildings which are to form part of school premises on the site. A 'site'[4] does not include playing fields but otherwise includes any site which is to form part of school premises. The interest of the LEA in the site and buildings on it which are to form part of the school premises (but not, it follows from the definition of 'site', in the playing fields) is to be conveyed to the trustees of the school.[5]

3.39 In the case of
(a) controlled schools, so much of the proceeds of sale of existing school premises on the site as the Secretary of State thinks just are to be paid to the LEA;[6]
(b) aided and special agreement schools, where a new site is provided and (i) work needs to be done on the site, the LEA and governing body may make an agreement under which the cost is borne by the LEA; (ii) there are buildings on the site of value for the school, they may make an agreement which has regard to the governing body's maintenance responsibilities (see para 3.34). Where any proper payment or adjustment has not been made the Secretary of State may give appropriate directions.[7]

---

1 1996 Act s 59(5) The LEA may assist the governing body under s 68 (see para 3.44).
2 1996 Act s 72. Exemption from registration under the Charities Act 1993 is granted where premises are the only endowment (Charities (Exemption of Voluntary Schools from Registration) Regulations 1960, SI 1960/2366).
3 1996 Act s 73. The governing body may retain the proceeds of hiring the school buildings, but charges for heat and light may be payable to the LEA.
4 1996 Act s 62(1).
5 1996 Act ss 60 and 61 (1) and (2). By sub-s (3) the Secretary of State settles any doubt about the proper recipients of the conveyance.
6 1996 Act s 60(4) and (5). 'Proceeds of sale' includes consideration for the creation or disposition of any kind of interest. By sub-s (6) a sum paid under sub-s (4) is to be treated for the purposes of the School Sites Act 1841 s 14 (see para 15.27) as a sum applied in the purchase of a site for the school; and by sub-s (7) the Secretary of State is not to make a determination under sub-s (4) in respect of any property the subject of a trust which has arisen under the Reverter of Sites Act 1987 s 1 (see Appendix 4 para 4) unless satisfied that the interests of beneficiaries under the trust are protected.
7 1996 Act s 61(4),(5) and (6).

3.40 Where premises which have been conveyed to trustees of a voluntary school are subsequently disposed of, the Secretary of State may require a specified proportion of the proceeds to be paid to the LEA.[8]

Financial assistance for controlled schools

3.41 The Secretary of State may by order direct that all or part of the expenses of establishing a new controlled school is to be met by the LEA where otherwise it would have to be met by the promoters. He may do this when the latter and the LEA satisfy him that the establishment of the school is required to provide accommodation in substitution for accommodation at another voluntary school (or a grant-maintained school which was formerly a voluntary school) which has been closed, or at which accommodation has otherwise ceased to be available.[9]

3.42 An LEA and the governing body of a controlled school may reach the conclusion that there should be a significant enlargement[10] of the school premises. The enlargement may be required wholly or mainly[11] to provide accommodation for pupils who would otherwise have attended another voluntary school which has been closed, or at which accommodation has otherwise ceased to be available (for example because of a change in its age-range). Alternatively it may be considered that enlargement would enhance primary or secondary education at the school and/or in the LEA's area generally. If the Secretary of State is satisfied, upon the application of LEA and governing body, that one of these sets of circumstances exists, and the governing body subsequently submit proposals for significant enlargement, he may, if he approves them, by order direct that the expenses are to be met by the LEA.[12]

Financial assistance by Secretary of State for aided and special agreement schools

3.43 The Secretary of State may make
(a) grants to governing bodies (or promoters), subject to any requirements he may impose, of up to 85 per cent (or as prescribed) of the cost of providing, altering or repairing premises, and of equipment; and he is to give

---

8 1996 Act s 62(2). By sub-s (3) 'premises' includes any interest in premises; by sub-s (4) the requirement does not apply where an institution is, or has been, within the further education sector. As to the effect of these provisions in relation to the disposal of premises on the transfer of a grant-maintained school to a new site see paras 4.14 and 4.93 ff.
9 1996 Act s 63. As to religious worship and education at controlled schools see paras 6.44 and 6.52 ff. Unless there is a trust deed denominational religious education cannot be given, so it has been the practice, where it is agreed that the school should be denominational, for LEAs to grant a 99 year lease to trustees (determinable if the school closes), the lease containing a clause securing denominational religious worship and education.
10 As to 'significant enlargement' see para 3.09.
11 'Mainly' probably means 'more than half'.
12 1996 Act s 64. Approval is under s 43 (see para 3.19).
    On one interpretation the LEA should hand over the money to the controlled school governing body and leave them to carry on as if they were an aided school governing body, buying the site (probably from the LEA) and erecting the buildings. On this interpretation the LEA would not recoup their expenditure if the school were to close. Normal practice has been for the LEA to carry out the enlargement but not to convey any additional land to the school trustees, which results in the enlarged site and buildings being in divided ownership.

3.43 Schools Maintained by Local Education Authorities

priority to supporting expenditure necessary for the performance by governing bodies of their duties.[13]

(b) grants of up to 85 per cent of preliminary expenditure on the planning and design work in relation to any scheme for (i) the transfer of an existing aided or special agreement school to a new site or the enlargement or alteration of school premises, or (ii) the provision of a site or buildings for a school either already established, or contemplated, by promoters which would be maintained by the LEA as an aided school on the submission and approval of formal proposals (see para 3.19). The Secretary of State has discretion to require repayment of grant if a school is closed at the instance of the governing body.[14]

(c) loans towards the governing body's share of the capital element of expenses (i) to be incurred in pursuance of a special agreement, (ii) of providing a site or school buildings grant-aided under (a) above, or (iii) of providing school buildings on a new site to which a school is transferred by order (see para 3.24). The Secretary of State is first to consult persons representing the governing body and satisfy himself that the governing body's share of these 'initial expenses' in connection with the school premises will involve capital expenditure, and that the expenditure ought properly to be met by borrowing. The amount of the loan, rate of interest and other terms and conditions are to be specified in an agreement made between the Secretary of State and the governing body with the consent of the Treasury.[15]

Assistance by LEAs for governing bodies of aided and special agreement schools and for promoters of new schools

3.44 LEAs may give assistance as they think fit to mitigate the obligations of governing bodies (a) on the implementation of proposals to establish or alter a school or transfer it to a new site (see para 3.21) or (b) in meeting their part of maintenance expenses (see para 3.34).[16] LEAs may similarly assist the promoters of new voluntary schools.[17] When the assistance of the LEA consists of the provision of premises, the authority are to convey their interest in them to the school trustees (who, on a sale, are to repay the net proceeds).[18]

GOVERNMENT OF LOCAL EDUCATION AUTHORITY SCHOOLS

3.45 Chapter IV of Part II of the 1996 Act (sections 76 to 100, Schedules 7 to 10) is concerned not with the conduct of schools (see para 3.88 ff below) but with constitutional matters, in particular the composition of governing bodies.

---

13 1996 Act s 65. See ss 48 and 58 (re-classification of voluntary schools).
14 1996 Act s 66. As to repayment of grant see s 173.
15 1996 Act s 67.
16 1996 Act s 68.
17 1996 Act s 69.
18 1996 Act s 70. If any doubt or dispute arises as to the persons to whom an LEA are required to make a conveyance, the Secretary of State determines the proper persons.

Instruments of government

3.46 Instruments of government regulate the constitution of the governing bodies of LEA schools. They are to be consistent with statutory provisions and comply with any trust deed relating to the school. They are made by order of the LEA, following consultation with governing body and head teacher.

3.47 In the case of voluntary schools, LEAs, before making an order, are to secure the agreement of the governing body, including that of the foundation governors (see para 3.48) to provisions in an instrument of particular concern to them, and to have regard to the way the school has been conducted. LEAs are also to consider proposals for alteration of an instrument made by the governing body or, as above, by foundation governors. In case of disagreement concerning a proposed order (or variation order) the Secretary of State gives a direction, having regard in particular to the status of the school, and he may modify a trust deed to ensure consistency with the order.[19]

Categories of governor

3.48 The categories[20] are
(a) co-opted governors, co-opted by those governors who have not been so appointed, and separate from co-opted parent governors;
(b) foundation governors (of voluntary schools) appointed, usually under a trust deed (and not by an LEA or minor authority), to maintain (as far as practicable) the character of a school and secure that it is conducted in accordance with the deed. The instrument is to name the appointor;
(c) parent governors, elected (or, exceptionally, co-opted) by parents of registered pupils at a school at a time when they themselves are parents of one or more registered pupils at the same school;
(d) teacher governors, elected by the teachers at the school at which they teach;
(e) governors appointed by the LEA;
(f) governors appointed by a minor authority;[1]
(g) sponsor governors, appointed by the sponsor, for certain aided secondary schools (see para 3.59);
(h) representative governors (see para 3.51 below);
(i) ex officio governors.

---

19 1996 Act ss 76 and 77. Section 76 has effect subject to the provisions relating to grouping of schools (see para 3.67 ff) and to temporary governing bodies (see para 3.70 ff). By s 88 governing bodies are to be constituted as bodies corporate under Sch 7, so that property, rights or liabilities attributable to the governing body immediately before incorporation vest in the body corporate; membership and proceedings etc are elaborated in Sch 8.
  See Circulars 7/87 (WO 12/87), 'Education (No 2) Act 1986: Further Guidance', E[333] and 15/93 (WO 68/93), 'The use of school premises and the incorporation of governing bodies of LEA maintained schools', E[2081].
20 1996 Act s 78 (which specifies the categories (a) to (d)) and Sch 8 paras 2 to 6. By sub-s(5) election of parent and teacher governors is subject to the provisions of s 93 which relate to grouped schools.
  See s 180 (para 15.24) as to the holding of property where a trust deed or other instrument was made before 1 July 1981.
1 Minor authorities are usually parish or (in Wales) community councils, or district councils, for the area served by the school (see Appendix 10).

3.49   *Schools Maintained by Local Education Authorities*

3.49   Arrangements for the election of parent and teacher governors are to be settled by LEAs (county, controlled and LEA special schools) or by governing bodies (aided and special agreement schools).[2]

Governing bodies of county, controlled and LEA special schools

3.50   Instruments determine the size of the governing body, which reflects the number of registered pupils. The membership is of specified numbers of appointees of the LEA, and of parent and teacher governors, together with the head teacher ex officio unless he chooses not to be a governor, foundation governors (for controlled schools) and co-opted members.[3]

3.51   Instruments are to provide that a 'representative' governor is to be appointed to the governing body of
(a)   a county or controlled primary school, by a minor authority, where the school serves the authority's area,
(b)   an LEA special school established in a hospital, by the Health Authority or NHS Trust,
(c)   a (non-hospital) LEA special school, by one or more voluntary organisations designated by the LEA (two representative governors if the school has 100 or more registered pupils), unless the LEA consider that there is no appropriate voluntary organisation.[4]

---

2   1996 Act Sch 8 para 7.
3   1996 Act s 79. The requirements are as follows.

County and LEA special schools

Category of governor	School with less than 100 registered pupils	School with 100 or more but less than 300 registered pupils	School with 300 or more but less than 600 registered pupils	School with 600 or more registered pupils
Parent governors	2	3	4	5
Governors appointed by the local education authority	2	3	4	5
Teacher governors	1	1	2	2
Co-opted governors	3	4	5	6

Controlled schools

Category of governor	School with less than 100 registered pupils	School with 100 or more but less than 300 registered pupils	School with 300 or more but less than 600 registered pupils	School with 600 or more registered pupils
Parent governors	2	3	4	5
Governors appointed by the local education authority	2	3	4	5
Teacher governors	1	1	2	2
Foundation governors	2	3	4	4
Co-opted governors	1	1	1	2

The instrument may provide that a school with 600 or more registered pupils is to be treated as having between 300 and 599 pupils.
By Sch 8 para 2, if no governor is a member of the local business community, or it is desired to increase that representation, a person is to be co-opted accordingly.

4   1996 Act s 80(1) to (6). The appointor is to be named in the instrument.

3.52 Where representative governors are appointed, if the school is a controlled school with less than 600 registered pupils there is to be no co-opted governor; otherwise the number of co-opted governors (excluding co-opted foundation governors) is to be reduced by the number of representative governors appointed.[5]

3.53 To fill vacancies for parent governors of county, controlled or LEA special schools, instruments are to provide for their appointment by the other governors, instead of election, where
(a) the school (other than a hospital special school) has at least 50 per cent boarders and the LEA consider election impracticable, or
(b) in a hospital special school, the LEA consider election likely to be impracticable, or
(c) there are not enough parents standing for election.

3.54 Where reasonably practicable the other governors are to appoint the parent of a registered pupil; otherwise the parent of a child of compulsory school age; but they are not to appoint as a parent governor an elected member or employee of the LEA or of the governing body of an aided school maintained by the LEA.[6]

3.55 The constitution of the governing body is to be reviewed by the LEA or governing body themselves as soon as reasonably practicable after the occurrence of a 'relevant event', namely
(a) implementation of specified proposals which increase the number of registered pupils arising from (i) an alteration of character or premises of a county or voluntary school or its transfer to a new site (see paras 3.08, 3.19 and 3.24), or (ii) a prescribed alteration to a maintained special school (see para 5.37), or
(b) the fourth anniversary of the current instrument or of the latest relevant event.

3.56 The review body are to consider whether the governing body are properly constituted and whether the existing instrument differs from the provision a new instrument would be required to make.[7]

3.57 Where there is an excess of governors in any category and the excess is not eliminated by resignation, the longest serving governor or governors in the category are to cease to hold office. If governors are of equal seniority lots are to be drawn. In the case of foundation governors of a controlled school the instrument itself is to provide a procedure for regularising the excess.[8]

Governing bodies of aided and special agreement schools

3.58 The instrument of government is to provide for the governing body to include

5 1996 Act s 80(7) to (9).
6 1996 Act s 81.
7 1996 Act s 82. Where the review is carried out by (a) the governing body (in all cases save in relation to proposals for significant change or transfer of site (see para 3.08) and to make a prescribed alteration to an LEA special school (see para 5.37)), they are to report any discrepancy to the LEA, (b) the LEA, they are to notify the governing body of the relevant implementation date.
8 1996 Act s 83.

3.58 *Schools Maintained by Local Education Authorities*

(a) the head teacher, ex officio (unless he chooses not to be a governor),
(b) at least one parent governor,
(c) at least one governor appointed by the LEA,
(d) one teacher governor (two if the school has 300 or more registered pupils),
(e) foundation governors (at least one of whom is the parent of a registered pupil), and
(f) at least one governor appointed by a minor authority (if any) whose area a primary school serves.

3.59   Foundation governors are to outnumber the other governors by a specified proportion. Instruments may provide for the inclusion of governors in addition to those mentioned;[9] and, if the Secretary of State so directs by order, the instruments for aided secondary schools are to name one or more sponsors, with power to appoint up to four persons to the governing body.[10]

Governing bodies: general

3.60   Instruments are to make provision so as to reflect the circumstances prevailing at the date when they are made. Where proposals have been implemented under para 3.55 (a) above the number of registered pupils at the school are, until the maximum number for which the proposals provide is reached, deemed to be that number, unless the LEA or governing body determine to the contrary.[11]

3.61   Instruments are to be revised to reflect a school's change of circumstances, but pending a review (see para 3.55), changes in the number of registered pupils (at county, controlled and LEA special schools) may be disregarded. An instrument may make provision in anticipation of change in a school's circumstances, but (in the case of county, controlled and LEA special schools) as respects the number of registered pupils at the school the provision is to have effect only after a review has established that revision is necessary.[12]

3.62   The main provisions relating to qualifications of governors and tenure of office are as follows.[13] The minimum age is 18. Governors (other than ex officio and sponsor governors) of county, controlled and LEA special schools hold office for a renewable term of four years. Sponsor governors hold office for from five to seven years. Regulations prescribe (and an instrument may provide) when a person is disqualified from holding office.[14] A governor may at any time

---

9   1996 Act s 84. See sub-ss (2) and (4), and s 85(7), as to the number of foundation governors.
10 1996 Act s 85. By sub-ss (2) and (3) a direction may be given only at the request or with the consent of the governing body (or after consulting them where a direction varies or revokes a previous direction) except (by sub-ss (4) and (5)) in the case of specified proposals approved under s 43 or published under s 52 (see paras 3.19 and 3.29). Where there are two or more sponsors see sub-s (6).
11 1996 Act s 86. The requirement is subject to Sch 10 para 5(2), which makes provision in relation to new schools. The determination is made by the governing body only when the proposals are under s 41(2)(a) or (b) for alteration of character or premises of a voluntary school or transfer to a new site.
12 1996 Act s 87. See sub-s (3) where s 86(2) has been disapplied by a determination under s 82(3).
13 1996 Act Sch 8 paras 8 to 13.
14 See the Education (School Government) Regulations 1989, SI 1989/1503. By Sch 8 para 21 in the case of conflict between instrument and regulations the latter are to prevail.

resign his office, and he may be removed from office (unless he was co-opted, or appointed by the other governors) by whoever appointed him (for instance because he ceases to possess the qualifications for which he was appointed). But the removal is to be fair,[15] and the appointing body may not validly dismiss governors for failure to comply with their wishes, because that would be to usurp the governors' functions.[16]

3.63 Meetings and proceedings of governing bodies are subject to regulations and are to follow specified requirements concerning, inter alia, election of chairman and vice-chairman, establishment of committees, delegation of functions and quorum. A vacancy in the governing body or defect in election or appointment does not invalidate their proceedings.[17] A governor ought not to participate in a decision in which he may have an interest;[18] indeed he may no longer even stay and listen to the discussion. Specified decisions of the governing body of an aided or special agreement school concerning its discontinuance, alteration or status take effect only if confirmed at a second meeting held not less than 28 days after the first.[19]

3.64 Articles of government (of other than aided schools) are to provide that where the clerk to the governing body fails to attend a meeting a governor may act as clerk without prejudice to his position as governor.[1]

3.65 The minutes of the proceedings of governing bodies are open to inspection by LEAs, and there is provision for minutes and other papers relating to meetings of governing bodies to be made available for general inspection at the school.[2]

3.66 Since 1 January 1994 governing bodies have become bodies corporate, in whom are vested subsisting property, rights and liabilities.[3] LEAs are to give governors, free of charge, information and training for the discharge of their functions and (in the case of schools without delegated budgets) pay them travelling and subsistence allowances, under a scheme made by the LEA.[4]

15 See *R v Brent London Borough Council, ex p Assegai* (1987) 151 LG Rev 891, F[100].
16 *R v Westminster Roman Catholic Diocese Trustee, ex p Andrews* (1989) Independent, 27 July, CA, F[93] and *Brunyate v Inner London Education Authority* [1989] 2 All ER 417, HL, F[101]. In *R v Warwickshire County Council, ex p Dill-Russell* (1990) 89 LGR 640 the Court of Appeal held that following local authority elections council-appointed governors could under s 8(5) lawfully be replaced in order to ensure that the number of governors nominated by each political party stayed in proportion to the representation of those parties on the council.
17 1996 Act Sch 8 paras 14 and 15, and SI 1989/1503.
18 *Noble v Inner London Education Authority* (1983) 82 LGR 291, CA, F[201]; *Bostock v Kay* (1989) 153 JP 549, CA, F[202]; and *R v Governors of Bacon's School, ex p Inner London Education Authority* [1990] COD 414. See SI 1989/1503 as amended by SI 1996/2050.
19 1996 Act Sch 8 para 16.
1 1996 Act s 135(8).
2 1996 Act Sch 8 paras 17 and 18, and SI 1989/1503, reg 24. The provisions about access to papers are applied by the Education (Grant-maintained Special Schools) Regulations 1994, SI 1994/653, reg 42, Schedule, Pt I; and by the Education (Special Schools Conducted by Education Associations) Regulations 1994, SI 1994/1084, reg 8(1), Sch 2, Pt I.
3 1996 Act s 88. Land was attributable to the governing body if it was held by or on behalf of any persons as members or former members of the governing body, and rights and liabilities were attributable if they were acquired or incurred on behalf of any such persons. See Circular 15/93, E[2081]. As to the incorporation of new governing bodies see Sch 7 paras 3 and 4.
4 1996 Act Sch 8 paras 19 and 20. See also para 12.43.

3.67 *Schools Maintained by Local Education Authorities*

Grouping of schools under a single governing body

3.67 LEAs may resolve to group schools they maintain for the purposes of government. Before a resolution is passed, however, governing bodies of county and special schools are to be consulted, and the consent of the governing body of a voluntary school and (with a limited exception relating to primary schools) of the Secretary of State is to be obtained. Where one of the schools has a sponsor, grouping is disallowed unless all the schools are secondary schools.[5] There are rules about the category of school into which a group is to be placed: the group is to be treated as (a) an aided school if it contains at least one such school; (b) a special agreement school if it contains at least one such school (and (a) does not apply); (c) a controlled school if it contains at least one such school (and neither (a) nor (b) applies); (d) as an LEA special school if it contains only such schools; (e) otherwise as a county school.[6] Grouped schools have a single governing body under a single instrument of government.[7]

3.68 Before making an order embodying the first instrument of government LEAs are to consult the governing body and head teacher of each constituent school. If the group contains one or more voluntary schools, LEAs are also (a) to obtain the consent of the governing bodies to the order and of foundation governors to provisions of particular concern to them, and (b) to have regard to how the schools have been conducted.[8] The instrument may provide for LEAs to determine voting rights for election of parent and teacher governors; where it does so it is to require the LEA to ensure that each school in the group has had the opportunity to participate in the election of at least one of the parent governors or teacher governors of the group.[9]

3.69 LEAs are to review the grouping of schools and consider termination in any one of a specified set of circumstances. If they consider that the grouping should be continued, and if the Secretary of State's consent was previously required, they are to report the results of the review and give him further information to enable him to consider whether to end the grouping.[10] He may do so by order. LEAs may end a grouping by resolution if the group does not contain

---

5 1996 Act ss 89 to 91. Consent may be given subject to conditions about the duration of grouping and to modifications of 1996 Act ss 79, 80, 81, 84 and Sch 8 para 2(2) (representation of local business community). As to the operation of ss 89 to 91 in relation to new schools (see para 3.70 ff) see s 100.

The exceptions to the requirement of consent are when the proposed grouping will consist only of two primary schools both of which serve substantially the same area, neither of the schools is a special school, and, where they are in Wales, there is no significant difference between them in their use of the Welsh language. Any dispute is to be settled by the Secretary of State. His consent to continued grouping is required if there is a change of circumstances.

By 1996 SI Act s 29 a resolution may not be passed if special measures (see para 8.30 ff) are required to be taken as respects any of the schools proposed to be grouped, and the Secretary of State may make an order ending any grouping which includes such a school.

6 1996 Act s 89(4).

7 On the incorporation under 1996 Act s 88 of a governing body constituted for two or more schools, Sch 7 para 4 provides that land, other property and other rights and liabilities are to be transferred to and vest in the new governing body.

8 1996 Act s 92. Section 77, modified, applies to subsequent orders.

9 1996 Act s 93.

10 1996 Act s 94. The circumstances are proposals under ss 35, 41, 52, 167 or 339 (see paras 3.08, 3.19, 3.29, 3.126 and 5.37 respectively), proposed orders under ss 46 or 47 (see paras 3.23 and 3.24), or orders by the Secretary of State under ss 50, 51, 57, 58(1) or 35(2)(b) (see paras 3.28, 3.31, 3.32 and 3.08 n 7 respectively).

a voluntary school, or (provided that there is no sponsor) even if it does but the governing body agree, or on one year's notice by either party.[11]

Government of new schools

3.70 LEAs are to make arrangements to constitute temporary governing bodies where the Secretary of State has approved their proposals (or they have determined to implement their own) for the establishment of a new county, or special school or the maintenance as a county school of a school which is neither a county school nor a voluntary school (see paras 3.08, 3.14, 3.16, 5.38 and 5.41). Where proposals have been published, or notice of them served, arrangements as above may be made in anticipation of approval (or determination). Arrangements come to an end if proposals are withdrawn, are rejected by the Secretary of State or if the LEA determine not to implement them; or in any event when the requirement for there to be an instrument of government for the school takes effect.[12]

3.71 Provisions to the same effect apply on approval of proposals for the establishment of a new voluntary school (see para 3.19). If it is to be (a) a controlled school the LEA are to consult the persons making the proposals on whether the LEA are to make anticipatory arrangements, and, if so, on what date, (b) an aided school the LEA and persons making the proposals are to consider the same question, and in case of disagreement the Secretary of State is to give the direction he thinks fit.[13]

3.72 Provision is made for, inter alia, the constitution of temporary governing bodies, the appointment of temporary governors, qualifications and tenure of office, meetings and proceedings, expenses and provision of information;[14] also for the conduct and staffing of new schools so as to anticipate the contents of articles of government.[15] LEA schemes for financial delegation and staffing powers (see below) apply with specified modifications.[16]

FINANCIAL DELEGATION TO GOVERNING BODIES

3.73 Chapter V of Part II of the 1996 Act (sections 101 to 126, Schedules 11, 12) begins with the general requirement that each LEA are to have a scheme,

---

11 1996 Act s 95. Once a group is brought to an end, or on expiry of the period for which it was established, the instrument of government is to be regarded as revoked. (Presumably the instruments of government of the constituent schools then revise). Schedule 7 makes provision for transfer of land etc on dissolution of the governing body in specified circumstances.
12 1996 Act s 96. By s 99 an instrument of government is required to take effect from the date of implementation of proposals (which the Secretary of State determines in case of dispute), and Sch 10 provides for the transition from temporary governing body to that constituted under the instrument. As to the effect of incorporation under s 88 of a governing body which immediately before the incorporation date was conducted by a temporary governing body, see 1996 Act Sch 7 para 3.
    See Circular 7/87, Annex 1, E[361].
13 1996 Act s 97.
14 1996 Act s 98 and Sch 9, under which temporary governing bodies are constituted broadly in accordance with the substantive provisions relating to county, controlled and maintained special schools, and aided schools respectively (see paras 3.50 and 3.58).
15 1996 Act s 166 and Sch 19.
16 1996 Act s 126 and Sch 12.

3.73 approved by the Secretary of State, for determining how they propose to allocate, among their county, voluntary and maintained special schools, as much as is available (the 'aggregated budget') of the amount they think appropriate for meeting the whole of the expenditure on all those schools (the 'general schools budget') in any financial year, exclusive of expenditure on provision for part-time education of persons over compulsory school age or full-time education for those of 19 and over.[17] The aggregated budget is to exclude amounts deducted in accordance with the scheme ('discretionary exceptions'), and (so far as taken into account in calculating the general schools budget) capital expenditure, repayment of loans for capital expenditure and other expenditure prescribed by the Secretary of State ('mandatory exceptions').[18]

3.74 In preparing their schemes for submission to the Secretary of State on or before the date he specifies by order, LEAs are to take into account his guidance; also to consult head teachers and governing bodies of LEA schools (and of grant-maintained schools and special schools unless the Secretary of State decides otherwise). Schemes are not to come into force until approved by the Secretary of State. He may give his approval subject to modifications (after consulting the LEA) and conditions; and he may, after consultation with the LEA and others, impose his own scheme upon an LEA who fail to submit a scheme, or who submit one which he believes cannot be brought into accord with his guidance.[19]

Provision by a scheme for determination of budget shares

3.75 Schemes are to provide for a share of the LEA's aggregated budget to be allocated to each school (the school's budget share), according to a formula—methods, principles and rules of any description. The formula (to be revised from time to time) is to take into account the numbers and ages of registered pupils at the school, and may also take into account other factors affecting the

---

17 1996 Act ss 101, 102 and 103. Schemes are also to provide for delegation of management of a school's 'budget share' to the governing body so far as specified (see para 3.76 below). See Circular 2/94, 'Local management of schools', E[2321].

It is lawful for a school's budget share to cover the cost of non-teaching support in accordance with a statement of special educational needs (*R v Oxfordshire County Council, ex p P* [1996] ELR 153).

By s 120 and the Education (Application of Financing Schemes to Special Schools) Regulations 1993, SI 1993/3104, the Secretary of State has required all schemes to cover LEA special schools.

See para 11.20 on the need to make provision in schemes for funding of permanently excluded pupils.

By s 126 and Sch 12 financial delegation is applied to new schools which have temporary governing bodies. See Circular 2/94 Annex D, E[2457.1].

Where the area of an LEA is affected by local government reorganisation see the Local Government Changes for England (Local Management of Schools) Regulations 1995, SI 1995/3114.

18 1996 Act s 105. The Education (Financial Delegation to Schools) (Mandatory Exceptions) Regulations 1995 (SI 1995/178) prescribe that expenditure attracting specified central government and other grants is to be left out of account in determining the aggregated budget. See Circular 2/94 Part 4, E[2333].

19 1996 Act s 104. Dates and guidance may apply generally or be specific. By s 571 guidance is to be published. By para 2 of Circular 7/88, 'Education Reform Act: Local Management of Schools' (superseded by 2/94), the Secretary of State directed all LEAs (save the Inner London Education Authority) to submit schemes for approval by 30 September 1989. The date specified for inner London borough councils was 30 September 1991. Provisions in ss 103 and 104 which are spent for existing LEAs will apply to new LEAs created as a result of local government reorganisation. See Circular 2/94 Part 2, E[2325].

needs of individual schools which are subject to variation from school to school, including in particular the number of pupils with special educational needs and the nature of the provision made for them. All amounts are to be determined initially before the beginning of the financial year. The formula is not to take into account provision for part-time education of persons over compulsory school age or full-time education for those of 19 and over.[20]

Provision by a scheme for financial delegation

3.76 Where a school is required to be covered by a scheme, the scheme is to delegate to the governing body responsibility for managing their own budget share; otherwise delegation of responsibility (conventionally referred to as 'local management of schools') is optional. Schemes may impose conditions, relating in particular to arrangements for managing expenditure, for keeping and audit of accounts and records, and submitting them and other documents and information to the LEA.[1] Delegation is to extend to LEA special schools, so far as prescribed.[2]

3.77 Schemes are to include a timetable for the introduction of delegation, and different dates may be specified for different schools or categories of school, but delegation is to start at the beginning of a financial year, and not more than three years after the scheme comes into force, unless the Secretary of State extends that initial period by order.[3]

Revision of schemes

3.78 An LEA may revise the whole or any part of a scheme, and the requirements mentioned in para 3.74 above apply.[4] Where the LEA propose to make a significant variation of the scheme they are first to consult governing bodies and head teachers and then seek the approval of the Secretary of State.[5] Where a proposed revision of a scheme does not in the opinion of the LEA vary it significantly they are to give brief particulars to the Secretary of State. Within two months of receiving notice of the proposal he may require a copy of the scheme as proposed to be revised; it is for him to determine whether the revision is a 'minor revision'.[6]

---

20 1996 Act s 106. In *R v Oxfordshire County Council, ex p P* [1996] ELR 153 it was held that the cost of non-teaching support for a Down's Syndrome pupil could properly be met from a school's budget share.
   See Circular 2/94, Part 6, E[2364].
1 1996 Act ss 103 and 107 to 109. By the 1988 Act s 41 and the Education (Financial Delegation for Primary Schools) Regulations 1991, SI 1991/1890, delegation was extended to all primary schools in England from 30th September 1991 and (by SI 1992/110, amending SI 1991/1890) in Wales from 30 September 1992.
2 1996 Act s 120. By the Education (Application of Financing Schemes to Special Schools) Regulations 1993, SI 1993/3104, the Secretary of State required all schemes to provide for financial delegation to governing bodies of LEA special schools in England.
3 1996 Act s 110. This section is disapplied in relation to LEA special schools by s 120(2). As to the effect of local government reorganisation see SI 1995/3114.
4 1996 Act s 111.
5 1996 Act s 112. Under sub-s (4) the Secretary of State may by order specify what descriptions of variations are to be regarded as significant. See Circular 2/94 paras 16 to 26 E[2326] and, at Annex B, E[2454], the Education (Significant Variations of Schemes for Financing Schools) Order 1993 (not an SI).
6 1996 Act s 113.

Schools Maintained by Local Education Authorities

3.79 After consulting the LEA and others as he thinks fit, the Secretary of State may by a direction revise the whole or part of any scheme from a specified date.[7]

Financial delegation under a scheme

3.80 Once a scheme is in operation, and financial delegation is required for any financial year, the LEA are to put the school's budget share at the disposal of the governing body to spend as they think fit for the purposes of the school in accordance with the scheme. The 'purposes of the school' do not include providing (a) part-time education suitable for persons of any age over compulsory school age and full-time education for persons of 19 and over and (b) initial teacher training courses.[8] The governing body may delegate their powers, so far as the scheme permits, to the head teacher. The only allowances governors may be paid from the 'delegated budget' are travelling and subsistence allowances. They are not personally liable for anything done in good faith.[9]

3.81 While a school has a delegated budget the governing body are responsible for the appointment, suspension, dismissal, duties, and remuneration of, and disciplinary and grievance procedures concerning, teaching and non-teaching staff (see para 13.18 ff).

Suspension of financial delegation

3.82 LEAs may suspend the delegation of the management of a school's budget share to the governing body for (a) failure substantially or persistently to comply with any of a scheme's requirements or (b) mismanaging the appropriation or expenditure of money. At least one month's written notice is to be given to the governing body (with a copy to the head teacher) specifying the grounds for the proposed suspension, except in circumstances of gross incompetence or mismanagement or other emergency, when the LEA are to notify the Secretary of State, giving their reasons.[10]

3.83 Suspension is to be reviewed by the LEA before the beginning of each financial year, and they are to give the governing body and head teacher an opportunity to make representations. If the LEA decide to revoke the suspension the revocation is to take effect from the beginning of the financial year following the review.[11]

3.84 The governing body may appeal against suspension (or failure to revoke it) to the Secretary of State, who in deciding whether to allow or reject the

---

7 1996 Act s 114.
8 1994 Act s 12(6). See also sub-s (7).
9 1996 Act ss 115 and 116. By SI 1993/3104, reg 2 these provisions apply to LEA special schools as well as to county and voluntary schools. See also s 125 (financial delegation apart from schemes) and s 489(2) (grants for education support and training), paras 3.87 and 11.06 respectively; and see Circular 2/94, E[2321].
10 1996 Act s 117. See Circular 2/94 paras 241 to 246, E[2445]. As regards suspension of the right to a delegated budget in the case of schools requiring special measures see para 8.32.
11 1996 Act s 118.

appeal is to have regard to the gravity of the default and the likelihood of its continuance or recurrence.[12]

Publication of schemes, financial statements etc

3.85 LEAs are to publish their schemes, in the manner prescribed, when they come into force and whenever the Secretary of State prescribes.[13] Once schemes are in force LEAs are to publish financial information statements about each of the county, voluntary and special schools covered, before the beginning and after the end of each financial year, in the form and manner, and at the time, prescribed. The end of year statement is to set out the planned financial provision for that year and the expenditure actually incurred for schools individually and as a whole.

3.86 LEAs are to send copies of statements (or prescribed parts) to governing bodies of schools in the scheme and of prescribed grant-maintained schools; governing bodies are to ensure that a copy is available for inspection at the school at all reasonable times and free of charge.[14] LEAs are to require the Audit Commission (for Local Authorities and the National Health Service in England and Wales) to make arrangements for certifying statements if the Secretary of State so directs. Copies of certified statements are to be sent to the Secretary of State.[15]

Financial delegation apart from schemes

3.87 At times when a county, voluntary or maintained special school does not have a delegated budget the LEA are to give the governing body money to spend (or to delegate to the head teacher for spending) on books, equipment, stationery and other heads of expenditure specified by the LEA (who may impose reasonable conditions) or prescribed by the Secretary of State in regulations he makes after consultation with local authority associations and (if he thinks desirable) individual local authorities.[16]

CONDUCT OF SCHOOLS

3.88 So much of Chapter VI of Part II of the 1996 Act (sections 127 to 166, Schedules 13 to 19) as is concerned with staffing of schools is mentioned in Chapter 13, in paras 13.18 to 13.34, and, as regards religious opinions of staff in para 13.69 ff. The remainder is outlined below.

12 1996 Act s 119.
13 1996 Act s 121. See the Education (Publication of Schemes for Financing Schools) Regulations 1993, SI 1993/3070 and Circular 2/94 Pt 12.
14 1996 Act s 122 and Sch 11 Pt I; and SI 1993/3104, reg 2. See (England) the Education (School Financial Statements) (Prescribed Particulars etc) Regulations 1995, SI 1995/208; and (Wales) SI 1994/323. By s 124 and Sch 11 Pt II similar requirements are imposed in relation to special schools not covered by statements under s 122. See the Education (Pre-Scheme Financial Statements) Regulations 1989, SI 1989/370.
15 1996 Act s 123. Certification is to be as specified in the direction under arrangements in accordance with s 29(1)(d) of the Local Government Finance Act 1982. A direction may relate to any LEA, to all LEAs or to a class of LEAs.
16 1996 Act s 125. The associations are presumably the Local Government Association and the Association of London Government. See Circular 2/94, para 44, E[2331].

3.89 *Schools Maintained by Local Education Authorities*

Articles of government

3.89 Articles of government, made by order of the LEA, regulate the conduct of LEA schools. Articles are to be consistent with statutory provisions (which relate, inter alia, to the allocation of functions between LEA, governing body and head teacher), and they are to comply with any trust deed relating to the school. (While a school has a delegated budget provisions in articles inconsistent with financial delegation are overridden and the articles are to be amended so as to indicate accordingly.)[17]

3.90 Before making an order embodying or varying articles, the LEA are to consult the governing body and the head teacher of the school concerned. In the case of voluntary schools, LEAs are to secure the agreement of the governing body and have regard to the way the school has been conducted. They are to consider proposals for alteration of articles made by a governing body. Where the LEA propose to make an order but cannot secure agreement, or refuse, in the case of a voluntary school, to make an order in response to a governing body's proposal, the matter may be referred to the Secretary of State, who is to give a direction as he thinks fit, having regard in particular to the status of the school; and he may modify a trust deed so as to make it consistent with an LEA's order.[18]

Conduct of schools: general

3.91 Articles are to place the conduct of LEA schools under the direction of the governing body, subject to statutory requirements and particular provisions in the articles.[19] Governing bodies may do anything necessary to carry out their statutory functions, subject to the instrument and articles and to any delegated budget provisions. In particular they may (a) acquire and dispose of land and any other property; (b) enter into contracts (but only governing bodies of aided schools may enter into contracts of employment); (c) invest sums not immediately required for the purposes of carrying on their activities; (d) accept gifts of money, land and other property and apply it, or hold and administer it on trust[20] for those purposes; and (e) do anything incidental to the conduct of the school.[1]

3.92 It is for the governing body to decide whether to provide part-time education of persons over compulsory school age or full-time education for those of 19 and over (but in the case of special schools, subject to the consent of the LEA). Save in prescribed circumstances, this education is not to be provided in a room where pupils are being taught.[2]

17 1996 Act ss 127 and 129.
18 1996 Act s 128.
19 1996 Act s 130. From the decision in *R v Manchester City Council, ex p Fulford* (1982) 81 LGR 292 DC, F[19] it appears that if a particular provision in the articles allocates a function to the governing body, it cannot also be exercised by the LEA. See Circular 7/87, para 5.9, E[333].
20 '... the only trusts which the governing body has power to administer are... charitable. They could not, for example, hold property on private trust for the benefit of particular individuals' (Government spokesman in Lords Committee on the Bill for the Education Act 1993: *Hansard*, 10 May 1993, col 1066).
1   1996 Act Sch 7 para 2. See Circular 15/93 (WO 68/93), E[2081].
2   1996 Act s 176. See the Education (Further Education in Schools) Regulations 1993, SI 1993/1987.

3.93 The Secretary of State has made regulations specifying when an LEA or head teacher may act as a matter of urgency without consulting the governing body if they cannot contact the chairman or vice-chairman.[3]

3.94 Where a school is organised in separate departments, each with a head teacher, those head teachers are to have the functions of a school head teacher, so far as is consistent with the school's articles.[4]

School terms, holidays and sessions

3.95 The governing bodies of county, controlled and special schools are to determine the timing of school sessions, ie when they are to begin and end on any day. But where governing bodies of those schools propose to change the times of school sessions they are to follow a procedure providing for consultation with the LEA, head teacher and parents; and the articles are to provide that the dates of school terms and holidays, which are at the discretion of the governing bodies of aided and special agreement schools, are to be decided by the LEA in the case of county, controlled and special schools.[5]

3.96 The procedure for changing the times of sessions, mentioned in the previous paragraph is, in outline, as follows. Governing bodies, having first consulted the LEA and head teacher in each instance, are to (a) prepare a statement specifying the proposed change and when it is proposed to take effect and (if the LEA so require) drawing attention, and responding, to any comment on the proposal made by the LEA, (b) provide an opportunity for discussion of the proposal by parents of registered pupils, teachers and others invited, (c) consider any comments made before deciding to act on or modify the proposal, (d) effect any change only at the beginning of a school year, and (e) inform the LEA, and so far as reasonably practicable parents, at least three months before a change comes into effect.

Control of school premises[6]

3.97 Articles of county and special schools are to provide for control of premises, outside school hours, by the governing body, subject to any directions given by the LEA. The governing body are to consider the desirability of community use of the premises and whether to enter into a transfer of control agreement with another body for that purpose (or for that purpose among

---

3 1996 Act s 131. The Education (School Government) Regulations 1989, SI 1989/1503, reg 23, gives the chairman or vice-chairman power to act in place of the governing body as a matter of urgency—when delay would be likely to be seriously detrimental to the interests of the school, of a registered pupil, his parent or an employee (see *R v Birmingham City Council ex p McKenna* (1991) Times, 16 May). Regulations 30 and 31 give the LEA power to act without consulting the governing body in matters of urgency affecting, respectively, exclusion of pupils from school and appointment of teachers at other than aided schools.
4 1996 Act s 132.
5 1996 Act s 147 and 148. As to (a) the duration of the school year and day see para 2.13 and the Education (Schools and Further Education) Regulations 1981, SI 1981/1086, reg 10, (b) new schools see Sch 19 Pt IV para 26, and (c) pupil referral units (see para 2.31) see the Education (Pupil Referral Units) (Application of Enactments) Regulations 1994, SI 1994/2103, reg 2, Sch 1, para 2(1).
6 Standards for school premises and requirements regarding new premises are mentioned in Chapter 15 para 15.04 ff.

3.97 *Schools Maintained by Local Education Authorities*

others). If they do so they are to secure, so far as is reasonably practicable, that control is exercised in accordance with the LEA's directions.[7]

3.98 A transfer of control agreement is to be taken to include terms under which (a) the governing body are to notify the controlling body of any LEA directions, (b) the controlling body agree to comply with those directions and to have regard to the desirability of the premises being made available for community use outside school hours, and (c) on reasonable notice the governing body may recover use of the premises for school purposes (unless the governing body, on entering into the agreement, made what they thought was better express provision for occasional use of the premises).

3.99 The occupation and use of voluntary school premises are under the control of the governing body, subject to (a) directions given by the LEA, (b) a transfer of control agreement,[8] and (c) statutory requirements other than in the 1996 Act.[9] In the case of

(i) controlled schools, an LEA's directions are to be as they think fit, except that the governing body may decide the use of all or part of the premises on Saturdays, so far as they are not required by the LEA for school purposes or for a purpose connected with education[10] or the welfare of the young; and the foundation governors may decide the use of all or part of the premises on Sundays.[11]

(ii) aided or special agreement schools, LEAs have power to direct governors to provide accommodation on the school premises (but not services, eg heating) on not more than three weekdays in any week, free of charge, for a purpose connected with education or the welfare of the young, and only when the premises (or part) are not needed for school purposes. LEAs are first to be satisfied that there is no suitable alternative accommodation in their area.[12]

---

7 1996 Act s 149. The similar test of a superseded provision was considered in *Islwyn Borough Council v Newport Borough Council* [1994] ELR 141, CA.
  By sub-s (5) 'school hours' means any time during a school session or during a break between sessions on the same day, a session being determined as mentioned in para 2.13 above; 'community use' means the use of school premises (when not required by or in connection with the school) by members of the local community; a 'transfer of control agreement' is one which provides for the use, subject to the terms mentioned, of all or specified parts of the school premises by, and under the control of, specified persons at specified times outside school hours; and 'the controlling body' means the body or person having control under the transfer of control agreement.
  See Circulars 15/93 (WO 68/93) E[2082], and 2/94, 'Local Management of Schools' para 227 E[2420].
8 1996 Act s 151. By 'transfer of control agreement' is meant an agreement entered into for the purpose or purposes mentioned in para 3.97 and the terms of which closely follow those outlined in para 3.98. An agreement is not to cover use of premises during school hours without the LEA's consent.
  A governing body may enter into a transfer of control agreement despite any contrary provision in a trust deed, but the use under the agreement is to be in accordance with any restrictions etc which would be imposed by the deed if they themselves were exercising control.
9 1996 Act s 150(1) and (2). By sub-s(3) where a trust deed provides for a person other than the governing body to control occupation and use of premises ss 150 to 153 apply to that person in place of the governing body. See Circular 15/93, E[2081].
10 An exhibition of work done by pupils is such a purpose (*Griffiths v Smith* [1941] AC 170).
11 1996 Act s 152(1) and (2).
12 1996 Act s 152(3). Section 150(3) (see n 9 above) applies.

3.100 All sums received by the governors or trustees of a voluntary school for use of part of school premises other than the school buildings are to be paid over to the LEA.[13]

Instruction or training outside school premises

3.101 The articles of government of LEA schools are to enable governing bodies to require pupils to attend elsewhere to receive instruction and training which is included in the secular curriculum.[14]

Discipline

3.102 In general the nature of school discipline turns on policies and decisions made under powers allocated to governing bodies or head teachers, or vested in LEAs, by articles of government.

> 'The authority of the schoolmaster is, while it exists, the same as that of the parent. A parent when he places his child with a schoolmaster delegates to him all his own authority so far as it is necessary for the welfare of the child.'

3.103 As will appear, this general rule (per Cockburn CJ in *Fitzgerald v Northcote*[15]) has been modified by statutory provision.

3.104 It was held in *Guardian of the Poor of Gateshead Union v Durham County Council*,[16] per Warrington LJ, that 'a child may be refused admission on reasonable grounds . . . as for example that he is in such a condition of person or health as to render contact with him offensive or dangerous to others, or is guilty of conduct prejudicial to good discipline'.

3.105 The objects of school disciplinary measures are to (a) promote among pupils self-discipline and proper regard for authority, (b) encourage good behaviour and respect for others on the part of pupils, (c) secure that the standard of behaviour of pupils is acceptable, and (d) otherwise regulate the conduct of pupils.[17]

3.106 Articles of government of LEA schools are to make the head teacher responsible for school disciplinary measures (including making and enforcing rules), subject to any written statement of general principles provided by the governing body and their guidance on particular matters. The head teacher is to determine (subject to the governing body) the acceptable standard of behaviour and to make his disciplinary measures known within the school. If those measures are likely to lead to increased expenditure, or affect the responsibilities of the LEA as employers, they are to be consulted.

3.107 LEAs have a reserve power to intervene (which includes giving directions to the governing body or head teacher) to prevent a breakdown, or

---

13 1996 Act s 73.
14 1996 Act s 153. For the application of this section, as modified, see the Education (Pupil Referral Units) (Application of Enactments) Regulations 1994, SI 1994/2103, reg 2 and Sch 1, para 2(1).
15 (1865) 4 F & F 656, F[53].
16 [1918] 1 Ch 146 at 163.
17 1996 Act s 154 (and as regards new schools, Sch 19 Pt IV para 27). See Circulars 8/94, 'Pupil Behaviour and Discipline', para 14 E[2805] and 10/94 para 12 E[2895].

3.107 *Schools Maintained by Local Education Authorities*

continuing breakdown, of discipline at county, controlled and special schools if (a) in their opinion the behaviour of registered pupils, or action taken by pupils or parents, is such as severely to prejudice the pupils' education, or is likely to do so in the immediate future, and (b) the governing body have been so informed in writing. If the same circumstances arise at aided or special agreement schools the governing body and head teacher are to consider the LEA's representations.[18]

Exclusion from school

3.108 Articles are to provide that only the head teacher may exclude a pupil from an LEA school on disciplinary grounds. Notwithstanding any provisions in articles, exclusion is not to be for an indefinite period or for fixed periods amounting to more than a total of 15 school days in any one term; but these restrictions are without prejudice to the power to exclude a pupil permanently.[19]

3.109 Where a head teacher excludes a pupil he is to take all the following steps without delay. He is to tell a parent (or the pupil if aged 18 or over) why, and for how long (or permanently), the pupil is being excluded, and likewise give an explanation when he decides to make permanent an exclusion that was originally for a fixed period. If the exclusion is to be (or to become) permanent, or is for more than five days in any one term, or if the pupil would because of exclusion lose the opportunity to take a public examination, he is to inform the LEA and governing body similarly. He is also to inform the parent (or the pupil if aged 18 or over) that he may make representations about exclusion to the governing body and to the LEA.[1]

3.110 The articles of government of county, controlled and special schools are to provide for reinstatement of pupils as follows.[2]

3.111 Where the LEA have been informed of a pupil's permanent exclusion from a school they are to consider whether reinstatement should take place, and if so when, after considering any views expressed by the governing body within the prescribed period. They are to inform the parent or pupil (if 18 or over) of

---

[18] 1996 Act s 155. For the application (with modifications) of this section to pupil referral units see the Education (Pupil Referral Units) (Application of Enactments) Regulations 1994, SI 1994/2103, reg 2, Sch 1, para 2.

[19] 1996 Act s 156. See *R v Newham London Borough Council, ex p X* [1995] ELR 303 (unfair expulsion), *R v Neale, ex p S* [1995] ELR 198, and *A v Staffordshire County Council, ex p Ashworth* (1996) Times, 18 October (adequacy of grounds for exclusion). The restriction on the power to exclude pupils is applied by the Education (Special Schools Conducted by Education Associations) Regulations 1994, SI 1994/1084, reg 8(1), Sch 2, Pt I. See Circular 10/94 (WO 60/94), 'Exclusions from school', E[2891].

[1] 1996 Act s 157. (Section 23 of the 1986 Act applies to pupils excluded before 1 November 1996). See *R v Governors of St Gregory's Roman Catholic Aided School, ex p Roberts* (1995) Times, 27 January.

For the application (with modifications) of this section to pupil referral units see SI 1994/2103, as above.

[2] 1996 Act s 158 and Sch 15 Pt I. As to the limited power of the LEA to direct the head teacher to reinstate the pupil without consulting the governing body if the exclusion would lose him the opportunity to take any public examination see the Education (School Government) Regulations 1989, SI 1989/1503, reg 30. For the application (with modifications) of this section to pupil referral units see SI 1994/2103, as above.

their decision, and if they decide that reinstatement should take place they are to give the appropriate direction to the head teacher. A direction for reinstatement may also be given by the governing body who, similarly, are to inform the parent or pupil.

3.112 Where a pupil is excluded for a fixed period of more than a total of five school days in any term, or where the exclusion would deprive him of the opportunity to take a public examination, the head teacher is to comply with any direction for reinstatement given by the LEA or governing body. Where the LEA have been informed of a fixed period exclusion and propose to give a direction they are first to consult the governing body; and where LEA or governing body give a direction they are to inform each other and also the parent or pupil.

3.113 In the case of both permanent and fixed-term exclusions if conflicting directions are given by the LEA and governing body the head teacher is to comply with the direction that leads to the earlier reinstatement of the pupil.

3.114 The articles of government of aided and special agreement schools are to provide as follows.[3]

3.115 Where the governing body have been informed of a pupil's permanent exclusion from a school they are to consider whether reinstatement should take place and, if so, when. If they decide that the pupil should be reinstated they are to give the appropriate direction to the head teacher; if they decide that he should not be reinstated they are to inform the LEA; in both cases they are to inform the parent or pupil of their decision.

3.116 Where a pupil is excluded for more than a total of five school days in any term, or where the exclusion would deprive him of the opportunity to take a public examination, the head teacher is to comply with any direction for reinstatement given by the LEA or governing body. Where the LEA propose to give a direction for reinstatement they are first to consider any views expressed by the governing body within the prescribed period. If conflicting directions are given by LEA and governing body the head teacher is to comply with the direction that leads to the earlier reinstatement of the pupil. Where LEA or governing body give a direction they are to inform each other and also the parent or pupil.

3.117 LEAs (governing bodies in the case of aided and special agreement schools) are to make arrangements for enabling parents of registered pupils (or pupils aged 18 or over) to appeal against failure to reinstate following permanent exclusion; also for governing bodies of county, controlled and special schools to appeal against an LEA's reinstatement direction. Appeals are to an appeal committee constituted in the same way as an admissions appeal

---

'Prescribed period' See Sch 15 para 14 and the Education (Exclusion from Schools) (Prescribed Periods) Regulations 1994, SI 1994/2093. Subject to prescribed exceptions, the LEA or governing body are not to be relieved of the duty to take any step which has not been taken within the prescribed period.

3 1996 Act s 158 and Sch 15 Pt II. See n 2 above as to 'prescribed period' and application of SI 1989/1503, reg 30.

3.117 *Schools Maintained by Local Education Authorities*

committee.[4] Their decision is binding on all concerned. If they direct reinstatement it is to be immediate or on a date specified.[5] Where articles of government of an LEA school provide a right of appeal by parents against exclusion to a specified person in circumstances beyond those mentioned above, his decision that the pupil be reinstated (or reinstated earlier than would otherwise be the case) binds the head teacher.[6]

Reports, meetings and information

3.118 Articles of government are to require governing bodies of LEA schools to prepare an annual report which includes a summary of how they have discharged their functions since the last annual report. As briefly as is reasonably consistent with the requirements, the report is also to contain (a) specified particulars relating to the annual parents' meeting (where one is held) and about the governors themselves; (b) information about arrangements for the next election of parent governors; (c) a financial statement; (d) the same information about public examinations etc, pupils' absences and their post-school careers as is required to be published in connection with school admission arrangements (see para 7.12); (e) information about educational provision and syllabuses at the school (see para 6.70); and (f) a description of the steps taken to strengthen the school's links with the community, including the police.[7] Beyond these requirements, governing bodies (except those of special schools) are obliged to include information in the annual report about admission arrangements for pupils with disabilities, and details of the steps taken to prevent those pupils from being treated less favourably than other pupils and of the facilities provided to assist their access to the school.[8]

---

4 See 1996 Act Sch 33 (see para 7.20).
   As to (a) the conduct of an appeal see *R v Governors of St Gregory's Roman Catholic Aided High School, ex p Roberts* (1995) Times, 27 January, (b) the procedure to be followed in connection with reinstatement see *R v Camden London Borough, ex p H (a minor)* [1996] ELR 360, CA and (c) judicial review see *R v Staffordshire County Council, ex p Ashworth* (1996) Times, 18 October.
   See also the Code of Practice on Procedure (1994) published by the Association of County Councils and Association of Metropolitan Authorities in conjunction with the Council on Tribunals and reprinted in *The Law of Education*.
5 1996 Act s 159. By sub-s (3) the governing bodies of two or more aided or special agreement schools maintained by the same LEA may make joint arrangements.
   By sub-s (4) Sch 16 regulates the conduct of exclusion and reinstatement appeals. See *R v Board of Governors of London Oratory School ex p Regis* [1989] Fam Law 67, F[91], and *R v Board of Governors of Stoke Newington School, ex p M* [1994] ELR 131, F[105]; also Circular 10/94 (WO 60/94), paras 68 to 76, E[2909].
6 1996 Act s 160.
7 1996 Act s 161(1) and (2), and Sch 17. The Secretary of State may amend the specified particulars etc by order—see the Education Act 1996 (Amendment) Order 1996, SI 1996/3210.
   The financial statement is (i) to reproduce or summarise that prepared under 1996 Act s 122 or 124 (see para 3.86), (ii) to indicate how the governing body have used any budget share (see para 3.80) or sum provided under s 125 (see para 3.87) (iii) to give details of the application of any gifts, and (iv) state the amount of any travelling and subsistence allowances paid to governors.
   As to the requirement to refer in the report to (i) a ballot on grant-maintained status see para 4.05, (ii) an 'action plan' relating to special measures see para 8.22, and (iii) pupils with special educational needs or disabled see para 5.11. See also the requirements mentioned at paras 6.70 and 7.12.
   See Circulars 11/96 and 12/96, 'School Prospectuses and Governors' Annual Reports in Primary/Secondary Schools'.
8 Children Act 1996 s 317(6) replacing the Disability Discrimination Act 1995 s 24(2). See Circular 3/97 (WO 20/97), 'What the Disability Discrimination Act 1997 means for Schools and LEAs'.

3.119 Articles are to empower governing bodies to produce their report in languages additional to English, and require them to do so in any other language the LEA direct. Governing bodies are to take reasonably practicable steps to see that parents of registered pupils and school employees are given free copies of the report (at least two weeks before an annual parents' meeting) and that copies are available for inspection at the school at all reasonable times.[9]

3.120 Articles are to require governing bodies to hold an annual parents' meeting, except when the school is a hospital special school or consists of at least 50 per cent boarders and, in either case, the governing body consider that it would be impracticable to hold a meeting in a particular school year. The meeting is to be open to parents of registered pupils, to the head teacher and to others the governing body invite. The purpose of the meeting is to provide an opportunity for discussion of the governors' report and the discharge of functions in relation to the school by the governing body, head teacher and LEA.[10]

3.121 The proceedings are to be under the control of the governing body. Resolutions may be passed, by simple majority, provided that parents are present at least equal in numbers to 20 per cent of the number of registered pupils. Only parents of registered pupils may vote (and who is to be treated as a parent for this purpose is a matter for the LEA or for the governing body in the case of aided and special agreement schools). Any resolutions are to be considered by governors, head teachers and LEA as appropriate to their subject matter, and a brief comment on them is to be included in the next governors' report.[11]

3.122 Where schools are grouped (see para 3.67 ff) governing bodies are to prepare separate reports for each of the schools unless they decide to hold a joint annual parents' meeting. At any such meeting voting is restricted to parents with pupils at the school or schools which a resolution concerns (as decided by the chairman of the governing body).[12]

3.123 Articles are to provide that governing bodies report on the discharge of their functions, regularly or from time to time, as the LEA require. Head teachers are to report similarly to the LEA or governing body when required to do so; and in the case of aided schools the LEA are to notify the governing body of any requirement they make and the head teacher is to provide the governing body with a copy of the report.[13]

Conduct of new schools

3.124 An LEA's order establishing articles of government for a new school is to be made once the requirement for the school to have an instrument of government takes effect. The LEA are to consult the temporary governing body (see

---

9 1996 Act s 161(3) and (4).
10 1996 Act ss 162 and 163. See Circular 8/86 (WO 56/86), 'Education (No 2) Act 1986', para 13, E[267].
11 1996 Act Sch 18.
12 1996 Act s 164.
13 1996 Act s 165. For the modified application of this section to pupil referral units, see SI 1994/2103, reg 2, Sch 1, para 2.

3.124 *Schools Maintained by Local Education Authorities*

para 3.70 ff) in advance. Before a governing body is constituted under the instrument the temporary governing body determine, as necessary, the conduct of the school, subject to statutory provision. There are requirements, mostly analogous to those relating to existing schools, about, in particular, (a) preparation of curriculum, (b) school terms, holidays and sessions, (c) discipline, (d) reports and information and (e) consultation between the LEA and governing body and head teacher on proposed expenditure on books etc where the new school is not to have a delegated budget.[14]

DISCONTINUANCE OF SCHOOLS

3.125 This is the subject matter of Chapter VII of Part II of the 1996 Act (sections 167 to 175).

Procedure for discontinuance of county, voluntary or nursery school by local education authority

3.126 Where an LEA intend to discontinue a county, voluntary or nursery school they are to publish their proposals in the same way, mutatis mutandis, as if they were proposing to establish a school (see para 3.08), and submit them to the Secretary of State. The same provisions about objections (and the publication of a statement explaining rights of objection) apply, as do the requirements for prior approval by the Secretary of State in specified circumstances (including contemporaneous proposals for acquisition of grant-maintained status) (see para 3.14) and concerning implementation of proposals.[15] The Secretary of State may modify a trust deed or other instrument as a necessary consequence of his approving a proposal, after consulting governors or other proprietors.[16]

3.127 Anticipatory action on proposals before the proper procedures have been complied with is expressly prohibited, except as may be permitted by the Secretary of State as reasonable in the circumstances of the case.[17]

---

14 1996 Act s 166 and Sch 19. By s 181 a 'new school' is a school (or proposed school) which is required to have a temporary governing body.

15 1996 Act ss 167 to 171. See *R v Secretary of State for Education and Science, ex p Birmingham District Council* (1984) 83 LGR 79, regarding the invalidity of proposals to close a school, and of the Secretary of State's approval of the proposals, when the date of closure is fixed by the chairman of a committee; *R v Gwent County Council, ex p Bryant* [1988] COD 19, in which it was held that the courts might not investigate the merits of a council's decision to close a school, but could only determine whether or not the decision was lawfully made; *Harvey v Strathclyde Regional Council* 1989 SLT 612, HL, F [48] as regards wishes of parents; *Milne v London Borough of Wandsworth* (see para 3.12 n 12); *R v Secretary of State for Education and Science, ex p Malik* [1992] COD 31; and *R v Northamptonshire County Council and Secretary of State for Education, ex p K* [1994] ELR 397, CA also Circular 23/94 (WO 13/95) on the supply of school places, E[3151], and para 1.17 ff as regards consultation with parents.

As to (a) rationalisation of school places by order of the Secretary of State see para 12.11 ff; (b) discontinuance of LEA schools involving the establishment of a further education corporation see para 10.55, (c) Church of England Schools see Diocesan Boards of Education Measure 1991 s 3, and (d) LEAs in Greater London see the London Government Act 1963 s 31(5).

16 1996 Act s 179. As to the powers of the Secretary of State where premises of a voluntary school have ceased to be used as such see s 554 and the Reverter of Sites Act 1987 (see paras 15.26 and 15.27).

17 1996 Act s 172. See Circular 23/94, paras 143 and 144 E[3190].

Discontinuance of voluntary school by governing body

3.128 Voluntary schools may, alternatively, be discontinued at the instance of the governing body. They are to serve on the Secretary of State and the LEA by whom the school is maintained not less than two years' notice of the intended discontinuance. Once given, notice may not be withdrawn save with the leave of the LEA; when it runs out the duty of the LEA to maintain the school as a voluntary school ceases. Where the procedure for acquisition of grant-maintained status is pending (see para 4.16 n 17) notice may not be served; nor may it be served except by leave of the Secretary of State if he or an LEA have incurred expenditure (beyond expenditure on repairs) on the premises. If leave is granted it may be subject to specified requirements he thinks just, including repayments and conveyance of premises to the LEA.[18]

3.129 If the governing body are unable or unwilling to carry on the school while the notice is in force the LEA may, if they wish, conduct the school as a county school on conditions which include the governing body's being entitled to residual use of the premises.[19]

3.130 Where a governing body intend to discontinue a voluntary school in connection with a proposal by a further education funding council or the Secretary of State to establish a further education corporation to conduct an educational institution in the same area, the provisions for discontinuance by governing bodies cease to apply. They are to publish statutory proposals as if for significant change in the character of the school (see para 3.09) which if approved end the maintenance obligations of the LEA.[20]

---

18 1996 Act s 173. Expenditure may have been incurred by an LEA in the case of controlled schools under s 63 or 64, and by the Secretary of State in the case of aided schools and special agreement schools under s 65 (or by provisions superseded by those sections).
  By sub-s (4) if discontinuing the school would affect facilities for full-time education for persons over compulsory school age but under 19, the governing body, before serving notice, are to consult the appropriate further education funding council.
  As to Church of England schools see Diocesan Boards of Education Measure 1991 s 3. As to cesser of use of voluntary school premises see 1996 Act s 554 and Reverter of Sites Act 1987, and note the possible application of the School Sites Acts (see Appendix 4). Failure to observe the provisions of s 173 might amount to a breach of trust.
  In *R v Secretary of State for Education and Science, ex p Inner London Education Authority* (1990) Times, 17 May, CA (*sub nom ILEA and Lewisham London Borough Council v Secretary of State for Education and Science and the Haberdashers Company* [1990] COD 412), it was held that the Secretary of State, when considering whether to require a school to repay capital expenditure to an LEA on giving leave to the school to discontinue as a controlled school, is not confined to considering financial matters relating to the value of the expenditure, but is entitled to take into account future educational requirements within the authority's area. See also *Re Hampstead Garden Suburb Institute* (1995) Times, 13 April.
19 1996 Act s 174.
20 1996 Act s 175.

Chapter 4

GRANT-MAINTAINED SCHOOLS

4.01 Part III of the 1996 Act (sections 183 to 311), with associated Schedules (20 to 25), largely re-enacts Part II of the 1993 Act, which in its turn consolidated, with amendments and additions, repealed provisions mainly in Chapter IV of Part I of the 1988 Act relating to grant-maintained schools.[1]

4.02 Chapter I (section 183) defines 'grant-maintained school' and provides for payment of annual grants by the funding authority under Chapter VI. Chapter II (sections 184 to 200) (with Part I of Schedule 20 and Schedule 21) specifies which schools are eligible for grant-maintained status and the procedure by which an existing school may acquire that status. A parental ballot may be initiated by a single resolution rather than by two as in the first place.

4.03 Special provision is made by regulation for the application of grant-maintained schools legislation to schools conducted by education associations, grant-maintained special schools and groups of grant-maintained schools.[2]

ACQUISITION OF GRANT-MAINTAINED STATUS

4.04 Grant-maintained schools, either primary or secondary,[3] may come into existence and be conducted by incorporated governing bodies under proposals either (a) to take over and manage an existing eligible (county or voluntary) school, provided that it is not subject to closure proceedings,[4] (b) to establish a

1 Grant-maintained schools are exempt charities under the Charities Act 1993 ss 3, 96 and Sch 2. Their governing bodies are public bodies for the purposes of the Local Authorities (Goods and Services) Act 1970 and the Welsh Language Act 1993.
2 See the Education (Schools Conducted by Education Associations) Regulations 1993, SI 1993/3103, the Education (Grant-maintained Special Schools) Regulations 1994, SI 1994/653, the Education (Groups of Grant-maintained Schools) Regulations 1994, SI 1994/1041 and the Education (Special Schools Conducted by Education Associations) Regulations 1994, SI 1994/1084. See also paras 5.36 ff and 8.40 ff.
3 Not to the exclusion of middle schools (see para 2.08). There are to be no new nursery schools, but nursery classes in primary schools are permissible (see para 4.86). As to grant-maintained special schools see para 5.36 ff.
4 1996 Act s 184 The proceedings are: (a) an LEA have published proposals to cease to maintain the school under the 1996 Act s 167 (see para 3.126) and these have been approved by the Secretary of State or are to be implemented without requiring approval; (b) the governing body of a voluntary school have given notice of intention to close the school under s 173 (see para 3.128) or have published proposals to do so under s 41 as applied by s 175(2)(b) (see para 3.130); (c) proposals for the closure of the school are pending under s 505(5), having been made by an LEA in response to a rationalisation order under s 500 or by the Secretary of State under s 502 (see para 12.11 ff).

new school, or (c) to conduct two or more existing schools as a group (see para 4.78 ff). Once a grant-maintained school is established it becomes the duty of the funding authority to pay annual grants to the governing body.[5]

4.05 The Secretary of State has made orders,[6] applying to all eligible schools in England and Wales, which require their governing bodies to consider, at least once in every school year,[7] holding a parental ballot on whether grant-maintained status should be sought, unless one was held in the preceding year. Governing bodies are to include reference in their annual reports to the consideration they have given to this requirement.[8]

4.06 The Secretary of State may finance all or part of the costs incurred by a governing body in connection with proposals for acquisition of grant-maintained status; and he may prohibit LEAs from incurring expenditure for the purpose of influencing the outcome of a ballot beyond that authorised by regulations.[9]

Acquisition procedure

4.07 There are three stages in the procedure for acquisition of grant-maintained status. The first starts with a resolution by the governing body[10] of an eligible school, or a request to the governing body by registered parents[11] numbering at least 20 per cent of the number of registered pupils (see para 7.35) at the school, to hold a ballot of parents on whether or not to seek grant-maintained status for the school. The ballot is to be held within ten weeks of the resolution or of the receipt of the request by parents. Within five working days of the resolution or request the governing body are to give notice of the ballot to the LEA and to the trustees of a voluntary school,[12] and disclose to parents, on request, the names and addresses of other registered parents[13]. A parent may procure his omission from the list, but this will not affect his right to vote. Ballots are not to be held more than once a year save with the Secretary of State's consent.[14]

See Circular 18/93 (WO 46/94), 'Education Act 1993: Grant-Maintained Schools: Acquisition, Transfer and Governance', E[2151].
5   1996 Act s 183.
6   See the Education (Annual Consideration of Ballot on Grant-Maintained Status) (England) Order 1993, SI 1993/3115, and Wales Order, SI 1994/1861.
7   'School year' is not defined but see 1996 Act s 551, para 2.13.
8   1996 Act s 185. As to annual reports see Sch 23 para 7.
9   1996 Act s 197. See the Education (Ballot Expenditure) Regulations 1995, SI 1995/628, which, by reg 4, require the keeping of a separate account of the expenditure and its submission to the Secretary of State.
10 Participation in discussion and voting by teacher governors and the head teacher is authorised by the Education (School Government) Regulations 1989, SI 1989/1503 reg 14 and Schedule, para 2(4). See regs 14 and 19 as to proceedings at a meeting at which the question of a ballot is to be discussed. As to action by headmaster and governors see *R v Knight, ex p Khan* [1989] COD 434.
11 'Registered' means shown in the register kept under the 1996 Act s 434 on the date the request is received. By s 576 'parent' in this context is restricted to an individual.
12 In the case of Church of England voluntary schools provision is made for the governing body to take advice from the Diocesan Board of Education (Diocesan Boards of Education Measure 1991 s 3(4)).
13 Disclosure is to take place only in connection with ballots and is to consist of making the list available for inspection by parents at the school at reasonable times free of charge, and supplying a copy for a limited fee.
14 1996 Act ss 186 to 188.

4.08 *Grant-Maintained Schools*

4.08 The holding of a ballot is the second stage. Taking into account any guidance given by the Secretary of State,[15] the governing body are to secure that arrangements for a secret postal ballot are made by the body prescribed[16] and that the body take reasonably practicable steps to give eligible voters—registered parents[17] of registered pupils—the prescribed information,[18] inform them of their entitlement to vote, and give them an opportunity to do so. (Each parent, whether single or one of a couple, has one vote, irrespective of how many children he or she may have at the school.) The governing body may, separately, promote the case for seeking grant-maintained status, and in doing so take into account the Secretary of State's guidance about what action he considers appropriate for the purpose.[19] If the votes cast are less than 50 per cent of eligible voters, or there is a tie, a second ballot is to be held within 14 days from the day after the result of the first ballot. The result of any second ballot is final.[20] In cases of irregularity[1] the Secretary of State may declare the ballot void and require a fresh one to be held.[2]

4.09 The third stage follows if a simple majority of votes is cast in favour of seeking grant-maintained status. Within four months of the result of the ballot the existing governing body are to publish their proposals, and submit them (with accompanying and annexed statements), to the Secretary of State, to whom specified interested persons, including any LEA concerned, may submit objections.[3] Proposals, once made, may be withdrawn only with the Secretary

---

15 By 1996 Act s 571 guidance is to be published by the Secretary of State in such manner as he thinks fit; and where the arrangements do not accord with the guidance the ballot may be declared void under s 192. See Circular 18/93 (WO 3/94), para 36, E[2157].
16 See the Education (Parental Ballots for Acquisition of Grant-maintained Status) (Prescribed Body) Regulations 1992, SI 1992/2598, prescribing Electoral Reform (Ballot Services) Ltd.
17 In this particular context 'registered' means shown in the school register on the date immediately following the end of the period of 14 days beginning with the date on which the relevant resolution was passed by the governing body or the request by parents was received by them.
18 See the Education (Acquisition of Grant-maintained Status) (Ballot Information) Regulations 1993, SI 1993/3189, and, as regards special schools, the Education (Maintained Special Schools becoming Grant-maintained Special Schools) (Ballot Information) Regulations 1994, SI 1994/1232. By the 1996 Act s 189(4) the governing body are to make the same information available free of charge to employees (see s 575) at the school.
19 1996 Act ss 189 and 190. See *R v Governors of Astley High School, ex p Northumberland County Council* [1994] COD 27 and *R v Governing Body of Irlam and Cadishead Community High School, ex p Salford City Council* [1994] ELR 81.
20 1996 Act s 191.
1 Irregularity occurs when it appears to the Secretary of State that requirements about ballots in ss 189 or 191 have been contravened or that the arrangements did not accord with his guidance; that the governing body have acted unreasonably in discharging their duties under those sections; that ineligible persons have purported to vote in a ballot or that ballot papers have been marked by unauthorised persons; that an eligible person has been prevented from, or hindered in, voting or voting freely; or that voting appears to the Secretary of State to have been influenced by false or misleading information. See the remarks of Woolf LJ in *R v Governors of Small Heath School, ex p Birmingham City Council* [1990] COD 23, CA, and of Owen J in *R v Secretary of State for Education and Science, ex p London Borough of Lambeth* (22 December 1992, unreported).
2 1996 Act s 192. Where the Secretary of State specifies a date for the fresh ballot which falls in the following school year the voters are to be those parents on the register at that date.
3 1996 Act s 193 and Sch 20. Together, the proposals and statements are to include information about, inter alia, (a) the existing size and character of the school, (b) arrangements proposed for admission of pupils, (c) the proposed date of implementation of the proposals and (d) the proposed initial governing body (the body appointed to oversee the school's transition to grant-maintained status, and therefore active before an instrument of government exists).

of State's consent and subject to conditions he may impose (which may include publication of further proposals).[4]

Approval and implementation of proposals

4.10 The Secretary of State may approve the proposals with or without modifications; if with modifications only after consultation with the existing governing body. If he rejects the proposals he may require further proposals to be published. From the date of approval of proposals, the persons named as initial governors and the existing head teacher are incorporated as the governing body of the school under the name given in the proposals. Between that date and the date of implementation (when the LEA's duty to maintain ceases and any special agreement lapses) they are known as the 'new' governing body. They have interim functions and are eligible to receive a grant. Between the incorporation date and the implementation date any statutory or other documentary reference to the school governing body outside Chapter V of the 1996 Act is to be read as referring to the 'old' governing body unless the new governing body is expressly specified.[5]

Proposals for alteration of county schools

4.11 Where the governing body of a county school have published proposals for grant-maintained status, but (a) the Secretary of State has yet to decide whether to approve them and (b) the LEA have published proposals for alteration of one or more county schools in the area (see para 3.08), the governing body may publish, in the manner specified and prescribed,[6] proposals for a significant change in the character of the school or significant enlargement of its premises, with the object of ensuring consistency of

---

    Where it is proposed to admit pupils for nursery education, see the Education (Publication of School Proposals and Notices) Regulations 1993, SI 1993/3113, reg 7 and Sch 2.
    As to proposals by the governing body of a Church of England voluntary school see Diocesan Boards of Education Measure 1991 s 5.
    Publication is by posting the proposals at and near the school and by making them available for inspection; and notice of the proposals is to be given in a local newspaper. Proposals 'published' are to be read as published with any modifications made by the Secretary of State, and published proposals are to be regarded as 'pending' until withdrawn or determined by the Secretary of State.
4 1996 Act s 194 and Sch 20. It was held in *R v Secretary of State for Education and Science, ex p Newham London Borough Council* [1991] COD 279 that it was open to the Secretary of State, when reaching a decision whether or not to approve proposals, to form the view that the experiment of grant-maintained status ought to be tried in an LEA's area, even though there was no evidence that the quality or range of teaching would improve if his approval were given. As to a claim that the Secretary of State's approval was irrational, see *R v Secretary of State for Education, ex p London Borough of Southwark* [1994] COD 298; also *R v Secretary of State for Education ex p Warwickshire County Council* (1996) unreported.
    Where further proposals are to be published, requirements in s 193 and Sch 20 para 2(1)(a) are modified. Where proposals are approved, the Secretary of State may make an order under s 302(1)(a) modifying any trust deed or other instrument relating to the school.
    For the procedure to be followed when there are simultaneous proposals for acquisition of grant-maintained status and discontinuance or alteration of the school see respectively ss 167 and 169, and 199.
5 1996 Act ss 195, 196 and Sch 21. See the Education (Acquisition of Grant-maintained Status) (Transitional Functions) Regulations 1993, SI 1993/3072.
6 See the Education (Publication of School Proposals and Notices) Regulations 1993, SI 1993/3113. Modifications are made in the requirements relating to alteration etc of grant-maintained schools (see para 4.49 ff).

4.11 Grant-Maintained Schools

provision in the area if the authority's proposals are implemented.[7] The Secretary of State is to consider the two sets of proposals in parallel (whether or not his approval would otherwise be required for an LEA's proposal) and determine the grant-maintained status proposals first. If he approves those proposals he may also approve the alteration proposals, but if he rejects the former he is also to reject the latter.[8]

PROPERTY, STAFF AND CONTRACTS

Transfer of property and staff

4.12 Chapter III (sections 201 to 210 of the 1996 Act) provides for the transfer of property, rights and staff where a school becomes grant-maintained. It imposes certain restrictions on the freedom of a local authority, while the procedure for acquisition of grant-maintained status is pending, (a) to enter into contracts relating to such matters, (b) to dispose of or change the use of land, or (c) to appoint, dismiss or move staff; and it imposes sanctions for the breach of those restrictions.

4.13 Subject to specified exceptions, the property, rights and liabilities attaching to a school which becomes grant-maintained—those of a local authority and of the existing governing body—are transferred to the new governing body on the implementation date—the date specified in the proposals as the date on which the school will be conducted as a grant-maintained school.[9] The exceptions are (a) rights and liabilities under contracts of employment; (b) land or other property vested in a local authority as trustees (which vests in the 'first governors'[10] on the existing trusts); (c) assets and liabilities excluded by agreement, before the implementation date, between the authority and the new governing body with the approval of the Secretary of State, or, in default of agreement, as directed by order of the Secretary of State;[11] (d) any liability of an

---

7 1996 Act s 198. The governing body may propose a middle school: see the Education (Middle Schools) Regulations 1980, SI 1980/918.
8 1996 Act s 199. Where the grant-maintained status proposals are approved along with proposals under s 198 for the school to become co-educational, the new governing body are to be treated as having applied for a transitional exemption order under the Sex Discrimination Act 1975 s 27, and Sch 2 para 1 of that Act is not to apply.
9 1996 Act s 201. The corresponding provisions in the 1988 Act s 74 were considered in *R v Tameside Metropolitan Borough Council, ex p Governors of Audenshaw High School* (1990) Times, 27 June, F[11]. By sub-s (8) any interest in a dwelling-house (see *Lewin v End* [1906] AC 299) used or held by the local authority for occupation by a person employed to work at the school is to be treated as an interest used or held for the purposes of the school. By sub-s (10) this section is subject to 1988 Act s 198 and Sch 10, which make further provision for the transfer of property, rights and liabilities, and in particular provides for the identification and apportionment of property, and for the part to be played by the Education Assets Board. References in those provisions to the 'transfer date' are to be read as referring to the date of implementation of the proposals.
   As to the Education Assets Board see 1988 Act ss 197 to 201 Sch 8 and Sch 10, and Appendix 5.
10 First governors are persons committed to the good government and continuing viability of the school. See the 1996 Act Sch 24 paras 7 and 12. See also para 4.31.
11 An agreement may provide for the property excluded from transfer to be used for the purposes of the grant-maintained school on such terms as may be specified in or determined under the agreement; and directions may confer rights or impose liabilities which could have been conferred or imposed by agreement. Orders are to be made by SI.

authority in respect of the principal of, or interest on, a loan; and (e) any liability to pay former employees of the authority or of the governing body compensation for premature retirement.

4.14 To protect the interests of trustees of voluntary schools where a voluntary school which has been moved to a new site becomes grant-maintained, it is provided[12]
(a) that the LEA will remain obliged (see para 3.38) to convey their interest in the new site and buildings to the trustees: thus if for any reason the property still remains in the hands of the LEA on the implementation date the obligation to provide new sites will continue to apply after the school becomes grant-maintained as if it were still a voluntary school of any kind;[13]
(b) that where immediately before the implementation date an LEA are under the duty to convey their interest in a new site to the trustees, or (where they have exercised their powers to provide premises for a voluntary school—see para 3.44), no interest in the site, buildings or premises will be transferred to the new governing body; and where the duty applies at a time when the procedure for acquisition for grant-maintained status is pending, the local authority will not be obliged to obtain consent before disposing of the site, buildings or premises or entering into a contract to do so;[14]
(c) that when immediately before the implementation date there is an agreement in force (see para 3.39) in relation to the site or buildings, the transfer will not apply to any rights or liabilities of the local authority under that agreement; and any directions given before the implementation date, so far as they relate to the existing governing body, are to have effect, on or after the implementation date, as if they related to the new governing body.[15]

4.15 Most of the staff working solely at the school are transferred automatically on the implementation date to the employment of the new governing body, who assume the contractual rights, liabilities etc of the former employer. The exceptions are school meals staff, unless they provide meals solely for consumption at the school; employees whose contract terminates on the day before the implementation date; and LEA employees assigned to work, from that date, solely at another school, or withdrawn from the school as from that date. Persons employed or assigned by the LEA to work at the school as from the implementation date are to be treated as if previously employed by the LEA to do similar work. Staff who work partly at the school and partly elsewhere may be transferred by order of the Secretary of State (which may designate individuals by name or a group of employees by description). An employee may terminate his contract (and claim 'constructive dismissal') if a substantial change to his detriment is made in his working conditions, but the mere change of employer does not count as such a change.[16]

---

12 1996 Act s 210.
13 1996 Act s 210(1) and (2).
14 1996 Act s 210(3). Sections 201(1)(a) and 204 are not to apply.
15 1996 Act s 210(4). Section 201(1)(a) is not to apply.
16 1996 Act s 202 (and see s 209).

4.16 *Grant-Maintained Schools*

Effect of pending procedure for acquisition of grant-maintained status on property disposals, contracts and staff changes

4.16 While the procedure for acquiring grant-maintained status is pending, local authorities are subject to the following restrictions in dealing with a school's land, entering into contracts and making staff changes.[17]

(a) Disposal of any land used by the school is prohibited (unless under a contract made or option granted before the procedure was initiated) without the consent of the existing governing body and the Secretary of State or, once grant-maintained status proposals have been approved, by the new governing body and, additionally, by the Secretary of State, if the value exceeds £6,000 or a sum he substitutes by order. Contracts for disposal, and disposals, of land entered into without consent are not invalid or void, but once proposals have been approved the Education Assets Board (see Appendix 5) may repudiate a wrongful contract or option or, if authorised by the Secretary of State, purchase compulsorily the interest in land disposed of, and then convey it to the new governing body, recovering its value, and costs, from the local authority.[18]

(b) A local authority may not, with specified exceptions, enter into a contract which would or might bind a new governing body without the consent of the existing governing body (and of the Secretary of State if outgoings would be £15,000 or more) or, after approval of grant-maintained status proposals, of the new governing body.[19] A contract

---

17 1996 Act s 203. Orders are to be made by SI. The procedure for acquisition of grant-maintained status is pending when it has been initiated and not terminated. The procedure is initiated when an LEA receive notice (a) under s 136, of a meeting of the governing body at which a motion is to be considered that it be resolved to hold a ballot on whether grant-maintained status for the school should be sought, no ballot having been held within the previous 12 months except with the consent of the Secretary of State; or (b) that a ballot is to be held following a written request under s 187. Subject to s 204(3) (see n 18 below) the procedure is terminated where the meeting is not held, the motion not moved or the resolution not passed; if a ballot (or second ballot) does not show a majority in favour; if the published proposals (or substituted proposals) are withdrawn or rejected by the Secretary of State without a requirement for further proposals being imposed; or on the date of implementation of the proposals.

18 1996 Act ss 204 and 205. By s 204(3) once approval of the proposals for grant-maintained status has been granted, the procedure for acquisition is to be deemed to continue, for the purposes of ss 204 and 205, until any agreement between the local authority and the Education Assets Board required by 1988 Act Sch 10, para 2(1), has been reached or the matter finally determined. Agreement is required (for example) about the identification of the land which is to transfer.
   Consent under s 204 is, by sub-s (7), in addition to any consent required by the Local Government Act 1972 s 123(2). Sections 204(8) and 205(9) provide that, for the purposes of those sections, references to disposing of land include granting or disposing of any interest in land; references to entering into a contract to dispose of land include granting an option to acquire land or an interest in land; and by s 204(9) a series of proposed disposals is to be treated as one disposal.
   Where the Education Assets Board acquire land compulsorily (under the Acquisition of Land Act 1981) the Compulsory Purchase Act 1965 s 11, or the Land Compensation Act 1973 s 52A, apply as respects compensation and any interest payable by the Board.

19 1996 Act s 206. The Secretary of State may give his consent, unconditionally or subject to conditions, in respect of a particular contract or contracts of any class or description; and he may amend the figure of £15,000 by order (made by SI). The section does not apply (a) to works contracts entered into in accordance with the Local Government, Planning and Land Act 1980, s 7 or the Local Government Act 1988, s 4 (which relate to competitive tendering); (b) to contracts to dispose of land, or to grant an option to dispose of land, or to grant an option to acquire land or an interest in land (as to which see s 204, above); or (c) to contracts of employment.

entered into without the required consent is not void, but once proposals have been approved, if it has not yet been performed, it may be repudiated by the Education Assets Board by notice in writing, and the local authority remain liable even after the implementation date.[20]

(c) A local authority may not remove land or other property from use by the school except with the consent of the existing governing body and of the Secretary of State, or (after approval of grant-maintained status proposals) of the new governing body. If the proposals are approved and the local authority have broken this requirement the change is nullified.[1]

(d) An LEA may not appoint, dismiss or withdraw staff except with the consent of the existing governing body and of the Secretary of State or, after approval of grant-maintained status proposals, of the new governing body. The staff affected are those whose posts are part of the complement determined for the school (see para 13.27), or who are employed to work solely at the school in some other post. Foundation governors may, however, dismiss reserved teachers.[2]

NEW GRANT-MAINTAINED SCHOOLS

Proposals for establishment

4.17 Chapter IV of the 1996 Act (sections 211 to 217) provides for new grant-maintained schools to be established. Proposals may come from a funding authority or from promoters, but not from LEAs.

4.18 When a funding authority, alone, or with an LEA, are responsible (see para 2.39), for providing sufficient primary or secondary education places (or both) in the LEA's area, and they intend to establish a new grant-maintained school, they are to publish proposals in the manner prescribed and submit them to the Secretary of State, first having had regard to any guidance he may give and after consulting appropriate persons.[3] When promoters propose to establish a grant-maintained school they are to follow the same procedures and consult, among others, the funding authority.[4]

4.19 Proposals may not relate to other than primary or secondary education unless it is either (a) part-time education for persons who are over compulsory school age or are junior pupils (ie aged under 12) or (b) full-time education for

20 1996 Act s 207.
1 1996 Act s 208.
2 1996 Act s 209.
3 1996 Act s 211. See the Education (Publication of School Proposals and Notices) Regulations 1993, SI 1993/3113, reg 4. By s 571 'guidance' is to be published in such manner as the Secretary of State thinks fit. As to compulsory purchase of land by the funding authority see Sch 2 para 3(1). See Circular 23/94 (WO 13/95), 'The Supply of School Places', E[3174].
4 1996 Act s 212. During parliamentary proceedings on the Bill for the 1993 Act the Government spokesman indicated that the criteria by which the Secretary of State would judge proposals submitted to him under this section would be those that apply to proposals for voluntary aided schools under (now) s 41. In particular account would be taken of the character of the proposed school, of the promoters' commitment to delivery of the National Curriculum, and of the demand for new school places in the area—the area for this purpose being a two mile radius from a proposed primary school and a three-mile radius from a proposed secondary school.

4.19 *Grant-Maintained Schools*

persons of 19 and over. Proposals are to be in a prescribed form, with supporting statements, and there are procedures for making objections and for obtaining approval of the proposed premises. Special requirements apply when promoters propose to substitute a grant-maintained school for an independent school.[5]

Approval and implementation of proposals

4.20 Proposals by promoters require the approval of the Secretary of State, as do those of the funding authority if (a) he so notifies the authority within two months of their submission, (b) objections have been made and not withdrawn, or (c) the proposals name a sponsor. The Secretary of State may reject the proposals or approve them with or without modifications; if with modifications only after consultation with the funding authority and the promoters (if any). Where proposals published by the funding authority do not require the approval of the Secretary of State, the funding authority are within four months to determine whether to adopt them or not, and notify the Secretary of State accordingly.[6]

4.21 If the proposals are approved or adopted the persons appointed in accordance with regulations as the initial first or foundation governors become a body corporate on the proposed incorporation date. The funding authority or promoters (as the case may be) are to implement the proposals in accordance with the particulars of the premises which have also been approved or adopted.[7]

4.22 Between the date of approval or adoption of proposals and the implementation date the governing body are to exercise their powers under Part III of the 1996 Act only for the purpose of, or in connection with, the conduct of the school on or after the implementation date. During the period between incorporation of the governing body and that date the funding authority may make them grants (and the provisions of Chapter VI—see para 4.37 ff—are not to apply). Grants are not to be for the provision of premises except when the proposals have been made by promoters, in which case they may amount to no more than 85 per cent of expenditure on the site (excluding playing fields) and buildings.

4.23 The authority may impose requirements which in the case of a school established by promoters are to include that the site or buildings are to be held in trust by trustees of the school.[8] Except where grant is in respect of premises, and the freehold in those premises is, or is to be, held on trust for the purposes of the school, the funding authority may, once any conditions specified in the requirements (eg as to use of the premises or equipment) are satisfied, require the governing body to pay back to them the amount of the grant, or so much of the current value of the premises or equipment in respect of which the grant was paid as is determined to be properly attributable to the payment of the grant, if that is greater.

5 1996 Act s 213 and Sch 20 Pt II.
6 1996 Act s 214. As respects a school in Wales, consultation with the funding authority is to take place only after the Schools Funding Authority for Wales have begun to exercise their functions.
7 1996 Act s 215 and the Education (Governors of New Grant-maintained Schools) Regulations 1994, SI 1994/654, regs 2 to 5. As to premises see Sch 20 para 12 and s 214(5) and (6).
8 1996 Act ss 216, 296(1) and (for England), pursuant to s 248(6) the Education (Grant-maintained and Grant-maintained Special Schools) (Finance) Regulations 1996, SI 1996/889. See *R v Funding Agency for Schools, ex p Bromley London Borough Council* 15 February (1996, unreported).

GOVERNMENT AND CONDUCT

4.24 Chapter V (sections 218 to 243, Schedules 22 to 24) specifies requirements relating to governing instruments and membership of governing bodies. In this part reference is also made to provisions relating specifically to exclusion from school and to admission and exclusion appeals.

Instruments and articles of government

4.25 For every grant-maintained school there is to be (a) an instrument of government defining the constitution of the governing body and (b) articles of government concerning conduct—about performance and delegation of functions, staff, curriculum, admission arrangements, admission and exclusion appeals, and annual reports and parents' meetings. Instrument and articles are both to comply with requirements under Chapter V but otherwise may make any provision which is authorised or may be necessary or desirable. Conduct is also to be in accordance with any trust deed relating to the school, subject to express provision in the instrument or articles.[9] The Secretary of State has power to modify by order any trust deed or other instrument relating to the school, to remove any inconsistency with instrument or articles.[10]

4.26 Notwithstanding any provisions in articles, the head teacher of a grant-maintained school may not exclude a pupil for an indefinite period or for fixed periods amounting to more than a total of 15 school days in any one term; but these restrictions are without prejudice to the power to exclude a pupil permanently.[11]

4.27 Under articles a committee is to be established to hear appeals against decisions on admissions and exclusions. Governing bodies are required (a) by regulation to advertise for lay members, and (b) to indemnify members of an appeal committee against the costs, incurred in good faith, of pursuing their functions.[12]

4.28 Initial instruments and articles are to be as prescribed, the instrument taking effect from the incorporation date and the articles from the implementation date (or, for some articles of new grant-maintained schools, the incorporation date). Before making regulations the Secretary of State is to consult specified church bodies where the school has foundation governors.[13]

---

9   1996 Act s 218 and Schs 22 and 23. See Circular 18/93, (WO 3/94).
    As to arrangements for admission and admission appeals see para 7.21, and as to admission numbers para 7.22 ff. As to exclusions see Circular 10/94 (WO 60/94), 'Exclusions from School'. Provision is made in Sch 22 para 14 for access to papers of governing bodies. As to appeal committees for exclusions see the Code of Practice (1994) published by the Department for Education.
10 1996 Act s 302(1).
11 1996 Act s 307.
12 1996 Act s 308, Sch 23 para 6(1) and the Education (Lay Members of Appeal Committees) Regulations 1994, SI 1994/1303. The indemnity is wide enough to cover professional charges and out-of-pocket expenses of solicitor and Counsel.
13 1996 Act s 219. See Sch 39 paras 24 to 26 where governing bodies were incorporated under Ch IV of Pt I of the 1988 Act; also the Education (Grant-maintained Schools) (Initial Governing Instruments) Regulations 1993, SI 1993/3102.

4.29 *Grant-Maintained Schools*

4.29 On the initiative of a governing body the Secretary of State may by order replace or modify instruments, or consent to their making or modifying new articles. Where the school has foundation governors the governing body are first to consult the person who appoints them and specified church authorities. The Secretary of State may on his own initiative by order modify instruments, or by direction require governing bodies to modify articles, and an order or direction may relate to all grant-maintained schools, to any category or to an individual school. Before making an order or giving a direction he is to consult (a) the governing body or bodies concerned; if the order or direction relates only to a school having foundation governors (b) the person who appoints them and specified church authorities; and if it relates to two or more schools any of which has foundation governors (c) an appropriate national representative body of the church in question.[14]

4.30 A new or modified instrument which would otherwise produce more governors in any of the categories than the instrument permits is to provide a means of eliminating the excess.

Governors

4.31 Governors fall into defined categories, and a distinction is drawn between those appointed to oversee the school's transition to grant-maintained status (the initial governors) and those who are to be governors on and after the incorporation date.[15] Initial and subsequent instruments of government are to provide that all governing bodies are to contain
(a) parent governors—for a secondary school five; for a primary school, three, four or five, initially as specified in the proposals (i) for acquisition of grant-maintained status or (ii) for establishment of a new grant-maintained school. If insufficient parents stand for election (except, in the case of (ii), where vacancies arise before the implementation date) the other governors are to fill vacancies by appointment of registered parents of registered pupils at the school, where reasonably practicable;

---

14 1996 Act ss 220 and 221. The powers under these sections apply also in respect of instruments and articles made under the 1988 Act and given effect by Sch 39 paras 24 and 25. The Secretary of State may by order under Sch 3 para 1 authorise the funding authority to exercise his powers under these sections. See also s 311(2) (Wales).

15 1996 Act s 222 and Sch 24.
  1996 Act ss 234 and 235 explain how the proposed initial governors of a school seeking to acquire grant-maintained status are to be selected. See the Education (Publication of School Proposals and Notices) Regulations 1993, SI 1993/3113, reg 6 and Education (Publication of Notices) (Special Schools) Regulations 1994, SI 1994/2167, reg 2.
  Provision is made under s 236 for the determination of initial first or foundation governors under s 237 for the replacement, before incorporation, of proposed initial parent and teacher governors, and under s 238 of proposed initial first or foundation governors. Section 239 contains supplementary provisions relating to elections and appointments required for determining initial governors of an elected category. Section 240 requires the Secretary of State to make regulations for the determination of initial sponsor governors and for them to be named (see the Education (Grant-maintained Schools) (Initial Sponsor Governors) Regulations 1993, SI 1993/3188). Section 241 requires the Secretary of State to make regulations for the appointment of initial governors of grant-maintained schools (see the Education (Governors of New Grant-maintained Schools) Regulations 1994 SI 1994/654, regs 2-5). By s 242 the proceedings of a governing body are not to be invalidated by any defect in any procedure required under Ch V in relation to the determination of an initial governor, or (Sch 22 para 11) by a vacancy in the governing body or defect in election or appointment.

otherwise persons who are parents of a child of compulsory school age;[16] and
(b) one or two teacher governors, initially as specified in the proposals;[17] and
(c) the head teacher ex officio;[18] and *either*
(d) first governors, if the school was a county school or established by the funding authority;[19] *or*
(e) foundation governors if it was voluntary or established by promoters;[20] and also,
(f) sponsor governors, in respect of a grant-maintained secondary school, where the proposals for acquisition of grant-maintained status or for establishment of a new school name a sponsor. (The sponsor may appoint up to four governors; if there is more than one sponsor the instrument or proposals are to specify how many governors each sponsor is separately to appoint.[1])

4.32 First governors, or foundation governors, are to outnumber the other governors.[2]

---

16 1996 Act s 223. Where an existing school acquires grant-maintained status sub-s (5), applying Sch 7 para 7, governs the initial election of parent governors to the new governing body, who are to inform the authority responsible for election arrangements of any vacancy for a parent governor. In the case of a new grant-maintained school, parent governors who satisfy prescribed requirements are to be appointed by the new governing body before the implementation date. See the Education (Governors of New Grant-maintained Schools) Regulations 1994, SI 1994/654 reg 6.
17 1996 Act s 224. The preceding note applies to the election of teacher governors as it applies to that of parent governors. See SI 1994/654 reg 7.
18 1996 Act s 225. Where an existing school acquires grant-maintained status, this means, up to the implementation date, the existing head teacher; in the case of a new grant-maintained school, a person who has been appointed as head teacher before the implementation date.
19 1996 Act s 226 and Sch 24, paras 7 and 12. At least two of the first governors are to be parents of registered pupils, and at least two, members of the local community, and some are to be business people. One person may satisfy two or more of the requirements. Where the school is established as a new grant-maintained school by the funding authority, first governors appointed before the implementation date need not include parents, and it will be for the authority, rather than the governing body, to appoint the first governors who are members of the local business community.
20 1996 Act s 228. The initial instrument is to provide for the number of foundation governors to be as specified in the proposals, and also, if the school was a voluntary school, that those who were entitled to appoint the foundation governors are to be entitled to appoint the new foundation governors; and, if the school is a new grant-maintained school established by promoters, for the promoters to appoint the foundation governors. Where the initial instrument provides for a foundation governorship to be held ex officio, it is to be an office specified in the proposals.
The instrument may provide for any foundation governorship, other than that of an additional governor appointed under s 230(2), to be held ex officio. Where it does so, the office is to be specified in the instrument; and any person or persons entitled to appoint a foundation governor are to be named in the instrument.
The instrument is also to provide that at least two foundation governors are, on the date of taking office, to be parents of registered pupils at the school, except in the case of appointments made before the implementation date for a school established by promoters. In the case of a former voluntary school, at least two initial foundation governors are to be parents on the date of their selection or appointment.
1 1996 Act s 229. In the case of a new grant-maintained school with a sponsor, the instrument of government is to be read as if it required the first appointments of sponsor governors to be made before the date of implementation.
2 1996 Act ss 226(2) and 228(2). Sponsor governors do not count as 'other governors' for the first governors' calculation.

4.33 *Grant-Maintained Schools*

4.33 The instrument of government is to give the Secretary of State power to replace first governors when (a) they fail to secure compliance with any statutory requirement, (b) an 'action plan' has followed an inspection report recommending special measures (see para 8.22), or (c) he thinks that the governing body's action or inaction is prejudicial to education at the school. The instrument is also to empower him to fill vacancies if the governing body omit to do so,[3] and to appoint one, or two, additional governors if he thinks that the governing body are not carrying out their responsibilities adequately. If he does so, those who appoint first or foundation governors may appoint an equal number of additional governors.[4]

Powers

4.34 Governing bodies have power to do anything necessary or expedient for the conduct of a grant-maintained school, or each school of a group, subject to provisions in the instrument or articles of government and to its remaining (if not new) a school of unchanged description unless change is authorised or does not require authorisation (see para 4.48 ff). In particular they may borrow from the Secretary of State or a funding authority (see para 4.45), acquire and (subject to the consent of the Secretary of State) dispose of land (but not grant a mortgage etc), enter into contracts (including contracts of employment—see para 13.32), invest sums not immediately required and accept gifts of land or other property or hold it on trust. If instruments or articles permit, the education provided may include education which is neither primary nor secondary if it is (i) part-time education for persons of over compulsory school age, (ii) full-time education for those of 19 and over, (iii) part-time education for junior pupils under five (and the school provides full-time education for those of the same age), or (iv), as agents of an LEA, other education which is neither primary nor secondary (eg adult education and youth and community provision).[5]

4.35 Two or more grant-maintained schools may enter into a 'joint scheme', so as to co-operate and seek economies of scale. The schools retain their own governing bodies but the scheme may authorise or require the establishment of joint committees, provide for their meetings and proceedings and for delegation of functions to them. Joint committees are to consist only of governors of the constituent schools and are to include a head teacher, a parent governor and a first or foundation governor. Functions to be exercised jointly, and expenses, are to be in accordance with the scheme. When a teacher is employed under a joint scheme the School Teachers' Pay and Conditions Act 1991 (see para 13.60 ff) is to apply as if the teacher were employed by the joint committee and that committee were a governing body.[6]

3 1996 Act s 227. A first governor appointed in any of the circumstances mentioned does not have to be a parent or member of the local (or local business) community. See Circular 17/93 (WO 64/93), 'Schools Requiring Special Measures', para 49, E[2132].
4 1996 Act s 230.
5 1996 Act s 231. See the Education (Transfer of Functions Relating to Grant-maintained Schools) Order 1997, SI 1997/294, under which consent to borrowing is to be exercised in, the Funding Agencies for Schools. By s 288 a single governing body conducting a group of schools has the same powers under this section in relation to each school in the group.
6 1996 Act s 232. A joint scheme overrides the provisions in the constituent schools' instruments and articles of government, but is not to affect any co-ordinated arrangements for admissions made under s 430 (see para 7.26).
    Under s 302(1)(b) the Secretary of State may, by order, modify any trust deed or other instrument to remove any inconsistency between it and a scheme under s 232.

4.36 A joint scheme does not come into force until the Secretary of State has approved it, and is to provide for its own termination if all the governing bodies so agree. A scheme may be varied by all the governing bodies if the variations are 'minor' as defined by order of the Secretary of State. He may approve a scheme or vary it, with modifications if he thinks fit, or give a direction to end it, but in each case only after consultations with the appropriate governing bodies.[7] A joint scheme is to be distinguished from the 'grouping' referred to in para 4.78 ff below.

FUNDING

4.37 Chapter VI of the 1996 Act (sections 244 to 258) deals with the grants payable to grant-maintained schools by the funding authorities (see para 2.35 ff) (including, in Wales, the Secretary of State until the establishment of the Schools Funding Council for Wales[8]) towards maintenance, special purpose and capital expenditure, loans to grant-maintained schools and the recovery from LEAs of sums paid out as maintenance grants. Governing bodies in receipt of grant are to comply with requirements specified in grant regulations.[9]

Maintenance grants

4.38 These are paid by the funding authority to governing bodies in accordance with grant regulations, which determine or redetermine their amount for each financial year. Grant is to be applied solely for 'the purposes of the school', which in this context do not include provision of part-time education suitable for persons over compulsory school age, or full-time education for those of 19 and over. This requirement is subject to any provision for the expenses of a joint scheme (see para 4.35), to any requirement of the funding authority (see para 4.41) and to any requirements in the articles of government about the application of maintenance grant.[10]

Special purpose grants

4.39 These are made (a) for the educational purposes specified in grant regulations, (b) to make any provision (of educational services or facilities or

7 1996 Act s 233. By order under Sch 3 para 1 the Secretary of State may authorise the funding authority to exercise his functions.
8 See ss 249 to 254 (para 4.44 below).
9 See, for Wales, the Education (Grant-maintained and Grant-maintained Special Schools) (Finance) (Wales) Regulations 1997, SI 1997/599, and, for England, the Education (Grant-maintained and Grant-maintained Special Schools) (Finance) Regulations 1996, SI 1996/889. The comparable powers to make grant regulations in s 79(1) and (2) of the 1988 Act were considered by Otton J in *R v Department of Education and Science, ex p Dudley Metropolitan Borough Council* [1992] Fam Law 483. See also *R v Secretary of State for Education and Science, ex p Birmingham City Council* [1992] RVR 218, DC.
10 1996 Act s 244. In relation to groups of schools see para 4.82. By the 1994 Act s 12(6) the provision of initial teacher training is not to be treated as being undertaken for the purposes of the school.
  During the passage of the Bill for the 1993 Act it was explained on behalf of the Government that annual maintenance grant was calculated to include three main elements. The core element was based on the financial delegation scheme of each school's former maintaining authority. To this was added a percentage to reflect that authority's spending record on services provided centrally to their remaining maintained schools. The third element was for school meals, again based on the spending of the individual LEA.

4.39 Grant-Maintained Schools

otherwise) required to meet any special needs of the population of the area served by the school, or (c) to meet any expenses which the governing body cannot reasonably be expected to meet from maintenance grant. Grants may be paid on a regular basis, in respect of recurrent expenditure, or to meet expenditure incurred or to be incurred on a particular occasion or during a particular period.[11]

Capital grants

4.40 These are made in respect of expenditure, past or future, of a capital nature (to be determined by or under the grant regulations) of any class or description there specified. When there are sponsor governors, the Secretary of State may, after consultation, direct the funding authority to pay a specified amount of capital grant to the governing body for specified purposes; but a direction may not be given more than 12 months after (a) the incorporation date in the case of an existing school acquiring grant-maintained status, if it has sponsor governors on that date, (b) the implementation date, in the case of a new grant-maintained school, if it has sponsor governors on that date or (c) in any other case, the date on which the instrument of government naming a person as sponsor of the school came into effect[12]

Grants: general

4.41 Grant regulations may authorise or require governing bodies to comply with specified requirements imposed by the funding authority, when payment is made or subsequently. Requirements may be directly imposed by the grant regulations, or determined in accordance with them. The funding authority may vary or remove requirements subject, in specified cases, to the consent of the Secretary of State.[13]

4.42 The grant regulations may, under specified conditions, require payments to be made to the funding authority of the amount of the grant, or of so much of the current value of the premises or equipment for which the grant was paid, as is determined to be properly attributable to the payment of grant, whichever

---

It was also explained that the restriction to 'the purposes of the school' was not intended to affect the power of the governing body to use maintenance grant to provide education for a pupil who had begun his education at the school when younger than 19 and continued with it—eg a pupil who retook his GCSE in his first year in the sixth form (year 12) and did so well that he went on to take 'A' levels over two years, attaining 19 in his third year; or a pupil with special educational needs for whom the school made special provision (where such a pupil aged over 16 began to attend a local college part-time while still at school to ease transition, the two institutions would be expected to make appropriate arrangements between them); and a pupil in his third year in the sixth form taking 'S' levels and preparing for Oxbridge entrance.

11 1996 Act s 245.
12 1996 Act s 246. Where capital grant is paid for providing a site or building for a school established by promoters, s 296(1) requires the imposition, under s 247, of a requirement to secure that they are held on trust by trustees of the school.
13 1996 Act s 247. During the passage of the Bill for the 1993 Act the Government spokesman explained the Department's policy on the recovery from voluntary aided and special agreement schools of assets which have been provided with, or enhanced by, the payment of grant aid, should those assets cease to be used for the purpose for which the grant was paid. Grant used on premises owned by trustees should not be recoverable by the Secretary of State but should be re-cycled for educational purposes 'through well-established mechanisms provided by existing education and charity law'.

is greater. But no such requirement may be imposed in relation to capital grant if it is made in respect of the provision, alteration or repair of the school premises, and the freehold is, or is to be, held on trust for the purposes of the school.

4.43 The funding authority determine the times and manner of payment of grant. Payments of maintenance grant may be made on the basis of an estimate before the precise amount has been determined under the regulations. Over-payments of maintenance grant, and payments of special purpose and capital grant, may be recovered by deduction from subsequent grant or otherwise.[14]

Wales

4.44 Once the Schools Funding Council for Wales begin to exercise their functions the provisions mentioned above will apply. Until then[15] the Secretary of State is to make annual maintenance grants to the governing bodies of grant-maintained schools in Wales, which, subject to grant regulations, any requirements under a joint scheme, and to articles of government, are to be applied 'for the purposes of the school' as indicated above.[16] He is also to make special purpose grants and capital grants for the purposes indicated above.[17] Governing bodies in receipt of grant are to comply with requirements similar to those mentioned above.[18] The times and manner of payment are to be determined similarly by the Secretary of State.[19]

Loans

4.45 The funding authority, or, in relation to Wales, the Secretary of State if the Schools Funding Council for Wales have not yet begun to exercise their functions, may make loans to governing bodies under regulation for prescribed purposes, and the lender may recover principal or interest by deduction from grant or otherwise.[20]

Recovery from local funds   Recoupment

4.46 Where the Secretary of State so determines, he recovers from an LEA, in respect of any financial year, the amount (or an estimate, if he thinks appropriate) of maintenance grants relating to some or all of the grant-maintained schools in their area. Subject to any provision in 'recoupment regulations' (not to be confused with inter-authority recoupment regulations), the amount recoverable is to be determined, and if necessary revised, by reference to the grant payable, and may be reduced to take account of any excess amount received for a previous year. Recovery may be made by requiring the LEA to pay all or part of the sums due, at a time or times the Secretary of State thinks fit, or by

---

14   1996 Act s 248.
15   1996 Act s 249.
16   1996 Act s 250 in place of s 244(1) and (3).
17   1996 Act s 251 in place of s 245(1), s 252 in place of s 246(1).
18   1996 Act s 253 in place of s 247.
19   1996 Act s 254 in place of s 248.
20   1996 Act s 255. Loans under this section do not require consent under s 231(6). See the Education (Grant-maintained Schools) (Loans) Regulations 1993, SI 1993/3073.

4.46 Grant-Maintained Schools

deduction from any grant or redistribution of non-domestic rates made to the LEA.[1]

4.47 When the Secretary of State has made a determination as mentioned above, an LEA may, under regulation, recoup so much of the amount recoverable as is attributable to extra-district pupils (see para 11.18) from the authorities to whose areas they belong, or (Scotland) with which they have connection. When a school is covered by a determination its governing body are to provide its LEA with the information about its pupils necessary to enable them to make a claim.[2]

ALTERATION ETC

4.48 Chapter VII (sections 259 to 266) deals with the procedure for making alterations in grant-maintained schools, including changes of character, enlargement of the premises and their transfer to a new site. Provision is made for the changes to be proposed by the governing body or by the funding authority, for the publication of the proposals, and for their adoption or approval, rejection or modification by the Secretary of State. For the most part the procedure follows that laid down for LEA schools. This Chapter of the Act also applies, with modifications, to proposals for alteration where the governing body of a county school seek grant-maintained status (see para 4.11).

Proposals

4.49 A governing body who intend
(a) to make a significant change in the character of a school,[3]
(b) to make significant enlargement of its premises, or
(c) to transfer the school to a new site (unless for a temporary period of up to three years),
are to publish proposals in the manner prescribed by regulations and send the Secretary of State a copy. Before doing so they are to obtain the consent of the trustees if any significant change in the religious character of the school is contemplated. They are also to consult appropriate persons, having regard to guidance given by the Secretary of State. The decision to publish proposals requires confirmation at a second meeting of the governing body held not less than 28 days after the first.

---

1 1996 Act ss 256 and 257. See, for Wales, SI 1997/599; and for England SI 1996/889, reg 42.
  In *R v Secretary of State for Wales, ex p Gwent County Council* [1995] ELR 87, the Court of Appeal held that deductions from revenue support grant under the 1988 Act s 81(8)(b) (now re-enacted in the 1996 Act s 256(6)) constituted 'expenditure' by the authority within the Local Government Finance Act 1992 s 43(2)(a) for the purpose of calculating their annual budget requirement and accordingly their liability to be 'capped'.
2 1996 Act s 258.
3 'Significant' means substantial in relation to function or size: 1996 Act s 573(5) (and see para 3.09). By s 573(4) 'change in the character' of a school includes change in the age-range or sex composition (see para 14.06) and the making or alteration of arrangements for admission by reference to ability or aptitude; but by s 266 it does not include a change resulting from (a) beginning or ceasing to provide part-time education for those over compulsory school age, or (b) part-time nursery education where full-time nursery education is provided, or (c) full-time education for those of 19 and over. By 1994 Act s 12(5) undertaking the provision of courses of initial teacher training is not 'a significant change of character'.

4.50 The proposals are to include particulars of the proposed implementation date and of the number of pupils to be admitted in each age group in the first school year in which the proposals will be wholly implemented. If pupils are to be admitted for nursery education, prescribed information must be given. The published proposals are to be accompanied by a statement dealing with the effect of the proposed changes on pupils with special educational needs and explaining the procedure for making objections.

4.51 Objections may be made to the Secretary of State within two months of the publication of proposals by (a) the appropriate further education funding council (if provision of full-time education for 16 to 18 year-olds is affected), (b) any ten or more local government electors for the area, (c) the governing body of any school affected by the proposals, and (d) any LEA concerned; and when the proposals are to transfer a school to a site in a different area, by any ten or more local government electors for that area.[4]

4.52 Where the Secretary of State has made an order transferring responsibility for providing some or all school places in the area of an LEA to a funding authority (see para 2.39), proposals for change of character etc as above may be made by the funding authority, who are to publish proposals in the manner prescribed and send the Secretary of State a copy. The particulars and procedure to be followed are as above, except that
(a) no proposals may be published to make a significant change in the religious character of a school, even if the trustees are prepared to consent,
(b) if the school is a Church of England, Church of Wales or Roman Catholic Church school having any foundation governor who is appointed by the appropriate diocesan authority, that authority is to be consulted, and
(c) objections are to be submitted to the funding authority, who are to send copies to the Secretary of State, with their observations, within a month from the end of the objection period, and may be submitted by the governing body of the school to which the proposals relate.[5]

4.53 Proposals published by the governing body of a grant-maintained school always require the approval of the Secretary of State. Those published by a funding authority require his approval only if he calls them in by notice to the authority, or if objections are made and not withdrawn within the two month period. The Secretary of State may reject the proposals or approve them, either without modification, or, after consulting the governing body and, where the

---

4 1996 Act s 259. See the Education (Publication of School Proposals and Notices) Regulations 1993, SI 1993/3113, regs 3 and 7.
  The Secretary of State may publish his 'guidance' as he thinks fit.
  If the school is a 'church school' as defined in the Diocesan Boards of Education Measure 1991 s 10 (as amended) the consent of the Diocesan Board of Education is also to be obtained (s 3(5) of the 1991 Measure as amended).
  As to the modifications in procedure where the Secretary of State has made an order under s 264, transferring functions to the funding authority, see para 4.56 below. See *R v Secretary of State for Education and the Governing Body of the Queen Elizabeth Grammar School, ex p Cumbria County Council* [1994] ELR 220.
5 1996 Act s 260. See the Education (Publication of School Proposals and Notices) Regulations 1993, SI 1993/3113, regs 3 and 7. By Sch 4 para 19 these powers may be used to secure the provision of boarding accommodation at boarding schools. Where the proposals are for the school to cease to be single sex, see s 552(3).

4.53 Grant-Maintained Schools

funding authority have made the proposals, that authority, with the modifications he thinks desirable. Where the Secretary of State's approval is not required, the funding authority have four months from publication in which to determine whether to adopt the proposals and are then to give notice of their determination to the Secretary of State and the governing body.[6]

4.54 Where a governing body publish proposals they are, if the funding authority so direct, to submit for their approval particulars of the means of access to and within school premises, and other particulars of the premises which the authority require, by reference to Design Note 18 or a document replacing it. Where proposals are published by the funding authority they are to prepare and adopt such particulars if they think the circumstances require them to do so.[7]

Implementation of proposals

4.55 The governing body of a grant-maintained school are to implement any proposals approved by the Secretary of State or adopted by the funding authority, in accordance with any approved particulars of the premises. At the request of the governing body the Secretary of State may modify any approved or adopted proposals, or, where the proposals were published by the funding authority, at the request of that authority after consulting the governing body. No governing body or other person may make significant changes in a grant-maintained school or transfer it to a new site (unless the transfer is intended to be for less than three years) or undertake to do so, unless proposals have been published and approved or adopted in accordance with the foregoing provisions. But pending the approval or adoption of proposals or particulars of premises the Secretary of State may allow the governing body to take anticipatory steps which he considers reasonable in the circumstances.[8]

4.56 So as to transfer some of his functions under this Part of the Act to the funding authority, the Secretary of State may make an order modifying the requirements relating to proposals published by a governing body as follows:
(a) a copy of the proposals is to be sent to the funding authority as well as to the Secretary of State;
(b) any objections are to be sent to the funding authority instead of to the Secretary of State;
(c) if any objections are made and not withdrawn within the two-month period, then, within one month thereafter, the funding authority are to send the Secretary of State copies of all objections not withdrawn, with their observations, and may also submit objections of their own;
(d) if objections are made and not withdrawn within the two-month period, or the Secretary of State calls the proposals in by notice to the authority, it will be for him to approve the proposals, and he will have power to modify them at the request of the governing body;

---

6 1996 Act s 261.
7 1996 Act s 262. 'Design Note 18' is entitled 'Access for Disabled People to Educational Buildings' and was published in 1984 on behalf of the Secretary of State. Any replacement document is to be prescribed by regulations under, or having effect as if made under, the Town and Country Planning Act 1990.
8 1996 Act s 263.

(e) if there are no objections (or they are all withdrawn within the two-month period) and the Secretary of State does not call the proposals in for his determination, the proposals will require the approval of the funding authority; they may reject them or approve them without modifications or (after consulting the governing body) with the modifications they think desirable; and they will have power to modify the proposals at the request of the governing body before they are implemented.

4.57 Approval and modification by the funding authority under a transfer order is deemed to be approval or modification by the Secretary of State. A transfer order is not to apply where the governing body of a school seeking grant-maintained status publish proposals for alteration of a school for the purpose of ensuring consistency in the educational provision made in the area (see para 4.11); and in those circumstances the Secretary of State retains his power to modify the proposals before implementation at the request of the governing body.[9]

4.58 Proposed changes in the character, enlargement of premises or transfer of site of a county or voluntary school, which have been approved but not implemented before it becomes grant-maintained, are to be implemented in accordance with any approved particulars of the premises. The right of trustees to have the LEA's interest in the site or buildings transferred to them is preserved.[10]

DISCONTINUANCE

4.59 Chapter VIII (sections 267 to 279) provides (a) for closure of a grant-maintained school following the publication and approval or adoption of proposals from the governing body or funding authority; (b) for the withdrawal of grant where the Secretary of State considers that a school is unsuitable to continue; and (c) for the winding up of the governing body and disposal of the school property.

Proposals for discontinuance

4.60 Before passing a closure resolution the governing body are to consult persons they think appropriate, having regard to any guidance published by the Secretary of State. If they confirm their intention by passing a second closure resolution, not sooner than 28 days after the first, they are to give the LEA notice as soon as practicable. Within six months of the second resolution they may publish proposals, in the manner prescribed, for closing the school on a specified date, and are to send a copy to the Secretary of State. The proposals are to be accompanied by a statement indicating whether there are any proposals for another school to use the premises, and explaining that objections may be submitted to the Secretary of State within two months of the publication date.

4.61 Objections may be made by (a) the appropriate further education

---

9 1996 Act s 264. An order under this section is by SI.
10 1996 Act s 265 (which applies s 210).

4.61 *Grant-Maintained Schools*

funding council (if provision of full-time education for 16 to 18 year-olds is affected), (b) any ten or more local government electors for the area, (c) the governing body of any school affected by the proposals, and (d) any LEA concerned.[11]

4.62 Where the Secretary of State has made an order (see para 2.39) transferring responsibility for providing some or all school places in the area of an LEA to the funding authority, the authority may make closure proposals (without need of a 'second resolution'). They are to publish them in the manner prescribed and send the Secretary of State a copy. The proposals are to be accompanied by a statement as mentioned in para 4.60. Before publishing the proposals the funding authority are to consult the persons they think appropriate (having regard to any guidance published by the Secretary of State), and also, if the school is a Church of England, Church in Wales or Roman Catholic Church school having any foundation governor who is appointed by the appropriate diocesan authority, that authority.

4.63 Objections may be made within two months of publication of the proposals by those mentioned in para 4.61 and also by the governing body of the school to which the proposals relate. Objections are to be submitted to the funding authority, who are to send copies to the Secretary of State, with their observations, within a month of the end of the objection period.[12]

4.64 Proposals published by the governing body of a grant-maintained school always require the approval of the Secretary of State. Those published by a funding authority require his approval only if he calls them in by notice to the authority, or if objections are made and not withdrawn within the two month period. The Secretary of State may reject the proposals or approve them, either without modification, or, after consulting the governing body and, in the case of funding authority proposals, that authority, with the substitution of a different closure date. If the Secretary of State approves the proposals he must notify the governing body and the funding authority (unless the school is in Wales and the Schools Funding Council for Wales have not begun to exercise their functions) and tell them the closure date. Where the Secretary of State's approval is not required, the funding authority have four months from publication in which to determine whether to adopt the proposals, and are then to give notice of their determination to the Secretary of State (with the closure date, if any) and the governing body.[13]

4.65 The governing body of a grant-maintained school may close it only in pursuance of proposals published and approved or adopted as above. Where proposals are approved the governing body are to cease to conduct the school on the closure date specified in the approved proposals or subsequently fixed by the Secretary of State.[14]

---

11 1996 Act s 267. See the Education (Publication of School Proposals and Notices) Regulations 1993, SI 1993/3113, reg 3. As to the modifications in procedure where the Secretary of State has made an order under s 271, transferring functions to the funding authority, see para 4.66 below.
12 1996 Act s 268. See SI 1993/3113, reg 3.
13 1996 Act s 269.
14 1996 Act s 270.

4.66 So as to transfer some of his functions under this Part of the Act to the funding authority, the Secretary of State may make an order modifying the requirements relating to proposals published by a governing body. The modifications follow those set out in para 4.56, with the exception that para (e) refers to approval of the proposals by the funding authority with a different closure date; and they have power to fix another closure date at the request of the governing body. If they approve the proposals they are to notify the governing body and tell them the closure date.

4.67 Approval by the funding authority under the Secretary of State's order is deemed to be approval by him.[15]

Unsuitable school   Withdrawal of grant

4.68 If the Secretary of State thinks that a school is too small to be educationally and financially viable, and, or additionally, that the governing body have seriously and persistently failed in their statutory duties, he is to give the governing body notice of the grounds and full particulars of the matters relevant to each. If the matters appear irremediable, and the Secretary of State so states in his notice, he is also to state the date on which the funding authority will cease to maintain the school. In other cases he is to specify the measures necessary to remedy the grounds of complaint and the time (not less than six months) within which they are to be taken, and state that grant will cease to be payable unless the matters of complaint are remedied. If the governing body fail to take those measures within the specified time the Secretary of State may either extend the time or, after consulting the LEA and, where relevant, the appropriate further education funding council, notify the governing body of the date on which the grant will cease. A copy of the notice is to be sent to the funding authority, and their duty and powers to pay grant cease on the date specified. If the school is in Wales, and the Schools Funding Council for Wales have not yet begun to exercise their functions, no copy of the notice has to be sent to the funding authority since it will be the Secretary of State who funds the school.[16]

4.69 The Secretary of State may by notice to the governing body (a) withdraw a notice of unsuitability or of grant withdrawal, (b) vary an 'irremediable' notice or a notice of grant withdrawal by substituting a later date for withdrawal of grant, and (c) vary the measures specified in an unsuitability notice, together with the time for taking them (as originally notified or as extended). An extension of time does not preclude a further extension being granted. Unless the school is in Wales and the Schools Funding Council for Wales have not yet begun to exercise their functions, the funding authority are to be notified of withdrawal of a notice, and, where the measures specified in a notice are varied, given a copy of the notice as varied.[17]

---

15 1996 Act s 271. An order under this section is by SI.
16 1996 Act s 272. Where responsibility for providing school places is shared with, or transferred to, the funding authority see the modifications made by Sch 4 para 22.
17 1996 Act s 273.

4.70 *Grant-Maintained Schools*

Winding up and disposal of property

4.70 When a grant-maintained school is to be closed the Secretary of State may make an order setting out a proposed timetable for winding-up the governing body and disposing of school property—in particular for securing that all property belonging to the governing body or held in trust for the purposes of the school is brought into their custody or control or that of the trustees; for discharging any liabilities of the governing body (including those mentioned in para 4.76); for making provision in connection with the transfer of school property (see para 4.73); and for the preparation and audit of the final accounts. The order may also provide for the exercise of the functions of the governing body during the winding-up period, requiring them to comply with the directions of the Secretary of State, authorising the delegation of functions to a specified member of the governing body, and providing for the authentication of their official seal. It may confer or impose functions on the governing body, and require them to terminate contracts of employment on a specified date.

4.71 The Secretary of State may by order appoint a date for dissolving the governing body once he is satisfied that all liabilities have been discharged (with the exception of liabilities for the loans mentioned at para 3.43 which were transferred to the governing body, see para 4.13), all costs of the winding-up have been paid and all necessary provisions made and things done.[18]

4.72 The funding authority may make grants to enable the governing body of a grant-maintained school in liquidation to discharge liabilities (with the exception mentioned above) and meet winding-up costs. The authority may impose requirements on the recipient governing body before, at, or after the time of payment.[19]

4.73 Subject to the provisions of the winding-up order, school property held by the governing body immediately before the dissolution date, other than that held on trust for the school, vests in the LEA on that date, or (in the case of a new grant-maintained school established by the funding authority) in that authority. The winding-up order may vest the school property, or part of it, in any specified person, either beneficially or on specified trusts. The order may require persons in whom property is vested other than the funding authority to pay to the Secretary of State or other specified person consideration not exceeding, for the school premises, market value, as determined by the Secretary of State as at the dissolution or transfer date or within six months before, and for other property a fair consideration determined by the Secretary of State. Where the property was held on trust otherwise than by the governing body the winding-up order is to require the person in whom it is vested to pay to the trustees the maximum consideration mentioned above.

4.74 The determination is to be set out in the order; any dispute as to the amount may be referred by transferor or transferee of the property, or the person receiving the consideration, to the Lands Tribunal for determination. If the Tribunal determines a different amount from that determined by the

---

18 1996 Act ss 274 and 275.
19 1996 Act s 276.

Secretary of State, he may vary the order accordingly. If the property has been vested in the funding authority or the Secretary of State free of consideration, and they subsequently dispose of all or part of the property, the Secretary of State may require the authority concerned to pay him or some other specified person the whole or part of the proceeds.

4.75 Nothing arising from the vesting of property in the LEA or funding authority, or in the winding-up order, is to affect any interest or right of any person in, to, or over any school property which is held otherwise than for the purposes of the school.[20]

4.76 Provision is made as follows for discharging or transferring the liabilities of the governing body in liquidation where the school premises are to be used for a new school.[1]
(a) Where a winding-up order vests all or part of the school premises (other than property held by trustees for the purposes of the school) in persons proposing to establish a new independent school, they may be required to discharge any liabilities of the governing body for redundancy payments, but may set them off against any consideration required.
(b) Where the school premises, in whole or part, are to be used for another grant-maintained school, the order may transfer to that school's governing body any rights or liabilities of the governing body in liquidation in connection with those premises.
(c) If the school was an aided or special agreement school before it became grant-maintained and proposals have been approved for an aided school to be established on the premises, liability for the loans mentioned at para 3.43 are to be transferred to the temporary governing body of the new school, subject to any variation in the terms of the loan agreed between them and the Secretary of State. But if no direction has been given that the school should be an aided school before the dissolution date those liabilities will terminate and their amount will be treated (see para 3.128) as expenditure incurred by the Secretary of State (otherwise than in connection with repairs) in respect of the premises of the new school.

4.77 Surplus money and investments held by or for a governing body in liquidation are to be transferred, after discharge of liabilities and winding-up costs (other than any not required to be discharged before the dissolution date is appointed), either to the Secretary of State or as he may direct. Where he is satisfied that they do not derive from grants paid by him or the funding authority, he may require that they go to an LEA or other person, beneficially or on trust as he specifies. Where premises are to be used for a new or existing grant-maintained school he may require that they go to its governing body.[2]

---

20 1996 Act s 277. By s 567 no stamp duty is chargeable on transfers to a funding authority, LEA or the governing body of a grant-maintained school.
1 1996 Act s 278.
2 1996 Act s 279. Investments under this section are those falling within the Financial Services Act 1986, Sch 11 paras 1 to 6, namely shares and stock, debentures, government and public securities, warrants and other instruments entitling the holder to subscribe for the above, certificates representing securities and units in a collective investment scheme and, by para 11, rights and interests in any of the above. Payments and transfers are to be free of trusts under which money or investments were formerly held; and, by s 567, stamp duty is not payable.

4.78 *Grant-Maintained Schools*

GROUPS OF SCHOOLS

4.78 Chapter IX (sections 280 to 290, Schedule 25) enables schools to acquire grant-maintained status, or to be conducted, as members of a group or 'cluster' of grant-maintained schools, with a single governing body. A group may consist of both primary and secondary schools.

Instruments and articles of government

4.79 Grant-maintained schools which are grouped are conducted under one instrument of government but with separate articles for each school. Trust deeds (if any) apply so far as consistent with instrument and articles. These are to comply with any requirements imposed under Chapter IX, and may make any provision it authorises, together with other necessary or desirable provisions.[3]

4.80 Initial instruments, having effect from the incorporation date of the governing body, and articles, effective from the implementation date of the grouping proposals, are prescribed by the Secretary of State. He may modify or replace them in the same way as he may those of schools which are not grouped, and the provisions relating to new and modifying articles (see para 4.14) also apply.[4] There are to be

(a) parent governors—not less than three and (subject to that requirment) not more than the number of schools in the group—elected for a term of four years by registered parents of registered pupils at schools in the group; but if any of the schools is in a hospital any of the parent governors may be appointed by the other governors; and if insufficient parents stand for election the other governors are to fill vacancies by appointment of registered parents of registered pupils at one of the schools, where practicable, otherwise persons who are parents of a child of compulsory school age;[5] and

(b) one or two teacher governors, elected for four years from teachers at schools in the group, who are the electorate;[6] and

(c) the head teacher ex officio, unless he chooses not to be a governor;[7] and

(d) core governors, who are to hold office for five, six or seven years, as specified in the instrument.[8] (For particulars of core governors see Appendix 6.)

4.81 The instrument is to give the Secretary of State power to replace all or any of the core governors (other than one externally appointed for a particular school) in the same circumstances as those in which he may he replace first

---

3 1996 Act s 280. Schedules 22 (para 14 excepted) and 23 are to have effect with any modifications prescribed by the Secretary of State. Subject to this Chapter and provisions made under it, any enactment applying to grant-maintained schools applies separately to each school in a group. See the Education (Groups of Grant-maintained Schools) Regulations 1994, SI 1994/1041. This Chapter applies as modified by the Education (Groups including Grant-maintained Special Schools) Regulations 1994, SI 1994/779 to enable grant-maintained special schools to join groups.
4 1996 Act s 281. See the Education (Groups of Grant-maintained Schools) (Initial Governing Instruments) Regulations 1994, SI 1994/2896. This section also applies to grant-maintained special schools: see SI 1994/779, reg 3(a).
5 1996 Act s 282.
6 1996 Act s 283.
7 1996 Act s 284.
8 1996 Act s 285, Sch 25.

governors of a single school (see para 4.33). The instrument is also to empower him to fill vacancies for core governors other than externally appointed governors if the governing body are unable or unwilling to do so,[9] and to appoint one, or two, additional governors if he thinks that the governing body are not carrying out their responsibilities adequately. If he does so, the governing body may appoint not more than the same number of additional governors.[10]

Powers   Maintenance grant

4.82 The governing body of a group have the same powers as those of a single governing body (see para 4.34).[11] In place of the maintenance grant provisions relating to single schools, the governing body of a group are to apply, for the purposes of each constituent school, the prescribed percentage of the maintenance grant they receive for each financial year, subject to any requirements imposed on them under the grant regulations and by the articles of government.[12]

Membership of groups

4.83 The Secretary of State may make regulations about (a) the formation of groups of grant-maintained schools, (b) individual schools joining an existing group, (c) the merger of groups, and (d) a school wishing to leave a group; and he may issue guidance additionally or instead about the requirements he would expect to be satisfied before approving proposals in relation to (a) to (d). Neither regulations nor guidance are to apply to nursery schools.[13] The regulations provide as follows.
(a) If a school wishes to acquire grant-maintained status as a member of a group the procedure includes a resolution by the existing governing body, a ballot of parents, the publication of the proposals and their approval by the Secretary of State, with or without modifications.
(b) A similar procedure, but without a ballot, is laid down where existing grant-maintained schools wish to form a new group. The modifications permitted may exclude a school only if the consent of the governing bodies of the other schools in the proposed group is obtained before the proposals are approved.
(c) Where proposals for a new group are approved, provision is made for determining the members of the initial governing body and their incorporation, and for provisions relating to governors (see paras 4.80 and 4.81) and the instrument of government to have effect, with prescribed modifications, before the proposals are implemented or before the instrument of government replacing the initial instrument comes into force.

9   1996 Act s 286. Any provision made by the instrument pursuant to Sch 25 is not to apply to any appointment of a core governor by the Secretary of State under this section.
10 1996 Act s 287. The terms of office for core governors, and Sch 25, do not apply to additional governors.
11 1996 Act s 288.
12 1996 Act s 289. By the Education (Groups of Grant-maintained Schools) (Finance) Regulations 1994, SI 1994/1195, 97.5 per cent is prescribed. During parliamentary proceedings the Government spokesman explained that normally regulations would provide for an element of the maintenance grant to be held centrally for the common purposes of the group. For groups including special schools SI 1994/779 applies this section with modifications.
13 1996 Act s 290. See SI 1994/1041, the Education (Government of Groups of Grant-maintained Schools) Regulations 1994, SI 1994/2281 and, for modifications of this section in relation to groups including special schools, SI 1994/779, reg 3.

(d) Where proposals are approved for two or more schools to acquire grant-maintained status in a new group, or for a school to acquire that status by joining an existing group, the LEA are to cease to be under a duty to maintain those schools, any relevant special agreement is to cease to have effect, and the functions of the new governing body between approval of proposals and their implementation are to be specified. The governing body's functions are also to be specified where proposals for two or more existing grant-maintained schools to form a group are approved.

4.84 In relation to schools seeking to become a new group or members of an existing group, or to the schools already in a group, regulations may apply provisions in Part III of the 1996 Act (except sections 280 to 290 and with modifications) and for the governing body of a group to be reconstituted when any change in membership occurs.

GENERAL AND MISCELLANEOUS

Middle schools

4.85 A proposal for the establishment of a new grant-maintained school (see para 4.17 ff) may be for a middle school as described at para 2.08.[14]

Nursery education

4.86 No nursery schools may be established under proposals for a new grant-maintained school or change of character of an existing school (see paras 4.17 ff and 4.49 respectively). But proposals may provide for nursery classes.[15]

Further education

4.87 Save in prescribed circumstances, the governing body of any grant-maintained school which provides part-time education for those over compulsory school age or full-time education for those of 19 or over are to secure that it is not provided in a room where school pupils are being taught.[16]

Teacher training

4.88 The governing body of a grant-maintained school have power to provide initial courses, either alone or with other eligible institutions.[17]

Provision of benefits and services

4.89 LEAs are subject to the following requirements and provisions in relation to grant-maintained schools:

14 1996 Act s 291. This section applies equally to significant change (see para 4.49).
15 1996 Act s 292.
16 1996 Act s 293.
17 1996 Act s 294. See 1994 Act s 12.

(a) in providing benefits and services—for example, the provision of transport (see para 12.24 ff)—for those receiving education at the schools they maintain and at grant-maintained schools, they are not to discriminate against the latter;[18]
(b) their powers are extended to enable them to provide clothing and board and lodging for pupils at grant-maintained schools in specified circumstances;[19]
(c) in extension of their powers under the Local Authorities (Goods and Services) Act 1970 the Secretary of State may by order permit them to supply goods and services to grant-maintained (and grant-maintained special) schools in their own or an adjacent area for two years at full cost.[20]

4.90 As to school meals etc for pupils at grant-maintained schools see para 12.32, and as to medical inspection and treatment see para 12.45.

Premises

4.91 As to use of premises for elections, and nuisance and disturbance, see paras 15.12 and 15.09 ff respectively. The following paragraphs concern transfer and disposal.

4.92 Where grant is paid by the funding authority for the provision of premises at a new grant-maintained school, or capital grant is paid for a similar purpose for a grant-maintained school to be established by promoters, a requirement is to be imposed to ensure that the site (not including playing fields) or buildings in question are held on trust by trustees of the school. Where buildings are to be provided which are to form part of the school premises and to be constructed partly on land held by the governing body and partly by trustees for the purposes of the school, the governing body are to transfer their land to the trustees. The consent of the Secretary of State is not required for this transaction.[1]

4.93 Where the funding authority pay capital grant on the transfer of a grant-maintained school to a new site, the governing body or trustees are to pay the Secretary of State the proceeds of disposal of premises formerly used for the school, or so much as is needed to repay the capital grant. The funding authority are to be regarded as paying capital grant for this purpose if they pay it for the acquisition of the new site or for the provision of school buildings on that site or any other buildings forming part of the school premises.[2]

18 1996 Act s 295.
19 1996 Act s 510(1) and (3) to (5), and s 514(1)(a). See also paras 12.29 ff and 12.35 ff.
20 1996 Act s 516. During proceedings on the Bill for the 1993 Act it was explained that, under the Local Government (Goods and Services Act) 1970, any LEA could provide services to any grant-maintained school in England and Wales, so long as they did not exceed the 'margins of capacity'. An order under this section would enable an LEA to operate temporarily beyond those margins.
1 1996 Act s 296. In ss 296 to 300 'trustees of the school' means (by s 301(2)) any person (other than the governing body) holding property on trust for the purposes of the school.
2 1996 Act ss 297(1) and 301(1). By s 301(3), for the purposes of ss 297 to 300 a governing body or trustees are to be regarded as disposing of any premises if those premises are acquired from them, compulsorily or otherwise (and including termination of a tenancy to which Pt II of the Landlord and Tenant Act 1954, relating to security of tenure for business, professional and other tenants, applies); and 'proceeds of disposal' means the compensation or purchase money (including, in the case of termination of any such tenancy, any compensation paid by the landlord, whether or not compensation is required to be paid under s 37 of the 1954 Act).

4.94 *Grant-Maintained Schools*

4.94 If any interest in the new site has vested in the trustees, the sum paid to the Secretary of State is to be regarded, for the purposes of the School Sites Act 1841, as a sum applied in the purchase of a site for the school.[3]

4.95 If the trustees are required to make a payment to the Secretary of State when an interest in the new site is to be held by the governing body, then if the trustees held a freehold interest in the old site, the governing body are to transfer their interest in the old site (not including playing fields) to the trustees; if the trustees held any other interest, or did not hold all the interests in the old site, the governing body are to transfer to the trustees their interest in the whole or part of the new site if the Secretary of State so directs.[4]

4.96 If trustees of a grant-maintained school are required to pay any sum to the Secretary of State as above in a case in which a sum is also due to the LEA in respect of disposal of the same premises (see para 3.40), the requirement is to have effect as if the reference to the purchase money paid for the premises referred to the balance remaining after deduction of the payment to the Secretary of State, and as if the premises conveyed by the authority were the premises transferred to the trustees in para 4.95 above.[5]

4.97 The Secretary of State, in granting consent to a governing body's request to dispose of (a) premises transferred to a grant-maintained school from a local authority, or (b) premises which were acquired wholly or partly with the proceeds of the sale of those premises (or of premises so acquired), may require the governing body to transfer the premises to a specified local authority on payment of the consideration he thinks appropriate, or to pay the authority all or part of the proceeds of sale. Where the occasion of disposal is a transfer to a new site in respect of which the funding authority have paid capital grant, the transfer requirement does not apply, and any payment to a local authority is to be reduced by the amount of repayment of capital grant to the Secretary of State.[6]

4.98 When premises have been transferred from a local authority to the governing body of a grant-maintained school on the acquisition of grant-maintained status, or have been acquired wholly or partly with the proceeds of the sale of those premises (or of premises so acquired) and then transferred by the governing body to the trustees of the school, the Secretary of State may require the trustees to pay a specified local authority all or part of the proceeds of sale if they dispose of them.[7]

4.99 In granting consent to a governing body's request to dispose of (a) premises provided for a grant-maintained school by the funding authority, or (b) premises which were acquired wholly or partly with the proceeds of the sale

---

3   1996 Act s 297(2).
4   1996 Act s 297(3).
5   1996 Act s 297(4).
6   1996 Act s 298. As under s 297, the funding authority are (by s 301(1)) to be regarded as having paid capital grant on a transfer to a new site if they have paid capital grant for the acquisition of the new site, or for the provision on that site of the school buildings or any other buildings forming part of the new school premises. By s 567 no stamp duty is chargeable on any transfer of premises to a local authority in the circumstances specified.
7   1996 Act s 299.

of those premises (or of premises so acquired), the Secretary of State may require the governing body to pay him or the funding authority all or part of the proceeds of the disposal.[8] Similarly, when the governing body have transferred any such premises, or premises on which capital grant was paid, to the school trustees, and the trustees dispose of the premises, they are, with specified exceptions, under the same obligation.[9]

Modification of instruments

4.100 A trust deed or other instrument relating to a school (including an independent school to be replaced by a new grant-maintained school) may be modified, after consultation with the governing body (or promoters in the case of an independent school) and trustess (if any), by order of the Secretary of State, or of the funding authority if he so authorises. The modification may be permanent or temporary, in consequence of the school becoming grant-maintained or a subsequent alteration or transfer to a new site, or for removing any inconsistency in the interests of the school.[10]

4.101 A provision in an instrument relating to land held for a voluntary school which confers on any person an option to acquire an interest in that land, or provides for the determination or forfeiture of any interest in that land if the school ceases to be a voluntary school or to be maintained by a specified LEA, is deferred until the school (having become a grant-maintained school) ceases to be either a grant-maintained or a voluntary school.[11]

Accounts

4.102 The accounts of grant-maintained schools are to be open to inspection by the Comptroller and Auditor General, who is required to report to the House of Commons, in each session, the results of any examinations relating to grant-maintained schools which he has carried out under the National Audit Act 1983, s 6. In exercising this function he is to have regard to the reports of any relevant Audit Commission studies.[12]

---

8   1996 Act s 300(1).
9   1996 Act s 300(2). The exceptions are transfers under ss 296 and 297.
10 1996 Act s 302 and Sch 3 para 1. By the Diocesan Boards of Education Measure 1991 s 6(3), before making any modifications relating to a school which was a Church of England voluntary school before it became grant-maintained, the Secretary of State is to consult, additionally, the Diocesan Board.
11 1996 Act s 303.
12 1996 Act s 310. As to Audit Commission reports see 1988 Act s 220. See also para 15.37.

Chapter 5

SPECIAL EDUCATIONAL NEEDS

5.01 Part IV of the 1996 Act (sections 312 to 349, Schedules 26 to 28) re-enacts Part III of the 1993 Act, which consolidated and re-enacted, with amendments and additions, almost all of the 1981 Act. That Act followed the publication in 1978 of 'Special Educational Needs', the report of the Committee of Enquiry into the Education of Handicapped Children and Young People, known as the 'Warnock Report' after their chairman, later Baroness Warnock.

5.02 The 1993 Act gave effect to the Government's proposals in Chapter 9 of the White Paper, *Choice and Diversity*, Cm 2021. It preserved the principle that, subject to certain conditions, a child with special educational needs should be educated at an ordinary school (ie a 'mainstream', not a special, school), but now the wishes of the child's parent are normally to prevail (see para 5.09).

CHILDREN WITH SPECIAL EDUCATIONAL NEEDS

5.03 Chapter I of Part IV (sections 312 to 336, Schedules 26 and 27) introduces a Code of Practice on the discharge of statutory functions, specifies general requirements regarding special education provision, provides for the identification and assessment of children with special educational needs and establishes a Special Educational Needs Tribunal.

Definitions

5.04 A 'child' in Part IV is a person under the age of 19 so long as he remains a registered pupil at a school. A child has 'special educational needs' if he has a 'learning difficulty' which calls for 'special educational provision' to be made for him. A learning difficulty exists if a child
(a) has a significantly greater difficulty in learning than the majority of children of his age; or
(b) has a disability which prevents or hinders him from using educational facilities generally provided for children of his age in schools within the LEA's area; or
(c) is under five, and is likely to fall within (a) or (b) when over five, or would be if special educational provision were not made or him.

5.05 Difficulty arising solely because the child is or will be taught in a language different from that spoken at home is specifically excluded.

5.06 'Special educational provision' for a child of two or over is educational provision additional to or different from that made generally for children of his age in maintained schools other than LEA special schools. Any kind of educational provision for a child under two is 'special'.[1]

Code of practice

5.07 To give practical guidance to LEAs and governing bodies the Secretary of State, after consultation on a draft, has published (and may revise), with the approval of Parliament, a Code of Practice on the discharge of their functions, to which they and those acting on their behalf are to have regard (as are the Special Educational Needs Tribunal).[2] LEAs are to keep their arrangements for special educational provision under review, and if need be consult the funding authority and school governing bodies in their area so as to co-ordinate provision.[3]

5.08 During proceedings in Parliament it was stated on behalf of the Government that the Code 'would deal with matters which are not susceptible to hard and fast rules, matters where an element of judgment is always required'. Bodies which assist LEAs, such as social service departments and district health authorities, would be required to have regard to the Code. The Code would deal with the identification and assessment of both children under five and those of school age who have special educational needs—both the 18 per cent who have such needs but do not require a statement and the 2 per cent whose needs are best met through a statement—*Hansard* (Lords), 29 April 1993, 485–492.

Special educational provision: general

5.09 Where a child with special educational needs should be educated in a school (whether or not he is the subject of a statement—see para 5.17) the school is not to be a special school if education in an 'ordinary' school is compatible with (a) the child getting the special provision he requires, (b) the provision of efficient education for the children with whom he will be educated and (c) the efficient use of resources. Notwithstanding that these conditions are

---

1 1996 Act s 312. 'Learning difficulty' is similarly defined for the purposes of s 15(5) (see para 10.87). On the interpretation of 'special educational provision', whether the applicant's dyslexia constituted a 'learning difficulty' and on the LEA's duty to remain open-minded on the possibility of making a discretionary grant, see *R v Hampshire Education Authority, ex p J* (1985) 84 LGR 547, F[87]. See also *R v Secretary of State for Education, ex p C* [1996] ELR 93.

2 1996 Act ss 313 and 314. See Circular 9/94 (WO 56/94), 'The education of children with emotional and behavioural difficulties', E[2831].

See the Education (Special Educational Needs Code of Practice) (Appointed Day) Order 1994, SI 1994/1414, which appointed 1 September 1994 for the coming into effect of the Code of Practice on the Identification and Assessment of Special Needs issued on 25 May 1994.

As to the obligations of LEAs towards disabled persons, see the Disability Discrimination Act 1995, the Disabled Persons (Services, Consultation and Representation) Act 1986 and *R v Merton London Borough Council, ex p Wiggins* [1996] ELR 332.

3 1996 Act s 315. See Circular 11/90 (WO 58/90), 'Staffing for children with special educational needs', E[1290] and Circular 6/94 (WO 49/94), 'The Organisation of Special Educational Provision', E[2654].

This section does not impose any duty concerning the progress of individual pupils. See *P v Harrow London Borough Council* [1993] 2 FCR 341.

5.09 *Special Educational Needs*

met, the obligation to educate the child in an ordinary school lapses if the parent prefers a special school; but subject to the parent's right of appeal to the Tribunal (see para 5.21), if the conditions *are* met the LEA retain a discretion to educate the child in an ordinary school.[4]

5.10 Governing bodies of ordinary maintained schools (LEAs in the case of nursery schools they maintain) are to use their best endeavours to secure (i) that special educational needs are met by appropriate provision, (ii) (where the LEA have informed the head teacher or responsible governor) that teachers are aware of needs in individual cases and (iii) that teachers are aware of the importance of identifying, and providing for, pupils with special needs. For co-ordination of provision there is to be consultation as necessary between LEA, governing bodies and funding authority. So far as reasonably practicable (and compatible with (a), (b) and (c) above) children with special needs are to engage in school activities with other children.[5]

5.11 The annual reports of governing bodies of maintained (including special, but not nursery) schools (see paras 3.118 and 4.25 as regards LEA and grant-maintained schools respectively) are to contain prescribed information about implementation of their policies for pupils with special educational needs, and also explain the arrangements for admission of disabled pupils, how they are to be protected against discriminatory treatment, and what facilities assist their access to the school.

5.12 LEAs may supply goods and services (a) to the governing bodies of maintained (including LEA and grant-maintained special) schools, within or outside their own areas to assist with special educational provision, on terms the Secretary of State prescribes, and (b) to authorities and persons (other than governing bodies) to assist them to make special educational provision to meet the learning difficulty of any child for whose education grants are made under arrangements applying under the 1996 Nursery Education etc Act.[6]

5.13 After consultation with parents, LEAs may make arrangements for children with learning difficulties to receive special educational provision (in whole

---

4 1996 Act s 316. During proceedings in Parliament it was stated on behalf of the Government that 'the crucial considerations determining the LEA's decision are that the placement should be appropriate to the child, appropriate to his peers and compatible with the efficient use of public resources. We cannot allow parents' views to override those wholly reasonable considerations: we cannot give parents a veto'.
  In *R v Mid-Glamorgan County Council, ex p Greig* (1988) Independent, 1 June, it was held that LEAs are under a duty to provide a suitable education, but not necessarily the most suitable. See also *R v Surrey County Council Education Committee, ex p H* (1984) 83 LGR 219, CA and *R v Secretary of State for Education, ex p C* [1996] ELR 93.
5 1996 Act s 317, applied by Sch 1 para 13 to pupil referral units and (with a modification regarding the annual report requirement) by the Education (Schools Conducted by Education Associations) Regulations 1993, SI 1993/3103 reg 2, Sch 1 and the Education (Special Schools Conducted by Education Associations) Regulations 1994, SI 1994/1084, reg 8, Sch 2, Pt I.
  Disabled pupils are disabled persons under the Disability Discrimination Act 1995.
  See the Education (Special Education Needs) (Information) Regulations 1994, SI 1994/1048.
6 1996 Act s 318. This section is without prejudice to the other powers of LEAs, eg s 516 and the Local Authorities (Goods and Services) Act 1970; and by Sch 1 para 13 it applies also to pupil referral units. See the Education (Payment for Special Educational Needs Supplies) Regulations 1994, SI 1994/650. As to the 1996 N Act see para 11.12 ff.

or part) elsewhere than in school, if they consider school to be inappropriate;[7] and they may arrange for those children for whom they maintain statements (see para 5.17) to attend establishments outside England and Wales, The arrangements may include contributing to, or paying, (a) fees charged by the institution, (b) maintenance expenses reasonably incurred, (c) travelling expenses, and (d) expenses reasonably incurred by an accompanying person while the child is travelling or staying at the institution.[8]

Identification and assessment of children with special educational needs

5.14 LEAs are to identify the children in their areas who have special educational needs of a kind that call for special educational provision to be determined by the authority, rather than left to be met by the schools at which they are pupils. LEAs are responsible in this respect for children who are (a) registered pupils in maintained, including LEA and grant-maintained special, schools, (b) being provided with education at other schools at the expense of an LEA or funding authority, (c) not within (a) or (b) but are registered school pupils and have been brought to the authority's attention as having (or probably having) special educational needs, or (d) not registered school pupils, are not under the age of two or over compulsory school age, and have been brought, as mentioned, to the authority's attention.[9]

5.15 A Health Authority or local authority whose help is requested by an LEA are to provide it unless they consider it unnecessary, or the Health Authority consider it unreasonable to comply because of prior claims on their resources, or the local authority consider the request incompatible with their statutory duties or unduly prejudicial to the discharge of any of their functions. Help with assessments and statements (see paras 5.16 and 5.17) is ordinarily to be given within a prescribed period.[10]

5.16 When an LEA provisionally identify a child for whom they are responsible (see para 5.14 above) as having special educational needs for which they should determine provision, they are to serve a preliminary notice on his parent, who then has an opportunity to make representations and give them evidence

---

7 1996 Act s 319. Where a child of compulsory school age will not receive suitable education unless arrangements are made for him to receive it otherwise than at school, the LEA are required by s 19 (see para 2.31) to make those arrangements.
8 1996 Act s 320. Specialist institutions include the Peto Institute in Budapest and the Institute for the Maximisation of Human Potential in Philadelphia.
9 1996 Act s 321. See *Holtom v Barnet London Borough Council* (1993) Times, 30 September as to the liability of an LEA for failing to make proper educational provision. As to (a) failure to disclose advice in the course of assessment see *R v Secretary of State for Education, ex p S* [1994] ELR 252, and (b) an allegation of negligence in assessment of needs etc *E (a minor) v Dorset County Council* [1994] 4 All ER 640, CA.
10 1996 Act s 322. These provisions replace the duty laid on a local authority by the Children Act 1989 s 27(4). A local authority in this context are a county council, county borough council, metropolitan district council, other district council where under local government reorganisation there is no county council, London borough council or the Common Council of the City of London. See *Brent and Harrow Health Authority, ex p Harrow London Borough Council* (8 October 1996, unreported).
  See the Education (Special Educational Needs) Regulations 1994, SI 1994/1047, reg 11(7) and (8); also Circular 14/96, 'Supporting Pupils with Medical Needs in School'.

5.16 Special Educational Needs

on the matter; after considering which they are to serve a further notice to tell the parent whether or not, and if so for what reasons, they have decided to make an assessment of the child's needs. Regulations make complementary provision about the medical and other advice which LEAs are to seek in making assessments and about the manner and timing of assessments. The LEA are to serve on the parent notice in specified terms requiring the child's attendance for examination (at which the parent may be present).[11]

5.17 If in the light of an assessment and any representations made by the parent the LEA conclude (or, on appeal, the Tribunal orders) that it is necessary for them to determine some form of special educational provision for a child, they are to make (and maintain) a statement of the child's special educational needs in the prescribed form. In particular the statement is to give details of the needs as assessed, and specify the special educational provision apt to meet them, including the type of school or other institution the LEA consider appropriate, naming it where required or where they consider appropriate; but before naming a maintained, including LEA or grant-maintained special, school they are first to consult the governing body and (if other) the maintaining LEA. Where they make arrangements for some or all of the provision to be made otherwise than in a school (see para 5.13) they are also to specify this where appropriate.[12]

---

11 1996 Act s 323 and Sch 26. See the Education (Special Educational Needs) Regulations 1994, SI 1994/1047, regs 5 to 11. A person who fails to comply with a notice is guilty of an offence, if the child is not over compulsory school age, and is liable on summary conviction to a fine not exceeding level 2 on the standard scale.

During proceedings in Parliament it was stated on behalf of the Government that once all the necessary procedures had been completed the assessment could proceed without waiting for the expiry of the period specified in the preliminary notice—eg if the parents indicated that they did not want to submit evidence or representations and wished the assessment to go ahead—*Hansard*, HC Standing Committee E, 26 January 1993, col 1118.

In *Re D (a minor)* [1987] 3 All ER 717, it was held that an LEA had a discretion not to proceed with an assessment if the High Court, in the exercise of its wardship jurisdiction, had decided what educational provision should be made for the child. *Quaere* whether this decision would be followed in the light of the absolute duty now laid on LEAs by s 323(3)(b).

In *R v Newham London Borough Council, ex p D* [1992] 1 FLR 395, it was held that no assessment was required of the educational needs of a child for whom the LEA had been providing special educational treatment before 1 April 1993 unless the child's parent requested it under (now) s 329.

See also *R v Secretary of State for Education and Science, ex p Lashford* [1988] 1 FLR 72, F[88] and *Knight v Dorset County Council* (1996) unreported.

By s 366(6), where it appears to a head teacher of a maintained school that a registered pupil has, or probably has, special educational needs, provision for which the responsible authority would be required to determine, that authority are to consider whether action under s 323 is required.

Where it appears to a local authority that a child within their area is in need, the authority may assess his needs for the purposes of the Children Act 1989 at the same time as any assessment of his needs is made under this Act (Children Act 1989 Sch 2 para 3).

In case of boundary or structural change affecting an LEA see the Local Government Changes for England (Education) (Miscellaneous Provisions) Regulations 1996, SI 1996/710, Part 3.

12 1996 Act s 324 and Sch 27. See the Education (Special Educational Needs) Regulations 1994, SI 1994/1047, reg 13 and Schedule, Pt B, and for the Welsh version of the statement the Education (Special Educational Needs) (Prescribed Forms) (Welsh Forms) Regulations 1995, SI 1995/45.

As to the scope of the LEA's duty see *R v Hillingdon London Borough Council, ex p Governing Body of Queensmead School* (1997) Times, 9 January.

By s 364 statements may exclude or vary the provisions of the National Curriculum.

5.18 Where an LEA maintain a statement for a child they are to arrange for the educational provision specified in the statement to be made, unless the parent has made suitable arrangements. They may also arrange for any specified non-educational provision to be made, in the manner they consider appropriate. The governing body of a named maintained, including special, school are required to admit the child (but this does not affect their power to exclude a child already registered).

5.19 There is no requirement to make and maintain a statement for every child who is found on assessment to have special educational needs calling for special educational provision: the obligation arises only where the LEA, or the Tribunal on appeal, regard it as 'necessary' that the LEA should determine the special educational provision that the child's learning difficulty calls for. (During proceedings in Parliament on the 1993 Act it was stated on behalf of the Government that some 18 per cent of children had special educational needs but only 2 per cent needed a statement.[13])

5.20 The courts have decided
(a) that an LEA are entitled, in their discretion, to conclude that there is no need for a statement if the High Court, in the exercise of its wardship jurisdiction, has determined what educational provision should be made for the child;[14]
(b) that once an LEA have decided that they are required to make *some* of the educational provision that should be made for a child, they are to make a statement for him setting out *all* his special educational needs, as assessed; and once the need has been specified, the special educational provision for it has also to be specified;[15]
(c) that an LEA's duty to provide a statement when the child attains 16 and

---

For the LEA's duty towards a child, in respect of whom they have made a statement, when he becomes 14, see the Disabled Persons (Services, Consultation and Representation) Act 1986 ss 5 and 6, and similarly entitled Circular 2/88 (WO 3/88).

Where a child is being looked after by a local authority, and the authority propose to provide accommodation for him in an establishment at which education is provided for children who are accommodated there, before doing so they are, so far as is reasonably practicable, to consult the appropriate LEA, namely, in the case of a child for whom a statement is being maintained, the LEA who maintain the statement (Children Act 1989 s 28).

The obligation of a governing body to admit a child to a named school is applied in relation to a pupil referral unit by 1996 Act Sch 1 para 13.

By 1996 Act s 424(3) ordinary admissions arrangements (see para 7.01 ff) do not apply in the case of a child for whom a statement is maintained.

13 *Hansard*, HL 29 April 1993, col 491. As to prima facie exclusion of certain categories of children from being the subject of a statement, see *R v Cumbria County Council, ex p B* [1996] ELR 65 and *R v Cumbria County Council, ex p P* [1995] ELR 337. See also *R v Oxfordshire County Council, ex p P* [1996] ELR 153, *R v Kent County Council ex p W* [1995] ELR 362 and *R v Hillingdon London Borough Council, ex p Governing Body of Queensmead School* (1997) Times, 9 January.
14 *Re D (minor)* [1987] 3 All ER 717. See also *R v Secretary of State for Education and Science, ex p Lashford* [1988] 1 FLR 72, F[88].
15 *R v Secretary of State for Education and Science, ex p E*[1992] 1 FLR 377, CA, F[102], as to which see the Department's Circular letter dated May 1991, E[1651]. See also *R v Wiltshire County Council, ex p D* [1994] 1 FCR 172 and *Jones v Dorset County Council* (25 January 1996, unreported).

5.20 *Special Educational Needs*

is no longer subject to compulsory education may or may not cease according to circumstances;[16]

(d) that naming a school in a statement may or may not, depending on the circumstances, render an LEA liable for all the fees at the school;[17]

(e) that educational considerations should prevail in the naming of a school outside England and Wales where no extra cost is imposed on the LEA;[18]

(f) that 'special educational provision' may include speech therapy and nursing;[19] but occupational therapy and physiotherapy may be non-educational.[20]

(g) that 'non-stressful' transport to school may be necessary to enable the pupil to benefit from the education provided,[21] as may, possibly, the provision of a lift in a school to assist a pupil's mobility;[1] and

(h) that failure of a health authority to make the necessary provision as required under a statement does not relieve the LEA of responsibility for doing so, the duty owed to the child not being delegable.[2]

5.21 Parents may appeal to the Tribunal against (a) an LEA's decision, following an assessment, not to make a statement;[3] and (b) the description, in a statement, of the child's special educational needs, the special educational provision specified, and any failure to name a school in the statement.[4]

---

16 *R v Dorset County Council, ex p Goddard* [1995] ELR 109, F[111.4] (in which it was held that the duty of the Further Education Funding Council under the 1992 FHE Act is secondary). See also *R v Oxfordshire County Council, ex p B* [1997] ELR 90, CA.

17 *R v Hackney London Borough, ex p GC* [1996] ELR 142, CA (The parents wished their child to attend a particular non-maintained school, which the LEA considered suitable for him, provided that the services of a special needs assistant, for which they were willing to pay, were made available. The court held that the naming of a particular school in the statement could not, in the circumstances, be elevated into an undertaking to pay all the fees at the school); but cf *R v Kent County Council, ex p W (a minor)* [1995] ELR 362.

18 *Cheshire County Council v C* [1996] 2 FCR 365.

19 *R v Lancashire County Council, ex p M* [1989] 2 FLR 279, CA, F[94]; and *Bradford Metropolitan Borough Council v A* (8 May 1996, unreported).

20 *B v Isle of Wight Council* (30 October 1996, unreported).

21 *R v Hereford and Worcester County Council ex p P* [1992] 2 FCR 732, F[212].

1 *R v Lambeth London Borough Council, ex p M* (1995) 160 LG Rev 61 (decided on regulations now revoked, but see para 14.11).

2 *R v Harrow Borough Council, ex p M* [1997] ELR 62.

3 1996 Act s 325. As to the *locus standi* of a foster parent see *Fairpo v Humberside County Council* [1997] 1 All ER 183..

No particular time is laid down within which the LEA are to make a decision following an assessment. They may even decide not to make a statement after serving on the parent a copy of the proposed statement under (now) Sch 27 para 2: *R v Isle of Wight County Council, ex p AS* [1993] 1 FLR 634, CA.

As to exclusion of judicial review see *R v Special Educational Needs Tribunal, ex p F*[1996] ELR 213.

4 1996 Act s 326. In *R v Secretary of State for Education and Science, ex p Davis* [1989] 2 FLR 190, F[96], a case under 1981 Act s 8 (replaced by s 326), the Divisional Court held that the initiation of an appeal against a statement did not require the LEA to suspend action on the arrangements to implement it. An appeal has no retrospective effect: it should address the issue of what is to be done for the child in the future.

See also *R v Inner London Education Authority, ex p F* (1988) Times, 16 June, F[46]; *R v Secretary of State for Education and Science, ex p E (a minor)* [1992] 1 FLR 377, F[102]; *R v Gloucestershire County Council, ex p P* [1993] COD 303; *R v Secretary of State for Education, ex p E*[1996] ELR 312; *S (a minor) v Special Educational Needs Tribunal and the City of Westminster* [1996] 2 FCR 292 *R v Hackney London Borough ex p GC* [1996] ELR 142; *R v Mid-Glamorgan County Council, ex p B* [1995] ELR 168 and *Sunderland City Council v P and C* [1996] ELR 283, QBD.

Children with Special Educational Needs 5.27

5.22 In the case of (a) the LEA are required to give notice of their decision and of the right of appeal to the child's parent. The Tribunal may dismiss the appeal, order the LEA to make and maintain a statement, or remit the case to them for reconsideration in the light of the Tribunal's observations.

5.23 In the case of (b) an appeal lies (i) when the statement is first made, (ii) when the description of special educational needs or provision is amended (unless the amendment is to the name of the school made at the request of the parent, or is an amendment made either on the order of the Tribunal on an appeal against ceasing to maintain the statement, or on the directions of the Secretary of State where a school attendance order is in force—see para 7.40 ff), and (iii) when the LEA, following a subsequent assessment, determine not to amend it. The Tribunal may dismiss the appeal, order the LEA to amend the description of the child's special educational needs or the provision specified and make consequential amendments, or order them to cease to maintain the statement. The Tribunal may not order the LEA to specify a school in the statement unless the parent has expressed a preference for it, or, in the proceedings, the parent, the LEA or both have proposed it. The Tribunal may, if the parties agree, correct deficiencies in the statement before determining the appeal.

5.24 LEAs have a right of access, at reasonable times, to (a) schools maintained by other LEAs and grant-maintained (including grant-maintained special) schools, for the purpose of monitoring the special educational provision which is being made for a child for whom they have made a statement,[5] and (b) non-maintained special schools and independent schools at which they have placed a child with special educational needs, under the regulations governing the approval of those schools (see paras 5.43 n 7 and 5.49 n 10).

5.25 The Secretary of State may make regulations prescribing, inter alia, how frequently assessments of children for whom statements are maintained are to be repeated, how reviews are to be conducted and who is to participate in them. The LEA are to carry out a further assessment (a) if a parent requests it and (b) one has not been carried out within the previous six months, and it is necessary. If (a) and (b) are satisfied, but the LEA decide not to comply with the request, they are to tell the parent and advise him of his right of appeal to the Tribunal against their decision. The Tribunal may dismiss the appeal or order the LEA to arrange an assessment.[6]

5.26 LEAs are to review a statement following an assessment and in any event within 12 months from when it was made or from the previous review.

5.27 Parents may request an LEA to arrange a formal assessment of a child

---

In *Re M* [1996] ELR 135, CA it was established that parents wishing to challenge the amendment of a statement proposed by an LEA are to appeal to the Tribunal, not to a court; judicial review is not available (see also *R v Newham London Borough Council, ex p R* [1994] COD 472 and *Re L* [1994] ELR 16).

As to cesser see *R v Cumbria County Council, ex p NB* [1996] ELR 65 and *R v Oxfordshire County Council, ex p Roast* [1996] ELR 381.

5   1996 Act s 327.
6   1996 Act s 328. The Education (Special Educational Needs) (Approval of Independent Schools) Regulations 1994, SI 1994/651, Sch 2 para 8(5) and the Education (Special Schools) Regulations 1994, SI 1994/652, Schedule para 19(2), relate to participation in reviews under this section. See also the Education (Special Educational Needs) Regulations 1994, SI 1994/1047, regs 15 to 17.

for whom they are responsible and for whom no statement is maintained; and the LEA are to comply if one has not been made within the previous six months and it is necessary. They are not obliged to make an assessment (or, *a fortiori*, maintain a statement) if they believe the child's needs can be met in an ordinary school. If they decide not to comply with the request the parent may appeal to the Tribunal as above.[7]

5.28 Where the governing body of a grant-maintained school have been directed (see para 7.27 ff) to admit a child, they may request a formal assessment if an LEA are responsible, but do not maintain a statement, for him. If he has not been assessed in the last six months the LEA are to serve a notice on his parent, as under para 5.16 above, giving not less than 29 days for submission of evidence and representations. On the expiry of that period the LEA are to decide whether or not to make an assessment and to notify the parent and governing body of their decision, with reasons if they decide to make one in the belief that a statement may be necessary.[8]

5.29 If an LEA consider that a child under two in their area has, or may have, special educational needs calling for a statement, they may make an assessment (in whatever manner they consider appropriate) if the parent consents, and are obliged to do so if he requests one. They may make and maintain a statement of his needs in the manner they consider appropriate.[9]

5.30 Where a Health Authority or National Health Service Trust form the opinion that a child under five has, or probably has, special educational needs, they are to inform the LEA, having first given the parent an opportunity for discussion. They are also to tell the parent if they think that any particular voluntary organisation is likely to be able to give him advice or assistance about any special educational needs the child may have.[10]

Special Educational Needs Tribunal

5.31 In accordance with the Government's proposals in chapter 9.3 of the White Paper *Choice and Diversity*, Cm 2021, the Tribunal were established for the first time under the 1993 Act, to hear appeals which would formerly have gone to an appeals committee of the LEA or to the Secretary of State.

5.32 The Lord Chancellor appoints a President of the Tribunal and a 'chairmen's panel' from whom a chairman for each tribunal is to be drawn. The Secretary of State appoints a 'lay panel' from whom two persons are to be drawn to make up the Tribunal; and he may also, with Treasury consent, provide staff and accommodation for the Tribunal. Regulations provide for the jurisdiction of the Tribunal to be exercised by a number of tribunals determined by the President, and make other provision the Secretary of State considers

---

7 1996 Act s 329. See *R v Secretary of State for Education and Science, ex p Lashford* [1988] 1 FLR 72, F[88]; *R v Surrey County Council ex p G* (1994) Times, 24 May; and *R v Hampshire County Council, ex p W* [1994] ELR 460.
8 1996 Act s 330.
9 1996 Act s 331. As to simultaneous assessment for the purposes of the Children Act 1989, see n 11 above.
10 1996 Act s 332.

necessary or desirable in connection with the establishment and continuation of the Tribunal.[11]

5.33 The qualification necessary for appointment as President of the Tribunal or member of the chairmen's panel is effectively seven years as a barrister or solicitor. Members of the lay panel are to satisfy the requirements prescribed. The Lord Chancellor may revoke the President's appointment if he is unfit to continue or incapable of performing his duties. Panel members hold and vacate office under the terms of their instrument of appointment. The President and members may resign and are eligible for reappointment.[12] The Secretary of State, with Treasury consent, determines the remuneration and allowances of the President and members of the Tribunal and defrays their expenses.[13]

5.34 Regulations make provision about the initiation of an appeal and the proceedings of the Tribunal, and may contain provisions corresponding to those in the Arbitration Act 1996. It is an offence to fail without reasonable excuse to comply with requirements imposed concerning discovery or inspection of documents, or to attend the Tribunal to give evidence or produce documents. On summary conviction the maximum fine is level 3 on the standard scale.[14] The Tribunal comes under the direct supervision of the Council on Tribunals. Appeals from it may be made to the High Court on a point of law. As an alternative to proceedings under the Tribunals and Inquiries Act 1992 the Tribunal may be required, by rules of court, to state and sign a case for the opinion of the High Court.[15]

SCHOOLS PROVIDING FOR SPECIAL EDUCATIONAL NEEDS

5.35 Chapter II of Part IV of the 1996 Act (sections 337 to 352, Schedule 28) is about the establishment and government of special schools, including their becoming grant-maintained and the grouping of grant-maintained special

---

11 1996 Act s 333. See the Special Educational Needs Tribunal Regulations 1995, SI 1995/3113. During proceedings in Parliament it was stated on behalf of the Government that the aim was to create a new system that would be 'quick, simple, impartial and independent; a system in which informality is the keyword but which at the same time gives parents complete confidence that their children's needs will be properly met and fully considered'. In practice the Tribunal sits as a number of regional tribunals.
12 1996 Act s 334. As to the seven year qualification see the Courts and Legal Services Act 1990 s 71.
13 1996 Act s 335.
14 1996 Act s 336. See the Special Educational Needs Tribunal Regulations 1995, SI 1995/3113. The Secretary of State, with Treasury consent, determines the amount of allowances payable for attendance at the Tribunal.
   During proceedings in Parliament it was stated on behalf of the Government that the Tribunal would not, as a general rule, award costs against an unsuccessful party. Its role was to make educational judgments. The power to award costs would be exercised only in exceptional circumstances, eg where one of the parties had acted in a frivolous, vexatious or otherwise unreasonable manner, thereby involving the other party and the Tribunal in a waste of time and money.
15 An appeal from a decision of the Tribunal should be brought under Order 55 of the Rules of the Supreme Court, under which the court may hear further evidence and make appropriate orders, and not be challenged by way of judicial review (*R v Special Educational Needs Tribunal, ex p South Glamorgan County Council* [1996] ELR 326. Only the child's parents or the LEA, and not the child himself, may appeal pursuant to s 11(1) of the Tribunals and Inquiries Act 1992 (*S v Special Educational Needs Tribunal* [1996] 2 All ER 286, CA).

5.35 Special Educational Needs

schools, and about independent schools providing special education. A special school is one specially organised to make special educational provision for pupils with special educational needs and approved as such by the Secretary of State (see para 5.39 ff). It may be maintained by an LEA or be grant-maintained, or fall into neither of those categories;[16] and it may be established in a hospital.

Establishment etc of special schools

5.36 Where an order (see para 2.39) applies, making the funding authority responsible for provision of school places in the area of an LEA (either alone or with the LEA), they may establish a grant-maintained special school in the area if the school is intended to provide primary or secondary education in the area.[17]

5.37 Where (a) the funding authority intend to establish a special school, or (b) they or the governing body wish to make prescribed alterations to a special school (including transfer to a new site) or (c) they or the governing body propose to close the school (ie cease to maintain it), one or other (as appropriate) are to serve notice on the Secretary of State and others he prescribes, after consultation (see para 5.39), giving prescribed information about their proposals.[18] (No proposals are to be made for a school to become a nursery school, but

---

As to (a) appeals by LEAs against schools named by the Tribunal see *Camden London Borough v Hadin and White* [1996] ELR 430, QBD, *Staffordshire County Council v J and J* [1996] ELR 418, QBD and *South Glamorgan County Council v L and M* [1996] ELR 400; (b) the powers of the Tribunal regarding choice of school see *Sunderland City Council v P and C* [1996] ELR 283, *Haringey London Borough Council v Special Educational Needs Tribunal* 10 September 1996, unreported and *South Glamorgan County Council v L and M* [1996] ELR 400; (c) jurisdiction of the Tribunal see *Alton Evans v Leicestershire Local Education Authority* (19 August 1996, unreported); (d) appeal time limits see *Phillips v Derbyshire County Council* (9 October 1996, unreported); (e) admissability of evidence to the Tribunal see *Duncan v Bedfordshire County Council* (1996) unreported; and (f) allegation of bias etc by tribunal see *Joyce v Dorset County Council* [1997] ELR 26.
  See also *R v Cheshire County Council, ex p Cherrih* 11 July 1996, unreported and *Staffordshire County Council v J and J* [1996] ELR 418.
16 1996 Act s 337. See Circular 3/94 (WO 36/94), 'The Development of Special Schools', E[2481].
17 1996 Act s 338.
18 1996 Act s 339. By Sch 4 para 19 the power of the funding authority to give notice of proposals may be exercised to secure provision of boarding accommodation at boarding schools; and by s 552(4) where an LEA serve notice of a proposal for a maintained special school to cease to be a one-sex school, the Secretary of State may make a transitional exemption order under the Sex Discrimination Act 1975.
  No proposals may be made by an LEA to alter or close a maintained special school where an order under 1996 SI Act s 33 has been made in respect of the school: see the Education (Special Schools Conducted by Education Associations) Regulations 1994, SI 1994/1084, reg 6; and reg 7 disapplies parts of s 339.
  Regulations may apply provisions from Pt III Ch IV (establishing new grant-maintained schools) (see para 4.17 ff) and Pt III Ch V (government, conduct etc of grant-maintained schools) (see para 4.24 ff) with or without modification, to the establishment of new grant-maintained special schools by the funding authority. See the Education (Special Schools) Regulations 1994, SI 1994/652, regs 9 to 11, the Education (Grant-maintained Special Schools) Regulations 1994, SI 1994/653, regs 12 to 13A, 24, 26 and 27, and the Education (Initial Government of Grant-maintained Special Schools) Regulations 1994, SI 1994/2003.
  Section 339 is applied in part by the Education (Groups of Grant-maintained Schools) Regulations 1994, SI 1994/1041, reg 45.
  The Local Government Changes for England (School Reorganisation and Admissions) See *R v Secretary of State for Wales, ex p Williams* [1997] ELR 10. Regulations 1995, SI 1995/2368, reg 3, apply ss 339 to 341 to transferee LEAs in England.
  See *R v Secretary of State for Wales, ex p Williams* [1997] ELR 100.

Schools Providing for Special Educational Needs 5.42

nursery classes are permissible.[19]) If the proposals are approved, they are to be implemented, and in the case of establishment the governing body will be incorporated on the date specified in the proposals.

5.38   An LEA who wish to establish, alter or close a special school are to serve notice in the same way. Once proposals for a new school have been approved the LEA are to implement them and (see para 3.70) make arrangements to constitute a temporary governing body.

5.39   Before serving notice as above, the body making proposals are to consult appropriately, having regard to any guidance given by the Secretary of State. At least two months are to be allowed for objections to be submitted to the body giving the notice, who within a further month are to send them on (if not withdrawn), with their observations, to the Secretary of State. He may reject the proposals or approve them, either as they stand or, having consulted the body making them (and in the case of proposals for alteration and closure, the governing body of the school), with the modifications he thinks desirable.[20]

5.40   The Secretary of State may also modify proposals after he has approved them, but (a) in the case of proposals by the funding authority for alteration or closure, only at the request of the governing body or of the funding authority after he has consulted the governing body, or (b) in any other case, at the request of the body making the proposals.

5.41   Particulars of the means of access to and within the proposed premises of a new LEA or grant-maintained special school, or of proposed prescribed alterations, together with other particulars the Secretary of State may require, are to be submitted for his approval by the body serving notice of the proposals. If approved they are to be implemented in accordance with the approved particulars.[1]

5.42   Regulations prescribe requirements to be complied with by approved special schools (including existing special schools and new maintained special

---

19   1996 Act s 343.
20   1996 Act s 340. As to publication of guidance see s 571.
   Where a notice is served by post under s 572, service is deemed to have been effected on the second day after the notice was posted.
   The requirements about modification of approved proposals are applied by the Education (Grant-maintained Special Schools) Regulations 1994, SI 1994/653, reg 6(2).
   This section is applied by the Education (Groups of Grant-maintained Schools) Regulations 1994, SI 1994/1041, reg 45(2).
   Where proposals for a prescribed alteration of a special school maintained by an LEA have been approved, and the school begins to be conducted by an education association (see para 8.35 ff) before they are implemented, see, for the application of Part IV of the Act, the Education (Special Schools Conducted by Education Associations) Regulations 1994, SI 1994/1084, reg 5.
   As to consultation with parents on closure of a boarding school for pupils with special educational needs see *R v Lambeth London Borough Council, ex p N* (1996) Times, 11 June.
1   1996 Act s 341. The requirements correspond to those in s 262 and Sch 20, para 12. The access particulars are to indicate the extent of conformity with Design Note 18 'Access for Disabled People to Educational Buildings' or any document replacing it which is prescribed by regulations under the Town and Country Planning Act 1990.
   The provisions of this section relating to alterations are applied by the Education (Groups of Grant-maintained Schools) Regulations 1994, SI 1994/1041, reg 45(3).
   As to exemption from Building Regulations see para 15.06.

5.42 *Special Educational Needs*

schools established under proposals approved as above) and provide for the withdrawal of approval at the instance of the proprietor or on failure to comply with a requirement. The regulations require that arrangements be approved by the Secretary of State, and that a school be organised as a primary or secondary school;[2] pupils are to receive religious education and attend religious worship, so far as practicable, subject to the usual right of withdrawal.[3] Where approval is withdrawn from a maintained special school the LEA or governing body are required to serve notice of proposals to close the school.[4]

5.43 The Secretary of State may approve non-maintained special schools, either before or after establishment, subject to prescribed requirements.[5]

Government etc of special schools

5.44 LEA special schools are to be conducted by governing bodies in compliance with an instrument and articles of government, and, so far as consistent with them, in accordance with any trust deed. Financial delegation schemes apply (see para 3.76).[6]

5.45 Initial instruments and articles of government of grant-maintained special schools are to be as prescribed, and have effect respectively from the incorporation date and the implementation date (see para 4.10). Provision is made for substitution and modification of instruments and articles at the instance of the governing body and with the approval of the Secretary of State, who may himself direct modification of instruments and articles. The governing body are to consist of the head teacher and parent, teacher and first governors (and the Secretary of State has power, in specified circumstances, to replace the last-mentioned). There may also, in specified circumstances, be sponsor governors and additional governors.[7]

Maintained schools becoming grant-maintained

5.46 The Secretary of State has made regulations providing for LEA-maintained special schools to become grant-maintained. The regulations impose a duty on the governing body to consider, annually, holding a ballot on grant-

---

2 Subject to any requirement imposed under regulations, by s 14(7) LEAs have discretion not to separate the provision of primary and secondary education in special schools.
3 1996 Act s 342(3) to (6). See the Education (Special Schools) Regulations 1994, SI 1994/652.
4 1996 Act s 342(7) and (8). These subsections are applied to grant-maintained special schools in groups by the Education (Groups of Grant-maintained Schools) Regulations 1994, SI 1994/1041, reg 45(4); and by the Education (Special Schools Conducted by Education Associations) Regulations 1994, SI 1994/1084, reg 7, the requirement to serve a notice (sub-s (7)) is disapplied where a special school is being conducted by an education association.
5 1996 Act s 342(1) and (2). See the Education (Special Schools) Regulations 1994, SI 1994/652, reg 4 and Schedule Pt I.
6 1996 Act s 344(1). But see the Education (Special Schools Conducted by Education Associations) Regulations 1994, SI 1994/1084, regs 7 to 9.
7 1996 Act s 344(2) and Sch 28. See the Education (Grant-maintained Special Schools) (Initial Governing Instruments) Regulations 1994, SI 1994/2104; also the Education (Grant-maintained Special Schools) Regulations 1994, SI 1994/653, the Education (Special Educational Needs) (Information) Regulations 1994, SI 1994/1048, reg 6, the Education (Initial Government of Grant-maintained Special Schools) Regulations 1994, SI 1994/2003, the Education (Grant-maintained Special Schools) (No 2) Regulations 1994, SI 1994/2247.

maintained status. Proposals if made are to be published and submitted by the governing body of the school to the Secretary of State, who, if he approves them, may do so as they stand or with modifications made before or after approval. A new governing body are to be incorporated on the date of approval. The regulations apply, with or without modification, provisions (a) in Part III of the 1996 Act relating (i) to acquisition of grant-maintained status, (ii) to property, staff and contracts, and (iii) to government, conduct etc of grant-maintained schools; and (b) elsewhere in the Act about the procedure for dealing with proposals for the establishment, alteration, change of site and discontinuance of LEA and grant-maintained special schools and of LEA schools generally (see paras 5.37 ff, 3.08 and 3.126).[8]

Grouping of grant-maintained special schools

5.47 Regulations may, by modifying Chapter IX of Part III of the 1996 Act (see para 4.78 ff), provide for groups ('clusters') of grant-maintained special schools (or grant-maintained special and ordinary schools) to be established under a single governing body. The regulations may also provide for an LEA-maintained special school to cease to be so maintained and to join a group, modifying for this purpose the provisions mentioned at paras 5.36 ff and 5.45 above.[9]

5.48 Where Chapter IX is applied by regulations to special schools, those conducted by the single governing body are to be known as grant-maintained special schools, not grant-maintained schools; and references in Chapter II of Part I of the 1996 SI Act (procedure for school inspections) to a group of grant-maintained schools include groups containing one or more grant-maintained schools and one or more grant-maintained special schools.

Independent schools

5.49 The Secretary of State may approve independent schools for children to whom statements apply, subject to requirements prescribed as a condition of approval. Regulations may also impose requirements about the conduct of schools while an approval is in force and for withdrawal of approval, either at the request of the proprietor or for breach of a prescribed requirement. The

---

8 1996 Act s 345. Incorporation is to be in accordance with Sch 28 (see para 5.45 above). See SI 1994/653. By 1996 SI Act s 30(2), regulations under s 345 do not apply at any time when an LEA special school is prohibited from holding a ballot and the governing body have received a copy of a report of a school inspection relating to the need for special measures. See also the Education (Maintained Special Schools becoming Grant-maintained Special Schools) Regulations 1994, SI 1994/1232.

9 1996 Act s 346. See the Education (Groups including Grant-maintained Special Schools) Regulations 1994, SI 1994/779 and the Education (Groups of Grant-maintained Schools) Regulations 1994, SI 1994/1041. Apart from paras 1, 2 and 4, the provisions in Sch 28 relating to the government and conduct of grant-maintained special schools do not apply (the Education (Government of Groups of Grant-maintained Schools) Regulations 1994, SI 1994/2281, reg 4).

Statutory references to grant-maintained schools do not apply to a group which are being conducted by an education association (Education (Schools Conducted by Education Associations) Regulations 1993, SI 1993/3103, reg 2, Sch 1, para 9). Section 346 does not apply in relation to the conduct of a school by an education association (Education (Special Schools Conducted by Education Associations) Regulations 1994, SI 1994/1084, reg 7).

5.49 *Special Educational Needs*

Secretary of State may impose conditions additional to those prescribed by the regulations, breach of which may entail withdrawal of approval.[10]

5.50 A child with special educational needs is not to be educated at an independent school unless it is for the time being approved by the Secretary of State or he gives his consent.[11]

5.51 Where special educational provision is made at a school which is not a maintained (including a grant-maintained special) school but is one which is named in a statement, or the LEA are satisfied that the child's interests require special educational provision to be made for him at a non-maintained school and that the particular school is appropriate, they are to pay all the fees, including, if need be, the cost of board and lodging.[12]

Variation of deeds

5.52 After consultation with school governing bodies or other proprietors, the Secretary of State may by order modify trust deeds and other instruments, permanently or temporarily, to make it possible to comply with regulations about the approval of special and independent schools.[13]

---

10 1996 Act s 347 (1) to (4). See the Education (Special Educational Needs) (Approval of Independent Schools) Regulations 1994, SI 1994/651. A school approved under this section does not have to be registered as a children's home under the Children Act 1989—see s 63(6) of that Act.
   In *P v Harrow London Borough Council* [1993] 1 FLR 723, Potter J held that the LEA were not liable in negligence for sexual abuse committed by the head master of an approved independent school on boys sent there by the LEA. When the Secretary of State is considering withdrawing approval he is ordinarily to consult the school's owner (*R v Secretary of State for Education and Employment, ex p McCarthy* (1996) Times, 24 July).
   See Departmental Special Education Letter, 28 February 1996, listing the schools approved, E[3501].
11 1996 Act s 347(5).
12 1996 Act s 348. This section comes into force on the making of a Commencement Order. See also para 12.40, *R v Inner London Education Authority, ex p F* (1988) Times, 16 June, F[46], and *R v Hampshire Education Authority, ex p J* (1985) 84 LGR 547, F[87].
   See the Letter mentioned at n 10 above.
13 1996 Act s 349.

Chapter 6

THE CURRICULUM

6.01 Part V of the 1996 Act[1] (sections 350 to 352) is about the school curriculum. Under Chapter I the Secretary of State, LEAs, school governing bodies and head teachers are all under a duty to exercise their functions—relating in particular to religious education and worship, and the National Curriculum—so as to secure that the curriculum of every maintained school is balanced and broadly based. The curriculum is to promote spiritual, moral, cultural, mental and physical development and prepare pupils for the opportunities, responsibilities and experiences of adult life.[2] These duties appear to derive from sections 1 and 7 of the 1944 Act, the former being replaced by the Secretary of State's duty under 1996 Act s 10 (see para 2.17). The new material comprises (a) the insertion of the word 'cultural', (b) the explicit reference to the curriculum, and (c) in relation to the curriculum, the partnership of four—Secretary of State, LEA, governing body and head teacher.

6.02 There is to be a basic curriculum which includes, for all registered pupils, (a) religious education, (b) sex education for those at secondary schools or receiving secondary education at special schools (except so far as exempted—see para 6.67), and (c) the National Curriculum. The general requirements are adapted for application in pupil referral units, grant-maintained special schools and special schools conducted by education associations (except hospital special schools).[3]

---

1 By 1996 Act s 350, in Pt V 'maintained school' does not include hospital special schools except where otherwise stated. By s 410 nothing in Pt V applies in relation to nursery schools or nursery classes in primary schools.
2 1996 Act s 351. The duty of LEAs does not extend to grant-maintained schools. As to the relationship between governors of a voluntary school and LEA see the remarks of Lord Haldane LC in *Gillow v Durham County Council* [1913] AC 54.
  Reference was made to the 1988 Act s 1 in *St Matthias Church of England School Board of Governors v Crizzle* [1993] ICR 401, F[37].
  By the 1996 Act Sch 1 para 6(2), in relation to pupil referral units the Secretary of State, the LEA and the teacher in charge are to exercise their functions with a view to securing that the curriculum for the unit satisfies the requirements of this section.
3 1996 Act s 352. It will be noted that the term 'basic curriculum' is broader than 'the National Curriculum'. Sex education includes education about AIDS and HIV and any other sexually transmitted disease.
  See, as to application of curriculum requirements, the Education (Pupil Referral Units) (Application of Enactments) Regulations 1994, SI 1994/2103, reg 2, Sch 1; the Education (Grant-maintained Special Schools) Regulations 1994, SI 1994/653, reg 42, Schedule Pt I; and the Education (Special Schools conducted by Education Associations) Regulations 1994, SI 1994/1084, regs 8(1) and 9.

6.03 *The Curriculum*

SECULAR EDUCATION

6.03 Chapter II (sections 353 to 374, Schedule 29) is about the National Curriculum both generally and in relation to special cases; it establishes the School Curriculum and Assessment Authority (SCAA) and its equivalent for Wales; and it specifies the general functions of LEAs, governing bodies and head teachers in relation to LEA schools.

The National Curriculum

6.04 The National Curriculum comprises core and other foundation subjects, for each of which there are to be attainment targets for pupils of different abilities and maturities, related to 'key stages' (see para 6.08) with associated programmes of study and assessment arrangements. Attainment targets relate to what pupils may be expected to know, do and understand by the end of each of the key stages.[4]

6.05 The core subjects of the National Curriculum are mathematics, English and science, and Welsh in Welsh-speaking schools in Wales. The other foundation subjects are (a) technology and physical education, (b) history, geography, art and music in the first three key stages, (c) a modern foreign language specified in an order of the Secretary of State in the third and fourth key stages; and (d) Welsh is a foundation subject in schools in Wales that are not Welsh-speaking.[5]

6.06 Technology and modern foreign languages are not foundation subjects for the fourth key stage until 1 August 1997 or 1 August 1996 for pupils entering the first year of that stage in 1996 (except that technology remains a foundation subject for pupils who entered the first year of the fourth key stage in 1993). Subject to the same exception for technology, in Wales the two subjects are not foundation subjects in relation to the fourth key stage.

6.07 The Secretary of State may change (and has changed) the requirements relating to core and foundation subjects by order (made by statutory instrument).[6] As a preliminary, he is to refer his proposals for the order to the appropriate curriculum authority (see para 6.14 ff) giving them a specified time within which to report to him, after they have consulted associations of LEAs, of governing bodies and of school teachers and others they think desirable (such as employers' organisations and representatives of minorities). The report, summarising the views expressed, making recommendations and giving other advice on the proposal, is to be published by them, having first been submitted

---

4 1996 Act s 353.
5 1996 Act s 354. In this section 'school' includes part of a school, and a school in Wales is Welsh-speaking if more than one half of the following subjects are taught in Welsh: (a) religious education; and (b) the subjects other than English and Welsh which are foundation subjects in relation to pupils at the school. See *R v Gwynedd County Council, ex p W* (1994) 158 LG Rev 201, DC about placing a pupil in classes to be taught in Welsh.
  By s 369 the Secretary of State may incur expenses on research, development and dissemination in connection with establishing or amending the National Curriculum in relation to Wales.
  See the Education (National Curriculum) (Modern Foreign Languages) Order 1991, SI 1991/2567.
6 1996 Act s 354(6). Orders are made by SI and are subject to affirmative resolution.

to the Secretary of State, who is to publish a draft order and any associated document (with a statement explaining any failure to follow the recommendations) and give those previously consulted by the authority not less than a month in which to respond. Then the Secretary of State makes the order.[7]

6.08 The key stages are identified ordinarily by reference to the age at which the majority of a pupil's class reach a specified age at the beginning or end of a school year. The stages are (i) from the beginning of a pupil's becoming of compulsory school age to seven, (ii) from 8 to 11, (iii) 12 to 14, and (iv) 15 to the end of compulsory school education. For individual pupils key stages are ordinarily defined by reference to the age of the majority of pupils in their class, but head teachers may treat particular pupils in accordance with their chronological age where it would not be appropriate, in relation to a particular subject, to use programmes of study and attainment targets suitable for the age of the majority.[8]

6.09 The Secretary of State may by order (a) alter the key stages, or (b) as respects the first two stages, substitute, for seven and eight, other ages less than 11 and 12, having in either case first observed the procedures mentioned at para 6.07 above.[9]

6.10 The Secretary of State was to establish the National Curriculum as soon as reasonably practicable, starting with the core subjects; and he is to revise it as necessary or expedient. He is empowered to make orders specifying (a) the attainment targets, (b) programmes of study and (c) assessment arrangements he considers appropriate for each foundation (including core) subject at each key stage, including the period leading up to the General Certificate of Secondary Education (GCSE) examination.[10]

6.11 Before making orders in relation to (a) and (b) the Secretary of State is

---

7 1996 Act s 368.
8 1996 Act s 355.
9 Orders are made by SI, in relation to (a) subject to affirmative and (b) to negative resolution.
10 1996 Act s 356. Orders may instead of containing the provisions refer to a document published by HMSO. Those relating to assessment arrangements are not laid before Parliament.
   As to application of this section to special schools conducted by education associations see n 3 above.
   Under sub-ss (2)(a) and (b) the Secretary of State has made the Education (National Curriculum) (Attainment Targets and Programmes of Study in...) Orders: English (No 2) 1990, SI 1990/423; Welsh 1990, SI 1990/1082; Mathematics 1991, SI 1991/2896; Science 1991, 1991/2897; Physical Education 1992, SI 1992/603; English 1995, SI 1995/51; Mathematics 1995, SI 1995/52; Science 1995, SI 1995/53; History (England) 1995, SI 1995/54; Geography (England) 1995, SI 1995/55; Technology 1995, SI 1995/56; Modern Foreign Languages 1995, SI 1995/57; Art (England) 1995, SI 1995/58; Music (England) 1995, SI 1995/59; Physical Education 1995, SI 1995/60; Welsh 1995, SI 1995/69; Music (Wales) 1995, SI 1995/70; Art (Wales) 1995, SI 1995/71; Geography (Wales) 1995, SI 1995/72, History (Wales) 1995, SI 1995/73.
   Under sub-s (2)(c) he has made the Education (National Curriculum) (Assessment Arrangements for . . .) Orders: the Core Subjects (Key Stage 1) (England) 1995, SI 1995/2071; the Core Subjects (Key Stage 2) (England) 1995, SI 1995/2072; the Core Subjects (Key Stage 3) (England) 1996, 1996/2116; English, Welsh, Mathematics and Science (Key Stage 1) 1995, SI 1995/2207; English, Welsh, Mathematics and Science (Key Stage 2) 1995, SI 1995/2208; English, Welsh, Mathematics and Science (Key Stage 3) 1996, SI 1996/2337.
   Circulars relating to orders under this section include 20/94 (WO 52/94) (Assessing 14 year-olds in 1995) and 21/94 (WO 51/94) (assessing 7 and 11 year-olds in 1995).

6.11 *The Curriculum*

to follow the procedures mentioned at para 6.07. Orders under (c) may authorise a named person or body to make assessment arrangements, and confer or impose functions on the governing body, head teacher and (except in the case of grant-maintained schools) the LEA, including the duty to permit authorised persons (i) to enter the school premises, (ii) to observe the implementation of the arrangements, and (iii) to inspect and take copies of documents and other articles. Provision is to be made by the order or in the arrangements to determine how far they achieve their purpose.

6.12 No order may require the school timetable to be organised so as to include separate lessons in each foundation subject, or specify the amount of time which should be spent on each; and science is not to include other than biological aspects of sex.

6.13 LEAs and governing bodies are to exercise their functions so as to secure—and it is the duty of head teachers to secure—that the National Curriculum is implemented; and until a subject it comprises is brought within the curriculum that subject is to be taught for a reasonable time during the relevant key stage.[11]

The Curriculum and Assessment Authorities

6.14 The SCAA have been established as a corporate body, superseding and taking over property and staff from the National Curriculum Council and the School Examinations and Assessment Council,[12] who themselves replaced pre-existing non-statutory bodies—the School Curriculum Development Committee and Secondary Examinations Council. The SCAA consist of between 10 and 15 members and are appointed by the Secretary of State. From their number he also appoints their chairman and may appoint a deputy chairman. He is to include persons with experience of and capacity in the provision of, or responsibility for the provision of (preferably, primary or secondary) education.[13]

6.15 The functions of the SCAA in relation to England, for the purpose of advancing education, are (a) keeping under review the maintained school curriculum, examinations and assessment, (b) advising the Secretary of State thereon, (c) giving him advice and assistance on research and development, (d) publishing information about the curriculum or examinations and assessment, (e) making arrangements with appropriate bodies for monitoring assessments, (f) advising the Secretary of State about approval of qualifications (see para 6.63), (g) advising him about other matters he specifies by order which are connected with the provision of education in maintained schools and in special schools not maintained by LEAs, and (h) carrying out the ancillary activities he directs.[14]

11 1996 Act s 357. This section is applied as in n 3 above.
12 1996 Act s 358 and Sch 39 para 36. Provision is made in Sch 29 for (a) the status and powers of the SCAA, (b) the appointment of a chief officer and the division of functions between him and the chairman, (c) the tenure of and payments to members, (d) staff, (e) finance, (f) committees, (g) delegation, (h) proceedings, (i) accounts, and (j) authentication of documents.
    The SCAA are an exempt charity: see the Charities Act 1993 Sch 2 para (da).
    Under the 1997 Act the SCAA (and the National Council for Vocational Qualifications) are to be superseded by the Qualifications and Curriculum Authority.
13 See *R v Croydon London Borough Council, ex p Leney* (1986) 85 LGR 466, F[90].
14 1996 Act s 359. No order (by SI) has yet been made. This section is applied by the Education (Grant-maintained Special Schools) Regulations 1994, SI 1994/653, reg 41.

6.16 The SCAA are to comply with the directions of the Secretary of State and act in accordance with any plans he approves, and so far as relevant are to have regard to the requirements which the curriculum for maintained schools is to satisfy (see para 6.01). They are to provide the Secretary of State with reports and other information he requires concerning their functions.

6.17 In relation to Wales the status, composition, functions and powers of the Curriculum and Assessment Authority for Wales (Awdurdod Cwricwlwm ac Asesu Cymru) (formerly the Curriculum Council for Wales) are similar to those of the SCAA.[15]

The National Curriculum: special cases

6.18 The Secretary of State may by direction waive or modify the requirements of the National Curriculum as respects a particular maintained school for a specified period so as to permit experiments and development work. A direction may apply generally or in specified cases. It may be given only on application by (a) in the case of county, controlled and LEA special schools, the governing body or LEA (with mutual agreement) or by the appropriate curriculum authority, with the agreement of both, (b) in the case of grant-maintained, aided or special agreement schools, the governing body or the appropriate curriculum authority with their agreement, the agreement of the LEA not being required. The Secretary of State may require reports from any of the above; and he may vary or revoke a direction.[16]

6.19 Having first observed the procedures mentioned at para 6.07 above, the Secretary of State may make regulations which specify the cases or circumstances in which all or part of the National Curriculum is not to apply, or to apply with modifications.[17]

6.20 Finally, in prescribed cases or circumstances, head teachers of maintained schools may direct that the National Curriculum shall not apply (or shall apply with modifications) to a particular pupil for a limited period. The Secretary of State is to consult appropriate persons before making regulations, under which the maximum period that may be specified in a direction (or in the variation of a direction) is to be six months; and the period specified may differ within the maximum in the case of successive directions. Regulations enable the head teacher to revoke a direction or to vary it, but not so as to extend the operative period.[18]

6.21 Where the head teacher gives or varies a direction he is to inform the

---

15 1996 Act ss 360, 361 and Sch 30. The Authority are retained by the 1997 Act s 27.
16 1996 Act s 362.
17 1996 Act s 363. See the Education (National Curriculum) (Exceptions) (Wales) Regulations 1990, SI 1990/2187; the Education (National Curriculum) (Exceptions) (Wales) Regulations 1991, SI 1991/1657; the Education (National Curriculum) (Exceptions in Welsh at Key Stage 4) Regulations 1994, SI 1994/1270; the Education (National Curriculum) (Exceptions) (Wales) Regulations 1995, SI 1995/1574; the Education (National Curriculum) (Exceptions) Regulations 1996, SI 1996/2083; and the Education (National Curriculum) (Exceptions) (Wales) Regulations 1996, SI 1996/2259.
18 1996 Act s 365. See the Education (National Curriculum) (Temporary Exceptions for Individual Pupils) Regulations 1989, SI 1989/1181 and Circular 15/89 (WO 46/89), similarly entitled, E[1040].

6.21 *The Curriculum*

governing body (also the LEA in the case of LEA schools) and the parent in the manner prescribed (a) that he has done so, and why, and about its effect, (b) of the provision made for the pupil's education while it is operative, and (c) *either* how he proposes thereafter fully to implement the National Curriculum in relation to the pupil, *or* indicate his opinion that the pupil has, or probably has, special educational needs by virtue of which the LEA would be required to determine special educational provision. In this last case the head teacher is to inform the 'responsible authority' for the pupil (see para 5.14) in the prescribed manner, and that authority are to consider whether they should carry out a statutory assessment (see para 5.16).[19]

6.22 When the head teacher gives, varies or revokes a direction, or fails to do so despite a parent's request, the parent has a right of appeal, in the manner prescribed, to the governing body, who may confirm the head teacher's decision or give him directions, within the regulations, as they think fit. How governing bodies are to conduct appeals is not specified.[20]

General functions of LEA, governing body and head teacher

6.23 LEAs are to (a) determine and keep under review their policy on the secular curriculum for the schools they maintain, and (b) make and keep up to date a written policy statement. In doing so they are to consider in particular the range and balance of the curriculum, and they are to have regard to the statement in carrying out all their statutory functions.[1]

6.24 Articles of government of county, controlled and LEA special schools are to require the governing body, in consultation with the head teacher, to consider (a) their authority's policy statement, (b) their own secular curriculum aims, and (c) how if at all the authority's policy on matters other than sex education should be modified in relation to their school; and to make, and keep up to date, their own statement.[2]

6.25 Articles are also to require the governing bodies of primary schools and LEA special schools (except in respect of pupils receiving secondary education at the latter) to consider separately, and having regard to the LEA's policy statement, whether sex education should form part of the secular curriculum. They are to make, and keep up to date, a separate statement indicating their policy about the relevant part of the curriculum or their conclusion that sex education be not given. Thus governing bodies of primary schools are free to decide whether or not to offer sex education, what it should include and (subject to para 6.66 below) how it should be taught, an option not open to governing bodies of secondary schools and special schools in respect of pupils receiving secondary education, who are obliged to offer it as part of the basic curriculum.

19 1996 Act s 366. See SI 1989/1181.
20 1996 Act s 367. See SI 1989/1181.
 1 1996 Act s 370. This section applies in relation to pupil referral units as it applies to county schools (Sch 1 para 6(1)). As to the provision of copies of statements see para 6.70.
 2 1996 Act s 371 and 404(3).
    For the application of this section (with modifications) to pupil referral units, see the Education (Pupil Referral Units) (Application of Enactments) Regulations 1994, SI 1994/2103, reg 2, Sch 1, para 2(1).

6.26 Governing bodies are to consider the matters mentioned on paras 6.24 and 6.25 above in consultation with the head teacher, and to take into account representations by persons connected with the community served by the school and the chief police officer; and they are to consult the LEA before making or varying the 'general' statement. Governing bodies are to review their conclusions (and make a fresh statement if they think appropriate) whenever they think fit and immediately following the implementation of any proposal (a) which, on the transfer of a voluntary school to a new site (see para 3.24), or on the establishment or alteration etc of a school (see paras 3.08 and 3.19) materially affects the school, and (b) which establishes, alters or discontinues an LEA special school (see para 5.36 ff).

6.27 The governing bodies of all maintained schools (including LEA special schools in hospitals providing secondary education) are to keep a separate statement indicating their policy on sex education. Copies are to be available for inspection by parents of registered pupils and to be provided free of charge at their request.[3]

6.28 Head teachers of county, controlled and LEA special schools are to be responsible under the articles for determining and organising the secular curriculum and securing that it is followed. Having taken into account the statements of the LEA and of the governing body and representations as above, they are to ensure that the curriculum is compatible with the authority's policy as modified by the governing body's statements and with the requirements of the Education Acts. On sex education, the obligation does not apply if the policy is incompatible with a public examination syllabus, or (in the case of secondary schools and education) is superseded by that mentioned in para 6.27 above[4]

6.29 Articles of government of aided and special agreement schools are to require the content of the secular curriculum to be under the control of the governing body. The governing body are to have regard to the LEA's policy statement and to representations as at para 6.26 above. The head teacher is to be allocated functions that will enable him, subject to the resources available, to determine and organise the curriculum and secure that it is followed.[5]

6.30 Articles of grant-maintained schools are to contain provisions for securing discharge of specified duties relating to the curriculum by the governing body and head teacher.[6]

RELIGIOUS EDUCATION AND WORSHIP

6.31 Chapter III of Part V of the 1996 Act (sections 375 to 399, Schedule 31)

---

[3] 1996 Act s 404(1) and (2). This provision is applied in relation to pupils receiving secondary education in grant-maintained special schools by the Education (Grant-maintained Special Schools) Regulations 1994, SI 1994/653, reg 40. For its application to pupil referral units see the Education (Pupil Referral Units) (Application of Enactments) Regulations 1994, SI 1994/2103, reg 2, Sch 1, para 4.
[4] 1996 Act ss 372 and 404(3). For application to pupil referral units see n 3 above.
[5] 1996 Act s 373.
[6] 1996 Act s 374 and Sch 23 para 4.

6.32 The Curriculum

is about agreed syllabuses for religious education, provision for religious education and for worship, and the constitution and functions of standing advisory councils on religious education (SACREs). Subject to the exceptions and special arrangements mentioned at para 6.58 ff, LEAs and governing bodies are to exercise their functions with a view to securing, and head teachers are to secure, that religious education is given in maintained schools as part of the school's basic curriculum, and that all pupils take part in daily collective worship.[7]

6.32   SACREs and conferences on agreed syllabuses are to be distinguished. Both are to give the public certain rights of access to meetings and documents. Regulations may make provision for meetings to be open to the public (subject to prescribed exceptions) and for them to have access to copies of agendas and reports.[8]

Agreed syllabuses

6.33   An 'agreed syllabus' is a syllabus of religious education to be used in the circumstances mentioned below. Agreed syllabuses have been prepared either in accordance with the 1944 Act (and remain in effect) or adopted by an LEA under Schedule 31 to the 1996 Act. Those adopted on or after 28 September 1988 are to 'reflect the fact that the religious traditions in Great Britain are in the main Christian, whilst taking account of the teaching and practices of the other principal religions represented in Great Britain'.[9]

6.34   Agreed syllabuses are prepared by a conference convened by an LEA and consisting of representatives of Christian and other religious traditions in the area (in numbers reflecting their strength) together with teacher and LEA representatives. Conferences are to reconsider (a) any syllabus adopted between 29 September 1988 and 1 April 1994 within five years of adoption, and (b) syllabuses (whenever adopted) from time to time thereafter and not later than five years from a date, falling after 31 March 1994, when the LEA adopted the syllabus or gave effect to a unanimous recommendation that the exisiting syllabus be retained. Whenever an agreed syllabus is reconsidered the governing body of any grant-maintained school in the LEA's area which uses it are to be consulted.[10]

6.35   Where a conference unanimously recommend an existing syllabus, or a new syllabus, the LEA may give effect to the recommendation if it appears to them that it reflects the fact that religious traditions in Great Britain are mainly Christian but takes account of the other principal religions represented. If the LEA report to the Secretary of State that they are not satisfied in that respect, or that the parties to the conference are unable to reach unanimous agreement, or if the Secretary of State thinks that an LEA have failed to give effect to a unanimously recommended syllabus, then he himself is to have a syllabus prepared by a representative body who are to consult the conference and the

---

7   1996 Act ss 384 and 388. See Circular 1/94 (WO 10/94), 'Religious education and collective worship', E[2221]. By s 410 religious education and worship are not mandatory in nursery schools and classes.
8   1996 Act s 397. See the Religious Education (Meetings of Local Conferences and Councils) Regulations 1994, SI 1994/1304.
9   1996 Act s 375.
10 1996 Act Sch 31. Special provisions apply when an order under s 27(1)(b) (see para 2.39) is in force.

parties to it. His syllabus is deemed to be the agreed syllabus adopted for the schools or pupils for which it was prepared.

Standing advisory councils on religious education

6.36 All LEAs are required to constitute a SACRE. The persons appointed as members are to be groups of representatives of (a) the Church of England[11] (except in Wales), (b) other religious traditions prevailing in the area (broadly reflecting their strength), (c) teachers' associations, and (d) the LEA, together with a person appointed to represent the governing bodies of grant-maintained schools which use an agreed syllabus and which were formerly county or controlled schools or which were established as 'non-religious' schools. Additionally, members may be co-opted by members who have not themselves been co-opted and on the terms those members set. Before making appointments LEAs are to take reasonable steps to assure themselves that potential members are indeed representative of the relevant religious interest.[12]

6.37 Members of a SACRE may resign at any time and may be removed if the LEA think they have ceased to be representative. The grant-maintained school representative may be removed by the governing bodies who appointed him.

6.38 On any question to be decided by a SACRE only the groups may vote, each having a single vote. In other respects SACREs and particular categories of members may regulate their own proceedings, the validity of which is not to be affected by vacancies or questions of 'representativeness'.

6.39 When the Secretary of State has made an order transferring responsibility for securing sufficient school places in an area to a funding authority alone (see para 2.39), the LEA are to constitute a new SACRE within six months. In place of the grant-maintained schools' representative mentioned at para 6.36 above the council are to include a group representing grant-maintained schools additional to the groups there mentioned. LEAs are to take all reasonable steps to ensure that persons appointed to represent grant-maintained schools are acceptable to the governing bodies of the majority of those schools. LEAs may remove any person who, in their opinion, ceases to be acceptable.[13]

6.40 The functions of SACREs are
(a) to advise, on their own initiative or at the LEA's request, about collective worship in county schools and the religious education to be given in accordance with an agreed syllabus, including in particular methods of teaching, choice of materials and provision of training for teachers; and
(b) those referred to at para 6.55 below.[14]

11 As to appointment of Church of England representatives see the Diocesan Boards of Education Measure 1991 s 6(1).
12 1996 Act ss 390 and 392. By the 1993 Act s 255(1) as from 1 October 1994 all LEAs were to constitute a new SACRE which broadly reflected the strength of denominations and religions in the area.
13 1996 Act s 393. Provided that the LEA have taken 'all reasonable steps' the proceedings of the SACRE cannot be invalidated on grounds of unacceptability of the persons concerned.
   This section is applied as in n 2 to para 6.24 above.
14 1996 Act s 391(1) and (2). Where functions are transferred on local government reorganisation see the Local Government Changes for England (Education) (Miscellaneous Provisions) Regulations 1996, SI 1996/710, reg 8.

6.41 *The Curriculum*

6.41 Groups (with the exception of that consisting of the LEA's representatives), each having a single vote, may by majority require an agreed syllabus to be reviewed, and thereupon a conference is to be convened (see para 6.34).[15]

6.42 SACREs are to publish annual reports about the exercise of their functions (in particular about any advice given) and any action taken by groups as above, and send a copy to the School Curriculum and Assessment Authority or the Curriculum and Assessment Authority for Wales (or their successors) as appropriate.[16] They are to send a copy of any advice given to the LEA (a) on religious worship to the head teachers of grant-maintained schools which were formerly county schools or which were established as 'non-religious' schools and (b) on religious education to the head teachers of grant-maintained schools which use an agreed syllabus or which were controlled schools before they became grant-maintained.[17]

Required provision for religious education

6.43 Religious education in *county schools* is non-denominational in accordance with an agreed syllabus. It is not to include any distinctive 'catechism or formulary'[18] though these may be studied as part of the syllabus included in the school's basic curriculum. Where parents wish pupils in a county secondary school to have denominational or other religious education but the school is so situated that arrangements cannot conveniently be made for it to be given elsewhere (see para 6.58), then if satisfactory arrangements have been made to provide it in the school the LEA are to provide the necessary facilities (but not at their own cost) unless special circumstances would make it unreasonable to do so.[19]

6.44 In *controlled schools*, unless parents specifically request otherwise, pupils receive religious education in accordance with an agreed syllabus. If parents request that religious education be given in accordance with a trust deed or the practice in the school before it became a controlled school, the foundation governors are to arrange to provide it, during not more than two periods a week, unless they are satisfied that special circumstances make it unreasonable to do so.[20]

6.45 Where there are more than two staff in a controlled school, the LEA are to appoint 'reserved' teachers (up to one fifth of the teaching staff including the head), selected for their fitness and competence to give religious education of the kind mentioned above; but the LEA may do so only after the foundation governors have satisfied themselves in each case of the fitness and competence in that respect of a person proposed to be appointed. And if the foundation governors think that any reserved teacher has not given religious education

---

15 1996 Act s 391(3) to (5) and Sch 31 para 4.
16 1996 Act s 391(6) (7) and (10).
17 1996 Act s 391(8) and (9).
18 These words derive from the 'Cowper Temple clause', in the Elementary Education Act 1870.
19 1996 Act s 376.
20 1996 Act s 377. By s 399 provisions in a trust deed which empower a specified authority to decide whether the religious education given is in accordance with the deed are to have effect.

efficiently and suitably they may require the LEA to dismiss him from employment as a reserved teacher at that school.[1]

6.46 In *aided and special agreement schools* religious education is to be under the control of the governing body and in accordance with the trust deed or, if none, with the practice in the school before it became a voluntary school.[2] If parents of any pupils desire an agreed syllabus for their children, and cannot with reasonable convenience[3] send them to a school which uses it, then unless the LEA think that special circumstances make it unreasonable, that syllabus is to be taught during religious education periods. The LEA are to make the arrangements if satisfied that the governing body are unwilling to do so.

6.47 Where a special agreement provides for the appointment of reserved teachers the LEA may, as in the case of controlled schools, make appointments only after the foundation governors have satisfied themselves in each case of the fitness and competence to give religious education of a person proposed to be appointed. Foundation governors of special agreement schools have the same powers of dismissal of reserved teachers as have the foundation governors of controlled schools.[4]

6.48 The governors of an aided school may without the consent of the LEA dismiss a teacher appointed to give religious education (other than on an agreed syllabus) if he fails to give that education efficiently and suitably.[5] In aided schools, unlike other voluntary schools, teachers are appointed by the governing body (see para 13.28) but may not be dismissed without the consent of the LEA save under this provision, which may be compared with the power of governing bodies of controlled and special agreement schools not to dismiss, but to require the dismissal of, reserved teachers.

6.49 In *grant-maintained schools* religious education requirements depend on the origins of the school. If before the school became grant-maintained it was
(a) a county school (or was established by a funding authority or by promoters with no particular provision for religious education) and no proposals for a change of religious character (see para 4.49) have been approved, religious education as part of the school's basic curriculum is to be given in accordance with the appropriate agreed syllabus, and there are requirements as regards secondary schools which follow those mentioned in para 6.43 above, the governing body adopting the

---

1   1996 Act s 143. The head teacher is not to count as a reserved teacher. Where there are no reserved teachers the arrangements made by the foundation governors may be the giving of instruction by a minister, or by the head, or by an assistant teacher if willing to do so (see para 13.71). The LEA may if they wish retain a dismissed reserved teacher on the school staff for other duties, or put him forward for employment as a reserved teacher in some other controlled school or in a special agreement school. As to dismissal of teachers generally see para 13.18 ff.
2   1996 Act s 378. See also s 399 (n 20) above. On the improper intervention of an LEA see *Re Wrexham Parochial Education Foundation; AG v Denbighshire County Council* (1910) 74 JP 198. See also para 4.16, and in circumstances of local government reorganisation n 14 above.
3   If another school is close at hand but a parent regards it as otherwise less satisfactory, it remains, arguably, not 'reasonably convenient'.
4   See the 1996 Act s 144 and Sch 5 para 4(1); also para 4.16.
5   1996 Act s 145. See *Harries v Crawfurd* [1918] 2 Ch 158 and *Smith v Macnally* [1912] 1 Ch 816.

6.49 *The Curriculum*

functions of the LEA.[6] The 'appropriate' agreed syllabus is the syllabus (or one of the syllabuses) adopted by the LEA for their area, or any agreed syllabus adopted by another LEA since 29th September 1988 and not replaced. A school in Wales is restricted to syllabuses adopted by LEAs in Wales.[7]

(b) a controlled school and no proposals for a change of religious character (see para 4.49) have been approved, religious education as part of the school's basic curriculum is to be given in accordance with the appropriate agreed syllabus (as above). Alternatively, if the parents of any pupils so request, the foundation governors are to arrange for not more than two periods of religious education a week to be given in accordance with the trust deed of the school, or if there is none, with practice before the school became grant-maintained, unless special circumstances make it unreasonable for them to do so.[8]

(c) an aided or special agreement school, or the school was established under proposals which include provision for religious education in accordance with a trust deed or the statement annexed to the proposals, and no proposals for a change of religious character (see para 4.49) have been approved, religious education is to be given in accordance with the the trust deed of the school, or if there is none, either in accordance with practice before the school became a grant-maintained school or with the statement mentioned above. Alternatively, if parents desire an agreed syllabus for their children, and cannot with reasonable convenience send them to a school which uses it, the governing body are to make arrangements for that syllabus to be taught during religious education periods, unless the governing body conclude that special circumstances make it unreasonable to do so. The agreed syllabus is to be that (or one of those) adopted by the LEA for their area, and the head teacher is to notify the SACRE of its use.[9]

6.50 When proposals have been approved to make a significant change in the religious character of a grant-maintained school (see para 4.53) so that the religious education as part of the school's basic curriculum is required to follow a particular religion or denomination, the substance of (c) above applies, to the exclusion of (a) or (b). Where the proposals have the opposite effect para (a) above applies, to the exclusion of (b) or (c).[10]

6.51 In *special schools* arrangements are to be made to secure that, so far as practicable, every pupil attending the school attends daily collective worship and receives religious education, or is withdrawn in accordance with the wishes of his parent.[11]

---

6 1996 Act s 379.
7 1996 Act s 382.
8 1996 Act s 380.
9 1996 Act s 381 and Sch 20 para 8. 'Reasonable convenience': see n 3 above. In circumstances of local government reorganisation n 14 above.
  Section 86(2) of the 1988 Act, from which s 381(2) derives, was referred to in *St Matthias Church of England School (Board of Governors) v Crizzle* [1993] ICR 401, F[37].
10 1996 Act s 383 (which also provides for concurrent changes in religious worship requirements).
11 1996 Act s 342(6) and the Education (Special Schools) Regulations 1994, SI 1994/652, Schedule, para 10. See Circular 1/94 (WO 10/94), Annex B, E[2297], and 3/94 (WO 36/94), 'The Development of Special Schools', para 125, E[2563].

Religious worship

6.52 On each school day, but not necessarily at the start, maintained (except special) school pupils are to take part in collective worship, either all together or in different age or school groups, and on school premises, but the governing bodies of aided, special agreement and grant-maintained schools may, after consultation with the head teacher, arrange for it to take place elsewhere on special occasions. In county schools and grant-maintained schools which were formerly county schools or established with no particular provision for religious education, the arrangements for collective worship are to be made by the head teacher after consultation with the governing body; in voluntary schools and other grant-maintained schools, by the governing body after consultation with the head teacher.[12]

6.53 In county schools, and grant-maintained schools established by a funding authority or by promoters with no particular provision for religious education, all or most acts of collective worship are, over a term, to be wholly or mainly of 'a broadly Christian character' and non-denominational. Worship is of a broadly Christian character if it reflects the broad traditions of Christian belief without being distinctive of any particular Christian denomination. The extent to which it is permissible for collective acts of worship not to comply with this requirement, or, in doing so, to reflect (and in what manner) the broad traditions of Christian belief, is to turn on the family background, age and aptitude of pupils.[13]

6.54 Where a SACRE determine, as in para 6.55 (or had determined before a school became grant-maintained), that it is inappropriate for collective worship at a school, or for some pupils, to be wholly or mainly of a broadly Christian character, the daily act of collective worship at the school or for those pupils is not to be distinctive of any particular Christian or other religious denomination, but may be of another faith. This provision applies only to county schools and grant-maintained schools established by a funding authority or by promoters with no particular provision for religious education.[14]

6.55 The head teacher of a school of the kind mentioned in the previous paragraph may request the SACRE to consider whether the Christian collective worship requirement should apply in the school or as respects some of the pupils there. Before doing so he is to consult the governing body, who may in turn decide to consult parents. In reaching their decision the SACRE are to take family backgrounds into account, and if they conclude that the requirement

---

12 1996 Act s 385. As to (a) special school pupils see para 6.51 above, (b) the consequences of a change in the religious character of a grant-maintained school see s 383. A 'school group' is any group in which pupils are taught or take part in other school activities. In *Marshall v Graham* [1907] 2 KB 112 it was held that Ascension Day was a special occasion for Church of England adherents. See Circular 1/94 (WO 10/94).
13 1996 Act s 386. These requirements apply to the grant-maintained schools mentioned when acts of collective worship take place off school premises.
  It was held in *R v Secretary of State for Education, ex p Ruscoe* (26 February 1993, unreported), F[111], that some non-Christian elements are permissible in collective worship. See also *R v Secretary of State for Education, ex p R and D* [1994] ELR 495.
14 1996 Act s 387.

6.55 *The Curriculum*

should not apply, in notifying the head teacher they are also to specify the date when disapplication takes effect.[15]

6.56 A determination to waive the requirement is to be reviewed by the SACRE on the application of the head teacher after consultation as above, or otherwise at not more than five-yearly intervals, when the head teacher, after the same consultation, is to be given the opportunity to make representations. The outcome of a review may be confirmation or revocation of the determination. If not confirmed a waiver determination lapses five years after the date it first took effect or was last confirmed.[16]

6.57 If the Secretary of State thinks that a SACRE are acting unreasonably with regard to the requirement for Christian worship, or are failing in their duty, he may give them appropriate directions.[17]

Exceptions and special arrangements

6.58 Attendance at a maintained school is not to be made conditional on a pupil's attending a Sunday school or place of religious worship, or abstaining from doing so. And at a parent's request he is to be excused, wholly or partly, from attending religious worship and, or alternatively, receiving religious education in accordance with the foregoing provisions. In those circumstances he may be withdrawn to receive religious education elsewhere than at the school if the responsible authority are satisfied on all of the following:
(a) the parent desires the pupil to have religious education of a kind not provided in the school while he is excused attendance,
(b) he cannot with reasonable convenience be sent to another maintained school where the alternative religious education is provided, and
(c) arrangements have been made for him to receive the alternative religious education during school hours elsewhere.

6.59 Withdrawal (for so long as is reasonably necessary) is to take place only at the beginning or end of a school session.[18]

6.60 Where the parent of a maintained boarding school pupil requests that he be permitted to attend religious worship on Sundays or other days of religious observance, or to receive religious education outside school hours, both of a kind not available at the school, the governing body are to arrange reasonable opportunities for him to do so. Facilities may be made available on the school premises but are not to entail expenditure by the responsible authority.

---

15 1996 Act s 394. By sub-s (8) where an application is made to a SACRE in respect of a county school which becomes a grant-maintained school before the application is determined, the application is to remain under consideration unless the head teacher withdraws it.
  In case of boundary or structural change affecting an LEA see the Local Government Changes for England (Education) (Miscellaneous Provisions) Regulations 1996 SI 1996/710, Pt 2.
16 1996 Act s 395.
17 1996 Act s 396. The directions are analogous to those which may be given under ss 496 and 497.
18 1996 Act ss 398 and 389. The excusal etc provisions do not apply to pupils at LEA special schools (as to whom see para 6.51). The 'responsible authority' are the LEA or the governing body in relation to county and voluntary, and grant-maintained, schools respectively. 'School session': see para 2.13.
  See *Re T and M (minors)* [1995] ELR 1.

MISCELLANEOUS AND SUPPLEMENTARY PROVISIONS

6.61 These constitute Chapter IV of Part V of the 1996 Act (sections 400 to 410).

Courses leading to external qualifications

6.62 Courses of study for external qualifications authenticated by a person other than a member of staff of the school concerned (an 'outside person') are to be provided for maintained school pupils of compulsory school age only if (a) approved by the Secretary of State or by a body he designates, such as the School Curriculum and Assessment Authority, and (b) a syllabus (or criteria for determining a syllabus) provided by an outside person has been approved by a designated body. It is the duty of the LEA and governing body to do their best to secure, and the head teacher is to secure, that these requirements are not contravened.

6.63 Approvals of qualifications and syllabuses may be given in relation to particular cases or generally, for example the GCSE, offered by nationally recognised school examination boards, and specialist qualifications (such as those for swimming, and graded music examinations) provided by national bodies, together with regional and local qualifications.[19]

6.64 After consultation the Secretary of State may by order extend his powers of approval to qualifications and syllabuses for (a) senior pupils of, or over, compulsory school age and (b) full-time further education (FE) students of, or over, that age but under 19, and he may exclude those qualifications from the ambit of the SCAA and designate another body to approve them. For the references above to maintained schools and head teachers there are substituted grant-aided further education institutions (see para 11.07) and institutions within the further education sector and principals or other heads. When an order is in force the requirements about provision of information (see para 6.70) to parents etc apply (with some modifications) to the FE students mentioned.[20]

Obligation to enter pupils for public examinations

6.65 At the time they think appropriate the governing bodies of maintained schools (including LEA hospital special schools) are to enter pupils for the prescribed public examinations[1] in each syllabus for which they are being prepared, unless either (a) they consider that there are educational reasons for not doing so, or (b) the parent so requests in writing. But (a) and (b) do not apply in relation to an examination which is part of a pupil's assessment arrangements for key stage 4. The obligation on governing bodies is limited to

---

19 1996 Act s 400. See Circular 4/97, 'Statutory approval of qualifications under s 400 of the Education Act 1996, for guidance on the statutory framework, explanation of the arrangements for approval of qualifications, lists of approved qualifications and syllabuses approved for use in maintained schools up to 31 July 1999, and explanation of arrangements for future approval of qualifications and for withdrawal of approval.
20 1996 Act s 401. An order (by SI) under this section is subject to the affirmative procedure in Parliament.
1 Defined in the 1996 Act s 462.

6.65 *The Curriculum*

one examination—they are not obliged to enter a pupil for another public examination with a corresponding syllabus. Governing bodies are to notify parents in writing whether or not it is intended to enter a pupil for a particular examination.[2] Parents are not to be charged for an entry (see para 7.55 n 18).

Sex education

6.66 LEAs, governing bodies and head teachers are to do what is reasonably practicable to ensure that sex education, where given, encourages registered pupils at maintained schools (including LEA hospital special schools) 'to have due regard to moral considerations and the value of family life'.[3] Local authorities are prohibited from promoting 'the teaching in any maintained school of the acceptability of homosexuality as a pretended family relationship'.[4]

6.67 Except so far as teaching about sex is part of the National Curriculum, parents have a right to exclude their children from sex education, which is defined to include reference to sexually transmitted diseases.[5] During the parliamentary proceedings on this provision when first introduced (in the 1986 Act) the Government spokesman said

> 'In primary schools the position will be similar to the current one: it will remain the responsibility of the governors to decide whether they wish to offer any sex education and, if they do, what it should cover and how it should be taught. There is, however, one important change. If parents do not wish their children to receive some or all of the sex education offered by a primary school, they will have the right to withdraw their children from that provision.
>
> In secondary schools sex education will be offered to all pupils. That provision will include education about sexually transmitted diseases including HIV and AIDS. It will be for governing bodies to decide, within that broad requirement, the content and organisation of sex education in their school. Parents will have the right to withdraw their children from some or all of that provision.
>
> There is an important proviso . . . Some aspects of what might generally be termed sex education, broadly speaking, the biology of human sexual development and reproduction will continue to form part of the National Curriculum. The parental right of withdrawal will not extend to these aspects; nor will governors have any discretion to allow children to be withdrawn from them.'

---

2 1996 Act s 402. See the Education (Prescribed Public Examinations) Regulations 1989, SI 1989/377.
3 1996 Act s 403. 'Sex education' is defined in para 6.02 n 3. See Circular 5/94 (WO 45/94), 'Education Act 1993. Sex education in schools', E[2609], paragraph 8 of which states that sex education must not be value-free, and mentions the Secretary of State's values, but does not recognise the contentious nature of moral considerations or the absence of a general consensus on the value of family life.
   By Sch 1 para 8, s 403 applies to pupil referral units.
   As to whether sex education should form part of the curriculum of a county, controlled or LEA special school see para 6.25 ff. See also paras 6.02 and 6.67.
4 Local Government Act 1986 s 2A. It was suggested by a Government spokesman during the passage of the Bill that this provision does not prevent the objective discussion of homosexuality in the classroom or the counselling of pupils concerned about their sexuality.
5 1996 Act s 405. As to the further application of this section see the Education (Pupil Referral Units) (Application of Enactments) Regulations 1994, SI 1994/2103, reg 2, Sch 1 para 3(2); and as respects specified special schools not established in hospitals, SI 1994/653, reg 42, Schedule, Pt I, and SI 1994/1084, reg 9.

Politics

6.68 LEAs, governing bodies and head teachers of maintained schools (including hospital special schools) are
(a) to forbid partisan political activities at a school by junior pupils, and the promotion of partisan political views in the course of teaching any subject; and
(b) to take reasonably practicable steps to secure balanced treatment of political issues where they arise in school and in the course of extra-curricular activities organised for pupils by or on behalf of the school.

6.69 The ban on activities under (a) does not apply outside school premises unless the arrangements for them are made by a member of the school staff or someone acting on the school's behalf.[6]

Information

6.70 The Secretary of State, after consultation, has made regulations requiring LEAs, governing bodies and head teachers of maintained schools to make available to parents and others (a) information about, in particular, the curriculum for maintained schools, the educational provision made for pupils at a school, syllabuses, and the achievements of pupils; and (b) copies, as prescribed, of the statements referred to at paras 6.23 and 6.24 and of the governing body's annual report (see paras 3.118 and 4.25). Information about the assessments of individual pupils is to be made available to parents and pupils and, only so far as relevant for performing their functions, to the school governing body, to the head teacher of the school to which a pupil has transferred and to the LEA.[7]

6.71 LEAs, governing bodies and head teachers may make reasonable charges for supplying copies of documents. LEAs are to do their best to secure that head teachers comply with the regulations.

Complaints and enforcement

6.72 After consulting governing bodies of aided and special agreement schools, LEAs are to set up arrangements, approved by the Secretary of State,

---

6 1996 Act ss 406 and 407. 'Partisan', 'political' and (in the shoulder note to s 406) 'indoctrination' are undefined. By Sch 1 para 8 these sections apply to pupil referral units as they apply to schools.
7 1996 Act s 408.
  See the Education (School Curriculum and Related Information) Regulations 1989, SI 1989/954, the Education (Individual Pupils' Achievements) (Information) Regulations 1993, SI 1993/3182, the Education (School Information) (Wales) Regulations 1994, SI 1994/2330, the Education (School Performance Information) (Wales) Regulations 1995, SI 1995/1904, the Education (School Performance Information) (England) Regulations 1996, SI 1996/2577, the Education (School Information) (England) Regulations 1996, SI 1996/2585 and the Education (Individual Pupils Achievements) (Information) (Wales) Regulations 1997, SI 1997/573.
  As to the further application of this section see SI 1994/653, reg 42, Schedule, Pt I, and SI 1994/1084, reg 9.
  See Circulars 8/96, (WO 23/96), 'The Parent's Charter: Publication of Information about Secondary School Performance in 1996'; 11/96 and 12/96, 'School Prospectuses and Governors' Annual Reports in Primary/Secondary Schools' and; 15/96, 'Publication of 1996 Key Stage 2 National Curriculum Assessment Results in Primary School Performance Tables' 1/97 and 2/97 (WO 11/97), 'Reports on Pupils' Achievements in Primary/Secondary Schools in 1996/7'.

6.72 *The Curriculum*

for dealing with complaints against the LEA or governing bodies in relation to LEA schools (other than hospital special schools). Complaints may be about unreasonableness in the exercise of powers and duties, or default, concerning matters such as (a) the National Curriculum, (b) collective worship, (c) religious education, (d) non-approved external qualifications or syllabuses and (e) the provision of information. The Secretary of State is not to entertain a complaint about any of those matters under sections 496 or 497 of the 1966 Act (see paras 12.05 and 12.09) until it has been dealt with under the LEA's arrangements.[8]

---

8 1996 Act s 409. The requirement was introduced by the 1988 Act for consideration of complaints made after 1 September 1989. By Sch 1, para 6(3), similar provision is made in relation to pupil referral units.

See Circular 1/89 (WO/26/89), 'Education Reform Act 1988: Local Arrangements for the Consideration of Complaints', E[857], and *R v Secretary of State for Education, ex p Ruscoe* (26 February 1993, unreported), F[111], concerning a complaint made to the Secretary of State, about religious worship, following its consideration under arrangements made in accordance with this section.

Chapter 7

SCHOOL ADMISSIONS, ATTENDANCE AND CHARGES

SCHOOL ADMISSIONS

7.01 Chapter I of Part VI of the 1996 Act (sections 411 to 436 Schedules 32 and 33) is about parental preferences; admission arrangements and numbers for maintained schools (including preserving the character of aided and special agreement schools); information about schools and admission arrangements; admission appeals; power to direct admission of a child to school; time for admission, and registration, of pupils; and withdrawal of pupils from LEA primary schools for secondary education.

7.02 These provisions, as they relate to parental preferences, preserving the character of aided and special agreement schools, information, and admission appeals relating to LEA schools, do not apply
(a) to nursery schools, or children under five at the time of their proposed admission to an LEA school unless the admission is for other than nursery education (ie is to a reception class);
(b) to special schools, except for the requirement (see para 7.12) under which the governing bodies of LEA special schools are to publish prescribed information about their schools and may publish other information as they think fit; or
(c) to children with special educational needs for whom statements are maintained (see para 5.17), with the same exception as in (b).[1]

Parental preferences

7.03 LEAs are to make (and publish information about—see para 7.12) arrangements to enable parents to express reasoned preferences about the county, voluntary or other schools to which they wish children in the area of the authority to be admitted. Application may be made to a school governing body when they are the admission authority, ie have been made responsible under the articles of government for admission arrangements to their school.[2]

1 1996 Act s 424.
2 1996 Act s 411(1) to (5). 'Child' in this section includes a person under 19. By s 436 'admission' includes admission to a reception class following nursery education. 'Other' schools include those with which the LEA have made arrangements under s 517 (see para 12.40) and those whose fees attract assistance under regulations made under s 518 (see para 12.41). A pupil referral unit is not a 'school' for the purposes of s 411: see the Education (Pupil Referral Units) (Application of Enactments) Regulations 1994, SI 1994/2103, reg 3, Sch 2, para 1.

7.04 School Admissions, Attendance and Charges

7.04 Arrangements are not restricted to the normal age of admission, and so are to take account of, for example, movements into the area, and a parent's desire to change his child's school. 'In the area of the authority' has been taken to refer to temporary as well as permanent residents, including gypsies and other itinerants and, subject to a number of qualifications, children from overseas;[3] moreover the duty of LEAs (as respects admission to LEA schools) extends to applications in respect of children not in the area of the authority and applications made in connection with school attendance orders (see para 7.43).

7.05 Subject to agreements between admission authorities for co-ordinating admissions to two or more schools (see para 7.26), LEAs and governing bodies of county and voluntary schools are to comply with parental preferences, unless to do so:
(a) would prejudice the provision of efficient education or the efficient use of resources; or
(b) would be incompatible with admission arrangements made between the authority and the governing body of an aided or special agreement school (see para 7.14); or
(c) would be incompatible with any arrangements for selection for admission to the school by ability and aptitude.

7.06 Where a parent requests the transfer of a child to a preferred school because of the racial mix of its pupils, the LEA are, other things being equal, to comply with the request, their duty not being qualified by s 18 of the Race Relations Act 1976 (see para 14.09).[4]

7.07 Provision of efficient education is not to be regarded as 'prejudiced' (para (a) above) until a school has admitted pupils up to the relevant standard number or any higher number that has been fixed (see para 7.15 ff).[5]

7.08 Some system of selection will be necessary to regulate admissions to schools which would otherwise be over-subscribed. In *R v Greenwich London Borough Council, ex p Governors of the John Ball Primary School*[6] Lloyd LJ said

---

A three-term (thrice yearly) entry scheme for an LEA's primary schools cannot be impugned as unfair or unreasonable; any unfairness to later applicants cannot properly found a challenge to the validity of the scheme – it is a blemish that must be accepted: *R v Hackney London Borough, ex p T* [1991] COD 454.

Applications for judicial review about admissions decisions are to be based on references to education law, and not other cases (*Ex p M (Judicial Review: Education)* (1994) Times, 22 March).

As to the provision of free transport to school in connection with the duty under this section, see para 12.24 ff.

See Circulars 11/88 (WO 47/88), 'Admission of Pupils to County and Voluntary Schools' E[782]; 6/91 (WO 14/91), 'Implementation of More Open Enrolment in Primary Schools', E[1377]; and 6/96 (WO 33/96), 'Admissions to Maintained Schools', E[1859].
3 See Circular 11/88, (WO 47/88), Part III, E[792].
4 See *R v Cleveland County Council, ex p Commission for Racial Equality* [1993] 1 FCR 597, F[36]. As to racial discrimination see para 14.08 ff.
5 1996 Act s 411(6) and (7). The burden of proving prejudice lies on the LEA (*R v South Glamorgan Appeal Committee, ex p Evans* (10 May 1984, unreported), F[43], approved in *R v Comr for Local Administration, ex p Croydon London Borough Council* [1989] 1 All ER 1033, F[44]).
6 [1990] Fam Law 469, CA, F[98]. See also *R v Dorset County Council, ex v p Greenwood[* 1990] COD 235, *R v Governors of the Buss Foundation Camden School for Girls, ex p Lukasiewicz* [1991] COD 98; *R v Hackney London Borough Council, ex p T* [1991] COD 454 and *R v Essex County Council, ex p Jacobs* [1997] ELR 190.

'I do not regard efficient education or the efficient use of resources as being the sole source of lawful policy ... In my judgment an LEA can have any reasonable policy they think fit, provided it does not conflict with their duties under section 6[of the 1980 Act], or any other enactment ... Sibling priority and the proximity rule are sound and lawful policies whether or not they promote efficient education.'

7.09 It has been held
(a) that random selection, although frowned on by the Secretary of State, was not unlawful in the circumstances prevailing;[7]
(b) that an over-subscribed voluntary aided school was entitled to operate an admissions policy intended to preserve the character of the school. The statutory duty to give effect to parental preference was disapplied because admitting all applicants would prejudice the provision of efficient education; it was open to the appeal committee (see para 7.20) to uphold reasonable criteria for selection among the applicants;[8]
(c) that it was not unlawful, in the circumstances, for an LEA to have a policy under which Roman Catholic children were considered for places at non-denominational county secondary schools only after other applicants had been placed;[9]
(d) that a system which, per se, favours children from within an authority's own area is unlawful;[10]
(e) that where schools are over-subscribed, LEAs are entitled to take into account traditional links between a school and the areas from which it draws its pupils;[11]
(f) that (a) in para 7.05 above applied where applicants were rejected for admission to a single-sex aided comprehensive school because it was over-subscribed, even though the school had taken lack of academic ability into account; (c) in para 7.05 refers to 'genuine academic selection'.[12]

Admission arrangements for county and voluntary schools

7.10 Where the governing body of a county or voluntary school are responsible under the articles of government for determining admissions arrangements, as is usual in the case of aided and special agreement schools, they (as admission authority) are to consult the LEA once in every school year on whether the

---

7 See Circular 6/93 (WO 47/94), Annex C, para 18, E[1897] and *R v Lancashire County Council, ex p West* (27 July, unreported), F[111.2].
8 *R v Governors of Bishop Challenor Roman Catholic Comprehensive School, ex p Choudhury* [1992] 3 All ER 277, HL, F[107]. See also *R v Governors of La Sainte Union Convent School, ex p T* [1996] ELR 98.
9 *R v Lancashire County Council, ex p Foster* [1995] 1 FCR 212, F[111.1].
10 See *R v Greenwich London Borough Council, ex p Governors of the John Ball Primary School* [1990] Fam Law 469, CA, F[98]; also *R v Bromley London Borough Council, ex p C* [1992] Fam Law 192; *R v Royal Borough of Kingston-upon-Thames, ex p Kingwell* [1992] Fam Law 193 and *ibid, ex p Emsden* (1994) 91 LGR 96, F[104]; *R v Rochdale Metropolitan Council, ex p Schemet* [1993] COD 113, F[213]; and *R v Wiltshire County Council, ex p Razazan* [1996] ELR 220 QBD. The principle applies in relation to the payment of awards under s 518: see *R v Lambeth London Borough, ex p G* [1994] ELR 207, F[49].
11 In the particular instance the long journeys which children living in the peripheral areas of Bradford would have to make if they could not go to their local school were relevant (*R v Bradford Metropolitan Borough Council, ex p Sikander Ali* [1994] ELR 299, F[109]).
12 See *R v Hasmonean High School (Governors), ex p N* [1994] ELR 343, CA, F[45]. As to sex discrimination see para 14.04 ff.

7.10 *School Admissions, Attendance and Charges*

arrangements are satisfactory, and before determining or varying them. Where the LEA are the admission authority they are to consult the governing body likewise.[13]

7.11 At the request of the governing body of an aided or special agreement school, LEAs are to make admission arrangements with them so as to preserve the character of the school. In default of agreement the terms of the arrangements are settled by the Secretary of State. In the absence of agreement on a proposal by either party to replace or modify the arrangements the Secretary of State, if so requested, may give an appropriate direction specifying when any new arrangements he settles come into effect.[14]

7.12 LEAs are to publish, for each school year, particulars of their arrangements (a) for admission of pupils to the schools they maintain other than aided and special agreement schools; (b) for provision of education at schools other LEAs maintain, and at schools not maintained by LEAs; and (c) for enabling parents to express preferences (see para 7.03) and to appeal against admission decisions (see para 7.20). The obligation to publish admission and appeal arrangements for aided and special agreement schools falls on governing bodies, but with their agreement LEAs may publish these and other information on their behalf.[15]

7.13 The particulars to be published are to include (a) admission numbers for each school,[16] (b) the respective admission functions of LEA and governing body, (c) the admissions policy (eg how priorities are determined when a school is over-subscribed and how a procedure for selection by ability or aptitude operates), (d) the arrangements made in respect of extra-district pupils, and (e) the criteria for offering places at schools not maintained by LEAs, and the names of, and number of places at, those with which the LEA have standing arrangements.

7.14 The Secretary of State has made regulations requiring prescribed information to be published by LEAs on their policies and arrangements (on, inter alia, transport to and from school) and by governing bodies of LEA schools

---

13 1996 Act s 412.
14 1996 Act s 413.
15 1996 Act s 414. See the Education (School Hours and Policies) (Information) Regulations 1989, SI 1989/398; the Education (School Curriculum and Related Information) Regulations 1989, SI 1989/954; the Education (Pupils' Attendance Records) Regulations 1991, SI 1991/1582; the Education (School Information) (Wales) Regulations 1994, SI 1994/2330; the Education (School Performance Information) (Wales) Regulations 1995, SI 1995/1904; the Education (School Performance Information) (England) Regulations 1996, SI 1996/2577; the Education (School Information) (England) Regulations 1996, SI 1996/2585; and as regards publication by governing bodies, the Education (Special Educational Needs) (Information) Regulations 1994, SI 1994/1048; and the Education (Pupil Referral Units) (Application of Enactments) Regulations 1994, SI 1994/2103.

See Circular 14/89, 'The Education (School Curriculum and Related Information) Regulations 1989', E[1019], and, as to publication requirements, Circulars 11/88 (WO 47/88), Part IV, E[796], and 6/96 (WO 33/96), 'Admisssion to Maintained Schools', Annex A.

For admission numbers for grant-maintained schools see para 7.22 ff.

16 The admission numbers are those applicable to the school in each school year in relation to the age groups in which pupils are normally admitted. They are the standard numbers applying to the school under 1996 Act ss 417 to 420 or (if higher) the admission numbers fixed by the admission authority in accordance with s 416 (see para 7.15 ff).

about their schools. Governing bodies may publish other information as they think fit. Information about the continuing education of pupils leaving a school, or their employment or training, is to be treated as information about the school.

Admission numbers for county and voluntary schools

7.15 The number of places available at a county or voluntary school for pupils of any age group in which they are normally admitted is to be not less than the 'standard number' for that school year, and at maximum may be limited only by the school's physical capacity ('open enrolment') despite any contrary provision in the articles of government. The number is fixed, after consultation between the governing body and LEA, by whoever of the two are the admission authority, but the other may propose a higher number. A proposal may relate to one or more relevant age groups and to a particular school year or to each school year within a specified period. Unless the admission authority reject the proposal within two months they are to give it effect. If they do reject it, the proposing authority may apply to the Secretary of State for an order (see para 7.17) increasing the standard number.[17]

7.16 The standard number for any school year after 1989 (secondary schools) or 1991 (primary schools) is the greater of (a) the school's existing standard number and (b) the number of pupils in the appropriate age group(s) admitted in 1989 to secondary, 1991 to primary, schools, except that where proposals made for establishing and altering schools (see paras 3.08 and 3.19) have fallen to be implemented, the standard number is that specified in the proposals (or varied by the Secretary of State when proposals are only partly implemented). The 'existing standard number' for secondary and primary schools is that applying in the school year beginning in 1989 and 1991 respectively, but in the case of primary schools recalculated so as to include all the children in a reception class but not children admitted for nursery education.[18]

7.17 The Secretary of State may by order vary any standard number that would otherwise apply to any class or description of county or voluntary school, or to any individual school. An admission authority may apply for an order increasing or reducing a school's standard number, in the latter case under a procedure similar to that outlined at para 3.08 ff). On application for an order increasing a standard number made by an admission authority, or by an LEA or governing body under para 7.15 above, the Secretary of State may increase the standard number to the number proposed or, after consultation

---

17 1996 Act ss 415 and 416. By s 436 the admission of a child to a school for nursery education is to be disregarded in references to the number of pupils admitted or intended to be admitted in any school year or for determining a 'relevant age group'; but those previously admitted for nursery education and transferred to a reception class are to be included.
   By the Local Government Changes in England (School Reorganisation and Admissions) Regulations 1995, SI 1995/2368. reg 5, a new LEA which is not the admission authority may make a proposal during the preliminary period.
   See, as to school attendance orders, para 7.40 ff.
   See Circulars 11/88 (WO 47/88), E[782], 6/91 (WO 14/91), E[1377], 23/94 'The Supply of School Places', E[3169] and 6/96 (WO/33/96), Annex C.
18 1996 Act ss 417 to 419. 'Existing standard numbers' were calculated by reference to the 1980 Act s 15 (repealed).

7.17 *School Admissions, Attendance and Charges*

with LEA and governing body, to a lower number he thinks desirable; or he may refuse to make an order.[19]

7.18 The admission authority are to keep a school's standard number or numbers under review having regard to changes, since they first applied, in the school's capacity to accommodate pupils, as a result of changes in the availability or use of accommodation or in requirements under prescribed standards for educational premises.[20]

New county and voluntary schools

7.19 The initial arrangements for the admission of pupils are to be made in the case of a new (a) county or controlled school, by the LEA, (b) aided school, by the temporary governing body or, if not yet constituted, by the promoters if they consider the matter urgent. Whoever make the arrangements are to have regard to the arrangements for admission to comparable schools in the area. The LEA are, in advance, to consult (county schools) the temporary governing body (except, if they have not yet been constituted, in case of urgency), or (controlled schools) the temporary governing body or the promoters if the governing body have not yet been constituted. The temporary governing body or promoters of a new aided school are to consult the LEA.[1]

Admission appeals relating to county and voluntary schools

7.20 LEAs are to make arrangements to enable parents to appeal against their decisions to allocate children (persons under 19) to particular schools (except a decision of the kind mentioned at para 7.27), or against a decision by the governing body of a county or controlled school to refuse a child admission. Governing bodies of aided and special agreement schools are to make similar arrangements, and may make them jointly for two or more schools maintained by the same LEA. The constitution and procedures of appeal committees are at Appendix 7. Their decisions are binding on the authority or governing body who took the original decision and, where the decision was taken by or on behalf of an LEA, on the governing body of a county or controlled school who are directed to offer a place.[2] Parents, however, may ask the Secretary of State

---

19 1996 Act s 420 and Sch 32. In the case of new LEAs see SI 1995/2368, regs 4 and 5.
  Only orders of general application are made by SI. See the Education (Variation of Standard Numbers for Primary Schools) Order 1991, SI 1991/410; also the Education (Publication of Proposals for Reduction in Standard Number) Regulations 1991, SI 1991/411.
20 1996 Act s 421. 'Prescribed standards': see para 15.04.
1 1996 Act s 422. In paras 7.03, 7.11, 7.12 and 7.20 the references to the governing body include reference to the person responsible for admissions under the initial arrangements.
2 1996 Act s 423 and Sch 33. The 1980 Act s 7 and Sch 2 were considered in *R v South Glamorgan Appeal Committee, ex p Evans* (10 May 1984, unreported), F[43], and *R v Comr for Local Administration, ex p Croydon London Borough Council* [1989] 1 All ER 1033, F[44]. See also *R v Education Appeal Committee of Leicestershire County Council, ex p Tarmohamed* [1997] ELR 48, [1996] COD 286 (allegation of improper procedure). As to the duty to give reasons see *R v Lancashire County Council, ex p Maycock* (1995) 159 LG Rev 201.
  A pupil referral unit is not a 'school' for the purposes of this section: see the Education (Pupil Referral Units) (Application of Enactments) Regulations 1994, SI 1994/2103, reg 3, Sch 2, para 1.

to overturn what they consider to be an unreasonable decision by an appeal committee (see para 12.05).

Admission arrangements for, and appeals relating to, grant-maintained schools

7.21 The articles of government of grant-maintained schools are to make the governing body responsible for (a) determining the arrangements for admitting pupils to the school, including the admissions policy; (b) making arrangements for appeals in relation to admission to an appeals committee (jointly, at option, with the governing body of one or more other grant-maintained schools); and (c) publishing particulars of the arrangements and procedures for admission and the arrangements for appeals by parents.[3]

Admission numbers for grant-maintained schools

7.22 The governing body of a grant-maintained school are not to fix the number of pupils in any relevant age group it is intended to admit to the school in any school year at a figure less than the approved admission number.[4] The 'approved admission number' is the number specified in the published proposals for acquisition of grant-maintained status, or for the establishment of the school (see, respectively, paras 4.09 and 4.18), except where proposals for significant alteration of the school or transfer to a new site have been approved or adopted (see para 4.53), when the number is that specified in the proposals as intended to be admitted in that age group in the first school year in which the proposals are wholly implemented. If the proposals are only partly implemented in any year, the Secretary of State may direct the substitution of a different number.[5]

7.23 The approved admission number for any age group may be varied with the approval of the Secretary of State, or of the funding authority where an order (see para 2.39) makes them wholly or jointly responsible for providing sufficient school places in the area of an LEA.

7.24 Where such an order
(a) has not been made, the Secretary of State may, by order, increase the admission number for any relevant age group in a grant-maintained

---

See Circular 11/88, (WO 47/88) para 51 ff, E[800], supplemented by Circular 6/96, 'Admissions to Maintained Schools', Annex D; also the Code of Practice 'County, Voluntary and Special School Appeals: Admissions...', published in 1994 by the Association of County Councils and the Association of Metropolitan Authorities with the support of the Council on Tribunals and reprinted in *The Law of Education* and reprinted as above.
3 1996 Act ss 425 and 429 and Sch 23 paras 5 and 6. See the Code of Practice 'Grant-maintained Schools: Appeal Committees: Admissions and Exclusions', published by the DFE. A [571]; also *R v Secretary of State for Education and the Governing Body of the Queen Elizabeth Grammar School, ex p Cumbria County Council* [1994] COD 30 (as to proposal for selective admission), *R v Governors of Pate's Grant-maintained Grammar School etc, ex p T* [1994] COD 297 (construction of 'admission arrangements'), and *R v Appeal Committee of Brighouse School, ex p G* [1997] ELR 39 (allegation of improper procedure), F[44.1].
4 As to the admission of a child to a school for nursery education see s 436 and n 17 above.
5 1996 Act s 426. See the Education (Schools Conducted by Education Associations) Regulations 1993, SI 1993/3103 reg 4 and Sch 3; and Circular 6/96 (WO 33/96), Annex C.

7.24 *School Admissions, Attendance and Charges*

school to the number specified in the order for any subsequent school year; but the order may not increase the admission number so as to change the character of the school significantly, or involve any alteration of its premises.[6]

(b) has been made, the funding authority may give a direction to the governing body of a grant-maintained school, increasing the approved admission number for any relevant age group to a specified number for any subsequent school year. If the increase involves any alteration in the school premises, the direction is to give particulars of the alteration. The governing body are to have the alteration made and will receive a grant from the funding authority to meet the reasonable cost of doing so. A direction may, however, not be given if it would involve a significant enlargement of the premises, or significantly change the character of the school; or to the governing body of a secondary school where an order relates only to primary education (and vice versa).

7.25 Before deciding to give a direction the funding authority are to consult the governing body, and, if the authority decide to proceed, are to serve a draft of the proposed direction on them. The governing body then have 15 days in which to refer the matter to the Secretary of State, informing the funding authority if they have done so. The Secretary of State may prohibit the direction or authorise it in the terms of the draft or as modified.[7]

Co-ordinated arrangements for admissions

7.26 Co-ordinated arangements for admission of pupils may be
(a) contained in an agreement, approved by the Secretary of State, between admission authorities (see para 7.10) for LEA schools (excluding hospital special schools) and grant-maintained schools, whether or not any LEA are a party. Agreements override (i) the obligation of LEAs and governors of county and voluntary schools to comply with parental preferences (see para 7.03) and (ii) conflicting provisions in a school's instrument or articles of government.
Alternatively, arrangements may be
(b) made in pursuance of a scheme made by the Secretary of State after consultation with governing bodies and, in the case of LEA schools, the LEAs themselves. Admission authorities may be required to (i) include specified provisions in their arrangements, or (ii) enter into, or modify, an existing, co-ordination agreement. A scheme may apply to all LEA and grant-maintained schools, or a specified category, or particular schools.[8]

Power to direct admission of a child to school

7.27 A child who has either been refused admission to, or permanently excluded from, each county, voluntary and grant-maintained school in the area

---

6 1996 Act s 427.
7 1996 Act s 428 and Sch 4 para 17(c). Building regulations under the Building Act 1984 (of which see s 4(1)(a)(iv) as substituted by the 1996 Act Sch 37 Pt I para 59) do not apply to buildings erected pursuant to a direction. As to the 'character' of a school see s 311(4).
8 1996 Act s 430. Schemes may be revoked or varied in the same way as orders of the Secretary of State (see para 1.28).

of an LEA which is a reasonable distance from his home and provides suitable education, may be the subject of a direction to be admitted to an equally accessible and suitable school in that area (save as mentioned in para 7.28) from which he is not permanently excluded. A direction is given by the LEA, or, if an order has been made making the funding authority solely responsible for providing school places (see para 2.39), the authority.

7.28 The parent and the governing body of the school proposed to be specified are to be consulted, as are also the maintaining authority if they are not the 'directing' authority, before a decision to give a direction is taken. If that decision is taken the LEA or funding authority are to serve notice accordingly on the governing body and head teacher of the specified school and, if different, the maintaining authority. Any of those notified may, within 15 days, refer the matter to the Secretary of State, who may decide which school (not necessarily in the child's home area) is to be required to admit the child. If he does so that school is to be specified in the direction. After the 15 days have elapsed, or the Secretary of State has made his decision, the LEA or funding authority are to notify the governing body and head teacher, and, if different, the maintaining authority, of the school specified in the direction.[9]

7.29 A school which has been directed to admit a child may subsequently exclude him as a pupil if his behaviour so justifies.

7.30 A direction may be given if the child 'has been refused admission' to each accessible suitable school—not if he has been refused admission and his parent's appeal against the refusal to admit was lodged within the time specified. It appears that there may be simultaneous moves (1) by the parent to appeal and (2) by the LEA or funding authority to consult before giving a direction. The direction-giving is unlikely to be concluded speedily because of the consultation requirement and right to refer to the Secretary of State.

7.31 A direction may specify a voluntary school. In parliamentary proceedings the Government spokesman said that the Secretary of State 'would only uphold a direction which would override the religious character of an aided school in exceptional circumstances where there was no other alternative within easy travelling distance.'

Time for admission of pupils

7.32 There is no obligation on
(a) the proprietor of a school (the governing body in the case of a county, voluntary or grant-maintained school) to admit children as pupils otherwise than at the beginning of a term, except (i) where a child was ill or for other circumstances beyond his parent's control at that time, or (ii) his parent was then resident at a place from which the school was not reasonably accessible, or

---

9 1996 Act ss 431 and 432. 'Suitable education' means full-time education suitable to age, ability and aptitude and any special educational needs. 'Maintaining authority' means an LEA or funding authority paying maintenance grant to a grant-maintained school.
  Section 423 (para 7.20 above) precludes an admission appeal by a parent where a direction has been given.

7.32 School Admissions, Attendance and Charges

(b) a parent to send a child of compulsory school age to school during any period when there is no obligation on the proprietor to admit him.[10]

7.33   In practice those provisions signify that a child's admission to primary school may be deferred until the term next after he attains the age of five (which includes a term beginning on his fifth birthday).

7.34   LEAs may give governing bodies general directions about the time of admission of children as pupils (which could relate to the admission of children under the age of five) except where the circumstances mentioned in (a) above apply, but not so as to prevent the admission of children eligible for nursery education grants (see para 11.12).

Registration of pupils

7.35   School proprietors (see para 7.32) are to arrange for the registration of pupils and to make prescribed returns to the Secretary of State, the funding authority and LEAs. Regulations require, inter alia,
(a) an admission register and (except in the case of an independent boarding school) an attendance register to be kept;
(b) the admission register to include the names and addresses of parents and the grounds on which a pupil's name is to be deleted;
(c) the names and addresses of pupils who fail to attend school regularly or are continuously absent for ten or more school days to be reported to the LEA, except in the case of absence due to ill-health or authorised as prescribed, or where the pupil is registered at and attending another school;
(d) registers to be open to inspection by HMIs, registered inspectors and, in respect of schools LEAs maintain, their officers.[11]

7.36   Breach of regulations entails, on summary conviction, a fine up to level 1 on the standard scale.

7.37   The admission register determines whether a pupil is a 'registered pupil' or a parent is a 'registered parent' for the purposes of the initiation by parents of the procedure for acquisition of grant-maintained status and eligibility to vote in the ballot (see para 4.08).

Withdrawal of pupils from a primary school for secondary education

7.38   LEAs may make arrangements under which they require junior pupils aged at least ten years six months registered at a primary school they maintain

---

10   1996 Act s 433. By s 448 where the intended school is grant-maintained and arrangements have been made for the child's admission at the start of the school term after he becomes five, the parent's obligation is likewise deferred. Section 448 is applied by the Education (Special Schools Conducted by Education Associations) Regulations 1994, SI 1994/1084, reg 8, Sch 2, Pt I.
11   1996 Act s 434. See the Pupils' Registration Regulations 1995, SI 1995/2089 and Circular 11/91 (WO 45/91), The Education (Pupils' Attendance Records) Regulations 1991, E[1581]. For application of these provisions see the Education (Grant-maintained Special Schools) Regulations 1994, SI 1994/653, reg 42, Schedule, Pt I; and SI 1994/1084, reg 8, Sch 2, Pt I.

to be withdrawn to receive secondary education (unless the school provides both primary and secondary education).[12]

SCHOOL ATTENDANCE

7.39 Chapter II of Part VI of the 1996 Act (sections 437 to 448) is about school attendance orders, offences in relation to school attendance and education supervision orders. For reference to exclusion and other disciplinary matters see paras 3.108 ff and 4.25 ff (LEA and grant-maintained schools respectively).

School attendance orders

7.40 If it appears[13] to an LEA that a child of compulsory school age in their area is not receiving suitable education (efficient full-time education suitable to his age, ability and aptitude and any special educational needs) by regular school attendance (see the cases at para 7.47 n 20) or otherwise (see para 2.10), and the parent, on 15 days' notice, fails to satisfy them that he is doing so, the LEA are to serve a school attendance order on the parent (if they think it expedient that the child should attend school) requiring his registration as a pupil at a school named in the order. The LEA are to inform the governing body and head teacher of a maintained school, and the governing body are to admit the child to the school. Unless revoked (see para 7.45) the order ordinarily remains in force so long as the child is of compulsory school age.[14]

7.41 When an LEA have to serve a school attendance order the following procedures apply in relation to choice of school, except in the case of a child who is the subject of a statement of special educational needs, to whom the procedure mentioned at para 5.14 ff applies.

7.42 The LEA are first to consult the governing body of any maintained school or schools one of which they intend to name in the order (and where appropriate another LEA) and then to give them and the head teacher notice of their decision, against which there is a right of appeal to the Secretary of State. Next, the LEA are to give the parent 15 days' notice of intention to serve the

---

12 1996 Act s 435.
13 See *Phillips v Brown* (20 June 1980, unreported), F[82]. The court also considered whether the LEA's judgment is a matter about which the court can enquire and, if so, whether there is sufficient evidence before the court, or any evidence, upon which it could be established that it did so appear to the LEA.
14 1996 Act s 437. 'Expedient': in *Phillips v Brown* Donaldson LJ said that in context it meant 'advantageous, fit, proper or suitable to the circumstances of the case'. 'Ordinarily': for exceptions see paras 7.46 and 7.51. The Education (School Attendance Order) Regulations 1995, SI 1995/2090 prescribe the form of the order. Where the school named is a pupil referral unit (see para 2.31) 1996 Act Sch 1 para. 14 applies.

When a parent has been prosecuted for failing to comply with a school attendance order, that order is spent, and if need be a new order has to be served: *Enfield London Borough Council v Forsyth and Forsyth* [1987] 2 FLR 126.

Note the exemption mentioned at para 2.11, and see para 7.51 and, generally, Circular 11/88 (WO 47/88), E[782].

Section 437 is applied in part by the Education (Special Schools Conducted by Education Associations) Regulations 1994, SI 1994/1084, reg 8, Sch 2, Pt I.

7.42 School Admissions, Attendance and Charges

order, which is to specify the school they intend to name or (in the case of an appeal as above) as the Secretary of State directs, and if the LEA (or the Secretary of State) think fit, one or more alternatives. The notice is not to specify a school from which the child is permanently excluded, and a school is not ordinarily to be proposed if the admission of the child would cause the number of pupils in the child's age group to exceed the number fixed (see paras 7.15 ff and 7.22 ff), unless the authority are responsible for admission of pupils to the school (see para 7.10). Exceptionally, the LEA may disregard the fact that a school is full if all accessible schools are up to their admissions numbers.[15]

7.43 If within the period of 15 days mentioned the parent selects one of the alternatives, or successfully applies for a place at (a) another maintained school, or (b) a school at which the fees are to be paid by the LEA (see para 12.40), or (c) some other school providing suitable education, the LEA are to name that school in the order instead. After an order is made, if the parent subsequently applies successfully for a place at a different school in one of the categories (a), (b) or (c) the order is to be amended accordingly.

7.44 When an LEA are obliged to serve a school attendance order in respect of a child for whom they maintain a statement of special educational needs (see para 5.17) the school named in the statement (by amendment if need be[16]) is to be named in the order, and the order is to be amended if the school named in the statement is changed.[17]

7.45 A parent may apply for a school attendance order to be revoked on the ground that arrangements have been made for the child to receive suitable education otherwise than at school (see para 2.10). The LEA are to comply unless they consider the arrangements unsatisfactory, in which case the parent may refer the question to the Secretary of State who determines it as he thinks fit. A parent for whose child a statement of special educational needs is maintained may not apply for revocation of an order if the institution is named in the statement; if it is not named the Secretary of State may direct amendment of the statement in consequence of his determination as above.[18]

School attendance: offences and education supervision orders

7.46 Failure to observe the requirements of a school attendance order is an offence unless the parent proves that the child is receiving suitable education otherwise than at school, in which case the court may (but need not) discharge the order; but the LEA are to take further action if circumstances change.[19]

---

15 1996 Act ss 438, 439 and 440. Where a parent selects a school in category (b), it is implicit that the LEA agree that the school is appropriate, whereas a place in a school in category (c) is likely to have been secured without the knowledge or backing of the LEA.
    See Sch 1 para 14 as to school attendance orders relating to pupil referral units and Sch 4 para 14(1) when an order has been made under s 27(1)(b) (see para 2.39).
16 In accordance with the 1996 Act Sch 27 para 10.
17 1996 Act s 441. See *R v Secretary of State for Education, ex p G* [1995] ELR 58.
18 1996 Act s 442.
19 1996 Act s 443.

7.47 An offence is also committed when a parent fails to ensure his child's regular attendance[20] at the school where he is a registered pupil, unless (where the child is not a boarder) the absence is (a) with leave,[1] or (b) due to sickness or other unavoidable cause,[2] or (c) on a day of religious observance by the religious body to which the parent belongs,[3] or the parent proves (d) that the school at which the child is registered is not within walking distance of his home and no suitable arrangements have been made by the LEA for transport,[4] for boarding accommodation, or for enabling him to become a registered pupil at a nearer school. Absence on 'reasonable' grounds is no excuse, but if the child has no fixed abode the parent is to be acquitted if his job involves travelling from place to place and the child has attended school as regularly as may be—at least 200 attendances over the previous 12 months if aged six or more.[5]

---

20 In *Spiers v Warrington Corpn* [1954] 1 QB 61, F[185] it was held that a parent's refusal to send a child to school dressed to meet the head teacher's reasonable requirements was failure to secure regular attendance; in *Hinchley v Rankin* [1961] 1 WLR 421, F[183], that frequent late arrival was the same failure; in *Crump v Gilmore* (1969) 68 LGR 56, F[186] that truancy of which the parent is unaware is no defence, although it may be accepted in mitigation; in *Jones v Rowland* (1899) 80 LT 630 it was held that it is no defence to send a child to a school of the parents' choice to which he is properly refused admission (see also *Bunt v Kent* [1914] 1 KB 207); and in *Fox v Burgess* [1922] 1 KB 623 that an offence is committed if a parent withholds his child from examination (as to cleanliness—see paras 12.48 and 12.49) and the child is in consequence excluded from school. As to the circumstances in which it is unreasonable to refuse a child admission see *Bowen v Hodgson* (1923) 93 LJKB 76. See para 2.14 and DFE Guidance, May 1994 (WO 53/94), 'School Attendance: Policy and Practice on Categorisation of Absence'.

1 By 1996 Act s 444(9) leave is to be granted by someone authorised by the governing body or proprietor of the school. By reg 8 of the Education (Pupil Registration) Regulations 1995, SI 1995/2089 (see para 2.14), leave of absence to undertake employment is not to be granted except as prescribed by that regulation. In *Happe v Lay* (1977) 76 LGR 313, F[189], it was held that a child is not absent from school 'with leave' if he is suspended because of his parents' refusal to return him to school.

2 *Jenkins v Howells* [1949] 2 KB 218, F[181], established that the 'unavoidable cause' must actually affect the child. The court held that sickness of a parent or 'family reponsibilities' did not count. See also *Walker v Cummings* (1912) 107 LT 304, *Symes v Brown* (1913) 109 LT 232, *LCC v Hearn* (1909) 78 LJKB 414 and *Jarman v Mid-Glamorgan Education Authority* (1985) Times, 11 February, F[190].

3 For example, Ascension Day for Church of England adherents (*Marshall v Graham, Bell v Graham* [1907] 2 KB 112).

4 'Walking distance' for a child under eight is two miles, otherwise three miles, by the nearest available route. A route does not cease to be 'available' because dangerous for an unaccompanied child if it is reasonably practicable for him to be accompanied. See *Shaxted v Ward* [1954] 1 All ER 336; *Essex County Council v Rogers* [1987] AC 66, F[209.1]; *George v Devon County Council* [1988] 3 All ER 1002, HL, F[209.2]; and *R v East Sussex County Council, ex p D* [1991] COD 374, F[214]. A bus pass having been granted may be withdrawn if on recalculation the distance is found to be less than walking distance (*Rootkin v Kent County Council* [1981] 2 All ER 227, CA, F[211]). In *Hares v Curtin* [1913] 2 KB 328 the measurement was made from a house porch to school porch, and 'road' (a narrower term than 'route') was held to include a cart track. It is not enough for the authority to pay for the transport of the child to within the limit (*Surrey County Council v Ministry of Education* [1953] 1 All ER 705, F[208]).

The meaning of 'suitable arrangements' was considered in *Surrey County Council v Minister of Education* [1953] 1 WLR 516, F[208], and in *R v Rochdale Metropolitan Borough Council, ex p Schemet* [1993] 1 FCR 306, F[213]. See also *R v East Sussex County Council, ex p D* [1991] COD 374, F[214], *R v Essex County Council ex p C* (1993) 93 LGR 10, CA, F[215] (not followed in *R v Dyfed County Council ex p S (minors)* [1995] 1 FCR 113, CA, in which it was stressed that 'suitable' qualifies the arrangements, not the school) *Re C (a minor)* [1994] ELR 273, CA, and *Re S (minors)* [1995] ELR 98, CA.

As to the provision of transport between home and school see para 12.24 ff.

5 1996 Act s 444. By Sch 1 para 14(6), where a child is registered as a pupil both at a pupil referral unit and at another school, the reference to the school at which he is registered as a pupil is to be read as reference to the unit.

7.48 A child who is a boarder has failed to attend regularly if he is absent without leave during part of a school term otherwise than on account of sickness or other unavoidable cause.

7.49 The fine, on summary conviction for school attendance offences, is up to level 3 on the standard scale.[6] There is a presumption that the child is of compulsory school age unless the parent proves otherwise.[7]

7.50 Proceedings may be brought only by an LEA,[8] and only after the LEA have considered whether it would be appropriate, alternatively or in addition, to apply for an education supervision order. If, in the event, proceedings are brought and a conviction is secured, the court may direct the LEA to apply for an education supervision order, unless the LEA have decided, after consulting the local authority responsible for the child's accommodation (or, otherwise, his home authority) that his welfare will be satisfactorily safeguarded without an order. If the LEA do so decide they are to inform the court of the reasons for their decision, ordinarily within eight weeks of the direction.[9]

7.51 Where an LEA propose to make an application for an education supervision order they are first to consult the appropriate local authority (as above). The court may make an order if it is satisfied that the child is of compulsory school age and is not being properly (ie suitably) educated and is not in the care of a local authority. Where a child is the subject of a school attendance order which has not been complied with or is a registered pupil at a school which he is not attending regularly it is to be asssumed, in the absence of proof to the contrary, that he is not being properly educated. If the child is subject to a school attendance order, and it is proved that he *is* being properly educated, the court may not make the supervision order and may discharge the attendance order. If a supervision order (or a care order) is made any subsisting attendance order lapses.[10]

7.52 The LEA designated in an education supervision order is to be the LEA for the area within which the child lives or, if different, in which the school at which he is a registerd pupil is situated, by agreement between the two LEAs.

CHARGES

7.53 These are the subject matter of Chapter III of Part VI of the 1996 Act (sections 449 to 462).[11] The restrictions on charges imposed in this chapter do

---

See DFE Guidance, May 1994, 'School Attendance: Policy and Practice on Categorisation of Absence', paras 23, 43 and 44, E[2741].
6 1996 Act ss 443(4) and 444(8).
7 1996 Act s 445. Section 565(1) (see para 15.35) does not apply.
8 1996 Act s 446. An LEA may not bring proceedings to make a child a ward of court: *Re Baker (Infants)* [1962] Ch 201, F[184], and *Re D (a minor)* [1987] 1 WLR 1400, CA.
9 1996 Act s 447. See *Essex County Council v B* [1993] 1 FLR 866.
10 Children Act 1989 s 36, Sch 3 Pt III and 1996 Act s 447(5). A 'good home', does not, as such, meet the requirement of 'proper education' (*Re S (a minor)* [1978] QB 120, F[187]). See also *Essex County Council v B* [1993] 1 FLR 866.
11 By the 1996 Act s 459 the Secretary of State may make regulations requiring LEA, governing body or head teacher to make available prescribed information about school hours relevant to charges. See the Education (School Hours and Policies) (Information) Regulations 1989, SI 1989/398.

not inhibit the soliciting by governing bodies and LEAs of voluntary contributions to schools; but it is to be made clear that there is no obligation to make any contribution, and that a parent's making or withholding a contribution will have no impact on his child as a registered pupil.

7.54 Charges made by persons other than a governing body or LEA, and charges to be paid by persons other than pupils or their parents, are unaffected by the provisions in Chapter III.[12]

Prohibition of charges

7.55 A charge may be made for admission to a maintained school for part-time education of persons over compulsory school age and full-time education for those of 19 and over, and for teacher training.[13] Otherwise no charge may be made
(a) for admission to a maintained school or for education provided during school hours[14] except for
   (i) tuition in playing a musical instrument, either individual or to a group of up to four, unless the tuition is required as part of the syllabus for a prescribed public examination,[15] provided to secure implementation of the National Curriculum or the religious education requirement in the basic curriculum; and
   (ii) part-time education for those over compulsory school age, or under five where the school provides full-time education for junior pupils of the same age, and full-time education for those of 19 and over, provided at a grant-maintained school acting as agent under arrangements made with an LEA;[16]
(b) (except as in (ii) above) for education outside school hours, which is required as part of the syllabus for a prescribed public examination, or provided to secure implementation of the National Curriculum or the religious education requirement in the basic curriculum;[17]
(c) for entrance charges to prescribed public examinations (but the entrance fee for any public examination paid by governing body or LEA may be recovered from a parent if without good reason the pupil fails to take it);[18]

   By s 461 sums payable by parents for wasted examination fees, optional extras and board and lodging at boarding schools are recoverable summarily as a civil debt.
   For application of the provisions relating to charges to (a) pupil referral units, see Sch 1 para 9(1); (b) education associations, see the Education (Schools Conducted by Education Associations) Regulations 1993, SI 1993/3103, Sch 1, para 2; (c) grant-maintained special schools, see the Education (Grant-maintained Special Schools) Regulations 1994, SI 1994/653, reg 42, Schedule, Pt I; and (d) special schools conducted by education associations, the Education (Special Schools Conducted by Education Associations) Regulations 1994, SI 1994/1084, reg 8(1), Sch 2, Pt I.
   See Circular 2/89 (WO 4/89), 'Education Reform Act 1988: Charges for School Activities', E[869], and Circular 2/94, para 147, E[2377].
12 1996 Act s 460.
13 1996 Act s 450(2).
14 1996 Act ss 450(1) and 451(1) and (2).
15 See the Education (Prescribed Public Examinations) Regulations 1989, SI 1989/377.
16 1996 Act s 451(3) and (5). See also para 4.34.
17 1996 Act ss 451(4) and 462. Examples are a field trip as part of a geography syllabus; a visit to a museum (history, technology), a concert, or a picture gallery.
18 1996 Act s 453. By s 461 sums payable by parents are recoverable summarily as a civil debt.

(d) for materials, books and equipment (but not clothing) associated with education and examinations; but charges may be raised for materials used in making articles at school which the parent wishes to keep;[19] and
(e) for transport incidental to free education, namely between school premises and to and from other places where education is provided, or in connection with a prescribed public examination.[20]

7.56 The method for establishing whether education which falls partly within and partly outside school hours, and education provided on residential trips,[1] should be considered as falling within or outside for charging purposes is as follows. If half or more of an educational activity (including travelling during school hours) falls during school hours then all the activity is to be treated as if it took place during school hours, and so no charge may be made. Conversely, if less than half of the activity and travelling time is in school hours all the activity is deemed to take place out of school hours, and so, subject to (b) above, charges may be made.[2]

7.57 The test for charging in relation to residential trips turns on the relationship between half-days (any period of 12 hours ending with noon or midnight) and school sessions. If the number of sessions occupied by the trip is 50 per cent or more of the total number of half-days on the trip then the whole trip is deemed to be within school hours and charges for education and transport are prohibited. A half-day and a school session are regarded as being spent on the trip if it takes up 50 per cent or more of one or the other.

Permitted charges

7.58 'Regulated charges' (which do not include those under the arrangements referred to under (a) (ii) above) may be made for education, transport or examination beyond the extent of free provision, if the parent has agreed to them as 'optional extras'; also (without parental agreement) for board and lodging on a residential trip. The cost of optional extras includes provision of staff and materials etc. Whether or not charges should be made is at the discretion of the governing body if provision is made from funds at their disposal; otherwise of the LEA, in which case the governing body may decide to relieve the parent in whole or part.[3]

7.59 LEAs and governing bodies are to settle, and keep under review, their policies on providing, and charging parents for, optional extras and board and lodging on residential trips (except under the arrangements referred to under (a) (ii)), and on remission of charges. Unless both have settled their charging and remissions policies no charges may be made. The remissions policies of governing bodies of other than grant-maintained schools are to set out the

19 1996 Act s 454(1) and (2).
20 1996 Act s 454(3) and (4). As to transport between home and school see para 12.24 ff.
 1 By 1996 Act s 462(2) a residential trip is one arranged for registered pupils at a maintained school which involves one or more overnight stays.
 2 1996 Act s 452.
 3 1996 Act ss 452(6), 455 and 456.

circumstances in which they propose to meet the charge payable to the LEA for an optional extra or a pupil's board and lodging.[4]

7.60 Remissions policies are to provide for complete remission of residential trip board and lodging charges when both (a) no charge is permissible for the education provided and (b) the pupils' parents are in receipt of specified allowances.

7.61 Parents are to pay the LEA (governing body in the case of grant-maintained schools) charges of up to the cost of providing pupils' board and lodging at maintained boarding schools. Where, however, suitable education cannot, in the opinion of a pupil's LEA, be provided for him otherwise than at (a) an LEA boarding school, the charges are to be wholly remitted (and reclaimed from another LEA if the pupil does not belong to the maintaining LEA), (b) a grant-maintained boarding school, the pupil's LEA, not the parent, are to pay the charges. Where the LEA believe that payment of full charges would cause the parent financial hardship they are to remit part or all of them, or pay them to the LEA maintaining the school or to the governing body in the case of grant-maintained schools.[5]

---

4 1996 Act s 457. The allowances specified are income support, family credit, an income-based jobseeker's allowance and disablity working allowance.
　By s 459 the Secretary of State may make regulations requiring LEA, governing body or head teacher to make available information about remissions policies. See SI 1989/398.
5 1996 Act s 458. Where (a) board and lodging are provided otherwise than at a boarding school see para 12.35, (b) an order under s 27 is in force (allocating responsibility to a funding authority) see Sch 4 paras 1(2) and 13(1)(a). As to payment of fees at other than LEA schools see para 12.40 ff.

Chapter 8

INSPECTION AND SPECIAL MEASURES

SCHOOL INSPECTIONS

8.01 Part I of the School Inspections Act 1996 (sections 1 to 25) provides for four kinds of inspection:
(a) ad hoc inspection of schools, carried out by the Chief Inspectors and Her Majesty's Inspectors of Schools (HMIs) at the request of the Secretary of State or on the initiative of the Chief Inspectors (see para 8.03 ff);
(b) periodical inspections of schools under Section 10, carried out by registered inspectors or HMIs acting in lieu (see para 8.08);
(c) inspections of religious education, carried out by persons chosen by school governors (see paras 8.27 and 8.28); and
(d) LEA inspections of schools in their areas, carried out by LEA officers (see para 8.29).

8.02 Part I of the Act, on school inspections, begins, in Chapter I, by recording the status and functions of Her Majesty's Inspectorate and registered inspectors. Chapter II is about procedure for inspections and Chapter III about other inspections—inspection of religious education and local authority inspection services.

Her Majesty's Inspectorate

8.03 By Order in Council there are appointed a Chief Inspector for Schools for England and his staff, Her Majesty's Inspectors of Schools. Together they form a non-ministerial government department, the Office for Standards in Education (OFSTED).[1] The same appointments are made for Wales.[2] Chief Inspectors are appointed for up to five years and may be reappointed. They may resign at any time and may be removed for incapacity or misconduct.

---

1 1996 SI Act s 1 and Sch 1. See the Education (Chief Inspector of Schools in England) Order 1994, SI 1994/1633 and the Education (Inspectors of Schools in England) Order 1992, SI 1992/1713 and 1996, SI 1996/2594; also Circular 7/93 (WO 44/93), 'Inspecting schools: a Guide etc', E[1921], as amended by DFE letter dated 24 September 1993.
  There is no explicit statutory reference to OFSTED, but it has been generally adopted as a collective description.
2 1996 SI Act s 4 and Sch 1. See the the Education (Chief Inspector of Schools in Wales) Order 1997, SI 1997/288 and the Education (Inspectors of Schools in Wales) Orders 1992, SI 1992/1740 and 1995, SI 1995/1628.

8.04 The duties of Chief Inspectors are to keep the Secretaries of State informed about (a) the quality of education provided by, and standards achieved in, schools, (b) whether the financial resources of schools are managed efficiently, and (c) the spiritual, moral, social and cultural development of pupils. On request each Chief Inspector is to advise his Secretary of State on matters specified (and may advise on his own initiative) and to inspect specified schools. He is also to (i) establish and maintain the register of inspectors (see para 8.09), (ii) give guidance about inspections under section 10 (see para 8.12 ff), (iii) keep under review the section 10 inspections system and the extent to which requirements relating to inspections are complied with, and (iv) promote efficiency by encouraging competition between registered inspectors in the provision of services; and he may be given additional, including teacher training, functions. He is to have regard to aspects of government policy as directed by the Secretary of State.[3]

8.05 Each Chief Inspector is to make an annual, and may make other, reports to the Secretary of State, who is to lay the former before Parliament. Reports are to be published as the Chief Inspector considers appropriate.[4]

8.06 Chief Inspectors have the right of entry to school premises, and to inspect and copy school records and other documents containing information about the school which they require for the purposes of inspections. Wilful obstruction of a Chief Inspector is an offence punishable on summary conviction by a fine up to level four on the standard scale.[5]

8.07 The Secretary of State may direct that a school is to be inspected by one or more HMIs, or arrange for HMIs to monitor an inspection under section 10 which is being conducted by a registered inspector. An HMI has the right of entry to school premises and to inspect and copy documents which 'he considers relevant to the discharge of his functions' (the analogous power of a registered inspector is in relation to any documents 'which he requires for the purposes of the inspection'). Wilful obstruction of an HMI is an offence punishable as above.[6]

Inspections by registered inspectors

8.08 Chief Inspectors are to secure that, with the exceptions to be mentioned, all maintained (including LEA nursery) schools, city colleges, special schools and independent schools approved for children with statements of special educational needs (see para 5.17) are to be inspected at prescribed intervals by registered inspectors, who are to report, in relation to particular schools, under the same headings, (a), (b) and (c), as in para 8.04. The exceptions are schools conducted by education associations (see para 8.35), and denominational education and the content of collective worship (see para 8.28).[7]

3 1996 SI Act s 2(1) to (6) and s 5(1) to (6). The Chief Inspector for England may attend but not vote at meetings (including committee meetings) of the School Curriculum and Assessment Authority (1996 Act Sch 29 para 16).
  As to the functions of Chief Inspectors and HMIs in relation to LEA further and higher education institutions see para 10.91.
4 1996 SI Act ss 2(7) and 5(7).
5 1996 SI Act ss 2(8) to (10) and 5(8) to (10).
6 1996 SI Act ss 3 and 6.
7 1996 SI Act s 10 and Sch 3. See the Education (School Inspection) (No 2) Regulations 1993, SI 1993/1986 and the Education (School Inspection) (Wales) (No 2) Regulations 1993, SI 1993/1982; also Circular 7/93 (WO 44/93). See also para 8.14.

8.09 *Inspection and Special Measures*

8.09 Persons are to be placed on the register of inspectors by a Chief Inspector if it appears to him that they are fit and proper persons for discharging the functions of a registered inspector and will be capable of conducting inspections competently and effectively. A Chief Inspector may register an applicant, refuse to do so, or register him subject to conditions applying generally or specifically. The register is to show the period for which the registration lasts; and application may be made for its continuation.[8]

8.10 A Chief Inspector may withdraw registration if he thinks an inspector (a) no longer meets the requirements mentioned, or (b) has significantly failed to comply with a condition of registration, or (c) has knowingly or recklessly produced a seriously misleading report. In those circumstances, or if the Chief Inspector otherwise considers that it would be in the public interest to do so, he may, alternatively, impose a condition on the registration or vary an existing one.[9] His decision in these respects, or his refusal to renew registration, is subject to a right of appeal to a tribunal; and it is ineffective until either (a) the appeal is disposed of or (b) the time for appealing (ordinarily 28 days) has expired, unless the circumstances appear to the Chief Inspector to be exceptional and he notifies the person concerned.

8.11 The appeal tribunal have power to confirm, vary or reverse the Chief Inspector's decision, or to remit the case to him with directions.[10]

Procedure for inspections

8.12 Having first consulted the appropriate authority—school governing body, LEA (where the school does not have a delegated budget) or proprietor (city colleges and independent schools approved for children with statements of special educational needs)—Chief Inspectors are to invite tenders to carry out periodic, 'section 10', inspections from at least two registered inspectors. The inspector selected is assisted by a team of fit and proper persons whom he chooses subject to requirements as to balance of skills and impartiality. Members of teams are ordinarily to have satisfactorily completed a training course approved by a Chief Inspector.[11]

8.13 Inspection procedures differ to some extent according to whether a school is either (a) a maintained (other than LEA nursery) school or a grant-maintained special school, or (b) an LEA nursery school, city college, non-LEA special school or an independent school approved for children with statements of special educational needs.[12]

---

8   1996 SI Act s 7. The Chief Inspector directs the manner of application for registration, which is to be accompanied by the prescribed fee (£150, under the Education (Registered Inspectors) (Fees) Regulations 1992, SI 1992/2025).
9   1996 SI Act s 8. Either Chief Inspector may have regard to action taken by the other.
10 1996 SI Act s 9 and Sch 2. See the Education (Registered Inspectors of Schools Appeal Tribunal) (Procedure) Regulations 1994, SI 1994/717.
11 1996 SI Act Sch 3 paras 1 to 5.
12 1996 SI Act s 11. See para 8.19 below. Provisions relating to inspectors' reports and action plans where special measures are required are contained in ss 16 to 19 (see para 8.21 ff) if the school falls within sub-s (2) (category (a)) and in ss 20 to 22 (see paras 8.25 and 8.26) if it falls within sub-s (3) (category (b)). See Circular 17/93 (WO 64/93), 'Schools requiring special measures' [E2113].

8.14 If no suitable registered inspector is available, a school may be inspected by an HMI, and so far as appropriate the same provisions apply as if the inspection were carried out by a registered inspector. The Chief Inspector may treat an ad hoc inspection by himself or an HMI (see paras 8.06 or 8.07) as if it were a periodic inspection under section 10.[13]

8.15 The appropriate authority (as in para 8.12) are to take reasonably practicable steps to inform parents of registered pupils and other prescribed persons when an inspection is to take place and to arrange a meeting at which parents can meet the inspector. The inspector has a right of entry to school premises and to inspect and copy records and documents required for the purposes of the inspection. Obstruction of an inspector or member of his team is an offence punishable on summary conviction by a fine of up to level four on the standard scale.[14]

8.16 Having completed a section 10 inspection a registered inspector is to prepare a written report and summary. Where in his opinion special measures are required—because the school is failing or likely to fail to give pupils an acceptable standard of education—he is to submit a draft of the report to the Chief Inspector, who may ask him for further information, and is to tell him whether he shares that opinion. Where the Chief Inspector disagrees but the inspector does not change his mind the latter is to report substantially in the terms of his draft, stating his own opinion; or he may submit a redraft for consideration by the Chief Inspector. His substantive report is to state whether or not the Chief Inspector agrees with his opinion as there expressed.[15]

8.17 If a registered inspector is of the opinion that special measures are not required but the latest inspection report stated that the Chief Inspector agreed that special measures *were* required (or an HMI expressed that opinion) the inspector's opinion is to be stated in the report.

8.18 Where an HMI submits a report on an ad hoc or section 10 inspection and is of opinion that special measures are required he is to prepare a written report and summary stating that opinion. If he is not of that opinion the substance of para 8.17 above applies with the substitution of 'HMI' for 'registered inspector'.[16]

8.19 A section 10 inspection and subsequent report by a registered inspector are to be completed within, respectively, a prescribed time and period. The prescribed time is two weeks and the period five weeks from the date of completion of inspection (extended by up to three months at the discretion of the Chief Inspector). The Chief Inspector's notice of extension is to be given to the inspector, and in the case of category (a) (see para 8.13) to the LEA and the governing body; in the case of category (b) to the appropriate authority (as in

---

By s 42 any person authorised to inspect records may inspect computers and associated apparatus and material, and may so far as reasonable require assistance in doing so.
13 1996 SI Act s 12.
14 1996 SI Act Sch 3 paras 6 to 8. See SI 1993/1986, reg 6 and SI 1993/1982, reg 6.
15 1996 SI Act s 13.
16 1996 SI Act s 14.

8.19 *Inspection and Special Measures*

para 8.12), and to the Secretary of State except where the school is an LEA nursery school.[17]

Destination of reports and special measures: schools within section 11(2)

8.20   In the case of these (category (a) in para 8.13) schools, namely maintained (other than LEA nursery) and grant-maintained special schools, copies of reports and summaries are to be sent by the person making the report to the following:
(a)   the appropriate authority (as in para 8.12),
(b)   the Secretary of State in the case of (i) a grant-maintained or grant-maintained special school, (ii) a county, voluntary or LEA special school where the opinion is expressed that special measures are required and (if not expressed by an HMI) is shared by the Chief Inspector and (iii) the report is made by an HMI in which he expresses the opinion that special measures are required,
(c)   the Chief Inspector (unless the report was by an HMI),
(d)   the head teacher,
(e)   in the case of a county, voluntary or LEA special school, whichever of the LEA and the governing body are not the appropriate authority,
(f)   the person appointing foundation governors (if any) and (if different) the appropriate diocesan authority,
(g)   any person named as sponsor in an instrument of government, and
(h)   in the case of any school in a group of grant-maintained schools in respect of which any person has power to appoint an externally appointed core governor (see Appendix 6), that person.

8.21   The appropriate authority (as in para 8.12) are to make public the report and summary, and parents are to receive copies of the latter.[18]

8.22   Where the appropriate authority receive a section 10 inspection report, or a report by an HMI recommending special measures, they are to prepare a statement in response (an 'action plan') and state the period within which they propose to take action. The plan is to be prepared within a prescribed period or, in specified circumstances, a shorter period the Secretary of State directs. The authority are to send copies of the plan to the Chief Inspector and others specified. It is to be made public and parents are to receive copies.[19]

8.23   Where the person making a report of an inspection of a county, voluntary or LEA special school which has a delegated budget expressed the opinion (shared by the Chief Inspector unless the person is an HMI) that special measures were required, and the LEA have received a copy of the action plan (or

---

17 1996 SI Act s 15. The requirements in this section do not apply in the case of inspections carried out by an HMI. See the Education (School Inspection) (No 2) Regulations 1993, SI 1993/1986, reg 7, and the Education (School Inspection) (Wales) (No 2) Regulations 1993, SI 1993/1982, reg 7 (under which the period for completion of the report is seven weeks if a translation is required).
18 1996 SI Act s 16. See SI 1993/1986, reg 8, or (Wales) SI 1993/1982, reg 8.
19 1996 SI Act s 17. 'Prescribed period': see SI 1993/1986, reg 7, or (Wales) SI 1993/1982, reg 7. The extent to which action plans have been carried into effect is to be referred to in governing bodies' reports (see paras 3.118 and 4.25).

one has not been prepared within the prescribed period), the LEA are to prepare a statement of the action they propose to take (within a period they specify) in the light of the report, or an explanation of why they do not propose to take any action. They are to send it to the Secretary of State, the Chief Inspector and, in the case of an aided or special agreement school, the person appointing foundation governors and (if different) the appropriate diocesan authority.[20]

8.24 Where (a) the person making an inspection report on a school in category (a) in para 8.13 expressed the opinion (shared by the Chief Inspector unless the person is an HMI) that special measures were required in relation to the school, (b) an action plan has been prepared (or has not been prepared within the prescribed period), and (c) in a later report by a registered inspector or an HMI that opinion was not repudiated, regulations may make provision to secure that measures for improving the standard of education are monitored by the appropriate authority; also by the LEA where the school has a delegated budget. Regulations may also, inter alia, authorise the Secretary of State to require the Chief Inspector to conduct further inspections, and provide for circumstances in which the grounds for the opinion that special measures are required have changed from one report to the next.[1]

Destination of reports and special measures: schools within section 11(3)

8.25 In the case of these (category (b) in para 8.13) schools, namely LEA nursery schools, city colleges, non-LEA special schools and independent schools approved for children with statements of special educational needs, copies of reports and summaries are to be sent by the person making the report to the following:
(a) the appropriate authority (as in para 8.12),
(b) the Chief Inspector (unless the report was by an HMI),
(c) the Secretary of State where (i) the person making the report expresses the opinion that special measures are required which (if not expressed by an HMI) is shared by the Chief Inspector, or (ii) the report is made by an HMI in which he expresses the opinion that special measures are required.

8.26 In the case of (a) a special school which is not maintained by an LEA or grant-maintained, or (b) an independent school approved for children with statements, the appropriate authority are to send a copy of any report or summary they receive to the funding authority, or any LEA paying a registered pupil's fees. They are to make public the report and summary, and parents are to receive copies of the latter.[2] They are also, mutatis mutandis, subject to the requirements in para 8.22;[3] and, with the same qualification, para 8.24 applies to schools in category (b) as it does to those in (a).[4]

---

20 1996 SI Act s 18. The statement is ordinarily to be prepared within the period prescribed in SI 1993/1986, reg 7, or (Wales) SI 1993/1982, reg 7. In case of urgency the Secretary of State may direct a shorter period.
1 1996 SI Act s 19.
2 1996 SI Act s 20.
3 1996 SI Act s 21.
4 1996 SI Act s 22.

8.27 *Inspection and Special Measures*

Inspection of religious education

8.27 Inspection, at prescribed intervals, of denominational education and collective worship (see para 6.43 ff) is the duty of the governing bodies of voluntary schools and of those grant-maintained schools which (a) were formerly voluntary schools, or (b) were established with specific provision for religious education, or (c) have been subject to a change of character under which religious education is to be given in accordance with tenets of a particular religion or denomination.

8.28 Inspection is to be conducted by a person chosen by governing bodies (or foundation governors in the case of a controlled school). He need not be a registered inspector. He may choose fit and proper persons as assistants. His report to the governing body on the quality of denominational education, or the content of collective worship, may refer to the spiritual, moral, social and cultural development of pupils. Provision is made for publication of reports and additional action plans.[5]

Local authority inspection services

8.29 LEAs may use their own officers to provide, at full cost, for the inspection, under paras 8.08 or 8.27, of schools in their areas (including those they do not maintain). Regulations may make provision about, inter alia, tenders and the keeping of accounts.[6]

SCHOOLS REQUIRING SPECIAL MEASURES

8.30 Part II of the School Inspections Act 1996 (sections 26 to 41, Schedule 5) describes the two sets of powers applying where special measures are needed in respect of schools, now set out in paras 8.31 to 8.34, and 8.35 ff respectively.

Miscellaneous powers and restrictions

8.31 The provisions mentioned in the following three paragraphs apply to county, voluntary and LEA special schools when (a) the report of an inspection contains the opinion (shared by the Chief Inspector unless the inspector is an HMI) that special measures need to be taken (see paras 8.16 and 8.18) in relation to the school, (b) that opinion has not been repudiated in a later report and

---

5 1996 SI Act s 23 and Sch 4. 'Denominational education' is religious education which is required to be included in a school's basic curriculum but is not in accordance with an agreed syllabus. See SI 1993/1986, regs 9 to 12 or (Wales) SI 1993/1982, regs 9 to 12. Denominational education is also subject to inspection at any grant-maintained school falling outside the three categories mentioned. Where a school is being conducted by an education association see the Education (Schools Conducted by Education Associations) Regulations 1993, SI 1993/3103 Sch 1, paras 3 and 4.
6 1996 SI Act s 24 and Sch 3 para 2. See SI 1993/1986, reg 13 or (Wales) SI 1993/1982, reg 13.
  The view has been expressed that local authority officers carrying out inspections under s 10 must be registered inspectors.
  As to inspection under s 25 to obtain information about an LEA school see para 2.24 n 1.

(c) the Secretary of State has not transferred responsibility for conducting the school to an education association (see para 8.35).[7]

8.32 When a special measures statement under section 17 or section 18—the former in the case of a school without a delegated budget—has been sent to the Secretary of State an LEA may
(a) appoint any number of additional governors to a county, controlled or LEA special school (the appropriate appointing authority of an aided or special agreement school appoint additional foundation governors instead),[8] and, or alternatively,
(b) suspend the right to a delegated budget of the governing body of a county, controlled or LEA special school (as in para 3.82 but without right of appeal);[9]

8.33 When an LEA have received a copy of the report of an inspection containing the opinion that special measures need to be taken at any county, voluntary or LEA special school, they may not include that school in a group (see para 3.67); and the Secretary of State having received a copy of the report may end a group which includes the school.[10]

8.34 Where the governing body of a county or voluntary school have received a copy of an inspection report containing the opinion that special measures need to be taken, they may not have a ballot held (see para 4.07) on prospective application for grant-maintained status. Similarly, in relation to LEA special schools, the route to becoming grant-maintained is barred by disapplication of regulations (see para 5.46 n 8).[11]

Education associations

8.35 In general terms, a school will be put under the management of an education association only where the LEA and governing body have manifestly failed to make improvements. The formal conditions precedent to the establishment, by order of the Secretary of State, of an association to conduct a county, voluntary or LEA special school, are that
(a) the report of an inspection contains the opinion (shared by the Chief Inspector unless the inspector is an HMI) that special measures need to be taken in relation to the school,
(b) that opinion has not been repudiated in a later report,

---

7 1996 SI Act s 26. See Circular 17/93 (WO 64/93), E[2113].
8 1996 SI Act s 27. Before the power of appointment can be exercised the LEA are to have received notice of receipt of the statement and at least ten days are to have elapsed since the date of the notice (or a shorter period set by the Secretary of State in relation to a particular school). The appointments take effect notwithstanding conflicting provisions in the 1996 Act s 79(1) or (2) (see para 3.50) relating to instruments etc of government.
    The provisions relating to aided and special agreement schools are similar. The 'appropriate appointing authority' are ordinarily the diocesan authority or other person who appoints the foundation governors.
9 1996 SI Act s 28. The notice of suspension, given to the governing body (with a copy to the head teacher), takes effect upon receipt, but before it can be given the LEA are to have received notice of receipt of the statement from the Secretary of State and at least ten days are to have elapsed since the date of the notice (or a shorter period determined by the Secretary of State).
10 1996 SI Act s 29.
11 1996 SI Act s 30.

8.35 Inspection and Special Measures

(c) the Secretary of State has received a special measures statement (see para 8.22) (or the time for preparing one has expired), and

(d) (in the case of a voluntary school) he has consulted appropriate persons including those who appoint foundation governors.

8.36 The Secretary of State is to give notice of the order to the governing body, the head teacher, the LEA and (except in Wales before the Schools Funding Council for Wales exercise their functions) the funding authority. On the transfer date named in the order the LEA's responsibility for maintenance ceases, and any special agreement lapses.[12]

8.37 An education association are a body corporate consisting of not less than five persons, including a chairman, appointed by order of the Secretary of State (after he has consulted the diocesan authority or foundation governors in the case of voluntary schools). Associations are to include at least one member who has had experience of, and shown capacity in, providing (or being responsible for providing) primary or secondary education, and in voluntary or special schools if the school to be conducted is one of such.[13] The association are to comply with the directions of the Secretary of State; he is to consult them in advance, except in case of urgency where it is not reasonably practicable for him to do so.[14]

8.38 The main function of an education association is to conduct a school of largely unchanged description so as to eliminate so far as practicable the deficiencies identified in the inspection report which prompted its establishment. If the school's articles of government permit, the association may provide education which is neither primary nor secondary, but is (a) part-time education for those over compulsory school age, (b) full-time education for those aged 19 and over, (c) part-time education for junior pupils who are under five (where the school provides full-time education for junior pupils of the same age), or (d) provided as agent for, and under arrangements made with, an LEA.[15]

---

12 1996 SI Act s 33 and see s 41. Orders under s 33 are made by SI but not subject to annulment by Parliament. See the Education (Schools Conducted by Education Associations) Regulations 1993, SI 1993/3103 and Circular 17/93 (WO 64/93), E[2113].
    LEA special schools are subject to the provisions relating to education associations as modified by the Education (Special Schools Conducted by Education Associations) Regulations 1994, SI 1994/1084. See also the Education (School Premises) Regulations 1996, SI 1996/360. Provision is made for modified application of s 37 and of s 345 of the 1996 Act (see para 5.46) to former LEA special schools being conducted by associations.

13 1996 SI Act s 31. Schedule 5 adds supplementary powers and provides for tenure of members; salaries, allowances and pensions; committees; delegation of functions; proceedings; and the application of the seal and proof of instruments.
    Where a school is being conducted by an association, for statutory references to the governing body or the foundation governors read 'education association'.
    'Experience': see *R v Croydon London Borough Council, ex p Leney* (1986) 85 LGR 466, F[90].
    Orders under s 31 are made by SI but not subject to annulment by Parliament. The North East London Education Association Order 1995, SI 1995/2037, established a body corporate to conduct Hackney Downs School from 1 September 1995.

14 1996 SI Act s 32. Directions are to be published as the Secretary of State thinks fit (ie they are to be in writing).

15 1996 SI Act s 35. 'Largely unchanged': changes in the character or premises not requiring authorisation under Ch VII of Pt III of the 1996 Act or authorised under that Chapter (see para 4.48 ff).

8.39 Education associations are to conduct schools in accordance with prescribed initial articles of government and any trust deed so far as the articles permit. Some of the articles may be brought into effect by regulation earlier than the transfer date. An association may modify the initial, or make new, articles with the consent of the Secretary of State, who has power to direct modification of articles of schools conducted by education associations, either generally or specifically, after consulting the association or associations concerned.[16]

8.40 Once an order has been made transferring a school to an education association it continues to be conducted by them until it becomes a grant-maintained school or is discontinued. Except as relating to new grant-maintained schools established by the funding authority or by promoters, and as respects section 10 inspection, the law relating to grant-maintained schools applies, subject to regulation, to schools conducted by education associations. In particular the funding authority are to make annual maintenance, and may pay special purpose, grants to associations, who are subject to requirements imposed by the authority.[17]

8.41 Where, following his inspection of a school conducted by an education association, an HMI concludes that special measures are no longer required, he is to state his opinion in a report and summary and send copies to the head teacher, the education association and the Secretary of State. He is also to make the report and summary available to the public, and parents are to receive copies of the latter.[18]

8.42 If having received the report the Secretary of State considers that the school should become grant-maintained, he is to give notice to the head teacher, the education association, the LEA and (except in Wales before the Schools Funding Council for Wales exercise their functions) the funding authority. The education association are within three months to publish proposals for acquisition of grant-maintained status (see para 4.09); and the provisions relating to procedure for acquisition of that status (see para 4.04 ff) and the government, conduct etc of grant-maintained schools (see para 4.24 ff) apply with the modifications specified or prescribed.[19]

8.43 Where the Secretary of State considers that a school conducted by an education association should be closed (the only alternative to grant-maintained status) he is to give notice accordingly to the education association, the LEA, the funding authority (except in Wales before the Schools Funding Council for Wales exercise their functions) and the further education funding council if the school provides full-time education for 16 to 18 year-olds. The Secretary of State fixes a closure date which, if he agrees, may be

---

16 1996 SI Act s 36. See the Education (Schools Conducted by Education Associations) (Initial Articles of Government) Regulations 1994, SI 1994/2849.
17 1996 SI Act ss 34 and 41. See the Education (Schools Conducted by Education Associations) Regulations 1993, SI 1993/3103. Regulation 2, Sch 1 paras 7 and 9 disapply, respectively, the provisions relating to a funding authority's responsibility for providing school places (see para 2.39) and power to form groups including grant-maintained special schools (see para 5.47).
18 1996 SI Act s 40.
19 1996 SI Act ss 37 and 41. Section 37 does not make provision for the possibility of the education association's failing to publish as required.

8.43 *Inspection and Special Measures*

changed at the request of the education association. He may make provision by order for disposal of school property and the discharge of the association's liabilities.[20]

8.44 The Secretary of State may by order dissolve an education association and transfer their property, rights and liabilities to himself where he has approved proposals for the school to become grant-maintained or he has given notice that it should close.[1]

---

20 1996 SI Act ss 38 and 41. Subject to regulations, the order may make the same provision as under 1996 Act ss 274 to 279 (see para 4.70 ff) except provision for the dissolution of the education association. As to exemption from stamp duty on transfers see s 44.
   In *R v Secretary of State for Education and Employment, ex p Morris* (1995) Times, 15 December it was held that in the circumstances of Hackney Downs School (see n 13 above) there was no obligation on the Secretary of State or the education association to consult before an order was made.
1 1996 SI Act s 39. Orders under s 39 are made by SI but not subject to annulment by Parliament. As to exemption from stamp duty on transfers see s 44.

Chapter 9

INDEPENDENT SCHOOLS

9.01 Chapter I of Part VII of the 1996 Act (section 463) defines an independent school as a school at which full-time education is provided for five or more pupils of compulsory school age, and which is neither LEA nor grant-maintained, nor a non-maintained special school.[1]

9.02 LEAs are under obligation to pay non-maintained school fees in full (including, if need be, for board and lodging) where they are satisfied that no place is available at a reasonably convenient LEA school at which suitable education can be provided. They may assist non-maintained schools and, in specified circumstances, pay the whole or part of the fees and expenses of pupils attending them.[2]

REGISTRATION

9.03 Chapter II of Part VII (sections 464 to 478, Schedule 34) is about registration, complaints, offences and the Independent Schools Tribunal.

Requirements

9.04 The proprietor (or person proposing to be the proprietor) of an independent school is to apply, as prescribed, to have his school included in either the register of independent schools for England or that for Wales. The registers are open to public inspection. An independent school is not to be registered if the proprietor or the premises are disqualified (see para 9.12 ff), and it is only provisionally registered until, after inspection, the Secretary of State notifies the proprietor that registration is final.[3]

---

1 1996 Act s 463. See as to (a) whether a pupil expelled from an independent school has a public law remedy *R v Fernhill Manor School, ex p A* [1994] ELR 67; (b) a claim against a parent for repayment of a scholarship *Church Education Corpn v McCoig and McCoig* (8 December 1995, unreported), Epsom County Court; (c) objection to a school take-over *Charters-Ancaster College v Girls Public Day School Trust (1872)* [1996] ELR 123; and (d) corporal punishment see para 15.15 ff.
2 1996 Act ss 16(1), 517(1) and (3) and 518 (see para 12.40 ff). As from a day to be appointed by the Secretary of State for 'LEA school' read 'maintained school'. A local authority who are not an LEA may establish a trust fund to provide free or assisted places at independent schools (*Manchester City Council v Greater Manchester County Council* (1980) 78 LGR 560).
3 1996 Act ss 464 and 465. See the Education (Particulars of Independent Schools) Regulations 1982, SI 1982/1730, which require, inter alia, numbers and particulars of pupils and teaching staff to be stated.

9.05   *Independent Schools*

9.05 It is an offence to conduct an independent school which is not registered or provisionally registered (unless an application for registration has been made within one month from when the school was first conducted) or to dissemble a provisionally registered school as a registered school.[4]

9.06 Regulations require the proprietor of a registered or provisionally registered school to submit prescribed particulars to the Registrar, in particular information required by the local authority to determine whether the school is a children's home. The particulars are contained in an annual return and include those required in the application for registration, and information about the number of pupils following examination courses. The proprietor is also to give the Registrar notice of certain changes—of proprietor, head teacher, name and location of the school and closure of the school; and he is to give the Secretary of State the facts of the case where a person is dismissed on grounds of misconduct, or would or might have been dismissed but for his resignation.[5]

9.07 If the Secretary of State is satisfied
(a) that the proprietor of a school has failed to comply with the requirements of the regulations, he may, on at least two months' notice in writing specifying the failings, order the deletion of the school from the register unless the proprietor satisfies him that the regulation in question has been complied with within the period of notice;[6]
(b) that the proprietor of, or a person employed at, a registered or provisionally registered school is prohibited or restricted under regulation, he may order that the school be struck off the Register, or that the Registrar not register the school in the first place.[7]

9.08 A school may also be deleted from the register by the Secretary of State if the proprietor fails to comply with regulations about providing and publishing information.[8]

Complaints about registered and provisionally registered schools   Independent Schools Tribunals

9.09 If the Secretary of State is satisfied that one or more specified grounds of complaint apply in repect of any registered or provisionally registered school, he is to serve notice of complaint on the proprietor, in which the grounds and

---

As to inspection, see the Inspection of Premises Children and Records (Independent Schools) Regulations 1991, SI 1991/1975 and para 8.29.
4   1996 Act s 466. As to proceedings see para 9.16.
5   1996 Act s 467(1) and (2). See SI 1982/1730 and para 12.57. An independent school is a 'children's home' under the Children Act 1989 s 63 when, in specified circumstances, accommodation is provided at the school, unless it is one approved by the Secretary of State under 1996 Act s 347 (see para 5.49).
6   1996 Act s 467(3). See SI 1982/1730.
7   1996 Act s 468. See the Education (Teachers) Regulations 1993, SI 1993/543, reg 10. In *R v Secretary of State for Education, ex p Standish* (1993) Times, 15 November, Potts J held that the Secretary of State should make express findings of fact and give reasons for his decision when debarring a teacher from his employment.
   By s 475 the Registrar is to act on an order striking a school off the Register as from the date when it takes effect.
8   1996 Act ss 467(4) and 537(9). See, as to regulations, para 12.57.

full particulars of the matters complained of are stated. The grounds specified are, briefly, as follows:
(a) the premises, in whole or part, are unsuitable;
(b) the accommodation is inadequate or unsuitable;
(c) efficient and suitable instruction[9] is not being provided;
(d) the proprietor of the school, teacher or other employee is personally unfit for that role;
(e) there has been a failure to comply with the duty under the Children Act 1989 section 87 regarding the welfare of a child accommodated at the school.

9.10 The Secretary of State's notice specifies how and by what time (not less than six months) the complaint is to be remedied unless he considers it irremediable. If the notice alleges that any teacher or other employee is not a proper person to be employed in any school the employee is to be named and the grounds of the allegation specified; and a copy of the notice is to be served on him. Notices are to specify the time (not less than one month) within which the complaint may be referred on appeal to an Independent Schools Tribunal.[10]

9.11 Appeals are made by sending the Secretary of State written notice stating the grounds, and if the complaint is that the employee is not a proper person (when employee, as well as proprietor may appeal) a copy of the notice is to be sent to the proprietor or employee (as the case may be). The Secretary of State then requests the Lord Chancellor and Lord President of the Council to constitute an Independent Schools Tribunal consisting of a chairman from the legal panel and two members from the educational panel.[11]

---

9 'Efficient and suitable instruction': a child's attendance at a registered independent school is not evidence that he is necessarily receiving suitable full-time education as required under 1996 Act s 7 (see AM 557). As from 30 April 1978 there has been no category of independent schools recognised as efficient by the Secretary of State; and most independent schools are no longer subject to statutory inspection (see para 8.08). Now the National Curriculum, although not applying as such to independent schools, may be relevant, throwing doubt on the decision in *Bevan v Shears* [1911] 2 KB 936, F[191].
  In *R v Secretary of State for Education and Science, ex p Talmud Torah Machzikei Hadass School Trust* (1985) Times, 12 April, F[85], Woolf J said that education catering for the special characteristics of a minority sect is suitable if it primarily equips a child for life within his own community, provided that it leaves him free in later years to adopt some other form of life.
10 1996 Act ss 469, 470(1) and 476. By s 469(6) 'employee' means a person whose employment brings him into regular contact with persons under 19. It seems that employment in an educational establishment which is not a school is not caught.
11 1996 Act Sch 34 and the Independent Schools Tribunal Rules 1958, SI 1958/519. Members of the legal panel are appointed by the Lord Chancellor and possess legal qualifications he considers suitable; members of the educational panel are appointed by the Lord President of the Council and possess experience he considers suitable in teaching or the conduct, management or administration of schools. No officer of a government department or a local government officer (other than a teacher) may be appointed to either panel. Remuneration is by the Secretary of State. The Lord Chancellor appoints a secretary to the Tribunal.
  Rules as to practice and procedure prescribe, inter alia, arrangements for the time and place of the hearings, rights of audience, procedures and interlocutory applications to the chairman. The decision of the Tribunal may be given orally at the hearing or in writing as soon as may be thereafter. The secretary sends a copy of the Tribunal's order with a statement of the findings to every appellant and to the Secretary of State. Part I of the Arbitration Act 1996 does not apply to proceedings before a Tribunal except so far as specifically applied by the rules.
  Tribunals are under the supervision of the Council on Tribunals (Tribunals and Inquiries Act 1992 s 1(1)(a), Sch 1 Pt I, para 15(a)). See also s 11 (appeals from a tribunal).

9.12 *Independent Schools*

9.12 Tribunals, after hearing evidence, may make one of five kinds of order:
(a) that the complaint be annulled;
(b) that the school be struck off the register;
(c) that the school be struck off unless it complies with the requirements of the notice (as may be modified by the order) within the period specified in the order and to the satisfaction of the Secretary of State;
(d) the premises be disqualified in whole or part for use as a school or from being used as accommodation for more than a number of pupils specified by age and sex;
(e) that the proprietor, teacher or other employee be disqualified from a position as such in any school.[12]

9.13 If notice of complaint is not referred by the proprietor to an Independent Schools Tribunal within the time specified, any of those orders may be made by the Secretary of State, unless the allegation is that a teacher or other employee is not a proper person to be employed as such in any school, in which case the Secretary of State may not make a disqualifying order if the employee refers the complaint in due time. Such an order, once made by Tribunal or Secretary of State, disqualifies the person concerned both from being proprietor of an independent school and from employment in any school, unless the order otherwise directs.[13]

9.14 It is an offence to use premises for purposes for which they are disqualified, and to act as the proprietor of an independent school or accept or attempt to obtain employment in a school while disqualified.[14]

9.15 If, on application, the Secretary of State is satisfied that any disqualification is no longer necessary by reason of change of circumstances, he may by order remove it. Should he fail to remove a disqualification the person aggrieved may appeal to an Independent Schools Tribunal in the same way as against a notice of complaint.[15]

9.16 Proceedings for an offence concerning registration or breach of a disqualification order may be instituted only by or on behalf of the Secretary of State. A person found guilty is liable on summary conviction to a fine not exceeding level 4 on the standard scale or up to three months' imprisonment, or both.[16]

---

12 1996 Act s 470(2). By s 477 an order made under the Education (Scotland) Act 1980 s 100 is of the same effect.
    By s 475 the Registrar is to act on an order striking a school off the register as from the date when it takes effect; by s 476(5) every order is to be registered by the Registrar and open to public inspection.
    For circumstances in which a proprietor was disqualified see *Byrd v Secretary of State for Education and Science* (1968) 112 Sol Jo 519, DC and (a teacher) *Gedge v Independent Schools Tribunal* (1959) Times, 7 October, DC.
13 1996 Act ss 471 and 472. By s 477 an order made under the Education (Scotland) Act 1980 s 100 is of the same effect.
14 1996 Act s 473.
15 1996 Act s 474.
16 1996 Act s 478.

ASSISTED PLACES AT INDEPENDENT SCHOOLS

9.17 The assisted places scheme is the subject matter of Chapter III of Part VII of the 1996 Act (sections 479 to 481, Schedule 35). The Education (Schools) Bill, introduced on 22 May 1997, proposes to bring the scheme to an end, while continuing to assist children who already hold assisted places.

The scheme

9.18 The Secretary of State operates the scheme, under regulations, to enable 'pupils who might not otherwise be able to do so to benefit from education at independent schools'. Participating schools are those registered independent schools, conducted for charitable purposes only, with which he has made a participation agreement. In deciding whether to enter into an agreement the Secretary of State is to have regard to the desirability of securing an equitable distribution of assisted places throughout England and Wales and as between boys and girls.[17]

9.19 A participation agreement is subject to conditions prescribed in regulations and may contain additional conditions. It refers to the number of assisted places at the school. The school remits the whole or part of fees of pupils selected for assisted places and is reimbursed by the Secretary of State. The fees covered are those for tuition, other fees which are a condition of attendance, and entrance fees for public examinations paid by the school, but not boarding fees and any other fees excluded under the agreement.

9.20 An agreement may be terminated only as provided: by school proprietors ordinarily on three years' notice, and by the Secretary of State on the same notice, or at any time if he (a) is satisfied that a condition has been contravened, or (b) is not satisfied about the educational standards of the school or about its compliance with the rule that a person is not to be excluded on grounds of his being exempted from corporal punishment (see para 15.15 ff). He is to state his reasons. Termination of an agreement is not adversely to affect a pupil holding an assisted place.[18]

9.21 Regulations, which give substance to the scheme, are to be the subject of prior consultation with the representatives of participating schools. Those regulations stating the conditions and extent of remission of fees are to be reviewed every two years. Each participating school is to publish particulars of the scheme, annual particulars of the number of places it is likely to offer, and examination results. Excluding pupils under the age of seven, at least 60 per cent of assisted pupils in any school year are to come from publicly maintained schools. The Secretary of State may require the submission of information and may specify the form of accounts, which are to be audited by an independent auditor.[19]

---

17 1996 Act s 479 as amended by the 1997 Act s 1. By sub-s (10) references to a school include proprietors and their agents.
18 1996 Act Sch 35.
19 1996 Act s 480 and the Education (Assisted Places) Regulations 1995, SI 1995/2016, as amended by SI 1996/2113, in which 'child' and other terms are defined.

9.22 *Independent Schools*

Eligibility for selection

9.22 To be eligible for selection[20] a child must satisfy conditions of which the following is an outline:

(a) he is either (i) to have been ordinarily resident in the British Islands throughout two years preceding 1 January in the calendar year in which his first assisted year begins, or (ii) to be a national of a state within the European Economic Area, ordinarily resident in that area throughout the same two years and entitled to equality of treatment under the EEC regulation (as extended by the EEA Agreement) on freedom of movement for workers, or (iii) to be a refugee who has not been ordinarily resident outside the British Islands since he, or his parent, was recognised as such or was granted leave to enter and remain;[1]

(b) he must have reached the age of five and, ordinarily, the normal school entry age, or will have reached both before 1 September at the end of his first assisted year;

(c) if following selection the child would be in the sixth form, either the participation agreement is to provide expressly for sixth form selection and the child satisfies any conditions specified, or, if he is already attending the school, the sixth form is to include assisted pupils admitted in an earlier school year;

(d) when applying to the school for an assisted place the parents are to provide information about their income; and

(e) a school is not to select a child for an assisted place unless satisfied that he is capable of benefiting from the education provided—the method of selection being at the school's discretion subject to any provisions in the participation agreement.

Remission of fees

9.23 The extent of remission of fees is governed by an income scale, and parents with a 'relevant income' below a certain figure are not required to make any payment towards the cost of the assisted place. Questions about entitlement to remission are settled by the school. The Secretary of State specifies various administrative arrangements, including the method of submitting and dealing with reimbursement claims.

Incidental expenses

9.24 Under separate regulations participating schools meet certain incidental expenses of assisted pupils and are reimbursed by the Secretary of State. Parents are paid grants for uniform and other (including sports) clothing, and towards

---

20 LEAs no longer have the power to veto the transfer of pupils from maintained schools to assisted places at independent schools. The revocation of that power by SI in 1983 followed a case in 1982 in which Derbyshire rejected the application by the father of a 17 year-old student who had applied to an independent school (and had been selected) for an assisted place to take a course which was not available at a maintained school. The Secretary of State then issued a direction under the 1944 Act s 68 requiring the authority to agree to the student's taking up the assisted place.

1 As to 'ordinary residence' see para 10.107. 'British Islands' means the United Kingdom, Channel Islands and Isle of Man (Interpretation Act 1978). The 'EEC regulation' is Council Regulation No 1612/68, Article 7(2) or (3) or 12.

expenditure on journeys actually made to and from school or to visit a parent, guardian or other relative, and to higher and further education establishments regarding admission. The amount of grant is determined by reference to parental relevant income and (travel grants) according as the pupil is a boarder or day pupil. Distance and mode of transport are also material in the calculation. The means of the parents also determine whether, or to what extent, a school remit part or the whole of charges they would otherwise make for meals provided for day pupils. Questions about the grants and remission of meals' charges are settled by the school in the same way as questions about remission of fees. Charges for specified field study courses leading to GCSE and 'A' level (and comparable) examinations are remitted if the parents are entitled to any remission of fees. There are general and administrative provisions along the lines of those in the principal regulations.[2]

CITY COLLEGES

9.25 These are the subject matter of Chapter IV of Part VII of the 1996 Act (sections 482 and 483).

9.26 The Secretary of State may enter into agreements under which he makes payments towards the establishment and running of independent schools to be known either as city technology colleges or as city colleges for the technology of the arts. The schools are (a) to be in an urban area, (b) to provide education for pupils of different abilities who are aged 11 or over and wholly or mainly drawn from that area, and (c) have a broad curriculum with an emphasis on science and technology or on the application of technology to the performing and creative arts. No charge is to be made for admission, or, except as permitted under the agreement, for education.

9.27 Requirements as to the training and teaching experience of teachers at city colleges who seek to become qualified teachers (see para 13.16) have effect. Other conditions and requirements may be imposed, for example that provision for religious worship and education is broadly in line with that in maintained schools, and that the National Curriculum is followed so far as is appropriate.[3]

9.28 Payments may relate to capital or current expenditure, or both, and are ordinarily (current expenditure) to be made for at least seven years, provided that conditions and requirements are met. Notice of discontinuance of an agreement is to be of equal length. In the event of a change of characteristics or discontinuance of a college the Secretary of State is to receive repayments calculated by reference to the value of the premises and other assets and to his contribution to those assets. An indemnity against expenditure incurred by the

---

2 1996 Act s 481 and the Education (Assisted Places) (Incidental Expenses) Regulations 1995, SI 1995/2017.
3 1996 Act s 482. In *R v Haberdashers' Aske's Hatcham College Trust (Governors), ex p Tyrell* [1995] ELR 350, it was held that decisions made by city technology colleges on pupil admissions are amenable to judicial review, because the Secretary of State is able to exercise some control over them.

9.28 *Independent Schools*

promoters (otherwise than to meet repayments as above) may be included in an agreement to cover its termination by the Secretary of State.[4]

9.29 The Secretary of State may by order authorise a funding authority to make and receive payments under agreements he has entered into, and any receipts are to be passed to him.[5]

---

4 1996 Act s 483. By s 485 the Secretary of State may also pay grants to the colleges. See the Education (Grants) (City Technology Colleges) Regulations 1987, SI 1987/1138.
5 1996 Act Sch 3 para 2. An order is to be made by SI.

Chapter 10

FURTHER AND HIGHER EDUCATION

10.01 The law derives mainly from two White Papers, *Education and Training for the 21st Century*, Cm 1536, 1991 and *Higher Education: a new framework*, Cm 1541, 1991. It is now chiefly, but by no means exclusively, to be found in the Further and Higher Education Act 1992, in two Parts on further and higher education respectively. Recent legislation has largely eroded the functions of LEAs. Those that remain are mentioned at para 10.87 ff.

10.02 Further education is full-time and part-time education for persons over compulsory school age (including vocational, social, physical and recreational training) and associated organised leisure-time occupation, unless it is higher education or (a) it is full-time, suitable for those under 19 and provided at a school for younger pupils or (b) it is provided for persons of 19 and over who began courses of secondary education before becoming 18. In those cases it is secondary education.[1] Higher education is defined by reference to specified courses, of which most lead to degrees and higher professional examinations.[2]

COUNCILS AND SECTORS

10.03 Funding councils have been established for both further and higher education (see paras 10.05 ff and 10.56 ff). They may act jointly if they consider it more efficient or effective to do so, and the Secretary of State may direct them to do so to monitor academic standards in the higher education sector (see para 10.04) institutions.[3]

10.04 The further education sector comprises institutions conducted by further education corporations (see para 10.20 ff) and the designated institutions mentioned at para 10.31 ff. The higher education sector comprises universities (see para 10.78 ff), institutions conducted by higher education corporations (see para 10.66 ff) and the designated institutions mentioned on para 10.74 ff.[4] The 'binary line' is erased.

1 1996 Act s 2. 'Organised leisure-time occupation' refers to cultural training and recreative activities for persons over compulsory school age.
2 1996 Act s 579 and 1988 Act Sch 6.
3 1992 FHE Act s 82. This section gives the Secretary of State reserve powers in respect of a proposed Quality Audit Unit in higher education. See *R v Universities Funding Council, ex p Institute of Dental Surgery* [1994] COD 147, DC.
4 1992 FHE Act s 91. By the 1988 Act s 157 the trust deeds of higher education corporations and designated institutions may be varied by the Privy Council.

10.05 *Further and Higher Education*

FURTHER EDUCATION

Further Education Funding Councils

10.05   Further Education Funding Councils, for England and for Wales, are appointed by the Secretary of State. The funding councils are corporate bodies, consisting of between (England) 12 and 15, (Wales) 8 and 12, members, including a chairman. In making appointments the Secretary of State is to take into account the desirability of including persons with experience of, and capacity in (a) providing, or having responsibility for providing, education (preferably, currently, further education) and (b) industrial, commercial or financial matters or the practice of any profession.[5]

10.06   The Secretary of State settles the amounts of the grants which finance the councils and the conditions of payment (which are not to apply to individual institutions).[6] The councils are to secure the provision of sufficient facilities for full-time education suitable for those of the 16 to 18 year-old population of their area who want it,[7] and adequate facilities for (i) part-time education for those over compulsory school age and (ii) full-time education for those of 19 and over through specified courses (which may be changed by order of the Secretary of State).[8]

10.07   The courses specified are at present those
(a)   which prepare students to obtain a vocational qualification approved by the Secretary of State;
(b)   which prepare students to qualify for a GCSE, A level or AS level (including special papers);
(c)   approved by the Secretary of State, which prepare students for entry to a course of higher education ('access courses');
(d)   which prepare students for entry to any of the courses listed above ('return to learn' courses);
(e)   for basic literacy in English;
(f)   to improve the knowledge of English of those for whom English is not the language spoken at home ('English for Speakers of Other Languages');
(g)   to teach the basic principles of mathematics;
(h)   (in Wales) for proficiency or literacy in Welsh; and
(i)   to teach independent living and communication skills to persons having learning difficulties, which prepare them for entry to another course falling within paragraphs (d) to (h) above.

10.08   Councils are to make the most effective use of their resources, avoid disproportionate expenditure and have regard to provision in (a) schools—where much of the full-time education of 16 to 18 year-olds continues to take place—and (b), as regards part-time education, institutions outside the further or higher education sector. There is a requirement to take account of different

---

5 1992 FHE Act s 1. Schedule 1 sets out the conditions which govern how each council are to function. It includes details of their powers, membership, status and operating procedures.
6 1992 FHE Act s 7.
7 1992 FHE Act s 2.
8 1992 FHE Act s 3 and Sch 2. Orders are to be made by SI.

abilities and aptitudes, and a power to provide education for those from outside their area.

10.09 There are special requirements with regard to persons with learning difficulties. Where facilities in institutions within the further or higher education sectors are inadequate for those who are over compulsory school age, councils have a *duty* to secure provision of education outside those sectors (ie in specialist institutions), with boarding accommodation if necessary, if the person is under 25 and it is in his best interests; otherwise they have a *power*.[9]

10.10 The funding councils may give financial support
(a) for the provision of facilities for (i) further education, to the governing bodies of further and higher education sector institutions, (ii) higher education, to the governing bodies of further education sector institutions, including in each case support for related facilities and activities;
(b) for the purposes of any educational institution to be conducted by a further education corporation, including its establishment, to that corporation;
(c) for persons with learning difficulties, to persons other than (i) LEAs, (ii) the governing bodies of grant-maintained schools and (iii) those maintaining or carrying on a city college; and
(d) for the provision of training, advice or the carrying on of research or other activities relevant to the provision of further education facilities, to any person.

10.11 Financial support may be by grants, loans or other payments, and on terms and conditions the council think fit, including (a) repayment in case of non-compliance and payment of interest on sums due, and (b) the publication of a 'disability statement' about the provision of facilities for the disabled at an institution.[10]

10.12 Before settling terms and conditions funding councils are to consult representative bodies and the governing bodies of particular institutions concerned. In exercising their functions they are to have regard to the desirability of not discouraging funding from other sources, and so far as they think appropriate are to maintain a balance between denominational and other institutions.[11]

10.13 The governing body of an institution outside the further education

---

9   1992 FHE Act s 4. 'Learning difficulty': see para 5.04. As to refusal by the Further Education Funding Council to fund a place for a student with learning difficulties see *R v Further Education Funding Council, ex p Parkinson* [1997] 2 FCR 67.
10 1992 FHE Act s 5. Although most further education which the councils fund is provided in or through further education sector institutions, they may also support further education in higher education institutions which provide some further education courses formerly funded by LEAs.
    See the Education (Disability Statements for Further Education Institutions) Regulations 1996, SI 1996/1664 and WO 48/96. (By the 1996 Act s 528 (not yet in force) every LEA are to publish 'disability statements', as prescribed, about the further education provision they make for disabled persons.)
    The provisions in (c) are applied by the Education (Grant-maintained Special Schools) Regulations 1994, SI 1994/653, reg 42, Schedule, Pt I; and by the Education (Special Schools Conducted by Education Associations) Regulations 1994, SI 1994/1084, reg 8(1), Sch 2, Pt I.
11 1992 FHE Act s 6(1) to (4).

10.13 *Further and Higher Education*

sector may ask the governing body of an institution within the sector (the sponsoring body) to apply on their behalf to a council for financial support for part-time or adult education courses of the description given at para 10.07; but only if there are no, or inadequate, alternative facilities in the area of the sponsoring body and it is one of a description specified by order of the Secretary of State.[12]

10.14 Each funding council are to
(a) give the Secretary of State information and advice when he asks for it or on their own initiative;
(b) keep activities eligible for funding under review;
(c) take over the Secretary of State's functions, at his direction, in respect of payments he made to institutions before the council were established (making any repayments to him immediately);
(d) undertake any supplementary functions the Secretary of State gives them by order; and
(e) report annually to the Secretary of State on the provision of further education for disabled students.[13]

10.15 The councils are to assess the quality of education in institutions they support through Quality Assessment Committees (to whom they may give other functions). The majority of committee members are not to be members of the council but are to be persons with successful experience and demonstrated capacity in further education provision, and preferably currently engaged or carrying responsibility in it. HM Chief Inspector of Schools for Wales is to assess the quality of education in further education sector institutions or other institutions to which the council for Wales give, or might give, financial support, if the council for Wales ask him to do so.[14]

10.16 Councils may by notice require the governing bodies of further education sector institutions which provide full-time education for 16 to 18 year-olds to provide for named individuals education appropriate to their abilities and aptitudes.[15]

10.17 Councils may require information from LEAs and governing bodies of (a) LEA institutions, grant-maintained schools and city colleges, (b) any institution in the further or higher education sector, and (c) any institution which receives or has received financial support as mentioned at paras 10.10 and 10.11 above. Governing bodies are to give LEAs the information they need to make recoupment claims (see para 11.17 ff).[16]

10.18 In exercising their functions councils are to comply with directions in

---

12 1992 FHE Act s 6(5) and (6). See the Further Education (Sponsoring Bodies) Order 1992, SI 1992/2400.
13 1992 FHE Act s 8. An order is to be by SI. 'Disabled students' are disabled persons under the Disability Discrimination Act 1995 (see para 14.11).
14 1992 FHE Act s 9 and Sch 1. Quality Assessment Committees are subject to the same provisions as apply to other committees established by a council.
15 1992 FHE Act s 52.
16 1992 FHE Act s 54. See, generally, Circular 9/96 'The Parent's Charter: Publication of Information about the Performance of Colleges in the Further Education Sector in 1996'.
   Section 54 is applied as in n 10 above.

an order made by the Secretary of State. Directions may be general or special, and the latter may relate in particular to financial support for activities carried on by particular institutions.[17]

10.19 No function of a funding council is to be construed as relating to any person detained, otherwise than at a school, in pursuance of an order made by a court or of an order of recall made by the Secretary of State.[18]

Further education corporations

10.20 Before the appointed day (30 September 1992) the Secretary of State specified by order the institutions which were to become further education corporations as from the operative date (1 April 1993), namely
(a) institutions maintained by LEAs with an enrolment number on 1 November 1990 of full-time and other (sandwich etc course) students following further or higher education courses (calculated in accordance with a formula[19]), not less than 15 per cent of their total enrolment number, and
(b) county, controlled and grant-maintained schools at which on 17 January 1991 not less than 60 per cent of the pupils were receiving full-time education suitable for 16 to 18 year-olds (sixth-form colleges).[20]

10.21 The Secretary of State may by order establish additional corporations to conduct institutions from a specified operative date
(i) subject in the case of existing institutions to the consent of the governing body, and not for an LEA institution or a grant-maintained school unless, at the time, it passes the 15 per cent test (as in (a) above) or is principally a sixth form college;
(ii) on the proposition of a funding council, to conduct an LEA institution or a grant-maintained school which is principally concerned with the provision of further or higher education or is a sixth-form college.[1]

10.22 Changes in the balance of a college's provision may bring it automatically within the criteria under (i) but even if it does not do so it may be proposed for further education corporation status if it meets the criteria under (ii).

10.23 The Secretary of State may, by order, dissolve a further education corporation, first having consulted the corporation and the funding council; and also thereby transfer property, rights and liabilities to (a) persons or corporate bodies engaged in the provision of education, or (b) a further or higher

---

17 1992 FHE Act s 56. Orders are to be made by SI. The reserve power to give directions reflects the Secretary of State's ultimate responsibility to Parliament for the Government's further education funding policy.
18 1992 FHE Act s 60. The section is analogous to s 562(1) of the 1996 Act (see para 15.02). It preserves the existing statutory position in relation to the education of prisoners, and means, in particular, that the councils' duties to secure the provision of further education under the 1992 FHE Act ss 2 and 3 do not apply to prisoners.
19 The formula is in the 1992 FHE Act Sch 3.
20 1992 FHE Act ss 15 and 17. The operative date was appointed under the Education (Further Education Corporations) Order 1992, SI 1992/2097. That order also specified institutions, as did subsequent SIs.
1 1992 FHE Act ss 16 and 17. The Secretary of State has made several orders, by SI. Section 16(2) has been applied as in n 10 above.

10.23 *Further and Higher Education*

education funding council (in either case with the consent of the person or body). Property is to be transferred on trust for exclusively educational charitable purposes.²

10.24 When a further education funding council make a proposal to the Secretary of State to establish or to dissolve a further education corporation they are to publish it in a prescribed form and consider representations made on it. Copies of the draft and of representations are to be sent to the Secretary of State. The Secretary of State is to publish the draft of an order establishing a further education corporation which does not derive from a council's proposal.³

10.25 The principal powers of further education corporations are provision of further and higher education and supply of related goods and services, which include those resulting from the use, or making available, of the corporation's facilities, or from the expertise or ideas of employees or the ideas of students.⁴

10.26 A corporation may do anything necessary or expedient which is ancillary to those powers. In addition to conducting an educational institution from the operative date on which it is established, they may, in particular, provide associated facilities (including boarding accommodation, recreational facilities and facilities for students with learning difficulties), acquire and dispose of land, enter into contracts (including contracts of employment), borrow (subject to the consent of the appropriate council), invest, accept gifts and do incidental things such as founding scholarships and giving prizes.⁵

10.27 Corporations are to conduct institutions in accordance with instruments and articles of government.⁶ These are prescribed, in the case of former grant-maintained schools, by the order incorporating them; otherwise by regulation. Existing members of a governing body may be made initial members of the corporation, or other arrangements prescribed to secure continuity.⁷ (The

2 1992 FHE Act s 27. Many orders have been made, by SI. Orders may apply 1992 FHE Act s 26 (see para 10.30), with modifications, so as to enable the Secretary of State to provide for transfer of staff. 'Charitable purposes': as defined in the Charities Act 1960.
3 1992 FHE Act s 51. See the Education (Publication of Draft Proposals and Orders) (Further Education Corporations) Regulations 1992, SI 1992/2361.
4 1992 FHE Act s 18.
5 1992 FHE Act s 19. The Department for Education and Employment take the view that despite the absence of an express power (as is in the 1988 Act s 124(2)) further education corporations may form other bodies corporate, because the terms of s 19(1) are slightly more open and because the supply of goods and services is a principal function of a further education corporation but not of a higher education corporation.
6 1992 FHE Act s 20 and Sch 4. The basic provisions in the instrument are the number of members of the corporation; eligibility for membership; arrangements for appointment of members; officers to be chosen from among the members; authentication of application of the seal; keeping of accounts; appointment of a principal; allocation of powers as between the corporation, its officers or committees and the principal; appointment, promotion, suspension and dismissal of staff; and admission, suspension and expulsion of students. There are also optional provisions, and detailed contents of instruments and articles are prescribed in orders or regulations.
7 1992 FHE Act s 21. In the case of former grant-maintained schools the existing statutory corporation is dissolved on the date the further education corporation begins to conduct the institution.
See the Education (Government of Further Education Corporations) (Former Sixth-Form Colleges) Regulations 1992, SI 1992/1957 and the Education (Government of Further Education Corporations) (Former Further Education Colleges) Regulations 1992, SI 1992/1963. Other regulations have been made relating to particular institutions.

Government intended that there should no longer be LEA representatives, but members or officers of a local authority could serve in a personal capacity.)

10.28 Corporations may replace or modify their initial instruments and articles with the consent, and (in the case of instruments) by order, of the Secretary of State. He is to consult the appropriate council on a draft instrument, or modification, submitted by a corporation, and not make one otherwise than in accordance with the draft without first consulting the corporation. On his own initiative he may, by order, modify instruments, having first consulted the council and corporations affected; and he may, by direction, and after consulting them, require corporations to modify articles and rules or bye-laws.[8]

10.29 Property, rights and liabilities are with some exceptions transferred to corporations on the operative date, without compensation, from LEAs and the governing bodies of their institutions and of grant-maintained schools. The exceptions—in the case of property etc formerly held by a local authority—are (a) their liabilities in respect of any loan (see para 10.42), and (b) land (with any related rights and liabilities) excluded by agreement, and with the Secretary of State's approval, before the operative date, or, in default of agreement, by order on his direction.[9]

10.30 Staff employed solely at an LEA institution or grant-maintained school which is transferred to a corporation automatically become their employees. Staff employed partly elsewhere are transferred only if the subject of a designation order. Contracts of employment continue to have effect as if made with the corporation, unless terminated by the employee on grounds of substantial worsening of working conditions.[10]

Designated institutions

10.31 The Secretary of State may by order designate, as also eligible to receive funds from a funding council, an educational institution which is principally concerned with providing full-time education for 16 to 18 year-olds, or courses of further or higher education (or both), and is either
(a) a voluntary aided school,

[8] 1992 FHE Act s 22.
[9] 1992 FHE Act ss 23 and 25. Agreements may include terms on which the land is to be used; directions may confer rights and liabilities to the same effect. The Further Education (Exclusion of Land from Transfer) Order 1993, SI 1993/901 and the (No 2) Order, SI 1993/937, relate to land held by specified local authorities.
By s 24 provision is made for (a) the transfer of rights and liabilities in relation to the supply of goods and services which arise as by-products of a college's educational activities (see para 10.94 ff), (b) the continuation of existing arrangements for the supply of goods and services by a local authority to a further education corporation supplied originally under competitive tendering agreements, and (c) the transfer of an interest in land owned by a local authority to a further education corporation under 1992 FHE Act s 23, whether or not it is by virtue of that interest that the land was used by the institution conducted by the corporation.
[10] 1992 FHE Act s 26. See the Education (Further Education Corporations) (Designated Staff) Order 1993, 1993/465 and the Education (Further Education Corporations) (Designated Staff) (Wales) Order 1993, 1993/612. There is an exception to automatic transfer relating to local authority direct service organisation staff: see the Further and Higher Education Act (Commencement No 1 and Transitional Provisions) Order 1992, SI 1992/831 as amended by SI 1992/2041.
As to the effect of EEC Business Transfers Directive 77/87 see *Kenny v South Manchester College* [1993] IRLR 265.

10.31 *Further and Higher Education*

(b) an institution (other than a school) assisted by an LEA, or
(c) an institution not maintained by an LEA which is, or is eligible to be, grant-aided.[11]

10.32 Institutions which are designated enter the further education sector, like those incorporated as above. Examples are voluntary aided sixth-form colleges, and colleges which provide long-term residential education for adults. The intention was broadly to retain their existing status and the composition of their governing bodies. The Secretary of State took power, as follows, however, to ensure that their government is consistent with the needs of the further education sector.

10.33 Institutions other than those conducted by companies or exempted unincorporated associations are to have instruments and articles of government. These are to be approved by the Secretary of State, having been in force before designation or made under a pre-existing regulatory instrument (or, in its absence, by the governing body); or he may make them himself by order. The governing body may modify an approved instrument or articles. The Secretary of State (and no other person without his consent) may also do so, after consultation so far as practicable with the governing body and any other persons having the power to make or modify.[12]

10.34 The articles of association of companies which conduct designated institutions are to incorporate instruments and articles of government. The Secretary of State may, after consulting the persons in charge, give them directions to amend the memorandum or articles of association and any rules or bye-laws. Any other amendments are subject to the Secretary of State's approval.[13]

10.35 Where an institution is in category (a) or (b) in para 10.31, the designating order provides for transfer, with some exceptions, of property, rights and liabilities from LEA to trustees or a company, as appropriate. The exceptions, and the consequential functions of the Secretary of State, are similar to those in relation to transfers to further education corporations (see para 10.20 ff above), with the substitution of 'designation date' for 'operative date'.[14] Some of the designated institutions already owned much of their land and property, but some leased or rented property from the local authority. The consequence of

---

11 1992 FHE Act s 28. By the 1996 Act s 579(6) 'assisted' means that the institution receives a grant from one or more LEAs. 'Grant-aided' refers to grants made by the Secretary of State, under the 1996 Act s 485 and the Education (Grant) Regulations 1990, SI 1990/1989.
  See the Education (Designated Institutions in Further Education) (Wales) Order 1993, SI 1993/215, the Education (Designated Institutions in Further Education) Order 1993, SI 1993/435 and the Education (Designated Institutions in Further Education) (No 2) Order 1993, SI 1993/562.
12 1992 FHE Act s 29. 'Exempted unincorporated associations' are bodies exempted by the designation order, such as the Workers' Educational Association, which are not colleges and do not have articles and instruments of government; 'a regulatory instrument' means any instrument or articles of government or other instrument of similar effect.
  See SI 1993/215 and SI 1993/435.
  Notwithstanding the provisions of s 29, by s 30 the instrument of government of a former voluntary aided sixth-form college is to provide for a majority of the governors to be 'foundation' governors (see para 3.48).
13 1992 FHE Act s 31.
14 1992 FHE Act s 32. The designation orders are SI 1993/215 and SI 1993/435.

this provision is that designated institutions have responsibility for managing and maintaining their capital assets.

10.36 Subject to the general provisions about property held on trust mentioned below (para 10.40), when trustees are the transferees the designation order specifies the trusts which are applicable under the trust deed. If there is no deed the property is held on trust for the general purposes of the institution. Trustees incur no personal liability in respect of transferred property but may apply property they hold on trust to meet liabilities. Any subsisting interest of a local authority in land used for the purposes of an institution is to be taken to be held for that purpose, whether or not the land is so used by virtue of that interest.[15]

Additional property for further education institutions

10.37 The Secretary of State was empowered to provide by order for local authority property to be made available to a further education sector institution where the property had been used within the preceding six months for further education and the LEA had ceased, or intended to cease, that use. The power was designed to meet circumstances in which an LEA had property adapted for courses (eg on basic skills) falling within the ambit of the funding councils, but had decided to take it out of use, although in the opinion of the governing body of the institution the courses were still needed for local people.[16]

10.38 It was provided that orders might transfer the property and associated rights or liabilities (except loan liabilities) to the governing body, and confer rights or liabilities. They might be made only when the governing body (a) needed the property for the purposes of the institution, (b) had been unable to secure its use by agreement with the local authority, and (c) applied to the Secretary of State within three years of the operative date for initial further education corporations (by 1 April 1996). Before making an order the Secretary of State was to consult the appropriate further education council, the local authority and the Education Assets Board (see Appendix 5).

10.39 Provision was made for continuity of employment of persons who ceased to be employed by a local authority in consequence of an order as above and who were recruited by the governing body of the transferred institution.[17]

General provisions about transfers to further education corporations and designated institutions

10.40 Where any land or other property or rights transferred were held on trust for the purposes of an institution immediately before the operative date (see paras 10.20 and 10.21) they continue to be so held by the transferee; and competitive tendering arrangements for supply of goods and services to an institution by a local authority take effect on the operative date as if contained in an agreement between the local authority and the further education corporation.[18]

15 1992 FHE Act s 33. The designation orders are SI 1993/215 and SI 1993/435.
16 1992 FHE Act s 34. Orders were made by SI.
17 1992 FHE Act s 35.
18 1992 FHE Act s 36. Together with Sch 5 (supplemented by Sch 7) this section also specifies the role of the Education Assets Board in settling differences of opinion between local authorities and institutions by identifying and apportioning property (see Appendix 5).

10.41 Provision is also made for the attribution to further education sector institutions of surpluses and deficits relating to LEA, and designated assisted, institutions which immediately before transfer were covered by a financial delegation scheme (see para 3.76).[19]

Excepted loan liabilities

10.42 The funding councils may make payments to local authorities in respect of the principal of, and interest on, 'excepted' loan liabilities—liabilities associated with property authorities have transferred to further education corporations and designated institutions. The Secretary of State has power to determine certain matters, such as rates of interest, by order.[20]

Control of disposals of land

10.43 Local authorities are to obtain the consent of the Secretary of State before disposing of land held, used or obtained from 21 March 1991 for the purposes of an institution which is to transfer to the further education sector.[1] Powers are granted to the Education Assets Board in case of wrongful disposal.[2]

Control of contracts

10.44 Local authorities entering into contracts between 21 March 1991 and 6 March 1992 (when the 1992 FHE Act was passed) were to obtain the prior consent of the governing body of an institution if the contract might bind them on its transferring to the further education sector; and where the contract had a value of £50,000 or more the local authority had also to obtain the consent of the Secretary of State.[3] The Education Assets Board were empowered to repudiate a contract made without consent before it was performed. If a contract was repudiated a claim could be made against the local authority.[4]

Collective worship and religious education

10.45 The governing body of every further education institution, except those which were colleges of further education on 30 September 1992, are to ensure

---

19 1992 FHE Act s 37. A 'designated assisted institution' is one designated by the Education (Schools and Further and Higher Education) Regulations 1989, SI 1989/351 Sch 1 (namely Cordwainers Technical College, London, and Morley College) dependent on an LEA for its maintenance.
   See the Further Education (Attribution of Surpluses and Deficits) Regulations 1993, SI 1993/609 and regulations applying to particular institutions, and *Birmingham City Council v Birmingham College of Food and Sutton Coldfield College* [1996] ELR 1 and (1996) 1 July, unreported.
20 1992 FHE Act s 38. The councils have been responsible, since 1 April 1992, for reimbursing debt charges to local authorities provided that (a) the relevant contract was entered into after 31 March 1991 (b) it has a value of £50,000 or more and (c) the total value of debts arising does not exceed the relevant annual capital guidelines and/or supplementary credit approvals for 1991-2 and 1992-3.
   See also Circular 1/93 (WO 15/93), 'The Further and Higher Education Act 1992', para 41, E[1815].
1 1992 FHE Act s 39.
2 1992 FHE Act s 40.
3 1992 FHE Act s 41. Consent could be given, unconditionally or subject to conditions, in respect of a particular contract or contracts of any class or description; and certain classes of contract were excepted.
4 1992 FHE Act s 42.

that a collective act of worship which students may attend is held at least once a week; and that religious education—which may include courses leading to examinations and qualifications—is provided for all who wish to receive it. Worship is to be wholly or mainly broadly Christian, and education is to reflect that religious traditions in Great Britain are mainly Christian; but provision may be made for worship reflecting other religious traditions prevalent in Great Britain, and education is to take them into account. Worship and education at former voluntary schools (including those which became grant-maintained schools) are to comply with any trust deed and reflect their traditions and practices.[5]

Variation of trust deeds

10.46 The Secretary of State may modify, by order, the trust deed or other instrument relating to, or regulating, an institution in the further education sector or relating to the land and other property held for the purposes of the institution, after first consulting, so far as practicable, the governing body of the institution, and any others with power to modify or replace the trust deed or instrument, including the trustees (if different).[6] The main purpose of this provision is to ensure that trust deeds of institutions are consistent with the principles governing the establishment of the further education sector or the conduct of other further education institutions, as appropriate.

Approval of new premises Health hazards

10.47 The requirements follow those mentioned at para 15.03 ff.[7]

Transfer of higher education institutions to the further education sector

10.48 Many colleges provide a mix of further and higher education. If the balance changes it may be appropriate to transfer an institution from one sector to the other.[8] The Secretary of State may by order provide for the transfer of a higher education corporation to the further education sector. The provisions relating to the constitution of a further education corporation have effect, as do those concerning initial instruments and articles; and those need, in particular, to conform to the general pattern prescribed for further education institutions (see para 10.27).[9]

---

5 1992 FHE Act ss 44 and 45. (These sections are not fully in force: see SI 1992/831 Sch 3.)
6 1992 FHE Act s 46. There is an analogous provision in relation to institutions conducted by higher education corporations (see para 10.66 ff).
7 1988 Act s 218 (1)(e), (7) and (10). See the Education (Schools and Further and Higher Education) Regulations 1989, SI 1989/351, regs 7 and 8.
8 For transfer from the further to the higher education sector see paras 10.68 and 10.74 n 15.
9 1992 FHE Act s 47. The order (by SI) may make any provision in relation to a higher education corporation that may be made in an order specifying a grant-maintained school under s 15 (see para 10.20).
   By sub-s (4) an order made under s 28 (which designates institutions as eligible to receive support from a further education funding council) may revoke any order made under the 1988 Act s 129 (which, as amended by the 1992 FHE Act s 72, designates institutions as eligible to receive support from a higher education funding council—see para 10.56 ff).

10.49 *Further and Higher Education*

Conditions of employment

10.49 The Secretary of State was empowered to authorise pay increases by LEAs, with an effective date later than 1 September 1992, to employees of institutions transferring to the further education sector except teachers in former sixth-form colleges (whose remuneration was set by a school teachers' pay and conditions order) (see para 13.63).

10.50 School teachers employed by an LEA or the governing body of a voluntary or grant-maintained school at an institution transferring to the sector whose pay and conditions were determined by a pay and conditions order immediately before the transfer, continue to be subject to those orders until such time as their contracts are varied.[10]

10.51 To give employers within the further education sector discretion to make decisions about redundancy, provision is made to annul any part of a contract which states that an employee may not be dismissed by reason of redundancy, or, if so dismissed is to be paid a sum in excess of the employer's liability under Part XI of the Employment Rights Act 1996; but contracts relating specifically to pending dismissal through redundancy are not rendered void.[11]

Information regarding institutions and their students

10.52 The Secretary of State may make regulations requiring the governing body of an institution within the further education sector to publish information about educational provision made or proposed; educational achievements of students on entry to, and while at, the institution; the financial resources of the institution and the use made of them; and the careers of their students after completing a course or leaving the institution. Conditions relating to the publication of the information may be prescribed, but no student is to be named.[12]

Accounts

10.53 The accounts of further education corporations and designated institutions are open to inspection by the Comptroller and Auditor General, who is head of the National Audit Office, so far as relating to moneys received under the 1992 Further and Higher Education Act.[13]

---

10 1992 FHE Act ss 43 and 48.
11 1992 FHE Act s 49.
12 1992 FHE Act s 50. See the Education (Further Education Institutions Information) (England) Regulations 1995, SI 1995/2065; and the Education (Further Education Institutions Information) (Wales) Regulations 1993, SI 1993/2169.
   Under the 1996 Act s 541 the Secretary of State may by regulations require information published under s 50 to be provided by (a) governing bodies and (b) proprietors of city colleges, to persons prescribed by the regulations (see para 12.62).
   See Circular 9/95, 'Local publication and distribution of information about the achievements of students in Further Education sector colleges'.
13 1992 FHE Act s 53. See the 1988 Act s 220(4) about advice by the Audit Commission on accounts.

Mismanagement and breach of duty

10.54 If the Secretary of State concludes that the affairs of a further education sector institution have been mismanaged, he may, by order, on the recommendation of a funding council, replace members of the governing body and modify the instrument of government. He may also by order give directions for the enforcement of any duty that a council or governing body have failed to discharge, has power to prevent unreasonable exercise of functions by a governing body, and may hold a local inquiry.[14]

Reorganisations of schools involving establishment of further education corporations

10.55 Provision is made for transfer of ownership of local authority land where closure or significant change in character or enlargement of premises of LEA schools in connection with their reorganisation involves the establishment of an institution to be conducted by a further education corporation, whether or not a new school or schools are to be established under the reorganisation.[15]

HIGHER EDUCATION

The Funding Councils

10.56 In succession to the Universities Funding Council and the Polytechnics and Colleges Funding Council the Secretary of State has appointed Higher Education Funding Councils, for England and for Wales. They are corporate bodies, consisting of (England) between 12 and 15, (Wales) 8 and 12, members, including a chairman. In making appointments the Secretary of State is to take into account the desirability of including persons with experience of, and capacity in (a) providing, or having responsibility for providing, higher education (preferably currently) and (b) industrial, commercial or financial matters or the practice of any profession.[16]

10.57 The councils are to have regard to the requirements of disabled persons.[17]

10.58 The Secretary of State finances the councils by grants, specifying the amounts and imposing conditions (on breach of which he may require repayments and interest on late payments). Conditions are to include the publication of disability statements by governing bodies. To promote his policies he may add requirements relating generally to the institutions (or a class of institutions) supported by the councils, but not terms and conditions relating to activities at

---

14 1992 FHE Act s 57. See the 1996 Act ss 496 and 507. In the case of an allegation that members of a governing body had acted ultra vires, application to the courts for judicial review was in order: see para 15.41 ff and *Herring v Templeman* [1973] 2 All ER 581, F[70].
15 1992 FHE Act s 58.
16 1992 FHE Act ss 62, 63 and 64. Schedule 1 sets out the conditions which govern how each council are to function. It includes details of their powers, membership, status and operating procedures. See the Education (PCFC and UGC Staff) Order 1993, SI 1993/434.
17 See the 1992 FHE Act s 62 (7A) and (7B).

10.58 *Further and Higher Education*

particular institutions; and the requirements are not to refer to particular courses of study or research programmes, or selection of staff and students.[18]

10.59 The property, rights and liabilities of the UFC and the PCFC were transferred to the funding councils for England and Wales. Staff were transferred to either of the new councils or to the Scottish Higher Education Funding Council.

10.60 The councils use their funds to make grants, loans or other payments, subject to the terms and conditions they specify (on breach of which repayments and interest on late payments may be required), for
(a) the purposes of education, research and connected activities, to the governing bodies of institutions within the higher education sector (having first consulted representative bodies and governing bodies as appropriate),
(b) providing services in support of the above, and
(c) the provision of prescribed courses of higher education at institutions maintained or assisted by LEAs or which are within the further education sector.

10.61 The councils are to consider the desirability of not discouraging funding from other sources (such as industry, commerce, benefactors, alumni and fee income), and, other things being equal, of keeping a balance between denominational and other institutions, and of maintaining the distinctive characteristics of institutions, for example the vocational emphasis of colleges and former polytechnics.[19]

10.62 The supplementary functions of councils are
(a) to give information and advice to the Secretary of State, if he requires it or on their own initiative,
(b) to keep the activities eligible for funding under review,
(c) to provide advice on higher education in Northern Ireland, on terms agreed with the appropriate Northern Ireland Departments,
(d) on the direction of the Secretary of State, to exercise his functions in relation to property in which he has an interest, and
(e) to undertake, on the order of the Secretary of State, additional supplementary functions—in effect taking over one or more of his own functions in relation to institutions (i) in the higher education sector, or (ii) in the further education sector or maintained or assisted by LEAs, at which prescribed courses of higher education are provided.[20]

10.63 Each council are to assess the quality of education in institutions they

18 1992 FHE Act ss 65 and 68.
19 1992 FHE Act ss 65 and 66. See the Education (Prescribed Courses of Higher Education) (Wales) Regulations 1993, SI 1993/481.
   By the 1988 Act s 133 the councils may make certain payments to persons of a prescribed description employed in further or higher education (see the Education (PCFC) (Prescribed Expenditure) Regulations 1991, SI 1991/2307); and the 1994 Act s 18 authorises them to reimburse specified institutions for safeguarding or supplementing salaries of certain training college etc teachers.
   As to failure to give reasons regarding an unsuccessful application for a research grant see *R v Higher Education Funding Council, ex p Institute of Dental Surgery* [1994] 1 WLR 242, DC.
20 1992 FHE Act s 69. Orders are to be made by SI.

support (or might support) through a Quality Assessment Committee, to whom they may give other functions. The majority of members of the committee are not to be members of the council but are to be persons with successful experience, and preferably currently engaged, in higher education sector provision. The committee are subject to the same provisions as apply to other committees established by a council.[1]

10.64 LEAs and governing bodies of institutions within the higher education sector or at which prescribed courses are provided are to give the councils information upon request.[2]

10.65 The Secretary of State may by order give general directions to a council; and if he thinks that the financial affairs of any higher education sector institution have been or are being mismanaged, he may, after consulting the council and the institution, give whatever directions he considers necessary or expedient about the provision of financial support in respect of the activities carried on at the institution.[3]

Higher education corporations

10.66 The Education Reform Act 1988 specified the polytechnics and colleges maintained by LEAs (institutions with a preponderance of students enrolled on advanced further education courses) that, by order of the Secretary of State, were to be conducted, from 1 April 1989, by higher education corporations.[4]

10.67 Property, rights and liabilities were, with some exceptions, transferred, without compensation, from LEAs.[5] Staff employed solely at a transferred institution automatically became the corporation's employees. Other staff were transferred only if the subject of a designation order. Contracts of employment continued to have effect as if made with the corporation, unless terminated by the employee on grounds of substantial worsening of working conditions.[6]

1 1992 FHE Act s 70 and Sch 1.
2 1992 FHE Act s 79.
3 1992 FHE Act s 81. Orders are to be made by SI. The 1996 Act s 496 (Secretary of State's power to prevent unreasonable exercise of functions) does not apply to higher education sector institutions.
4 1988 Act s 121. Higher education corporations are exempt charities under the Charities Act 1993.
   See the Education (Higher Education Corporations) Order 1988, SI 1988/1799 and the Education (Higher Education Corporations) (No 5) Order 1989, SI 1989/17; also the 1988 Act Sch 9 as to determination of full-time equivalent enrolment numbers.
   By the 1988 Act s 137 LEAs had to obtain the consent of the Secretary of State before disposing of land held, used or obtained for the purposes of an institution before 22 July 1987 which was to transfer to the higher education sector (listed in Annex C to the White Paper, *Higher Education: Meeting the Challenge* Cm.114, 1987). Section 137 was considered in *R v Tameside Metropolitan Borough Council, ex p Governors of Audenshaw High School* (1990) Times, 27 June, F[11]. See also s 138. By s 201 powers were granted to the Education Assets Board (see Appendix 5) in case of wrongful disposal.
5 1988 Act s 126. The exceptions are (a) rights and liabilities under a contract of employment, (b) liabilities in respect of any loan, and (c) liability for compensation for premature retirement. See s 138 for construction of references to 'land' and s 198 regarding transfers generally; also Appendix 5 as regards the functions of the Education Assets Board.
6 1988 Act s 127. See the Education (Higher Education Corporations) (Designated Staff) Order 1989, 1989/369. Other orders have been made in respect of particular institutions.

10.68 Additional LEA institutions with a full-time equivalent enrolment number for courses of higher education exceeding 55 per cent of their total full-time equivalent enrolment number may, by order of the Secretary of State, and subject to the same transfer provisions, become higher education corporations.[7] The Secretary of State may also, by order, transfer further education corporations with an enrolment number as above to the higher education sector,[8] and dissolve higher education corporations. Before making a dissolution order the Secretary of State is to consult the corporation and the funding council. The order transfers property, rights and liabilities to (a) persons or corporate bodies engaged in the provision of education (with their consent), or (b) a higher or further education funding council. Property is to be transferred on trust for exclusively educational charitable purposes.[9]

10.69 The powers of a corporation are, principally, to provide higher and further education, and to carry out research and publish the results and connected material. They may also do anything necessary or expedient which is related to their principal powers, including employing staff, making contracts, acquiring and disposing of land and any other property, forming a corporate body for any of those purposes, founding scholarships and giving prizes.[10]

10.70 The constitution of higher education corporations (whose members are known as boards of governors) differs according to when they were established. Those which were established
(a) before 6 May 1992 are subject to provisions specifying the initial constitution of the corporation, initial and subsequent appointments, determination of membership numbers, qualifications for, and tenure of, office, allowances to members, election of chairman, committees and proceedings, accounts etc;[11]
(b) on or after 6 May 1992 are to conduct institutions in accordance with instruments of government prescribed by order of the Privy Council, who may also replace or modify them. Orders are to make provision to secure continuity of government. Instruments are to comply with provisions similar to those specified for pre-existing corporations, and may make any other provision considered necessary or desirable. The validity of proceedings of a corporation is not affected by a vacancy in membership or a defect in appointment or nomination.[12]

---

7 1988 Act s 122. See also s 123 for supplementary provisions. Orders have been made by SI in respect of several institutions.
8 1988 Act s 122A. The Secretary of State appoints the first members of new higher education corporations, who are subject to ss 124A and 125 (see below) as respects instruments and articles of government. Orders have been made, by SI, in respect of several institutions.
9 1988 Act s 128. Many orders have been made, by SI. Orders may apply s 127, with modifications, so as to enable the Secretary of State to provide for transfer of staff. 'Charitable purposes': see the Charities Act 1993.
10 1988 Act s 124.
11 1988 Act s 123 and Sch 7. By s 124A(3), an order of the Privy Council may substitute an instrument embodying a constitution as in para (b). As to accounts, see also the 1992 FHE Act s 78.
12 1988 Act s 124A and Sch 7A, part of which is subject to amendment or repeal by the Secretary of State. By the 1988 Act s 124C the Secretary of State appoints the first members of the corporation, at least half of whom are to be independent members. The corporation themselves determine subsequent membership in accordance with Sch 7A. Section 124D specifies the formalities under which the Privy Council act.

10.71 Corporations are to keep proper accounts and related records, and prepare an annual statement of accounts. This is to give a true and fair account of the corporation's affairs at the end of, and their income and expenditure during, a financial year, and is to comply with the funding council's procedural directions. Copies of the statement are to be available to the public. The accounts and statement are to be audited by a person qualified as specified and, in respect of the first financial year, appointed after consultation with, and receipt of any advice from, the Audit Commission. [13]

10.72 The conduct of institutions is regulated by articles of government made by the corporation and approved by the Privy Council. Articles (a) are to allocate functions between the board of governors, the principal and the academic board; (b) may regulate the constitution and functions of committees and of the academic board, and provide for delegation by the board of governors and academic board to the chairman of the board or the principal; (c) are to make provision for procedure for meetings and appointment of members of the corporation; (d) may make provision for procedures for (i) appointment, promotion, suspension and dismissal of staff, (ii) admission, suspension and expulsion of students, and (iii) the appointment and functions of a clerk to the board of governors; and (e) may make provision for the board of governors to make bye-laws about the conduct of the institution.

10.73 The corporation may vary, revoke and replace articles with the approval of the Privy Council, who may by direction, after consultation with the board of governors, amend articles and secure amendment of bye-laws made by the board.[14]

Designated institutions

10.74 The Secretary of State may by order designate, as eligible to receive support from higher education funding council funds, institutions (a) with a preponderance of students enrolled on higher education courses, and (b) conducted by successor companies to higher education corporations.[15]

10.75 If an LEA formerly assisted an institution, the designating order

---

13 1988 Act s 124B. The 'first financial year' extends from the date on which the corporation is established to the second succeeding 31 March. Subsequent financial years end on 31 March unless, by 1992 FHE Act s 78, the Secretary of State directs otherwise.
14 1998 Act s 125. As to the expulsion of a student see *R v Sheffield Hallam University (Board of Governors), ex p R* [1995] ELR 267, F[235].
15 1988 Act s 129. By the 1992 FHE Act s 74(2) designated institutions in the further education sector may be removed by order under s 129 into the higher education sector; and (vice versa) an order under this section may, by 1992 Act s 47(4), be revoked by s 28 of that Act (see para 10.31).
   'A preponderance' exists where the full-time equivalent enrolment number for courses of higher education (see Sch 9) exceeds 55 per cent of its total full-time equivalent enrolment number.
   'Successor companies' are companies with charitable objects (exempt charities under the Charities Act 1993) which are limited by guarantee, the memorandum and articles of association of which have been approved by the Secretary of State, and the corporation have been dissolved under s 128.
   See the Education (Designated Institutions) Order 1989, SI 1989/282, the Education (Designated Institutions) (Wales) Order 1992, SI 1992/2622, and the Education (Designated Institutions) Order 1993, SI 1993/404.

10.75 *Further and Higher Education*

provides for transfer, as appropriate, to a corporate body or to trustees specified in the order, of LEA land or other property and rights attaching to the institution, and also liabilities except (a) those in respect of any loan, and (b) compensation payable in respect of premature retirement of employees. Except where land etc was vested in the LEA for the purposes of the institution, transferees who are trustees hold it on trusts under a specified trust deed (if any) relating to the institution; in the absence of a deed it is held for the purposes of the institution. Property so held may be applied towards meeting liabilities transferred, for which transferees incur no personal liability.[16]

10.76 The government and conduct of designated institutions differs according to their status. Institutions other than those (a) established by Royal Charter, and (b) conducted by companies, are to have instruments and articles of government approved by the Privy Council, which were either (a) in force when the designation took effect, or (b) made under a regulatory instrument, or (c) made in the absence of any regulatory instrument by the persons responsible for managing the institution. Those persons (who include a governing body) may modify any such instrument or articles; no other person may do so without the Privy Council's consent. The Council may themselves modify instruments and articles by order, after consultation so far as practicable with the governing body and any other persons having power under a regulatory instrument to make or modify them.[17]

10.77 The articles of association of companies which conduct designated institutions are to incorporate instruments and articles of government. The Privy Council may, after consulting the persons in control, give them directions to amend the memorandum or articles of association and any rules or bye-laws. Any other amendments are subject to the Privy Council's approval.[18]

Universities and degrees

10.78 A university characteristically derived its constitution and powers as a corporation from a Royal Charter, granted through the Privy Council, and statutes deriving therefrom; but the 1992 Act provided that if power exists for the name of an institution within the higher education sector to be changed with the consent of the Privy Council, the Council may consent to the word 'university' being included, after which the institution is to be treated as a university for all purposes.[19] Thus in 1992 and 1993 former polytechnics and some other higher education institutions became universities, the Privy Council having been required to have regard to the need to avoid confusing names.

10.79 The Privy Council may by order specify institutions which provide

---

16 1988 Act s 130. The supplementary provisions formerly contained in Sch 10 para 3 are in effect replaced by the 1992 FHE Act Sch 8 paras 62 to 64, which give functions to the Education Assets Board (see Appendix 5) and the Education Assets Board (Transfers under the Education Reform Act 1988) Regulations 1992, SI 1992/1348.
   See s 138 for construction of references to 'land' and s 198 regarding transfers generally.
17 1988 Act s 129A. A 'regulatory instrument' means any instrument of government or articles of government and any other instrument relating to or regulating the institution.
18 1988 Act s 129B.
19 1992 FHE Act s 77.

higher education as competent to grant degrees and other awards to those who successfully complete taught courses and research. Subsidiary powers include the granting of honorary degrees, the authorisation of other institutions to grant awards on behalf of the institution, and the power to rescind an award.[20] The Council for National Academic Awards has been dissolved.[1]

10.80 University Commissioners were appointed in 1988 to secure that provision was made in the statutes of (then existing) universities (and other chartered bodies awarding degrees) for dismissal of academic staff[2] for
(a) redundancy, defined so as to make it possible to dismiss staff where it can be shown that they were appointed for the purposes of a particular activity and that activity is no longer being carried on, or fewer staff are needed to maintain it (but dismissal of a senior member of staff for replacement by a junior does not count as dismissal for redundancy);
(b) good cause, a reason relating to conduct, capability or qualifications.

10.81 Disciplinary procedures were to be established to deal with complaints made against staff, as were procedures to enable staff to appeal against dismissal or other disciplinary measures, and to seek redress for other grievances relating to appointment or employment.

10.82 In exercising their functions the Commissioners were to have regard to the need
(a) to ensure that academic staff had freedom within the law 'to question and test received wisdom, and to put forward new ideas and controversial or unpopular opinions, without placing themselves in jeopardy of losing their jobs or the privileges they may have at their institutions',
(b) to enable institutions to operate efficiently and economically, and
(c) 'to apply the principles of justice and fairness'.

10.83 The Commissioners were given powers to modify statutes subject to the approval of Her Majesty in Council. Modifications to facilitate dismissal for redundancy apply only to staff who entered into contracts of employment or were appointed on or after 20 November 1987 (when the Bill for the 1988 Act was introduced) or who are promoted on or after that date (whether or not the promotion is backdated). Temporary or titular promotions do not compromise tenure.[3]

10.84 The exclusive jurisdiction of the Visitor in disputes over the appointment, employment or dismissal of a member of the academic staff has been ended, but if the Commissioners have so decided in relation to particular

---

20 1992 FHE Act s 76. An order is to be by SI. The 1988 Act s 124D states the formalities under which the Privy Council act.
1 1992 FHE Act s 80. See the Education (Dissolution of the Council for National Academic Awards) Order 1993, SI 1993/924.
2 See the 1988 Act ss 202 and 203. Schedule 11 is about the appointment, powers, proceedings etc of the Commissioners.
   Dismissal includes removal from office and, in relation to employment under a contract, is to be construed in accordance with Part X of the Employment Rights Act 1996. 'Academic staff' includes 'academic-related staff'—those with similar conditions of employment.
3 1988 Act ss 204 and 207. Section 205 is about the procedure for the exercise of the Commissioners' powers.

10.84 *Further and Higher Education*

institutions the Visitor may determine appeals and redress grievances.[4] In consequence, actions may now be brought in the courts for wrongful dismissal (as well as before industrial tribunals for unfair dismissal) until a reference has been made to and accepted by the Visitor if the Commissioners have given him jurisdiction.[5]

10.85 To outlaw courses in preparation for examinations to qualify for a false title of 'bachelor, master or doctor', any person who in the course of business grants, offers to grant or issues any invitation relating to an unrecognised award—a bogus degree—now commits an offence (punishable by a fine not exceeding level 5 on the standard scale) unless he can show that he took reasonable steps not to pass the award off as a recognised award granted by a UK institution.[6] Proceedings may be brought by local weights and measures authorities and chief police officers.[7]

10.86 Recognised awards are those (a) made or sanctioned by universities or other bodies authorised to grant degrees or (b) designated by order of the Secretary of State. The Secretary of State, by order, designates as 'recognised bodies' those mentioned under (a) above, and lists bodies which provide degree courses under the auspices of a recognised body or which are constituents of a university which is a recognised body. A UK-based institution which awards degrees under a licence from a foreign institution (eg a branch of a US university in Britain) does not commit an offence.

LOCAL EDUCATION AUTHORITY FUNCTIONS

10.87 The obligations of LEAs have been severely curtailed by those now placed upon the further education funding councils. Nevertheless LEAs have a remaining duty to secure the provision of adequate facilities for further education which falls outside the responsibilities of the funding councils (see para 10.03) for persons from their own and, at their option, other areas. This duty

---

4   1988 Act ss 206 and 207.
    The use of the Visitor's discretion in investigating the administration of a university is not ordinarily subject to judicial review (*R v HM the Queen in Council, ex p Vijayatunga* [1990] 2 QB 444, CA, F[95]; and *R v Lord President of the Privy Council, ex p Page* [1993] AC 682 F[233]). A Visitor may decline to impugn the professional judgment of examiners; but the court has assumed a supervisory jurisdiction on an allegation of impropriety by a board of examiners (*R v Manchester Metropolitan University, ex p Nolan* [1994] ELR 380, F[234]).
5   See *Pearce v University of Aston in Birmingham* [1991] 2 All ER 461, CA, F[232].
6   1988 Act ss 214 and 216.
    'Any person', in the case of a company includes (in addition to the company itself) a director, manager or secretary etc, if his consent, connivance or neglect is proved.
    See the Education (Recognised Awards) Order 1988, SI 1988/2035, the Education (Recognised Awards) (Richmond College) (No 2) Order 1996, SI 1996/2564, the Education (Recognised Bodies) Order 1997, SI 1997/1 and the Education (Listed Bodies) Order 1997, SI 1997/54.
7   1988 Act s 215. Local weights and measures authorities are, in England, county, unitary and metropolitan district, and London Borough, councils, the Common Council of the City of London (for the City and the Temples) and the Council of the Isles of Scilly; and in Wales, the county and county borough councils (Weights and Measures Act 1985 s 69(7)). The enforcing authorities are to report to the Secretary of State on their work as he directs. Their officers have powers of entry and search, power to require the production of documents, including computer print-outs, and powers of seizure. In proper circumstances justices of the peace may issue entry warrants. The Trade Descriptions Act 1968, s 29 (penalty for obstruction of authorised officers) is applied.

extends to vocational, social, physical and recreational training and organised leisure-time occupation associated with education. LEAs may also secure the provision of specified courses of part-time education for those over compulsory school age and full-time education of those of 19 and over. In pursuing their further education functions LEAs are to take account of facilities available from other sources and of the requirements of those over compulsory school age who have learning difficulties (see para 5.04).[8]

10.88 LEAs also have power to secure the provision of higher education, but are to take into account other facilities available.[9]

10.89 LEAs may make provision as they think fit for the government of the further and higher education institutions which they maintain and which are outside the further and higher education sectors, including replacing instruments and articles of government; and they may delegate financial and other functions to governing bodies.[10]

10.90 Governors of LEA further and higher education institutions are to be aged 18 or over, unless they are students at the institution. The Secretary of State may make regulations which place restrictions on students' participating as members of governing bodies, and instruments of government may make further restrictions authorised by the regulations.[11] Regulations may also require documents and information relating to meetings of governing bodies to be made available as prescribed.[12]

10.91 HM Chief Inspectors of Schools are required to keep the Secretary of State informed about the quality of education in institutions other than schools which are maintained or assisted by LEAs, the educational standards achieved and the efficiency of financial management. On request they are to advise the Secretary of State about LEA institutions and other matters relating to further education, and to inspect institutions specified by the Secretary of State. Their school inspection powers, and those of HMIs (see para 8.03), are extended for those purposes.[13]

10.92 LEAs are to keep under review the quality of education provided at maintained and assisted institutions, the standards achieved and financial management; and may authorise their own inspections by suitably qualified persons. They are to publish 'disability statements', as prescribed, about the further education provision they make for disabled persons.[14]

---

8   1996 Act s 15. The 'specified courses' are those listed in the 1992 FHE Act Sch 2 (see para 10.07). As to (a) LEA administration of European Social Fund grants see *R v Cheshire County Council, ex p Halton College* (30 July 1996, unreported), (b) the obligation of an LEA towards a student with learning difficulties see *R v Islington Borough Council, ex p Rixon* [1997] ELR 66, *R v Bradford Metropolitan District Council, ex p Parkinson* (1996) Times, 31 October.
9   1988 Act s 120.
10 1992 FHE Act s 85. LEAs were newly empowered by this section to establish governing bodies for wholly part-time institutions.
11 1986 Act s 61. There are no subsisting regulations.
12 1986 Act s 62.
13 1992 FHE Act s 55. 'Assisted': by a grant or payment for providing facilities (1996 Act s 579(6)). Wilful obstruction of authorised inspection is an offence for which on summary conviction a fine is payable not exceeding level 4 on the standard scale.
14 1996 Act s 528 (not yet in force).

10.93 The Secretary of State may require governing bodies of LEA further and higher education institutions providing full-time education to make reports and returns and give him any other information he requires.[15] He may make regulations requiring LEAs, or governing bodies on their behalf, to publish information on educational provision and students' achievements (examination results etc) at LEA maintained and assisted institutions which provide full-time further or higher education.[16]

10.94 Through the further and higher education institutions they maintain, LEAs may enter into agreements to supply specified goods or services, and may make loans for those purposes, to
(a) further and higher education corporations;
(b) the governing bodies or companies conducting
  (i) institutions in the further or higher education sectors which are not conducted by further or higher education corporations,
  (ii) institutions which provide further education or higher education and are assisted by an LEA; and
(c) bodies corporate in which a corporation or company mentioned in (a) or (b) hold 20 per cent or more of the voting shares.

10.95 The goods specified are those that result from (a) the institution's educational activities, (b) the use of its facilities and the expertise of its employees, and (c) the ideas of employees and students; and the services are those (a) provided by making its facilities and expertise available, and (b) which result from its educational activities or the ideas mentioned.[17]

10.96 Where a local authority have entered into an agreement in relation to the supply of goods and services, or for that purpose hold shares in a company, the authority's rights and liabilities transfer to a further education corporation where one has been established to conduct the institution in place of the LEA.[18]

FREEDOM OF SPEECH

10.97 All those concerned in the government of universities and further and higher education establishments (within the relevant sector or maintained by an LEA) are to take reasonably practicable steps to ensure that freedom of speech within the law is secured for members, students, employees and visiting speakers. The duty includes ensuring, so far as reasonably practicable, that use of premises, including those occupied by students' unions, is not denied on account of beliefs or policies. Governing bodies are to issue and keep up to date codes of practice on conduct and procedures to be followed by members, students and employees in connection with the organisation of meetings and other activities; and compliance with the codes (together, if

---

15 1988 Act s 158. This section is analogous to the 1996 Act s 29(1).
16 1988 Act s 159. No regulations have yet been made.
17 1985 Act ss 1 and 2. In s 3 there are detailed financial and accounting provisions. 'Educational activities' are the provision of teaching and industrial and vocational training, the carrying out of research, and incidental or ancillary activities.
18 1992 FHE Act s 24(1) and (2).

need be, with disciplinary measures) is the responsibility of those concerned in the government of the establishment, including, where appropriate, the LEA.[19]

STUDENTS' UNIONS

10.98 A 'students' union' is an association of the students at an establishment whose principal purposes include promoting the general interests of its members as students. Associations concerned with a single purpose, such as sport, are excluded. A union exists when open to the generality of students, or of students of a particular description (eg full-time students), irrespective of whether or not a majority are in fact members, and it includes a representative body, such as a Student Representative Council, whose principal purposes include representing the generality of students in matters relating to the government of an establishment.[20]

10.99 Associations and bodies consisting of, or representing, only undergraduates, or graduates, or the students at a particular hall of residence are also included, as are associations or bodies which consist of other students' unions or representatives of them, if they fulfil the functions of a students' union at a particular establishment. This brings in associations such as the university-wide unions at Oxford and Cambridge which comprise the Junior Common Rooms which are themselves 'students' unions' for the purposes of the Act. The definition is further extended to include a single union serving a number of establishments, as at Loughborough, but not all the establishments in England, Scotland or Wales, or the whole of the United Kingdom.

10.100 Governing bodies of (in the main—see para 10.103) universities and institutions within the further and higher education sectors are, so far as reasonably practicable, to secure that students' unions operate in a fair and democratic manner and are accountable for their finances. 'Democratic' is an unusual word to find in a statute, and presumably means, in context, giving all students opportunity to express their opinions and to be elected to office in the union.

10.101 The requirements upon unions are, in general, that
(a) each should have a written constitution, which is subject to approval and review by the governing body,
(b) students should have the right not to belong (and not be disadvantaged as a result),
(c) appointment to major union offices should be by election in a secret ballot, fairly conducted to the satisfaction of the governing body,
(d) sabbatical or paid office should be limited to two years,

---

19 1986 Act s 43. See also the 1994 Act s 22(4)(c) (see para 10.102). In *R v University of Liverpool, ex p Caesar-Gordon* [1991] 1 QB 124 the Divisional Court granted a declaration that a university should not take into account any risk of public disorder outside its precincts by members of the public over whom the university had no control unless that disorder gave rise to a risk of disorder in the university precincts or affected its property, students or members, or the risk of disorder occasioned by persons over whom it did have control. See also *R v University College London, ex p Riniker* [1995] ELR 213.
20 1994 Act s 20.

10.101 *Further and Higher Education*

(e) governing bodies should monitor unions' financial affairs, and financial reports should be published at least annually,
(f) the procedure for allocating resources to groups or clubs should be fair and accessible,
(g) relationships with external organisations should be made public and open to review, and
(h) there should be a complaints procedure for students.

(Paragraphs (c) and (g) apply only in part to open and distance learning establishments.)

10.102 Governing bodies are to prepare, issue and keep up to date a code of practice explaining how the requirements are to be met, and bring it to the attention of students at least annually, along with notice of charity law restrictions on union activities and freedom of speech obligations. Prospectuses of the institutions to which the requirements apply are to mention the right of students not to belong to the union, and how non-members are to be provided with services of the kind available to members.[1]

10.103 The establishments in England and Wales to which the requirements apply are
(a) universities receiving financial support from the higher education funding councils;
(b) higher education institutions, formerly maintained by LEAs, but now conducted by higher education corporations incorporated under the 1988 Act; and further education and sixth-form colleges now conducted by further education corporations incorporated under the 1992 FHE Act;
(c) higher education institutions designated under the 1988 Act s 129 as eligible to receive funds from a higher education funding council (these are the higher education colleges, mostly in the voluntary sector, which were not incorporated under the 1988 Act);
(d) institutions designated under the 1992 FHE Act s 28 as eligible to receive funds from a further education funding council (these are institutions which were formerly voluntary aided sixth-form colleges, and specialist institutions such as long term residential colleges for adults, formerly funded by grants from the Secretary of State or LEAs);
(e) institutions outside the further education sector providing part-time or adult further education, substantially (ie for more than 25 per cent of their income) dependent on support from a further education funding council via a sponsoring institution within the further education sector (currently Sutton College of Liberal Arts and Richmond Adult and Community College);
(f) institutions, or categories of institution, designated by order of the Secretary of State; and
(g) colleges, schools or halls in collegiate and federal universities or in any other of the establishments mentioned above, including any institution in the nature of a college (eg Christ Church, Oxford).[2]

1 1994 Act s 22. As to the restrictions imposed by the law relating to charities see *A-G v Ross* [1985] 3 All ER 334 in which Scott J followed *London Hospital Medical College v IRC* [1976] 2 All ER 113, and the guidance on permissible expenditure published by the Charity Commission.
2 1994 Act s 21. Para (a) relates to support under the 1992 FHE Act s 65 (not received by the University of Buckingham). An order under para (f) is to be made by SI.

FEES, AWARDS AND LOANS

Fees

10.104 Regulations may, with some exceptions, require or authorise the charging of higher fees to students who lack a relevant United Kingdom connection at (a) universities, university colleges and colleges, schools and halls of universities, (b) institutions within the further or higher education sectors, (c) institutions providing higher or further education which are either maintained by LEAs or are substantially dependent on public funds and are specified under the regulations, and (d) teacher training institutions eligible for funding under the 1994 Act (see para 13.04).[3]

10.105 The Secretary of State has a general power to regulate course fees at institutions (a) providing higher or further education which are within the further education sector or maintained by LEAs, and (b) within the higher education sector and supported by a funding council.[4]

LEA awards

10.106 LEAs are under a duty to make awards, in accordance with regulations, to persons ordinarily resident in their areas who attend prescribed courses leading to a first degree, Diploma in Higher Education or Higher National Diploma, or which constitute initial teacher training, and other courses comparable to a first degree course, provided at a university or other institution in the UK (or in conjunction with a foreign institution). The regulations prescribe the conditions under which awards are bestowed, the exceptions to the duty to bestow, the nature and circumstances of payment, and the power to suspend or terminate awards. In the case of courses comparable to first degree courses the regulations may prescribe qualifications upon which awards are conditional.[5] When a student has a spouse or child the Secretary of State may supplement the LEA award.[6]

---

3 1983 Act s 1. The exceptions include nationals of European Union states who have been ordinarily resident (see para 10.107) in the European Economic Area, refugees and recently arrived immigrants. See the Education (Fees and Awards) Regulations 1994, SI 1994/3042, which grants exemption from the provisions of the Race Relations Act 1976 under s 41(1) of that Act.
4 1988 Act s 218(9)(a), (10) and (11). Fees are not at present subject to regulation.
5 1962 Act ss 1 and 4, Sch 1. A revised set of mandatory awards regulations has been made for each academic year. The Education (Mandatory Awards) Regulations 1997, SI 1997/431, come into force on 1 September 1997.
   The 1988 Act s 209 requires the Secretary of State to reimburse LEAs for mandatory awards made under the this section.
   'First degree' see *R v Secretary of State for Education and Science, ex p Royal Institute of British Architects* [1991] COD 281.
   In *Shah v Barnet London Borough Council* [1983] 2 AC 309 it was held that where the court grants relief by way of judicial review of a decision by an LEA to refuse an application for an award under 1962 Act s 1 the appropriate remedy is an order of certiorari quashing the refusal to make an award and an order of mandamus requiring the authority to reconsider the application. The court cannot make a declaration of the person's entitlement or right to an award or of the authority's duty to make an award, since to do so would be to assume the authority's function.
   As to (a) a claim for a maintenance grant for a first degree course see *R v Rotherham Metropolitan Borough Council, ex p Croft* (29 April 1996, unreported), (b) income support for a student temporarily withdrawn from a course see *Chief Adjudication Officer v Clarke* [1995] ELR 259, CA, and (c) whether maintenance payments are part of a student's own income see *R v Sheffield City Council, ex p Parker* [1993] 2 FLR 907.
6 1973 Act s 3. This power has been exercised in the Education (Mandatory Awards) Regulations 1995, SI 1995/3321, Sch 2, Pt III and Sch 4.

10.107 *Further and Higher Education*

10.107 A person is ordinarily resident in the area of an LEA, subject to the awards regulations, when he belongs to that area. Belonging to an area is, however, mainly defined by reference to 'ordinary residence'.[7] This term, the House of Lords has held,[8] is to be given its natural and ordinary meaning: the question is whether the applicant for an award has habitually and normally resided in the United Kingdom from choice and for a settled purpose throughout the prescribed period of three years, apart from temporary and occasional absences. The regulations except from eligibility for a mandatory award those who for any part of the three years have been resident wholly or mainly for the purposes of receiving full-time education.

10.108 LEAs may also, at their discretion, make awards to persons attending the prescribed courses who are not eligible for mandatory awards, because, for example, the course is for a second degree.[9] Additionally they have power to make awards to persons over compulsory school age (including those training as teachers) for attendance at courses (eg part-time courses at further education institutions) other than those (a) prescribed or (b) of primary or secondary education. Except as regards teacher training this power is not available in respect of prescribed postgraduate courses at universities and elsewhere (but none has yet been prescribed).[10] LEAs may, with prescribed exceptions, restrict discretionary awards to persons having a relevant connection ('ordinary residence', as above) with the United Kingdom.[11]

---

7 See the Education (Areas to which Pupils and Students Belong) Regulations 1996, SI 1996/615. Under the 1996 Act s 579(4) any dispute is to be settled by the Secretary of State.
8 See *Shah* (n 5 above) and the Departmental circular letter, 30 March 1983, on 'ordinary residence', E[192.1]; also *R v Hampshire County Council, ex p Martin* (1982) Times, 20 November, F[78], *MacMahon v Department of Education and Science* [1983] Ch 227, F[76], *R v Hereford and Worcester County Council, ex p Wimbourne* (1983) 82 LGR 251 (the three year residence requirement applies to a British citizen), *R v Inner London Education Authority, ex p Hinde* (1984) 83 LGR 695 (European Union nationals eligible under Council Regulation 1612/68, art 7), *R v Lancashire County Council, ex p Huddleston* [1986] 2 All ER 941, *R v Hertfordshire County Council, ex p Cheung* (1986) Times, 4 April, CA, F[81], *R v Nottinghamshire County Council, ex p Jain* [1989] COD 442 (two ordinary residences) and *R v Redbridge London Borough Council, ex p East Sussex County Council* [1993] COD 256.
9 1962 Act s 1(6). In *R v Bexley London Borough, ex p Jones* [1995] ELR 42, F[111.3], it was held (1) that the LEA had unlawfully fettered their discretion by adopting a policy of always refusing discretionary awards and not affording applicants an opportunity to request special consideration, (2) that a discretionary award had to be a full award (as for mandatory awards) and could not, for example, be limited to the amount of fees payable. Cf *R v Warwickshire County Council, ex p Williams* [1995] ELR 326, F[111.6], and *R v Southwark London Borough Council, ex p Udu* [1995] ELR 390, CA, F[111.3]. See also *R v Bexley London Borough Council, ex p Jones* [1994] COD 393, and *R v Shropshire County Council, ex p Jones* (23 August, 1996, unreported).
10 1962 Act ss 2 and 4. See also para 12.41.
As to the obligation on LEAs to be willing to depart in special circumstances from a general policy of refusing discretionary awards, see *R v Warwickshire County Council, ex p Collymore* [1995] ELR 217, F[111.6], ibid *ex p Williams* [1995] ELR 326 F[111.6]; and *R v Southwark London Borough Council, ex p Udu* [1995] ELR 390, F[111.7].
11 1983 Act s 2. Discretionary awards are those made under 1962 Act ss 1(6) and 2 or specified in regulations. The restriction is not to extend to 'excepted candidates', who include the children of European Economic Area migrant workers and others prescribed. Similar rules apply in connection with awards by research councils (see para 10.112) and certain other institutions, and postgraduate agricultural studentships. See SI 1994/3042. Exemption from the provisions of the Race Relations Act 1976 is granted under s 41(1) of that Act.

Awards by the Secretary of State and others

10.109 The Secretary of State may, under regulation, bestow awards (a) (state studentships and state bursaries) on persons attending designated postgraduate or comparable courses in Britain or elsewhere who satisfy him about their educational qualifications, and (b) (state bursaries for adult education) on persons aged 20 and over in respect of courses at institutions supported by grants (see para 11.07) and which are designated as colleges providing long term residential courses of full-time education for adults. Candidates for awards are to meet fitness and residence requirements.[12]

10.110 State studentships (at present administered by the British Academy as agent for the Secretary of State) are tenable for full-time humanities courses leading to higher degrees at universities and other institutions in England and Wales, other courses designated by the Secretary of State in the United Kingdom or abroad, and courses at the European University Institute. State bursaries (but not studentships) are tenable for courses, mainly professional or vocational in character, designated by the Secretary of State. The maximum period of a state studentship or bursary is ordinarily three years but it may be suspended or cancelled for unsatisfactory progress or conduct.

10.111 The Secretary of State may also award, or by making payments enable other persons to award, industrial scholarships tenable for relevant full-time higher education courses including sandwich courses at universities, colleges or other institutions in the United Kingdom.[13]

10.112 Awards (variously described) for education, training and research are made by Research Councils and specified institutions and further education establishments. They may be confined, with prescribed exceptions, to those who have a relevant connection with the UK and Islands or with Great Britain and (apart from postgraduate agricultural studentships) made subject to further specified restrictions.[14]

Loans

10.113 Students attending specified higher education courses of first degree and comparable standard may be eligible for loans, under regulation, towards their maintenance costs, but not fees. Eligible students are those attending courses lasting at least one academic year at institutions which are publicly supported, or designated by regulation. The Secretary of State may make arrangements (a) for (public sector) loans to be made by the Student Loans Company—a company with two shareholders, the Secretary of State for Education and Employment and the Secretary of State for Scotland, or (b) to pay subsidies to institutions such as banks and building societies to enable them to make (private sector) loans on the same favourable terms as those made by the Student Loans Company.[15]

---

12 1962 Act ss 3 and 4. See the State Awards Regulations 1978, SI 1978/1096 and the State Awards (State Bursaries for Adult Education) (Wales) Regulations 1979, SI 1979/333.
13 1980 Act s 20. The scholarships (last awarded in 1986) were known as National Engineeering Scholarships, and were funded jointly by the Department and industry.
14 See SI 1994/3042, Pt IV, which defines 'relevant connection'.
15 1990 Act s 1, Schs 1 and 2 and 1996 SL Act s 1 and Sch 1. See the Education (Student Loans) Regulations 1996, SI 1996/1812.

Chapter 11

GRANTS AND OTHER FINANCIAL MATTERS

11.01 LEAs are financed mainly by revenue support grant, which is a general grant to local authorities, unallocated to particular functions, from the aggregate of which, before it is distributed, deductions are made to meet expenditure incurred by certain national educational (and other) bodies.[1]

11.02 LEAs receive full reimbursement of expenditure on mandatory awards for students on first degree and comparable courses (see para 10.06), and payments by Health Authorities in respect of expenditure incurred in performing functions for the benefit of disabled persons.[2] Local authorities may in certain circumstances receive grants from the European Social Fund for educational purposes.[3]

11.03 Part VIII of the 1996 Act specifies the several kinds of grant payable by the Secretary of State under that Act, the circumstances in which he is obliged to pay school fees and expenses, and the arrangements for recoupment of expenses by one LEA from another.

GRANTS

11.04 The regulations under which most of the specific grants mentioned below are paid from the Exchequer to LEAs and others may make payment depend on the meeting of conditions and provide for compliance with requirements or requests.[4] But special provision is made for grants in respect of nursery education (see para 11.12); and grants for the Fellowship of Engineering and the Further Education Unit[5] and in respect of ethnic minorities (see para 11.15) are not made under regulation.

---

1 Local Government Finance Act 1988, Pt V. See the Revenue Support Grant (Specified Bodies) Regulations 1992, SI 1992/89, under which deductions from revenue support grant finance, inter alios, the National Foundation for Educational Research and the National Institute of Adult Continuing Education.
2 National Health Service Act 1977 s 28A.
3 See *Birmingham City Council v Birmingham College of Food* [1996] ELR 1 in which reference was made to the essential principles of specificity and additionality.
4 1996 Act s 489(1) and (grants for teacher training etc) 1986 Act s 50(3).
5 1986 (No 1) Act s 1.

Grants for training of teachers and others

11.05 To facilitate the training of teachers and others in prescribed classes the Secretary of State or the Teacher Training Agency (see para 13.06) pay grants, under regulation, to prescribed persons other than LEAs. 'Training' includes further (not necessarily post-qualification) training, the provision of experience beneficial to a person's employment, training for a change of employment in education and the study of matters related to education.[6]

Grants for education support and training

11.06 The Secretary of State pays education support and training grant on an annual (financial year) basis to LEAs in aid of expenditure on activities which he wishes to encourage. Regulations (a) prescribe the type of expenditure eligible; (b) determine the rate of grant, and when and how it is payable;[7] and (c) may oblige LEAs to delegate to prescribed persons decisions about spending on education support and training.[8] England and Wales may be treated differently.

Grants in aid of educational services or research

11.07 The Secretary of State pays grants under regulation to persons other than LEAs in respect of educational services and research as follows:[9]
(a) non-LEA special schools,
(b) a special, limited, category of further and higher education institutions,
(c) specified bodies providing tuition for adult education courses,
(d) educational services provided by national adult education associations,
(e) vocational, social, physical and recreational training,
(f) specified courses for training youth leaders and community centre wardens,
(g) expenditure on certain educational services and research,
(h) training abroad of teachers and others,
(i) certain music and ballet schools, to reimburse them for operating the

---

6 1986 Act s 50 and 1994 Act s 13. See the Education (Welsh Medium Teacher Training Incentive Supplement) Regulations 1990, SI 1990/1208; the Education (Grant) Regulations 1990, SI 1990/1989; and the Education (Bursaries for Teacher Training) Regulations 1994, SI 1994/2016.
7 1996 Act s 484. See the Education (Grants for Education Support and Training: Nursery Education) (England) Regulations 1996, SI 1996/235 (grant is set at 100 per cent), the Education (Grants for Education Support and Training) (England) Regulations 1997, SI 1997/514, and the Education (Grants for Education Support and Training) (Wales) Regulations 1997, SI 1997/390. SI 1997/390 and SI 1997/514 prescribe multiple purposes for, or in connection with, which grants are payable, and set the rate of grant, ordinarily at 60 per cent, from 1 April 1997.
   In case of boundary or structural change affecting an LEA see the Local Government Changes for England (Education) (Miscellaneous Provisions) Regulations 1996, SI 1996/710, Pt 4.
   See Circular 13/96 (WO 31/96), 'Grants for Education Support and Training 1997–98'.
8 1996 Act s 489(2).
9 1996 Act s 485. See, in respect of the grants mentioned in:
   (a) to (h) and (m), the Education (Grant) Regulations 1990, SI 1990/1989 the Education (Grant) (Henrietta Barnett School) Regulations 1994, SI 1994/156, the Education (Grant) (Bishop Perowne High School) Regulations 1995, SI 1995/1688 and the Education (Grants) (Purcell School) Regulations 1996, SI 1996/757.
   (i) the Education (Grants) (Music, Ballet and Choir Schools) Regulations 1995, SI 1995/2018,
   (j) the Education (Grants) (City Technology Colleges) Regulations 1987, SI 1987/1138,
   (k) the Education (Grants) (Voluntary Aided Sixth-Form Colleges) Regulations 1992, SI 1992/2181, and
   (l) the Education (Grants) (Higher Education Corporations) Regulations 1992, SI 1992/3237.

11.07 *Grants and Other Financial Matters*

   aided pupils scheme for pupils at those schools, and the Choir Schools' Association Bursary Trust,
(j) city technology colleges (see para 9.25 ff),
(k) voluntary aided sixth-form colleges, preparatory to their entering the further education sector (see para 10.31),
(l) higher education corporations (see para 10.66 ff) for a limited period after establishment.
(m) proprietors of independent schools in respect of education provided to certain five-year-old children.

11.08 The Secretary of State may by order modify an institution's trust deed or other regulating instrument, after consulting the persons responsible for its management, to enable them to comply with the requirements of regulations.[10]

Grants to bodies whose objects are promoting of learning or research

11.09 The Secretary of State pays grants under regulation to bodies other than LEAs whose main object is the promotion of learning or research.[11]

Grants for education in Welsh

11.10 The Secretary of State pays grants under regulation to LEAs and other persons in aid of the teaching of the Welsh language or the teaching of other subjects in that language.[12]

Grants for education of travellers and displaced persons

11.11 The Secretary of State pays grants under regulation to LEAs or institutions within the further education sector in aid of prescribed descriptions of expenditure on the education of persons
(a) whose (or whose parents') way of life is, or was recently, such that they either have no fixed abode or leave their main abode to live elsewhere for significant periods each year; or
(b) who are for the time being resident in accommodation provided for refugees or displaced or similar persons.[13]

Grants in respect of nursery education

11.12 Nursery education is education provided at school or elsewhere for children from a prescribed time up to their first school term after reaching the

---

10 1996 Act s 489(3) and (4).
11 1996 Act s 486. See the Education (Grant) Regulations 1990, SI 1990/1989, reg 14.
12 1996 Act s 487. See the Grants for Welsh Language Education Regulations 1980, SI 1980/1011. In WO 37/83 it was stated that 'the bulk of grant payments should be made to LEAs in respect of projects related to the maintained education system...in recognition of the fact that LEAs in Wales already show significant expenditure in Welsh language education'.
13 1988 Act s 210 and 1996 Act s 488. See the Education (Grants) (Travellers and Displaced Persons) Regulations 1993, SI 1993/569. The rate of grant is 65 per cent of approved expenditure in England, 75 per cent in Wales.
  In case of boundary or structural change affecting an LEA see SI 1996/710, Pt 4.
  See also Circular 10/90 (WO 52/90), 'The Education Reform Act 1988: Specific Grant for the Education of Travellers and of Displaced Persons', E[1259], and Circular 11/92 (same title), E[1762], replacing Circular 10/90, Pt A.

age of five (or, if they do not attend school, similarly as prescribed). The Secretary of State may make (or delegate the task of making) arrangements for grants in respect of nursery education to be paid (a) to LEAs for nursery education provided at their schools and (b) to others as prescribed. The amount of grant and related matters are settled by regulation, and the recipients are to comply with requirements imposed by the arrangements, which, under conditions the requirements specify, may call for repayment of grant. Breach of a prescribed condition about calculation of the amount of grant in relation to a child may justify refusal to provide a nursery education place at a maintained, or grant-maintained special, school, without right of appeal.[14]

11.13 Those providing or employed in providing funded nursery education are to have regard to the code of practice which gives guidance about children wih special educational needs (see para 5.04). If necessary the Secretary of State is to publish an additional document about their nursery education needs.[15]

11.14 Chief Inspectors of Schools in England and in Wales have functions in respect of nursery education analogous to their general functions. They are to establish registers of nursery education inspectors whose duties and qualifications are similar to those of registered inspectors of schools. There are also provisions relating to reports of inspections, and the annual reports of Chief Inspectors are to refer to their nursery education functions.[16]

Grants in respect of special provision for ethnic minorities

11.15 The Secretary of State may pay grants to city colleges and to governing bodies of grant-maintained schools and of institutions within the further education sector towards approved expenditure on employing extra staff where, in his opinion, they make special provision to meet the needs of persons belonging to ethnic minorities within the locality of the school or institution whose language or customs differ from those of the rest of the community. Where the grant is payable in respect of city colleges or grant-maintained schools the Secretary of State may by order transfer his responsibility to a funding authority.[17]

---

14 1996 N Act ss 1 to 3. This is the so-called 'voucher scheme'. Section 6 and Sch 2 provide for supply of social security information to civil servants and others concerned, under penalty for its wrongful disclosure.
  See the Education (Grants for Nursery Education) (England) Regulations 1996, SI 1996/353 (made under the 1944 Act s 100) and the Nursery Education Regulations 1996, SI 1996/2086, which as amended by SI 1996/3117, define 'nursery education' for the purposes of the Act.
15 1996 N Act s 4.
16 1996 N Act s 5 and Sch 1.
17 1988 Act s 211 and 1996 Act s 490 and Sch 3 para 3, an order under which is made by SI.
  Under the Local Government Act 1966 s 11, local authorities may in the same circumstances apply for grant towards expenditure on staff in respect of any of their functions.
  See, as regards grant payments, and whether they should be included in the calculation of an annual maintenance grant for a grant-maintained school, *R v Department of Education and Science, ex p Dudley Metropolitan Borough Council* (1992) 90 LGR 296.
  Grant is administered by the Home Office, in accordance with that Department's Circular No 78/1990.
  These provisions are applied by the Education (Grant-maintained Special Schools) Regulations 1994, SI 1994/653, reg 42(1), Schedule, Pt I and the Education (Special Schools conducted by Education Associations) Regulations 1994, SI 1994/1084, reg 8(1), Sch 2, Pt I.

11.16 Grants and Other Financial Matters

PAYMENT OF SCHOOL FEES AND EXPENSES

11.16 The Secretary of State is to make provision, by regulation, to pay all or part of the fees and expenses of children attending fee-paying schools so as to enable them to take advantage of the educational facilities without hardship to themselves or their parents. Payment depends on compliance with prescribed conditions and requirements.[18]

RECOUPMENT

Adjustment between LEAs and cross-border provisions

11.17 To settle responsibility for expenditure as between LEAs the Secretary of State has made regulations to establish the area to which a person receiving education belongs: this is normally the area of the LEA in which he is ordinarily resident (see para 10.107); otherwise that in which he is resident for the time being.[19]

11.18 Under separate regulations one LEA are to recoup from another the costs of providing education (and related benefits and services) for (a) children with statements of special educational needs, (b) persons attending special schools, and (c) persons under 19 receiving education in hospital special schools or otherwise than in school. The amounts are to be agreed between the LEAs or, failing agreement, determined by the Secretary of State. The amounts may, but are not required to, reflect average costs incurred by LEAs. In all other cases of primary, secondary and further education and part-time education of under-fives recoupment is voluntary and depends on agreement between the LEAs concerned.[20]

11.19 The Secretary of State may make regulations to meet cases where education is provided by an LEA in England and the paying authority is in Scotland, and vice versa, but he has not yet done so.[1]

Excluded pupils

11.20 Where a pupil is permanently excluded (see paras 3.108 ff and 4.26) from a maintained school and transfers to another maintained school (including

---

18 1996 Act s 491. See regulations mentioned under n 9 above. Otherwise in practice reliance is placed upon LEAs who have power to make similar provision under 1996 Act s 518 (see para 12.41).
19 1996 Act s 579(4) and the Education (Areas to which Pupils and Students Belong) Regulations 1996, SI 1996/615. See Circular 1/96 (WO 17/96), 'The Belonging Regulations', E[3551]. In case of boundary or structural change affecting an LEA see SI 1996/710, Pt 5.
20 1996 Act s 492 and the Education (Inter-authority Recoupment) Regulations 1994, SI 1994/3251. Expenditure on further education which is 'pooled' under the Local Government, Planning and Land Act 1980 Sch 10 para 6 is not subject to recoupment. As to the effect of recoupment on recovery by the Secretary of State from LEAs of maintenance grant he has paid to grant-maintained schools, see paras 4.46 and 4.47.
  See Circular 2/95 (WO 1/95), 'Arrangements for Inter-Authority Recoupment after 1 April 1995', E[3301], and 1/96 (WO 17/96)' E[3551].
1 1996 Act s 493. See Circular 3/94, 'The Development of Special Schools', para 88 and Circular 2/95, para 3.

a pupil referral unit) or a grant-maintained special school, or an LEA provides education outside school, the former provider is to pay any new provider an amount for the balance of the financial year determined under regulation.[2]

11.21 Regulations determine the transfer of funds from the excluding school, the calculation being based on the relevant age-weighted pupil unit under the financial delegation scheme (see para 3.75) of the LEA for the area of the excluding school. In the case of exclusions from grant-maintained special schools the unit is that of the LEA which formerly maintained the school. Schemes are to be revised, if need be, to provide that where a pupil is permanently excluded the school's budget share is reduced accordingly for that financial year, and that the admitting school is, conversely, compensated.

11.22 Disputes about whether an LEA or the governing body of a grant-maintained school are entitled to payment are determined by the Secretary of State.

---

2 1996 Act s 494. See the Education (Amount to Follow Permanently Excluded Pupil) Regulations 1994, SI 1994/1697 and Circular 17/94, 'Arrangements for money to follow pupils who have been permanently excluded from school', E[3061].

Chapter 12

ANCILLARY FUNCTIONS

12.01 Part IX of the 1996 Act is about the ancillary functions of the Secretary of State, LEAs and governing bodies.

ANCILLARY FUNCTIONS OF THE SECRETARY OF STATE

12.02 The functions specified in Chapter I of Part IX (sections 495 to 507), with the exception mentioned at para 2.23, and an addition, are as follows.

Determination of disputes

12.03 In the absence of other express provision the Secretary of State is to determine disputes between LEAs about responsibility for the education of pupils, and between LEAs and governing bodies of schools and of LEA further and higher education institutions about their respective powers and duties, 'despite [in the case of schools] any enactment which makes the exercise of the power or the performance of the duty contingent upon the opinion of the authority or of the governing body'.[1] The obligation upon the Secretary of State may or may not oust or limit the jurisdiction of the courts, according to circumstances;[2] and they may require him to carry out his obligations.[3]

12.04 The Secretary of State is also to decide disputes between LEAs and a funding authority as to which should exercise a function (see para 2.40).[4]

---

1 1996 Act s 495 and 1988 Act s 219 as substituted by 1996 Act Sch 37 para 77. These provisions are apt for determination of disputes arising under instruments and articles of government, but not, by s 560(7), in relation to work experience powers (see para 15.32) or (eg) on whether governors are disqualified from voting on a proposal that a school should seek grant-maintained status: *R v Governors of Small Heath School, ex p Birmingham City Council* [1990] COD 23 CA. As to disputes about recoupment see para 11.18.
2 In *Blencowe v Northamptonshire County Council* [1907] 1 Ch 504 a disputed direction by the LEA concerning the hour of secular instruction was held to be outside the jurisdiction of the court, as was, in *West Suffolk County Council v Olorenshaw* [1918] 2 KB 687, a dispute about a school cleaner's wages; but in *Wilford v West Riding County Council* [1908] 1 KB 685, F[66], a disputed direction (in effect) to change the character of a school was held to be within jurisdiction. These decisions were made in relation to schools not provided by the LEA on provisions in the Education Act 1902 similar to the 1996 Act s 495, but are now of doubtful authority.
3 In *Board of Education v Rice* [1911] AC 179, F[67], the House of Lords held that the duty of an LEA (in a dispute with managers) to keep efficient a school they did not provide was a matter which could and should be determined by the Board of Education.
4 1996 Act s 28.

Power to prevent unreasonable exercise of functions

12.05 If the Secretary of State is satisfied, either on complaint or otherwise, that an LEA or governing body have acted, or are proposing to act, unreasonably in the exercise of any of their powers or duties, he may give such directions as he considers expedient[5] and may do so 'despite any enactment which makes the exercise of the power or the performance of the duty contingent upon the opinion of the authority or of the governing body'. It has been held that this power excludes the jurisdiction of the courts,[6] except where ultra vires, for example breach of the rules of natural justice, is alleged.[7]

12.06 The use of 'otherwise' above, indicates that the Secretary of State may act on his own initiative, and the use of the subjective terminology 'is satisfied' gives him, prima facie, unqualified discretion in determining what is unreasonable. But in *Secretary of State for Education and Science v Metropolitan Borough of Tameside*,[8] the court applied the '*Wednesbury*' test,[9] and concluded that on the facts the authority were not guilty, in Lord Diplock's words, of 'conduct which no sensible authority acting with due appreciation of its responsibilities would have decided to adopt'. Therefore the Secretary of State could not properly have reached the conclusion that the LEA had acted unreasonably; and in consequence his direction to the council was ultra vires. Although the wording was subjective, in the words of Lord Wilberforce

'If a judgment requires, before it can be made, the existence of some facts, then, although the evaluation of those facts is for the Secretary of State alone, the court

---

5   1996 Act s 496 and 1988 Act s 219 as substituted by 1996 Act Sch 37 para 77. The 'governing bodies' are those of a maintained school and LEA further or higher education institution.
   Section 496 has been extended by the 1992 FHE Act s 56 (as amended by the 1996 Act Sch 37, paras 112 and 113) to apply to a further education funding council and to the governing body of an institution within the further education sector, and by the 1996 Act s 24 applies to a funding authority. See also paras 14.07 and 14.10 (about, respectively, sex and racial discrimination).
   As to (a) limitations on the power of the Secretary of State see para 6.72 and (pupil referral units) the 1996 Act Sch 1 para 6; (b) prior consultation with the intended recipient of a direction see *R v Secretary of State for Education and Science, ex p Chance* (26 July 1982, unreported), F[77] (see n 10 below); (c) enforcement of directions, in the *Tameside* case (see n 8 below) Lord Wilberforce said that s 68 of the 1944 Act imposed a statutory duty to comply, enforceable by order of mandamus.
   Section 496 is applied in relation to grant-maintained special schools by the Education (Grant-maintained Special Schools) Regulations 1994, SI 1994/653, reg 42, Schedule, Pt I; and by the Education (Special Schools Conducted by Education Associations) Regulations 1994, SI 1994/1084, reg 8(1), Sch 2, Pt I.
6   See *Cumings v Birkenhead Corpn* [1972] Ch 12, F[42] and *R v Powys County Council, ex p Smith* (1982) 81 LGR 342.
7   See *Herring v Templeman* [1973] 2 All ER 581, F[70].
8   [1977] AC 1014, F[73], F[73.1]. Following an election and change of power the LEA withdrew plans to introduce 'comprehensive' secondary education. The Secretary of State directed that they should adhere to the plans: to change them when they were 'designed to come into effect less than three months later would in his opinion give rise to considerable difficulties'. He subsequently applied, properly (according to Lord Wilberforce) but unsuccessfully, for an order of mandamus. See also *Norwich City Council v Secretary of State for the Environment* [1982] 1 All ER 737.
9   See *Associated Provincial Picture Houses v Wednesbury Corpn* [1948] 1 KB 223, F[68], and *Secretary of State for Employment v Associated Society of Locomotive Engineers and Firemen (No 2)* [1972] 2 QB 455 at 493, per Lord Denning MR. Cf *R v Secretary of State for Education and Employment, ex p M* [1996] ELR 162, CA.

12.06 *Ancillary Functions*

must inquire whether those facts exist, and have been taken into account, whether the judgment has been made upon a proper self-direction as to those facts, whether the judgment has not been made upon other facts which ought not to have been taken into account. If these requirements are not met, then the exercise of the judgment, however bona fide it may be, becomes capable of challenge.'

12.07 It is not enough that the Secretary of State regards an action as misguided. 'He must be very careful then not to fall into the error—a very common error—of thinking that anyone with whom he disagrees is being unreasonable . . . He must ask himself: Is this person so very wrong? May he not quite reasonably take a different view?'—per Lord Denning MR.

12.08 Despite the limited scope for intervention by the Secretary of State his use of s 68 of the 1944 Act went unchallenged by Derbyshire County Council in 1982 when he directed that a sixth-former should be allowed to take up an assisted place at an independent school, and by Brent London Borough Council in 1986 when he directed the council to drop disciplinary proceedings against a teacher.

General default powers

12.09 If the Secretary of State is satisfied, either on complaint or otherwise, that an LEA or governing body have failed to discharge a statutory duty, he may make an order declaring the default and giving directions for enforcing performance. If need be he may apply for mandamus.[10] This recourse ordinarily excludes application to the courts,[11] but if a person suffers special damage as a result of breach of statutory duty he may apply to the court for damages or an injunction.[12] It appears that if the court entertain an application for judicial

---

10 1996 Act s 497 and 1988 Act s 219 as substituted by 1996 Act Sch 37 para 77. The governing bodies are those of a maintained school and LEA further or higher education institution.
   Section 497 is applied by s 24 to a funding authority. See also paras 14.07 and 14.10 (respectively sex and racial discrimination). As to limitations on the power of the Secretary of State see n 5 above.
   'Statutory duty': see *Board of Education v Rice* [1911] AC 179, F[67].
   'Declaring . . . and giving directions': in *R v Secretary of State for Education and Science, ex p Gray* (20 July 1988, unreported), Henry J remarked obiter that it seemed to him that it was open to the Secretary of State to make a direction simpliciter, though if he thought it expedient, having made a declaration, he might give directions in addition.
   In *R v Secretary of State for Education and Science, ex p Chance* (26 July 1982, unreported), F[77] it was held that although there is no obligation to consult a complainant before giving a direction under ss 68 and 99, it is the normal practice of the Secretary of State to consult the recipient before doing so. It was also held that the Secretary of State ought to reconsider his decision, since he had not properly addressed the facts and in consequence had declined to make a default order (on an allegation that an LEA had failed to provide special educational treatment for a dyslexic child).
   Section 497 is applied in relation to grant-maintained special schools by the Education (Grant-maintained Special Schools) Regulations 1994, SI 1994/653, reg 42, Schedule, Pt I; and by the Education (Special Schools Conducted by Education Associations) Regulations 1994, SI 1994/1084, reg 8(1), Sch 2, Pt I.
11 In *R v Northampton County Council, ex p Gray* (1986) Times, 10 June, an application for judicial review was rejected where a person sought to challenge the propriety of the election of parent governors to the governing body of a county school.
12 See *Meade v Haringey London Borough Council* [1979] 1 WLR 637, CA, F[75]. This was a private law claim: where no private rights are affected the general rule applies that the specific statutory remedy should be sought.

review they are unlikely to act so as to overrule the Secretary of State's decision, but may direct him to review it if he failed to give proper consideration to its consequences.[13]

Appointment of governors etc

12.10 Where the Secretary of State considers that by default there is no properly constituted governing body he may make appointments and give directions so as to secure one, and he may validate acts and proceedings which are defective in consequence of the default.[14]

Rationalisation of school places

12.11 Where the Secretary of State thinks that the provision for primary or secondary education in LEA schools in any area is excessive, he may by order direct the exercise of powers by (a) the LEA to propose the establishment, alteration or discontinuance (see paras 3.08, 3.126 and 5.38) of any of their schools; or (b) the governing body of a voluntary school to propose the alteration of their school (see para 3.19); or (c) the funding authority (where an appropriate order applies—see para 2.39) to propose the establishment, alteration or discontinuance of grant-maintained (including special) schools (see paras 4.18, 4.52, 4.62 and 5.37). The proposals are (i) to be published (or notice of them served) by the date specified in the order, and (ii) to apply the principles the Secretary of State specifies. An order under (a) or (c) may not require proposals to relate to any named school. Proposals once made may be withdrawn only with the consent of the Secretary of State, who may impose conditions.[15]

12.12 No order may require any significant change to be made in the religious character of a voluntary school. Where the governing body of a voluntary school make proposals the persons appointing foundation governors are to be among those who may submit objections. The LEA are to reimburse the governing body's reasonable costs in making proposals, and where their proposals are approved the LEA are to meet the cost of implementation.

---

13 See *R v Secretary of State for the Environment, ex p Ward* [1984] 2 All ER 556.
14 1996 Act s 498 and 1988 Act s 219 as substituted by 1996 Act Sch 37 para 77. The governing bodies are those of maintained schools and LEA further or higher education institutions. As to the proper constitution of governing bodies see paras 3.50 ff (county, controlled and LEA special schools), 3.58 (voluntary aided and special agreement schools), 4.31 (grant-maintained schools), and 10.89 (LEA institutions of further or higher education).
15 1996 Act ss 500 and 505. In ss 500 to 504 (a) the powers of governing bodies of voluntary schools to make proposals for alteration means their powers to publish proposals under s 41(2); and (b) the powers of LEAs and funding authorities to make proposals for establishment, alteration or discontinuance of schools refer (i) to publication under ss 35 and 167 (LEAs) and 211, 260 or 268 (funding authorities) and (ii) to serving notice of proposals relating to special schools under s 339 (see paras 5.37 and 5.38). Where under s 339 the proposals are for a school to cease to be single sex see para 14.06 n 7.
 The power of the Secretary of State to approve or reject proposals made pursuant to a s 500 order is modified: s 37(4), (7) and (8) (or 43(3)–(5)) (see paras 3.14 and 3.19) do not apply to proposals under s 35(1)(c) or (d) or 41(2).
 A school is not eligible for grant-maintained status if the LEA or Secretary of State have made proposals under s 500 or s 502 repectively, and the proposals have not been withdrawn or determined.
 See Circular 23/94 on the Supply of School Places, para 38, E[3162].

12.13   Ancillary Functions

12.13 During parliamentary proceedings a Government spokesman said 'An example of the type of principle that the Secretary of State might wish to set would be that in bringing forward proposals the LEA should have regard to the need, to the desirability, of protecting and, where possible, enhancing schools of particular popularity with parents . . . [T]he direction and the principles would have to be within the purpose of the provisions of the Act in reasonably leading to the removal of surplus places. Further, the principles could not be ones that the authority could not itself put forward in fulfilment of its statutory duties'. A second Government spokesman said 'We must ensure that there is a sufficient, but not excessive, provision of places in each LEA area. We will want popular schools to expand in order to satisfy parental choice. If there is a perceived surplus capacity, the number of places should be reduced to a reasonable level'.

12.14 Where the Secretary of State has conferred on a funding authority sole responsibility for provision of sufficient school places in an LEA's area, (see para 2.39) but thinks that a given number of extra places is needed, he may by order direct (a) the authority to propose the establishment, alteration, or discontinuance of schools (without naming a particular school), or (b) the governing body of a voluntary school to propose the alteration of their school, so as (in either case) to make room for the number of extra pupils specified in the order. As with excessive provision, the proposals are (i) to be published (or notice of them served) by the date specified in the order, and (ii) to apply the principles the Secretary of State specifies.[16]

12.15 If the time allowed by an order for publication or service of notice of proposals relating to excessive provision has expired, the Secretary of State may make his own proposals in the manner prescribed. The proposals are to include (a) proposed implementation times, (b) (except where they relate to school closures or to a special school) particulars of numbers of pupils proposed to be admitted in each relevant age group in the first school year of full implementation, and (c) (in the case of pupils proposed to be admitted to a grant-maintained (including special) school for nursery education) prescribed information. Admission to an LEA school for nursery education is not to be regarded as an age at which pupils are normally admitted, but transfer to a nursery class is to be treated as admission.

12.16 The proposals are to be accompanied by a statement indicating what their effect will be upon school provision for pupils with special educational needs, and who has a statutory right of objection, namely
(a)   if the proposals affect full-time education for 16 to 18 year-olds, the further education funding council,
(b)   ten or more local government electors for the area,
(c)   the governing body of any school affected by the proposals and the persons entitled to appoint foundation governors of a voluntary school (see para 3.48),
(d)   any LEA concerned, and

---

16   1996 Act s 501. An order applying to an LEA may not require proposals to relate to a named school. Para 12.12 above applies. An order having been made, Sch 4 para 7 (under which the powers of LEAs to establish and maintain schools are modified where they share responsibilities for providing school places with the funding authority – see para 2.39) is disapplied in relation to the implementation of proposals under s 35 (see para 3.08).

(e) the funding authority if they have functions in the area (see para 2.39).[17]

12.17 If objections are made and not withdrawn the Secretary of State is to submit his proposals to a public inquiry, which is also to consider any outstanding proposals of his which are not opposed, and related proposals by the LEA, the funding authority or the governing body of a voluntary school. He may decide to withhold from the inquiry any proposals he thinks ought to be implemented in advance of it, but on reconsideration (if, for example, circumstances have changed) may decide to refer them to the inquiry after all. An inquiry is not to question the principles specified in (excessive, or additional provision) orders.[18]

12.18 Having considered the inquiry report the Secretary of State may abandon his own, or reject other, proposals, and/or adopt or approve either, with or without modification, or make his own further proposals, which he has subsequently to decide whether or not to adopt, with or without modification, in the light of further objections received (but without another public inquiry). Proposals adopted by the Secretary of State take effect as if approved by him under his powers in relation to LEAs and governing bodies of voluntary schools outlined at paras 3.13, 3.19, 3.126 and 5.39.[19]

Medical examinations

12.19 The Secretary of State may serve notice on parents to submit pupils for medical examination by a duly qualified practitioner to help him settle questions referred to him about revocation of school attendance orders (see para 7.45) and determination of disputes (see para 12.03). Failure to comply without reasonable excuse incurs a fine on summary conviction not exceeding level 1 on the standard scale.[20]

Local inquiries

12.20 The Secretary of State may cause a local inquiry to be held for the purposes of section 57 of the 1992 FHE Act (see para 10.54) and any of his functions under the 1996 Act.[1]

---

17 1996 Act s 502. See the Education (Publication of School Proposals and Notices) Regulations 1993, SI 1993/3113, regs 5 and 7(2).
  Objections are to be made within one month from the date on which the prescribed requirements are satisfied.
  'School year' is undefined in s 502, but in s 355(5) means the period beginning with the first school term to begin after July and ending with the beginning of the next school year.
  See Circular 23/94, para 40, E[3162].
18 1996 Act s 503. This section does not apply to 'further proposals' under s 504 (see below). The provisions of the Local Government Act 1972 s 250(2) to (5) (see n 1) apply to inquiries under this section.
  See Circular 23/94, para 43, E[3162].
19 1996 Act s 504. It might be appropriate for the Secretary of State to make further proposals if, for example, the inquiry inspector puts forward compromise proposals which do not entirely reflect any of the proposals which were before the inquiry.
20 1996 Act s 506.
1 1996 Act s 507. The Local Government Act 1972 s 250(2) to (5) (about giving evidence and costs) applies to the inquiry.

12.21   *Ancillary Functions*

Schools in the European Union

12.21 The Secretary of State has an obligation regularly to provide information about educational developments in England and Wales to persons managing schools elsewhere in the European Union which are (a) for resident British pupils between the ages of 5 and 18 inclusive, (b) have a curriculum broadly similar to that in maintained schools, and (c) have other characteristics which he may prescribe. If the school's management so requests, he is to arrange, at their expense, for inspections of such schools to be made from time to time by, or under the direction of, HMIs.[2]

ANCILLARY FUNCTIONS OF LOCAL EDUCATION AUTHORITIES AND GOVERNING BODIES

12.22 Most of these functions derive from Chapters II and III of Part IX of the 1996 Act (sections 508 to 536), but some from employment and health legislation.

Recreation and social and physical training

12.23 LEAs are to secure that adequate facilities for recreation and social and physical training are part of the provision for primary, secondary and further education for their areas. They may establish, maintain and manage camps, holiday classes, playing fields, play centres, and other places, including playgrounds, gymnasiums and swimming baths not appropriated to any school or other educational institution; or they may give assistance for those purposes. They may organise games, expeditions and other activities, and defray, or contribute towards, the expenses. In making their arrangements LEAs are to have regard to the expediency of co-operating with voluntary bodies.[3] There are other, general, powers to provide recreational facilities.[4]

Transport

12.24 LEAs are to make the arrangements they consider necessary, or as the Secretary of State directs, to provide free transport and otherwise to facilitate attendance at schools and specified further and higher education institutions, not discriminating between pupils at LEA schools and persons in other specified categories, including those in the further education sector and pupils at grant-maintained schools.[5]

---

2   1988 Act s 226.
3   1996 Act s 508. See also the Activity Centres (Young Persons' Safety) Act 1995 and Circular 22/94, 'Safety in Outdoor Activity Courses', E[3101].
4   Local Government (Miscellaneous Provisions) Act 1976 s 19.
5   1996 Act s 509(1), (2), (5) and (6). See Departmental Circular Letter, 29 January 1994, 'School Transport'.
     Transport should be 'non-stressful' (*R v Hereford and Worcester County Council, ex p P* [1992] 2 FCR 732 F[212] and *R v Gwent County Council, ex p Harris* [1995] 1 FCR 551, [1995] ELR 27). Failure to appoint supervisory staff may constitute negligence (*Shrimpton v Hertfordshire County Council* (1911) 104 LT 145, F[115]), but supervision by prefects may be adequate (*Jacques v Oxfordshire County Council* (1967) 66 LGR 440, F[140]). An LEA were held not liable for the negligence of a taxi driver who was their independent contractor (*Myton v Wood* (1980) 79 LGR 28).
     As to publication of information about arrangements for transport see the Education (School Information) (England) Regulations 1996, SI 1996/2585, reg 6 and Sch 1, para 7, and the Education (School Information) (Wales) Regulations 1994, SI 1994/2330, reg 7 and Sch 1, para 8.

12.25 'Spare seats' on school buses may be used to carry fare-paying passengers, who may, but need not, be pupils who are not entitled to free transport.[6] Where seat belts are not fitted three seated children each of whom is under 14 count as two passengers.[7]

12.26 In considering whether they are obliged to make arrangements for a particular person authorities are to have regard, inter alia, to the parent's wishes as regards religious education, and to the age of the person and the nature of the route or alternative routes he could reasonably be expected to take.[8] A route does not cease to be available because dangerous for an unaccompanied child if it is reasonably practicable for him to be accompanied.[9]

12.27 If a pupil's home is not within walking distance of his school and the LEA have not made suitable transport arrangements for him, his parent has a valid excuse for failing to secure his attendance (see para 7.47). Provision of the minimum arrangements which would be necessary to defeat the excuse is now regarded as an obligation upon LEAs, independent of any actual non-attendance. But a parent's choice of school beyond walking distance does not oblige an authority to make transport arrangements for the pupil if a place is available at a suitable nearer school, the suitability of the school not being wholly a matter of parental preference.[10]

12.28 LEAs may consider arrangements 'necessary' which go beyond the minimum, so providing, for example, free transport for those who live within walking distance of school but have health problems; and where 'arrangements' have not been made they have power to pay the whole or part of reasonable travelling expenses.[11]

Clothing

12.29 LEAs may provide clothing for pupils (a) boarding at LEA institutions and grant-maintained schools, (b) attending LEA nursery schools or nursery classes at maintained schools, (c) being provided with board and lodging elsewhere than at an institution they maintain, (d) for whom the LEA are making special educational provision, and (e) who do not fall within any of those categories but who, because of inadequate or unsuitable clothing, are unable to take full advantage of education at maintained schools or LEA and other special schools.

12.30 LEAs may also provide clothing for physical training at maintained schools, LEA further and higher education institutions and (pupils under 19) institutions in the further education sector, and to enable use to be made of the facilities they make available under their provision for recreation (see para

---

Sub-s (5) is applied by the Education (Grant-maintained Special Schools) Regulations 1994, SI 1994/653, reg 42, Schedule, Pt I, and by the Education (Special Schools Conducted by Education Associations) Regulations 1994, SI 1994/1084, reg 8(1), Sch 2, Pt I.
6 Public Passenger Vehicles Act 1981 s 46.
7 The Public Service Vehicles (Carrying Capacity) Regulations 1984, SI 1984/1406.
8 1996 Act s 509(4).
9 See the cases cited at para 7.47 n 4.
10 See the cases cited at para 7.47 n 4.
11 1996 Act s 509(3).

12.30 *Ancillary Functions*

12.23). Additionally, LEAs may make arrangements to provide clothing as in (e) above for pupils at non-maintained (other than special) schools, if the proprietor consents, on agreed financial and other terms. The expense is not to exceed, so far as practicable, that which would have been incurred had the pupil been at one of their schools.[12]

12.31 Provision of clothing may confer a right of property, or of user, at the option of the providing LEA unless the Secretary of State prescribes one way or the other. The LEA may, as prescribed, require the parent to pay as much of the cost of provision as he can without financial hardship, or a lesser sum, or nothing at all. Those aged 18 or over who are not registered school pupils pay instead of the parent.[13]

Meals and milk

12.32 LEAs and governing bodies of grant-maintained schools may provide registered pupils with milk, meals or other refreshment, either on school premises or elsewhere where education is being provided; and they are to provide facilities for consumption of food and drink brought to school by pupils. They are to make a charge, which is to be the same for all, except that free midday provision is to be made for pupils whose parents (or who themselves) receive income support or an income-based jobseeker's allowance. The same conditions (but without eligibility for free provision) apply in respect of persons receiving education at maintained schools who are no longer 'pupils', having reached the age of 19.[14]

12.33 The governing bodies of LEA schools are to give LEAs the facilities they need in connection with provision of school meals etc, and allow LEAs to make use of premises and equipment and make any necessary alterations to school buildings; but governors are not to be required to incur expenditure. Where there is financial delegation to governing bodies (see para 3.76) and they provide refreshments they are to charge for doing so and make no price discrimination between the recipients.[15]

12.34 LEAs may provide refreshments at non-LEA schools on terms agreed with the proprietor. So far as practicable the expense of doing so is not to exceed that which would have been incurred had the pupils been at one of their own schools.[16]

Board and lodging

12.35 An LEA may make arrangements to provide board and lodging for a pupil where they are satisfied

---

12 1996 Act s 510. See the Education (Provision of Clothing) Regulations 1980, SI 1980/545.
   This section is applied in part by the regulations mentioned at n 5 above.
13 1996 Act s 511. Payments under this section may be recovered summarily as a civil debt. See SI 1980/545.
14 1996 Act ss 512 and 534. 'Income support': see the Social Security Contributions and Benefits Act 1992 ss 123-127 and the Social Security Administration Act 1992 ss 105-108; 'income-based jobseeker's allowance': see the Jobseekers Act 1995 s 1. See also Circular 2/94, 'Local Management of Schools', E[2321], Annex E.
   This section is applied by the regulations mentioned at n 5.
15 1996 Act s 533.
16 1996 Act s 513.

(a) that primary or secondary education suitable to his age, ability and aptitude and any special educational needs he may have can best be provided at a particular maintained school, or special school, which is not a boarding school, and suitable education cannot otherwise be provided (for example because it is not within reasonable distance of the pupil's home); or
(b) that a pupil with special educational needs requires boarding accommodation to enable him to receive special educational provision.

12.36 So far as practicable the LEA are to respect the wishes of the parent about the religion or denomination of the person with whom the pupil is to reside.[17]

12.37 The cost of providing board and lodging is recoverable from the parent (so far as not to cause him financial hardship) unless the LEA have no other means of providing the pupil with suitable education. The exception does not apply where the Secretary of State has made an order under which responsibility for providing sufficient school places is transferred wholly to the funding authority or shared with the LEA (see para 2.39). Sums payable are recoverable summarily as a civil debt.[18]

Teaching services for day nurseries

12.38 With the agreement of a teacher employed in a nursery school or in a primary school with a nursery class, LEAs may make arrangements to make his services available in a day nursery provided by a local social services authority. In the case of a voluntary school the concurrence of the governing body is necessary. At the request of, and on terms approved by, the LEA, the governing bodies of county and voluntary primary schools may make the same arrangements. While at the day nursery the teacher remains a member of the school staff and subject to the general directions of his head teacher.[19]

12.39 Arrangements may provide for the supply of associated equipment; for regulating the respective functions of the teacher concerned, his head teacher and the person in charge of the day nursery; and for incidental matters, including financial adjustments between authorities where the school and day nursery are in different LEA areas.

17 1996 Act s 514(1) to (3). By Sch 4 para 13, s 514 does not apply where the Secretary of State has made an order under which responsibility for providing sufficient school places is transferred wholly to the funding authority (see para 2.39).
   Suitable education: see para 2.10 n 12.
   A general duty to have regard to the expediency of securing the provision of boarding accommodation in relation to primary and secondary schools, whether in boarding schools or otherwise, is imposed by s 14(6)(c) (see para 2.30).
18 1996 Act s 514(4) to (7) and Sch 4 para 1(2). Contrast 'could not otherwise be provided' with 'can *best* be provided' in s 514(1).
   See para 12.40 as to payment of fees for board and lodging at boarding schools.
   Sch 4 para 1(2) (relating to an order by the Secretary of State) is applied by the Education (Special Schools Conducted by Education Associations) Regulations 1994, SI 1994/1084, reg 8(1), Sch 2, Pt I.
19 1996 Act ss 515 and 535. Day nurseries are provided under the Children Act 1989 s 18. By s 29 local social services authorities may make a reasonable charge for services other than advice, guidance or counselling. See, as to the closure of a day nursery, *R v Barnet London Borough Council, ex p B* [1994] 1 FLR 592.

12.40 *Ancillary Functions*

Payment of fees   Expenses

12.40 Where LEAs make arrangements for pupils to receive primary or secondary education at non-LEA schools, to make special educational provision for them or otherwise, they are to pay the whole of the fees
(a) where the pupil fills a place put at the disposal of the LEA by a school in receipt of a 'direct grant'; or
(b) where the LEA are satisfied that education suitable to the age, ability and aptitude of the pupil and any special educational needs he may have cannot be provided at an LEA school to which he could be sent with reasonable convenience, because of shortage of places; or
(c) where neither (a) nor (b) apply and the pupil has special educational needs for which it is expedient in his interests that provision should be made at a non-LEA school; and
(d) for board and lodging (at school or elsewhere) where they are satisfied that otherwise they cannot provide education suitable as described in paragraph (b) at any school.[20] This provision is consistent with that applying exceptionally where board and lodging is provided otherwise than at a boarding school (see para 12.37).

12.41 So as to avoid hardship to persons using educational facilities or their parents, the Secretary of State has made regulations under which LEAs may
(a) defray expenses (such as purchase of uniform or other clothing, or transport costs) of those attending maintained schools or non-LEA special schools to enable them to take part in school activities;
(b) pay the whole or part of the fees and expenses related to attendance of children at fee-paying schools (including fees for board and lodging); and
(c) grant scholarships etc and other allowances to those at school over compulsory school age and on further education correspondence courses.

12.42 Payments may be made only to relieve financial hardship, and (excepting the correspondence courses) are to be related to means; and LEAs are to be satisfied that the education to which a payment relates is suitable for the pupil.[1]

---

20 1996 Act s 517. As from a day appointed by order of the Secretary of State (made by SI) these provisions are modified so as, in effect, to substitute 'maintained school' for 'LEA school', to include grant-maintained special schools and to disapply para (d) where the LEA pay fees under s 348(2) (see para 5.51).

The 'arrangements' are made under s 18 or Pt IV (special educational needs); 'direct grant' is payable under s 485; 'education suitable': see para 2.10 n 12; 'shortage of places' could be a general shortage of places affecting a range of pupils, or in respect of an individual pupil with some special (for example, musical) ability.

As to para (b), in *Watt v Kesteven County Council* [1955] 1 QB 408, F[41], it was held that where an LEA had fulfilled their duty under the 1944 Act s 8 to secure that sufficient schools were available for their area by making arrangements for the payment of full tuition fees at an independent school, they were not under an obligation to pay the whole tuition fees at some other independent school chosen by the parent.

The duty under para (c) was considered in *R v Hampshire Education Authority, ex p J* (1985) 84 LGR 547, F[87], and in *R v Inner London Education Authority, ex p F* (1988) Times, 16 June, F[46]. See also *R v Hackney London Borough, ex p GC* [1996] ELR 142, CA.

By 1996 Act Sch 4 para 13 (1)(c), para (b) does not apply where the Secretary of State has made an order under which responsibility for providing sufficient school places in the LEA's area has been transferred wholly to the funding authority (see para 2.39).

1 1996 Act s 518. See the Direct Grant Grammar Schools (Cessation of Grant) Regulations 1975, SI 1975/1198 and the Scholarships and Other Benefits Regulations 1977, SI 1977/1443. Compare the similar power of the Secretary of State (para 11.16). See also para 10.108.

Allowances for governors

12.43 LEAs may make schemes for paying travelling and subsistence allowances to governors of (a) LEA schools without delegated budgets, and (b) LEA higher or further education institutions. Schemes may make different provision as between categories of schools and institutions, but not between different categories of governor at the same school or institution.[2]

12.44 LEAs may also pay travelling and subsistence allowances to their representatives on governing bodies of (a) institutions of higher or further education or special schools which they do not maintain, and (b) independent schools, unless, in either case there is some other source of reimbursement, or if the LEA have failed to make a scheme, or, where a scheme has been made, the arrangements would provide for allowances more generous than any under the scheme.

Medical inspection and treatment   Notifiable disease

12.45 LEAs and governing bodies of grant-maintained schools are to make arrangements for encouraging and assisting pupils, with their parents' agreement, to take advantage of National Health Service medical and dental inspection and treatment. The Secretary of State (in practice, the Secretary of State for Health) has a complementary duty to provide medical inspection and treatment and, so far as he considers reasonably necessary, dental inspection and treatment, and education in dental health.[3]

12.46 By arrangement with LEAs the Secretary of State may also provide medical or dental inspection or treatment, or education in dental health, for senior pupils in LEA full-time further education institutions (if the governors agree), and for children and young persons receiving primary or secondary education otherwise than at school (see para 2.31). Arrangements may also be made, for junior and senior pupils, with proprietors of educational establishments not maintained by LEAs, by whom payments may be required.

12.47 A child suffering from a notifiable disease, or having been exposed to infection, is to be kept away from school, and the person having care of the child commits an offence if he attends in those circumstances.[4]

The 1944 Act s 81 was considered in *R v Inner London Education Authority,ex p F*[1988] Times, 16 June, F[46]. See also *R v Lambeth London Borough, ex p G* [1994] ELR 207, F[49], in which Potts J held that it was unlawful for an LEA to have a policy of making awards to persons attending schools outside their area only where there was no suitable course available within their area.

2 1996 Act s 519. No allowances are to be paid to governors otherwise than under this section. By Sch 9 para 19, s 519 applies to members of a temporary governing body. See Circular 2/94 'Local management of Schools', para 236, E[2443].

3 1996 Act ss 520 and 536, and National Health Service Act 1977 s 5 and Sch 1. LEAs, and governors of voluntary and grant-maintained schools, are to provide the necessary accommodation at their schools.

These sections are applied by the Education (Grant-maintained Special Schools) Regulations 1994, SI 1994/653, reg 42, Schedule, Pt I; and by the Education (Special Schools Conducted by Education Associations) Regulations 1994, SI 1994/1084, reg 8(1), Sch 2, Pt I.

4 Public Health (Control of Disease) Act 1984, ss 10, 21 and 22.

12.48 *Ancillary Functions*

Cleanliness

12.48 LEAs may by directions in writing authorise a medical officer of the authority to have the persons and clothing of pupils at maintained schools examined in the interests of cleanliness. Directions may apply to some or all schools in the LEA's area. Examinations are to be made by a person authorised by the LEA. The examination or subsequent cleansing of a girl is to be carried out only by a qualified medical practitioner or a woman authorised by an LEA. If a pupil or his clothing is found to be infested with vermin or in a foul condition, any officer of the LEA may serve a notice requiring his parent to have him and his clothing cleansed. The notice is to convey that unless the cleansing has been carried out satisfactorily within a stated period (not less than 24 hours) it will be done under the LEA's arrangements; and if need be the medical officer may by order direct accordingly. The order may cover removing the pupil to, and keeping him at, the premises where the cleansing is to be carried out.[5]

12.49 The LEA are to make arrangements for suitable premises, persons and appliances for undertaking the cleansing. Where district councils[6] have premises and appliances for cleansing from vermin the LEA may require permission to use them, on terms settled by agreement or, in default, by the Secretary of State [for Health].[7] Where there is a delay in carrying out an examination or cleansing the medical officer may, on his own account, if he thinks it necessary, direct that a pupil be excluded from school in the meantime; and the direction is a defence to proceedings for non-attendance (see para 7.47) unless made necessary by wilful default of pupil or parent.[8] If, after cleansing, the pupil or his clothing is again found to be in need of cleansing, and this is proved to be due to the parent's neglect, on summary conviction the parent incurs a fine at level 1 on the standard scale. Where the child lives with both parents the court may, on the facts of the case, hold one or other liable.[9]

Educational research and conferences

12.50 To improve the educational facilities for their areas LEAs may make provision for, or assist, the conduct of research; and at reasonable cost they may organise or participate in organising conferences for discussion of educational questions, paying the expenses of those they authorise to attend as well as speakers' fees and expenses.[10]

The Youth Service

12.51 LEAs rely on their recreation and training and further education powers (see paras 10.87 and 12.23), to set up and run youth clubs and centres,

---

5   1996 Act ss 521 and 522. These sections are applied as noted above. See AM 156.
6   Does not apply in Wales where district councils have been superseded.
7   1996 Act s 523. This section is applied as noted above.
8   1996 Act s 524. See *Fox v Burgess* [1922] 1 KB 623. This section is applied as noted above.
9   1996 Act s 525. See *Plunkett v Alker* [1954] 1 All ER 396, F[182], distinguishing *LCC v Stansell* (1935) 154 LT 241.
    This section is applied as noted above.
10 1996 Act ss 526 and 527.

Careers services

12.52 Careers services consist of providing information about persons seeking, obtaining or offering employment, training and education; offering advice and guidance; and supporting services.[11]

12.53 The Secretary of State has a duty to secure the provision of careers services for those in full-time education (except in the higher education sector) and in part-time vocational education. He may do so for others and make a charge. The object is to help those concerned (a) to decide what forms of employment will be suitable and available for them, and what available training or further education they will need; and (b) to obtain employment, training or further education.

12.54 The Secretary of State may make arrangements with LEAs or others to provide, or arrange the provision of, the services, jointly or separately; or he may give directions to LEAs (which may include a requirement to transfer any relevant records) on how they should do so. In either case he is to have regard to the requirements of disabled persons. Arrangements may include (a) the Secretary of State's paying grants or loans (but LEAs may meet their costs otherwise), and (b) requirements that his general guidance be followed, and that he be given the information he specifies or facilities for obtaining it.

12.55 Subject to any directions given, LEAs may provide or arrange for provision of services in accordance with arrangements or directions by whatever means they consider appropriate (which may include the formation of companies). They may employ officers and provide facilities accordingly. With the consent of the Secretary of State services may be provided more extensive than those authorised under the arrangements or required by the directions.

PROVISION OF INFORMATION BY GOVERNING BODIES AND SCHOOL PROPRIETORS

12.56 The following obligations derive from Chapter IV of Part IX of the 1996 Act (sections 537 to 541).

12.57 The Secretary of State has made regulations requiring proprietors of independent schools and governing bodies of maintained schools and non-LEA special schools (but not nursery schools) to provide the information he prescribes to assist parents to choose schools for their children, to show the quality

---

11 Employment and Training Act 1973, ss 8 to 10 (as substituted by the Trade Union Reform and Employment Rights Act 1993, s 45). Directions given may be varied or revoked by another direction. Section 10A (inserted by s 46) specifies the powers of LEAs to enter into agreements for the provision of ancillary goods and services.

12.57 *Ancillary Functions*

of education provided and standards achieved, and to assist in assessing the efficiency of financial resource management. No pupil is to be named. Prescribed information may extend to information about continuing education and employment or training for school-leavers.[12]

12.58 The Secretary of State has powers, and may make requirements, under regulation, concerning publication of information and its provision to prescribed persons by governing bodies of maintained schools, proprietors of city colleges and LEAs. Where the proprietor of an independent school fails to comply with requirements under the regulations the Secretary of State may order its deletion from the register of independent schools.

12.59 Governing bodies of LEA schools are to make reports and returns, and give the Secretary of State the information he requires for the exercise of his education functions.[13]

12.60 Governing bodies of grant-maintained schools are to publish prescribed information, and provide the Secretary of State, the funding authority and any LEA affected with reports, returns and information relevant to their functions, in particular to enable LEAs to co-operate in the obligatory triennial review of day care provision for children in need aged five or under and not yet attending school.[14]

12.61 When the governing bodies of maintained schools providing primary education (including LEA (non-hospital) special schools and, additionally, grant-maintained special schools) receive requests from the governing bodies of schools providing secondary education about the free distribution of information about those schools to parents, they are not to discriminate as between secondary schools as to the services they provide and the terms on which they provide them.[15]

---

12 1996 Act s 537. Although this section refers to parents 'choosing' schools, the substantive provision on school admissions, s 411 (see para 7.03), refers only to expressing a 'preference', which may or may not be complied with according to circumstances.

See the Education (School Performance Information) (England) Regulations 1996, SI 1996/2577; the Education (School Information) (England) Regulations 1996, SI 1996/2585; the Education (School Information) (Wales) Regulations 1994, SI 1994/2330; the Education (School Performance Information) (Wales) Regulations 1995, SI 1995/1904; and also as regards publication by governing bodies, the Education (Special Educational Needs) (Information) Regulations 1994, SI 1994/1048; and the Education (Pupil Referral Units) (Application of Enactments) Regulations 1994, SI 1994/2103.

See also regulations made under s 408 (para 6.70) and Circular 8/96, (WO 23/96) 'The Parent's Charter: Publication of Information about Secondary School Performance in 1996'.

The requirements concerning publication and provision of information are applied by the Education (Grant-maintained Special Schools) Regulations 1994, SI 1994/653, reg 42, Schedule, Pt I and by the Education (Special Schools Conducted by Education Associations) Regulations 1994, SI 1994/1084, reg 8(1), Sch 2, Pt I.

13 1996 Act s 538.

14 1996 Act s 539 and the Children Act 1989 s 19(1)(a). See the Education (Special Educational Needs) (Information) Regulations 1994, SI 1994/1048; the Education (School Information) (England) Regulations 1996, SI 1996/2585; the Education (School Information) (Wales) Regulations 1994, SI 1994/2330; and the Education (School Performance Information) (Wales) Regulations 1995, SI 1995/1904.

Section 539 is applied by the Education (Special Schools Conducted by Education Associations) Regulations 1994, SI 1994/1084, reg 8, Sch 2, Pt I.

15 1996 Act s 540.

12.62 The Secretary of State has made regulations requiring (a) governing bodies of maintained schools providing secondary education (including LEA (non-hospital) special schools and, additionally, grant-maintained special schools), and (b) proprietors of city colleges, to distribute, to the pupils mentioned, information about institutions in the further education sector which their governing bodies are already required to publish.[16]

---

16 1996 Act s 541. The information is published under 1992 FHE Act s 50 (see para 10.52).
　　See the Education (Distribution by Schools of Information about Further Education Institutions) (England) Regulations 1995, SI 1995/2065 and the Education (Distribution by Schools of Information about Further Education Institutions) (Wales) Regulations 1994, SI 1994/1321; also Circular 9/95, 'Local publication and distribution of information about the achievements of students in Further Education sector colleges'.

Chapter 13

TEACHERS AND OTHER STAFF

TRAINING

13.01 Teacher training is the subject matter of Part I of the Education Act 1994 (sections 1 to 19). There are a few other relevant statutory provisions.

General

13.02 The Secretary of State is to make arrangements for securing sufficient facilities for the training of teachers in (a) maintained schools, (b) further education sector institutions, and (c) LEA further and higher education institutions.[1] Courses of initial teacher training require his approval, under regulation; and he may also bring courses to an end and control the number and categories of students to be admitted.[2]

13.03 To facilitate the training of teachers the Secretary of State or Teacher Training Agency (see para 13.06 ff below) pay grants to prescribed persons other than LEAs (see para 11.05). The Secretary of State may make loans under regulation (otherwise than to LEAs) towards the capital expenditure of teacher training colleges.[3]

13.04 The governing bodies of maintained schools may provide courses of initial training for school teachers, either alone or in association with other 'eligible institutions'—those within the further and higher education sectors, other schools, and other bodies designated by order of the Secretary of State; also any association etc of eligible institutions or body established to carry on 'qualifying activities'. These are the provision of (a) teacher training, (b) supporting activities approved by governing bodies, and (c) related services, by any person.[4]

---

1 1994 Act s 11A. Applied by the Education (Grant-maintained Special Schools) Regulations 1994, SI 1994/653, reg 42, Schedule, Pt I; and by the Education (Special Schools Conducted by Education Associations) Regulations 1994, SI 1994/1084, reg 8(1), Sch 2, Pt I.
2 1988 Act s 218(9)(b) and (c), (10) and (11). See the Education (Schools and Further and Higher Education) Regulations 1989, SI 1989/351, regs 11 to 13 and Sch 2, in which initial teacher training courses are designated as those leading to the degree of B Ed, the Certificate of Education, the Post-graduate Certificate in Education or a comparable UK university award.
3 1967 Act s 4.
4 1994 Act ss 4 and 12. Entry to initial training courses is limited to graduates of a UK or foreign institution. (Students are eligible for the awards referred to in para 10.106; as to fees see para 10.104). The governing body's supplementary and incidental powers apply, and any conflicting provisions in the school's instrument or articles of government are overridden.

13.05 Providing or ceasing to provide a course of teacher training does not constitute a significant change in the character of the school and thus give rise to the procedures mentioned at paras 3.08, 3.19 and 4.49; nor is providing a course to be treated for budgetary purposes as being undertaken 'for the purposes of the school'—and this prevents the governing body from spending, for training, funds which they receive as part of their delegated budget or annual maintenance grant.

The Teacher Training Agency

13.06 A corporate non-departmental public body, the Teacher Training Agency have the main functions of providing information and advice about teaching as a career, and, in England, of funding teacher training and related facilities and activities.[5]

13.07 The Secretary of State appoints between 8 and 12 members of the Teacher Training Agency (including their chairman) who are ordinarily to have had either successful experience of teaching, or providing education, in schools or in higher education (whether or not in teacher training), and are preferably doing so currently. Some members are preferably to have experience of (a) denominational institutions, (b) special educational needs, and (c) industrial, commercial or financial matters or the practice of a profession.[6]

13.08 In Wales, the Higher Education Funding Council for Wales are the funding agency. The two funding agencies (to be distinguished from the Funding Agency for Schools and the Schools Funding Council for Wales) are responsible for administering funds made available by the Secretary of State and others to provide financial support for eligible institutions to carry on qualifying activities. The Secretary of State determines any dispute about which funding agency are to act.[7]

13.09 The Secretary of State may, after due consultation, by order give the Teacher Training Agency additional functions which are consistent with their general objectives (see para 13.10 below); and he may give the Council for Wales supplementary functions, namely those of his own relating to an eligible institution or its activities. He may direct both the Agency and the Council

---

By s 4(3) the Secretary of State is given power to provide by order for references to the governing body to be read as references to any company conducting an institution, or to both the company and the governing body, thus enabling requirements in s 5 about grants and loans etc to be imposed on the appropriate body. See the Education (Funding for Teacher Training) Designation Order 1995, SI 1995/1704 (City Technology Colleges Trust Ltd), SI 1996/1832 (Centre for British Teachers Maryvale Institute and the Urban Learning Foundation) and SI 1997/515 (Titan Partnership, Solihull Metropolitan Borough Council and Essex County Council). By s 4(4) the 'governing body' of an LEA nursery school are the LEA.

Section 12 does not affect the ability of a school to provide training for its teaching staff, or to participate in a teacher training course provided by another institution, as an ordinary incident of the conduct of the school. This section is applied by the Education (Grant-maintained Special Schools) (No 2) Regulations 1994, SI 1994/2247.

5 1994 Act s 1(1). By sub-s (4) the Agency are to have regard to the requirements of disabled persons under the Disability Discrimination Act 1995.
6 1994 Act s 2 and Sch 1, which provides for such matters as the supplementary powers of the Agency, their chief officer, members and staff, committees, proceedings, accounts, annual report and status.
7 1994 Act s 3. By sub-s (2) the institutions include the Open University.

13.09 *Teachers and Other Staff*

to carry out ancillary activities.⁸ He has conferred on the Agency functions concerning (a) the licensing etc of unqualified teachers, (b) teachers at city colleges aspiring to be qualified, and (c) (additionally on the Council for Wales) the accreditation of institutions as providing courses satisfying criteria he specifies.⁹

13.10 The objectives of the Agency in exercising their functions are to (a) contribute to raising the standards of teaching, (b) promote teaching as a career, (c) improve the quality and efficiency of all routes into the teaching profession, and (d) secure the involvement of schools in all courses for the initial training of school teachers, and 'generally to secure that teachers are well fitted and trained to promote the spiritual, moral, social, cultural, mental and physical development of pupils for the opportunities, responsibilities and experiences of adult life'. Except where otherwise provided (eg in relation to funding) the Agency's functions may be exercised in relation to both England and Wales, but in relation to Wales only at the request of the Secretary of State.¹⁰

13.11 The Agency have both an obligation and a power to give the Secretary of State information and advice; the Agency and the Higher Education Council for Wales are to give each other information about teacher training; and the governing bodies of teacher training institutions and LEAs are to give relevant information to the Agency and the Council upon request.¹¹

The activities of the Agency   Funding

13.12 The agencies may make grants, loans and other payments to governing bodies of eligible institutions for qualifying activities, and to persons providing related services, subject to terms and conditions which may include, on non-compliance, the requirement to repay sums paid and pay interest on sums outstanding. Agencies are to have regard to (a) forecasts of demand for newly-qualified teachers received from the Secretary of State, and (b) assessments of the quality of education provided by particular institutions made by HM Chief Inspectors of Education or from other specified sources.¹²

13.13 In providing financial support the agencies are to have regard to the desirability of (a) keeping an appropriate balance between school-centred and other courses, and between denominational and other institutions, (b) maintaining the distinctive characteristics of eligible institutions, and (c) not discouraging alternative sources of support. Before agencies impose terms and conditions they are to consult bodies representing eligible institutions, and also the governing bodies of any particular institutions concerned. The agencies are

---

8 1994 Act s 16. See the Teacher Training Agency (Additional Functions) Order 1995, SI 1995/601.
9 1988 Act s 218(2A) inserted by the 1994 Act s 14. See the Education (Teachers) Regulations 1993, SI 1993/543, Sch 3, para 2(1A).
10 1994 Act s 1(2) and (3). The functions mentioned were formerly carried out by the Teaching as a Career Unit (whose property etc was transferred to the Agency under s 17 and the Teaching as a Career Unit (Transfer of Property, Rights and Liabilities) Order 1994, SI 1994/2463) and by the Higher Education Funding Council for England.
11 1994 Act s 15.
12 1994 Act s 5. Terms and conditions are not to relate to sums received otherwise than from funding agencies.

to secure that governing bodies make information available about the initial teacher training courses funded.[13]

13.14 The Secretary of State may make grants to funding agencies subject to terms and conditions which include their imposing requirements to be complied with by institutions (or classes of institution) before financial support is provided. On non-compliance with terms or conditions, repayment of sums paid and payment of interest on sums outstanding may be required. Terms and conditions are not to relate to activities carried on by particular institutions, or to be framed by reference to particular courses or research programmes, or to criteria for appointment of staff and admission of students.[14]

13.15 Funding agencies are to comply with directions made by order of the Secretary of State. Directions may be general or, if he considers that the financial affairs of an eligible institution are being mismanaged, specific. Before giving a specific direction the Secretary of State is to consult the agency and the institution.[15] Agencies may
(a) exercise their functions jointly with the other funding agency, the Higher Education Funding Council for England, a further education funding council or a funding authority for schools, so as to improve efficiency or discharge their functions more effectively,[16]
(b) arrange for efficiency etc studies to be undertaken at an institution receiving financial support,[17] and
(c) carry out or commission research into training of teachers and standards of teaching.[18]

QUALIFICATIONS, FITNESS, APPRAISAL

13.16 The requirements are mainly those prescribed by the Secretary of State.[19] In outline they are as follows:

13 1994 Act s 6. A 'school-centred' course is one which is provided by a school or schools, or by a body established by a school or institutions consisting wholly or mainly of schools. It does not include a course provided mainly by an institution of higher education.
14 1994 Act s 7.
15 1994 Act s 8. Orders are to be by SI and, by s 23, may be revoked or varied by orders giving subsequent directions.
16 1994 Act s 9. Funding authorities for schools are the Funding Agency for Schools and the Schools Funding Council for Wales (see para 2.35).
17 1994 Act s 10. The person or body carrying out the studies has power to require the governing body of the institution to furnish information and make accounts and other documents available for inspection so far as reasonably required for the purpose of the studies.
18 1994 Act s 11.
19 1988 Act s 218 and the Education (Teachers) Regulations 1993, SI 1993/543. The regulations apply to maintained schools and to non-maintained (including grant-maintained) special schools. Regulation 10 (barring by the Secretary of State) applies also to the proprietors of independent schools.
    By regs 14 to 16 (with an exception for temporary employment in reg 17) teachers of pupils with impaired sight or hearing are to possess additional qualifications. Schedule 3 defines 'qualified teacher' and Sch 2 specifies the cases and circumstances in which unqualified teachers may be employed at schools.
    As to overseas teachers see *Hampson v Department of Education and Science* [1990] 2 All ER 513, HL and *Bleis v Ministère de l'Education Nationale*: C–4/91 [1991] ECR I–5627, ECJ.
    See Circulars 13/93 'Physical and mental fitness to teach of teachers and entrants to initial teacher training' and 14/93, (WO 62/93) 'The initial training of primary school teachers: new criteria for courses'.

13.16 *Teachers and Other Staff*

(a) teachers at maintained schools and special schools (whether or not maintained) are, with minor exceptions, *either* to be qualified teachers (those who (i) having obtained at least GCSE Grade C in English and mathematics, have completed successfully an approved initial training course leading to the degree of B Ed, the Certificate of Education, the Postgraduate Certificate in Education or a comparable UK university qualification; or (ii) hold a UK or foreign degree or equivalent qualification and have successfully completed an initial training course at an accredited institution (see para 13.09) *or* to fall within specified excepted categories (including persons whom the Secretary of State or the Teacher Training Agency license, or in the case of overseas trained teachers authorise, to teach);

(b) teachers at further education institutions maintained by LEAs, or within the further education sector, are to possess appropriate qualifications;

(c) teachers at the schools and institutions mentioned in (a) and (b) are no longer required to serve probationary periods;

(d) '. . . a staff of teachers suitable and sufficient in numbers for . . . securing the provision of education appropriate to . . . ages, abilities and aptitudes and needs . . .' is to be employed at the schools and institutions mentioned in (a) and (b)[20] ('supply' teachers are employed to stand in for those absent from school in case of (eg) sickness, on a day-to-day or other short term basis[1]);

(e) the health and physical capacity of teachers and other persons regularly in contact with those aged under 19 employed at the schools and institutions mentioned in (a) and (b) and at institutions in the higher education sector which are funded by the Higher Education Funding Council (or, if employed by LEAs, elsewhere) are to meet specified standards; and

(f) the employment or further employment by LEAs, governing bodies and proprietors of independent schools of those mentioned in (e), on medical grounds, in cases of misconduct, and (teachers) on educational grounds, is prohibited or restricted, and in misconduct cases the facts are to be reported to the Secretary of State.[2]

13.17 Regular appraisal may be required by LEAs and others, under regulation, of the performance of teachers in discharging their duties and other activities. Regulations are to be made after consultation with representative bodies of local authorities and teachers. They apply at present to teachers at maintained schools. Governing bodies of LEA schools are, so far as reasonably practicable, to secure compliance with the appraisal arrangements. Teachers are to receive a copy of the 'appraisal statement', on which they have a prior opportunity to comment. Appraisal records may be used in connection with pay, promotion, dismissal or discipline.[3]

---

20 See *R v Liverpool City Council, ex p Ferguson* (1985) Times, 20 November, F[86].
1 See Circular 7/96 (WO 38/96) 'Supply Teachers'.
2 In *R v Secretary of State for Education, ex p Standish* (1993) Times, 15 November, it was held that the Secretary of State should make express findings of fact and give reasons when debarring a teacher from his employment. See Circulars 9/93 (WO 54/93) 'Protection of Children: Disclosure of Criminal Background . . .', 10/95, 'Protection of Children from Abuse—Role of the Education Service' and 11/95, 'Misconduct of Teachers and Workers with Children and Young Persons', E[3451].
3 1986 Act s 49. See the Education (School Teacher Appraisal) Regulations 1991, SI 1991/1511 and Circular 12/91 (WO 43/91) 'School Teacher Appraisal', E[1597].

APPOINTMENT AND DISMISSAL

13.18 Once a county, controlled or special agreement school has a delegated budget (see para 3.76) the powers of governing bodies are enhanced: the LEA remain the employer but decisions about appointment and dismissal etc are for the governing body; and within five years of the date when an LEA school first has a delegated budget the articles of government are to be amended to include a statement to the effect that the provisions mentioned in paras 13.21 to 13.26 below supersede those mentioned in para 13.27.[4] Also the Secretary of State may, after consultation as specified, by order suitably modify employment law.[5]

13.19 Where a county or voluntary school at which non-school activities take place on the premises under the management or control of the governing body (a 'community school') has a delegated budget, members of staff may be treated as taking part in school activities even if not employed, or only partly employed, on those activities.[6]

13.20 Arrangements for appointment and dismissal[7] etc of staff in maintained schools vary according to the status of the school, and there are special provisions relating to teachers of religious education (see para 13.33 below). Schools fall into several categories, as follows.

LEA (except aided) schools with delegated budgets

13.21 When a vacancy arises for a head or deputy head teacher the governing body are to notify the LEA, advertise the vacancy nationally and appoint a selection panel to recommend who should fill it. An acting appointment may be

---

4 1996 Act ss 136 and 141. As to new schools see s 166 and Sch 19. For application to LEA special schools see s 142 and the Education (Application of Financing Schemes to Special Schools) Regulations 1993, SI 1993/3104. Where schools are affected by local government reorganisation see the Local Government (Changes for England) (Local Management of Schools) Regulations 1995, SI 1995/3114.
   See Circular 2/94 'Local Management of Schools . . .', Pt 8, E[2405].
5 1996 Act s 178. See the Education (Modification of Enactments Relating to Employment) Order 1989, SI 1989/901 and Circulars 13/89, (WO 37/89) 'Local Management of Schools . . .: Order under s 222 of the Education Reform Act 1988', E[1010], and 2/94 para 185, E[2410].
6 1996 Act s 140. See Circular 2/94 paras 184, E[2409] and 229, E[2420].
7 In *R v Birmingham City Council, ex p McKenna* (1991) Times, 16 May, it was held that a selection panel should not operate with fewer than its full complement: if it did not sit as constituted it did not amount to a selection panel.
   See the Education (School Government) Regulations 1989, SI 1989/1503 and Circular 7/87 (WO 12/87) 'Education (No 2) Act 1986: Further Guidance', para 5.13, E[357].
   As to (a) staffing of new schools see Sch 19, (b) the invalidity of an appointment where the procedure was improper see *Noble v Inner London Education Authority* (1983) 82 LGR 291, CA and *Champion v Chief Constable of the Gwent Constabulary* [1990] 1 All ER 116, HL F[97] (in which a parent governor who was a police constable was held to be as such not disqualified from sitting on an appointments committee), (c) cases on dismissal see *Watts v Monmouthshire County Council* (1967) 66 LGR 171, CA, *R v Governors of Litherland High School, ex p Corkish* (1982) Times, 4 December, CA. *R v Powys County Council, ex p Smith* (1982) 81 LGR 342, *McGoldrick v Brent London Borough* [1987] IRLR 67, CA, *Gunton v Richmond-upon-Thames London Borough Council* (1980) 79 LGR 241 CA, *Winder v Cambridgeshire County Council* (1978) 76 LGR 549 CA, (procedure on dismissal of a further education teacher), *Blanchard v Dunlop* [1917] 1 Ch 165, *Malloch v Aberdeen Corpn* [1971] 1 WLR 1578, HL and *Scott v Aberdeen Corpn* 1975 SLT 167 (right to a non-statutory hearing before dismissal), and (d) suspension see *Gorse v Durham County Council* [1971] 1 WLR 775 and *Whitley v Harrow London Borough Council* (1988) Guardian, 29 March.

13.21 *Teachers and Other Staff*

made. Procedures are specified in case of disagreement within a selection panel, and between panel and governing body, on settlement of which the authority are to appoint the person recommended by the governing body unless he fails to meet the qualification and fitness requirements, in which case the selection panel may be reactivated.[8]

13.22 To fill any other vacant teaching post (other than temporarily) the governing body are to decide a specification for it in consultation with the head teacher and advertise it, unless they accept the LEA's nomination or recommend that it be filled by an existing member of staff. The governing body may delegate their appointing functions to one or more of their number or to the head teacher (or to both acting together). Procedures are specified for settling disagreements, and appointments are to be made as above.

13.23 Non-teaching staff and clerks to governing bodies are also to be appointed by authorities on the recommendation of governing bodies. School meals staff are excluded from these provisions if less than 50 per cent of their remuneration derives from the school's budget share.

13.24 The governing body control staff discipline, and are to be supported when necessary by the LEA. Both governing body and head teacher have power to suspend (without loss of emoluments) employees whose exclusion from school appears to be required. Only governing bodies have power to reinstate. Before a governing body decide that a person should cease to work at a school (as contrasted with suspension) or that their clerk should be dismissed, they are to give him the opportunity to make representations, and, if those fail, a right of appeal. Once a decision is made, the governing body are to give the LEA a reasoned explanation, and if the person works solely at the school the authority are to dismiss him by notice under his contract of employment, or without notice if his conduct entitles them to do so. Where the dismissal is required in the case of misconduct, or on medical or educational grounds, these procedures are superseded by regulation.[9]

13.25 The governing body decide upon the level of compensation (if any) to be paid by the LEA to a member of staff on his dismissal or agreement to resign, except where the LEA make a payment by virtue of a contract not made in contemplation of impending dismissal or resignation. The LEA may deduct compensation costs from the school's budget share only if they have 'good reason'—which does not include a policy of not dismissing for redundancy. But the costs incurred by an LEA in respect of the premature retirement of a member of staff occurring on or after 21 March 1997 are to be met from the school's budget share, except so far as the LEA agree to the contract.[10]

13.26 Chief education officers and head teachers are to be consulted and have the right to attend meetings on appointments of teachers. Head teachers are to be consulted on appointment of non-teaching staff, as are chief education officers in the case of those who are to work at the school for 16 hours a week or more.

---

8 1996 Act Sch 14. See Circular 2/94 Pt 8, E[2405].
9 See the Education (Teachers) Regulations 1993, SI 1993/543, regs 9 and 10.
10 1996 Act s 139 and 1997 Act s 50. See Circular 2/94 paras 175 to 180, E[2406]. As to premature retirement see para 13.74 below. See, as to dismissal for redundancy para 13.46 ff.

Both chief education officers and head teachers are entitled to attend meetings about dismissals (except where a head teacher is the person concerned).[11]

LEA schools (except aided schools) without delegated budgets

13.27 Few if any schools now fall within this category. The appointment and dismissal procedures are outlined in Appendix 8, but in brief they are as follows. The LEA are to determine the complement of posts, which includes all full-time teaching posts and part-time teaching posts where employment is confined to a particular school, together with non-teaching posts apart from the authority's school meals and midday supervisory staff. Appointment and dismissal of staff are under the control of the authority subject to the articles of government of the school, to provisions relating to the appointment and dismissal of the clerk to the governing body and to the conduct and staffing of new schools; and, as regards 'reserved' teachers at controlled and special agreement schools, to the provisions outlined in para 13.33 below.[12]

Voluntary aided schools

13.28 The contract of service is between teacher and governing body.[13]

13.29 When the governing body have a delegated budget, appointment, suspension and dismissal are entirely at their discretion, subject to the articles of government. They may, however, agree with the LEA that the authority's chief education officer should have advisory rights (or, in default of agreement, those rights may be determined by the Secretary of State). The advice may extend to the appointment or dismissal of all teachers (or both) or may be restricted to head teachers and, or alternatively, deputy head teachers. While the rights subsist the chief education officer, or an officer nominated by him, is entitled to attend all relevant proceedings of the governing body. The governing body are to notify the LEA of the reason for dismissing any member of staff.[14] Para 13.25 above applies with regard to compensation.

13.30 Where there is no delegated budget, the functions of LEAs and governing body are to be determined by the articles of government, which are to provide that
(a) the LEA decide teacher numbers,
(b) the governing body appoint teachers,
(c) the LEA may prohibit the dismissal of teachers without the authority's consent[15] (with the exception mentioned at para 13.34 below),

---

11 1996 Act Sch 14 paras 16, 17 and 26.
12 1996 Act ss 133 and 135, and Schs 13 and 19.
13 See *Hannam v Bradford City Council* [1970] 1 WLR 937. As to status of governors, see *National Union of Teachers v Governors of St Mary's Church of England Aided Junior School* [1995] ICR 317 EAT.
14 1966 Act ss 137 and 138. The diocesan director of education has the same rights in respect of Church of England aided schools (Diocesan Boards of Education Measure 1991 s 9).
  The dismissal or withdrawal from school of any member of the staff who is employed by the LEA is to be in accordance with the procedures under paras 23 to 28 of Sch 14 (as in the case of staff in other LEA schools with delegated budgets).
  See, as to the appointment of a head teacher, *St Matthias Church of England School (Board of Governors) v Crizzle* [1994] ICR 401, EAT, F[37].
15 See *Jones v Lee* [1980] ICR 310, CA.

13.30 *Teachers and Other Staff*

(d) the LEA are to be able to require the dismissal of any teacher, and
(e) by agreement between LEA and the governing body (or in default as determined by the Secretary of State) the LEA are to be enabled to prohibit the appointment without their consent of teachers to be employed for giving secular education, and to direct what are to be the educational qualifications of those so employed.[16]

13.31 Only when a school does not have a delegated budget may an LEA give directions to the governing body regarding the number and conditions of service of persons employed to maintain the school premises.[17]

Grant-maintained schools

13.32 Contracts of employment are made between the governing body and teachers and other staff.[18]

Appointment and dismissal of teachers of religious education

13.33 The appointment of 'reserved' teachers at controlled and special agreement schools to give denominational religious education is to be made by LEAs only with the approval of the foundation governors, who are to be satisfied about their competence for that purpose. Foundation governors may also require the LEA to dismiss reserved teachers from employment as such if of the opinion that they have failed to give that education efficiently and suitably.[19]

13.34 If a teacher at an aided school appointed to give (denominational) religious education otherwise than in accordance with an agreed syllabus (see para 6.33) fails to give that education efficiently and suitably the governing body may dismiss him without the consent of the LEA.[20]

CONDITIONS OF EMPLOYMENT: GENERAL LEGISLATION

13.35 Legislation of general effect governs the employment of teachers and supporting staff. Aspects which particularly affect them and which are briefly

---

16 1996 Act s 134(1) to (4). See *Hannam* (n 13 above). As to the effect of failure to communicate a resolution of appointment see *Powell v Lee* (1908) 99 LT 284.
17 1996 Act s 134(5). By sub-s (6) for 'governing body' substitute 'a person specified in a trust deed' where control over occupation and use of school premises is transferred by the deed to him from the governing body.
18 1996 Act s 231(5) (e). Under Sch 21 para 2 a new governing body may enter into contracts of employment for teachers and other staff between the incorporation date and the implementation date (see para 4.10).

   As to dismissal of a teacher from a grant-maintained school see *R v Secretary of State for Education, ex p Prior* [1994] ELR 231.

   Section 231 is applied to the governing bodies of grant-maintained special schools by Sch 28 para 12 and the Education (Grant-maintained Special Schools) Regulations 1994, SI 1994/653, reg 16.
19 1996 Act s 143 (under which the number of reserved teachers at controlled schools is specified, and it is provided that the head teacher is not to be a reserved teacher) and s 144.
20 1996 Act s 145.

mentioned here are (a) time off work, (b) health and safety at work, (c) dismissal, (d) redundancy, (e) sex and racial discrimination, and (f) disability discrimination. The following outline is not comprehensive.

13.36 As will appear, disputes are in most cases subject to the jurisdiction of industrial tribunals, from whom appeal lies only on a point of law; but successful application has been made for judicial review (see para 15.41 ff) where there was procedural ultra vires.[1]

Time off work

13.37 Employees are to be given time off during working hours (a) to perform duties as members of specified public bodies, including governing bodies of LEA educational establishments, grant-maintained schools and further and higher education corporations,[2] (b) on redundancy (to look for work or training),[3] (c) for ante-natal care,[4] (d) as pension scheme trustees,[5] and (e) as employee representatives.[6] All the 'time off' rights can be asserted by complaint to an industrial tribunal.[7]

13.38 There is also provision, subject to specified conditions, for maternity leave and the right to return to work thereafter.[8]

Health and safety at work

13.39 Employers are to ensure the health, safety and welfare of employees and others, such as school pupils, so far as reasonably practicable. This duty includes provision of systems of work that are without risk to health, provision of information, training and supervision, and a safe and healthy place of work and working environment.[9] Employees are to take reasonable care for the

1 See *R v Birmingham City Council, ex p National Union of Public Employees* (1984) Times, 24 April.
2 Employment Rights Act 1996 s 50. The duties are attendance at meetings and taking part in the discharge of the functions of the body; the amount of time off is to be reasonable having regard to (a) the time needed to perform the duties, (b) how much time off the employee has already been permitted under this section and for trade union activities under the Trade Union and Labour Relations (Consolidation) Act 1992 ss 168 and 170, and (c) the circumstances of the employer's business and the effect of the employee's absence.
   See *Corner v Buckinghamshire County Council* (1978) 77 LGR 268 (time off to carry out duties as JP), and *Borders Regional Council v Maule* [1993] IRLR 199, EAT.
3 Ibid ss 52 and 53.
4 Ibid ss 55 and 56.
5 Ibid ss 58 and 59.
6 Ibid ss 61 and 62.
7 Ibid ss 51, 54, 57, 60 and 63.
8 Ibid ss 71 to 85. The right (a) to maternity leave (which implements European Union Council Directive 92/85) is irrespective of length of service or number of hours worked, (b) to return to work applies to women who, 11 weeks before the expected confinement, have been employed continuously (see s 210ff and n 12 below) for at least two years, and may be exercised between the end of maternity leave and 29 weeks after childbirth.
9 Health and Safety at Work etc Act 1974, ss 2–4. As to enforcement of the Act, obtaining disclosure of information, and offences, see ss 18 ff, 27 to 28 and 33 ff. See also Environment and Safety Information Act 1988.
   Pupils etc are owed a duty even though (because not employees or self-employed) they are not doing 'work' or 'at work'—defined at s 52, as extended by regulations made thereunder. As to whether an employee was at work when involved in a car accident on the work site see *Coult v Szuba* [1982] ICR 380.

13.39 *Teachers and Other Staff*

safety of themselves and others likely to be affected by their acts and omissions at work, and co-operate with their employers regarding statutory obligations.[10]

13.40 Breaches of health and safety requirements do not as such give rise to civil liability, but the circumstances of an accident or injury to health may be actionable in separate proceedings.[11]

Dismissal

13.41 The length of notice to be given to an employee on dismissal varies according to his length of service. Employees are to give at least a week's notice if employed continuously for a month or more.[12] An employee is entitled to receive a written statement giving particulars of the reasons for his dismissal provided that he has been continuously employed for two years; unreasonable refusal to provide a statement, or inadequate or untrue particulars, may give grounds for complaint to an industrial tribunal.[13]

13.42 A common law claim for redress upon wrongful dismissal[14] is to be distinguished from the right granted by statute not to be unfairly dismissed.[15] Dismissal, for the purposes of statutory protection,[16] arises
(a) when the employer terminates a contract of employment with or without notice;
(b) when a fixed term contract expires;[17]

---

10 Ibid s 7.
11 Ibid s 47.
12 Employment Rights Act 1996 s 86. See also, as to 'notice', ss 87 to 91.
  'Continuous employment' is explained and computed in accordance with s 210 ff. In calculating its length only service with the 'dismissing' authority counts (*Merton London Borough Council v Gardiner* [1981] ICR 186). By s 216 periods on strike do not count. There is a presumption of continuity, and a period of employment with the same employer is ordinarily continuous even though the capacity in which the employee works and his terms of employment change (*Wood v York City Council* [1978] ICR 840, CA). Breaks in employment between July and September, when a teacher has been employed year by year over a series of academic years, do not break the continuity of employment within the period of employment as a whole (*Ford v Warwickshire County Council* [1983] ICR 273, HL). As to a series of fixed term contracts, see *Pfaffinger v City of Liverpool Community College* [1996] IRLR 508, EAT. A teacher 'starts work' at the beginning of employment under the contract, not later when she actually begins teaching (*General of the Salvation Army v Dewsbury* [1984] ICR 498, EAT).
13 Ibid ss 92 and 93. As to what constitutes an adequate statement see *Kent County Council v Gilham* [1985] ICR 227, CA.
14 See the cases cited at para 13.20 n 7(c).
15 Ibid s 94. By ss 108 and 109 the right does not in general extend to those who have been continuously employed (see n 12) by the same employer for less than (normally) two years, or who have reached the normal retiring age for the position held or the age of 65 (see *Nothman v London Borough of Barnet* [1978] IRLR 1489, CA; affd [1979] IRLR 35, HL, *Waite v Government Communications Headquarters*[1983] IRLR 161, CA, *Secretary of State for Education and Science v Birchall*[1994] IRLR 630, EAT, and *Milligan v Securicor Cleaning* [1995] IRLR 288 EAT); nor, by s 197, does it extend to those who have agreed in writing to exclude the right before the end of a fixed term contract of one year or more.
16 Ibid s 95.
17 As to the distinction between a fixed term contract and a contract for a specific task see *Wiltshire v National Association of Teachers in Further Education and Guy*[1980] IRLR 198, *Ford v Warwickshire County Council* [1983] ICR 273, HL, and *Brown v Knowsley Borough Council* [1986] IRLR 102.

Conditions of Employment: General Legislation **13.44**

(c) when the employee, properly, terminates the contract of employment by reason of the employer's conduct;[18] and
(d) when, with specified exceptions, a woman is not permitted to return to work after childbirth.[19]

13.43 Where the employers are the governors of an aided school and dismissal is required by the LEA,[20] the unfair dismissal provisions apply as if the LEA were the employer.[1]

13.44 Complaint against unfair dismissal is made to an industrial tribunal, and if successful may lead to reinstatement, re-engagement or the award of compensation.[2] To resist the claim, employers have first to state the reason (or principal reason) for dismissal and show that it meets one of a number of specified requirements; if they can do so, whether or not the dismissal counts as unfair depends on whether or not in the circumstances (including the employer's size and administrative resources) they acted reasonably in treating the reason as sufficient to justify dismissal. The question is to be determined 'in accordance with equity and the substantial merits of the case'.[3]

---

18 As to constructive dismissal see *Bridgen v Lancashire County Council* [1987] IRLR 58.
19 Ibid s 96.
20 Under the 1996 Act s 134(3). See para 13.30.
1 Employment Rights Act 1996 s 134.
2 See ibid s 111 ff, and (as to conciliation to anticipate proceedings before a tribunal) the Industrial Tribunals Act 1996 s 18. As to appeal from a tribunal on a point of law see Pt II of that Act.
   As to (a) the time limit for making a claim see *Biggs v Somerset County Council* [1995] IRLR 452, EAT, and (b) the method of calculating compensation see *Gilham v Kent County Council (No 3)* [1986] ICR 52, EAT.
3 Ibid s 98. The (alternative) requirements are
   (a) that the reason specifically related to the capability or qualifications of the employee for performing work of the kind for which he was employed (see *Cohen v London Borough of Barking* [1976] IRLR 416); or
   (b) that it related to his conduct (see, as to dismissal following a strike, *Haddow v Inner London Education Authority* [1979] ICR 202; as to indecency, *Gardiner v Newport County Borough Council* [1974] IRLR 262, *Nottinghamshire County Council v Bowly* [1978] IRLR 252), and *Wiseman v Salford City Council* [1981] IRLR 202; misconduct by teacher, *Neale v Hereford and Worcester County Council* [1986] ICR 471; drugs offences *Norfolk County Council v Bernard* [1979] IRLR 220); or
   (c) that the employee was redundant (see s 105 and definition at s 139 and *National Union of Teachers v Governing Body of St. Mary's Church of England (Aided) Junior School* [1997] ICR 334, CA); or
   (d) that he could not continue to work in the position that he held without some statutory provision being contravened (this reason was advanced, erroneously, it was held, in *Birmingham City Council v Elson* (1979) 77 LGR 743 and *Sandhu v Department of Education and Science* and *London Borough of Hillingdon* [1978] IRLR 208); or
   (e) that some other reason existed so substantial as to justify dismissal (see, as respects the expiry of a fixed term contract, *Terry v East Sussex County Council* [1976] ICR 536, EAT, *Beard v Governors of St. Joseph's School* [1979] IRLR 144 and *North Yorkshire Council v Fay* [1985] IRLR 247, CA; reasonableness of request to teacher, *Redbridge London Borough Council v Fishman* (1978) 76 LGR 408; dismissal by mistake, *Pendlebury v Christian Schools North West Ltd* [1985] ICR 174; unsatisfactory probation *Inner London Education Authority v Lloyd* [1981] IRLR 394; and dismissal followed by offer of new engagement *Gilham v Kent County Council (No 2)* [1985] ICR 233, CA).
   As to whether the employer acted 'reasonably' see ACAS Code of Disciplinary Practice and Procedure, brought into effect by the Employment Protection Code of Practice (Disciplinary Practice and Procedures) Order 1977, SI 1977/867. See *R v Hertfordshire County Council, ex p National Union of Public Employees* (NUPE) [1985] IRLR 258, CA and *R v Birmingham City Council, ex p NUPE* (1984) Times, 24 April.

13.45 *Teachers and Other Staff*

13.45 Pressure put on employers by threat of industrial action is to be discounted in determining whether or not dismissal was unfair.[4] Dismissal is to be regarded as unfair in specified circumstances relating to an employee's taking part, or failing to take part, in trade union activities.[5] Dismissal on grounds of pregnancy is ordinarily unfair.[6]

Redundancy

13.46 Redundancy can come about through closure of a teaching establishment or reduction in the need for staff there, or in LEA institutions as a whole.[7] The legislation is modified to apply to employees who by statute are remunerated otherwise than by the employer—in the present context those who are remunerated by LEAs but employed by the governors of aided schools.[8]

13.47 An LEA or other employer proposing to dismiss[9] employees as redundant are to consult representatives of (ordinarily) the relevant trade unions, and comply with other specified requirements, provided that they are reasonably practicable in the circumstances.[10] A union may complain to an industrial tribunal against non-compliance.[11] Multiple dismissals are to be notified to the Secretary of State.[12]

13.48 An employee who has been continuously employed (see para 13.41 n 12) for at least two years by one or more LEAs, or by certain other bodies, and who is dismissed wholly or mainly by reason of redundancy, may be

---

4 Employment Rights Act 1996 s 107. Refusal to work during a strike is not 'self-dismissal' (*Simmons v Hoover* [1976] IRLR 266).
5 Trade Union and Labour Relations (Consolidation) Act 1992 s 152.
6 Employment Rights Act 1996 s 99.
7 Redundancy is defined at ibid s 139. Failure to renew a fixed-term contract constitutes dismissal, but does not necessarily prove redundancy. See *Lee v Nottinghamshire County Council* [1980] IRLR 284, CA (redundancy established even though the lecturer knew on appointment that a run-down of staff was taking place), *North Yorkshire County Council v Fay* [1985] IRLR 247, *Brown v Knowsley Borough Council* [1986] IRLR 102, EAT and *National Union of Teachers v Solihull Metropolitan Borough Council* (unreported).

By the 1988 Act s 221 any term in a contract made after 20 November 1987 which would have conferred on an employee the right not to be made redundant, or to compensation in excess of the statutory entitlement, is ineffective; but a contract may be made to pay enhanced redundancy compensation to a person who is actually being dismissed by reason of redundancy.

See application by the Education (Grant-maintained Special Schools) Regulations 1994, SI 1994/653, reg 42, Schedule Pt I and the Education (Special Schools Conducted by Education Associations) Regulations 1994, SI 1994/1084, reg 8(1), Sch 2, Pt I.
8 Employment Rights Act 1996 s 173.
9 As to the circumstances of dismissal see ibid s 136, and *Pickwell v Lincolnshire County Council* [1993] ICR 87, EAT.
10 Trade Union and Labour Relations (Consolidation) Act 1992, ss 188 and 282. See *National Associationn of Teachers in Further and Higher Education v Manchester City Council* [1978] ICR 1190, EAT, *National Union of Teachers v Avon County Council* [1978] IRLR 55, EAT and the cases mentioned at n 7 above. An agreement was reached in 1976 between the Council of Local Education Authorities and teachers' organisations regarding consultation between LEAs and local teachers' representatives in advance of the introduction of local redundancy and premature retirement arrangements. The agreement is in Appendix VIII to the Burgundy Book (see para 13.67) and supplements statutory consultation requirements.
11 Trade Union and Labour Relations (Consolidation) Act 1992 s 189.
12 Ibid ss 193 and 194.

entitled to a lump sum redundancy payment from his employers of between a half, and one and a half, week's pay for each year of up to 20 years of continuous employment. Teachers and others who have served more than one LEA or governing body have their periods of employment aggregated.[13]

13.49 No redundancy payment is due to employees age 65 or more (or less if normal retiring age is under 65) or in other specified circumstances, including summary dismissal and where re-engagement or renewal of suitable employment is offered but not accepted.[14] In certain circumstances, where the employee has pension or compensation rights, payment may be excluded or reduced.[15] Questions about the right to a redundancy payment or its amount are determined by industrial tribunals.[16]

Sex and racial discrimination

13.50 Men and women engaged upon like or equivalent work are to be given equal treatment disregarding any special legal protection or treatment enjoyed by women. An 'equality clause' to secure the right, if not expressly included in a contract of employment, is deemed to be included. Disputes are to be determined by industrial tribunals.[17]

13.51 With specified exceptions it is unlawful to discriminate between men and women (a) in arrangements for recruitment of staff; (b) in the terms on which employment is offered; (c) by refusing or deliberately omitting to offer employment; (d) by the way access is given (or not given) to promotion, transfer or training or other benefits, etc; and (e) by dismissing a person, or

---

13 Employment Rights Act 1996 s 218(7), and the Redundancy Payments (Local Government) (Modification) Order 1983, SI 1983/1160. The 'other bodies' include the governing body of a voluntary school and of an assisted or grant-aided further education establishment.
   As to calculation of payment due to part-time, hourly paid, teachers see *Cole v Birmingham City District Council* [1978] ICR 1004.
   Retirement under an early retirement scheme does not constitute dismissal for redundancy (*University of Liverpool v Humber and Birch* [1984] IRLR 54).
   As to employees in Lancashire see the Redundancy Payments (Exemption) Order 1980, SI 1980/1052.
   See also para 13.74 below.
14 Ibid ss 156, 140 and 141. In *Taylor v Kent County Council* [1969] 2 QB 560, it was held that an offer to a former headmaster of a post at the same salary in a mobile pool of teachers was not suitable because not substantially equivalent to the employment that had ceased; and in *Spencer and Griffin v Gloucestershire County Council* [1985] IRLR 59 that, the council having to reduce their costs and lower school cleaning standards, it was not unreasonable for school cleaners to refuse re-engagement for rather fewer hours a week than they had previously worked on the ground that they would be unable to do their work to a standard satisfactory to themselves.
15 See the Redundancy Payments Pensions Regulations 1965, SI 1965/1932. See ibid s 158 and, as regards set-off of redundancy payments against compensation granted under certain statutory provisions, the Redundancy Payments Statutory Compensation Regulations 1965, SI 1965/1988.
16 Employment Rights Act 1996 s 163 and the Industrial Tribunals Act 1996.
17 Equal Pay Act 1970 ss 1, 2, 2A and 6. Discriminatory practices under the 1970 Act (contractual terms of employment) are in general not to be challenged under the Sex Discrimination Act 1975 (non-contractual). See *Pearse v City of Bradford Metropolitan Council* [1988] IRLR 379 in which a woman part-time lecturer unsuccessfully claimed that she had suffered 'indirect' discrimination (as to which see para 14.04); and see *Scullard and Knowles v Southern Regional Council for Education and Training* [1996] IRLR 344, in which Art 119 of the Treaty of Rome was invoked.

13.51 Teachers and Other Staff

submitting him or her to any other detriment, on grounds of sex.[18] Terms in collective agreements are to be non-discriminatory.[19]

13.52 It is lawful to discriminate where sex is a genuine occupational qualification for a job. Among the circumstances specified are where, for reasons stated, 'the job needs to be done by a man to preserve decency or privacy' and where 'the holder of the job provides individuals with personal services promoting their welfare or education . . . and those services can most effectively be provided by a man'.[20]

13.53 The law against racial discrimination in employment follows closely that relating to sex discrimination. It is unlawful to discriminate on racial grounds in relation to (a) to (e) in para 13.51 above.[1] There are fewer exceptions for genuine occupational qualifications, but there is a 'personal services' exception of which an LEA might wish to take advantage, for example to employ an educational welfare officer of the same racial group as form a significant proportion of the pupils at a school.[2]

13.54 A complaint of unlawful sex or racial discrimination as respects employment is to be made to an industrial tribunal,[3] and may be the subject of conciliation by an ACAS conciliation officer to endeavour to promote a settlement in advance of a tribunal hearing.[4] The remedy granted by a tribunal for a well-founded complaint is to be whichever (one or more) of the following they consider just and equitable: (a) an order declaring rights; (b) an order for monetary compensation; and (c) a recommendation that the respondent take action to obviate or reduce the adverse effect of the act of discrimination on the complainant.[5]

13.55 The Equal Opportunities Commission and the Commission for Racial Equality may prepare, for approval by Parliament and the Secretary of State, codes of practice designed, respectively, to promote equality of opportunity and eliminate unlawful discrimination in the field of employment; and an industrial tribunal may take codes into account when considering any question to which they are relevant.[6]

18 Sex Discrimination Act 1975 s 6. 'Sex discrimination' is defined in ss 1 and 2 (see para 14.04). The specified exceptions are mostly in Pt V of the Act.
   The 'other detriment' includes sexual harrassment (*Porcelli v Strathclyde Council* [1985] ICR 177, EAT, and *Jackson v Helsey Group* (Case No 40121/95 1996 Industrial Tribunal).
   Exemplary damages may be awarded by an industrial tribunal against a local authority found to have unlawfully discriminated on grounds of sex or race against an applicant for a post at a college for which the authority had responsibility (*Bradford City Metropolitan Council v Arora* [1991] 2 QB 507).
19 See Sex Discrimination Act 1986 s 6, applying Sex Discrimination Act 1975 s 77.
20 Sex Discrimination Act 1975 s 7, and see also s 46 (communal accommodation). 'Job' is not defined but in the Employment Rights Act 1996 s 235 (1) means the nature of the work which the employee is employed to do in accordance with his contract, and the capacity and place in which he is so employed.
1 Race Relations Act 1976 s 4. 'Racial discrimination' is defined in ibid ss 1 and 3 (see para 14.08).
2 Ibid s 5.
3 Sex Discrimination Act 1975 s 63; Race Relations Act 1976 s 54.
4 Industrial Tribunals Act 1996 s 18.
5 Sex Discrimination Act 1975 s 65; Race Relations Act 1976 s 56.
6 Sex Discrimination Act 1975 s 56A; Race Relations Act 1976 s 47. Codes of practice under both sections have come into effect: see the Sex Discrimination Code of Practice Order 1985, SI 1985/387, and the Race Relations Code of Practice Order 1983, SI 1983/1081.

Disability discrimination

13.56 By Part II of the Disability Discrimination Act 1995[7] employers are not to discriminate unjustifiably against employeees or prospective employees in recruitment, training, promotion, dismissal and other aspects of the relationship (but 'positive discrimination' is not demanded). Also, to remove substantial disadvantage to disabled persons, employers are to make reasonable adjustments to their premises and arrangements generally. Whether an adjustment is 'reasonable' turns, in particular, on (a) how far an alteration will help the employee, (b) how easy it is to make the adjustment, (c) its cost, financial, and in terms of disruption, (d) the employer's (ie ordinarily the LEA's) resources, and (e) the availability of financial or other help.

13.57 Less favourable treatment of disabled persons can be justified if the reason for it is material to the circumstances of the case and is substantial, for example inability to do the job for reasons connected with the disability which no reasonable adjustments could remedy. Examples of reasonable adjustments are altering premises, reallocation of duties, changing place of work and making changes to equipment. Adjustments are not required if the disadvantage suffered is only minor, and where the employer is, reasonably, ignorant of the disability.

13.58 Part II of the 1995 Act does not apply to employers with fewer than 20 employees, so small voluntary aided, grant-maintained and grant-maintained special schools are exempt, as are, similarly, small independent schools, including city colleges, and non-maintained special schools.

13.59 Complaint may be made to an industrial tribunal alleging unlawful discrimination or refusal to make reasonable adjustments. If the complaint is upheld the tribunal may recommend the employer to take appropriate action, or pay compensation. LEAs are the employers of teachers and other staff in LEA schools (except aided schools, but costs may fall to the LEA as part of maintenance). It is intended to provide that where governing bodies have delegated staffing powers (see paras 13.18 and 13.29) they will be respondents in industrial tribunal cases, but decisions and orders of the tribunal, except for re-instatement or re-engagement, shall take effect against the LEA. As regards costs associated with dismissal see para 13.25.

CONDITIONS OF EMPLOYMENT: EDUCATION PROVISIONS

13.60 The School Teachers' Pay and Conditions Act 1991 and regulations made under that Act are the main source of statutory provision. Separate legislation provides safeguards for teachers in relation to religious worship and education, and governs superannuation and early retirement.

---

7 See ss 4 to 8. 'Disabled persons' are defined at s 1 (see para 14.11). See also Circular 3/97 (WO 20/97), 'What the Disability Discrimination Act 1995 means for Schools and LEAs'.

13.61 *Teachers and Other Staff*

Negotiation and review

13.61 Conditions of employment, including remuneration, of teachers in further education institutions, are ordinarily negotiated, outside a statutory framework, by representative bodies of employers and staff.

13.62 The conditions of employment of teachers in maintained schools are partly regulated by statute:[8] a review body appointed by the Prime Minister from time to time examines their remuneration, professional duties and working time. The Secretary of State may give the review body directions as to 'considerations to which they are to have regard' and as to the time within which they are to report. The review body are to consult representative bodies of employers and teachers (and any LEA with whom consultation appears desirable) and give them the opportunity to submit evidence and make representations. The review body's report is to contain their recommendations and advice on any matter referred to them.[9]

13.63 After consultation with the same parties the Secretary of State may make a pay and conditions order implementing the review body's recommendation, with or without modifications, or as he thinks fit. The order may contain the provisions to be made, or alternatively (as is current practice) refer to a document under which pay scales and allowances are settled and which determines, inter alia, the number or proportion of teachers in a school to be paid on specified scales, and matters on which LEAs or governing bodies may exercise discretion. The Secretary of State may make a pay and conditions order without reference to the review body if he considers (after consultation as above and with the chairman or deputy chairman of the review body) that the provision proposed to be made by the order is not significant enough for referral.[10]

13.64 The governing bodies of county and voluntary schools with delegated budgets (see paras 13.18 and 13.29) exercise discretion in place of LEAs, as do the governing bodies of grant-maintained schools. The latter may, however, after consulting teachers, apply for exemption by order from statutory requirements altogether.[11]

8 School Teachers' Pay and Conditions Act 1991, which is to be construed with the 1996 Act, and of which ss 496 and 497 apply. See Circular 4/96 'School Teachers' Pay and Conditions of Employment 1996'.
  The whole of the 1991 Act is applied by the Education (Grant-maintained Special Schools) Regulations 1994, SI 1994/653, reg 42, Schedule, Pt I; and by the Education (Special Schools Conducted by Education Associations) Regulations 1994, SI 1994/1084, reg 8(1), Sch 2, Pt I.
  By the 1991 Act s 3A when an independent school becomes a maintained school statutory pay and conditions do not apply to teachers employed there unless they so choose. See the Transfer of Undertakings (Protection of Employment) Regulations 1981, SI 1981/1794.
9 1991 Act s 1 and Sch 1. The report is made to both Prime Minister and Secretary of State and is published by the latter.
10 1991 Act s 2. Pay and conditions orders are made by SI and are subject to annulment by parliamentary resolution if materially modifying the review body's recommendations. See the Education (School Teachers' Pay and Conditions) (No 2) Order 1996, SI 1996/1816, giving effect to the School Teachers' Pay and Conditions Document 1996 from 1 September 1996 and the 1997 Order SI 1997/755 amending the 1996 Document from 1 April 1997; and Circular 4/96.
  See *Lewis v Dyfed County Council* (1978) 77 LGR 339, CA, F[73.2], as to the interpretation of a remuneration order.
11 1991 Act s 3. Orders are made by SI.

Contracts and duties

13.65 The conditions of service settled under a pay and conditions order form part of the contracts of employment of teachers in maintained schools. Head teachers are responsible for the internal organisation, management and control of schools, subject to overriding provisions in statute, articles of government and trust deeds etc. Their professional duties are specified, but not comprehensively. In carrying them out they are to consult LEA, governing body, staff and parents of pupils, as appropriate. Deputy head teachers have duties, supplementing those of teachers in general, which include carrying out professional duties assigned or reasonably delegated to them by the head teacher.[12]

13.66 With some exceptions the professional duties of full-time teachers include being available for 195 days in any year, and for 1,265 hours during those days; but the limit on hours may need to be exceeded for marking, preparation, directed time etc. 'Cover' for absent colleagues is a professional duty, provided, ordinarily, that it does not exceed a short, specified, period. (In advance of the statutory requirement, teachers who failed to comply with a direction to cover for absent colleagues were held to be in breach of contract, so that it was proper to make a deduction from their salaries, by way of equitable set-off.[13])

13.67 Subject to the statutory requirements, contracts may incorporate national collective agreements or include terms agreed between employers and local branches of unions. The collective agreements now incorporated in *Conditions of Service for Schoolteachers in England and Wales* (known as the *Burgundy Book*) were negotiated by a joint committee of the Council of Local Education Authorities and the school teacher unions. They are concerned with practical arrangements for appointment, resignation and retirement (ordinarily by the age of 65); collective disputes which involve more than one school; maternity leave and pay; leave for examinations, jury and other public service and union activities; union facilities; insurance for teachers in respect of assaults, loss or damage to personal property, death and personal loss or injury sustained during out-of-school activities; and travelling allowances.

13.68 Teachers are not to be required to undertake midday supervision, but may do so under a separate contract. Under the 1996 Act (see para 12.38) LEAs and governing bodies of county and voluntary schools may make arrangements for teachers employed by them to serve in day nurseries provided by local social services authorities.[14]

---

12 1991 Act s 2, and see n 10 above. In the case of a strike, where the teacher does not work for the whole or part of the school day no pay is due in respect of the strike period. See *Henthorn and Taylor v Central Electricity Generating Board*[1980] IRLR 361 and *Hereford and Worcester County Council v National Association of Schoolmasters/Union of Women Teachers* (1988) Independent, 1 March. Teachers' refusal to carry out National Curriculum tasks because of the excessive workload was a trade dispute protected by the Trade Union and Labour Relations (Consolidation) Act 1992 (*Wandsworth London Borough Council v National Association of Teachers/Union of Women Teachers* [1993] IRLR 344, CA).
13 See *Sim v Rotherham Metropolitan Borough Council*[1987] Ch 216, F[231], and *Royle v Trafford Metropolitan Borough Council* [1984] IRLR 184.
14 See the Children Act 1989 s 18.

13.69 *Teachers and Other Staff*

Religious education and worship
Savings for teachers and others

13.69 No person is to be disqualified from being a teacher or otherwise employed at (a) a county school, or (b) a voluntary controlled or special agreement school (unless as a reserved teacher), or (c) a grant-maintained school that was formerly a county school (or is a new non-denominational school) because of his religious opinions or because he attends or omits to attend religious worship. Nor are any teachers so employed to be disadvantaged (for example, in relation to pay or promotion) on those grounds or because they do or do not give religious education.[15]

13.70 No person is to be disqualified from being employed (otherwise than as a teacher) at a grant-maintained school which was formerly a voluntary school (or is a new school where the trust deed or published statement makes special provision for religious education) on account of his religious opinions, or attending or failing to attend religious worship.[16]

13.71 Only (a) teachers at aided schools, (b) reserved teachers at controlled or special agreement schools, and (c) teachers at grant-maintained schools which were formerly voluntary schools (or are new schools where the trust deed or published statement makes special provision for religious education) may be required to give religious education. They are not to be paid less or otherwise discriminated against because they *do* give religious education or by reason of their religious opinions or attendance at religious worship; but it appears that they may be paid less or be deprived or disqualified for promotion etc for *not* giving religious education or attending religious worship.[17]

13.72 Without prejudice to paras 13.70 and 13.71 above, teachers who are employed in grant-maintained schools which were formerly voluntary schools continue, while they remain in the same employment, to be entitled to the safeguards applying to their former employment.[18] Where the religious character of a grant-maintained school is formally changed (see para 4.49 ff) teachers become subject to para 13.71 instead of para 13.69 (or vice versa) as appropriate, save that where special provision for religious education is introduced para 13.69 continues to apply to teachers employed at the school before the change while they remain in the same employment.[19]

---

15 1996 Act ss 146 and 304. A teacher is not entitled to break a contract of employment to attend a religious service (*Ahmad v Inner London Education Authority* [1978] QB 36). See Circular 1/94, paras 142 to 144, E[2290].
    See also the Education (Grant-maintained Special Schools) Regulations 1994, SI 1994/653, reg 38, the Education (Special Schools Conducted by Education Associations) Regulations 1994, SI 1994/1084, reg 8, Sch 2, Pt I, and, as to religious freedom for teachers in special schools, the Education (Special Schools) Regulations 1994, SI 1994/652, Schedule, Pt II, para 16.
16 1996 Act s 305(2).
17 1996 Act ss 146 and 305(3).
18 1996 Act s 305(4).
19 1996 Act s 306.

Superannuation   Early retirement   'Safeguarding'

13.73 There is a statutory superannuation scheme for teachers[20] but they may elect not to join it.[1] The scheme is extremely complex. In bare outline its main provisions are as follows:
(a) those eligible to join are mostly full-time teachers in maintained schools and further education establishments who are over 18 and under 55 when they begin teaching;
(b) teachers in service which counts towards the reckoning of benefits (reckonable service) pay contributions of 6 per cent of salary, and employers pay sufficient to keep the account in balance;
(c) subject to minimum qualifying periods, the basic benefits, related to the amount of reckonable service, are a pension and lump sum on retirement at 60 or over, or earlier on health breakdown, or on the teacher's being prematurely retired;
(d) there is also a death gratuity, a widow's pension payable while the widow is on her own, and pensions for dependent children;
(e) pensions are indexed to the cost of living; and
(f) there are arrangements to deal with breaks in service, for 'freezing' pension benefits when a teacher leaves employment with enough qualifying service before a pension falls due, for transfer values 'out' and 'in' and for repayment of contributions on leaving employment covered by the scheme; also for reconciling the scheme with the national insurance system.

13.74 Teachers aged between 50 and 59 (inclusive) who retire prematurely on grounds of redundancy (see also para 13.46 ff), or in the interests of the efficient discharge of their employers' functions, may be eligible for a pension and lump sum. 'Extra service' may be credited by the employer.[2] Also certain further education teachers and teachers at teacher training establishments who suffered loss of employment or diminution of emoluments became eligible for compensation in prescribed circumstances.[3] And compensation

---

20 Superannuation Act 1972 s 9. See the Teachers' Superannuation (Consolidation) Regulations 1988, SI 1988/1652 and the Teachers' Superannuation (Provision of Information and Administrative Expenses etc) Regulations 1996, SI 1996/2282; also, as regards grant-maintained schools, Circular 21/89 'Grant-maintained Schools: Financial Arrangements', E[1090].
1 Pension Schemes Act 1993 s 160.
2 The Teachers' Superannuation (Consolidation) Regulations 1988, SI 1988/1652 (made under the Superannuation Act 1972 s 9) and the Teachers' (Compensation for Redundancy and Premature Retirement) Regulations 1997, SI 1997/311 (made under ibid s 24). As to the latter see Circular 7/89 (so entitled), E[985].
   See as regards non-teaching staff pensionable under the Local Government Superannuation Regulations 1986, SI 1986/24, the Local Government (Compensation for Premature Retirement) Regulations 1982, SI 1982/1009, the Local Government (Compensation for Redundancy and Premature Retirement) Regulations 1984, SI 1984/740, and the Local Government Reorganisation (Compensation) Regulations 1986, SI 1986/151.
   As to liability for pension enhancement payments see *Cooke v Birmingham City Council* (14 November 1996, unreported) CA.
3 See the Teachers' (Compensation) (Advanced Further Education) Regulations 1983, SI 1983/856 and the Colleges of Education (Compensation) Regulations 1975, SI 1975/1092 (both made under the Superannuation Act 1972, s 24), and Circulars 5/83 (WO 43/83) 'Reduction of Teaching Posts in Advanced Further Education: Redundancy Compensation' and 6/75 respectively; also the Pensions Increase (Compensation to Staff of Teacher Training Establishments) Regulations 1975, SI 1975/1478, made under the Pensions (Increase) Act 1971 s 5(2), *Pearson v Kent County Council* (1979) 77 LGR 604, QBD and, as to calculation of emoluments, *Leeds City Council v Pomfret* [1983] ICR 674.

13.74 *Teachers and Other Staff*

is payable to specified persons adversely affected by local government reorganisation.[4]

13.75 Following the reorganisation of teacher training in the 1970s, arrangements were made under the 'Crombie' scheme to 'safeguard' (ie make up to their former level) the salaries of certain employees who lost their jobs in teacher training as a result of directions made by the Secretary of State. Similar arrangements have been made by provisions under which higher education funding councils may reimburse employing bodies for payments to former and serving staff, those bodies supplying information required for the purpose.[5]

---

4 See the Local Government Reorganisation (Compensation for Redundancy or Loss of Remuneration) (Education) Regulations 1996, SI 1996/1240.
5 1988 Act s 133 and 1994 Act s 18. See the Education (Polytechnics and Colleges Funding Council) (Prescribed Expenditure) Regulations 1991, SI 1991/2307.

Chapter 14

WRONGDOINGS

14.01 In this chapter a brief account is given of the law relating to unlawful discrimination on grounds of race, sex or disability, and of the torts to which educational activities have given rise. Even more briefly, litter offences are noted.

UNLAWFUL DISCRIMINATION

14.02 The Equal Opportunities Commission and the Commission for Racial Equality may make formal investigations into possible contraventions by LEAs and others of, respectively, the Sex Discrimination Act 1975 and the Race Relations Act 1976, and are to give the Secretary of State notice of acts in respect of which he could exercise his powers under the 1996 Act ss 496 (unreasonable exercise of functions) and 497 (default). See para 12.05 ff.[1] Disability discrimination is covered by the Act of 1995 so entitled, but the National Disability Council established by that Act has no power to investigate complaints or institute proceedings.

14.03 Improper discrimination in relation to employment has been mentioned above at para 13.50 ff. Here reference is made to provisions applying otherwise in the field of education.

Sex discrimination

14.04 Sex discrimination is defined as treating a person less favourably on the grounds of his or her sex (direct discrimination), or applying a requirement or condition which (a) is such that a considerably smaller proportion of persons of one, than of the other, sex can comply with it, (b) cannot be shown to be justifiable irrespective of the sex of the person to whom it is applied, and (c) is to his

---

1 Sex Discrimination Act 1975 ss 57, 60 and 67(6); Race Relations Act 1976 ss 48, 51 and 58(6). Several formal investigations have been made. Article 14 of the European Human Rights Convention, and the law of the European Union, in particular Council Directive 76/207 on sex discrimination, may also be relevant.

223

14.04 *Wrongdoings*

or her detriment because he or she cannot comply with it (indirect discrimination).[2]

14.05 It is unlawful for an LEA, governing body or proprietor of an educational establishment (the 'responsible body') to discriminate against a pupil on the grounds of his or her sex:
(a) in the terms of an offer of admission;
(b) by refusal or deliberate omission of acceptance of an application for admission;
(c) in the way in which they afford access to any benefits, facilities or services, or by refusing or deliberately omitting to afford access to them, or by excluding him or her from the establishment, or by subjecting him or her to any other detriment;[3] or
(d) by way of victimisation.[4]

14.06 An LEA also act unlawfully, as do a funding council or a funding authority, if they do any act that constitutes sex discrimination in carrying out other functions;[5] and there is a general duty, applying also to other responsible bodies, the funding councils and authorities and the Teacher Training Agency, to provide facilities for education and ancillary benefits and services without sex discrimination, with exceptions for single-sex establishments and physical education and training courses.[6] There are also exceptions for single-sex establishments turning co-educational: the responsible body may apply for a transitional exemption order.[7]

14.07 Complaints about sex discrimination may be made to the Secretary of State, seeking action by use of his powers concerning unreasonable

---

2 Sex Discrimination Act 1975 ss 1 and 2. 'Treats less favourably': see *Debrell, Sevket and Teh v London Borough of Bromley* (12 November 1984, unreported), F[31]; *R v Secretary of State for Education and Science, ex p Keating* (1985) 84 LGR 469, F[33]; *Birmingham City Council v Equal Opportunities Commission* [1989] AC 1155, F[34]; and *R v Birmingham City Council, ex p EOC (No 2)* [1994] ELR 282, CA. See also *Pearse v City of Bradford Metropolitan Council* [1988] IRLR 379, EAT in which a woman part-time lecturer unsuccessfully claimed that she had suffered 'indirect' discrimination; *Bullock v Alice Ottley School* [1993] ICR 138 in which a female member of the school's domestic staff claimed discrimination in relation to retirement age; and *O'Neill v Governors of St. Thomas More Roman Catholic Voluntary Aided Upper School* [1997] ICR 33, in which a teacher of religious education was held to have been constructively dismissed.
3 Sex Discrimination Act 1975 ss 22, 22A and 24. 'In the way it offers her access to any benefits, facilities or services': see *Debell* above.
4 Discrimination by victimisation is defined in Sex Discrimination Act 1975 s 4.
5 Sex Discrimination Act 1975 ss 23, 23A and 23C. Section 23 was considered in *R v Secretary of State for Education and Science, ex p Keating* (1985) 84 LGR 469, F[33] (closure of a boys' school held to be unlawful discrimination because two girls' schools survived); *Birmingham City Council v Equal Opportunities Commission* [1989] AC 1155, F[34]; *R v Northamptonshire County Council, ex p K* [1994] ELR 397, F[110]; and *R v Birmingham City Council, ex p Equal Opportunities Commission (No 2)*[1992] 2 FLR 133 (in performance of their statutory duty to ensure that places at their grammar schools were allocated without sex discrimination, the LEA were obliged to take into consideration places available for boys at a grant-maintained school). See also *R v Secretary of State for Education and Science, ex p Malik* [1992] COD 31; *R v Northamptonshire County Council and Secretary of State for Education, ex p K* [1994] ELR 397, CA; *R v Secretary of State for Education and Science, ex p Malik* [1994] ELR 121, and *Kingsbury v Northamptonshire Education Department* [1994] COD 114, CA.
6 Sex Discrimination Act 1975 ss 25, 26 and 28. Section 25 was considered in *Birmingham City Council v Equal Opportunities Commission* [1989] AC 1155, F[34].
7 Sex Discrimination Act 1975 s 27 and Sch 2, and 1996 Act s 552.

exercise of functions or default, or claims may be pursued in tort in the county court.[8]

Racial discrimination

14.08 Racial discrimination exists when a person is treated less favourably on racial grounds (direct discrimination), or a requirement or condition is imposed which applies or would apply to persons not of the person's racial group but which (a) is such that a considerably smaller proportion of persons of that racial group, than not of that group, can comply with it, (b) cannot be shown to be justifiable irrespective of the colour, race, nationality or ethnic or national origins of the person to whom it is applied, and (c) is to his detriment because he cannot comply with it (indirect discrimination).[9]

14.09 LEAs act unlawfully, as do other responsible bodies, the funding councils and authorities and the Teacher Training Agency, if they do any act that constitutes racial discrimination in carrying out the functions mentioned under (a) to (d) in para 14.05 above or other functions;[10] and there is a general duty, applying to LEAs and other responsible bodies, to provide facilities for education and ancillary benefits and services without racial discrimination.[11] There are limited exceptions to the duty, including giving a particular racial group access to educational facilities to meet their special needs.[12] Unless for this purpose the 'bussing' of children is probably unlawful.

14.10 Recourse against racial discrimination is similar to that against sex discrimination (see para 14.07).[13]

Disability discrimination

14.11 Provision of education is not caught by Part III of the Disability

8 Sex Discrimination Act 1975 ss 25 and 66, and 1996 Act ss 496 and 497. The European Convention on Human Rights, Art 14, and European Union Directive 76/07 are also material.
9 Race Relations Act 1976 s 1. See *Hampson v Department of Education and Science* [1991] 1 AC 171, F[35].
  'Racial grounds', 'racial group', 'ethnic or national origins': see s 3 and *Mandla v Dowell Lee* [1983] 1 All ER 1062, F[30]; and *Orphanos v Queen Mary College* [1985] AC 761, F[32]. The Sikhs constitute a group defined by ethnic origins. See *Mandla* per Lord Templeman at 1072. In that case a headmaster's refusal to admit a Sikh boy to school unless he removed his turban was held illegal under s 1(1)(b).
  'Justifiable': governors of an aided church school may justifiably require that the applicants for the post of head teacher should be committed communicant Christians despite the discriminatory effect on applicants of Asian origin (*St Matthias Church of England School Board of Governors v Crizzle* [1993] IRLR 472, EAT, F[37]). See also *R v Bradford Metropolitan Borough Council, ex p Sikander Ali* [1994] ELR 299.
  As to discrimination by way of victimisation see s 2.
10 Ibid, ss 17, 17A, 18, 18A and 18C. Compliance by an LEA with parental preference under 1996 Act s 411 (see para 7.03 ff) does not constitute racial discrimination (*R v Cleveland County Council, ex p Commission for Racial Equality* [1994] ELR 44, CA, F[36]. See also *R v Neale, ex p S* [1995] ELR 198.
11 Ibid, s 19. See *Race Relations Board v Ealing London Borough (No 2)* [1978] 1 All ER 497.
12 Ibid, ss 27, 34, 35 and 42.
13 Ibid, ss 19 and 57, and 1996 Act ss 496 and 497; and see *Orphanos* (n 9 above). The European Convention on Human Rights, Art 14, and European Union law, may also be material.

14.11 *Wrongdoings*

Discrimination Act 1995.[14] 'Education' is undefined, but it probably excludes child care. It probably includes not only nursery and further education but field trips and other extra-curricular activities which contain an element of education and are not merely leisure-time activities. LEAs and other specified bodies are, however, not to discriminate against disabled persons—those who have 'a physical or mental impairment which has a substantial and long-term adverse effect on . . . ability to carry out normal day-to-day activities'—when providing non-educational services—by refusing to provide a service altogether, making it difficult for a disabled person to make use of it (by failure to make adjustments), or providing the service to a lower standard or on less favourable terms.

14.12 Non-educational services include the provision of goods and facilities, in particular access to schools, which may, for example, be required by parents and for meetings of the governing body, and for use of sports facilities and for fund-raising events. Responsibility for complying with rights of access falls on the 'service provider', among whom may be the school governing body, the LEA, some other department of the local authority or the Parent Teacher Association. There are limited circumstances in which it is justifiable to treat a disabled person unfavourably, for example to protect his own health and safety or that of others. Positive requirements to improve rights of access for disabled persons are not yet in force.

14.13 On breach of the requirements of the Act relating to the provision of services the disabled person may have recourse to civil proceedings in tort, and recover compensation for financial loss.

LITTER

14.14 Leaving litter on the land of educational institutions is an offence carrying a fine not exceeding level 4 on the standard scale, and a duty falls on governing bodies to keep land clear of litter so far as is practicable. Failure on their part to comply with an abatement notice incurs the same penalty.[15]

TORT AND BREACH OF STATUTORY DUTY

14.15 Reference to false imprisonment and to trespass to the person is made at para 15.14 ff. Negligence has been the tort most subject to judicial consideration.

Negligence

14.16 Failure to observe the standard of care of a reasonably prudent man in reasonably foreseeable circumstances (*M'Alister (or Donoghue) v Stevenson*)[16]

---

14 See ss 19, 20, 21 (which requires providers of services to make reasonable adjustments) and 25. The Disability Discrimination (Services and Premises) Regulations 1996, SI 1996/1836, exempt some services closely related to education, such as provision of a youth service and the activities of voluntary organisations concerned with educational and personal development.
  As to employment of disabled persons see para 13.56 ff.
  See also Circular 3/97 (WO 20/97), 'What the Disability Discrimination Act 1995 means for Schools and LEAs'.
15 Environmental Protection Act 1990 ss 86 to 98.
16 [1932] AC 562, F[120].

alleged against a teacher in relation to pupils, has given rise to most of the actions in tort in the field of education. Between an LEA or governing body and a teacher or other employee there ordinarily exists a master and servant relationship. Thus the authority or body are vicariously liable for torts committed by employees within the scope of their duties (*Smith v Martin and Kingston-upon-Hull Corpn*),[17] including the negligent exercise of professional skills (*E v Dorset County Council* and *X (minors) v Bedforshire County Council* and associated cases).[18]

14.17 *Williams v Eady*[19] established the *in loco parentis* rule—'the schoolmaster was bound to take such care of his boys as a careful father of his boys . . . he was bound to take notice of the ordinary nature of young boys, their tendency to do mischievous acts and their propensity to meddle with anything that came in their way.' Other cases in which a teacher or other employee failed to meet this standard, and hence negligence was found, include *Ralph v LCC*,[20] *Gibbs v Barking Corpn*[1] (distinguished in *Wright v Cheshire County Council*),[2] *Moore v Hampshire County Council*,[3] *Shrimpton v Hertfordshire County Council*,[4] *Ellis v Sayers Confectioners Ltd*,[5] *Toole v Sherbourne Pouffes Ltd*,[6] *Camkin v Bishop*[7] and *Black v Kent County Council*.[8]

14.18 The 'careful father' (or 'prudent parent') test is a rather subjective one; moreover it does not fit all circumstances, but it is still used where appropriate; and the Department have expressed the view that 'teachers and other school staff in charge of pupils are under a common law duty to act as any reasonably prudent parent would to make sure that pupils are healthy and safe on school premises. This might, in exceptional circumstances, extend to administering medicine and/or taking action in an emergency. The duty also extends to teachers leading activities taking place off the school site, such as educational visits, school outings or field trips'.[9]

14.19 The following general propositions about negligence in and around schools and other educational institutions, derived from the decisions of the courts, illustrate some particular circumstances in which the duty of care has existed and the qualifications which have been placed upon it. Over the years opinion about the appropriate standard of care has changed, and it is not so demanding as to exclude all possibility of mishap.
(1) Unless *res ipsa loquitur* it is for the plaintiff to prove that the defendant has been negligent. However serious a mishap, unless failure to take

17 [1911] 2 KB 775, F[116].
18 [1995] 3 All ER 353, HL, F[154].
19 (1893) 10 TLR 41, CA, F[54].
20 (1947) 111 JP 548, CA, F[129].
1 [1936] 1 All ER 115, CA, F[123].
2 [1952] 2 All ER 789, CA, F[130].
3 (1981) 80 LGR 481, CA, F[149].
4 (1911) 104 LT 145, HL, F[115].
5 (1963) 61 LGR 299, CA, F[136].
6 (1971) 70 LGR 52, CA, F[147].
7 [1941] 2 All ER 713.
8 (1983) 82 LGR 39, CA, F[150].
9 See Circular 14/96, 'Supporting Pupils with Medical Needs in Schools', in which it is also suggested that the Children Act 1989 s 3(5) can give protection to teachers acting reasonably in emergency situations.

14.19 *Wrongdoings*

proper care is proved, the injured party—pupil or teacher (see *Watts v Monmouthshire County Council*[10])—has no right to any recompense at common law. Accidents can happen without negligence, or with negligence by the victim only (*Jones v LCC*,[11] *Conrad v Inner London Education Authority*,[12] *Crisp v Thomas*,[13] *Perry v King Alfred School Society*,[14] *Jacques v Oxfordshire County Council*[15] and *Cahill v West Ham Corpn*[16]).

(2) Only a reasonable standard of supervision of pupils is required; their age will be relevant to what is reasonable; continuous supervision may not be called for (*Ricketts v Erith Borough Council*,[17] *Rawsthorne v Ottley*,[18] *Clark v Monmouthshire County Council*,[19] *Ward v Hertfordshire County Council*,[20] *Chilvers v LCC*,[1] and *Nwabudike v Southwark London Borough Council*[2]); and warnings given to children may be material in assessing what is adequate. Removal of all potential sources of danger goes beyond what is reasonable (*Rich v LCC*,[3] distinguishing *Jackson v LCC and Chappell*[4]); the proper development of children entails their taking some risks and this applies to even quite young children (*Suckling v Essex County Council*,[5] *Jefferey v LCC*[6]). The child may be 'the author of his own misfortune' (*Trevor v Incorporated Froebel Institute*[7]). The duty to supervise does not ordinarily extend beyond school hours (*Mays v Essex County Council*[8]).

(3) Where a pupil is injured by another pupil, and in some other circumstances, the 'careful father' test may be inappropriate. The question may be rather whether there was any departure from the standard of care that would have been prudent in the circumstances and whether the consequences of that departure were reasonably foreseeable. The 'ordinary language of the law of negligence' (per Geoffrey Lane J) was applied in *Beaumont v Surrey County Council*,[9] and see also *Gillmore v LCC*,[10] *Langham v Wellingborough School Governors and Fryer*,[11] *Affutu-Nartoy v Clarke*[12] and *Smoldon v Whitworth*, in which it was held that a referee may owe a duty of care to a player.[13]

10 (1967) 66 LGR 171.
11 (1932) 96 JP 371, CA, F[122].
12 (1967) 65 LGR 543, CA, F[141].
13 (1890) 63 LT 756, CA.
14 [1961] CLY 5865, CA.
15 (1967) 66 LGR 440, F[140].
16 (1937) 81 Sol Jo 630.
17 [1943] 2 All ER 629, F[128].
18 [1937] 3 All ER 902, F[126].
19 (1954) 118 JP 244, F[133].
20 [1970] 1 All ER 535, F[146].
1 (1916) 80 JP 246, F[119].
2 [1997] ELR 35.
3 [1953] 2 All ER 376, F[131].
4 (1912) 76 JP 217, CA, F[117].
5 (1955) Times, 27 January.
6 (1954) 119 JP 45, F[134].
7 (1954) Times, 11 February.
8 (1975) Times, 11 October, F[148].
9 (1968) 66 LGR 580, F[143].
10 [1938] 4 All ER 331, F[127].
11 (1932) 101 LJKB 513, CA, F[121].
12 (1984) Times, 9 February, F[151].
13 (1996) Times, 18 December, CA, F[155].

(4) It is not always necessary for the plaintiff to show that any particular teacher was at fault—a system of supervision or arrangements with regard to safety on school premises may be defective (*Barnes v Hampshire County Council*[14], and *Fowles v Bedfordshire County Council*[15] where contributory negligence was also found)). In assessing the arrangements what is reasonably practicable for the smooth running of a school will be material, and whether practice is in accordance with that generally adopted and approved in schools (*Wright v Cheshire County Council*[16] and *Van Oppen v Clerk to the Bedford Charity Trustees*[17]).

(5) What kind of accident is reasonably foreseeable turns in part on the age of pupils and their experience in the activity in which they are engaged at the time of the accident (*Crouch v Essex County Council*,[18] *Martin v Middlesbrough Corpn*[19] and *Butt v Cambridgeshire and Isle of Ely County Council*[20]). Against an older pupil employers may be able to plead *volenti non fit injuria* (*Smerkinich v Newport Corpn*,[1] distinguished in *Butt v Inner London Education Authority*[2]). An accident to a third party where inadequate care is exercised over a child may be held to be reasonably foreseeable (*Carmarthenshire County Council v Lewis*[3]).

(6) The more dangerous the article in the school the higher the standard of care required (*King v Ford*[4]). Articles such as teapots and oilcans are not dangerous per se (*Wray v Essex County Council*[5]).

(7) A pupil does not become a servant of the teacher's employers (and hence potentially render them vicariously liable for his negligence) just because from time to time he does some act in support of the life of the school community (*Watkins v Birmingham City Council*[6]); and it is reasonable that pupils should be required to perform such acts (*Smith v Martin and Kingston-upon-Hull Corpn*[7]).

14.20 Negligence of a different kind was alleged in *Palmer v Harrow London Borough Council*.[8] The authority, in exercise of their duty in respect of special educational needs, sent children to a special school in Shropshire, at which they were subjected to sexual abuse, but no breach of the duty of care was found.

Breach of statutory duty

14.21 LEAs are under no direct liability at common law in relation to the exercise of statutory discretions conferred on them by the Education Acts (*X*

14 [1969] 3 All ER 746, HL, F[144]. Compare *Nwabudike v Southwark London Borough Council* [1997] ELR 35.
15 [1996] ELR 51, CA, F[153].
16 [1952] 2 All ER 789, CA, F[130].
17 [1989] 3 All ER 389, CA, F[152].
18 (1966) 64 LGR 240, F[139].
19 (1965) 63 LGR 385, CA, F[138].
20 (1969) 68 LGR 81, CA, F[145].
1 (1912) 76 JP 454, F[118].
2 (1968) 66 LGR 379, F[142].
3 [1955] 1 All ER 565, HL, F[132].
4 (1816) 1 Stark 421, F[112].
5 [1936] 3 All ER 97, CA, F[124].
6 (1976) 126 NLJ 442, CA.
7 [1911] 2 KB 775, F[116].
8 [1992] PIQR P 296.

14.21 *Wrongdoings*

(minors) v Bedforshire County Council and associated cases[9]). An action for breach of statutory duty may be brought only when the statute is intended to prevent the kind of harm that has been suffered, the plaintiff is one of a class the statute is intended to protect and no special remedy is provided by the statute for the protection of the person injured.

14.22 The main relevant statutory provisions are
(a) the 1996 Act s 542, which, subject to s 543 (relaxation of standards in special cases), requires LEAs and governing bodies of grant-maintained schools to secure that the premises of their schools conform to the standards prescribed by regulations. The material regulation is now reg 17 of the Education (School Premises) Regulations 1996, under which school buildings are to be such as reasonably to assure the safe escape of occupants in case of fire and other aspects of health, safety and welfare. See *Ching v Surrey County Council*,[10] *Morris v Carnarvon County Council*,[11] *Lyes v Middlesex County Council*,[12] *Reffell v Surrey County Council*[13] and *Abbott v Isham*,[14] all decided under comparable earlier legislation;
(b) the Occupiers' Liability Act 1957 s 2, which places a 'common duty of care' on the occupier of premises, namely 'to take such care as in all the circumstances of the case is reasonable to see that the visitor [an invitee or licensee under the common law which was superseded by the 1957 Act] will be reasonably safe in using the premises for the purposes for which he is invited or permitted by the occupier to be there'. LEAs or governing bodies are occupiers and potentially liable at the suit of visitors—pupils and others such as parents—in case of default (*Fryer v Salford Corpn*[15]). Liability will not arise for injuries to a pupil if he is one of those taken to apparently safe premises staffed by competent and careful persons, and uses equipment apparently safe and under the control of those persons (*Brown v Nelson*[16]);
(c) the Health and Safety at Work etc Act 1974 s 4, under which it is the duty of employers (including LEAs) to ensure, so far as reasonably practicable, the health, safety and welfare of employees and others, such as school pupils.[17] But breach of duty under that section does not as such give rise to civil liability.

14.23 Cases decided on common law principles may assist in the interpretation of a statutory duty, because the circumstances which give rise to a breach of duty may equally support an action for negligence (*Reffell v Surrey County Council*,[18] *Ward v Hertfordshire County Council*);[19] and it doubtful whether, despite strict liability, in practice statutory duty is likely to be any more demanding than the common law.

9 [1995] 3 All ER 353, HL F[154].
10 [1910] 1 KB 736, CA, F[113].
11 [1910] 1 KB 840, CA, F[114].
12 (1962) 61 LGR 443, F[135].
13 [1964] 1 All ER 743, F[137].
14 (1920) 90 LJKB 309.
15 [1937] 1 All ER 617, CA, F[125].
16 (1970) 69 LGR 20.
17 See Circular 14/96, 'Supporting Pupils with Medical Needs in Schools'.
18 [1964] 1 WLR 358.
19 [1970] 1 All ER 535, F[146].

Nuisance

14.24 In *Dunton v Dover District Council*[20] a children's playground in a housing estate was used from dawn to dusk by children of all ages. It was adjacent to the garden of a hotel, whose owner was awarded damages for noise nuisance and was granted an injunction against the Council, stipulating that the playground should be open only at specified times, and to children under the age of 12. See also *Matheson v Northcote College Board of Governors*,[1] in which English case law and authorities were reviewed.

Defamation

14.25 Most of the reported cases concern allegations against school teachers in their calling, and the defence has often been that of qualified privilege. Cases involving (a) head teachers include *Ripper v Rate*,[2] *Jones v Jones*,[3] *Baraclough v Bellamy*,[4] and *Hardwick v Daily Express*;[5] (b) assistant teachers include *Hume v Marshall*,[6] *Goslett v Garment*,[7] *Reeve v Widderson*,[8] *Milne v Bauchope*[9] and *M'Carogher v Franks*;[10] and (c) pupils include *Bridgman v Stockdale*[11] (an allegation of cribbing).

14.26 Remarks written by teachers on reports to parents or made, for example, to a doctor or social worker, and references, are also covered by qualified privilege.

---

20 (1977) 76 LGR 87.
1 [1975] 2 NZLR 106.
2 (1919) Times, 17 January.
3 [1916] 2 AC 481.
4 (1928) Times, 18 July.
5 (1972) Times, (a news item) 22 December.
6 (1877) 37 LT 711.
7 (1897) 13 TLR 391.
8 (1929) Times, 24 April.
9 1867 SC 1114.
10 (1964) Times, 25 November.
11 [1953] 1 WLR 704.

Chapter 15

CONCLUSION

15.01 This account of education law is concluded mainly by reference to the miscellaneous and general provisions in Part X of the 1996 Act (sections 542 to 583, Schedule 36),[1] but with the addition of passages on, in particular, the law concerning employment of children and young persons, and on the means of making complaints and seeking redress against LEAs and others.

15.02 Under Part X Chapter V (sections 561 and 562), the 1996 Act does not apply (a) to children and young persons in the service of the Crown provided that the Secretary of State certifies that the exercise of his powers and duties, or those of LEAs or parents, is unnecessary; or (b) to persons in custody.[2] Chapter VI is about the exemptions from stamp duty otherwise payable on transfers under the Education Acts;[3] the provisions relating to orders, regulations and directions;[4] the publication of guidance and service of documents.[5]

EDUCATIONAL PREMISES

15.03 Chapter I of Part X (sections 542 to 547) is about required standards of educational premises, control of potentially harmful materials and apparatus and nuisance or disturbance on educational premises. Reference is also made under this heading to exceptional use of school premises.

Standards

15.04 LEAs and the governing bodies of grant-maintained schools are to secure that the premises of all maintained schools conform to prescribed standards. The Secretary of State may prescribe different standards for different types of school. He may also, in the following circumstances, give a direction that, although a particular requirement is not satisfied, school premises shall be deemed to conform to the prescribed standards as respects matters, and subject to conditions, specified in the direction. The circumstances are (a) it would be unreasonable to require conformity having regard to the nature of the existing

---

1 For construction of the Act see ss 573 to 580 and Appendix 10.
2 1996 Act ss 561 and 562. LEAs have discretion to arrange for prisoners to receive the benefit of educational facilities.
3 1996 Act s 567.
4 1996 Act ss 568 to 570. See paras 1.28, 1.30 and 1.20.
5 1996 Act s 572. See para 1.31.

site or buildings, or other special circumstances affecting the school premises; or (b) shortage of suitable sites (where the school is to have an additional or new site); or (c) the need to control public expenditure (where the school is to have additional buildings or is to be transferred to a new site and existing or temporary buildings are to be used).[6]

15.05 Proposals submitted to the Secretary of State for establishment and alteration of county and voluntary schools are to be accompanied, for his approval, by any particulars he requires of the premises (see paras 3.08 and 3.19). Otherwise proposed new premises, or alteration of premises, for the following are subject to his approval (or that of the funding authority if he so prescribes) under regulation, namely (a) maintained schools, all special schools, LEA further and higher education institutions and institutions within the further education sector; and (b) any boarding hostel provided by an LEA for persons receiving education at those schools or institutions.[7]

15.06 On approval having been given by the Secretary of State to plans or particulars of a building, it is exempt from building regulations[8] and, so far as the Secretary of State directs by order, from local Acts and byelaws.[9]

15.07 For the needs of disabled persons, buildings for most schools and educational institutions are to be provided, so far as practicable and reasonable, with appropriate (a) means of access to and within the building, (b) parking facilities, and (c) sanitary conveniences.[10]

Control of potentially harmful materials and apparatus

15.08 The Secretary of State has made regulations requiring his approval to be obtained for the use of specified materials or apparatus which involve serious health hazards in maintained schools, all special schools and LEA further

---

6 1996 Act ss 542 and 543. See the Education (School Premises) Regulations 1996, SI 1996/360 and Circular 10/96 (WO 30/96) (similarly entitled). Many of the detailed requirements of the revoked 1981 regulations no longer apply.
   The duty is an absolute one and its breach may thus give rise to an action for damages without proof of negligence if injury is sustained. But failure to comply with the duty is otherwise enforceable only by the Secretary of State under s 497 (see para 12.09). See *Reffell v Surrey County Council* [1964] 1 WLR 358, F[137], *Bradbury v Enfield London Borough Council* [1967] 1 WLR 1311 and *Ward v Hertfordshire County Council* [1970] 1 All ER 535, F[146].
   Sections 542 and 543 are applied by the Education (Grant-maintained Special Schools) Regulations 1994, SI 1994/653, reg 42, Schedule, Pt I; and by the Education (Special Schools Conducted by Education Associations) Regulations 1994, SI 1994/1084, reg 8(1), Sch 2, Pt I.
7 1988 Act s 218(7) and (10) and 1996 Act s 544. See the Education (Schools and Further and Higher Education) Regulations 1989, SI 1989/351. Hostels are subject to inspection under the regulations.
8 Building Act 1984 s 4(1).
9 1996 Act s 545. 'Approval': under (a) s 39 or 44 (see paras 3.17 and 3.19); (b) SI 1989/351; or (c) s 428(2)(b) (see para 7.24).
10 Chronically Sick and Disabled Persons Act 1970, s 8, and see Circular 2/82 'Re: Disabled Persons Act 1981', E[144].
   The schools and other educational instututions are: (a) universities, university colleges and colleges, schools and halls of universities, (b) institutions within the higher education sector, (c) LEA schools and maintained and assisted further and higher education institutions, and (d) institutions in the further education sector.

15.08 *Conclusion*

and higher education institutions, and institutions in the further education sector.[11]

Nuisance or disturbance on educational premises

15.09 A person who without lawful authority is on the premises of a maintained school, or of an LEA further or higher institution, commits an offence if he causes or permits nuisance or disturbance to the annoyance of those who lawfully use the premises. Proceedings may be brought only by a police constable, LEA (with the consent of the governing body of a voluntary or grant-maintained school) or person authorised by the governing body of an aided, special agreement or grant-maintained school. On summary conviction a fine not exceeding level 2 on the standard scale may be imposed.[12] (An offence occurs only in the limited circumstances stated; otherwise the remedy is a civil action in trespass.)

15.10 The following may remove the person concerned from the premises if they have reasonable cause to suspect that an offence is being, or has been, committed: (a) a police constable (ie any police officer), (b) a person authorised by an LEA (in the case of voluntary or grant-maintained schools, with the consent of the governing body), or (c) a person authorised by the governing body of an aided, special agreement or grant-maintained school.

15.11 It appears to be for the LEA or governing body (or, for example, the head teacher on their behalf) to determine who may lawfully be present on premises, but it may be that the presence of parents on school premises for a legitimate purpose is lawful unless and until a person authorised by the LEA or governing body has asked them to leave, or told them not to call except by appointment, or (perhaps) posted a notice to the same effect.

Exceptional use of school premises

15.12 Special provision is made for rooms in maintained schools to be used for elections. A candidate in a parliamentary or European Assembly election may on giving reasonable notice use a suitable room at reasonable times (not including times of use for educational purposes) for holding public meetings. Use of the room is free of charge but the candidate is to defray expenses incurred and the cost of making good any damage done. Arrangements are to be made with the LEA or governing body of a grant-maintained school.

---

11 1988 Act s 218(1)(e) and (10) and 1996 Act s 546. See the Education (Schools and Further and Higher Education) Regulations 1989, SI 1989/351, reg 7.
12 1996 Act s 547 and Local Government (Miscellaneous Provisions) Act 1982 s 40 (2) to (5) as substituted by the 1996 Act Sch 37, para 55.
   The offence is committed whether or not the persons disturbed etc are present at the time. It might consist, for instance, in the fouling of school playing fields by dogs at any time. See *Sykes v Holmes* [1985] Crim LR 791, DC, where the inhalation of solvents on school premises outside school hours and unobserved by pupils or staff was held to be an offence under this section.
   'Premises' includes playgrounds, playing fields and other premises for outdoor recreation.
   'Remove[the person concerned] from the premises'. It is implicit that where the offender is present the police constable or person authorised should first ask him to leave the premises; and that if that request is not complied with the degree of force used to effect his removal should be no more than is reasonable in the circumstances.

Questions about entitlement to use etc are determined by the Secretary of State. Similar provisions apply to the use of rooms as polling stations and in respect of local government elections. Schools used as polling stations do not necessarily have to close for the election.[13]

15.13 If a parish (in Wales a community) do not have their own meeting room, a suitable room in maintained school premises may be used free of charge for specified meetings about parish affairs. Use is to take place at reasonable times and after reasonable notice, and when the room is not required for educational purposes. Expenses and the cost of making good any damage done are to be met by the parish or community council. The Secretary of State determines what is reasonable or suitable if any question arises.[14]

PUNISHMENT

15.14 LEAs are vicariously liable if expressly or by implication they have authorised any improper punishment. Although punishment should not be indiscriminate, blanket detention of a whole class may be justified as a last resort if there is joint responsibility for indiscipline. If a parent formally withdraws permission to detain, a claim for false imprisonment may succeed.[15]

Corporal punishment

15.15 This is the subject matter of Chapter II of Part X of the 1996 Act (sections 548 to 550). 'Corporal punishment', given by, or on the authority of, a member of school staff, means doing anything to punish a pupil (whether or not there are other reasons for doing it) which, apart from any justification, would constitute battery. It follows that, as well as caning, slapping, throwing missiles such as chalk and rough handling are included.[16] Reasonable force to avert immediate danger to person or property is not corporal punishment. Following a decision in the European Court of Human Rights[17] the law[18] was amended so that corporal punishment of pupils under 18 now gives rise to civil (but not criminal) liability in maintained schools, all special schools, and independent schools where there is an element of public funding for school or pupils; also where an LEA provides education otherwise than at school.[19]

---

13 Representation of the People Act 1983 ss 23, 36, 95, 96, Sch 1, Pt III, para 22, and Sch 5, and rules and regulations made thereunder. 'Room' includes a hall, gallery or gymnasium. LEAs are to keep lists of suitable rooms and make them available for inspection at the appropriate time.
14 Local Government Act 1972 s 134.
15 See *Mansell v Griffin* [1908] 1 KB 947, CA, F[55]; *Terrington v Lancashire County Council* Blackpool County Court (28 August 1986, unreported), F[56]; *Price v Wilkins* (1888) 58 LT 680. See also paras 2.31 and 3.102 ff.
16 Recent cases on the ingredients of trespass to the person and battery are *Wilson v Pringle*[1987] QB 237, CA, and *F v West Berkshire Health Authority*[1989] 2 All ER 545 at 563j, per Lord Goff, HL.
17 *Campbell and Cosans v United Kingdom* (1982) 4 EHRR 293, F[18].
18 See *R v Hopley* (1860) 2 F & F 202, F[14], *Gardner v Bygrave* (1889) 53 JP 743, F[15], *Cleary v Booth* [1893] 1 QB 465, F[16], *R v Newport (Salop) Justices, ex p Wright*[1929] 2 KB 416, F[17] and *Mansell v Griffin* [1908] 1 KB 947, CA, F[55].
19 1996 Act ss 548 and 549. See Circular 7/87 'Education (No 2) Act 1986: Further Guidance', para 3.1, E[335].

15.16 Conclusion

15.16 An 'element of public funding' exists where
(a) an independent school is maintained, or assisted by, a Minister of the Crown (including a school of which a government department is the proprietor) or is assisted by an LEA, and in either case falls within a prescribed class,[20] or
(b) at any other independent school
  (i) a pupil holds an assisted place (see para 9.17 ff), or
  (ii) any fees or expenses are paid by the Secretary of State under the 1996 Act section 491, or by an LEA under section 517 (see paras 11.16 and 12.40), or by an LEA or the funding authority under Schedule 4 paragraph 9 or 10, or
  (iii) fees are payable by an LEA under section 518 (see para 12.41), or
  (iv) a person falls within a prescribed category of persons (at present those whose fees are paid by local social service authorities in England and Wales or equivalent bodies in Scotland and Northern Ireland).[1]

15.17 Corporal punishment cannot be justified by virtue of a member of staff's position as such, or if it is inhuman or degrading.[2] 'Member of the staff' means a teacher at the school (or, where an LEA provide education, some other place) and any other person working there who has lawful control or charge of a pupil. In determining whether punishment is 'inhuman or degrading' regard is to be had to all the circumstances of the case, including the reason for giving it, how soon after the event it is given, its nature, the manner and circumstances in which it is given, the persons involved and its mental and physical effects.

15.18 A person is not to be debarred from receiving education (whether by refusal of admission, suspension or otherwise) because the law is as stated above with the consequence that he is exempt from corporal punishment.[3]

EDUCATIONAL TRUSTS

15.19 Section 1 of the 1973 Act (with Schedule 1) revised the powers of the Secretary of State in relation to educational trusts generally. It first repealed section 2 of the Charities Act 1960 and the Endowed School Acts 1869–1948 so

---

As to corporal punishment at independent schools where there is no element of public funding, see *Y v United Kingdom (No 14229/88)* (1992) 17 EHRR 238, ECt HR, and *Costello-Roberts v United Kingdom* [1994] 1 FCR 65, where the European Court of Human Rights held, by five votes to four, that corporal punishment consisting of three whacks with a rubber-soled gym shoe on the bottom of a seven year-old boy by the head teacher of an independent school was not severe enough to constitute 'degrading punishment', even though it was imposed automatically as part of the school's disciplinary system, the boy had been at the school for only five weeks, and the punishment was administered three days after the boy had been told that he would be corporally punished.

20 See the Education (Abolition of Corporal Punishment) (Independent Schools) Regulations 1987, SI 1987/1183.
1 See the Education (Abolition of Corporal Punishment) (Independent Schools) (Prescribed Categories of Persons) Regulations 1989, SI 1989/1825.
2 The words 'inhuman or degrading' are taken from Art 3 of the European Convention on Human Rights.
3 1996 Act s 550. If the Secretary of State is not satisfied that this requirement is being complied with he may terminate an assisted places participation agreement (see para 9.20). See Circular 7/87, para 3.1.6.

that he might no longer exercise concurrently the functions of the Charity Commissioners[4] regarding charitable trusts, or make new educational endowment schemes; and his approval became no longer required for the appointment of new trustees under a scheme made before the Education Act 1918 came into operation.[5]

15.20 Secondly (now by re-enactment[6]) it enables the Secretary of State, after consultation with the governing body or other proprietor, by order to modify a trust deed or other instrument relating to a school to take account of
(a) implementation of proposals for establishment or alteration of a county or voluntary school (see paras 3.18 and 3.22),
(b) a transfer of the school to a new site (see paras 3.08 and 3.19),
(c) establishment of a new voluntary school in substitution for an old one (see para 3.23),
(d) transfer of a voluntary school to a new site (see para 3.24), or
(e) implementation of proposals for discontinuance of a county or voluntary school or LEA nursery school (see para 3.126).[7]

15.21 Modifications may be permanent or for a period specified.

15.22 Similarly, after consultation with those managing an institution concerned with the provision of educational services or research, he may modify a trust deed or other instrument to comply with the conditions or requirements of regulations.[8]

15.23 Trust deeds concerning property used for educational purposes in specified establishments may, on the application of the trustees, or of the proprietor or governing body, and subject to specified conditions, be amended by the Secretary of State so as to advance education without sex discrimination.[9]

15.24 To provide a safeguard against the consequences of changes affecting governing bodies which were brought about by the 1980 Act, where governors of a voluntary school are expressed to be trustees of property held for the school under a provision in a trust deed or other instrument made before 1 July 1981, the provision is to apply as if restricting trusteeships to foundation governors and those appointed by the LEA and any minor authority, but without prejudice to any power to amend the provision.[10]

15.25 Where under a scheme made under the (repealed) Endowed Schools Acts 1869 to 1948 there was a requirement for the approval or order of any person additional to the trustees to be obtained for the application of property to which the scheme relates, that requirement is retrospectively waived, but any such person may apply to the Secretary of State for a direction that the

---

4 'Charity Commissioners' : see Charities Act 1993 s 1.
5 1918 Act s 47 as amended by 1973 Act s 1(4) and Sch 2.
6 1996 Act s 179.
7 Unless the Secretary of State makes an appropriate order, on discontinuance of a school an LEA will remain bound by a trust created by a conveyance of land to their predecessors in title.
8 See the Education (Grant) Regulations 1990, SI 1990/1989, especially regs 11 and 15, having effect under the 1996 Act s 485.
9 Sex Discrimination Act 1975 s 78.
10 1996 Act s 180. See Circular 4/81 (WO 27/81), E[87].

15.25 Conclusion

requirement is to continue to have effect. No liability arises for previous failure to have obtained approval.[11]

RELIGIOUS EDUCATIONAL TRUSTS — THE SCHOOL SITES ACTS

15.26 Where the premises of a voluntary or grant-maintained school have ceased, or are likely to cease, to be used for school purposes, the Secretary of State may by order make new provision for the use of endowments which have been held wholly or partly for religious education or, subject to specified requirements, used for that purpose. 'Religious education' means education in accordance with the tenets of a particular religion or denomination.[12] No order may be made without the application of the appropriate authority of the religion or denomination concerned. The Secretary of State is to give at least one month's notice of any proposed order to the trustees and other interested persons, and take into account representations received.[13] With the object of enabling the religion or denomination to participate more effectively in the statutory system of education, an order may require or authorise the disposal of land or other property and establish a scheme which provides for endowments to be used for religious educational purposes in connection with voluntary or grant-maintained schools, or partly in other ways related to the locality served by the disused premises.[14]

15.27 If the Secretary of State fails to make an order—perhaps because a school was provided to advance 'Christian' education but not attached to a particular denomination—the School Sites Acts may apply to land no longer used for the purposes for which it was granted.[15] Where he does make an order he may extinguish rights to land or other property under a trust if he is satisfied that the beneficiary, or potential beneficiary, cannot be found or, having been found, has consented to relinquish his rights gratuitously or otherwise.[16]

15.28 The trustees of certain endowments which are regulated by a scheme (in force on 1 January 1994) made as above or under the 1973 Act section 2, or under the Endowed Schools Acts, as applied by the 1944 Act section 86, may resolve, in the manner provided, to adopt specified 'uniform statutory trusts' as the trusts on which the endowments are to be held. They are to send a copy of their resolution to the Secretary of State. The relevant endowments are those held under a scheme which provides for capital or income or both to be applicable for the provision of religious education (or premises for it) at voluntary or grant-maintained schools (or some, but not particular, schools) in a diocese or

---

11 1996 Act s 553.
12 1996 Act s 554. An order is to be made by SI.
  Before the enactment of the 1973 Act s 2 (repealed), the 1944 Act s 86 (repealed by the 1973 Act, but under which schemes are still operating) provided the statutory basis for redistributing the assets of denominational bodies. The Endowed Schools Acts 1869 to 1948 (which included s 2 of, and Sch 1, Pt II to, the Education (Miscellaneous Provisions) Act 1948 were also repealed by the 1973 Act.
13 1996 Act s 555.
14 1996 Act s 556.
15 See the School Sites Acts 1841, 1844, 1849, 1851 and 1852, and the Reverter of Sites Act 1987. See further, as to reverter and the School Sites Acts, Appendix 4.
16 See the Reverter of Sites Act 1987 s 5.

other geographical area. Endowments which constitute a religious education fund (which includes a Sunday school fund) are excluded, and specified rights are not to be affected where the uniform statutory trusts are adopted.[17]

EMPLOYMENT OF CHILDREN AND YOUNG PERSONS

15.29 This part derives not only from Chapter IV of Part X of the 1996 Act (sections 558 to 560) but also from provisions in employment legislation.

15.30 For the purposes of the enactments relating to the prohibition or regulation of employment of children and young persons, a child is a person who is not over compulsory school age.[18] Children under the age of 13 may not be employed.[19] The performance of children in entertainments for which a charge is made, and some other performances, are specifically prohibited (with limited exceptions) unless a licence is granted by an LEA.[20] Permission may be granted for employment abroad for a specified purpose by licence of a police magistrate.[1]

15.31 By notice served on an employer, LEAs may prohibit or restrict the employment of county, voluntary and special school pupils if they consider the employment to be prejudicial to health or to the pupil's obtaining full benefit from education. To ascertain whether this is the case they may, by notice served on parent or employer, obtain information about the employment. Contravention of a requirement is an offence, for which on summary conviction the penalty is a fine not exceeding level 1 on the standard scale or one month's imprisonment, or both.[2]

15.32 To give children work experience in the last compulsory school year, LEAs and governing bodies of grant-maintained schools may lift statutory restrictions where employment is under arrangements made or approved by them. (A child is in his last year of compulsory schooling from the beginning of the term at his school which precedes the beginning of the school year in which he would cease to be of compulsory school age.) But no child is to be employed contrary to (a) an enactment which in terms applies to persons of less than, or not over, a specified age, or (b) other enactments specified. Nor are any

---

17 1996 Act s 557. Schedule 36 sets out the uniform statutory trusts.
18 1996 Act s 558. The enactments include the Children and Young Persons Act 1933 ss 18, 20, 21 and 23 to 30 (see also ss 96 and 97); the Young Persons (Employment) Act 1938; the Factories Act 1961 ss 86 to 119; the Children and Young Persons Act 1963 ss 34 to 44; and the Employment of Children Act 1973 (not in force).
  As to leave of absence from school for employment see para 15.32.
19 Children Act 1972 s 1.
20 Children and Young Persons Act 1963 ss 37 to 39 (which lay down the conditions under which licences are to be granted).
1 Children and Young Persons Act 1933 s 25.
2 1996 Act s 559. (This section ceases to have effect when the Employment of Children Act 1973 s 2 comes into force, but it is understood that implementation has been postponed indefinitely.) As respects powers of entry see Children and Young Persons Act 1933 s 28(1) and (3).
  To prove an offence an LEA need to adduce, for example, evidence of a decline in a pupil's work performance. See *Margerison v Hind* [1922] 1 KB 214. Section 559 is applied by the Education (Pupil Referral Units) (Application of Enactments) Regulations 1994, SI 1994/2103, reg 2, Sch 1, para 1.

15.32 *Conclusion*

arrangements to permit a child to be employed contrary to enactments prohibiting or regulating the employment of young persons: these apply to children employed under the arrangements.³

EDUCATIONAL RECORDS

15.33 This topic is the first in Chapter VI of Part X. The Secretary of State may make regulations with respect to the keeping, disclosure and transfer of educational records about persons receiving education at (a) maintained schools and all special schools, (b) LEA further and higher education institutions, and (c) institutions in the further education sector. Regulations also determine to whom, and under what circumstances, the records may be supplied, and authorise the charging of a fee, which is not to exceed the cost of supply.⁴

CERTIFICATES OF BIRTH AND REGISTRARS' RETURNS

15.34 Where age is required to be proved for the purposes of the 1996 Act (for example, in school attendance proceedings (see para 7.50), or the enactments relating to the employment of children and young persons), any person may obtain a copy of the entry in the register of births certified by a registrar, upon payment of a fee of £2; and an LEA may obtain particulars of entries in the register of births and deaths free of charge.⁵

EVIDENCE

Presumption as to age

15.35 The general rule is that where a person bringing proceedings under the 1996 Act needs to prove someone's age, but, unable to adduce evidence, has

---

3 1996 Act s 560. In this section 'enactments' includes byelaws, regulations and other provisions having effect under statute; 'statutory restrictions' are those in the enactments mentioned in n 18 above; the 'other enactments specified' are the Employment of Women, Young Persons and Children Act 1920 s 1(2) and the Merchant Shipping Act 1995 s 55(1) (prohibition of employment of children in ships); and the 'enactments . . . regulating . . . young persons' include the Children and Young Persons Acts 1933 to 1969.
  Sections 495 and 496 (see para 12.03 ff) do not apply to the powers of LEAs and governing bodies under this section.
  See Circular 7/74 (WO 135/74) 'Work Experience'.
  As to application, see the Education (Grant-maintained Special Schools) Regulations 1994, SI 1994/653, reg 42, Schedule, Pt I, and the Education (Special Schools Conducted by Education Associations) Regulations 1994, SI 1994/1084, reg 8(1), Sch 2, Pt I.
4 1988 Act s 218(1)(f), (4) and (10) and 1996 Act s 563. See the Education (School Records) Regulations 1989, SI 1989/1261, and (with the same title) Circular 17/89 (WO 40/89), E[1054].
5 1996 Act s 564. 'Enactments relating to the employment of children and young persons': see n 18 above.
  A written requisition is to be made in the form specified in the Certificates of Births, Deaths and Marriages (Requisition) Regulations 1937, SR & O 1937/885.

nevertheless satisfied the court that he has used all due diligence in the attempt to do so, the court may presume that the age is as alleged unless the contrary is proved. In proceedings relating to school attendance, however, the child is to be presumed to have been of compulsory school age unless the parent proves otherwise.[6]

Documents

15.36 In legal proceedings the following are to be received in evidence and accepted for what they purport to be unless the contrary is proved: (a) documents issued by LEAs and signed by any authorised officer, (b) extracts from minutes of proceedings of governing bodies of county and voluntary schools signed by their chairman or clerk, (c) attendance certificates signed by head teachers, and (d) certificates signed by LEA medical officers. Extracts and certificates under (b), (c) and (d) are to be evidence of the matters stated.[7]

AUDIT COMMISSION SERVICES

15.37 The Audit Commission for Local Authorities in England and Wales may, at request, and at full cost, promote or undertake studies designed to improve the economy, efficiency and effectiveness of a higher education funding council or an institution within the higher education sector; a teacher training funding agency (or a governing body they support); a further education funding council or an institution within the further education sector; the Funding Agency for Schools, the Schools Funding Council for Wales; or the governing body of a grant-maintained school.[8]

COMPLAINTS AND REMEDIES

15.38 The bodies and institutions which this book is about are subject to the common law of contract and tort, and reference is made at appropriate places to statutory provisions for appeals to LEAs, the courts and tribunals. Three special opportunities for redress require mention.

The Secretary of State

15.39 Complaints may be made to the Secretary of State, inviting him to use his powers, mentioned at para 12.05 ff, to find that an LEA or other body have acted unreasonably or are in default, but he is not to consider using those powers in relation to complaints falling within an LEA's arrangements mentioned at para 6.72 unless those arrangements have first been utilised.

---

6   1996 Act ss 445(3) and 565.
    The main burden of proof is that of establishing that an offence has been committed. See *R v Carr-Briant*[1943] KB 607, *R v Dunbar*[1958] 1 QB 1 and *R v Hudson*[1966] 1 QB 448.
7   1996 Act s 566. In *Hinchley v Rankin* [1961] 1 WLR 421, F[183], a certificate signed by a head teacher was produced in evidence.
8   1988 Act s 220.

15.40 *Conclusion*

The Local Ombudsman

15.40 The jurisdiction of the Local Commissioners for Administration (Ombudsmen) to investigate maladministration[9] extends to the school admission and exclusion appeal committees for maintained schools (see paras 4.25 n 9 and 7.20 n 2), but investigation of instruction in schools and other educational establishments, and conduct, curriculum, internal organisation, management and discipline are outside their jurisdiction. The Ombudsman is not ordinarily to investigate a complaint if other rights of appeal are available, but has discretion to do so. It has been held that if it becomes apparent during an Ombudsman's investigation that the issues are appropriate to be resolved in a court of law he should exercise his discretion to consider whether he should proceed with his investigation.[10]

Judicial review

15.41 Where statute grants a right of appeal the court is concerned with the merits of an issue; on judicial review the question is whether an action is or is not lawful. The distinction is one which laymen may find difficult to make in principle, and which lawyers may find equally difficult in practice. Judicial review cannot be used as an oblique means of appeal.[11]

15.42 The grounds upon which administrative action is subject to review were classified by Lord Diplock[12] as 'illegality', 'irrationality' (or 'Wednesbury unreasonableness') and 'procedural impropriety' (of which failure to act fairly and consistently, and failure to observe the rules of natural justice are examples). Cases for the most part not already mentioned in the text include

HTV Ltd v Price Commission (duty of a public body to act fairly and consistently);[13]

R v Department of Education and Science, ex p Kumar (denial of natural justice where a teacher was not shown allegations made against him in reports prepared by school inspectors);[14]

R v Secretary of State for Wales and Clwyd County Council, ex p Russell (no breach of natural justice where objectors were not shown the observations of the LEA on their objections to proposals under the 1980 Act s 12);[15]

R v Gwent County Council, ex p Perry (whether LEA complied with the requirements of fairness in deleting a child's name from a school's admission register);[16]

---

9 Local Government Act 1974 s 25. As to the meaning of 'maladministration' see *R v Comr for Administration for the North and East Area of England, ex p Bradford Metropolitan City Council* [1979] QB 287, F[200].
10 See *R v Comr for Local Administration, ex p Croydon London Borough Council* [1989] 1 All ER 1033, F[44], in which the court granted an application for judicial review of the Ombudsman's conclusion that an appeal committee had been guilty of maladministration in considering an appeal.
11 See *R v Secretary of State for Education, ex p Banham* [1992] Fam Law 435.
12 See *Council of Civil Service Unions v Minister for the Civil Service*[1985] AC 374 at 410.
13 [1976] ICR 170, F[72].
14 (1982) Times, 23 November,. F[79].
15 (28 June 1983, unreported), F[80].
16 (1985) 129 Sol Jo 737, CA, F[192].

R v Educational Services Committee of Bradford City Metropolitan Council, ex p Professional Association of Teachers (procedural impropriety constituting breach of the rules of natural justice);[17]
R v Board of Governors of the London Oratory School, ex p Regis (whether breach of natural justice in proceedings of governors' meeting to consider a pupil's expulsion);[18]
R v Secretary of State for Education and Science, ex p Avon County Council (No 2) (whether Secretary of State acted ultra vires in rejecting proposals under 1980 Act ss 12 and 13);[19]
R v Board of Governors of Stoke Newington School, ex p M (impropriety—likelihood of bias—in exclusion procedure, constituting breach of the rules of natural justice);[20]
R v Headmaster of Fernhill Manor School, ex p Brown (pupil had no public law remedy on expulsion from independent school); and[1]
R v Leicestershire Education Authority ex p C (provision of information to divorced father).[2]

15.43 Judicial consideration has also been given to the circumstances in which the courts may entertain an application for judicial review where the applicant has an alternative remedy or alternative avenue for redress.[3]

---

17 (1986) Independent, 16 December, F[92].
18 [1989] Fam Law 67, F[91].
19 (1990) 88 LGR 737n, F[99].
20 [1994] ELR 131, F[105].
 1 (1992) Times, 5 June, F[91.1].
 2 [1991] FCR 76, DC.
 3 See *R v Devon County Council, ex p Baker* [1995] 1 All ER 73, CA, F[13]; *Cumings v Birkenhead Corpn* [1972] Ch 12, F[42]; and *Meade v London Borough of Haringey* [1979] 2 All ER 1016, F[75].

Appendix 1
THE EDUCATION ACTS

The 18 Education Acts (those listed in the 1996 Act s 578, together with the 1997 Act), preceded by abbreviations used in the text, are as follows. Many have been heavily amended.

1962 Act: Education Act 1962

Awards and grants for students at further and higher education institutions.

1967 Act: Education Act 1967

Loans for capital expenditure on teacher training institutions.

1973 Act: Education Act 1973

Educational trusts and supplementation of 1962 Act awards.

1980 Act: Education Act 1980

(Largely repealed.)

1983 Act: Education (Fees and Awards) Act 1983

Fees and awards in respect of non-UK students at (mostly) higher education institutions.

1985 Act: Further Education Act 1985

Supply of goods and services by LEAs through further education institutions.

1986 (No 1) Act: Education Act 1986

Grants payable by the Secretary of State to the Fellowship of Engineering and the Further Education Unit; and pooling adjustments.

1986 Act: Education (No 2) Act 1986

Largely repealed. Extant provisions relate to teacher appraisal and further and higher education.

1988 Act: Education Reform Act 1988

Further and higher education and miscellaneous provisions.

1990 Act: Education (Student Loans) Act 1990

Loans towards maintenance of higher education students.

Appendix 1

1991 Act: School Teachers' Pay and Conditions Act 1991

(As indicated by title.)

1992 FHE Act: Further and Higher Education Act 1992

(As indicated by title.)

1994 Act: Education Act 1994

Teacher training and students' unions.

1996 SL Act: Education (Student Loans) Act 1996

Payment of subsidy in respect of private sector loans.

1996 N Act: Nursery Education and Grant-Maintained Schools Act 1996

Grants in respect of nursery education.

1996 Act: Education Act 1996

Consolidation of education law exclusive of provisions here listed.

1996 SI Act: School Inspections Act 1996

Consolidation of the law relating to school inspections and powers over schools requiring special measures.

1997 Act: Education Act 1997

Extension of disciplinary powers; expansion of the assisted places scheme to cover primary schools; and other miscellaneous provisions.

* * *

The following 18 Education Acts were repealed in their entirety by Schedule 38 to the 1996 Act and Schedule 7 to the 1996 SI Act, and, as previously amended, are re-enacted in those Acts. References to these 18 (and earlier) Education Acts are also abbreviated in the text to 'the 1944 Act' etc.

Education Act 1944
Education Act 1946
Education (Miscellaneous Provisions) Act 1948
Education (Miscellaneous Provisions) Act 1953
Education Act 1959
Education Act 1964
Education Act 1968
Education (Handicapped Children) Act 1970
Education (Work Experience) Act 1973
Education Act 1975
Education (School-leaving Dates) Act 1976
Education Act 1976
Education Act 1979
Education Act 1981
Education (Grants and Awards) Act 1984
Education (Amendment) Act 1986 (repealed by Local Government and Housing Act 1989 Sch 12 and SI 1996/1857)
Education (Schools) Act 1992 (except in relation to Scotland)
Education Act 1993

Appendix 2

DERIVATION OF THE PROVISIONS OF THE EDUCATION ACT 1996 AND OF THE SCHOOL INSPECTIONS ACT 1996

EDUCATION ACT 1996

Notes

1. This table shows the derivation of the provisions of the Act.
2. The following abbreviations are used in the Table:-

Acts of Parliament

1944	=	Education Act 1944 (c 31)
1946	=	Education Act 1946 (c 50)
1948	=	Education (Miscellaneous Provisions) Act 1948 (c 40)
1953	=	Education (Miscellaneous Provisions) Act 1953 (c 33)
1962	=	Education Act 1962 (c 12)
1964	=	Education Act 1964 (c 82)
1967	=	Education Act 1967 (c 3)
1968	=	Education Act 1968 (c 17)
1972LG	=	Local Government Act 1972 (c 70)
1973EWE	=	Education (Work Experience) Act 1973 (c 23)
1973NHSR	=	National Health Service Reorganisation Act 1973 (c 32)
1976	=	Education Act 1976 (c 81)
1978IA	=	Interpretation Act 1978 (c 30)
1980	=	Education Act 1980 (c 20)
1981	=	Education Act 1981 (c 60)
1982LG(MP)	=	Local Government (Miscellaneous Provisions) Act 1982 (c 30)
1984	=	Education (Grants and Awards) Act 1984 (c 11)
1986	=	Education (No 2) Act 1986 (c 61)
1988	=	Education Reform Act 1988 (c 40)
1992FHE	=	Further and Higher Education Act 1992 (c 13)
1992(S)	=	Education (Schools) Act 1992 (c 38)
1993	=	Education Act 1993 (c 35)
1994LG(W)	=	Local Government (Wales) Act 1994 (c 19)
1994	=	Education Act 1994 (c 30)
1995HA	=	Health Authorities Act 1995 (c 17)
1996ER	=	Employment Rights Act 1996 (c 18)
1996N	=	Nursery Education and Grant-Maintained Schools Act 1996 (c 50)

Appendix 2

Subordinate legislation

SI 1968/1699	=	Secretary of State for Social Services Order 1968
SI 1977/293	=	Local Authorities etc (Miscellaneous Provisions) Order 1977
SI 1991/1890	=	Education (Financial Delegation for Primary Schools) Regulations 1991
SI 1992/110	=	Education (Financial Delegation for Primary Schools) (Amendment) Regulations 1992
SI 1992/1548	=	Education (National Curriculum) (Foundation Subjects at Key Stage 4) Order 1992
SI 1993/1975	=	Education Act 1993 (Commencement No 1 and Transitional Provisions) Order 1993
SI 1993/3106	=	Education Act 1993 (Commencement No 2 and Transitional Provisions) 1993
SI 1994/507	=	Education Act 1993 (Commencement No 3 and Transitional Provisions) Order 1994
SI 1994/1814	=	Education (National Curriculum) (Foundation Subjects at Key Stage 4) Order 1994
SI 1994/2038	=	Education Act 1993 (Commencement No 5 and Transitional Provisions) Order 1994
SI 1994/2092	=	Education (No 2) Act 1986 (Amendment) (No 2) Order 1994
SI 1996/951	=	Deregulation (Length of the School Day) Order 1996

3. The abbreviation 'Law Com Rec No' followed by a number refers to a recommendation set out in the paragraph of that number in Appendix 1 to the Report of the Law Commission (Cm 3251).

4. By virtue of the Secretary of State for Education and Science Order 1964 (SI 1964/490) all the functions of the Minister of Education were transferred to the Secretary of State for Education and Science. By virtue of further Transfer of Functions Orders (SIs 1970/1536, 1978/274 and 1995/2986) all the functions so transferred are now exercisable by the Secretary of State at large. The effect of these Orders is not separately acknowledged in the Table against each of the provisions affected.

5. The Table also does not separately acknowledge the provisions of general effect contained in the Criminal Law Act 1977 and the Criminal Justice Act 1982 which secure that, where the maximum fine that may be imposed on the commission of a summary offence was originally expressed as a particular amount (or one particular amount on a first conviction and another on subsequent convictions), the amount of the maximum fine is now a particular level on the standard scale.

Provision	Derivation
1(1)	1944 s 7.
(2) to (4)	Drafting.
2(1)	1944 ss 8(1)(a), 114(1) ('primary education'); 1948 s 3(2).
(2)	1944 ss 8(1)(b), 114(1) ('secondary education'); 1992FHE ss 10(1), 14(2), Sch 8 para 13(2).
(3)	1944 ss 41(3), (4), 114(1) ('further education'); 1992FHE s 11, Sch 8 para 13(2).
(4)	1992FHE s 14(1).
(5)	1992FHE s 14(3).
(6)	1944 s 41(5); 1992FHE s 11.
(7)	1992FHE s 14(4).
3(1)	1944 s 114(1) ('pupil'); 1992FHE s 14(6), Sch 8 para 13(2).
(2)	1944 s 114(1) ('junior pupil'; 'senior pupil').
(3)	1992FHE s 14(6).

Derivation of Education Act 1996 & School Inspections Act 1996

Provision	Derivation
4(1)	1944 s 114(1) ('school'); 1992FHE s 14(5); 1993 s 304(1).
(2)	Law Com Rec No 2.
(3)	1992FHE s 91(3).
(4)	1992FHE s 91(5).
5(1)	1994 s 114(1) ('primary school'); 1992FHE Sch 8 para 13(2); 1993 s 304(2).
(2)	1994 s 114(1) ('secondary school'); 1992FHE Sch 8 para 13(2); 1993 Sch 19 para 24(1).
(3)	Drafting.
(4)	1964 s 1(2); 1980 Sch 3 para 12.
(5)	1964 s 1(3); 1993 Sch 19 para 38(3).
6(1)	1944 s 9(4).
(2)	1993 s 182(1).
7	1944 s 36; 1981 s 17.
8	1993 s 277.
9	1944 s 76; 1993 Sch 19 para 20; 1996N Sch 3 para 1.
10	1993 s 1.
11	1993 s 2.
12(1)	1944 ss 6(1), 114(1) ('county'; 'local education authority'); 1972LG ss 179(2), 192(1); SI 1977/293; 1994LG(W) s 21(2).
(2)	1944 s 114(1) ('local education authority'); 1972LG s 192(1); SI 1977/293 art 4; Local Government Changes for England Regulations 1994 (SI 1994/867) reg 5(6); Local Government Changes for England (Amendment) Regulations 1996 (SI 1996/611) reg 2.
(3)	London Government Act 1963 (c 33) s 30(1)(a); 1988 s 163.
(4)	1988 ss 163, 235(4).
(5)	1944 ss 6(1), 114(1) ('local education authority'); 1972LG s 192(1); SI 1977/293; 1994LG(W) s 21(1), (2).
(6)	Drafting.
13(1)	1944 s 7.
(2)	1992FHE s 91(2), (4), Sch 8 para 2.
14(1)	1944 s 8(1); 1992FHE s 10(1).
(2), (3)	1944 s 8(1).
(4)	1980 s 24(2).
(5)	1944 s 8(1A); 1992FHE s 10(2).
(6)	1944 s 8(2); 1981 s 2(1); 1992FHE s 10(3).
(7)	1944 s 8(2) proviso; 1964 s 1(3).
15(1) to (3)	1944 s 41(1), (2); 1992FHE s 11.
(4)	1944 s 41(6); 1992FHE s 11.
(5)	1944 s 41(7), (8); 1992FHE s 11.
(6), (7)	1944 s 41(9), (10); 1992FHE s 11.
(8)	1944 s 41(2), (11); 1992FHE s 11.

Appendix 2

Provision	Derivation
16 (1)	1944 s 9(1); 1992FHE Sch 8 para 4.
(2)	1944 s 9(6).
(3)	1944 s 9(7); 1992FHE s 12(1).
17 (1)	1980 s 24(1).
(2)	1980 s 24(2).
18	1953 s 6(1).
19 (1) to (4)	1993 s 298(1) to (4).
(5) to (7)	1993 s 298(6) to (8).
20	1993 s 3.
21	1993 s 4.
22	Drafting.
23	1993 s 8.
24	1993 s 9.
25	1993 s 6.
26	1993 s 5.
27	1993 s 12.
28	1993 s 20.
29 (1)	1944 s 92.
(2)	1993 s 7(3).
(3), (4)	1993 s 21(2), (3).
(5)	1980 s 8(5B), (7); 1992(5) Sch 4 para 4.
(6)	1980 s 9(1).
30 (1), (2)	1993 s 7(1), (2).
(3)	1993 s 7(4).
(4)	1993 s 21(1).
(5)	1993 s 21(3).
31 (1), (2)	1994 s 9(2).
(3)	1994 s 9(2); 1993 s 298(5).
32 (1)	1944 s 15(1).
(2)	1944 s 15(2); 1986 Sch 4 para 1.
(3), (4)	Drafting.
(5)	1944 s 114(1), Sch 3 para 11.
(6)	Drafting.
33	Drafting.
34 (1)	1944 s 114(1) ('maintain'), (2); 1993 s 305(1) ('local education authority'); drafting.
(2)	1944 s 114(2).

Derivation of Education Act 1996 & School Inspections Act 1996

Provision	Derivation
(3)	1944 s 114(2); 1946 Sch 1 para 1.
(4)	1944 s 114(2); 1946 Sch 1 para 1.
(5)	Rating and Valuation Act 1961 (c 45) s 12(6).
35(1)	1980 s 12(1); 1993 s 229(1).
(2)	1980 s 16(1A); 1993 Sch 19 para 78; Law Com Rec No 3.
(3)	1980 s 12(2).
(4)	1980 s 12(2A); 1988 s 31(4).
(5)	1980 s 12(1A); 1993 s 229(1).
(6)	1992FHE s 59(3), (4).
(7)	1993 ss 272(6), 273(1).
(8)	1993 s 273(2).
36(1)	1980 s 12(3); 1993 s 229(2).
(2)	1980 s 12(3).
(3)	1993 s 229(3).
(4)	1980 s 12(3).
(5), (6)	1980 s 16(3A), (3B); 1988 Sch 12 para 81.
37(1)	1980 s 12(4), (5); 1993 s 273(4).
(2)	1980 s 12(4).
(3)	1980 s 12(5).
(4)	1993 s 273(3).
(5)	1980 s 12(6).
(6)	1980 s 12(4).
(7)	1993 s 273(4).
(8)	1993 s 273(5).
(9)	1993 s 273(6).
38(1), (2)	1980 s 12(7).
(3)	1980 s 12(8).
39(1), (2)	1980 s 14(1).
(3)	Drafting.
40(1)	1980 s 12(9).
(2)	1980 s 14(3).
(3)	1980 s 12(9).
(4), (5)	1980 s 16(1).
41(1)	1980 s 13(1).
(2)	1980 s 13(1); 1993 s 230(1).
(3)	1980 s 16(1A); 1993 Sch 19 para 78; Law Com Rec No 3.
(4)	1980 s 13(1A); 1992FHE s 12(2).
(5), (6)	1980 s 13(2); 1988 s 31(5).
(7)	1980 s 13(1B); 1993 s 230(1).
(8)	1992FHE s 59(3), (4).
(9)	1993 s 273(2).
42(1)	1980 s 13(3); 1993 s 230(2).
(2)	1980 s 13(3).
(3)	1980 s 13(3A); 1993 s 230(3)
(4)	1980 s 230(6).
(5), (6)	1980 s 16(3A), (3B); 1988 Sch 12 para 81.

Appendix 2

Provision	Derivation
43(1), (2)	1980 s 13(4).
(3) to (6)	1993 s 273(3) to (6).
(7)	Law Com Rec No 4.
44(1)	1980 s 14(1); 1993 Sch 19 para 77.
(2)	1980 s 14(1).
(3), (4)	1980 s 14(2); Law Com Rec No 4.
45(1)	1980 s 13(5); Law Com Rec No 4.
(2)	1980 s 13(6); 1993 s 230(4).
(3)	1980 s 14(3).
(4)	1980 s 13(7).
(5), (6)	1980 s 16(1).
(7)	1980 s 13(8); 1993 s 230(5).
46(1)	1944 s 16(2); 1980 Sch 3 para 1.
(2)	1944 s 16(2).
(3)	1944 s 16(2).
(4)	1944 s 16(3).
(5)	1944 s 16(3).
47(1)	1944 s 16(1).
(2)	1946 Sch 1 para 2(1); Law Com Rec No 5.
(3), (4)	1944 s 16(3).
48(1)	1944 s 15(2); 1986 Sch 4 para 1.
(2)	1944 s 15(2); 1993 Sch 19 para 7.
(3)	1944 s 105(3).
(4)	1944 s 105(3); 1993 Sch 19 para 23(b).
49	1964 s 1(1); 1968 s 2; 1980 Sch para 11.
50(1)	1946 s 2(1).
(2)	1946 s 2(1), (7).
(3)	1946 s 2(7).
(4)	1946 s 2(2); 1980 Sch 3 para 7.
(5)	1946 s 16(1) ('department').
51(1)	1946 s 2(1).
(2), (3)	1946 s 2(3), (4).
(4)	1946 s 2(1), (7).
(5)	1946 s 2(7).
(6)	1946 s 2(2); 1980 Sch para 7.
(7)	1946 s 2(8).
(8)	1946 s 16(1) ('department').
52(1)	1986 s 54(3).
(2)	1986 s 54(4).
(3)	1986 s 54(3).
53(1), (2)	1986 s 54(5).
(3), (4)	1986 s 54(13), (14); 1988 Sch 12 para 102.
54(1)	1986 s 54(1).
(2)	1986 s 54(2); Law Com Rec No 6.

Provision	Derivation
(3)	1986 s 54(7).
(4)	1986 s 54(6).
(5), (6)	1986 s 54(12).
55	1986 s 54(8) to (11).
56(1)	1986 s 55(1), (2).
(2)	1986 s 55(2).
(3)	1986 s 55(1).
(4), (5)	1986 s 55(3), (4).
57(1)	1944 s 15(4); 1946 s 2 (5), Sch 1 para 2(1).
(2)	1944 s 15(4); 1946 Sch 1 para 2(1).
(3)	1944 s 15(4A); 1946 Sch 1 para 2(2); 1993 s 282(2), (4).
(4)	1944 s 15(4); 1946 s 2(5), Sch 1 para 2(1); drafting.
58(1)	1944 s 15(5).
(2)	1944 s 15(5); 1993 Sch 19 para 7.
(3)	Drafting.
59(1)	1944 s 15(3).
(2)	1944 s 15(3); 1946 Sch 2 Pt II.
(3)	1944 s 15(3); 1946 Sch 2 Pt II.
(4)	1944 s 15(3); 1946 Sch 2 Pt II.
(5)	1946 Sch 1. para 2(1).
60(1)	1946 Sch 1 para 1; 1980 Sch 3 para 8.
(2), (3)	1946 Sch 1 para 6.
(4) to (6)	1946 Sch 1 para 7.
(7)	Reverter of SitesAct 1987 (c 15) s 8(1).
61(1)	1946 Sch 1 para 1; 1980 Sch 3 para 8.
(2), (3)	1946 Sch 1 para 6.
(4)	1946 Sch 1 para 3.
(5)	1946 Sch 1 para 4.
(6)	1946 Sch 1 para 5.
62(1)	1946 s 16(1) ('site').
(2), (3)	1946 Sch 1 para 8.
(4)	1946 Sch 1 para 9; 1992FHE Sch 8 para 14.
63(1)	1953 s 2; 1980 Sch 3 para 9.
(2)	1953 s 2.
(3)	1953 s 2; 1988 s 114, Sch 12 para 8.
64(1)	1946 s 1(1); 1953 s 3; 1968 Sch 1 para 6; 1980 Sch 3 para 6.
(2)	1946 s 1(1).
(3)	1946 s 1(1); 1953 s 3; 1967 s 2.
65	1993 s 281.
66	1988 s 212.
67(1), (2)	1944 s 105(1).
(3)	1944 s 105(2); 1968 Sch 1 para 4(2); 1993 Sch 19 para 23(a).

Appendix 2

Provision	Derivation
(4)	1944 s 105(2); 1993 Sch 19 para 23(a).
68	1993 s 282(1).
69	1993 s 283.
70	1993 s 284.
71	1944 s 99(3).
72	1944 s 65.
73	1946 s 4(1).
74	1946 s 6.
75	1993 s 285.
76 (1)	1986 s 1(1).
(2)	1986 s 1(2).
(3), (4)	1986 s 1(3), (5).
(5)	1986 s 1(6).
77 (1) to (7)	1986 s 2.
(8)	Drafting.
78 (1)	1986 s 65(1) ('co-opted governor').
(2)	1944 s 114(1) ('foundation governors'); 1980 Sch 1 para 13(a).
(3)	1986 s 65(1) ('parent governor').
(4)	1986 s 65(1) ('teacher governor').
(5)	1986 s 65(1) ('parent governor'; 'teacher governor').
79 (1), (2)	1986 s 3(1) to (5).
(3), (4)	1986 s 3(6), (7).
80 (1)	1986 s 7(1).
(2)	1986 s 7(2); National Health Service and Community Care Act 1990 (c 19) Sch 9 para 31; 1995HA Sch 1 para 112.
(3) to (5)	1986 s 7(3) to (5).
(6)	1986 s 7(6).
(7)	1986 s 7(6).
(8)	1986 s 7(6).
(9)	1986 s 7(7).
81 (1)	1986 s 5(1).
(2)	1986 s 5(3).
(3)	1986 s 5(2).
(4), (5)	1986 s 5(4).
82 (1)	1986 s 11(1).
(2)	1986 s 11(2).
(3)	1986 s 11(2); 1993 Sch 19 para 91(a); Law Com Rec No 3.
(4)	1986 s 11(3); 1993 Sch 19 para 91(d); Law Com Rec No 7.
(5), (6)	1986 s 11(4), (5).
(7)	1986 s 11(6); Sch 19 para 91(d); Law Com Rec No 7.

Derivation of Education Act 1996 & School Inspections Act 1996

Provision	Derivation
83	1986 s 14.
84(1)	1986 s 4(1), (2).
(2)	1986 s 4(3).
(3)	1986 s 4(2).
(4) to (6)	1986 s 4(4) to (6).
85	1986 s 4A; 1993 s 271(1).
86	1986 s 13(1) to (3).
87(1)	1986 s 13(4).
(2)	1986 s 13(7), (9).
(3)	1986 s 13(8).
(4)	1986 s 13(5).
(5)	1986 s 13(6), (9).
88(1)	1993 s 238(1), (8); drafting.
(2)	Drafting.
89(1)	1986 s 9(1).
(2)	1986 s 9(1A); 1993 s 271(3)(a).
(3)	1986 s 9(2).
(4)	1986 s 9(3).
(5), (6)	1986 Sch 1 para 1(1), (2).
90(1), (2)	1986 s 10(1).
(3)	1986 s 10(3).
(4)	1986 s 10(2).
(5)	1986 s 10(4).
(6)	1986 s 10(7).
91(1)	1986 s 10(5).
(2)	1986 s 10(6).
92(1)	1986 Sch 1 para 2(1).
(2)	1986 Sch 1 para 2(1).
(3)	1986 Sch 1 para 2(2).
(4)	1986 Sch 1 para 2(3).
93	1986 Sch 1 para 3.
94(1)	1986 s 9(4).
(2)	1986 s 9(5); 1993 Sch 19 para 90; Law Com Rec No 8.
(3)	1986 s 9(4).
95(1)	1986 s 9(6).
(2)	1986 s 9(7).
(3)	1986 s 9(7); 1993 s 271(3)(b).
(4)	1986 s 9(8).
96(1)	1986 s 12(1); 1993 Sch 19 para 92(a).
(2)	1996 s 12(2); 1993 Sch 19 para 92(b).
(3)	1986 s 12(4); 1993 Sch 19 para 92(d).
(4)	1986 Sch 2 para 5(2); 1993 Sch 19 para 109(c).

Appendix 2

Provision	Derivation
(5)	1986 Sch 2 para 5(1).
97 (1)	1986 s 12(1), (2), (9).
(2)	1986 s 12(4).
(3)	1986 ss 12(5), (9), 65(1) ('promoters'); Law Com Rec No 9.
(4)	1986 ss 12(6), (9), 65(1) ('promoters'); Law Com Rec No 9.
(5)	1986 ss 12(7), 65(1) ('promoters'); Law Com Rec No 9.
(6)	1986 s 12(8).
(7)	1986 Sch 2 para 5(2).
(8)	1986 Sch 2 para 5(1).
98	Drafting.
99 (1)	1986 Sch 2 para 3(1).
(2)	1986 Sch 2 para 3(7).
(3)	Drafting.
100 (1), (2)	Law Com Rec No 10.
(3)	1986 Sch 2 para 3(6).
(4)	1986 Sch 2 para 3(6); drafting.
101 (1)	1988 s 51(2)(a)(i); 1993 s 274(4).
(2)	1988 s 51(2)(a)(ii).
(3)	1988 s 33(2), (4); 1992FHE s 12(5).
(4)	1988 s 33(4); 1992FHE s 12(5).
(5)	1988 s 33(5).
(6)	1988 s 51(2)(b).
102	1988 s 33(3).
103	1988 s 33(1), (2).
104 (1), (2)	1988 s 34(1), (2).
(3)	1988 s 34(4); 1993 s 274(1).
(4) to (6)	1988 s 34(5) to (7).
105 (1)	1988 s 33(4).
(2)	1988 s 33(5).
(3)	1988 ss 33(4), 38(4), 51(1) ('expenditure of a capital nature').
106 (1)	1988 s 38(1).
(2)	1988 s 38(1), (2).
(3)	1988 s 38(2).
(4)	1988 s 38(3).
(5)	1988 s 38(3A); 1992FHE s 12(7).
(6)	1988 s 33(5).
107 (1)	1988 s 39(1); SI 1991/1890; SI 1992/110.
(2)	1988 s 39(4); SI 1991/1890; SI 1992/110.
108	1988 s 39(10).
109 (1)	1988 s 39(11).
(2)	1988 s 39(12).
(3)	1988 s 39(11).

Derivation of Education Act 1996 & School Inspections Act 1996

Provision	Derivation
110 (1)	1988 s 40(1).
(2)	1988 s 40(2); 1993 s 274(3).
(3) to (5)	1988 s 40(3) to (5).
111	1988 s 35(1), (2); 1993 s 274(2).
112 (1) to (3)	1988 s 35(3); 1993 s 274(2).
(4)	1988 s 35(4); 1993 s 274(2).
113 (1), (2)	1988 s 35(5); 1993 s 274(2).
(3), (4)	1988 s 35(6); 1993 s 274(2).
(5)	1988 s 35(4); 1993 s 274(2).
114	1988 s 35(7), (8); 1993 s 274(2).
115	1988 s 33(6)(a), (b).
116 (1) to (3)	1988 s 36(1) to (3).
(4)	1988 s 36(4); 1993 Sch 19 para 125(a).
(5)	1988 s 36(5).
(6)	1988 s 36(5A); 1992FHE s 12(6).
(7)	1988 s 36(5B); 1993 Sch 19 para 125(b).
(8)	1988 s 36(6).
117 (1)	1988 s 37(1).
(2), (3)	1988 s 37(2).
(4), (5)	1988 s 37(3).
(6)	1988 s 37(4).
118 (1) to (3)	1988 s 37(5).
(4), (5)	1988 s 37(6), (7).
119	1988 s 37(8), (9).
120	1988 s 43; 1993 s 276.
121	1988 s 42(1).
122 (1), (2)	1988 s 42(2), (3).
(3)	Drafting.
(4)	1988 s 42(4); 1993 s 275(1)(c).
(5)	1988 s 42(7).
(6)	1988 s 42(8); 1993 s 275(1)(d).
(7)	1988 s 42(9).
123	1988 s 42A; 199 s 275(2).
124 (1)	1988 s 50(2), (5).
(2)	1988 s 50(3).
(3)	Drafting.
(4)	1988 s 50(6).
(5)	1988 s 50(10).
(6) to (8)	1988 s 50(7) to (9).
125 (1)	1988 s 49(1).

Appendix 2

Provision	Derivation
(2), (3)	1988 s 49(2).
(4)	1988 s 49(3).
126	Drafting.
127(1), (2)	1986 s 1(1), (2).
(3), (4)	1986 s 1(4), (5).
128(1) to (3)	1986 s 2(1) to (3).
(4) to (6)	1986 s 2(5) to (7).
(7)	Drafting.
129(1)	1988 s 51(3).
(2), (3)	1988 s 51(4), (5).
(4)	1988 s 51(4).
(5)	1988 s 51(6).
130	1986 s 16(1).
131	1986 s 16(2).
132	1986 s 16(3); Law Com Rec No 11.
133(1) to (3)	1986 s 34.
(4)	Drafting.
(5)	1986 s 35(1).
(6)	Drafting.
134(1)	1944 s 24(2).
(2), (3)	1944 s 24(2), proviso (a).
(4)	1944 s 24(2), proviso (b).
(5)	1944 s 22(4); 1986 Sch 4 para 2; 1993 Sch 13 para 4(6).
(6)	1944 s 22(5); 1993 Sch 13 para 4(4).
(7)	Drafting.
135(1) to (4)	1986 s 40(1) to (4).
(5), (6)	1986 s 40(6), (7).
(7)	Drafting.
(8)	1986 s 40(5).
136(1), (2)	1988 s 44(1), (2); Law Com Rec No 12.
(3)	1988 s 44(3), (5).
137(1), (2)	1988 s 45(1), (2).
(3), (4)	1988 s 45(3).
(5)	1988 s 45(9).
(6)	1988 s 45(10).
138(1)	1988 s 45(1), (4).
(2)	1988 s 45(6).
(3)	1988 s 45(5).
(4)	1988 s 45(7).
(5)	1988 s 45(8).
139(1), (2)	1988 s 46(2).

Derivation of Education Act 1996 & School Inspections Act 1996

Provision	Derivation
(3) to (6)	1988 s 46(3) to (6).
(7)	1988 s 235(2)(f); 1996ER Sch 1 para 37(5).
140	1988 s 47.
141 (1)	1988 ss 44(4), 45(11).
(2)	1988 s 44(4); Law Com Rec No 12.
(3)	1988 s 45(11).
(4)	1988 s 51(6).
142	Drafting.
143 (1), (2)	1944 s 27(2).
(3)	1944 s 27(2) proviso.
(4) to (6)	1944 s 27(3) to (5); 1988 Sch 1 para 2(1).
(7)	Drafting.
144 (1), (2)	1944 s 28(3), Sch 3 para 7; 1988 Sch 1 para 3(2).
(3)	1944 s 28(4); 1988 Sch 1 para 3(2).
(4)	Drafting.
145	1944 s 28(2); 1988 Sch 1 para 3(2).
146 (1)	1944 s 30.
(2) to (4)	1944 s 30; 1988 Sch 1 para 4(b).
147 (1)	1986 s 21(1); 1988 s 115; SI 1996/951 art 3(1).
(2)	1986 s 21(4); 1988 s 115.
(3)	1986 s 21(4); 1988 s 115; SI 1996/951 art 3(1).
148 (1) to (4)	SI 1996/951 art 3(2) to (5).
(5)	Drafting.
149 (1), (2)	1986 s 42(1), (2); 1993 Sch 13 para 5.
(3), (4)	1986 s 42(3); 1993 Sch 13 para 5.
(5)	1986 s 42(4); 1993 Sch 13 para 5; SI 1996/951 art 5.
150 (1)	1944 s 22(3); 1993 Sch 13 para 4(2), (6).
(2)	1944 s 22(1).
(3)	1944 s 22(5); 1993 Sch 13 para 4(4).
151 (1) to (3)	1944 s 22(3A) to (3C); 1993 Sch 13 para 4(3).
(4), (5)	1944 s 22(3D); 1993 Sch 13 para 4(3).
(6)	1944 s 22(3E); 1993 Sch 13 para 4(3).
(7)	1944 s 22(6); 1978IA s 17(2)(a); 1993 Sch 13 para 4(5).
(8)	Drafting.
152 (1), (2)	1944 s 22(1); 1993 Sch 13 para 4(6).
(3), (4)	1944 s 22(2); 1993 Sch 13 para 4(6).
(5)	Drafting.
153	1986 s 21(5); 1988 s 115.
154 (1)	1986 s 22.
(2)	1986 s 22(d).

Appendix 2

Provision	Derivation
(3)	1986 s 22(a); 1993 Sch 19 para 95.
(4)	1986 s 22(b).
(5)	1986 s 22(c).
(6)	1986 s 22(e).
155	1986 s 28.
156 (1)	1986 s 22(f).
(2), (3)	1993 s 261(1), (2).
157 (1)	Law Com Rec No 13.
(2)	1986 s 23(a); Law Com Rec No 13.
(3)	1986 s 23(b).
(4)	1986 s 23(a), (b); Law Com Rec No 13.
(5)	1986 s 23(a); Law Com Rec No 13.
158	Drafting.
159 (1) to (4)	1986 s 26(1) to (4).
(5), (6)	1986 s 26(5).
(7)	1986 s 26(1), (2)
160	1986 s 27.
161 (1)	1986 s 30(1).
(2)	Drafting.
(3)	1986 s 30(3).
(4)	1986 s 30(4).
162 (1), (2)	1986 s 31(1), (2).
(3)	Drafting.
163	1986 s 31(7), (8).
164 (1)	1986 Sch 1 paras 4, 5.
(2)	1986 Sch 1 para 4(1).
(3)	1986 Sch 1 para 4(2).
(4) to (7)	1986 Sch 1 para 5.
165	1986 s 32.
166	Drafting.
167 (1)	1980 s 12(1).
(2)	1980 s 12(2).
(3)	1993 s 273(1).
(4)	1980 s 12(1A); 1993 s 229(1).
(5)	1992FHE s 59(3), (4).
(6)	1993 s 273(2).
168 (1)	1980 s 12(3); 1993 s 229(2).
(2)	1980 s 12(3).
(3)	1993 s 229(3).
(4)	1980 s 12(3).
(5), (6)	1980 s 16(3A), (3B); 1988 Sch 12 para 81.

Derivation of Education Act 1996 & School Inspections Act 1996

Provision	Derivation
169(1)	1980 s 12(4), (5); 1993 s 273(4).
(2)	1980 s 12(4).
(3)	1980 s 12(5).
(4)	1993 s 273(3).
(5)	1980 s 12(6).
(6)	1993 s 273(4), (5)(a).
170(1), (2)	1980 s 12(7).
(3)	1980 s 12(8).
171	1980 s 12(9).
172	1980 s 16(1).
173(1)	1944 s 14(1).
(2)	1944 ss 14(1), 114(1) ('former authority'); 1946 Sch 2 Pt II.
(3)	1944 s 14(1); 1946 Sch 2 Pt II.
(4)	1992FHE s 59(3), (4).
(5)	1993 s 273(2).
(6)	1944 s 14(2).
(7)	1944 s 14(5).
(8)	Drafting.
174(1)	1944 s 14(3).
(2), (3)	1944 s 14(4).
175	1992FHE s 59(1), (2).
176	1986 s 16A; FHE1992 s 12(3).
177	Drafting.
178	1988 s 222.
179(1)	1973 s 1(2); 1980 Sch 3 para 17; Law Com Rec No 3.
(2)	1973 s 1(2).
180	1980 s 5.
181(1)	1986 Sch 2 para 1 ('new school'); 1988 s 48(2).
(2)	1986 Sch 2 para 1 ('relevant proposal'); 1988 s 48(2).
(3)	1988 s 48(2) ('temporary governing body'); drafting.
182	1986 s 65(2).
183	1993 s 22.
184	1993 s 23.
185	1993 s 24.
186	1993 s 25.
187	1993 s 26.

Appendix 2

Provision	Derivation
188	1993 s 27.
189	1993 s 28.
190 (1) (2) (3)	1993 s 29(1). 1993 s 29(2); Law Com Rec No 14. 1993 s 29(3).
191	1993 s 30.
192	1993 s 31.
193	1993 s 32.
194	1993 s 33.
195	1993 s 34.
196	1993 s 35.
197	1993 s 36.
198 (1) to (5) (6)	1993 s 272(1) to (5). 1964 s 1(1); 1993 Sch 19 para 38.
199 (1) to (3) (4)	1993 s 273(3) to (5). 1993 s 273(7).
200	1993 s 37.
201 (1) to (8) (9) (10)	1993 s 38(1) to (8). 1993 s 155(8). 1993 s 38(9).
202	1993 s 39.
203	1993 s 40.
204	1993 s 41.
205	1993 s 42.
206	1993 s 43.
207	1993 s 44.
208	1993 s 45.
209	1993 s 46.
210	1993 s 47(1) to (4).
211	1993 s 48.
212	1993 s 49(1) to (3).

Derivation of Education Act 1996 & School Inspections Act 1996

Provision	Derivation
213	1993 s 50.
214	1993 s 51.
215	1993 s 52.
216	1993 s 53.
217	1993 s 54.
218	1993 s 55.
219 (1) to (3) (4)	1993 s 56. 1993 s 301(5).
220	1993 s 57.
221	1993 s 58.
222	1993 s 59.
223	1993 s 60.
224	1993 s 61.
225	1993 s 62.
226	1993 s 63.
227	1993 s 64.
228	1993 s 65.
229	1993 s 66.
230	1993 s 67.
231 (1) to (4) (5) to (7) (8)	1993 s 68(1) to (4). 1993 s 68(5) to (7); 1996N s 7(2) to (4). 1993 s 68(8).
232	1993 s 69.
233	1993 s 70.
234	1993 s 71.
235	1993 s 72.
236	1993 s 73.
237	1993 s 74.
238	1993 s 75.

Appendix 2

Provision	Derivation
239	1993 s 76.
240	1993 s 77.
241	1993 s 78.
242	1993 s 79.
243	1993 s 80.
244	1993 s 81.
245	1993 s 82.
246	1993 s 83.
247	1993 s 84.
248	1993 s 85.
249	1993 s 86.
250	1993 s 87.
251	1993 s 88.
252	1993 s 89.
253	1993 s 90.
254	1993 s 91.
255	1993 s 92.
256	1993 s 93(1) to (6).
257	1993 s 94.
258	1993 s 95.
259	1993 s 96; Law Com Rec No 3.
260	1993 s 97; Law Com Rec No 3.
261	1993 s 98.
262	1993 s 99.
263	1993 s 100; Law Com Rec No 3.
264	1993 s 101.
265	1993 s 102.
266	1993 s 103(2) (3).

Derivation of Education Act 1996 & School Inspections Act 1996

Provision	Derivation
267	1993 s 104.
268	1993 s 105.
269	1993 s 106.
270	1993 s 107.
271	1993 s 108.
272	1993 s 109.
273	1993 s 110.
274	1993 s 111.
275	1993 s 112.
276	1993 s 113.
277	1993 s 114.
278	1993 s 115.
279	1993 s 116.
280	1993 s 117.
281	1993 s 118.
282	1993 s 119.
283	1993 s 120.
284	1993 s 121.
285	1993 s 122.
286	1993 s 123.
287	1993 s 124.
288	1993 s 125.
289	1993 s 126.
290 (1) to (7) (8), (9) (10), (11) (12) (13)	1993 s 127(1) to (7). 1993 s 127(8). 1993 s 127(9), (10). 1993 s 305(1). 1993 s 127(11).
291	1964 s 1(1); 1993 Sch 19 para 38.
292 (1)	1993 s 231(1); drafting.

Appendix 2

Provision	Derivation
(2)	1993 s 232(2).
293	1993 s 128.
294	Drafting.
295	1993 s 129.
296 (1)	1993 s 130(1).
(2)	1993 s 130(2); 1996N Sch 3 para 11.
297	1993 s 131.
298	1993 s 132.
299	1993 s 133.
300	1993 s 134.
301	1993 s 135.
302	1993 s 136.
303	1993 s 137.
304	1993 s 143.
305	1993 s 144.
306	1993 s 145.
307 (1), (2)	1993 s 261(1), (2).
308 (1)	1993 ss 267(1), 268(1).
(2)	1993 s 267(2).
(3)	1993 s 268(2).
309	1993 s 152.
310	1993 s 154.
311 (1)	1993 ss 155(1) ('premises'), 305(1) ('Church in Wales school'; 'Church of England School'; 'Roman Catholic Church school').
(2)	1993 s 305(4).
(3)	1993 s 155(2).
(4)	1993 s 155(3).
(5)	1993 s 155(6).
(6)	1993 s 155(7).
(7)	Drafting.
(8)	1993 s 155(11).
312 (1) to (4)	1993 s 156(1) to (4).
(5)	1993 ss 156(5), 305(1) ('maintained school').
313 (1) to (4)	1993 s 157.

Derivation of Education Act 1996 & School Inspections Act 1996

Provision	Derivation
(5)	Drafting.
314	1993 s 158.
315	1993 s 159.
316	1993 s 160.
317 (1) to (5)	1993 s 161(1) to (5).
(6), (7)	1993 s 161(6), (7); Disability Discrimination Act 1995 (c 50) s 29(2).
318(1), (2)	1993 s 162(1), (2)
(3)	1993 s 162(2A); 1996N Sch 3 para 12.
(4)	1993 s 162(3).
319	1993 s 163.
320	1993 s 164.
321	1993 s 165.
322 (1)	1993 s 166(1); 1995HA Sch 1 para 124(2).
(2)	1993 s 166(2).
(3)	1993 s 166(3); 1995HA Sch 1 para 124(2).
(4)	1993 s 166(4).
(5)	1993 s 166(5); 1994LG(W) Sch 16 para 105(1); Local Government Changes for England Regulations 1994 (SI 1994/867) reg 5(6); Local Government Changes for England (Amendment) Regulations 1996 (SI 1996/611) reg 2.
323	1993 s 167.
324	1993 s 168.
325	1993 s 169.
326	1993 s 170.
327	1993 s 171.
328	1993 s 172.
329	1993 s 173.
330	1993 s 174.
331	1993 s 175.
332	1993 s 176; 1995HA Sch 1 para 124(3).
333	1993 s 177.
334	1993 s 178.

Appendix 2

Provision	Derivation
335	1993 s 179.
336	1993 s 180; Arbitration Act 1996 (c 23) Sch 3 para 59.
337 (1)	1993 s 182(1).
(2)	Drafting.
(3), (4)	1993 s 182(2), (3).
338 (1)	1993 s 183(1).
(2)	Drafting.
339	1993 s 183(2) to (10).
340	1993 s 184.
341	1993 s 185.
342	1993 s 188.
343	1993 s 231.
344 (1)	Drafting.
(2)	1993 s 182(4).
345	1993 s 186.
346	1993 s 187.
347	1993 s 189.
348	1993 s 190.
349	1993 s 191.
350 (1)	1988 s 25(1) ('maintained school'); 1993 s 245(5).
(2)	1988 s 25(1) ('assess').
351 (1)	1988 s 1(2).
(2) to (5)	1988 s 1(1).
352 (1)	1988 ss 2(1), 8(2); 1993 s 241(1), Sch 19 para 114.
(2)	1988 s 2(3).
(3)	1944 s 114(1) ('sex education'); 1993 s 241(2).
353	1988 s 2(2); 1993 ss 240(1), 245(5).
354 (1)	1988 s 3(1).
(2)	1988 s 3(2); SI 1992/1548 art 2; SI 1994/1814 art 2(2) to (4).
(3) to (5)	1988 s 3(2A), (2B); SI 1994/1814 art 2(5).
(6)	1988 s 3(4).
(7)	1988 s 3(6) ('school').
(8)	1988 s 3(7).
355 (1)	1988 s 3(3); 1993 Sch 19 para 113.
(2)	1988 s 3(4).

Derivation of Education Act 1996 & School Inspections Act 1996

Provision	Derivation
(3)	1988 s 3(5).
(4)	1988 s 3(5A); 1993 s 240(2).
(5)	1988 s 3(6) ('class'; 'school year'); 1993 s 240(3).
356 (1) to (4)	1988 s 4(1) to (4).
(5) to (8)	1988 s 4(5) to (8); 1993 s 240(4).
(9)	1993 s 241(4).
357 (1)	1988 s 10(2).
(2)	1988 s 10(3).
358	1993 s 244.
359 (1)	1993 s 245(1).
(2)	1993 s 245(4).
(3)	1993 s 245(3).
(4)	1993 s 245(2).
(5)	1993 s 245(5).
360 (1)	1988 s 14(1); 1993 s 253(1).
(2) to (4)	1988 s 14(2); 1993 Sch 15 para 4(3), Sch 19 para 118(a).
(5)	1988 s 14(7).
361 (1)	1988 s 14(3); 1993 Sch 15 para 4(3), Sch 19 para 118(b); Education (School Curriculum and Assessment Authority) (Transfer of Functions) Order 1994 (SI 1994/645); Education (School Curriculum and Assessment Authority) (Transfer of Functions) Order 1995 (SI 1995/903).
(2)	1988 s 14(5); 1993 Sch 15 para 4(3), Sch 19 para 118(c).
(3), (4)	1988 s 14(6); 1993 Sch 15 para 4(3), Sch 19 para 118(d).
(5)	Drafting.
362 (1), (2)	1988 s 16(1), (2).
(3), (4)	1988 s 16(3); 1993 Sch 19 para 119(a).
(5), (6)	1988 s 16(4), (5).
(7)	1988 s 16(6); 1993 Sch 15 para 4(4), Sch 19 para 119(b).
363	1988 s 17.
364	1988 s 18; 1993 Sch 19 para 120.
365 (1)	1988 s 19(1).
(2) to (4)	1988 s 19(2).
(5)	1988 s 19(1).
(6)	1988 s 19(10).
366 (1)	1988 s 19(3).
(2)	1988 s 19(4).
(3)	1988 s 19(4); 1993 Sch 19 para 121(a); Law Com Rec No 15.
(4)	Law Com Rec No 15.
(5)	1988 s 19(5); Law Com Rec No 15.
(6)	1988 s 19(6); 1993 Sch 19 para 121(b); Law Com Rec No 15.
(7)	Law Com Rec No 15.
367 (1)	1988 s 19(7).

Appendix 2

Provision	Derivation
(2), (3)	1988 s 19(8).
(4)	1988 s 19(9).
368 (1)	1988 ss 20(1), 21(1).
(2)	1988 ss 20(2), 21(2); 1993 s 243.
(3)	1988 ss 20(3), 21(3); 1993 s 243.
(4), (5)	1988 ss 20(4), 21(3A); 1993 s 243.
(6), (7)	1988 ss 20(5), 21(3B); 1993 s 243.
(8)	1988 ss 20(6), 21(4).
(9)	1993 s 242(1), (3).
(10)	1988 ss 20(2), 21(2); 1993 Sch 15 para 4(5), Sch 19 para 122; drafting.
369	1988 s 227(1).
370 (1)	1986 s 17(1).
(2), (3)	1986 s 17(2), (3).
371 (1), (2)	1986 s 18(1).
(3)	1986 s 18(2).
(4)	1986 s 18(3).
(5)	1986 s 18(7); 1993 Sch 19 para 94.
(6)	1986 s 18(8).
(7)	1986 s 18(7); Law Com Rec No 3.
(8)	Drafting.
372 (1)	1986 s 18(5).
(2) to (4)	1986 s 18(6).
(5)	Drafting.
373 (1), (2)	1986 s 19.
374	Drafting.
375 (1)	Drafting.
(2)	1944 s 114(1) ('agreed syllabus'); 1988 Sch 1 para 6.
(3)	1988 s 8(3).
(4)	1944 s 114(1) ('agreed syllabus'), Sch 5 para 11; 1988 Sch 1 para 6.
(5)	1988 s 8(3).
376 (1)	1944 s 26(1); 1988 Sch 1 para 1.
(2)	1944 s 26(2); 1988 Sch 1 para 1.
(3)	1944 s 26(3), (4); 1988 Sch 1 para 1; 1993 Sch 19 para 9.
377 (1)	1944 s 27(6); 1988 Sch 1 para 2(2).
(2)	1944 s 27(1); 1988 Sch 1 para 2(1).
378 (1)	1944 s 28(1); 1988 Sch 1 para 3(1).
(2), (3)	1944 s 28(1B); 1988 Sch 1 para 3(1).
(4)	1944 s 28(1C); 1988 Sch 1 para 3(1).
(5)	1944 s 28(1A); 1988 Sch 1 para 3(1).
379 (1)	1993 s 138(1).
(2) to (4)	1993 s 138(9) to (11).

Derivation of Education Act 1996 & School Inspections Act 1996

Provision	Derivation
380	1993 s 139.
381	1993 s 140.
382	1993 s 142.
383	1993 s 141.
384	1988 s 10(1).
385 (1)	1988 s 6(1), (7).
(2)	1988 s 6(2).
(3)	1988 s 6(7).
(4)	1988 s 6(3); 1993 s 138(8); Law Com Rec No 16.
(5)	1988 s 6(4).
(6)	1988 s 6(5); Law Com Rec No 16.
(7)	1988 s 6(6).
386 (1)	1988 s 7(1); 1993 s 138 (1).
(2)	1988 s 7(1); 1993 s 138 (2).
(3)	1988 s 7(2); 1993 s 138 (3).
(4)	1988 s 7(3); 1993 s 138 (4).
(5)	1988 s 7(4); 1993 s 138 (5).
(6)	1988 s 7(5); 1993 s 138 (6).
(7)	1993 s 138(12).
387	1988 s 7(6); 1993 s 138(7).
388	1988 s 10(1).
389 (1)	1988 s 9(3).
(2)	1988 s 9(9).
(3)	1988 s 9(4).
(4)	1988 s 9(6).
(5)	1988 s 9(7); 1993 Sch 19 para 115.
(6)	1988 s 9(8).
(7)	1988 s 9(2), (5).
390 (1)	1988 s 11(1).
(2)	1988 s 11(3), (4); 1993 s 147(1).
(3)	1988 ss 11(3), 13(4).
(4)	1988 s 11(4); 1993 Sch 19 para 116(a).
(5)	1988 s 11(5).
(6)	1988 s 11(5); 1993 s 255(2).
(7)	1988 s 11(6).
391 (1)	1988 s 11(1).
(2)	1988 s 11(2).
(3)	1988 s 11(7).
(4)	1988 s 11(7).
(5)	1988 s 11(8).
(6)	1988 s 11(9).
(7)	1988 s 11(10).
(8), (9)	1988 s 11(11), (12); 1993 s 147(2).
(10)	1988 s 11(13); 1993 Sch 15 para 4(2), Sch 19 para 116(b).

Appendix 2

Provision	Derivation
392 (1)	1988 s 11(1).
(2)	1988 s 13(1); 1993 Sch 19 para 117.
(3)	1988 s 13(2); 1993 Sch 19 para 117.
(4)	1988 s 13(3).
(5)	1988 s 13(4).
(6)	1988 s 13(5).
(7)	1988 s 13(6).
(8)	1988 s 13(7); 1993 Sch 19 para 117.
393	1993 s 16.
394 (1)	1988 ss 11(1), 12(1); 1993 s 148(a).
(2), (3)	1988 s 12(2), (3).
(4)	1988 s 12(4); 1993 s 148(b).
(5)	1988 s 12(1).
(6)	1988 s 12(9); 1993 s 148(c).
(7)	1988 s 12(10).
(8)	1988 s 12(11); 1993 s 148(d).
395 (1)	1988 s 12(5).
(2)	1988 s 12(6).
(3), (4)	1988 s 12(7).
(5)	1988 s 12(8).
(6)	1988 s 12(5), (6).
(7)	1988 s 12(9); 1993 s 148(c).
(8)	1988 s 12(10).
396 (1)	1988 s 12A(1), (3); 1993 s 257.
(2)	1988 s 12A(2); 1993 s 257.
397	1993 s 258.
398	1988 s 9(1), 9(1A); 1992FHE s 12(4); 1994 Sch 2 para 8(2).
399	1944 s 67(3); 1988 Sch 1 para 4, Sch 12 para 4.
400 (1), (2)	1988 s 5(1).
(3)	1988 s 5(2).
(4)	1988 s 10(2).
(5)	1988 s 5(3).
401 (1)	1988 s 24(1); 1992FHE Sch 8 para 28.
(2)	1988 s 24(2); 1993 Sch 19 para 124.
(3), (4)	1988 s 24(3), (4).
(5)	1988 s 235(2)(c).
402 (1)	1988 s 117(1).
(2)	1988 s 117(2); 1993 s 240(5).
(3) to (5)	1988 s 117(3) to (5).
(6)	1988 s 118(7), (8).
403 (1)	1986 ss 46, 46A; 1988 Sch 12 para 34.
(2)	1986 s 46.
404 (1), (2)	1993 s 241(5).

Derivation of Education Act 1996 & School Inspections Act 1996

Provision	Derivation
(3)	1993 s 241(6).
405	1988 s 17A; 1993 s 241(3).
406 (1), (2)	1986 ss 44(1), (2), 46A; 1988 Sch 12 para 34.
(3)	1986 s 44(1).
407 (1)	1986 ss 45, 46A; 1988 Sch 12 para 34.
(2)	1986 s 45.
408 (1)	1988 s 22(1).
(2)	1988 s 22(2); 1992(S) Sch 4 para 6(2).
(3)	1988 s 22(3); 1993 Sch 19 para 123.
(4)	1988 s 22(1); Law Com Rec No 17.
(5)	1988 s 22(4).
(6)	1988 s 22(5); 1992(S) Sch 4 para 6(3), (4).
(7), (8)	1988 s 22(6); (7).
409 (1) to (3)	1988 s 23(1).
(4)	1988 s 23(2).
410	1988 s 25(2); Law Com Rec No 17.
411 (1), (2)	1980 s 6(1), (2).
(3)	1980 s 6(3); 1988 s 30(2).
(4)	1980 s 6(4).
(5)	1980 s 6(5); 1971IA s 17(2)(a).
(6)	1988 s 26(9).
(7)	1988 s 26(10).
(8)	1980 s 38(4).
412	1986 s 33.
413 (1)	1980 s 6(6); 1988 s 30(3).
(2) to (4)	1980 s 6(7) to (9); 1993 s 270.
414 (1), (2)	1980 s 8(1), (2).
(3), (4)	1980 s 8(3); 1988 s 31(2).
(5)	1980 s 8(4).
(6) to (8)	1980 s 8(5), (5A), (6); 1992(S) Sch 4 para 4(1).
(9)	1980 s 8(7).
415	Drafting.
416 (1)	1988 s 26(1).
(2) to (7)	1988 s 26(3) to (8).
(8)	1988 s 26(1), (3), (4).
417 (1)	1988 ss 27(1), (2), 32(4).
(2), (3)	1988 s 27(3).
(4), (5)	1988 s 27(9).
418 (1)	1988 ss 27(1), (2), 32(4); Education Reform Act 1988 (Commencement No 9) Order 1991 (SI 1991/409).
(2)	1988 s 27(3).

Appendix 2

Provision	Derivation
(3)	1988 s 27(3), (9).
419 (1)	1988 s 29(7).
(2) to (5)	1988 s 29(1) to (4).
420 (1) to (3)	1988 s 27(4) to (6).
(4), (5)	1988 s 27(7).
421 (1)	1988 s 27(8).
(2)	1988 s 32(1).
422 (1) to (6)	1986 Sch 2 para 19.
(7)	1986 s 65(1) ('promoters'), Sch 2 para 1; drafting; Law Com Rec No 9.
423 (1)	1980 s 7(1); 1993 Sch 19 para 73.
(2), (3)	1980 s 7(2), (3).
(4)	1980 s 7(4).
(5)	1890 s 7(5).
(6)	1980 s 38(4).
424 (1)	1980 s 9(1); 1988 s 31(3).
(2)	1980 s 9(1A); 1988 s 31(3).
(3)	1980 s 9(2); 1981 Sch 3 para 14; 1992(S) Sch 4 para 4(2); 1993 Sch 19 para 74.
425	Drafting.
426	1993 s 149(1) to (4).
427	1993 s 150.
428	1993 s 151.
429	Drafting.
430 (1) to (8)	1993 s 260.
(9)	1993 s 305(1) ('maintained school').
431 (1) to (6)	1993 s 13(1) to (6).
(7), (8)	1993 ss 13(7), (8), 305(1) ('maintained school').
432	1993 s 14.
433 (1), (2)	1948 s 4(2).
(3)	1948 s 4(3).
(4)	1948 s 4(3A); 1996N Sch 3 para 2.
(5)	1948 s 4(2).
434 (1)	1944 s 80(1).
(2)	1944 s 80(1A); 1988 Sch 12 para 58.
(3)	1948 s 4(6).
(4)	1944 s 80(1); 1993 Sch 19 para 21.
(5)	1944 s 114(1); 1993 s 155(1), Sch 19 para 24(a)(ii).
(6)	1944 s 80(2).

Derivation of Education Act 1996 & School Inspections Act 1996

Provision	Derivation
435	1948 s 4(1).
436 (1)	1980 s 9(1A); 1988 ss 29(5), 31(3); 1993 s 155(6).
(2)	1988 s 29(5), (6); 1993 s 149(5).
437 (1) to (7)	1993 s 192(1) to (7).
(8)	1993 ss 192(8), 197(6), 198(4), 305(1) ('maintained school').
438	1993 s 193.
439	1993 s 194.
440	1993 s 195.
441	1993 s 196.
442	1993 s 197(1) to (5).
443 (1) to (3)	1993 s 198(1) to (3).
(4)	1993 s 201(2).
444 (1) to (4)	1993 s 199(1) to (4).
(5)	1993 s 199(5); Units of Measurement Regulations 1995 (SI 1995/1804) reg 3.
(6), (7)	1993 s 199(6), (7).
(8)	1993 s 201(2).
(9)	1993 s 199(8).
445	1993 s 200.
446	1993 s 201(1).
447	1993 s 202.
448	1993 s 203.
449	1988 s 118(7).
450 (1)	1988 s 106(1).
(2)	1988 s 106(1A); 1992FHE s 12(9); 1994 Sch 2 para 8(3).
451 (1), (2)	1988 s 106(2).
(3)	1988 s 106(3), (4); 1993 s 280.
(4)	1988 s 106(4).
(5)	1988 s 106(3), (4); 1993 Sch 19 para 127.
452 (1) to (4)	1988 s 107(1) to (4).
(5)	1988 s 107(5), (6).
(6)	1988 s 106(9).
453 (1)	1988 s 106(5).
(2), (3)	1988 s 108.
454 (1)	1988 s 106(6).
(2)	1988 s 118(3).

Appendix 2

Provision	Derivation
(3), (4)	1988 s 106(7), (8).
455 (1)	1988 s 109(1).
(2)	1988 s 109(2).
(3)	1988 ss 109(2), 110(5).
456 (1)	1988 s 109(3); 1978IA s 17(2)(a).
(2) to (8)	1988 s 109(4) to (10).
457 (1)	1988 s 110(1); 1993 Sch 19 para 128.
(2), (3)	1988 s 110(2).
(4)	1988 s 110(3); Disability Living Allowance and Disability Working Allowance Act 1991 (c 21) Sch 3 para 12; Job-seekers Act 1995 (c 18) Sch 2 para 17.
(5)	1988 s 110(4).
458 (1) to (4)	1988 s 111(1) to (3) and (5); 1993 Sch 19 para 129.
(5)	1988 s 111(6).
459	1988 s 118(5).
460 (1), (2)	1988 s 118(1), (2).
(3)	1988 s 118(4).
461	1988 s 118(6).
462 (1)	1988 s 118(7)(a), (e).
(2)	1988 s 106(10).
(3)	1988 s 106(11).
(4)	1988 s 118(7)(d).
(5)	1988 s 118(7)(d), (8).
463	1944 s 114(1) ('independent school'); 1980 s 34(1); 1988 Sch 12 para 7.
464 (1) to (3)	1944 s 70(1); Transfer of Functions (Education and Employment) Order 1995 (SI 1995/2986) art 11(2).
(4)	Drafting.
465 (1)	1944 s 70(1).
(2)	1944 s 70(1) proviso (a).
(3)	1944 s 70(1) proviso (b).
(4)	1944 s 114(1) ('provisionally registered school'; 'registered school').
466 (1)	1944 s 70(3).
(2)	1944 s 70(3A); 1980 s 34(6).
(3)	1944 s 70(3).
467 (1)	1944 s 70(4); 1980 s 34(7).
(2)	1944 s 70(4A); 1993 s 292(2).
(3)	1944 s 70(4); 1980 s 34(7).
(4)	Drafting.
468	1944 s 71(4); 1993 s 290(1).

Derivation of Education Act 1996 & School Inspections Act 1996

Provision	Derivation
469 (1)	1944 s 71(1); Children Act 1989 (c 41) Sch 13 para 9; 1993 s 290(2).
(2), (3)	1944 s 71(1).
(4)	1944 s 71(2); 1993 s 290(2).
(5)	1944 s 71(3).
(6)	1944 s 71(5); 1993 s 290(1).
470 (1)	1944 s 72(1).
(2)	1944 s 72(2); 1993 s 290(2).
471 (1)	1944 s 72(3).
(2)	1944 s 72(3) proviso; 1993 s 290(2).
472	1944 s 72(4); 1993 s 290(2).
473 (1)	1944 s 73(2).
(2)	1944 s 73(3); 1993 s 290(2).
474	1944 s 74.
475	1944 s 73(1).
476 (1)	Drafting.
(2), (3)	1944 s 75(1).
(4)	1944 s 75(2); Arbitration Act 1996 (c 23) Sch 3 para 4.
(5)	1944 s 75(3).
477	1944 s 73(5); 1946 Sch 2 Pt I; 1978IA s 17(2)(a).
478 (1)	1944 s 73(4).
(2)	1944 ss 70(3), 73(2), (3); Criminal Justice Act 1982 (c 48) Sch 3.
479 (1) to (3)	1980 s 17(1) to (3).
(4)	1980 s 17(2).
(5)	1980 s 17(4), (5).
(6), (7)	1980 s 17(10).
480 (1), (2)	1980 s 17(6), (7).
(3)	1980 s 17(9).
(4)	1980 s 17(8), (9).
481	1980 s 18.
482 (1)	1988 s 105(1).
(2)	1988 s 105(2).
(3)	1988 s 105(1), (2).
(4)	1988 s 105(3).
(5)	1988 s 218(2B); 1993 s 291; 1994 Sch 2 para 8(4).
483 (1), (2)	1988 s 105(4).
(3), (4)	1988 s 105(5), (6).
484 (1)	1984 s 1(1), (2); 1993 s 278(2).
(2)	1984 s 1(2), (6).
(3), (4)	1984 s 1(3), (4); 1993 s 278(2).

Appendix 2

Provision	Derivation
(5)	1984 s 1(5).
(6)	1984 s 1(7).
(7)	Drafting.
485	1944 s 100(1)(b); 1988 s 213(3).
486	1988 s 213(1); Transfer of Functions (Science) Order 1995 (SI 1995/2985) Sch para 5.
487	1980 s 21(1).
488	1988 s 210.
489 (1)	1944 s 100(3); 1980 s 21(2); 1984 s 1(4); 1988 ss 210(3), 213(2).
(2)	1984 s 1(4A); 1993 s 278(4).
(3), (4)	1973 s 1(2).
490	1988 s 211; 1978IA s 17(2)(a).
491 (1)	1944 s 100(1)(c).
(2)	1944 s 100(3).
492 (1) to (4)	1986 s 51(1) to (4); 1993 s 279(1).
(5)	1986 s 51(11); 1993 Sch 19 para 103(d).
(6)	1986 s 51(7), (8); 1993 Sch 19 para 103(a).
493 (1)	1986 s 52(1); 1992FHE Sch 8 para 25.
(2)	1986 s 52(2); 1993 Sch 19 para 104.
(3)	1986 s 52(3); 1992FHE Sch 8 para 25.
(4)	1986 s 52(4).
494	1993 s 262.
495 (1), (2)	1944 s 67(1).
(3)	1944 s 67(2).
496 (1)	1944 s 68.
(2)	1944 s 68; 1988 s 219(2).
497 (1)	1944 s 99(1).
(2)	1944 s 99(1); 1988 s 219(3).
(3)	1944 s 99(1).
498 (1)	1944 s 99(2).
(2)	1944 s 99(2); 1988 s 219(3).
499	1993 s 297.
500	1993 s 232.
501	1993 s 233.
502	1993 s 234.
503 (1) to (6)	1993 s 235(1) to (6).

Derivation of Education Act 1996 & School Inspections Act 1996

Provision	Derivation
(7)	1993 s 235(8).
504	1993 s 236.
505 (1) to (7)	1993 s 237(1) to (7).
(8)	1993 ss 237(8), 305(1) ('maintained school').
506	1944 s 69(2); Criminal Justice Act 1967 (c 80) Sch 3; 1978IA s 7(2)(a); Medical Act 1983 (c 54) Sch 6 para 11.
507 (1)	1944 s 93.
(2)	1944 s 93; 1972LG s 272(2); 1993 s 235(7).
508 (1)	1944 s 53(1).
(2)	1944 s 53(1); 1948 Sch 1 Pt I; 1988 Sch 12 para 54.
(3)	1944 s 53(2).
509 (1), (2)	1944 s 55(1); 1992FHE Sch 8 para 5.
(3)	1944 s 55(2); 1948 Sch 1 Pt I; 1988 Sch 12 para 55; 1992FHE Sch 8 para 5.
(4)	1944 s 55(3); 1986 s 53; 1992FHE Sch 8 para 5; 1993 Sch 19 para 15.
(5)	1944 s 55(4); 1992FHE Sch 8 para 5.
(6)	1944 s 55(5); 1992FHE Sch 8 para 5.
510 (1)	1948 s 5(1); 1988 s 100(4).
(2)	1948 s 5(1); 1953 Sch 1; 1981 Sch 3 para 7.
(3)	1948 s 5(2); 1988 s 100(4).
(4)	1948 s 5(3); 1980 s 29(1); 1988 s 100(4), Sch 12 para 61; 1992FHE Sch 8 para 16.
(5)	1948 s 5(4); 1988 s 100(4).
(6)	1948 s 5(4).
511 (1)	1948 s 5(5).
(2), (3)	1948 s 5(6).
(4)	1948 s 5(6A); 1980 s 29(2).
512 (1)	1980 s 22(1); Social Security Act 1986 (c 50) s 77(1).
(2)	1980 s 22(2); Social Security Act 1986 (c 50) s 77(2).
(3)	1980 s 22(3); Social Security Act 1986 (c 50) s 77(2); Jobseekers Act 1995 (c 18) Sch 2 para 3.
(4)	1980 s 22(1).
(5)	1980 s 22(3B); 1992FHE Sch 8 para 17.
513	1944 s 78(2).
514 (1)	1944 s 50(1); 1946 Sch 2 Pt I; 1981 Sch 3 para 3; 1988 s 100(2).
(2)	1944 s 50(1); 1948 Sch 1 Pt I; 1981 Sch 3 para 3.
(3)	1944 s 50(2); 1946 Sch 2 Pt I; 1993 Sch 19 para 12.
(4)	1944 s 52(1).
(5)	1944 s 52(1) proviso; 1981 Sch 3 para 4.
(6)	1944 s 52(2).
(7)	1944 s 52(3).
515 (1)	1980 s 26(1).

Appendix 2

Provision	Derivation
(2)	1980 s 26(3).
(3)	1980 s 26(4).
(4)	1980 s 26(5); 1978IA s 17(2)(a).
(5)	1980 s 26(6).
516	1993 s 295.
517 (1)	1953 s 6(2); 1993 Sch 19 para 31(a).
(2)	1953 s 6(2)(a)(i).
(3)	1953 s 6(2)(a)(ii); 1981 Sch 3 para 8.
(4)	1953 s 6(a)(iii).
(5)	1953 s 6(2)(b); 1981 Sch 3 para 8.
(6)	1993 Sch 19 para 31(b) to (f).
(7)	1993 s 308(3).
518	1944 s 81; 1988 Sch 12 para 6; 1992FHE Sch 8 para 11.
519 (1)	1986 s 58(1); 1988 Sch 12 para 103; 1993 Sch 19 para 106.
(2)	1986 s 58(2).
(3)	1986 s 58(5); 1988 Sch 12 para 103.
(4), (5)	1986 s 58(6).
(6)	1986 s 58(7).
520 (1), (2)	1944 s 48(4); 1973NHSR Sch 4 para 7; National Health Service Act 1977 (c 49) Sch 15 para 2; 1978IA s 17(2)(a).
(3)	Drafting.
521 (1), (2)	1944 s 54(1).
(3)	1944 s 54(2), (8); Medical Act 1983 (c 54) Sch 6 para 11.
(4)	1944 s 54(1); 1993 Sch 19 para 14(a).
522 (1)	1944 s 54(2).
(2) to (4)	1944 s 54(3).
(5)	1944 s 54(5).
523 (1), (2)	1944 s 54(4); SI 1968/1699 art 5; 1972LG s 179(3).
(3)	1944 s 54(9); 1994LG(W) Sch 16 para 8.
(4)	1944 s 54(8); Medical Act 1983 (c 54) Sch 6 para 11.
524 (1), (2)	1944 s 54(7).
(3)	1944 s 54(7); 1993 Sch 19 para 14(c).
525 (1)	1944 s 54(6).
(2)	1944 s 54(6).
(3)	1944 s 54(6); 1993 Sch 19 para 14(b).
526	1944 s 82.
527	1944 s 83.
528	1944 s 41(2A), (2B); Disability Discrimination Act 1995 (c 50) s 30(8).
529 (1)	1944 s 85(1).
(2), (3)	1944 s 85(2), (3); 1980 Sch 3 para 3.

Derivation of Education Act 1996 & School Inspections Act 1996

Provision	Derivation
530 (1)	1944 s 90(1); Acquisition of Land (Authorisation Procedure) Act 1946 (c 49) Sch 4; 1948 s 10(1); 1988 Sch 12 para 59.
(2)	1944 s 90(1) proviso; Acquisition of Land (Authorisation Procedure) Act 1946 (c 49) Sch 4.
(3)	1944 s 90(1A); 1993 s 282(3).
531 (1)	1948 s 10(2); 1972LG s 272(2); 1988 Sch 12 para 62.
(2)	1948 s 10(3).
532	1944 s 88; 1978IA s 17(2)(a).
533 (1), (2)	1980 s 22(4).
(3)	1980 s 22(4A); 1993 Sch 19 para 79.
534 (1) to (4)	1980 s 22(3A); 1988 Sch 12 para 24.
(5)	1980 s 22(3B); 1992FHE Sch 8 para 17.
535 (1)	1980 s 26(2).
(2)	1980 s 26(3).
(3)	1980 s 26(4).
(4)	1980 s 26(5); 1978IA s 17(2)(a).
(5)	1980 s 26(6).
536 (1), (2)	1944 s 48(4); 1973NHSR Sch 4 para 7; National Health Service Act 1977 (c 49) Sch 15 para 2; 1978IA s 17(2)(a); 1988 Sch 12 para 2.
537 (1) to (6)	1992(S) s 16(1) to (6).
(7)	1992(S) s 16(7); 1993 s 263.
(8) to (10)	1992(S) s 16(8) to (10).
(11)	1992(S) s 19(2).
(12), (13)	1992(S) s 16(11), (12).
538	1986 s 56, Sch 2 para 13(2).
539	1993 s 153.
540 (1)	1993 s 264(1).
(2)	1993 ss 264(2), 305(1) ('maintained school').
541 (1) to (3)	1993 s 265.
(4)	1993 ss 264(1), 305(1) ('maintained school').
542 (1)	1944 s 10(1); 1988 Sch 12 para 1.
(2) to (4)	1944 s 10(2); 1988 Sch 12 para 1.
543	1944 s 10(2) proviso; 1948 s 7(1); 1968 s 3(3).
544 (1)	1988 s 218(7); 1992FHE Sch 8 para 49; 1993 Sch 19 para 136.
(2)	1988 s 218(7).
(3)	1988 s 218(12).
545 (1)	1944 s 63(2); 1993 Sch 19 para 18.
(2)	1988 s 218(8); 1993 Sch 19 para 19.

Appendix 2

Provision	Derivation
546 (1)	1988 s 218(1)(e).
(2)	1988 s 218(12).
547 (1)	1982LG(MP) s 40(1).
(2)	1982LG(MP) s 40(2); 1988 Sch 12 para 29.
(3)	1982LG(MP) s 40(3).
(4), (5)	1982LG(MP) s 40(4), (5); 1988 Sch 12 para 29.
(6)	1982LG(MP) s 40(6).
(7), (8)	1982LG(MP) s 40(7), (8); 1988 Sch 12 para 29.
548 (1)	1986 s 47(1); 1993 s 293(2).
(2)	1986 s 47(1A); 1993 s 293(2).
(3)	1986 s 47(5); 1988 Sch 12 para 35; 1993 s 293(3), Sch 19 para 101(a).
(4)	1986 s 47(6); 1993 Sch 19 para 101(b).
(5)	1986 s 47(7).
(6)	1986 s 47(4).
549 (1), (2)	1986 s 47(2), (3).
(3)	1986 s 47(1B); 1993 s 293(2).
(4)	1986 s 47(10).
(5)	1986 s 47(5); 1993 s 293(3).
550	1986 s 47(8).
551(1)	1988 s 218(1)(g).
(2)	1988 s 218(12).
552 (1)	1993 Sch 19 para 62(5).
(2), (3)	1993 Sch 19 para 62(2), (3).
(4)	1993 Sch 19 para 62(1).
(5)	1993 Sch 19 para 62(4).
(6)	1993 Sch 19 para 62(6).
553	1988 s 113.
554 (1)	1973 s 2(1); 1988 s 112(2).
(2)	1973 s 2(1); 1988 s 112(2); 1993 Sch 19 para 52(a).
(3)	1973 s 2(1A); 1988 s 112(2); 1993 Sch 19 para 52(b).
(4)	1973 s 2(1C); 1988 s 112(2); 1993 Sch 19 para 52(c).
(5)	1973 s 2(1B); 1988 s 112(2).
(6)	1973 s 2(8).
555 (1)	1973 s 2(2); 1993 Sch 19 para 52(c).
(2) to (4)	1973 s 2(2).
(5)	1973 s 2(1B); 1988 s 112(2).
556 (1)	1973 s 2(3); 1993 s 288(3).
(2)	1973 s 2(4); 1988 s 112(3); 1993 Sch 19 para 52(c).
(3)	1973 s 2(4); 1993 s 288(2), Sch 19 para 52(c).
(4)	1973 s 2(5).
(5)	1973 s 2(5A); 1993 s 288(4).
(6), (7)	1973 s 2(6), (7).
(8)	1973 s 2(1B); 1988 s 112(2).

Derivation of Education Act 1996 & School Inspections Act 1996

Provision	Derivation
557	1993 s 287.
558	1944 s 58.
559 (1), (2)	1944 s 59(1), (2).
(3), (4)	1944 s 59(3).
(5)	1944 s 59(4).
(6)	Employment of Children Act 1973 (c 24) s 3(4).
560 (1)	1973EWE s 1(1); 1988 Sch 12 para 14.
(2)	1973EWE s 1(4); Employment Act 1990 (c 38) s 14.
(3)	1973EWE s 1(2); Merchant Shipping Act 1995 (c 21) Sch 13 para 48.
(4), (5)	1973EWE s 1(3).
(6)	Drafting.
(7)	1973EWE s 1(4).
561	1944 s 115.
562	1944 s 116; 1948 Sch 1 Pt I; 1993 Sch 19 para 25.
563 (1)	1988 s 218(1)(f); 1992FHE Sch 8 para 49.
(2)	1988 s 218(4).
(3)	1988 s 218(12).
564 (1)	1944 s 94(1); SI 1968/1699 art 5; Registration of Births, Deaths and Marriages (Fees) Order 1995 (SI 1995/3162) Sch.
(2)	1944 s 94(1).
(3)	1944 s 94(2); SI 1968/1699 art 5.
(4)	1944 s 94(3); 1978IA s 17(2)(a).
565 (1)	1944 s 95(1).
(2)	1993 s 200(3).
566	1944 s 95(2).
567 (1), (2)	1993 s 299(1), (2).
(3)	1993 ss 299(3), 305(1) ('maintained school').
(4), (5)	1993 s 299(4), (5).
568 (1)	1973 s 2(1); 1986 s 63(1); 1988 s 232(1); 1993 s 301(1); Law Com Rec No 19.
(2)	1986 ss 4A(8), 63(1); 1988 s 232(2); 1993 ss 271(1), 301(2).
(3)	1986 s 63(2); 1988 s 232(4); 1993 s 301(3).
(4)	1988 s 232(3).
(5)	1986 s 63(3); 1988 s 232(5); 1993 s 301(6); Law Com Rec No 18.
(6)	1988 s 232(6); Law Com Rec No 18.
569 (1)	Statutory Instruments Act 1946 (c 36) s 1(2); 1948 s 12; 1980 s 35(1); 1984 s 3(1); 1986 s 63(1); 1988 s 232(1); 1992(S) s 19(1); 1993 s 301(1); Law Com Rec No 18.
(2)	1944 s 112; Statutory Instruments Act 1946 (c 36) s 5(2); 1948 s 12; 1980 s 35(3); 1984 s 3(3); 1986 s 63(2); 1988 s 232(4); 1992(S) s 19(2); 1993 ss 279(2)(a), 301(3).

Appendix 2

Provision	Derivation
(3)	1980 s 35(2); 1986 s 63(2A); 1993 ss 279(2)(b), 301(4).
(4)	1980 s 35(4); 1984 s 3(4); 1986 s 63(3); 1988 s 232(5); 1992(S) s 19(3); 1993 s 301(6), Sch 19 para 107(a); Law Com Rec No 18.
(5)	1944 s 111A; 1980 s 35(5); 1988 ss 229(1), 232(6); Law Com Rec No 18.
(6)	1980 s 35(5).
570 (1), (2)	1944 s 111; SI 1968/1699 art 5; 1993 s 301(7).
(3)	1944 s 111 proviso.
571	1980 ss 12(1B), 13(1C); 1988 s 34(3); 1993 ss 229(1), 230(1), 300.
572	1944 s 113; 1946 Sch 2 Pt I.
573 (1)	Drafting.
(2)	1944 s 114(1) ('alterations'); 1968 Sch 1 para 5(a); 1993 s 305(1).
(3)	1944 s 114(1) ('enlargement'); 1968 Sch 1 para 5(b).
(4)	1980 s 16(2); 1993 s 103(1).
(5)	1944 s 114(1) ('significant'); 1968 Sch 1 para 5(c).
(6)	1944 s 67(4); 1968 Sch 1 para 3; 1988 Sch 12 para 4.
574	1968 s 1(1); 1980 Sch 3 para 15; 1993 Sch 19 para 41.
575 (1), (2)	1988 s 235(1); 1993 s 305(1); 1996ER Sch 1 paras 37(5), 59.
(3)	1988 s 235(3); 1993 s 155(9), (10).
(4)	1988 s 235(1); 1993 s 305(1) 1996ER Sch 1 paras 37(5), 59.
576 (1)	1944 s 114(1D); Children Act 1989 (c 41) Sch 13 para 10.
(2)	1944 s 114(1E); Children Act 1989 (c 41) Sch 13 para 10; 1993 Sch 19 para 24(b).
(3), (4)	1944 s 114(1F); Children Act 1989 (c 41) Sch 13 para 10.
577	1944 s 114 ('minor authority'); 1972LG s 192(4); Local Government Changes for England (Education) (Miscellaneous Provisions) Regulations 1996 (SI 1996/710) reg 19.
578	1992FHE s 90(1) ('the Education Acts'); 1993 s 305(1) ('the Education Acts'); 1996N Sch 3 para 8.
579 (1)	'boarder': 1986 s 65(1). 'child': 1944 s 114(1). 'clothing': 1944 s 114(1). 'exclude': 1986 s 65(1). 'financial year': 1984 s 1(6); 1988 s 235(1), Sch 2 para 18; 1993 s 305(1), Sch 14 para 20. 'functions': 1988 s 235(1); 1993 s 305(1). 'governing body'; 'governor': 1944 s 114(1); 1980 Sch 1 para 13. 'higher education': 1944 s 114(1); 1988 s 120(9). 'land': 1988 s 235(1); 1993 s 306(1). 'liability': 1988 s 235(1); 1993 s 305(1). 'local authority': 1988 s 235; 1993 s 305(1); 1994LG(W) Sch 16 paras 83, 105(2). 'the local education authority': 1944 s 114(1); 1988 s 118(7)(b); 1993 s 305(1). 'local government elector': 1944 s 114(1); 1972LG s 272(2).

Derivation of Education Act 1996 & School Inspections Act 1996

Provision	Derivation
	'medical officer': 1944 s 114(1); 1973NHSR Sch 4 para 8; Medical Act 1983 (c 54) Sch 6 para 11.
	'modifications': 1988 s 235(1); 1993 s 305(1).
	'premises': 1944 s 114(1).
	'prescribed': 1944 s 114(1); 1993 s 305(1).
	'proprietor': 1944 ss 80(1), 114(1); 1988 Sch 12 para 5.
	'reception class': 1980 s 38(5A)(b); 1988 ss 31(6), 119(1)(b); 1993 s 155(1).
	'relevant age group': 1980 s 16(3); 1988 s 32(2); 1993 s 155(4).
	'school buildings': 1946 s 4(2); 1973NHSR Sch 4 para 9; National Health Service Act 1977 (c 49) Sch 15 para 3; 1978IA s 17(2)(a).
	'school day': 1986 s 65(1).
	'trust deed': 1944 s 114(1).
	'young person': 1944 s 114(1).
(2)	1988 s 235(3)(g); 1993 s 305(2).
(3)	1980 s 38(5A); 1988 ss 31(6), 119(1)(a); 1993 s 155(5).
(4)	1980 s 38(5); 1986 s 51(10); 1993 Sch 19 para 103.
(5)	1944 s 114(2)(b).
(6)	1944 s 114(2)(b); 1988 s 234(2)(a), (3)(a).
(7)	1944 s 114(2A); 1988 s 234(2)(b); 1992FHE Sch 8 para 13(4).
580	—
581	1944 s 118; SI 1977/293 art 4; Law Com Rec No 19.
582	—
583	—
Sch 1	1993 Sch 18.
Sch 2	
para 1	1993 Sch 1 para 16.
paras 2 to 8	1993 Sch 1 paras 1 to 7.
para 9	1993 Sch 19 paras 46 to 48.
paras 10 to 14	1993 Sch 1 para 8 to 12.
para 15	1993 Sch 1 para 15.
paras 16 to 17	1993 Sch 1 paras 13, 14.
Sch 3	
para 1	1993 s 17; 1996N Sch 3 para 10.
para 2	1993 s 18.
para 3	1993 s 19.
Sch 4	
para 1	1993 Sch 2 para 1, s 305(1) ('maintained school').
paras 2 to 23	1993 Sch 2 paras 2 to 23.
Sch 5	
para 1	—
para 2	1944 Sch 3 para 8.
para 3	1944 Sch 3 paras 4, 5; 1948 Sch 1, Pt I; 1980 Sch 3 para 5.
para 4	1944 Sch 3 para 7; drafting.
para 5	1944 Sch 3 para 9.

Appendix 2

Provision	Derivation
para 6	1944 Sch 3 para 10.
Sch 6	1944 Sch 2.
Sch 7	
para 1	1993 s 238(5) to (7).
para 2	1993 s 239.
para 3	1993 Sch 13 para 2.
para 4	1993 Sch 13 para 1.
para 5	1993 Sch 13 para 3.
paras 6 to 10	1993 Sch 13 paras 8 to 12.
paras 11, 12	1993 Sch 13 paras 14, 15.
Sch 8	
para 1	Drafting.
para 2	1986 ss 6, 15(12), (13); drafting.
para 3	1986 s 15(11).
para 4	1986 s 15(7).
para 5	1986 s 15(1).
para 6	1986 s 15(8).
para 7	Drafting; 1986 s 15(2) to (6), (15).
para 8	1986 s 15(14).
para 9	1986 s 15(10).
para 10	1986 ss 8(6), (9), 15(9).
para 11	1986 s 8(2), (3); 1993 s 271(2).
para 12	1986 s 8(4).
para 13	1986 s 8(5).
para 14	1986 s 8(1).
para 15	1986 s 8(6), (7), (9); 1988 s 116; drafting.
para 16	1986 s 8(11), (12); Law Com Rec Nos 3, 20.
para 17	1986 s 8(8).
para 18	1986 s 62.
para 19	Drafting.
para 20	1986 s 57.
para 21	1986 s 8(10).
Sch 9	
para 1	1986 s 65(1) ('promoters'), Sch 2 para 1; Law Com Rec No 9.
para 2	1986 Sch 2 para 2(1), (2); 1993 Sch 19 para 109(a), (b)(i).
para 3	1986 Sch 2 para 6.
para 4	1986 Sch 2 para 7(1).
para 5	1986 Sch 2 para 8(1).
para 6	1986 Sch 2 para 7(2) to (5).
para 7	1986 Sch 2 paras 7(6), (7), 8(2).
para 8	1986 Sch 2 para 9(1), (2); 1993 Sch 19 para 109(e).
para 9	1986 Sch 2 paras 2(3), 11(4), (5).
para 10	1986 Sch 2 para 11(3).
para 11	1986 Sch 2 para 11(6).
para 12	1986 Sch 2 para 11(1), (2).
para 13	1986 Sch 2 para 10(4).
para 14	1986 Sch 2 para 10(2).
para 15	1986 Sch 2 paras 10(1), 26(3).
para 16	1986 Sch 2 para 10(4).
para 17	1986 Sch 2 para 2(4).
para 18	1986 Sch 2 para 10(3).

Derivation of Education Act 1996 & School Inspections Act 1996

Provision	Derivation
para 19	1986 Sch 2 para 27.
para 20	1986 Sch 2 para 28.
para 21	1986 Sch 2 para 30(1).
para 22	1986 Sch 2 para 29.
Sch 10	
para 1	1986 Sch 2 para 3(4).
para 2	1986 Sch 2 para 3(5).
para 3	1986 Sch 2 para 4.
para 4	1986 Sch 2 para 13(3), (4).
para 5	1986 Sch 2 paras 2(2), 3(2), (3); 1993 Sch 19 para 109(b)(i).
para 6	1986 Sch 2 para 13(3), (5).
Sch 11	
para 1	Drafting.
para 2	1988 ss 33(6), 42(4)(a) to (d).
para 3	1988 s 42(4)(e), (5)(a).
para 4	1988 s 42(4)(j).
paras 5 to 7	1988 s 50(5); 51(1) ('expenditure of a capital nature').
para 8	1988 s 50(10).
Sch 12	
para 1	1988 s 48(2) ('temporary governing body').
para 2	1988 Sch 4 para 1(2)(a), (b).
para 3	1988 Sch 4 paras 1(1), 2(1).
para 4	1988 Sch 4 para 2(2) to (5).
para 5	1988 Sch 4 para 2(6); SI 1991/1890; SI 1992/110.
para 6	1988 Sch 4 para 2(8).
para 7	1988 Sch 4 para 2(9).
para 8	1988 Sch 4 para 3.
para 9	1988 Sch 4 para 6.
para 10	1988 Sch 4 para 5.
Sch 13	
para 1	1986 s 36(1).
para 2	1986 s 36(2).
para 3	1986 s 37.
para 4	1986 s 39.
para 5	1986 s 38(1), (2).
para 6	1986 s 38(3).
para 7	1986 s 38(4).
para 8	1986 s 38(6).
para 9	1986 s 38(5).
para 10	1986 s 35(2).
para 11(1), (2)	1986 s 41(1)(a).
(3)	1986 s 41(3).
(4) to (7)	1986 s 41(1)(b) to (e).
(8)	1986 s 41(3).
Sch 14	
para 1	1988 Sch 3 paras 1(1), (2), (6), 2(1), 4(1), 5(1), 6(1), 7(1), 8(1), 10(1), 11(3); 1978IA s 17(2)(a).
para 2	1988 Sch 3 para 1(1).
para 3	1988 Sch 3 para 1(3).
para 4	1988 Sch 3 para 1(4), (5), (12).

Appendix 2

Provision	Derivation
para 5	1988 Sch 3 para 1(7).
para 6	1988 Sch 3 para 1(8) to (10).
para 7	1988 Sch 3 para 1(11), (13).
para 8	1988 Sch 3 para 2(1).
para 9	1988 Sch 3 para 2(2), (3).
para 10	1988 Sch 3 para 2(4).
para 11	1988 Sch 3 para 2(5).
para 12	1988 Sch 3 para 2(6), (7).
para 13	1988 Sch 3 para 2(8), (9).
para 14	1988 Sch 3 para 2(10), (11).
para 15	1988 Sch 3 para 2(12).
para 16	1988 Sch 3 para 3(1) to (3).
para 17	1988 Sch 3 para 3(4).
para 18	1988 Sch 3 para 4(1) to (3), (5).
para 19	1988 Sch 3 para 4(4).
para 20	1988 Sch 3 para 5.
para 21	1988 Sch 3 para 6.
para 22	1988 Sch 3 para 7.
para 23	1988 Sch 3 para 8(1) to (3), (6).
para 24	1988 Sch 3 para 8(4), (5).
para 25	1988 Sch 3 para 8(7), (8).
para 26	1988 Sch 3 para 8(9).
para 27	1988 Sch 3 para 9; 1978IA s 17(2)(a).
para 28	1988 Sch 3 para 10; 1993 Sch 19 para 142.
Sch 15	
para 1	1986 s 24.
para 2	1986 s 24(a), (h); 1993 Sch 13 para 97.
para 3	1986 s 24(b), (f), (g).
para 4	1986 s 24(h).
para 5	1986 s 24(b), (g).
para 6	1986 s 24(d), (h).
para 7	1986 s 24(h).
para 8	1986 s 25.
para 9	1986 s 25(a), (h).
para 10	1986 s 25(b).
para 11	1986 s 25(b), (g).
para 12	1986 s 25(c), (h); 1993 Sch 19 para 98.
para 13	1986 s 25(h).
para 14	1993 Sch 19 para 99.
para 15	Drafting.
Sch 16	
para 1	1986 Sch 3 paras 1, 2; SI 1994/2092.
para 2	1986 Sch 3 para 3; SI 1994/2092.
para 3	1986 Sch 3 para 3A; SI 1994/2092.
para 4	1986 Sch 3 para 4; drafting.
para 5	1986 Sch 3 para 16.
para 6	1986 Sch 3 para 6.
para 7	1986 Sch 3 para 6A; SI 1994/2092.
para 8	1986 Sch 3 para 7; Education (No 2) Act 1986 (Amendment) (No 2) Order 1993 (SI 1993/2827) art 2.
para 9	1986 Sch 3 para 8; Education (No 2) Act 1986 (Amendment) Order 1993 (SI 1993/2709) art 2.
para 10	1986 Sch 3 para 9; SI 1994/2092 art 8.

Derivation of Education Act 1996 & School Inspections Act 1996

Provision	Derivation
para 11	1986 Sch 3 para 13.
para 12	1986 Sch 3 para 14.
para 13	1986 Sch 3 para 11.
para 14	1986 Sch 3 para 12; SI 1994/2092 art 9.
para 15	1986 Sch 3 para 15.
para 16	1986 Sch 3 para 17; SI 1994/2092 art 10.
para 17	Drafting.
para 18	1986 Sch 3 para 5.
Sch 17	
para 1	1986 s 30(2).
para 2	1986 s 30(2)(a).
para 3	1986 s 30(2)(b).
para 4	1986 s 30(2)(c) to (e).
para 5	1986 s 30(2)(g).
para 6	1986 s 30(2)(h); 1988 s 51(9); Education (No 2) Act 1986 (Amendment) Order 1994 (SI 1994/692) art 2.
para 7	1986 s 30(2)(i); Education (No 2) Act 1986 (Amendment) (No 3) Order 1994 (SI 1994/2732).
para 8	1986 s 30(2)(j).
para 9	1986 s 30(2)(k); 1978IA s 17(2)(a).
para 10	1986 s 30(5); 1992(S) Sch 4 para 5.
Sch 18	
para 1	1986 s 31(4)(a).
para 2	1986 s 31(4)(b), (9).
para 3	1986 s 31(3).
para 4	1986 s 31(4)(c), (d).
para 5	1986 s 31(5), (6).
Sch 19	
para 1	1986 Sch 2 paras 4, 12(1).
para 2	1988 Sch 4 para 7.
para 3	1986 Sch 2 para 12(2).
para 4	1986 Sch 2 para 12(3).
para 5	1986 Sch 2 para 20(5).
para 6	1986 Sch 2 para 21.
para 7	1986 Sch 2 para 22.
para 8	1986 Sch 2 para 23.
para 9	1986 Sch 2 para 25.
para 10	1986 Sch 2 para 24.
para 11	1986 Sch 2 para 26(1), (2).
para 12	1986 Sch 2 para 30(2).
para 13	Drafting.
para 14	1986 Sch 2 para 20(1).
para 15	1986 Sch 2 para 20(2), (3); Law Com Rec No 9.
para 16	1986 Sch 2 paras 20(4), 30(3).
para 17	1986 Sch 2 para 28.
para 18	1988 Sch 4 para 1.
para 19	1988 Sch 4 para 4(1), (4), (5).
para 20	1988 Sch 4 para 4(2).
para 21	1988 Sch 4 para 4(3); Education (Application of Financing Schemes to Special Schools) Regulations 1992 (SI 1992/164).
para 22	1988 Sch 4 para 4(7).
para 23	1988 Sch 4 para 4(8).

Appendix 2

Provision	Derivation
para 24	1988 Sch 4 para 4(6).
para 25	1986 Sch 2 para 15.
para 26	1986 Sch 2 para 16; 1988 Sch 12 para 106.
para 27	1986 Sch 2 para 17.
para 28	1986 Sch 2 paras 13(1), 14.
para 29	1986 Sch 2 para 18; 1988 Sch 4 para 2(10).
Sch 20	
para 1	1993 Sch 3 para 1(1) to (4); drafting.
paras 2 to 12	1993 Sch 3 paras 2 to 12.
Sch 21	1993 Sch 4.
Sch 22	
paras 1 to 13	1993 Sch 5 paras 1 to 13.
para 14	1986 s 62; 1988 Sch 12 para 37.
paras 15, 16	1993 Sch 5 paras 14, 15.
Sch 23	
paras 1 to 3	1993 Sch 6 paras 1 to 3.
para 4	1993 Sch 6 para 7.
para 5	1993 Sch 6 paras 4, 6.
para 6	1993 Sch 6 paras 5, 6.
para 7, 8	1993 Sch 6 paras 8, 9.
Sch 24	1993 Sch 7.
Sch 25	1993 Sch 8.
Sch 26	1993 Sch 9.
Sch 27	1993 Sch 10.
Sch 28	
paras 1 to 14	1993 Sch 11, paras 1 to 14.
para 15	1993 s 261(1), (2), (5).
Sch 29	
paras 1 to 16	1993 Sch 14 paras 1 to 16.
para 17	1993 Sch 14 para 17; 1993 Sch 15 para 6(2).
paras 18 to 22	1993 Sch 14 paras 18 to 22.
Sch 30	
paras 1 to 5	1988 Sch paras 2 to 6; 1993 Sch 15 para 4(6).
paras 6, 7	1988 Sch 2 para 7; 1993 Sch 15 para 4(6).
para 8	1988 Sch 2 para 8; 1993 Sch 15 para 4(6), Sch 19 para 141.
paras 9, 10	1988 Sch 2 para 10; 1993 Sch 15 para 4(6).
para 11	1988 Sch 2 para 11; 1993 s 249, Sch 15 para 4(6).
paras 12, 13	1988 Sch 2 paras 12, 13; 1993 Sch 15 para 4(6).
para 14	1988 Sch 2 para 13A; 1993 s 250, Sch 15 para 4(6).
paras 15, 16	1988 Sch 2 paras 14, 15; 1993 Sch 15 para 4(6).
para 17	1988 Sch 2 para 18; 1993 s 251(3), Sch 15 para 4(6).
paras 18, 19	1988 Sch 2 paras 16, 17; 1993 Sch 15 para 4(6).

Derivation of Education Act 1996 & School Inspections Act 1996

Provision	Derivation
Sch 31	
para 1	1944 Sch 5 para 12(1), (3); 1993 s 256(1).
para 2	1944 Sch 5 para 12(4); 1993 s 256(1).
para 3	1988 s 11(8).
para 4	1944 Sch 5 paras 2, 5; 1988 Sch 1 para 7; 1993 s 254(3), Sch 19 para 27.
para 5, 6	1944 Sch 5 paras 7, 8.
para 7	1944 Sch 5 para 3; 1988 Sch 1 para 7; 1993 Sch 19 para 27.
paras 8, 9	1944 Sch 5 para 4; 1993 Sch 19 para 27.
para 10	1944 Sch 5 para 13; 1988 Sch 1 para 7; 1993 s 256(2).
para 11	1993 s 146.
para 12	1944 Sch 5 paras 10, 13(4); 1988 Sch 1 para 7.
para 13	1944 Sch 5 para 11; 1988 Sch 1 para 7.
para 14	1944 Sch 5 para 11.
para 15	1993 s 15.
Sch 32	
para 1	1988 s 28(1).
para 2	1988 s 28(2).
para 3	1988 s 28(3), (4).
para 4	1988 s 28(5).
para 5	1988 ss 28(6), (7), 32(1).
para 6	1988 s 28(8).
para 7	1988 s 119(2), (3).
Sch 33	
para 1	1980 Sch 2 para 1; 1993 Sch 16 para 2.
para 2	1980 Sch 2 para 2; 1993 Sch 16 para 3.
para 3	1980 Sch 2 para 3.
para 4	1980 Sch 2 para 4; Local Government and Housing Act 1989 (Commencement No 11 and Savings) Order 1991 (SI 1991/344) Sch para 1.
para 5	1980 Sch 2 para 4A; 1993 Sch 16 para 4.
para 6	1993 s 267.
para 7	1993 s 268.
para 8	Drafting.
paras 9 to 11	1980 Sch 2 paras 5 to 7.
para 12	1980 Sch 2 para 10.
para 13	1980 Sch 2 para 8.
para 14	1980 Sch 2 para 9.
para 15	1980 Sch 2 para 11.
Sch 34	
para 1	1944 Sch 6 para 1.
para 2	1944 Sch 6 para 2.
para 3	1944 Sch 6 paras 3, 3A; Judicial Pensions and Retirement Act 1993 (c8) Sch 6 para 51.
para 4	1944 Sch 6 para 4.
para 5	1976 s 6(1).
Sch 35	
paras 1 to 3	1980 Sch 4 paras 1 to 3.
para 4	1980 Sch 4 para 4; 1986 s 47(9).
paras 5, 6	1980 Sch 4 paras 5, 6.

Appendix 2

Provision	Derivation
Sch 36	1993 Sch 17.
Schs 37, 38	—
Sch 39	
para 1	—
para 2	1993 s 303.
para 3	1944 s 2(1).
para 4	1944 s 120(1).
paras 5 to 9	—
para 10(1)	—
(2)	1980 s 1(4).
para 11	1986 Sch 5 para 1.
paras 12 to 16	—
para 17(1)	—
(2)	1993 s 274(3).
(3)	1993 s 274(5).
para 18	Law Com Rec No 12.
para 19	SI 1996/951 art 4.
paras 20 to 23	—
para 24	1993 Sch 20 para 1; SI 1993/3106 Sch 2 paras 8, 9.
para 25	1993 Sch 20 para 1; SI 1993/3106 Sch 2 para 10.
para 26	SI 1993/3106 para 11.
para 27	SI 1993/3106 Sch 2 para 14.
para 28	1993 Sch 20 para 5.
para 29	1993 Sch 20 para 6.
para 30	SI 1993/1975 Sch 2 para 4(2).
para 31	1993 Sch 20 para 2; SI 1994/507 Sch 3 para 10.
para 32	SI 1994/507 Sch 3 para 11.
para 33	SI 1994/507 Sch 3 para 12.
para 34	SI 1994/2038 Sch 4 paras 2(7), 4(3).
para 35	SI 1994/507 Sch 3 para 5.
paras 36 to 42	—
para 43	SI 1993/507 Sch 3 para 7.
para 44	1993 Sch 20 para 4.
para 45	1946 s 13(1).
para 46	—
para 47	1944 s 120(5).
para 48	—
para 49	1973 Sch 1 para 3.
para 50	—
Sch 40	—

SCHOOL INSPECTIONS ACT 1996

Notes

1. This Table shows the derivation of the provisions of the Act.
2. The following abbreviations are used in the Table:-

    1992 = Education (Schools) Act 1992 (c 38)
    1993 = Education Act 1993 (c 35)

3. The abbreviation 'Law Com Rec No' followed by a number refers to a recommendation set out in the paragraph of that number in Appendix 1 to the Report of the Law Commission (Cm 3251).

Derivation of Education Act 1996 & School Inspections Act 1996

Provision	Derivation
1	1992 s 1.
2 (1) to (6)	1992 s 2.
(7)	1992 s 4.
(8) to (10)	Law Com Rec No 22.
3	1992 s 3.
4	1992 s 5.
5 (1) to (6)	1992 s 6.
(7)	1992 s 8.
(8) to (10)	Law Com Rec No 22.
6	1992 s 7.
7 (1) to (9)	1992 s 10.
(10)	Drafting.
8	1992 s 11.
9	1992 s 12.
10 (1), (2)	1992 s 9(1), (2).
(3)	1992 s 9(3); 1993 Sch 19 para 173(1)(a).
(4)	1993 s 227(4).
(5), (6)	1992 s 9(4), (5).
(7)	Drafting.
(8)	1992 s 9(6); 1993 Sch 19 para 173(1)(b).
(9)	1992 s 9(7); 1993 Sch 19 para 173(1)(c).
11 (1)	1992 s 9(7); 1993 s 204(1), (4), Sch 19 para 173(1)(c).
(2)	1993 s 204(1).
(3)	1992 s 9(7); 1993 s 204(4), Sch 19 para 173(1)(c).
(4)	1993 s 204(2).
(5)	1992 Sch 2 para 1.
(6)	1992 Sch 2 para 1; 1993 s 204(2), Sch 19 para 173(3).
12 (1), (2)	1992 Sch 2 para 12(1), (2); 1993 s 205(1), (2), Sch 19 para 173(7); Law Com Rec No 23.
(3), (4)	1992 Sch 2 para 12(3); 1993 s 205(3), Sch 19 para 173(7); Law Com Rec No 23.
13 (1) to (8)	1992 Sch 2 para 9; 1993 s 206, Sch 19 para 173(5).
(9)	1992 Sch 2 para 1; 1993 s 204(3), Sch 19 para 173(3).
14	1992 Sch 2 para 9A; 1993 s 207, Sch 19 para 173(5).
15 (1), (2)	1992 Sch 2 para 9B(1), (2); 1993 s 208(1), (2), Sch 19 para 173(5).
(3)	1993 s 208(3).
(4)	1992 Sch 2 para 9B(3); 1993 Sch 19 para 173(5).
(5)	1992 Sch 2 para 9B(4); 1993 s 208(4), Sch 19 para 173(5).
16	1993 s 209.

Appendix 2

Provision	Derivation
17	1993 s 210.
18	1993 s 211.
19	1993 s 212.
20 (1) (2) (3), (4)	1992 Sch 2 para 9C(1), (3); 1993 Sch 19 para 173(5). 1992 Sch 2 para 9C(2); 1993 Sch 19 para 173(5). 1992 Sch 2 para 9C(4), (5); 1993 Sch 19 para 173(5).
21	1992 Sch 2 para 10; 1993 Sch 19 para 173(6).
22	1992 Sch 2 para 11; 1993 Sch 19 para 173(6).
23 (1) to (4) (5) to (7) (8) (9), (10)	1992 s 13(1) to (3A); 1993 s 259(2). 1992 s 13(4) to (6). 1992 s 13(7); 1993 s 259(3). 1992 s 13(8), (9).
24	1992 s 14.
25	1992 s 15.
26	1993 s 213.
27 (1) to (8) (9) (10)	1993 s 214(1) to (8). 1993 s 204(2). 1993 s 214(9).
28	1993 s 215.
29	1993 s 216.
30	1993 s 217.
31	1993 s 218.
32	1993 s 219.
33	1993 s 220.
34	1993 s 221.
35	1993 s 222.
36	1993 s 223.
37	1993 s 224.
38	1993 s 225.
39	1993 s 226.
40	1993 s 227(1) to (3).

Derivation of Education Act 1996 & School Inspections Act 1996

Provision	Derivation
41 (1), (2)	1993 s 228(1).
(3) to (5)	1993 s 228(2) to (4).
42	1992 s 18(3).
43	1992 s 20(2).
44 (1)	1993 s 299(1) to (4).
(2)	1993 s 299(5).
45 (1)	1992 s 19(1); 1993 s 301(1), (2).
(2)	1992 s 19(2); 1993 s 301(3).
(3), (4)	1992 s 19(3); 1993 s 301(6); Law Com Rec No 24.
46 (1)	1992 s 18(1); Interpretation Act 1978 (c 30) s 17(2)(a) ('denominational education'); 1992 Sch 2 para 1 ('member of the Inspectorate'); 1993 ss 204(2), 305(1), Sch 19 para 173(3).
(2)	Drafting.
(3)	1992 s 18(2).
(4)	1992 s 18(4).
	1993 s 305(3).
47	Drafting.
48 (1), (2)	Drafting.
(3)	1992 s 21(4); 1993 s 308(4); drafting.
(4)	1992 s 21(6); drafting.
(5)	Drafting.
Sch 1	
paras 1, 2	1992 Sch 1 paras 1, 2.
para 3	1992 Sch 1 para 3; The Transfer of Functions (Treasury and Minister for the Civil Service) Order 1995 (SI 1995/269) Art 3, Sch para 19.
para 4	1992 Sch 1 para 5.
para 5	1992 Sch 1 para 6; Law Com Rec No 22.
para 6	1992 Sch 1 para 7.
Sch 2	
para 1	1992 Sch 3 para 1; Judicial Pensions and Retirement Act 1993 (c 8) Sch 6 para 67.
para 2	1992 Sch 3 para 2.
para 3	1992 Sch 3 para 3(1).
Sch 3	
para 1	1992 Sch 2 para 1; 1993 Sch 19 para 173(3).
paras 2, 3	1992 Sch 2 paras 2, 3; 1993 Sch 19 para 173(4).
para 4(1)	1992 Sch 2 para 4(1); 1993 Sch 19 para 173(4).
(2)	1992 Sch 2 para 4(3).
(3)	1992 Sch 2 para 4(2).
para 5(1)	1992 Sch 2 para 5(1); 1993 Sch 19 para 173(4).
(2)	1992 Sch 2 para 5(3).
(3)	1992 Sch 2 para 5(2).
paras 6, 7	1992 Sch 2 paras 6, 7; 1993 Sch 19 para 173(4).
para 8	1992 Sch 2 para 8.

Appendix 2

Provision	Derivation
Sch 4	
para 1	1992 Sch 2 para 13.
para 2	1992 Sch 2 para 14; 1993 Sch 19 para 173(8).
para 3	1992 Sch 2 para 15; Interpretation Act 1978 (c 30) s 17(2)(a) ('governors' report'); 1993 Sch 19 para 173(9).
Sch 5	1993 Sch 12.
Sch 6	
para 1	1992 Sch 1 para 8.
paras 2, 3	1992 Sch 1 para 9.
paras 4 to 7	Drafting.
Sch 7	Drafting.
Sch 8	Drafting.

Appendix 3

DESTINATION TABLE TO THE EDUCATION ACT 1996 AND THE SCHOOL INSPECTIONS ACT 1996

EDUCATION ACT 1996: DESTINATION TABLE

This table shows in column (1) the enactments repealed by the Education Act 1996 and in column (2) the provisions of that Act corresponding thereto.

In certain cases the enactment in column (1), though having a corresponding provision in column (2) is not, or not wholly, repealed as it is still required, or partly required, for the purposes of other legislation.

A 'dash' in the right hand column means that the repealed provision to which it corresponds in the left hand column is spent, unnecessary or for some other reason not specifically reproduced.

† Not repealed
* Repealed in part

Education Act 1944 (c 31)	Education Act 1996 (c 56)
s 1(1)	Rep 1993 c 35, s 307(1), (3), Sch 19, paras 3, 4, Sch 21, Pt II
s 1(2)	—
s 1(3), (4)	Rep SI 1964/490, art 3 (1), Schedule
s 2(1)	—
s 2(2)	Rep 1948 c 40, s 11, Sch 2
s 3(1)–(3)	—
s 3(4)	Rep SI 1964/490, art 3 (1), Schedule
ss 4, 5	Rep 1986 c 61, ss 59, 60(1), 67(6), Sch 6, Pt I
s 6(1)	s 12(1), (5)
s 6(2)	Rep 1993 c 35, ss 296, 307(3), Sch 21, Pt II
s 6(3), (4)	—
s 7	ss 1(1), 13(1)
s 8(1)	ss 2(1), (2), 14(1)–(3)
s 8(1A)	s 14(5)
s 8(2)	s 14(6), (7)
s 8(3)	Rep 1992 c 13, s 93, Sch 8, Pt I, paras 1, 3, Sch 9
s 9(1)	s 16(1)
s 9(2)	s 31
s 9(4)	s 6(1)
s 9(5)	Rep 1993 c 35, s 307(1), (3), Sch 19, paras 3, 6, Sch 21, Pt I

Appendix 3

Education Act 1944 (c 31)	Education Act 1996 (c 56)
s 9(6)	s 16(2)
s 9(7)	s 16(3)
s 10(1)	s 542(1)
s 10(2)	ss 542(2)–(4), 543
ss 11–13	Rep 1980 c 20, s 38(6), Sch 7
s 14(1)	s 173(1)–(3)
s 14(2)	s 173(6)
s 14(3)	s 174(1)
s 14(4)	s 174(2), (3)
s 14(5)	s 173(7)
s 15(1)	s 32(1)
s 15(2)	ss 32(2), 48(1), (2)
s 15(3)	s 59(1)–(4)
s 15(4)	s 57(1), (2), (4)
s 15(4A)	s 57(3)
s 15(5)	s 58(1), (2)
s 15(6)	Rep 1946 c 50, s 14(1), Sch 2, Pt II
s 16(1)	s 47(1)
s 16(2)	s 46(1)–(3)
s 16(3)	ss 46(4), (5), 47(3), (4)
ss 17–21	Rep 1986 c 61, s 67(6), Sch 6, Pt I
s 22(1)	ss 150(2), 152(1), (2)
s 22(2)	s 152(3), (4)
s 22(3)	s 150(1)
s 22(3A)	s 151(1)
s 22(3B)	s 151(2)
s 22(3C)	s 151(3)
s 22(3D)	s 151(4), (5)
s 22(3E)	s 151(6)
s 22(4)	s 134(5)
s 22(5)	ss 134(6), 150(3)
s 22(6)	s 151(7)
s 23	Rep 1986 c 61, s 67(6), Sch 6, Pt I
s 24(1)	Rep 1986 c 61, s 67(6), Sch 6, Pt I
s 24(2)	s 134(1)–(4)
s 24(3)	Rep 1975 c 65, s 83, Sch 6
s 25	Rep 1988 c 40, s 237(2), Sch 13, Pt II
s 26(1)	s 376(1)
s 26(2)	s 376(2)
s 26(3), (4)	s 376(3)
s 27(1)	s 377(2)
s 27(2)	s 143(1)–(3)
s 27(3)	s 143(4)
s 27(4)	s 143(5)
s 27(5)	s 143(6)
s 27(6)	s 377(1)
s 28(1)	s 378(1)
s 28(1A)	s 378(5)
s 28(1B)	s 378(2), (3)
s 28(1C)	s 378(4)
s 28(2)	s 145
s 28(3)	s 144(2)
s 28(4)	s 144(3)
s 29(1)	—
s 29(2)–(4)	Rep 1988 c 40, s 237(2), Sch 13, Pt II

Destination Table to Education Act 1996 & School Inspections Act 1996

Education Act 1944 (c 31)	Education Act 1996 (c 56)
s 30	s 146
s 31(1)	Rep 1980 c 20, s 38(6), Sch 7
s 31(2)–(4)	—
s 32	Rep 1980 c 20, s 38(6), Sch 7
ss 33, 34	Rep 1981 c 60, s 21, Sch 4
s 35	Cf Sch 40, para 1
s 36	s 7
s 37	Rep 1993 c 35, s 307(1), (3), Sch 19, paras 3, 11, Sch 21, Pt I
3 38	Rep 1981 c 60, s 21, Sch 4
ss 39, 40	Rep 1993 c 35, s 307(1), (3), Sch 19, paras 3, 11, Sch 21, Pt I
s 40A	Rep 1969 c 54, s 72(4), Sch 6
s 41(1)	s 15(1)
s 41(2)(a)	s 15(2), (3)
s 41(2)(b)	s 15(8)
s 41(2A)	s 528
s 41(2B)	s 528
s 41(3), (4)	s 2(3)
s 41(5)	s 2(6)
s 41(6)	s 15(4)
s 41(7), (8)	s 15(5)
s 41(9)	s 15(6)
s 41(10)	s 15(7)
s 41(11)	s 15(8)
ss 42–46	Rep 1988 c 40, ss 120(5), 237(2), Sch 13, Pt II
s 47	—
s 48(1)–(3)	Rep 1973 c 32, s 57, Sch 5
s 48(4)	ss 520, 536
s 48(5)	Rep 1973 c 32, s 57, Sch 5
s 49	Rep 1980 c 20, s 38(6), Sch 7
s 50(1)	s 514(1), (2)
s 50(2)	s 514(3)
s 51	Rep 1948 c 40, s 11, Sch 2
s 52(1)	s 514(4), (5)
s 52(2)	s 514(6)
s 52(3)	s 514(7)
s 53(1)	s 508(1), (2)
s 53(2)	s 508(3)
s 53(3)	Rep 1948 c 40, s 11, Sch 2
s 53(4)	Rep SLR Act 1950
s 54(1)	s 521(1), (2), (4)
s 54(2)	ss 521(3), 522(1)
s 54(3)	s 522(2)–(4)
s 54(4)	s 523(1), (2)
s 54(5)	s 522(5)
s 54(6)	s 525
s 54(7)	s 524
s 54(8)	ss 521(3), 523(4)
s 54(9)	s 523(3)
s 55(1)	s 509(1), (2)
s 55(2)	s 509(3)
s 55(3)	s 509(4)
s 55(4)	s 509(5)
s 55(5)	s 509(6)

Appendix 3

Education Act 1944 (c 31)	Education Act 1996 (c 56)
s 56	Rep 1993 c 35, s 307(1), (3), Sch 19, paras 3, 16, Sch 21, Pt II
ss 57–57B	Rep 1970 c 52, s 2, Schedule
s 58	s 558
s 59(1)	s 559(1)
s 59(2)	s 559(2)
s 59(3)	s 559(3), (4)
s 59(4)	s 559(5)
ss 60, 61	Rep 1988 c 40, s 237(2), Sch 13, Pt II
s 62(1)	—
s 62(2)	Rep 1988 c 40, s 237, Sch 12, Pt III, para 56, Sch 13, Pt II
s 63(1)	Rep 1984 c 55, s 133(2), Sch 7
s 63(2)	s 545(1)
s 64	Rep 1961 c 45, ss 12, 29(2), Sch 5, Pt I
s 65	s 72
s 66	Rep 1980 c 20, s 38(6), Sch 7
s 67(1)	s 495(1), (2)
s 67(2)	s 495(3)
s 67(3)	s 399
s 67(4)	s 573(6)
s 67(4A)	Rep 1992 c 13, s 93, Sch 8, Pt I, paras 1, 8, Sch 9
s 68	s 496
s 69(1)	Rep 1973 c 32, s 57, Sch 5
s 69(2)	s 506
s 70(1)	ss 464(1)–(3), 465(1)–(3)
s 70(2)	Rep 1980 c 20, s 34(2)
s 70(3)	ss 466(1), (3), 478(2)
s 70(3A)	s 466(2)
s 70(4)	s 467(1), (3)
s 70(4A)	s 467(2)
s 70(5)	Rep SI 1995/2986, art 11, Schedule, para 1
s 71(1)	s 469(1)–(3)
s 71(2)	s 469(4)
s 71(3)	s 469(5)
s 71(4)	s 468
s 71(5)	s 469(6)
s 72(1)	s 470(1)
s 72(2)	s 470(2)
s 72(3)	s 471
s 72(4)	s 472
s 73(1)	s 475
s 73(2)	ss 473(1), 478(2)
s 73(3)	ss 473(2), 478(2)
s 73(4)	s 478(1)
s 73(5)	s 477
s 74	s 474
s 75(1)	s 476(2), (3)
s 75(2)	s 476(4)
s 75(3)	s 476(5)
s 76	s 9
s 77	Rep 1992 c 13, s 93, Sch 8, para 10; 1992 c 38, s 21, Sch 5
s 78(1)	Rep 1973 c 32, s 57, Sch 5
s 78(2)	s 513
s 79	Rep 1973 c 32, s 57, Sch 5

Destination Table to Education Act 1996 & School Inspections Act 1996

Education Act 1944 (c 31)	Education Act 1996 (c 56)
s 80(1)	ss 434(1), (4), 579(1)
s 80(1A)	s 434(2)
s 80(2)	s 434(6)
s 80(3)	Rep 1948 c 40, ss 4(5), 11, Sch 2
s 81(a)–(c)	s 518
s 81(d)	—
s 82	s 526
s 83	s 527
s 84	Rep 1988 c 40, s 237(2), Sch 13, Pt II
s 85	s 529
s 86	Rep 1973 c 16, s 1(4), Sch 2, Pt II
s 87	Rep 1960 c 58, ss 38(1), 48(2), Sch 7, Pt II
s 88	s 532
s 89	Rep 1965 c 3, s 7(6)
s 90(1)	s 530(1), (2)
s 90(1A)	s 530(3)
s 90(2), (3)	Rep 1980 c 20, s 38(6), Sch 7
s 91	Rep 1972 c 70, s 272, Sch 30
s 92	s 29(1)
s 93	s 507
s 94(1)	s 564(1), (2)
s 94(2)	s 564(3)
s 94(3)	s 564(4)
s 95(1)	s 565(1)
s 95(2)	s 566
s 96	—
s 97	Rep 1980 c 20, s 38(6), Sch 7
s 98	—
s 99(1)	s 497
s 99(2)	s 498
s 99(3)	s 71
s 100(1)(a)	—
s 100(1)(b)	s 485
s 100(1)(c)	s 491(1)
s 100(2)	Rep 1958 c 55, s 67, Sch 9, Pt II
s 100(3)	ss 489(1), 491(2)
s 100(4)	Rep 1973 c 16, s 1(4), Sch 2, Pt II
s 100(5)	—
s 101	Rep 1958 c 55, s 67, Sch 9, Pt II
ss 102, 103	Rep 1993 c 35, s 307(1), (3), Sch 19, paras 3, 22, Sch 21, Pt II
s 104	Rep 1967 c 3, s 1(5)(b)
s 105(1)	s 67(1), (2)
s 105(2)	s 67(3), (4)
s 105(3)	s 48(3), (4)
s 106	Rep SL(R) Act 1975
s 107	Rep SL(R) Act 1978
ss 108–110	Rep SL(R) Act 1975
s 111	s 570
s 111A	s 569(5)
s 112	s 569(2)
s 113	s 572
s 114(1)	ss 2(1)–(5), 3(1), (2), 4(1), 5(1), (2), 12(1), (2), (5), 32(5), 34(1), 78(2), 312(1), (4), 352(3), 375(2), (4), 434(5), 463, 465(4), 573(2), (3), (5), 577, 579(1)

Appendix 3

Education Act 1944 (c 31)	Education Act 1996 (c 56)
s 114(1A)–(1C)	Rep 1992 c 13, s 93, Sch 8, paras 1, 13(3), Sch 9
s 114(1D)	s 576(1)
s 114(1E)	s 576(2)
s 114(1F)	s 576(3), (4)
s 114(2)(a)	s 34(1)–(4)
s 114(2)(b)	s 579(5), (6)
s 114(2A)	s 579(7)
s 114(3)	Rep 1980 c 20, s 38(6), Sch 7
s 114(4)	Rep SL(R) Act 1975
s 114(5)	Rep 1946 c 50, s 8(4)
s 114(6)	Rep 1976 c 5, s 3(3), Schedule
s 114(7)	—
s 114(8)	—
s 115	s 561
s 116	s 562
s 117	Rep 1963 c 33, s 93(1), Sch 18, Pt II
s 118	s 581
s 119	Rep 1973 c 16, s 1(4), Sch 2, Pt I
ss 120–122	See Sch 39, paras 1(2), 4, 47
Sch 1, Pts I, II	Rep 1993 c 35, ss 296, 307, Sch 19, paras 3, 26, Sch 20, para 4, Sch 21, Pt II
Sch 1, Pt III	Rep 1972 c 70, s 272(1), Sch 30
Sch 2	Sch 6
Sch 3, paras 1, 2	—
para 3	Rep 1980 c 20, s 38(6), Sch 7
para 4	Sch 5, para 3(1)
para 5	Sch 5, para 3(2), (3)
para 6	—
para 7	s 144(1), Sch 5, para 4(1)
para 8	Sch 5, para 2(1)
para 9	Sch 5, para 5
para 10	Sch 5, para 6
para 11	Cf s 32(5)
Sch 4	Rep 1980 c 20, s 38(6), Sch 7
Sch 5, para 1	—
para 2	Sch 31, para 4(1)–(3)
para 3	Sch 31, para 7
para 4	Sch 31, paras 8, 9
para 5	Sch 31, para 4(1)
para 6	—
para 7	Sch 31, para 5
para 8	Sch 31, para 6
para 9	—
para 10	Sch 31, para 12
para 11	Sch 31, paras 13, 14
para 12(1), (3)	Sch 31, para 1
para 12(4)	Sch 31, para 2
para 12(5)	—
para 13(1)	Sch 31, para 10(1)
para 13(2), (3)	Sch 31, para 10(2)
para 13(4)	Sch 31, para 10(3)
Sch 6, para 1	Sch 34, para 1
para 2	Sch 34, para 2
para 3	Sch 34, para 3(1)
para 3A	Sch 34, para 3(2)

Destination Table to Education Act 1996 & School Inspections Act 1996

Education Act 1944 (c 31)	Education Act 1996 (c 56)
para 4	Sch 34, para 4
Sch 7	Rep SL(R) Act 1975
Sch 8, Pt I	—
Sch 8, Pt II	Rep SL(R) Act 1978
Sch 9	Rep 1973 c 16, s 1(4), Sch 2, Pt I

Acquisition of Land (Authorisation Procedure) Act 1946 (c 49)	Education Act 1996 (c 56)
Sch 4*	s 530(1), (2)

Education Act 1946 (c 50)	Education Act 1996 (c 56)
s 1(1)	s 64
s 1(2)	Rep 1968 c 17, s 1(3), Sch 2
s 2(1)	ss 50(1), (2), 51(1), (4)
s 2(2)	ss 50(4), 51(6)
s 2(3)	s 51(2)
s 2(4)	s 51(3)
s 2(5)	s 57(1)
s 2(6)	—
s 2(7)	ss 50(2), (3), 51(4), (5)
s 2(8)	s 51(7)
s 3	—
s 4(1)	s 73
s 4(2)	s 579(1)
s 5	Rep SL(R) Act 1975
s 6	s 74
s 7	Rep 1988 c 40, s 237(2), Sch 13, Pt II
s 8(1), (2)	Rep 1962 c 12, ss 9(5), (6), 13(1), Sch 2
s 8(3)	Rep 1988 c 40, s 237(2), Sch 13, Pt II
s 8(4)	Rep SL(R) Act 1978
s 9	Rep 1948 c 40, s 11(2), Sch 2
s 10	Rep 1972 c 70, s 272(1), Sch 30
s 11	Rep 1948 c 26, s 147, Sch 2
s 12	Rep 1972 c 70, s 272(1), Sch 30
s 13(1)	See Sch 39 para 45
s 13(2)	Rep 1972 c 70, s 272(1), Sch 30
s 14(1)	—
s 14(2)	Rep 1972 c 70, s 272(1), Sch 30
s 14(3)	Rep 1964 c 75, s 26(2), Sch 3
s 15	Rep SL(R) Act 1978
s 16(1)	ss 50(5), 51(8), 62(1)
s 16(2)	—
s 17	—
Sch 1, para 1	ss 34(3), 60(1), 61(1)
para 2(1)	ss 34(4), 47(2), 57(1), (2), (4), 59(5)
para 2(2)	s 57(3)
para 3	s 61(4)
para 4	s 61(5)
para 5	s 61(6)
para 6	ss 60(2), (3), 61(2), (3)
para 7	s 60(4)–(6)

Appendix 3

Education Act 1946 (c 50)	Education Act 1996 (c 56)
para 8	s 62(2), (3)
para 9	s 62(4)
Sch 2	ss 59(2)–(4), 173(2), 477, 514(1), (3), 572

Education (Miscellaneous Provisions) Act 1948 (c 40)	Education Act 1996 (c 56)
s 1	Rep 1960 c 58, s 48(2), Sch 7, Pt I
s 2	Rep 1973 c 16, s 1(4), Sch 2, Pt II
s 3(1)	—
s 3(2)	s 2(1)
s 3(3)	Rep 1992 c 13, s 93, Sch 8, Pt I, para 15, Sch 9
s 4(1)	s 435
s 4(2)	s 433(1), (2), (5)
s 4(3)	s 433(3)
s 4(3A)	s 433(4)
s 4(4), (5)	—
s 4(6)	s 434(3)
s 5(1)	s 510(1), (2)
s 5(2)	s 510(3)
s 5(3)	s 510(4)
s 5(4)	s 510(5), (6)
s 5(5)	s 511(1)
s 5(6)	s 511(2), (3)
s 5(6A)	s 511(4)
s 5(7)	—
s 6	Rep 1980 c 20, s 38(6), Sch 7
s 7(1)	s 543(1)–(4)
s 7(2), (2A)	Rep 1980 c 20, s 38(6), Sch 7
s 7(3)	—
s 8	Rep 1959 c 72, s 149(2), Sch 8, Pt I
s 9	Rep 1993 c 35, s 307(1), (3), Sch 19, para 30, Sch 21, Pt I
s 10(1)	s 530(1)
s 10(2)	s 531(1)
s 10(3)	s 531(2)
s 11(1)	—
s 11(2)	Rep SLR Act 1950
s 12	s 569(1), (2)
s 13	Rep SL(R) Act 1978
s 14	—
Sch 1	ss 508(2), 509(3), 514(2), 562, Sch 5, para 3(2), (3)
Sch 2	Rep SLR Act 1950

Education (Miscellaneous Provisions) Act 1953 (c 33)	Education Act 1996 (c 56)
s 1	Rep 1967 c 3, s 1(5)(c), (6)
s 2	s 63
s 3	s 64(1), (3)
s 4	Rep 1973 c 32, ss 57, 58, Sch 5

Destination Table to Education Act 1996 & School Inspections Act 1996

Education (Miscellaneous Provisions) Act 1953 (c 33)	Education Act 1996 (c 56)
s 5	Rep 1956 c 75, ss 6(3), 13 (2), Sch 2
s 6(1)	s 18
s 6(2)	s 517(1)–(5)
s 6(3)	s 564(1), (3)
s 7	Rep 1980 c 20, s 38(6), Sch 7
s 8(1)	—
s 8(2)	Rep 1967 c 3, s 1(5)(c), (6)
s 8(3)	—
s 9	Rep 1980 c 20, s 38(6), Sch 7
s 10	Rep 1993 c 35, s 307(1), (3), Sch 19, para 32, Sch 21, Pt I
s 11	Rep 1969 c 54, s 72(4), Sch 6
s 12	Rep 1980 c 34, ss 32(5), 69, Sch 9, Pt I
s 13	Rep SL(R) Act 1978
s 14	Rep 1973 c 16, s 1(4), Sch 2, Pt I
s 15	Rep 1960 c 58, s 48(2), Sch 4, Pt II
s 16	Rep 1980 c 20, s 38(6), Sch 7
s 17(1)	—
s 17(2)	Rep 1973 c 16, s 1(4), Sch 2, Pt I
s 18	—
s 19	Rep SL(R) Act 1978
s 20	—
Sch 1	s 510(2)
Sch 2	Rep 1973 c 16, s 1(4), Sch 2, Pt I

Town and Country Planning Act 1959 (c53)	Education Act 1996 (c 56)
Sch 4, para 4	—

Education Act 1959 (c 60)	Education Act 1996 (c 56)
s 1(1)–(3)	Rep 1967 c 3, s 1(5)(d), (6)
s 1(4)	—
s 1(5)–(8)	Rep 1967 c 3, s 1(5)(d), (6)

Rating and Valuation Act 1961 (c 45)	Education Act 1996 (c 56)
ss 1–11	Rep 1967 c 9, s 117(1), (11), Sch 14, Pt I
s 12(1)–(5)	Rep 1967 c 9, s 117(1), Sch 14, Pt I
s 12(6)	s 34(5)
ss 13–23	Rep 1967 c 9, s 117(1), Sch 14, Pt I
ss 24–27	Rep 1967 c 9, s 117(1), Sch 14, Pt I
s 28(1), (4), (5)	Rep 1967 c 9, s 117(1), Sch 14, Pt I
s 28(2)	Rep 1963 c 33, s 93(1), Sch 18, Pt II
s 28(3)	Rep 1966 c 42, s 43(2)(a), Sch 6, Pt I
s 29(1)–(3)	Rep 1967 c 9, s 117(1), Sch 14, Pt I, 1975 c 7, Sch 13, Pt I
s 29(4)	—
Schs 1, 2	Rep 1967 c 9, s 117(1), Sch 14, Pt I, 1975 c 7, Sch 13, Pt I

Appendix 3

Rating and Valuation Act 1961 (c 45)	Education Act 1996 (c 56)
Sch 3, paras 1–4, 6	Rep 1966 c 42, ss 38(3), 43(2), Sch 4, para 26(b), Sch 6, Pt III
para 5	Rep 1967 c 9, s 117(1), Sch 14, Pt I
Sch 4, paras 1–14	Rep 1967 c 9, s 117(1), Sch 14, Pt I
para 15	Rep 1963 c 33, s 93(1), Sch 18, Pt II
para 16	Rep 1967 c 9, s 117(1), Sch 14, Pt I
Sch 5	Rep 1967 c 9, s 117(1), Sch 14, Pt I

Education Act 1962 (c 12)	Education Act 1996 (c 56)
ss 9, 13(4), 14(2)	—

Children and Young Persons Act 1963 c 37	Education Act 1996 (c 56)
s 38(2)	—

Education Act 1964 (c 82)	Education Act 1996 (c 56)
s 1(1)	ss 49, 198(6), 291
s 1(2)	s 5(4)
s 1(3)	s 5(5)
s 2	Rep 1976 c 5, s 3(3), Schedule
ss 3, 4	Rep SL(R) Act 1978
s 5	—

Education Act 1967 (c 3)	Education Act 1996 (c 56)
s 2	s 64(3)
s 6(1)*	—

Criminal Justice Act 1967 (c 80)	Education Act 1996 (c 56)
Sch 3, Pt I*	—

Education Act 1968 (c 17)	Education Act 1996 (c 56)
s 1(1)	s 574
s 1(2)	Rep 1980 c 20, s 38(6), Sch 7
s 1(3)–(5)	—
s 2	s 49
s 3(1), (2)	Rep 1980 c 20, s 38(6), Sch 7
s 3(3)	s 543(4)
s 3(4)	Rep 1993 c 35, ss 286, 307(3), Sch 21, Pt Ii
ss 4–6	—
Sch 1, para 1	Rep 1993, c 35, s 307(3), Sch 21, Pt II
para 2	—
para 3	s 573(6)
para 4	Rep 1993 c 35, s 307(3), Sch 21, Pt II

Destination Table to Education Act 1996 & School Inspections Act 1996

Education Act 1968 (c 17)	Education Act 1996 (c 56)
para 5	s 573(2), (3), (5)
para 6	s 64
para 7	Rep 1980 c 20, s 38(6), Sch 7
para 8	See Sch 37, para 9
Sch 2	—
Sch 3, Pt A	Rep 1980 c 20, s 38(6), Sch 7
Sch 3, Pt B	—
Sch 3, Pt C	—

Greater London Council (General Powers) Act 1968 (c xxxix)	Education Act 1996 (c 56)
s 56	—

Local Authority Social Services Act 1970 (c 42)	Education Act 1996 (c 56)
Sch 1*	—

Education (Handicapped Children) Act 1970 (c 52)	Education Act 1996 (c 56)
ss 1, 2, Schedule	—

Local Government Act 1972 (c 70)	Education Act 1996 (c 56)
s 192(1)	s 12(1), (2), (5)
s 192(2), (3)	—
s 192(4)	s 577
s 192(5), (6)	—

Education Act 1973 (c 16)	Education Act 1996 (c 56)
s 1(2)	ss 179, 489(3), (4)
s 2(1)	ss 554(1), (2), 568(1)
s 2(1A)	s 554(3)
s 2(1B)	ss 554(5), 555(5), 556(8)
s 2(1C)	s 554(4)
s 2(2)	s 555(1)–(4)
s 2(3)	s 556(1)
s 2(4)	s 556(2), (3)
s 2(5)	s 556(4)
s 2(5A)	s 556(5)
s 2(6)	s 556(6)
s 2(7)	s 556(7)
s 2(8)	s 554(6)
s 2(9)	—
s 5(1)*	—
Sch 1, para 3	See Sch 39 para 49

Appendix 3

Education (Work Experience) Act 1973 (c 23)	Education Act 1996 (c 56)
s 1(1)	s 560(1)
s 1(2)	s 560(3)
s 1(3)	s 560(4), (5)
s 1(4)	s 560(2), (7)
s 2	—

Education Act 1975 (c 2)	Education Act 1996 (c 56)
ss 1, 2	Rep 1980 c 20, s 38(6), Sch 7
ss 3, 4	—
s 5(1)–(3)	
s 5(4)	Rep 1980 c 20, s 38(6), Sch 7
s 5(5), (6)	—
Schedule	—

Sex Discrimination Act 1975 (c 65)	Education Act 1996 (c 56)
s 82(1)*	—

Education (School-leaving Dates) Act 1976 (c 5)	Education Act 1996 (c 56)
	—

Race Relations Act 1976 (c 74)	Education Act 1996 (c 56)
s 78(1)*	—

Education Act 1976 (c 81)	Education Act 1996 (c 56)
ss 1–3	Rep 1979 c 49, s 1(1)
ss 4, 5	Rep 1980 c 20, s 38(6), Sch 7
s 6(1)	Sch 34, para 5
s 6(2)	—
ss 7–9	Rep 1980 c 20, s 38(6), Sch 7
s 10	Rep 1981 c 60, s 21, Sch 4
ss 11, 12	—

National Health Service Act 1977 (c 49)	Education Act 1996 (c 56)
Sch 14, para 13*	ss 520(1), (2), 536(1), (2), 579(1)
Sch 15, para 2	ss 520, 536
para 3	s 579(1)

Education Act 1979 (c 49)	Education Act 1996 (c 56)
ss 1, 2	ss 520(1), (2), 536(1), (2), 579(1)

Destination Table to Education Act 1996 & School Inspections Act 1996

Education Act 1980 (c 20)	Education Act 1996 (c 56)
s 1	—
ss 2–4	Rep 1986 c 61, s 67(6), Sch 6, Pt I
s 5	s 180
s 6(1)	s 411(1)
s 6(2)	s 411(2)
s 6(3)	s 411(3)
s 6(4)	s 411(4)
s 6(5)	s 411(5)
s 6(6)	s 413(1)
s 6(7)	s 413(2)
s 6(8)	s 413(3)
s 6(9)	s 413(4)
s 7(1)	s 423(1)
s 7(2)	s 423(2)
s 7(3)	s 423(3)
s 7(4)	s 423(4)
s 7(5)	s 423(5)
s 7(6)	Rep 1992 c 53, s 18(2), Sch 4, Pt I
s 7(7)	—
s 8(1)	s 414(1)
s 8(2)	s 414(2)
s 8(3)	s 414(3), (4)
s 8(4)	s 414(5)
s 8(5)	s 414(6)
s 8(5A)	s 414(7)
s 8(5B)	s 29(5)
s 8(6)	s 414(8)
s 8(7)	ss 29(5), 414(9)
s 9(1)	ss 29(6), 424(1)
s 9(1A)	ss 424(2), 436(1)
s 9(2)	s 424(3)
ss 10, 11	Rep 1993 c 35, s 307(1), (3), Sch 19, paras 72, 75, Sch 21, Pt I
s 12(1)(a), (b), (d)	s 35(1)
s 12(1)(c), (e)	s 167(1)
s 12(1A)	ss 35(5), 167(4)
s 12(1B)	s 571
s 12(2)	ss 35(3), 167(2)
s 12(2A)	s 35(4)
s 12(3)	ss 36(1), (2), (4), 168(1), (2), (4)
s 12(4)	ss 37(1), (2), (6), 169(1), (2)
s 12(5)	ss 37(1), (3), 169(1), (3)
s 12(6)	ss 37(5), 169(5)
s 12(7)	ss 38(1), (2), 170(1), (2)
s 12(8)	ss 38(3), 170(3)
s 12(9)	ss 40(1), (3), 171
s 13(1)	s 41(1), (2)
s 13(1A)	s 41(4)
s 13(1B)	s 41(7)
s 13(1C)	s 571
s 13(2)	s 41(5), (6)
s 13(3)	s 42(1), (2)
s 13(3A)	s 42(3)
s 13(4)	s 43(1), (2)
s 13(5)	s 45(1)

Appendix 3

Education Act 1980 (c 20)	Education Act 1996 (c 56)
s 13(6)	s 45(2)
s 13(7)	s 45(4)
s 13(8)	s 45(7)
s 14(1)	ss 39(1), (2), 44(1), (2)
s 14(2)	s 44(3), (4)
s 14(3)	ss 40(2), 45(3)
s 14(4)	Rep 1993 c 35, s 307(1), (3), Sch 19, paras 72, 77, Sch 21, Pt II
s 15	Rep 1988 c 40, ss 31(1), 237(2), Sch 13, Pt II
s 16(1)	ss 40(4), (5), 45(5), (6), 172
s 16(1A)	ss 35(2), 41(3)
s 16(2)	s 573(4)
s 16(3)	s 579(1)
s 16(3A)	ss 36(5), 42(5), 168(5)
s 16(3B)	ss 36(6), 42(6), 168(6)
s 16(4)–(7)	—
s 17(1)	s 479(1)
s 17(2)	s 479(2), (4)
s 17(3)	s 479(3)
s 17(4), (5)	s 479(5)
s 17(6)	s 480(1)
s 17(7)	s 480(2)
s 17(8)	s 480(4)
s 17(9)	s 480(3), (4)
s 17(10)	s 479(6), (7)
s 18	s 481
s 21(1)	s 487
s 21(2)	s 489(1)
s 22(1)(a)	s 512(1)
s 22(1)(b)	s 512(4)
s 22(2)	s 512(2)
s 22(3)	s 512(3)
s 22(3A)	s 534(1)–(4)
s 22(3B)	ss 512(5), 534(5)
s 22(4)	s 533(1), (2)
s 22(4A)	s 533(3)
s 22(5)	—
s 24(1)	s 17(1)
s 24(2)	ss 14(4), 17(2)
s 24(3)	—
s 26(1)	s 515(1)
s 26(2)	s 535(1)
s 26(3)	ss 515(2), 535(2)
s 26(4)	ss 515(3), 535(3)
s 26(5)	ss 515(4), 535(4)
s 26(6)	ss 515(5), 535(5)
s 28	—
s 29(1)	s 510(4)
s 29(2)	s 511(4)
s 30	—
s 33(3)	—
s 34(1)	s 463
s 34(2)–(5)	—
s 34(6)	s 466(2)
s 34(7)	s 467(1), (3)

Destination Table to Education Act 1996 & School Inspections Act 1996

Education Act 1980 (c 20)	Education Act 1996 (c 56)
s 35(1)	s 569(1)
s 35(2)	s 569(3)
s 35(3)	s 569(2)
s 35(4)	s 569(4)
s 35(5)	s 569(5), (6)
s 37	—
s 38(2)	—
s 38(4)	ss 411(8), 423(6)
s 38(5)	s 579(4)
s 38(5A)(a)	s 579(3)
s 38(5A)(b)	s 579(1)
s 38(6)	—
Sch 1, paras 1–9	—
para 10	Rep 1993 c 35, s 307(1), (3), Sch 19, paras 72, 80, Sch 21, Pt II
paras 11, 12	—
para 13(a)	s 78(2)
para 13(b)	—
paras 14–24	—
para 25	Rep 1988 c 40, s 237(2), Sch 13, Pt II
para 26	s 179
paras 27–29	—
para 30	Rep 1996 c 18, s 242, Sch 3, Pt I
para 31	—
Sch 2, Pt I, para 1(1)	Sch 33, para 1(1)
para 1(2)	Sch 33, para 1(2)
para 1(2A)	Sch 33, para 1(5)
para 1(2B)	Sch 33, para 1(4)
para 1(3)	Sch 33, para 1(3)
para 1(4)	Sch 33, para 1(6)
para 1(5)	Sch 33, para 1(7)
para 1(6)	Sch 33, para 1(8)
para 1(7)	Sch 33, para 1(9)
para 2(1)	Sch 33, para 2(1)
para 2(2)	Sch 33, para 2(2)
para 2(2A)	Sch 33, para 2(6)
para 2(2B)	Sch 33, para 2(4)
para 2(3)	Sch 33, para 2(3)
para 2(4)	Sch 33, para 2(5)
para 2(5)	Sch 33, para 2(7)
para 2(6)	Sch 33, para 2(8)
para 2(7)	Sch 33, para 2(9)
para 3	Sch 33, para 3
para 4	Sch 33, para 4
para 4A	Sch 33, para 5
Pt II, para 5	Sch 33, para 9
para 6	Sch 33, para 10
para 7	Sch 33, para 11
para 8	Sch 33, para 13
para 9	Sch 33, para 14
para 10	Sch 33, para 12
para 11	Sch 33, para 15
Sch 3, para 1	s 46(1)
para 2	—
para 3	s 529(2), (3)

Appendix 3

Education Act 1980 (c 20)	Education Act 1996 (c 56)
para 4	Rep 1993 c 35, s 307(3), Sch 21, Pt II
para 5	Sch 5, para 3(2), (3)
para 6	s 64
para 7	ss 50(4), 51(6)
para 8	ss 60(1), 61(1)
para 9	s 63(1)
para 10	—
para 11	s 49
para 12	s 5(4)
para 13	Rep 1993 c 35, s 307(3), Sch 21, Pt II
para 14	Rep 1988 c 40, s 237(2), Sch 13, Pt II
para 15	s 574
para 16	—
para 17	s 179
para 18	—
Sch 4, para 1	Sch 35, para 1
para 2	Sch 35, para 2
para 3	Sch 35, para 3
para 4(1)	Sch 35, para 4(1)
para 4(2)	Sch 35, para 4(2)
para 5	Sch 35, para 5
para 6	Sch 35, para 6
Sch 7	—

Local Government, Planning and Land Act 1980 (c 65)	Education Act 1996 (c 56)
s 2(3)	—

Education Act 1981 (c 60)	Education Act 1996 (c 56)
s 1	Rep 1993 c 35, s 307(1), (3), Sch 19, para 82, Sch 21, Pt I
s 2(1)	s 14(6)
s 2(2)–(7)	Rep 1993 c 35, s 307(1), (3), Sch 19, para 82, Sch 21, Pt I
s 11(1)	—
s 11(2), (3)	Rep 1993 c 35, s 307(1), (3), Sch 19, para 82, Sch 21, Pt I
ss 12–16	Rep 1993 c 35, s 307(1), (3), Sch 19, para 82, Sch 21, Pt I
s 17	s 7
ss 18, 19	Rep 1993 c 35, s 307(1), (3), Sch 19, para 82, Sch 21, Pt I
Sch 2, para 1	—
paras 2–8	Rep 1993 c 35, s 307(1), (3), Sch 19, para 82, Sch 21, Pt I
Sch 3, paras 1, 2	Rep 1993 c 35, s 307(1), (3), Sch 19, para 82, Sch 21, Pt I
para 3	s 514(1), (2)
para 4	s 514(5)
para 5	Rep 1988 c 40, s 237(2), Sch 13, Pt II
para 6	—

Destination Table to Education Act 1996 & School Inspections Act 1996

Education Act 1981 (c 60)	Education Act 1996 (c 56)
para 6A	Rep 1993 c 35, s 307(1), (3), Sch 19, para 82, Sch 21, Pt I
para 7	s 510(2)
para 8	s 517(3), (5)
para 9	Rep 1989 c 41, s 108(7), Sch 15
para 10	Rep 1993 c 35, s 307(1), (3), Sch 19, para 82, Sch 21, Pt I
paras 11, 12	See Sch 37, paras 31, 39
para 13	Rep 1993 c 35, s 307(1), (3), Sch 19, para 82, Sch 21, Pt I
para 14	s 424(3)
paras 15, 16	Rep 1993 c 35, s 307(1), (3), Sch 19, para 82, Sch 21, Pt I
Sch 4	—

Criminal Justice Act 1982 (c 48)	Education Act 1996 (c 56)
s 3*	s 478(2)

Education (Grants and Awards) Act 1984 (c 11)	Education Act 1996 (c 56)
s 1(1)	s 484(1)
s 1(2)	s 484(1), (2)
s 1(3)	s 484(3)
s 1(4)(a)	s 484(4)
s 1(4)(b), (c)	s 489(1)
s 1(4A)	s 489(2)
s 1(5)	s 484(5)
s 1(6)	ss 484(2), 579(1)
s 1(7)	s 484(6)
s 2	Rep 1989 c 42, s 188
s 3(1)	s 569(1)
s 3(2)	Rep 1993 c 35, ss 278(5), 307(3), Sch 21, Pt II
s 3(3)	s 569(2)
s 3(4)	s 569(4)
s 3(5)	Rep 193 c 35, ss 278(5), 307(3), Sch 21, Pt II
ss 4–6	—

Further Education Act 1985 (c 47)	Education Act 1996 (c 56)
s 8(2)	—

Social Security Act 1986 (c 50)	Education Act 1996 (c 56)
s 77*	s 512(1)–(3)

Appendix 3

Education (No 2) Act 1986 (c 61)	Education Act 1996 (c 56)
s 1(1)	ss 76(1), 127(1)
s 1(2)	ss 76(2), 127(2)
s 1(3)	s 76(3)
s 1(4)	s 127(3)
s 1(5)	ss 76(3), (4), 127(3), (4)
s 1(6)	s 76(5)
s 2(1)	ss 77(1), 128(1)
s 2(2)	ss 77(2), 128(2)
s 2(3)	ss 77(3), 128(3)
s 2(4)	s 77(4)
s 2(5)	ss 77(5), 128(4)
s 2(6)	ss 77(6), 128(5)
s 2(7)	ss 77(7), 128(6)
s 3(1)–(5)	s 79(1), (2)
s 3(6)	s 79(3)
s 3(7)	s 79(4)
s 4(1), (2)	s 84(1), (3)
s 4(3)	s 84(2)
s 4(4)	s 84(4)
s 4(5)	s 84(5)
s 4(6)	s 84(6)
s 4A(1)	s 85(1)
s 4A(2)	s 85(2)
s 4A(3)	s 85(3)
s 4A(4)	s 85(4)
s 4A(5)	s 85(5)
s 4A(6)	s 85(6)
s 4A(7)	s 85(7)
s 4A(8)	ss 85(8), 568(2)
s 5(1)	s 81(1)
s 5(2)	s 81(3)
s 5(3)	s 81(2)
s 5(4)	s 81(4), (5)
s 6	Sch 8, para 2(2)
s 7(1)	s 80(1)
s 7(2)	s 80(2)
s 7(3)–(5)	s 80(3)–(5)
s 7(6)	s 80(6)–(8)
s 7(7)	s 80(9)
s 8(1)	Sch 8, para 14
s 8(2), (3)	Sch 8, para 11
s 8(4)	Sch 8, para 12
s 8(5)	Sch 8, para 13
s 8(6)	Sch 8, paras 10(1), 15(1)
s 8(7)	Sch 8, para 15(3)
s 8(8)	Sch 8, para 17
s 8(9)	Sch 8, paras 10(2), 15(2), (3)
s 8(10)	Sch 8, para 21
s 8(11), (12)	Sch 8, para 16
s 9(1)	s 89(1)
s 9(1A)	s 89(2)
s 9(2)	s 89(3)
s 9(3)	s 89(4)
s 9(4)	s 94(1), (3)

Destination Table to Education Act 1996 & School Inspections Act 1996

Education (No 2) Act 1986 (c 61)	Education Act 1996 (c 56)
s 9(5)	s 94(2)
s 9(6)	s 95(1)
s 9(7)	s 95(2), (3)
s 9(8)	s 95(4)
s 9(9)	—
s 10(1)	s 90(1), (2)
s 10(2)	s 90(4)
s 10(3)	s 90(3)
s 10(4)	s 90(5)
s 10(5)	s 91(1)
s 10(6)	s 91(2)
s 10(7)	s 90(6)
s 11(1)	s 82(1)
s 11(2)	s 82(2), (3)
s 11(3)	s 82(4)
s 11(4)	s 82(5)
s 11(5)	s 82(6)
s 11(6)	s 82(7)
s 11(7)	Rep 1993 c 35, s 307(1), (3), Sch 19, paras 88, 91, Sch 21, Pt I
s 12(1)	ss 96(1), 97(1)
s 12(2)	ss 96(2), 97(1)
s 12(3)	Rep 1993 c 35, s 307(1), (2), Sch 19, paras 88, 92, Sch 21, Pt I
s 12(4)	ss 96(3), 97(2)
s 12(5)	s 97(3)
s 12(6)	s 97(4)
s 12(7)	s 97(5)
s 12(8)	s 97(6)
s 12(9)	s 97(1)
s 12(10)	—
s 13(1)–(3)	s 86
s 13(4)	s 87(1)
s 13(5)	s 87(4)
s 13(6)	s 87(5)
s 13(7)	s 87(2)
s 13(8)	s 87(3)
s 13(9)	s 87(2), (5)
s 14	s 83
s 15(1)	Sch 8, para 5
s 15(2)–(6), (15)	Sch 8, para 7
s 15(7)	Sch 8, para 4
s 15(8)	Sch 8, para 6
s 15(9)	Sch 8, para 10(3)
s 15(10)	Sch 8, para 9
s 15(11)	Sch 8, para 3
s 15(12), (13)	Sch 8, para 2
s 15(14)	Sch 8, para 8
s 15(15)	Sch 8, para 7(1)
s 16(1)	s 130
s 16(2)	s 131
s 16(3)	s 132
s 16A	s 176
s 17(1)	s 370(1)

Appendix 3

Education (No 2) Act 1986 (c 61)	Education Act 1996 (c 56)
s 17(2)	s 370(2)
s 17(3)	s 370(3)
s 17(4)	Rep 1988 c 40, s 237(2), Sch 13, Pt II
s 18(1)	s 371(1), (2)
s 18(2)	s 371(3)
s 18(3)	s 371(4)
s 18(4)	Rep 1988 c 40, s 237(2), Sch 13, Pt II
s 18(5)	s 372(1)
s 18(6)	s 372(2)–(4)
s 18(7)	s 371(5), (7)
s 18(8)	s 371(6)
s 19(1)	s 373(1)
s 19(2)	s 373(2)
s 19(3)	Rep 1988 c 40, s 237(2), Sch 13, Pt II
s 20	Rep 1988 c 40, s 237(2), Sch 13, Pt II
s 21(1)	s 147(1)(a), (3)
s 21(2), (3)	Rep SI 1996/951, art 2(1)
s 21(4)	s 147(2), (3)
s 21(5)	s 153
s 22(a)–(e)	s 154
s 22(f)	s 156(1)
s 23	s 157
s 24	Sch 15, paras 1–7
s 25	Sch 15, paras 8–13
s 26(1)	s 159(1)
s 26(1)	s 159(1)
s 26(2)	s 159(2)
s 26(3)	s 159(3)
s 26(4)	s 159(4)
s 26(5)	s 159(5), (6)
s 27	s 160
s 28	s 155
s 29	Rep 1988 c 40, ss 51(8), 237(2), Sch 13, Pt II
s 30(1)	s 161(1), Sch 17, para 1
s 30(2)(a)	Sch 17, para 2
s 30(2)(b)	Sch 17, para 3
s 30(2)(c)–(f)	Sch 17, para 4
s 30(2)(g)	Sch 17, para 5
s 30(2)(h)	Sch 17, para 6
s 30(2)(i)	Sch 17, para 7
s 30(2)(j)	Sch 17, para 8
s 30(2)(k)	Sch 17, para 9
s 30(3)	s 161(3)
s 30(4)	s 161(4)
s 30(5)	Sch 17, para 10
s 31(1)	s 162(1)
s 31(2)	s 162(2)
s 31(3)	Sch 18, para 3
s 31(4)(a)	Sch 18, para 1
s 31(4)(b)	Sch 18, para 2(1)
s 31(4)(c), (d)	Sch 18, para 4
s 31(5)	Sch 18, para 5(1)
s 31(6)	Sch 18, para 5(2)
s 31(7)	s 163(1)

Destination Table to Education Act 1996 & School Inspections Act 1996

Education (No 2) Act 1986 (c 61)	Education Act 1996 (c 56)
s 31(8)	s 163(2)
s 31(9)	Sch 18, para 2(2)
s 32	s 165
s 33	s 412
s 34(1)	s 133(1)
s 34(2)	s 133(2)
s 34(3)	s 133(3)
s 35(1)	s 133(5)
s 35(2)	Sch 13, para 10
s 36(1)	Sch 13, para 1
s 36(2)	Sch 13, para 2
s 37	Sch 13, para 3
s 38(1), (2)	Sch 13, para 5
s 38(3)	Sch 13, para 6
s 38(4)	Sch 13, para 7
s 38(5)	Sch 13, para 9
s 38(6)	Sch 13, para 8
s 39(1)–(3)	Sch 13, para 4
s 39(4)	—
s 40(1)	s 135(1)
s 40(2)	s 135(2)
s 40(3)	s 135(3)
s 40(4)	s 135(4)
s 40(5)	s 135(8)
s 40(6), (7)	s 135(5), (6)
s 41	Sch 13, para 11
s 42(1)	s 149(1)
s 42(2)	s 149(2)
s 42(3)	s 149(3), (4)
s 42(4)	s 149(5)
s 44	s 406
s 45	s 407
s 46	s 403
s 46A	ss 403, 406, 407
s 47(1)	s 548(1)
s 47(1A)	s 548(2)
s 47(1B)	s 549(3)
s 47(2)	s 549(1)
s 47(3)	s 549(2)
s 47(4)	s 548(6)
s 47(5)	ss 548(3), 549(5)
s 47(6)	s 548(4)
s 47(7)	s 548(5)
s 47(8)	s 550
s 47(9)	Sch 35, para 4(1)
s 47(10)	s 549(4)
s 47(11)	—
s 51(1)–(4)	s 492(1)–(4)
s 51(5), (6)	Rep 1992 c 13, s 93, Sch 8, Pt I, para 24(b), Sch 9
s 51(7), (8)	s 492(6)
s 51(9)	Rep 1993 c 35, s 307(1), (3), Sch 19, paras 88, 103, Sch 21, Pt II
s 51(10)	s 579(4)
s 51(11)	s 492(5)

Appendix 3

Education (No 2) Act 1986 (c 61)	Education Act 1996 (c 56)
s 51(12)	—
s 51(13)	Rep 1993 c 35, s 307(1), (3), Sch 19, paras 88, 103, Sch 21, Pt II
s 52	s 493
s 53	s 509(4)
s 54(1)	s 54(1)
s 54(2)	s 54(2)
s 54(3)	s 52(1), (3)
s 54(4)	s 52(2)
s 54(5)	s 53(1), (2)
s 54(6)	s 54(4)
s 54(7)	s 54(3)
s 54(8)	s 55(1)
s 54(9)	s 55(2)
s 54(10)	s 55(3)
s 54(11)	s 55(4)
s 54(12)	s 54(5), (6)
s 54(13)	s 53(3)
s 54(14)	s 53(4)
s 55(1)	s 56(1), (3)
s 55(2)	s 56(1), (2)
s 55(3)	s 56(4)
s 55(4)	s 56(5)
s 56	s 538
s 57	Sch 8, para 20
s 58(1)	s 519(1)
s 58(2)	s 519(2)
s 58(3), (4)	Rep 1992 c 13, s 93, Sch 8, Pt I, para 26, Sch 9
s 58(5)	s 519(3)
s 58(6)	s 519(4), (5)
s 58(7)	s 519(6)
ss 59, 60	—
s 62(1)*	Sch 8, para 18(1), Sch 22, para 14(1)
s 62(2)†	Sch 8, para 18(2), Sch 22, para 14(2)
s 63(1)*	ss 568(1), 569(1)
s 63(2)†	ss 568(3), 569(2)
s 63(2A)	s 569(3)
s 63(3)†	ss 568(5), 569(4)
s 65(1)	ss 78(1), (3)–(5), 422(7), 579(1), Sch 9, para 1
s 65(2)†	s 182
s 67(2), (5), (6)	—
Sch 1, para 1(1)	s 89(5)
para 1(2)	s 89(6)
para 2(1)	s 92(1), (2)
para 2(2)	s 92(3)
para 2(3)	s 92(4)
para 3	s 93
para 4	s 164(2)–(3)
para 5(1)	s 164(4)
para 5(2)	s 164(5)
para 5(3)	s 164(6)
para 5(4)	s 164(7)
Sch 2, Pt I, para 1	s 181(1), (2), 422(7) Sch 9, para 1
para 2(1)	Sch 9, para 2(1)

Destination Table to Education Act 1996 & School Inspections Act 1996

Education (No 2) Act 1986 (c 61)	Education Act 1996 (c 56)
para 2(2)	Sch 9, para 2(2), Sch 10, para 5(2)
para 2(3)	Sch 9, para 9(2), (3)
para 2(4)	Sch 9, para 17
Pt II, para 3(1)	s 99(1)
para 3(2), (3)	Sch 10, para 5
para 3(4)	Sch 10, para 1
para 3(5)	Sch 10, para 2
para 3(6)	s 100(3), (4)
para 3(7)	s 99(2)
para 4	Sch 10, para 3, Sch 19, para 1
para 5(1)	ss 96(5), 97(8)
para 5(2)	ss 96(4), 97(7)
para 6	Sch 9, para 3
para 7(1)	Sch 9, para 4
para 7(2)–(5)	Sch 9, para 6
para 7(6), (7)	Sch 9, para 7(1), (2)
para 8(1)	Sch 9, para 5
para 8(2)	Sch 9, para 7(3)
para 9	Sch 9, para 8
para 10(1)	Sch 9, para 15(1)
para 10(2)	Sch 9, para 14
para 10(3)	Sch 9, para 18
para 10(4)	Sch 9, paras 13, 16
para 11(1), (2)	Sch 9, para 12
para 11(3)	Sch 9, para 10
para 11(4), (5)	Sch 9, para 9(1), (3)
para 11(6)	Sch 9, para 11
Pt III, para 12(1)	Sch 19, para 1(1)
para 12(2)	Sch 19, para 3
para 12(3)	Sch 19, para 4
para 13(1)	Sch 19, para 28(1)
para 13(2)	s 538
para 13(3)	Sch 10, paras 4(1), 6(1)
para 13(4)	Sch 10, para 4(2)
para 13(5)	Sch 10, para 6(2)
para 14(1)	Sch 19, para 28(2)
para 14(2)	Sch 19, para 28(3)
para 15	Sch 19, para 25
para 16	Sch 19, para 26
para 17	Sch 19, para 27
para 18	Sch 19, para 29(1)
para 19	s 422(1)–(6)
para 20(1)	Sch 19, para 14
para 20(2)	Sch 19, para 15(1)
para 20(3)	Sch 19, para 15(2)
para 20(4)	Sch 19, para 16(1)
para 20(5)	Sch 19, para 5
para 21	Sch 19, para 6
para 22	Sch 19, para 7
para 23	Sch 19, para 8
para 24	Sch 19, para 10
para 25	Sch 19, para 9
para 26(1)	Sch 19, para 11(1)
para 26(2)	Sch 19, para 11(2)

Appendix 3

Education (No 2) Act 1986 (c 61)	Education Act 1996 (c 56)
para 26(3)	Sch 9, para 15(2)
Pt IV, para 27	Sch 9, para 19
para 28	Sch 9, para 20, Sch 19, para 17
para 29	Sch 9, para 22
para 30(1)	Sch 9, para 21
para 30(2)	Sch 19, para 12
para 30(3)	Sch 19, para 16(2)
Sch 3, para 1	Sch 16, para 1(1)
para 2	Sch 16, para 1(2)
para 3	Sch 16, para 2
para 3A	Sch 16, para 3
para 4	Sch 16, para 4
para 5	Sch 16, para 18
para 6	Sch 16, para 6
para 6A	Sch 16, para 7
para 7	Sch 16, para 8
para 8	Sch 16, para 9
para 9	Sch 16, para 10
para 10	—
para 11	Sch 16, para 13
para 12	Sch 16, para 14
para 13	Sch 16, para 11
para 14	Sch 16, para 12
para 15	Sch 16, para 15
para 16	Sch 16, para 5
para 17	Sch 16, para 16
Sch 4, para 1	ss 32(2), 48(1)
para 2	s 134(5)
para 5	—
Schs 5, 6	—

Reverter of Sites Act 1987 (c 15)	Education Act 1996 (c 56)
s 8(1)	s 60(7)

Education Reform Act 1988 (c 40)	Education Act 1996 (c 56)
s 1(1)	s 351(2)–(5)
s 1(2)	s 351(1)
s 2(1)	s 352(1)
s 2(2)	s 353
s 2(3)	s 352(2)
s 3(1)	s 354(1)
s 3(2)	s 354(2)
s 3(2A)	s 354(3), (4)
s 3(2B)	s 354(5)
s 3(3)	s 355(1)
s 3(4)	ss 354(6), 355(2)
s 3(5)	s 355(3)
s 3(5A)	s 355(4)
s 3(6)	ss 354(7), 355(5)

Destination Table to Education Act 1996 & School Inspections Act 1996

Education Reform Act 1988 (c 40)	Education Act 1996 (c 56)
s 3(7)	s 354(8)
s 4(1)	s 356(1)
s 4(2)	s 356(2)
s 4(3)	s 356(3)
s 4(4)	s 356(4)
s 4(5)	s 356(5)
s 4(6)	s 356(6)
s 4(7)	s 356(7)
s 4(8)	s 356(8)
s 5(1)	s 400(1), (2)
s 5(2)	s 400(3)
s 5(3)	s 400(5)
s 6(1)	s 385(1)
s 6(2)	s 385(2)
s 6(3)	s 385(4)
s 6(4)	s 385(5)
s 6(5)	s 385(6)
s 6(6)	s 385(7)
s 6(7)	s 385(1), (3)
s 7(1)	s 386(1), (2)
s 7(2)	s 386(3)
s 7(3)	s 386(4)
s 7(4)	s 386(5)
s 7(5)	s 386(6)
s 7(6)	s 387
s 8(1)	—
s 8(2)	s 352(1)
s 8(3)	s 375(3), (5)
s 9(1), (1A)	s 398
s 9(2)	s 389(7)
s 9(3)	s 389(1)
s 9(4)	s 389(3)
s 9(5)	s 389(7)
s 9(6)	s 389(4)
s 9(7)	s 389(5)
s 9(8)	s 389(6)
s 9(9)	s 389(2)
s 9(10)	—
s 10(1)	ss 384, 388
s 10(2)	ss 357(1), 400(4)
s 10(3)	s 357(2)
s 11(1)	ss 390(1), 391(1), 392(1), 394(1)
s 11(2)	s 391(2)
s 11(3)	s 390(2), (3)
s 11(4)	s 390(2), (4)
s 11(5)	s 390(5), (6)
s 11(6)	s 390(7)
s 11(7)	s 391(3), (4)
s 11(8)	s 391(5), Sch 31, para 3
s 11(9)	s 391(6)
s 11(10)	s 391(7)
s 11(11)	s 391(8)
s 11(12)	s 391(9)
s 11(13)	s 391(10)

Appendix 3

Education Reform Act 1988 (c 40)	Education Act 1996 (c 56)
s 12(1)	s 394(1), (5)
s 12(2)	s 394(2)
s 12(3)	s 394(3)
s 12(4)	s 394(4)
s 12(5)	s 395(1), (6)
s 12(6)	s 395(2), (6)
s 12(7)	s 395(3), (4)
s 12(8)	s 395(5)
s 12(9)	ss 394(6), 395(7)
s 12(10)	ss 394(7), 395(8)
s 12(11)	s 394(8)
s 12A(1)	s 396(1)
s 12A(2)	s 396(2)
s 12A(3)	s 396(1)
s 13(1)	s 392(2)
s 13(2)	s 392(3)
s 13(3)	s 392(4)
s 13(4)	ss 390(3), 392(5)
s 13(5)	s 392(6)
s 13(6)	s 392(7)
s 13(7)	s 392(8)
s 14(1)	s 360(1)
s 14(2)	s 360(2)–(4)
s 14(3)	s 361(1)
s 14(4)	Rep 1993 c 35, s 307(3), Sch 21, Pt II
s 14(5)	s 361(2)
s 14(6)	s 361(3), (4)
s 14(7)	s 360(5)
s 15	—
s 16(1)	s 362(1)
s 16(2)	s 362(2)
s 16(3)	s 363(3), (4)
s 16(4)	s 362(5)
s 16(5)	s 362(6)
s 16(6)	s 362(7)
s 17	s 363
s 17A	s 405
s 18	s 364
s 19(1)	s 365(1), (5)
s 19(2)	s 365(2)–(4)
s 19(3)	s 366(1)
s 19(4)	s 366(2), (3)
s 19(5)	s 366(5)
s 19(6)	s 366(6)
s 19(7)	s 367(1)
s 19(8)	s 367(2), (3)
s 19(9)	s 367(4)
s 19(10)	s 365(6)
s 20(1)	s 368(1)
s 20(2)	s 368(2), (10)
s 20(3)	s 368(3)
s 20(4)	s 368(4), (5)
s 20(5)	s 368(6), (7)
s 20(6)	s 368(8)

Destination Table to Education Act 1996 & School Inspections Act 1996

Education Reform Act 1988 (c 40)	Education Act 1996 (c 56)
s 21(1)	s 368(1)
s 21(2)	s 368(2), (10)
s 21(3)	s 368(3)
s 21(3A)	s 368(4), (5)
s 21(3B)	s 368(6), (7)
s 21(4)	s 368(8)
s 22(1)	s 408(1), (4)
s 22(2)	s 408(2)
s 22(3)	s 408(3)
s 22(4)	s 408(5)
s 22(5)	s 408(6)
s 22(6)	s 408(7)
s 22(7)	s 408(8)
s 23(1)	s 409(1)–(3)
s 23(2)	s 409(4)
s 24(1)	s 401(1)
s 24(2)	s 401(2)
s 24(3)	s 401(3)
s 24(4)	s 401(4)
s 25(1)	s 350
s 25(2)	s 410
s 26(1)	s 416(1), (8)
s 26(2)	—
s 26(3)	s 416(2), (8)
s 26(4)	s 416(3), (8)
s 26(5)	s 416(4)
s 26(6)	s 416(5)
s 26(7)	s 416(6)
s 26(8)	s 416(7)
s 26(9)	s 411(6)
s 26(10)	s 411(7)
s 27(1)	ss 417(1), 418(1)
s 27(2)(a)	s 417(1)
s 27(2)(b)	s 418(1)
s 27(3)	ss 417(2), (3), 418(2), (3)
s 27(4)	s 420(1)
s 27(5)	s 420(2)
s 27(6)	s 420(3)
s 27(7)	s 420(4), (5)
s 27(8)	s 421(1)
s 27(9)	ss 417(4), (5), 418(3)
s 28(1)	Sch 32, para 1
s 28(2)	Sch 32, para 2
s 28(3)	Sch 32, para 3(1)
s 28(4)	Sch 32, para 3(2)
s 28(5)	Sch 32, para 4
s 28(6)	Sch 32, para 5(1)
s 28(7)	Sch 32, para 5(2)
s 28(8)	Sch 32, para 6
s 29(1)	s 419(2)
s 29(2)	s 419(3)
s 29(3)	s 419(4)
s 29(4)	s 419(5)
s 29(5), (6)	s 436

Appendix 3

Education Reform Act 1988 (c 40)	Education Act 1996 (c 56)
s 29(7)	s 419(1)
s 30(1)	—
s 30(2)	s 411(3)(b)
s 30(3)	s 413(1)
s 32(1)	s 421(2), Sch 32, para 5(3)
s 32(2)	s 579(1)
s 32(3)	—
s 32(4)	ss 417(1), 418(1)
s 33(1)	s 103(1)
s 33(2)	ss 101(3), 103(2)
s 33(3)	s 102
s 33(4)	ss 101(3), (4), 105(1), (3)
s 33(5)	ss 101(5), 105(2), 106(6)
s 33(6)	s 115, Sch 11 para 2
s 34(1)	s 104(1)
s 34(2)	s 104(2)
s 34(3)	s 571
s 34(4)	s 104(3)
s 34(5)	s 104(4)
s 34(6)	s 104(5)
s 34(7)	s 104(6)
s 35(1)	s 111(1)
s 35(2)	s 111(2)
s 35(3)	s 112(1)–(3)
s 35(4)	ss 112(4), 113(5)
s 35(5)	s 113(1), (2)
s 35(6)	s 113(3), (4)
s 35(7)	s 114(1)
s 35(8)	s 114(2)
s 36(1)	s 116(1)
s 36(2)	s 116(2)
s 36(3)	s 116(3)
s 36(4)	s 116(4)
s 36(5)	s 116(5)
s 36(5A)	s 116(6)
s 36(5B)	s 116(7)
s 36(6)	s 116(8)
s 37(1)	s 117(1)
s 37(2)	s 117(2), (3)
s 37(3)	s 117(4), (5)
s 37(4)	s 117(6)
s 37(5)	s 118(1)–(3)
s 37(6)	s 118(4)
s 37(7)	s 118(5)
s 37(8)	s 119(1)
s 37(9)	s 119(2)
s 38(1), (2)	s 106(1)–(3)
s 38(3)	s 106(4)
s 38(3A)	s 106(5)
s 38(4)	s 105(3)
s 39(1)	s 107(1)
s 39(2), (3)	Rep SI 1991/1890, reg 2
s 39(4)	s 107(2)
s 39(5)	—

Destination Table to Education Act 1996 & School Inspections Act 1996

Education Reform Act 1988 (c 40)	Education Act 1996 (c 56)
s 39(6)–(9)	Rep SI 1991/1890, reg 2
s 39(10)	s 108
s 39(11)	s 109(1), (3)
s 39(12)	s 109(2)
s 40	s 110
s 41	—
s 42(1)	s 121
s 42(2)	s 122(1)
s 42(3)	s 122(2)
s 42(4)(a)–(d)	Sch 11, para 2
s 42(4)(e)	Sch 11, para 3(1)
s 42(4)(f)–(i)	Rep 1993 c 35, ss 275(1), 307(3), Sch 21, Pt II
s 42(4)(j)	Sch 11, para 4
s 42(5)(a)	Sch 11, para 3(2)
s 42(5)(b)	Rep 1993 c 35, ss 275(1), 307(3), Sch 21, Pt II
s 42(6)	s 122(4)
s 42(7)	s 122(5)
s 42(8)	s 122(6)
s 42(9)	s 122(7)
s 42A	s 123
s 43	s 120
s 44(1)	s 136(1)
s 44(2)	s 136(2)
s 44(3)	s 136(3)
s 44(4)	s 141(1), (2)
s 44(5)	s 136(3)
s 45(1)	s 137(1), 138(1)
s 45(2)	s 137(2)
s 45(3)	s 137(3), (4)
s 45(4)	s 138(1)
s 45(5)	s 138(3)
s 45(6)	s 138(2)
s 45(7)	s 138(4)
s 45(8)	s 138(5)
s 45(9)	s 137(5)
s 45(10)	s 137(6)
s 45(11)	s 141(1), (3)
s 46(1)	Rep 1991 c 49, s 6(3), Sch 2
s 46(2)	s 139(1), (2)
s 46(3)	s 139(3)
s 46(4)	s 139(4)
s 46(5)	s 139(5)
s 46(6)	s 139(6)
s 47	s 140
s 48(1)	—
s 48(2)	s 181, Sch 12, para 1
s 49(1)	s 125(1)
s 49(2)	s 125(2), (3)
s 49(3)	s 125(4)
s 50(1)	—
s 50(2)	s 124(1)
s 50(3)	s 124(2)
s 50(4)	—
s 50(5)	s 124(1), Sch 11, paras 5–7

Appendix 3

Education Reform Act 1988 (c 40)	Education Act 1996 (c 56)
s 50(6)	s 124(4)
s 50(7)	s 124(6)
s 50(8)	s 124(7)
s 50(9)	s 124(8)
s 50(10)	s 124(5), Sch 11, para 8
s 51(1)	s 105(3)(a), (b), Sch 11, paras 5(2), 6(1)
s 51(2)(a)	s 101(1), (2)
s 51(2)(b)	s 101(6)
s 51(2)(c)–(i)	—
s 51(3)	s 129(1)
s 51(4)	s 129(2), (4)
s 51(5)	s 129(3)
s 51(6)	ss 129(5), 141(4)
s 51(7)	Rep SI 1991/1890, reg 2
s 51(8)	—
s 51(9)	Sch 17, para 6
ss 52–99	Rep 1993 c 35, s 307(1), (3), Sch 19, paras 112, 126, Sch 21, Pt I
s 100(1)	Rep 1993 c 35, s 307(1), (3), Sch 19, paras 112, 126, Sch 21, Pt I
s 100(2)	s 514(1)(a)
s 100(3)	Rep 1993 c 35, s 307(1), (3), Sch 19, paras 112, 126 Sch 21, Pt I
s 100(4)(a)	s 510(1)
s 100(4)(b)	s 510(3)–(5)
ss 101–104	Rep 1993 c 35, s 307(1), (3), Sch 19, paras 112, 126, Sch 21, Pt I
s 105(1), (2)	s 482(1)–(3)
s 105(3)	s 482(4)
s 105(4)	s 483(1), (2)
s 105(5)	s 483(3)
s 105(6)	S 483(4)
s 106(1)	s 450(1)
s 106(1A)	s 450(2)
s 106(2)	s 451(1), (2)
s 106(3), (4)	s 451(3)–(5)
s 106(5)	s 453(1)
s 106(6)	s 454(1)
s 106(7)	s 454(3)
s 106(8)	s 454(4)
s 106(9)	s 452(6)
s 106(10)	s 462(2)
s 106(11)	s 462(3)
s 107(1)	s 452(1)
s 107(2)	s 452(2)
s 107(3)	s 452(3)
s 107(4)	s 452(4)
s 107(5), (6)	s 452(5)
s 108(1)	s 453(2)
s 108(2)	s 453(3)
s 109(1)	s 455(1)
s 109(2)	s 455(2), (3)
s 109(3)–(10)	s 456
s 110(1)	s 457(1)

Destination Table to Education Act 1996 & School Inspections Act 1996

Education Reform Act 1988 (c 40)	Education Act 1996 (c 56)
s 110(2)	s 457(2), (3)
s 110(3)	s 457(4)
s 110(4)	s 457(5)
s 110(5)	s 455(3)
s 111(1)	s 458(1)
s 111(2)	s 458(2)
s 111(3)	s 458(3)
s 111(4)	Rep 1993 c 35, s 307(1), (3), Sch 19, paras 112, 129, Sch 21, Pt II
s 111(5)	s 458(4)
s 111(6)	s 458(5)
s 112(1)	—
s 112(2)	s 554(1)–(5), 555(5), 556(8)
s 112(3)	s 556(2)
s 113	s 553
s 114	s 63(3)
s 115	ss 147, 153
s 116	Sch 8, para 15(3)
s 117(1)	s 402(1)
s 117(2)	s 402(2)
s 117(3)	s 402(3)
s 117(4)	s 402(4)
s 117(5)	s 402(5)
s 118(1)	s 460(1)
s 118(2)	s 460(2)
s 118(3)	s 454(2)
s 118(4)	s 460(3)
s 118(5)	s 459
s 118(6)	s 461
s 118(7)	ss 402(6), 449, 462(1), (4), (5), 579(1)
s 118(8)	s 462(5)
s 119(1)(a)	s 579(3)
s 119(1)(b)	s 579(1)
s 119(2)	Sch 32, para 7(1)
s 119(3)	Sch 32, para 7(2)
s 120(5)	—
s 120(9)(a)(i)	s 579(1)
s 120(9)(a)(ii)	Rep 1992 c 13, s 93, Sch 8, paras 27, 30, Sch 9
s 120(9)(b)	Rep 1992 c 13, s 93, Sch 8, paras 27, 30, Sch 9
s 210(1)*	s 488(1)
s 210(2)†	s 488(2)
s 210(3)(a)†, (b)†	s 488(3)
s 210(3)(c)†	s 489(1)
s 210(3)(d)*	s 489(1)
s 211*	s 490
s 212	s 66
s 213(1)	s 486
s 213(2)	s 489(1)
s 213(3)	s 485
s 218(1)(e)*	s 546(1)
s 218(1)(f)*	s 563(1)
s 218(1)(g)	s 551(1)
s 218(2B)†	s 482(5)
s 218(4)†	s 563(2)

Appendix 3

Education Reform Act 1988 (c 40)	Education Act 1996 (c 56)
s 218(7)*	s 544(1), (2)
s 218(8)	s 545(2)
s 218(12)†	ss 544(3), 546(2), 551(2), 563(3)
s 218(13)	—
s 222(1), (2)	s 178(1)
s 222(3)	s 178(2)
s 225	—
s 227(1)	s 369
s 227(2)–(4)	Rep 1992 c 13, s 93, Sch 8, Pt I, paras 27, 54
s 229(1)	s 569(5)
s 230(1)*	—
s 232(1)†	ss 568(1), 569(1)
s 232(2)†	s 568(2)
s 232(3)	s 568(4)
s 232(4)*	ss 568(3), 569(2)
s 232(5)†	ss 568(5), 569(4)
s 232(6)†	ss 568(6), 569(5)
s 234(1)	—
s 234(2)(a)	s 579(6)
s 234(2)(b)	s 579(7)
s 234(3)	s 579(6)
s 234(4)	—
s 235(1)*	ss 575(1), (2), 579(1)
s 235(2)(c)†	s 401(5)
s 235(2)(g)†	s 579(2)
s 235(3)†	s 575(3)
s 236(1)*, (2), (3)	—
s 238(2)	—
Sch 1, paras 1–4	—
para 5	—
paras 6, 7	—
para 8	—
para 9	Rep 1993 c 35, s 307(1), (3), Sch 19, paras 112, 140, Sch 21, Pt I
Sch 2, para 1	Rep 1993 c 35, s 307(3), Sch 21, Pt II
paras 2–6	Sch 30, paras 1–5
para 7(1)	Sch 30, para 6
para 7(2)	Sch 30, para 7
para 8	Sch 30, para 8
para 9	Rep 1993 c 35, s 307(3), Sch 21, Pt II
para 10(1)–(4)	Sch 30, para 9
para 10(5)–(7)	Sch 30, para 10
para 11	Sch 30, para 11
para 12	Sch 30, para 12
para 13	Sch 30, para 13
para 13A	Sch 30, para 14
para 14	Sch 30, para 15
para 15	Sch 30, para 16
para 16	Sch 30, para 18
para 17	Sch 30, para 19
para 18(1)	Sch 30, para 17(1)
para 18(1A)	Sch 30, para 17(2)
para 18(2)	Sch 30, para 17(3)
para 18(3)	s 579(1)

Destination Table to Education Act 1996 & School Inspections Act 1996

Education Reform Act 1988 (c 40)	Education Act 1996 (c 56)
Sch 3, para 1(1)	Sch 14, paras 1(1), 2
para 1(2)	Sch 14, para 1(2)
para 1(3)	Sch 14, para 3
para 1(4)	Sch 14, para 4(1)
para 1(5)	Sch 14, para 4(2)
para 1(6)	Sch 14, para 1(3)
para 1(7)	Sch 14, para 5
para 1(8)	Sch 14, para 6(1)
para 1(9)	Sch 14, para 6(2)
para 1(10)	Sch 14, para 6(3)
para 1(11)	Sch 14, para 7(1)
para 1(12)	Sch 14, para 4(3)
para 1(13)	Sch 14, para 7(2)
para 2(1)	Sch 14, para 8
para 2(2)	Sch 14, para 9(1)
para 2(3)	Sch 14, para 9(2)
para 2(4)	Sch 14, para 10
para 2(5)	Sch 14, para 11
para 2(6)	Sch 14, para 12(1)
para 2(7)	Sch 14, para 12(2)
para 2(8)	Sch 14, para 13(1)
para 2(9)	Sch 14, para 13(2)
para 2(10)	Sch 14, para 14(1)
para 2(11)	Sch 14, para 14(2)
para 2(12)	Sch 14, para 15
para 3(1)	Sch 14, para 16(1)
para 3(2)	Sch 14, para 16(2), (3)
para 3(3)	Sch 14, para 17
para 4(1)	Sch 14, para 18(1)
para 4(2)	Sch 14, para 18(2)
para 4(3)	Sch 14, para 18(3)
para 4(4)	Sch 14, para 19
para 4(5)	Sch 14, para 18(4)
para 5	Sch 14, para 20
para 6	Sch 14, para 21
para 7(1)	Sch 14, para 22(1)
para 7(2)	Sch 14, para 22(2)
para 7(3)	Sch 14, para 22(3), (4)
para 7(4)	Sch 14, para 22(5)
para 8(1)	Sch 14, para 23(1)
para 8(2)	Sch 14, para 23(2)
para 8(3)	Sch 14, para 23(3)
para 8(4)	Sch 14, para 24(1)
para 8(5)	Sch 14, para 24(2)
para 8(6)	Sch 14, para 23(4)
para 8(7)	Sch 14, para 25(1)
para 8(8)	Sch 14, para 25(2)
para 8(9)	Sch 14, para 26
para 9	Sch 14, para 27
para 10	Sch 14, para 28
para 11(1), (2)	—
para 11(3)	Sch 14, para 1(4)
Sch 4, para 1(1)	Sch 12, para 3, Sch 19, para 18
para 1(2)	Sch 12, para 2, Sch 19, para 18

Appendix 3

Education Reform Act 1988 (c 40)	Education Act 1996 (c 56)
para 2(1)	Sch 12, para 3
para 2(2)	Sch 12, para 4(1)
para 2(3)	Sch 12, para 4(2)
para 2(4)	Sch 12, para 4(3)
para 2(5)	Sch 12, para 4(4)
para 2(6)	Sch 12, para 5
para 2(7)	Rep SI 1991/1890, 1992/110
para 2(8)	Sch 12, para 6
para 2(9)	Sch 12, para 7
para 2(10)	Sch 19, para 29(2)
para 3	Sch 12, para 8
para 4(1), (4), (5)	Sch 19, para 19
para 4(2)	Sch 19, para 20
para 4(3)	Sch 19, para 21
para 4(6)	Sch 19, para 24
para 4(7)	Sch 19, para 22
para 4(8)	Sch 19, para 23
para 5	Sch 12, para 10
para 6	Sch 12, para 9
para 7	Sch 19, para 2
Sch 12, Pt I, paras 1–7	—
para 8	s 63
para 14	s 560(1)
para 17	—
para 24	s 534(1)–(4)
para 25	—
para 34, 35, 37	—
Sch 12, Pt III, para 54–62	—
para 69(4)	—
paras 76, 77	—
para 81, 82	—
para 87(3)	—
para 99	—
para 102, 103	—
para 106	—

Children Act 1989 (c 41)	Education Act 1996 (c 56)
Sch 13, para 9	s 469(1)
Sch 13, para 10	s 576

Local Government and Housing Act 1989 (c 42)	Education Act 1996 (c 56)
s 13(9)*	—
s 188	—

Education (Student Loans) Act 1990 (c 6)	Education Act 1996 (c 56)
s 4(2)	—

Destination Table to Education Act 1996 & School Inspections Act 1996

National Health Service and Community Care Act 1990 (c 19)	Education Act 1996 (c 56)
Sch 9, para 31	s 80(2)
Employment Act 1990 (c 38)	Education Act 1996 (c 56)
s 14	s 560(2)
s 18(2)*	—
Disability Living Allowance and Disability Working Allowance Act 1991 (c 21)	Education Act 1996 (c 56)
Sch 3, Pt II, para 12	s 457(4)
School Teachers' Pay and Conditions Act 1991 (c 49)	Education Act 1996 (c 56)
s 6(2)	—
Diocesan Boards of Education Measure 1991 (No 2)	Education Act 1996 (c 56)
s 10(1)*	—
Further and Higher Education Act 1992 (c 13)	Education Act 1996 (c 56)
s 10(1)	ss 2(2), 14(1)
s 10(2)	s 14(5)
s 10(3)	s 14(6)
s 11	ss 2(3), (6), 15
s 12(1)	s 16(3)
s 12(2)	s 41(4)
s 12(3)	s 176
s 12(4)	s 398
s 12(5)	s 101(3), (4)
s 12(6)	s 116(6)
s 12(7)	s 106(5)
s 12(8)	—
s 12(9)	s 450(2)
s 13	Rep 1993 c 35, s 307(1), (3), Sch 19, para 168, Sch 21, Pt I
s 14(1)	s 2(4)
s 14(2)	s 2(2)
s 14(3)	s 2(5)
s 14(4)	s 2(7)
s 14(5)	s 4(1)
s 14(6)	s 3(1)

Appendix 3

Further and Higher Education Act 1992 (c 13)	Education Act 1996 (c 56)
s 59(1)	s 175(1)
s 59(2)	s 175(2)
s 59(3), (4)	ss 35(6), 41(8), 167(5), 173(4)
s 59(5)	Rep 1993 c 35, s 307(1), (3), Sch 19, para 169, Sch 21, Pt I
s 91(3)†	s 4(3)
s 91(5)†	s 4(4)
s 94(2)	—
Sch 8, Pt I, para 1	—
para 2	s 13(2)
para 3	—
para 4	s 16(1)
para 5(a)	s 509(1), (2)
para 5(b)	s 509(3)
para 5(c)	s 509(4)
para 5(d)	s 509(5)
para 5(e)	s 509(6)
paras 6–10	—
para 11	s 518
para 12	—
para 13(1)	—
para 13(2)(a), (b)	—
para 13(2)(c)	s 5(1)
para 13(2)(d)–(f)	—
para 13(2)(g)	s 5(2)
para 13(3)	—
para 13(4)	s 579(7)
para 14	s 62(4)
para 15	—
para 16	s 510(4)
para 17	ss 512(5), 534(5)
para 24	—
para 25	s 493(1), (3)
para 26	—
para 28	s 401(1)
para 43(b)	—
para 49(a)†	s 563(1)
para 49(b)†	s 544(1)
paras 50, 53, 54, 56, 57, 82	—

Education (Schools) Act 1992 (c 38)	Education Act 1996 (c 56)
s 16(1)	s 537(1)
s 16(2)	s 537(2)
s 16(3)	s 537(3)
s 16(4)	s 537(4)
s 16(5)	s 537(5)
s 16(6)	s 537(6)
s 16(7)	s 537(7)
s 16(8)	s 537(8)
s 16(9)	s 537(9)
s 16(10)	s 537(12)

Destination Table to Education Act 1996 & School Inspections Act 1996

Education (Schools) Act 1992 (c 38)	Education Act 1996 (c 56)
s 16(11)	s 537(10)
s 16(12)	s 537(13)
s 19(1)†	s 569(1)
s 19(2)†	s 569(2)
s 19(3)†	ss 537(11), 569(4)
Sch 4, para 1	—
para 4(1)	ss 29(5), 414(6)–(8)
para 4(2)	s 424(3)
para 5	Sch 17, para 10
para 6(1)	—
para 6(2)	s 408(2)
para 6(3), (4)	s 408(6)

Judical Pensions and Retirement Act 1993 (c 8)	Education Act 1996 (c 56)
Sch 6, para 51	Sch 34, para 3(1), (2)

Charities Act 1993 (c 10)	Education Act 1996 (c 56)
Sch 2*	—

Education Act 1993 (c 35)	Education Act 1996 (c 56)
s 1	s 10
s 2	s 11
s 3	s 20
s 4	s 21
s 5	s 26
s 6	s 25
s 7(1)	s 30(1)
s 7(2)	s 30(2)
s 7(3)	s 29(2)
s 7(4)	s 30(3)
s 8	s 23
s 9	s 24
ss 10, 11	—
s 12	s 27
s 13	s 431
s 14	s 432
s 15(1)	Sch 31, para 15(1)
s 15(2), (3)	Sch 31, para 15(2)
s 15(4)	Sch 31, para 15(3)
s 15(5)	Sch 31, para 15(4), (5)
s 15(6)	Sch 31, para 15(6), (7)
s 15(7)	Sch 31, para 15(8)
s 16	s 393
s 17	Sch 3, para 1
s 18	Sch 3, para 2
s 19	Sch 3, para 3
s 20	s 28

Appendix 3

Education Act 1993 (c 35)	Education Act 1996 (c 56)
s 21(1)	s 30(4)
s 21(2)	s 29(3)
s 21(3)	ss 29(4), 30(5)
s 22	s 183
s 23	s 184
s 24	s 185
s 25	s 186
s 26	s 187
s 27	s 188
s 28	s 189
s 29	s 190
s 30	s 191
s 31	s 192
s 32	s 193
s 33	s 194
s 34	s 195
s 35	s 196
s 36	s 197
s 37	s 200
s 38(1)	s 201(1)
s 38(2)	s 201(2)
s 38(3)	s 201(3)
s 38(4)	s 201(4)
s 38(5)	s 201(5)
s 38(6)	s 201(6)
s 38(7)	s 201(7)
s 38(8)	s 201(8)
s 38(9)	s 201(10)
s 39	s 202
s 40	s 203
s 41	s 204
s 42	s 205
s 43	s 206
s 44	s 207
s 45	s 208
s 46	s 209
s 47(1)–(4)	s 210
s 47(5)–(9)	—
s 48	s 211
s 49(1)–(3)	s 212
s 49(4)	—
s 50	s 213
s 51	s 214
s 52	s 215
s 53	s 216
s 54	s 217
s 55	s 218
s 56(1)	s 219(1)
s 56(2)	s 219(2)
s 56(3)	s 219(3)
s 57	s 220
s 58	s 221
s 59	s 222
s 60	s 223
s 61	s 224

Destination Table to Education Act 1996 & School Inspections Act 1996

Education Act 1993 (c 35)	Education Act 1996 (c 56)
s 62	s 225
s 63	s 226
s 64	s 227
s 65	s 228
s 66	s 229
s 67	s 230
s 68	s 231
s 69	s 232
s 70	s 233
s 71	s 234
s 72	s 235
s 73	s 236
s 74	s 237
s 75	s 238
s 76	s 239
s 77	s 240
s 78	s 241
s 79	s 242
s 80	s 243
s 81	s 244
s 82	s 245
s 83	s 246
s 84	s 247
s 85	s 248
s 86	s 249
s 87	s 250
s 88	s 251
s 89	s 252
s 90	s 253
s 91	s 254
s 92	s 255
s 93(1)–(6)	s 256
s 93(7)	—
s 94	s 257
s 95	s 258
s 96	s 259
s 97	s 260
s 98	s 261
s 99	s 262
s 100	s 263
s 101	s 264
s 102	s 265
s 103(1)	s 573(4)
s 103(2), (3)	s 266
s 104	s 267
s 105	s 268
s 106	s 269
s 107	s 270
s 108	s 271
s 109	s 272
s 110	s 273
s 111	s 274
s 112	s 275
s 113	s 276
s 114	s 277

Appendix 3

Education Act 1993 (c 35)	Education Act 1996 (c 56)
s 115	s 278
s 116	s 279
s 117	s 280
s 118	s 281
s 119	s 282
s 120	s 283
s 121	s 284
s 122	s 285
s 123	s 286
s 124	s 287
s 125	s 288
s 126	s 289
s 127(1)	s 290(1)
s 127(2)	s 290(2)
s 127(3)	s 290(3)
s 127(4)	s 290(4)
s 127(5)	s 290(5)
s 127(6)	s 290(6)
s 127(7)	s 290(7)
s 127(8)	s 290(8), (9)
s 127(9)	s 290(10)
s 127(10)	s 290(11)
s 127(11)	s 290(13)
s 128	s 293
s 129	s 295
s 130	s 296
s 131	s 297
s 132	s 298
s 133	s 299
s 134	s 300
s 135	s 301
s 136	s 302
s 137	s 303
s 138(1)	ss 379(1), 386(1)
s 138(2)	s 386(2)
s 138(3)	s 386(3)
s 138(4)	s 386(4)
s 138(5)	s 386(5)
s 138(6)	s 386(6)
s 138(7)	s 387
s 138(8)	s 385(4)
s 138(9)	s 379(2)
s 138(10)	s 379(3)
s 138(11)	s 379(4)
s 138(12)	s 386(7)
s 139	s 380
s 140	s 381
s 141	s 383
s 142	s 382
s 143	s 304
s 144	s 305
s 145	s 306
s 146	Sch 31, para 11
s 147(1)	s 390(2)
s 147(2)	s 391(8), (9)

Destination Table to Education Act 1996 & School Inspections Act 1996

Education Act 1993 (c 35)	Education Act 1996 (c 56)
s 148(a)	s 394(1)
s 148(b)	s 394(4)
s 148(c)	ss 394(6), 395(7)
s 148(d)	s 394(8)
s 149(1)	s 426(1)
s 149(2)	s 426(2)
s 149(3)	s 426(3)
s 149(4)	s 426(4)
s 149(5)	s 436(2)
s 150	s 427
s 151	s 428
s 152	s 309
s 153	s 539
s 154	s 310
s 155(1)	ss 311(1), 434(5), 579(1)
s 155(2)	s 311(3)
s 155(3)	s 311(4)
s 155(4)	s 579(1)
s 155(5)	s 579(3)
s 155(6)	ss 311(5), 436(1)
s 155(7)	s 311(6)
s 155(8)	s 210(9)
s 155(9)	s 575(3)
s 155(10)	s 575(3)
s 155(11)	s 311(8)
s 156	s 312
s 157(1)	s 313(1)
s 157(2)	s 313(2)
s 157(3)	s 313(3)
s 157(4)	s 313(4)
s 158	s 314
s 159	s 315
s 160	s 316
s 161(1)	s 317(1)
s 161(2)	s 317(2)
s 161(3)	s 317(3)
s 161(4)	s 317(4)
s 161(5)	s 317(5)
s 161(6)	s 317(6)
s 161(7)	s 317(6), (7)
s 162(1)	s 318(1)
s 162(2)	s 318(2)
s 162(2A)	s 318(3)
s 162(3)	s 318(4)
s 163	s 319
s 164	s 320
s 165	s 321
s 166	s 322
s 167	s 323
s 168	s 324
s 169	s 325
s 170	s 326
s 171	s 327
s 172	s 328
s 173	s 329

Appendix 3

Education Act 1993 (c 35)	Education Act 1996 (c 56)
s 174	s 330
s 175	s 331
s 176	s 332
s 177	s 333
s 178	s 334
s 179	s 335
s 180	s 336
s 181	—
s 182(1)	ss 6(2), 337(1)
s 182(2)	s 337(3)
s 182(3)	s 337(4)
s 182(4)	s 344(2)
s 183(1)	s 338(1)
s 183(2)–(10)	s 339
s 184	s 340
s 185	s 341
s 186	s 345
s 187	s 346
s 188	s 342
s 189	s 347
s 190	s 348
s 191	s 349
s 192	s 437
s 193	s 438
s 194	s 439
s 195	s 440
s 196	s 441
s 197(1)–(5)	s 442
s 197(6)	s 437(8)
s 198(1)–(3)	s 443(1)–(3)
s 198(4)	s 437(8)
s 199(1)–(7)	s 444(1)–(7)
s 199(8)	s 444(9)
s 200	s 445
s 201(1)	s 446
s 201(2)	ss 443(4), 444(8)
s 202	s 447
s 203	s 448
ss 204–228	See the destination table to 1996 c 57 below
s 229(1)	ss 35(1), (5), 167(4), 571
s 229(2)	ss 36(1), (2), (4), 168(1), (2), (4)
s 229(3)	ss 36(3), 168(3)
s 230(1)	ss 41(1), (2), (7), 571
s 230(2)	s 42(1), (2)
s 230(3)	s 42(3)
s 230(4)	s 45(2)
s 230(5)	s 45(7)
s 230(6)	s 42(4)
s 231(1)	ss 292(1), 343(1)
s 231(2)	ss 292(2), 343(2)
s 232	s 500
s 233	s 501
s 234	s 502
s 235(1)	s 503(1)
s 235(2)	s 503(2)

Destination Table to Education Act 1996 & School Inspections Act 1996

Education Act 1993 (c 35)	Education Act 1996 (c 56)
s 235(3)	s 503(3)
s 235(4)	s 503(4)
s 235(5)	s 503(5)
s 235(6)	s 503(6)
s 235(7)	s 507(2)
s 235(8)	s 503(7)
s 236	s 504
s 237	s 505
s 238(1)	s 88(1)
s 238(2)–(4)	—
s 238(5)	Sch 7, para 1(1)
s 238(6)	Sch 7, para 1(2)
s 238(7)	Sch 7, para 1(3)
s 238(8)	—
s 238(9), (10)	—
s 239	Sch 7, para 2
s 240(1)	s 353
s 240(2)	s 355(4)
s 240(3)	s 355(5)
s 240(4)	s 356(5)–(8)
s 240(5)	s 402(2)
s 241(1)	s 352(1)
s 241(2)	s 352(3)
s 241(3)	s 405
s 241(4)	s 356(9)
s 241(5)	s 404(1), (2)
s 241(6)	s 404(3)
s 242(1)	s 368(9)
s 242(2)	—
s 242(3)	s 368(9)
s 243	s 368(2)–(7)
s 244	s 358
s 245(1)	s 359(1)
s 245(2)	s 359(4)
s 245(3)	s 359(3)
s 245(4)	s 359(2)
s 245(5)	ss 350(1), 353, 359(5)
ss 246–248	—
s 249	Sch 30, para 11
s 250	Sch 30, para 14
s 251(1)	—
s 251(2)	Sch 30, para 17(1)
s 251(3)	Sch 30, para 17(2)
s 252	—
s 253(1)	s 360(1)
s 253(2)	—
s 254(1), (2)	—
s 254(3)	Sch 31, para 4(4)
s 255(1)	—
s 255(2)	s 390(6)
s 256(1)	Sch 31, paras 1, 2
s 256(2)(a)	Sch 31, para 10(2)
s 256(2)(b)	Sch 31, para 10(3)
s 257	s 396
s 258	s 397

Appendix 3

Education Act 1993 (c 35)	Education Act 1996 (c 56)
s 259	—
s 260	s 430(1)–(8)
s 261(1)	ss 156(2), 307(1), Sch 28, para 15
s 261(2)	ss 156(3), 307(2), Sch 28, para 15
s 261(3), (4)	—
s 261(5)	Sch 28, para 15
s 262	s 494
s 263	s 537(7)
s 264(1)	s 540(1)
s 264(2)	s 540(2)
s 265(1)	s 541(1), (4)
s 265(2)	s 541(2)
s 265(3)	s 541(3)
s 266	—
s 267(1)	s 308(1), Sch 33, para 6
s 267(2)	s 308(2), Sch 33, para 6
s 268(1)	s 308(1), Sch 33, para 7
s 268(2)	s 308(3), Sch 33, para 7
s 269	—
s 270	s 413(2)–(4)
s 271(1)	ss 85, 568(2)
s 271(2)	Sch 85, para 11(2)
s 271(3)(a)	s 89(2)
s 271(3)(b)	s 95(3)
s 272(1)–(5)	s 198(1)–(5)
s 272(6)	s 35(7)
s 273(1)	ss 35(7), 167(3)
s 273(2)	ss 35(8), 41(9), 167(6), 173(5)
s 273(3)	ss 37(4), 43(3), 169(4), 199(1)
s 273(4)	ss 37(1), (7), 43(4), 169(1), (6), 199(2)
s 273(5)	ss 37(8), 43(5), 169(6), 199(3)
s 273(6)	ss 37(9), 43(6)
s 273(7)	s 199(4)
s 274(1)	s 104(3)
s 274(2)	ss 111, 112, 113, 114
s 274(3)	—
s 274(4)	s 101(1)
s 274(5)	—
s 275(1)(a), (b)	—
s 275(1)(c)	s 122(4)
s 275(1)(d)	s 122(6)
s 275(2)	s 123
s 275(3)	—
s 276	s 120
s 277	s 8
s 278(1)	—
s 278(2)	s 484(1), (3), (4)
s 278(3)	—
s 278(4)	s 489(2)
s 278(5), (6)	—
s 279(1)	s 492(1)–(4)
s 279(2)(a)	s 569(2)
s 279(2)(b)	s 569(3)
s 280	s 451(3)
s 281	s 65

Destination Table to Education Act 1996 & School Inspections Act 1996

Education Act 1993 (c 35)	Education Act 1996 (c 56)
s 282(1)	s 68
s 282(2)	s 57(3)
s 282(3)	s 530(3)
s 282(4)	s 57(3)
s 283	s 69
s 284	s 70
s 285	s 75
s 286	—
s 287	s 557
s 288(1)	—
s 288(2)	s 556(3)
s 288(3)	s 556(1)
s 288(4)	s 556(5)
s 289	—
s 290(1)	ss 468, 469(6)
s 290(2)	ss 469(1), (4), 470(2), 471(2), 472, 473(2)
s 290(3)	—
s 291	s 482(5)
s 292(1)	—
s 292(2)	s 467(2)
s 293(1)	—
s 293(2)	ss 548(1), (2), 549(3)
s 293(3)(a)	ss 548(3), 549(5)
s 293(3)(b)	s 549(5)
s 294	Applies to Scotland
s 295	s 516
s 296	—
s 297	s 499
s 298(1)–(4)	s 19(1)–(4)
s 298(5)	s 31(3)
s 298(6)–(8)	s 19(5)–(7)
s 299	s 567
s 300	s 571
s 301(1)	ss 568(1), 569(1)
s 301(2)	s 568(2), and see 1996 c 57, s 45(1)
s 301(3)	ss 568(3), 569(2), and see 1996 c 57, s 45(2)
s 301(4)	s 569(3)
s 301(5)	s 219(4)
s 301(6)	ss 568(5), 569(4)
s 301(7)	s 570
ss 302, 303	—
s 304(1)	s 4(1)
s 304(2)	s 5(1)
s 305(1)	ss 34(1)–(4), 290(12), 311(1), 312(5), 430(9), 431(7), (8), 437(8), 505, 540(2), 541(1), (4), 567(3), 573(2), 575(1), (2), (4), 579(1), Sch 4, para 1(3)
s 305(2)	s 579(2)
s 305(3)	—
s 305(4)	s 311(2)
s 306	—
s 307	—
s 308	—
Sch 1, paras 1–7	Sch 2, paras 2–8
paras 8–12	Sch 2, paras 10–14
para 13	Sch 2, para 16

Appendix 3

Education Act 1993 (c 35)	Education Act 1996 (c 56)
para 14	Sch 2, para 17
para 15	Sch 2, para 15
para 16	Sch 2, para 1
Sch 2, para 1(1)	Sch 4, para 1(1)
para 1(2)	Sch 4, para 1(2), (3)
paras 2–23	Sch 4, paras 2–23
Sch 3	Sch 20
Sch 4	Sch 21
Sch 5, paras 1–13	Sch 22, paras 1–13
para 14	Sch 22, para 15
para 15	Sch 22, para 16
Sch 6, para 1	Sch 23, para 1
para 2	Sch 23, para 2
para 3	Sch 23, para 3
para 4	Sch 23, para 5(1)
para 5(1)	Sch 23, para 6(1)
para 5(2)	Sch 23, para 6(2)
para 6	Sch 23, paras 5(2), 6(3)
para 7	Sch 23, para 4
para 8	Sch 23, para 7
para 9	Sch 23, para 8
Sch 7	Sch 24
Sch 8	Sch 25
Sch 9	Sch 26
Sch 10	Sch 27
Sch 11	Sch 28, paras 1–14
Sch 12	See the destination table to 1996 c 57 below
Sch 13, para 1	Sch 7, para 4
para 2	Sch 7, para 3
para 3	Sch 7, para 5
para 4(1)	—
para 4(2)	s 150(1)
para 4(3)	s 151(1)–(6)
para 4(4)	ss 134(6), 150(3)
para 4(5)	s 151(7)
para 4(6)	ss 134(5), 150(1), 152(1), (3), (4)
para 5	s 149
paras 6, 7	—
paras 8–12	Sch 8, paras 6–10
para 13	—
para 14	Sch 7, para 11
para 15	Sch 7, para 12
Sch 14, paras 1–9	Sch 29, paras 1–9
para 20(1)	Sch 29, para 20(1)
para 20(2)	Sch 29, para 20(2)
para 20(3)	Sch 29, para 20(3)
para 20(4)	s 579(1)
para 21	Sch 29, para 21
para 22	Sch 29, para 22
Sch 15, paras 1–3	—
para 4(1)	—
para 4(2)	s 391(10)
para 4(3)	ss 360, 361, passim
para 4(4)	s 362(7)
para 4(5)	s 368(10)

Destination Table to Education Act 1996 & School Inspections Act 1996

Education Act 1993 (c 35)	Education Act 1996 (c 56)
para 4(6)	Sch 30 passim
para 5	—
para 6(1)	—
para 6(2)	Sch 29, para 17
para 6(3)	—
Sch 16, para 1	—
para 2(1)	Sch 33, para 1(2), (4), (5)
para 2(2)	Sch 33, para 1(3)
para 2(3)	—
para 2(4)	Sch 33, para 1(7)
para 3(1)	Sch 33, para 2(2), (4), (6)
para 3(2)	Sch 33, para 2(3)
para 3(3)	Sch 33, para 2(5)
para 4	Sch 33, para 5
Sch 17	Sch 36
Sch 18	Sch 1
Sch 19, paras 1, 2	—
para 3	—
paras 4–6	—
para 7	ss 48(2), 58(1), (2)
para 8	—
para 9	s 376(3)
paras 10, 11	—
para 12(a)	—
para 12(b)	s 514(3)
para 13	—
para 14(a)	s 521(4)
para 14(b)	s 525(3)
para 14(c)	s 524(2), (3)
para 15	s 509(4)
paras 16, 17	—
para 18	s 545(1)
para 19	s 545(2)
para 20	s 9
para 21	s 434(1), (4)
para 22	—
para 23(a)	s 67(3), (4)
para 23(b)	s 48(3), (4)
para 24(a)(i), (iii), (iv)	—
para 24(a)(ii)	s 434(5)
para 24(b)	s 576(2)
para 25	s 562(1)
para 26	—
para 27(a), (b)	Sch 31, para 4(2)
para 27(c)	Sch 31, para 7
para 27(d)	Sch 31, paras 8, 9
para 28	—
para 29	—
para 30	—
para 31(a)	s 517(1)
para 31(b)–(f)	s 517(6)
paras 32–37	—
para 38(1)	—
para 38(2)	ss 198(6), 291
para 38(3)	s 5(5)

Appendix 3

Education Act 1993 (c 35)	Education Act 1996 (c 56)
para 39, 40	—
para 41	s 574
paras 42–45	—
para 46	Sch 2, para 9(1)
para 47	Sch 2, para 9(2)
para 48	Sch 2, para 9(3)
paras 49–51	—
para 52(a)	s 554(2)
para 52(b)	s 554(3)
para 52(c)	ss 554(4), 555(1), 556(2), (3)
para 52(d)	—
para 53	—
para 54	s 560(2)
para 55	—
para 56	Rep 1996 c 50, s 10, Sch 4
paras 57–61	—
para 62(1)	s 552(4)
para 62(2)	s 552(2)
para 62(3)	s 552(3)
para 62(4)	s 552(5)
para 62(5)	s 552(1)
para 62(6)	s 552(6)
para 63	—
para 64	Rep 1996 c 50, s 10, Sch 4
paras 65–68	—
para 69	Rep 1996 c 50, s 10, Sch 4
paras 70, 71	—
para 72	—
para 73	s 423(1)
para 74	s 424(3)
para 75	—
para 76	—
para 77(a)	s 44(1), (2)
para 77(b)	—
para 78	ss 35(2), 41(3)
para 79	s 533(3)
para 80	—
para 81	Sch 33, para 1(3)
paras 82, 83	—
para 84	Rep 1996 c 50, s 10, Sch 4
paras 85–89	—
para 90	s 94(2)
para 91(a)	s 82(3)
para 91(b)	—
para 91(c)	—
para 91(d)	s 82(4), (7)
para 91(e)	—
para 92(a)	s 96(1)
para 92(b)	s 96(2)
para 92(c)	—
para 92(d)	s 96(3)
para 93	—
para 94	s 371(5), (7)
para 95	s 154(3)
para 96	—

Destination Table to Education Act 1996 & School Inspections Act 1996

Education Act 1993 (c 35)	Education Act 1996 (c 56)
para 97(a)	Sch 15, para 2(1)
para 97(b)	—
para 97(c), (d)	—
para 98(a)	Sch 15, para 12(1)
para 98(b)	—
para 99	Sch 15, para 14
para 100	—
para 101(a)	s 548(3)
para 101(b)	s 548(4)
para 102	—
para 103(a)	s 492(6)
para 103(b)	—
para 103(c)	s 579(4)
para 103(d)	s 492(5)
para 103(e)	—
para 104	s 493(2)
para 105	—
para 106	s 519(1)
paras 107, 108	—
para 109(a)	Sch 9, para 2(1)
para 109(b)	Sch 9, para 2(2)
para 109(c)	s 96(4)
para 109(d)	—
para 109(e)	Sch 9, para 8(1), (3)
paras 110–112	—
para 113(a)	—
para 113(b)	s 355(1)
para 114	s 352(1)
para 115	s 389(5)
para 116(a)	s 390(4)
para 116(b)	s 391(10)
para 117	s 392(2), (3), (8)
para 118(a)	s 360(2)
para 118(b)	s 361(1)
para 118(c)	s 361(2)
para 118(d)	s 361(3), (4)
para 118(e)	—
para 119(a)	s 362(3), (4)
para 119(b)	s 362(7)
para 120	s 364
para 121(a)	s 366(2), (3)
para 121(b)	s 366(6)
para 122	s 368(10)
para 123	s 408(3)
para 124	s 401(2)
para 125(a)	s 116(4)
para 125(b)	s 116(7)
para 126	—
para 127	s 451(5)
para 128	s 457(1)
para 129(a)	s 458(1)
para 129(b)	s 458(2)
para 129(c)	s 458(3)
para 129(d)	—
para 129(e)	s 458(4)

Appendix 3

Education Act 1993 (c 35)	Education Act 1996 (c 56)
para 130	—
para 131	Rep 1996 c 50, s 10, Sch 4
paras 132–135	—
para 141	Sch 30, para 8
para 142	Sch 14, para 28
paras 143–169	—
para 170	Rep 1996 c 50, s 10, Sch 4
paras 171, 172	—
para 173	See the destination table to 1996 c 57 below
paras 174, 175	See Sch 37, paras 118, 120
Sch 20, para 1	See Sch 39, paras 24, 25
para 2	See Sch 39, para 31
para 3	—
para 4	See Sch 39, para 44
paras 5, 6	See Sch 39, paras 28, 29
Sch 21	—

Local Government (Wales) Act 1994 (c 19)	Education Act 1996 (c 56)
s 21(1)	s 12(5)
s 21(2)	s 12(1), (5)
s 21(3)	—
Sch 16, para 8	s 523(3)
para 105(1)	s 322(5)
para 105(2)	s 579(1)

Education Act 1994 (c 30)	Education Act 1996 (c 56)
s 27(2)	—
Sch 2, para 5(2), 4(a)	See Sch 37, paras 32, 35
para 6(2), (4)(a)	See Sch 37, paras 40, 42
para 8(2)	s 398
para 8(3)	s 450(2)
para 8(4)(a)	s 482(5)
para 8(4), (5)	—

Health Authorities Act 1995 (c 17)	Education Act 1996 (c 56)
Sch 1, Pt III, para 112	s 80(2)
para 124(1)	—
para 124(2)	s 322(1), (3)
para 124(3)	s 332

Jobseekers Act 1995 (c 18)	Education Act 1996 (c 56)
Sch 2, para 3	s 512(3)
para 17	s 457(4)

Merchant Shipping Act 1995 (c 21)	Education Act 1996 (c 56)
Sch 13, para 48	s 560(3)

Destination Table to Education Act 1996 & School Inspections Act 1996

Children (Scotland) Act 1995 (c 36)	Education Act 1996 (c 56)
Sch 4, para 10(a)	—
Disability Discrimination Act 1995 (c 50)	Education Act 1996 (c 56)
s 29(1)	—
s 29(2)	s 317(6), (7)
s 30(7)	—
s 30(8)	s 528
s 30(9)	—
Education (Student Loans) Act 1996 (c 9)	Education Act 1996 (c 56)
s 4(2)	—
Employment Rights Act 1996 (c 18)	Education Act 1996 (c 56)
Sch 1, para 59	s 575(1), (4)
Arbitration Act 1996 (c 23)	Education Act 1996 (c 56)
Sch 3, para 4	s 476(4)
para 59	s 336(4)
Nursery Education and Grant-Maintained Schools Act 1996 (c 50)	Education Act 1996 (c 56)
s 7(1)	—
s 7(2)	s 231(5)
s 7(3)	s 231(6)
s 7(4)	s 231(7)
Sch 3, para 1	s 9
para 2	s 433(4)
paras 3–8	—
para 10	Sch 3, para 1(2)
para 11	s 296(2)
para 12	s 318(3)
paras 13, 14	—
para 15	See Sch 37, para 125
Local Authorities etc (Miscellaneous Provisions) Order 1977 (SI 1977/293)	Education Act 1996 (c 56)
art 4(1)	ss 12, 581
art 4(5)	—
Education (Financial Delegation for Primary Schools) Regulations 1991 (SI 1991/1890)	Education Act 1996 (c 56)
	—

Appendix 3

Education (Financial Delegation for Primary Schools) (Amendment) Regulations 1992 (SI 1992/110)	Education Act 1996 (c 56)
	—
Education (National Curriculum) (Foundation Subjects at Key Stage 4) Order 1992 (SI 1992/1548)	Education Act 1996 (c 56)
art 1	—
art 2	s 354(2)
Education (No 2) Act 1986 (Amendment) Order 1993 (SI 1993/2709)	Education Act 1996 (c 56)
art 1	—
art 2	Sch 16, para 9(2)
Education (No 2) Act 1986 (Amendment) (No 2) Order 1993 (SI 1993/2827)	Education Act 1996 (c 56)
art 1	—
art 2	Sch 16, para 8(2)
Education (No 2) Act 1986 (Amendment) Order 1994 (SI 1994/692)	Education Act 1996 (c 56)
art 1	—
art 2	Sch 17, para 6
art 3	—
Education (National Curriculum) (Foundation Subjects at Key Stage 4) Order 1994 (SI 1994/1814)	Education Act 1996 (c 56)
arts 1, 2(1)–(3)	—
art 2(4)—(5)	s 354(2)–(5)
Education (No 2) Act 1986 (Amendment) (No 2) Order 1994 (SI 1994/2092)	Education Act 1996 (c 56)
arts 1, 2	—
art 3	Sch 16, para 1(1)
art 4	Sch 16, para 1(2)

Education (No 2) Act 1986 (Amendment) (No 2) Order 1994 (SI 1994/2092)	Education Act 1996 (c 56)
art 5	Sch 16, para 2(1), (2)
art 6	Sch 16, para 3
art 7	Sch 16, para 7
art 8	Sch 16, para 10(2)
art 9	Sch 16, para 14
art 10	Sch 16, para 16
art 11	—
Education (No 2) Act 1986 (Amendment) (No 3) Order 1994 (SI 1994/2732)	Education Act 1996 (c 56)
art 1	—
art 2	Sch 17, para 7
art 3	—
Local Government Changes for England (Education) (Miscellaneous Provisions) Regulations 1996 (SI 1996/710)	Education Act 1996 (c 56)
reg 19	s 577(1)
Deregulation (Length of the School Day) Order 1996 (SI 1996/951)	Education Act 1996 (c 56)
arts 1, 2	—
art 3(1)	s 147(1), (3)
art 3(2)	s 148(1)
art 3(3)	s 148(2)
art 3(4)	s 148(3)
art 3(5)	s 148(4)
art 4	see Sch 39, para 19
art 5	s 149(5)
art 6	—

† Not repealed
* Repealed in part

SCHOOL INSPECTIONS ACT 1996: DESTINATION TABLE

This table shows in column (1) the enactments repealed by the School Inspections Act 1996 and in column (2) the provisions of that Act corresponding thereto.

In certain cases the enactment in column (1), though having a corresponding provision in column (2) is not, or not wholly, repealed as it still required, or partly required, for the purposes of other legislation.

A 'dash' in the right hand column means that the repealed provision to which it corresponds in the left hand column is spent, unnecessary or for some other reason not specifically reproduced.

Appendix 3

Education (Schools) Act 1992 (c 38)	School Inspections Act 1996 (c 57)
s 1	s 1
s 2	s 2(1)–(6)
s 3	s 3
s 4	s 2(7)
s 5	s 4
s 6	s 5(1)–(6)
s 7	s 6
s 8	s 5(7)
s 9(1)	s 10(1)
s 9(2)	s 10(2)
s 9(3)	s 10(3)
s 9(4)	s 10(5)
s 9(5)	s 10(6)
s 9(6)	s 10(8)
s 9(7)	ss 10(9), 11(1), (3)
s 10	s 7(1)–(9)
s 11	s 8
s 12	s 9
s 13(1)	s 23(1)
s 13(2)	s 23(2)
s 13(3)	s 23(3)
s 13(3A)	s 23(4)
s 13(4)	s 23(5)
s 13(5)	s 23(6)
s 13(6)	s 23(7)
s 13(7)	s 23(8)
s 13(8)	s 23(9), 11(1), (3)
s 13(9)	s 23(10)
s 14	s 24
s 15	s 25
s 18(1)	s 46(1)
s 18(2)	s 46(3)
s 18(3)	s 42
s 18(4)	s 46(4)
s 19(1)	s 45(1)
s 19(2)	s 45(2)
s 19(3)	s 45(3), (4)
s 20(1)	—
s 20(2)	s 43
s 21(1)–(4), (6)–(8)	—
Sch 1, para 1	Sch 1, para 1
para 2	Sch 1, para 2
para 3	Sch 1, para 3
para 4	—
para 5	Sch 1, para 4
para 6	Sch 1, para 5(1), (2)
para 7	Sch 1, para 6
paras 8, 9	Sch 6, paras 1–3
Sch 2, para 1	ss 11(5), (6), 13(9), 46(1), Sch 3, para 1
paras 2, 3	Sch 3, paras 2, 3
para 4(1)	Sch 3, para 4(1)
para 4(2)	Sch 3, para 4(3)
para 4(3)	Sch 3, para 4(2)
para 5(1)	Sch 3, para 5(1)

Destination Table to Education Act 1996 & School Inspections Act 1996

Education (Schools) Act 1992 (c 38)	School Inspections Act 1996 (c 57)
para 5(2)	Sch 3, para 5(3)
para 5(3)	Sch 3, para 5(2)
paras 6–8	Sch 3, paras 6–8
para 9	s 13(1)–(8)
para 9A	s 14
para 9B(1)	s 15(1)
para 9B(2)	s 15(2)
para 9B(3)	s 15(4)
para 9B(4)	s 15(5)
para 9C(1), (3)	s 20(1)
para 9C(2)	s 20(2)
para 9C(4)	s 20(3)
para 9C(5)	s 20(4)
para 10	s 21
para 11	s 22
para 12	s 12
para 13	Sch 4, para 1
para 14	Sch 4, para 2
para 15	Sch 4, para 3
Sch 3, para 1(1)–(3)	Sch 2, para 1(1)–(3)
para 2	Sch 2, para 2
para 3(1)	Sch 2, para 3
para 3(2)	—
Sch 4, paras 2, 3	Rep 1992 c 53, s18(2), Sch 4, Pt I
para 7	—
Sch 5	—

Judicial Pensions and Retirement Act 1993 (c 8)	School Inspections Act 1996 (c 57)
Sch 6, para 67	Sch 2, para 1(3)

Education Act 1993 (c 35)	School Inspections Act 1996 (c 57)
s 204(1), (4)	s 11(1)–(3)
s 204(2)	ss 11(4), (6), 27(9), 46(1)
s 204(3)	s 13(9)
s 205	s 12
s 206	s 13(1)–(8)
s 207	s 14
s 208(1)	s 15(1)
s 208(2)	s 15(2)
s 208(3)	s 15(3)
s 208(4)	s 15(5)
s 209	s 16
s 210	s 17
s 211	s 18
s 212	s 19
s 213	s 26
s 214(1)–(8)	s 27(1)–(8)
s 214(9)	s 27(10)
s 215	s 28

Appendix 3

Education Act 1993 (c 35)	School Inspections Act 1996 (c 57)
s 216	s 29
s 217	s 30
s 218	s 31
s 219	s 32
s 220	s 33
s 221	s 34
s 222	s 35
s 223	s 36
s 224	s 37
s 225	s 38
s 226	s 39
s 227(1)–(3)	s 40
s 227(4)	s 10(4)
s 228(1)	s 41(1), (2)
s 228(2)–(4)	s 41(3)–(5)
s 259(1)	—
s 259(2)	s 23(1)–(4)
s 259(3)	s 23(8)
s 299(1)–(4)*	s 44(1)
s 299(5)*	s 44(2)
s 301(1), (2)†	s 45(1)
s 301(3)†	s 45(2)
s 301(6)†	s 45(3), (4)
s 305(1)†	s 46(1)
s 305(3)†	s 46(4)
s 306*	—
Sch 12	Sch 5
Sch 19, para 173(1)(a)	s 10(3)
para 173(1)(b)	s 10(8)
para 173(1)(c)	ss 10(9), 11(1)
para 173(2)	—
para 173(3)	ss 11(6), 13(9), 46(1), Sch 3, para 1
para 173(4)	Sch 3, paras 2, 3(5), 4(1), 5(1), 6, 7
para 173(5)	ss 13(1)–(8), 14, 15(1), (2), (4), (5), 20
para 173(6)	ss 21, 22
para 173(7)	s 12
para 173(8)	Sch 4, para 2(4)
para 173(9)	Sch 4, para 3(3)

Appendix 4

REVERTER AND THE SCHOOL SITES ACTS

1   As mentioned in Chapter 1, in the early nineteenth century the established and dissenting churches took the initiative in attempting to secure elementary education for the populace. To facilitate the acquisition of land for the charitable purpose of providing schools the School Sites Act 1841 made possible the conveyance of sites of up to one acre for schools and school teachers' houses out of a landowner's estate or manor where the grantor was not the absolute owner or was under some other legal disability. The legislation also provided a simplified form of conveyance (which could also be used by an absolute owner) for such sites; and where the grantees were an incumbent and parish officers they were treated as a corporate body; so that they and their successors became ex officio trustees of a charity. It also included provisos that if the land ceased to be used for the purposes for which it had been granted it would immediately and automatically revert.[1]

2   The School Sites Acts 1844, 1849, 1851 and 1852 were passed to explain the 1841 Act and (the 1852 Act) to extend its provisions to schools for 'the sons of yeomen and tradesmen and others' and to theological training colleges. This legislation preserved the right of reverter. Its exercise has given rise to complex problems and remains a live issue because many voluntary schools which may in due course be discontinued still occupy the sites conveyed under the School Sites Acts. There may be more than 2,000 of these sites. The Reverter of Sites Act 1987 resolves the major difficulty identified by a Law Commission working party[2] as follows.

3   It is not disputed that trustees under the School Sites Act hold a legal estate determinable when the circumstances come about that give rise to reverter. Before the 1925 property legislation the legal estate would automatically have shifted from the trustees to the person entitled on reverter. Subsequently it is arguable that despite saving provisions in the Law of Property Act 1925 s 7(1) and (3), the effect of s 3(3) is that only the equitable, beneficial, interest passes. If this is the case the trustees are not divested of the legal estate but continue to hold it on trust, not now for the charity but for the person entitled on reverter until, when the person entitled is ascertained, they convey the legal estate as required by s 3(3). So it was held in *Re Clayton's Deed Poll*[3], but there is more recent authority, also at first instance, (in *Re Rowhook Mission Hall, Horsham*[4]) that, as before the 1925 legislation, on reverter the trustees lose the entirety of their interest. Nourse J's conclusion in the last-mentioned case is consistent with two earlier decisions.

1   See *Dennis v Malcolm* [1934] Ch 244 and *Re Cawston's Conveyance* [1939] 4 All ER 140. In *A-G v Shadwell* [1910] 1 Ch 92 it was held that land having been granted for use as a day school reverted on change of use to a Sunday School.
2   *Property Law. Rights of Reverter* (Law Commission No 111, Cmnd 8410). November 1981.
3   [1980] Ch 99.
4   [1985] Ch 62.

Appendix 4

In *Re Ingleton Charity*[5] a school the subject of the 1841 Act was closed in 1929. In 1952 the premises were sold by the trustees (no reverter claim having been made). The court held that the statutory limitation period had run and that the trustees held a possessory title free from the right of reverter, but that they had at all times been trustees for charitable (educational) purposes, and that the proceeds could not be diverted from those purposes. In *Re Chavasse's Conveyance*[6] a former school site bombed during the Second World War was afterwards compulsorily purchased for other purposes by Birmingham Corporation. The court held that the trustees were not entitled to the purchase money because reverter had operated so as to leave them nothing to convey.

4   The Reverter of Sites Act 1987 repealed s 3(3) of the Law of Property Act 1925 and amended s 7(1). Section 1 of the 1987 Act provides that on land ceasing to be used for the purposes for which it was conveyed under the School Sites Acts no right of reverter arises, but the land becomes vested in the trustees on a trust for sale. (The provision is retrospective in applying to land in respect of which a right of reverter has already arisen.) The trustees then hold the land, or the proceeds of sale, as trustees for the reverter. If they wish to apply to the Charity Commissioners under s 2 to establish a scheme which extinguishes the rights of beneficiaries they must first, under s 3, take steps to trace the revertee (unless any claim has already become statute-barred). If after three months they have failed to trace him they may make an application. The scheme will require the trustees to hold the property on trust for the charitable purposes specified in the Commissioners' order—purposes as similar in character as practicable to those for which the land was previously held, but the Commissioners are given a broad discretion. If a beneficiary makes a valid claim within five years of the making of the Commissioners' order he is to receive the value of his rights as compensation.

5   Section 2 also requires the Charity Commissioners to give notice of, and invite representation on, their proposed scheme, and, by s 4, once the order is made it too is to be published, and it is subject to a right of appeal to the High Court.

6   The substitution of a trust for sale, under the 1987 Act, for reverter does not, it seems, wholly dismiss the following questions: (a) when does reverter occur, (b) what reverts, and (c) to whom (or what) does the land revert.

7   The answer to (a)—immediately upon cesser of the charitable use—leaves open the question of fact: what constitutes cesser? In *Re Chavasse* it was held that cesser did not take place when the school was bombed but some years later, upon intentional permanent discontinuance of the school. In practice there may be a dispute as to the date of permanent discontinuance.

8   Question (b)—what reverts—is material if part only of the land in question ceases to be used for the charitable purpose. It is arguable on the wording of the 1841 Act that the whole of the land reverts, but in the absence of authority the Law Commission working party took the better view to be that part-cesser leads to part-reverter—a conclusion that is not problem-free if the site is built upon, and, for example, the upper floor but not the ground floor remains in use for charitable purposes.

9   The 1841 Act states that the land 'shall . . . revert to and become a portion of the said estate in fee simple or otherwise, or of any manor or land as aforesaid . . .' But this is no complete answer to question (c) if only because as in *Re Cawston's Conveyance*[7] the site of the redundant school may be an isolated one. In that case the charitable trustees argued that since the site did not form part of the land, reverter did not arise. The Court of Appeal, however, interpreted the Act so that reverter operated in favour of

---

5 [1956] Ch 585.
6 1954 unreported, but see Cmnd 8410 at p 6.
7 [1939] 4 All ER 140. See also *Marchant v Onslow* [1994] 2 All ER 707.

the grantor's personal representatives. This decision raises the major question whether, as a fixed general rule, a site, even if it is not isolated, always reverts to the grantor's representatives (or to the settlement under which he held it) rather than rejoins the 'estate' from which it was severed (which over the years may have been split into numerous plots in different ownerships and which may not all be contiguous). Whatever the answer, identification of the persons entitled under the reverter may well be difficult.

10   There are additional uncertainties. Section 14 of the 1841 Act has been understood, despite ambiguous limiting words in the reverter provisos, to give trustees the power of sale of land given or acquired under the Act so as to move the school, as an existing insititution, to another site; but there is no direct authority on the point. It does seem clear, however, that trustees cannot exercise their power once the reverter proviso has taken effect. Also, events occurring between the grant and reverter may throw up problems on which the courts have not spoken. For example, the donor may have been tenant for life of an entailed estate and the entail may subsequently have been broken. It is not clear how a site devolves in those circumstances. Nor is it clear whether rights of common lost by the grant revive upon reverter.

11   Section 6 of the 1987 Act confirms that the power conferred by s 14 of the 1841 Act is exercisable at any time in relation to land which might otherwise become the subject of a trust under s 1; and the exercise of that power prevents a section 1 trust from arising.

12   The court and the Charity Commissioners have powers, pre-dating the 1987 Act, to make *cy-près* schemes for charitable purposes—but the circumstances which point to the need for a scheme may be those in which reverter comes about; and once reverter has occurred the land is released from charitable trusts and it is too late to make a scheme which affects the revertee's rights. There are other complications, some related to the *Clayton* decision, which may make court and Commissioners reluctant to act.

13   Where court and Commissioners—more frequently the latter—do make a scheme it will reflect the original trust purpose—normally to benefit a particular locality. (See *A-G v Price*[8], in which the Court of Appeal held that following the closure of a denominational school a *cy-près* scheme should not permit the premises to be let at a rent to be applied to church purposes generally, but that the premises should be used for the education of the poor in the locality which was the subject of the original grant.)

---

8   [1912] 1 Ch 667.

Appendix 5

THE EDUCATION ASSETS BOARD

1   The Education Assets Board were foreshadowed, under a different name, in the White Paper, '*Higher Education: Meeting the Challenge*', Cm 114 (1987), para 4.26 of which stated their main task as being to 'resolve any difficulties in the apportionment of assets to transferred institutions and to assist them to make arrangements as quickly as possible for the holding of their own assets'. The Board were established by the 1988 Act s 197 to deal with such matters arising from the transfer of property, rights and liabilities from LEAs to grant-maintained schools and to instititions in the polytechnics and colleges sector (now superseded by the higher education sector). The 1992 FHE Act s 36 extended their role to deal with property transfer to the new further education sector, and the 1993 Act replaced the provisions in the 1988 Act relating to grant-maintained schools. The 1993 Act provisions were superseded by those in the 1996 Act.

Composition and administration

2   The Board are established under s 197 of the 1988 Act. They are a body corporate consisting of a chairman and between two and ten other members appointed by the Secretary of State, who is to have regard to the desirability of including persons with successful experience in property management, local government or education. He may make them grants, and they are to comply with his directions. They do not enjoy Crown status. They may require information from LEAs and from governing bodies of LEA and grant-maintained schools and of institutions in the further and higher education sectors. Schedule 8 to the 1988 Act
(a)   gives the Board incidental powers, including the power to enter into contracts, ie employment and business contracts,
(b)   provides that one of the Board's members is to be their chief officer (appointed on the first occasion by the Secretary of State but subsequently by the Board with his approval),
(c)   relates to the tenure of office, salaries, allowances and pensions of members, who are disqualified from membership of the House of Commons,
(d)   empowers the Board to appoint staff and settle terms of service,
(e)   empowers the Board to appoint committees, which may include a joint consultative committee with local authority representatives, and a committee to represent the voluntary colleges' interest,
(f)   authorises delegation of functions to chairman, committee or chief officer,
(g)   authorises the Secretary of State to be represented at meetings, but otherwise gives the Board power to regulate their own procedure,
(h)   relates to application of seal and proof of documents, and
(i)   provides for the keeping of accounts under the supervision of the Comptroller and Auditor General.

Functions

3   The principal functions of the Board are those mentioned below, which were conferred or imposed by the 1988 Act ss 198, 199 and 201 and Sch 10; the 1992 FHE Act ss 36 (with Sch 5 and supplemented by Sch 7), 40 and 42; and provisions in the 1993 Act now superseded by the 1996 Act ss 205 and 207. The Board may carry on ancillary activities.

Transfers of property etc to grant-maintained schools and higher education institutions

4   The 1988 Act s 198 with Sch 10 (as amended, in particular, by the 1992 FHE Act Sch 8, paras 61 to 64) applies to transfers, under the 1996 Act s 201, and the 1988 Act ss 126 and 130 (see paras 4.13, 10.67 and 10.75 respectively), of property, rights and liabilities from LEAs to grant-maintained schools,[1] higher education corporations and institutions designated under the 1988 Act s 129 for funding by a higher education funding council, and also, if 1988 Act s 228 is applied, to transfers to corporations conducting grant-aided higher education institutions in Wales. Where Sch 10 gives functions to the Board they are not to be performed by the transferee, on whose behalf the Board act. The Board are to give the higher education funding council particulars of property etc transferred.

5   Schedule 10 is concerned with (a) the identification and allocation of shared property, rights and liabilities so as to enable institutions and authorities properly to discharge their respective functions, (b) documents of title and construction of transfer agreements, and (c) the position of third parties affected by transfers.

Excepted loan liabilities: higher education institutions

6   By the 1988 Act s 199 the Board and the LEA concerned are to attempt to agree how a loan in relation to higher education corporations and institutions designated under s 129 is to be repaid to the LEA by the body or persons to whom the liability would have been transferred by ss 126 or 130 had it not been excepted under those sections. Whatever the terms agreed the loan may be discharged by a single lump sum. The Board are to notify the Secretary of State of likely failure to agree, upon which he may determine the matter after consulting the authority and with the assistance of the Board. See the Education Assets Board (Transfers under the Education Reform Act 1988) Regulations 1992, SI 1992/1348.

Transfers of property to further education institutions

7   The 1992 FHE Act s 36 and Sch 5 (supplemented by Sch 7) apply to transfers of land, property or other rights to further education corporations under s 23 and to designated institutions under s 32. Sch 5 has a similar compass to the 1988 Act Sch 10. Where Sch 5 gives functions to the Board they are not to be performed by the transferee, on whose behalf the Board act. The Board are to give the further education funding council particulars of property etc transferred.

---

1   See *Secretary of State for Education ex p London Borough of Southwark* [1995] ELR 308.

Appendix 5

Wrongful disposals and contracts: grant-maintained schools

8   By the 1996 Act s 205, where a local authority have made a wrongful disposal of land under s 204 and the contract has not been executed, or consists of granting an option to acquire the land or an interest in it, the Board may, by notice, repudiate the contract or option. Where the transaction has been carried through and an interest in land has been granted or disposed of, the Board may be authorised by the Secretary of State to acquire that interest compulsorily under the Acquisition of Land Act 1981, and they are then to convey it to the new governing body of the school. The Board may recover any compensation and interest they have to pay in respect of the purchase, together with their costs and expenses, from the local authority. (These compulsory purchase powers were not contained in the 1988 legislation.)

9   By the 1996 Act s 207, a contract entered into without the required consent under s 206 may, before it is performed, be repudiated by the Board by notice in writing. If the contract is repudiated after the proposals have been implemented, repudiation takes effect as if the local authority (and not the governing body) were party to the contract, and they assume liabilities.

10   The provisions of the 1996 Act ss 205 and 207 apply with modifications under the Education (Schools Conducted by Education Associations) Regulations 1994, SI 1993/3103, reg 4, Sch 3, and the Education (Special Schools Conducted by Education Associations) Regulations 1994, SI 1994/1084, reg 3, Sch 1.

Wrongful disposals: higher education institutions

11   The 1988 Act s 201 applied to disposals, in contravention of s 137, of land which until 22 July 1987 was obtained, used, or held, for the purposes of higher education institutions maintained by LEAs (see para 10.66 n 4).

12   Where an LEA entered into a contract wrongfully to dispose of land or to grant or dispose of an interest in land, or grant an option to acquire land, the Board had power to repudiate it, and the repudiation took effect as if made by the LEA, so that the latter incurred any liability to damages.

13   Where the wrongful disposal was the granting or disposing of any interest in land, the Board were empowered, if so authorised by the Secretary of State, to purchase it compulsorily and the legislation on compulsory purchase procedures and compensation applied. On completion of compulsory purchase the Board were to transfer the interest purchased to the appropriate transferee—the higher education corporation or designated institution. The Board were entitled to recover from the LEA concerned the amount of the compensation on compulsory purchase, and their costs.

Wrongful disposals and contracts: further education institutions

14   Where a local authority have made a wrongful disposal of land in contravention of the 1992 FHE Act s 39 (control of disposals of land destined for an institution in the further education sector), s 40 applies, in the same terms as the 1988 Act s 201.

15   Where a local authority have entered into a contract in contravention of the 1992 FHE Act s 41 which might bind the new governing body (see para 10.44) the Board may, by s 42, repudiate the contract by notice in writing at any time before performance, and the repudiation takes effect as if made by the local authority

Appendix 6
CORE GOVERNORS FOR GROUPS OF GRANT-MAINTAINED SCHOOLS

1   References made to core governors at para 4.80(d). The following summary derives from Schedule 25 to the 1996 Act, brought into effect by section 285.

2   Core governors may be appointed either by the governing body or externally appointed. Externally appointed governors may be either (a) appointed in respect of a particular school in the group, being a school which was (i) a voluntary school immediately before it became grant-maintained or (ii) newly established under the 1996 Act s 212; or (b), where the group consists only of such schools, appointed in respect of the group otherwise than by the governing body.

3   Core governors appointed under (a) above are to be appointed by persons named for that purpose in the instrument, and, if the school has a specific religious character, or there is a trust deed, are required to be appointed so as to secure that character or comply with the deed. Core governors other than those externally appointed in respect of a particular school in the group are to be persons with the characteristics of 'first' governors (see para 4.31 n 19). A member of the staff at any of the schools in the group may become a core governor only by external appointment.

4   Core governors appointed under (b) above are (i) to number at least one more than the number of governors who are not externally appointed (including a notional head teacher where the head chooses not to be a governor); and (ii) there is to be the same number of externally appointed governors in respect of each school in the group. The total number of externally appointed core governors for the group as a whole is to be not less than the highest number, not exceeding the number under (i), which is consistent with (ii).

5   In the case of groups not appointed under (b) above, (i) there is to be an externally appointed governor in respect of each school in the group which falls under (a) above; and (ii) at least two core governors (or if all but one of the schools in the group fall within (a) above, at least one) are to be parents of registered pupils; and the same requirement as regards numbers applies as respects members of the local community, but one person may satisfy both requirements. In appointing core governors the governing body are to secure that they include members of the local business community (who may also satisfy one or both of the foregoing requirements). The number of core governors is not to be less than five, or, consistent with this requirement, more than the number of schools in the group, but is to be large enough to secure that the core governors and the parent governors together outnumber the other governors (including a notional head teacher where the head chooses not to be a governor).

Appendix 7

CONSTITUTION AND PROCEDURE OF ADMISSION APPEAL COMMITTEES

1 Admission appeals relating to (a) county and voluntary schools are mentioned at para 7.20, (b) grant-maintained schools, at para 7.21.

Constitution

2 Where arrangements for admission appeals are made by LEAs[1], appeals are heard by appeal committees comprising three, five or seven members nominated by the authority.[2] Committees are to include one lay member—a person without personal experience in managing or providing education at a school otherwise than in a voluntary capacity. The Secretary of State may require authorities to advertise for lay members and to consider the applications received.

3 The following rules apply: (a) lay members are not to be members or employees of the LEA, or to have any connection with the LEA (or members or employees of the LEA) which puts their impartiality in doubt; (b) members of the LEA are not to outnumber the other members of a committee; (c) members or employees of the LEA are not to be committee chairmen; and (d) a person may not consider on appeal a decision in which he has been personally concerned or if he is a teacher at the school in question.

4 With the exception of the lay member, committees are drawn from a panel comprising members of the LEA and other persons who have experience in education,[3] are acquainted with educational conditions in the area, or are parents of registered pupils at a school. The panel are not to include any person employed by the authority otherwise than as a teacher.

Procedure

5 The grounds of an appeal are to be set out in writing. The appellant is to be given an opportunity to make his case orally and may be accompanied by a friend or be represented. The appeal committee are to take into account, inter alia, parental preference

1 Under 1996 Act s 423. Arrangements made by governing bodies of aided and special agreement schools appeal committees (and panels) are similar. As to grant-maintained schools see s 429 and Sch 23.
2 1996 Act Sch 33. By para 6, requirements regarding lay members are in the Education (Lay Members of Appeal Committees) Regulations 1994, SI 1994/1303. By para 7, members of committees are to be indemnified against legal costs and expenses reasonably incurred in good faith. As to voting rights see the Local Government and Housing Act 1989 s 13. As to allowances payable see ibid s 18 and the Local Authorities (Members' Alowances) Regulations 1991, SI 1991/351.
3 See *R v Croydon London Borough Council, ex p Leney* (1986) 85 LGR 466, F [90].

Constitution and Procedure of Admission Appeal Committes

(see para 7.03) and published arrangements for admissions (see para 7.12). One member of a committee may not drop out during the course of an appeal, to be replaced by another[4]. Appeals are to be heard privately unless those who made the arrangements direct otherwise. A member of the (a) LEA may attend as observer where the LEA made the arrangements, (b) Council on Tribunals may attend any appeal as observer.

6 Decisions of an appeal committee are to be by simple majority, the chairman having a casting (second) vote. Decisions, reasoned, are to be sent to the appellant and LEA. Subject to the requirements mentioned, matters relating to the procedure on appeals, including the time within which they are to be brought, are to be decided by the LEA who made the arrangements. Local authority committee procedures[5] do not apply.

7 Appeal committees have been brought within the jurisdiction of Local Government Ombudsmen,[6] and they are under the direct supervision of the Council on Tribunals.[7]

---

4 See *R v Camden Education Appeal Committee, ex p X* [1991] COD 195, F[103].
5 Under Local Government Act 1972 s 106 or Sch 12 para 44.
6 1996 Act Sch 37 para 27. (See para 15.40.)
7 See the Tribunals and Inquiries Act 1992, s 1(1)(a) and Sch 1. There is no right of appeal to the High Court under s 11 on a point of law.

Appendix 8

STAFFING OF LEA SCHOOLS (EXCEPT AIDED SCHOOLS) WITHOUT DELEGATED BUDGETS

1   The arrangements for staffing county, controlled, special agreement and LEA special schools without delegated budgets (see para 13.27) are provided for in the 1996 Act Sections 133 and 135, and in Schedules 13 and 19.

2   Articles are to provide for a selection panel to be constituted to consider the appointment of the head teacher. The panel is to consist of not less than three persons appointed by the LEA and not less than three governors appointed by the governing body; and the number appointed by the governing body is not to be less than that appointed by the LEA. Members of the panel may be replaced at any time. Regulations govern the meetings and proceedings of selection panels.[1] The chief education officer of the LEA (or a member of his department) is to have the right to attend all panel proceedings, including interviews, to advise the members.[2]

3   Articles are to require the LEA to appoint an acting head teacher, after consulting the governing body, on a vacancy occurring; and the vacancy for the substantive post is to be advertised in publications circulating throughout England and Wales which the LEA consider appropriate. The selection panel are to interview applicants as they think fit, and if they fail to agree about who is to be interviewed the governor members may nominate one or two applicants for interview and the other members one or two different applicants. If the panel are unable to agree to recommend the LEA to appoint any of the applicants interviewed they are to consider interviewing other applicants. If they do so and are still unable to make a recommendation, or if they decide not to do so, they may require the LEA to re-advertise the vacancy. If the LEA decline to appoint a person recommended, the panel are to consider interviewing applicants not previously interviewed and recommending one of them, and if necessary request the LEA to re-advertise the vacancy. The LEA are to comply with that request, and may re-advertise on their own account if, the post having been duly advertised, the panel have failed to make an acceptable recommendation or a request to re-advertise, after having had sufficient time to carry out their functions.[3]

4   Articles are to provide for deputy head teachers to be appointed either (a) under the arrangements for head teachers as above (but articles do not to have make provision for an acting deputy), and the head teacher, if not a member of the panel, is entitled to be present to advise at their proceedings, including interviews, and is in any event to be

1   1996 Act Sch 13 paras 1 and 2. See the Education (School Government) Regulations 1989, SI 1989/1503.
    A selection panel (See SI 1989/1503, reg 29) cannot operate without their full complement (*R v Birmingham City Council ex p McKenna* (1991) Times, 16 May.
2   1996 Act Sch 13 para 3(11).
3   Ibid para 3.

consulted before a recommendation is made to the LEA; or (b) in accordance with the arrangements described in the following paragraph.[4]

5   Articles are to require LEAs to deal with vacancies in the school complement by first deciding whether to retain an existing post, and then, if they decide to do so or the post is a new one, either advertising the vacancy or filling it with an existing or prospective employee. (The procedures do not apply in the case of a temporary appointment made pending (a) the return to work of the holder of the post or (b) the taking of any steps the articles require concerning the vacancy.)[5]

6   When the post is advertised, much the same procedures apply as in the case of a head teacher, but advertisement does not have to be nationwide and the governing body fill the role of the panel; and once the post has been advertised an LEA may make an appointment only after the proper procedures have been followed or they decide to fill it with an existing or prospective employee. When the post is not advertised the governing body are entitled to determine a specification for it in consultation with the head teacher. The LEA are to have regard to the specification and to consult the governing body and the head teacher when considering whom to appoint. Whether the post is advertised or not, articles are to enable the governing body to delegate their functions to one or more governors or to the head teacher, or to both acting together.[6]

7   In case of urgent need to appoint a particular person in their employ to a teaching post an LEA may act without consulting the governing body if they are unable to contact the chairman or vice-chairman.[7]

8   Articles are to require the LEA to consult the governing body and head teacher before appointing any person to work at the school otherwise than as (a) a teacher, (b) in a non-teaching post in its complement, or (c) solely in connection with meals and/or midday supervision.[8]

9   Articles are to require the LEA to consult the governing body and head teacher (except where he is the person concerned) before dismissing any person (except a reserved teacher, see para 13.33) holding a post in the school complement or working solely at the school in any other post (save in the provision of school meals and midday supervision) or otherwise requiring him to cease work at the school, or permitting him to retire so that he would be entitled to premature retirement compensation (see para 13.74). The LEA are to consult similarly before extending a teacher's initial period of probation (if any) or deciding whether he has completed it successfully; and to consider the recommendation of a governing body that a person should cease to work at the school. It does not follow from the requirement to consult that the LEA may act only on the recommendation of the governing body.[9] Both governing body and head teacher are to have power to suspend (without loss of emoluments) any person from working at the school when one or other are of the opinion that his exclusion is required, and on doing so the one is to inform the other and the LEA, who may direct the end of suspension.[10] This provision appears to be without prejudice to the LEA's power to suspend an employee.

---

4   Ibid para 4.
5   Ibid para 5.
6   Ibid paras 6 to 9.
7   SI 1989/1503, reg 31.
8   1996 Act Sch 13, para 10.
9   See *Curtis v Manchester City Council* (1976) Times, 27 May, *Honeyford v Bradford Metropolitan City Council* [1986] IRLR 32, CA and *Dyke v Hereford and Worcester County Council* [1989] ICR 800.
10 1996 Act Sch 13, para 11. As to cases on dismissal see 13.20 n 7(c).

Appendix 8

9   Articles are to provide that the clerk to the governing body is to be appointed by the LEA in accordance with arrangements determined by them in consultation with the governing body, except in the case of controlled and special agreement schools where the articles already make provision for his appointment. The LEA may dismiss a clerk only in accordance with like arrangements and with the same exception. The LEA are to consider any representations by the governing body as to their clerk's dismissal.[11]

11   1996 Act s 135.

Appendix 9

EDUCATION ACT 1997

Chapter 44

Arrangement of Sections

Part I

Assisted Places Scheme

Section
1   Extension of assisted places scheme to schools providing only primary education.

Part II

School Discipline

Responsibility for discipline

2   Responsibility for discipline: LEA-maintained schools.
3   Responsibility for discipline: grant-maintained and grant-maintained special schools.

Power to restrain pupils

4   Power of members of staff to restrain pupils.

Detention

5   Detention outside school hours lawful despite absence of parental consent.

Exclusion of pupils from school

6   Variation of limit on fixed-period exclusions: all maintained schools.
7   Exclusion or re-instatement appeals: LEA-maintained schools.
8   Exclusion appeals: grant-maintained and grant-maintained special schools.

LEA plans

9   LEA plans relating to children with behavioural difficulties.

Appendix 9

Part III

School admissions

Chapter I

County and voluntary schools

Partially-selective schools

10 Restriction of right to refuse admission to partially-selective school.

Children permanently excluded from two or more schools

11 No requirement to admit children permanently excluded from two or more schools.
12 Appeals in the case of children permanently excluded from two or more schools.

Home-school partnership documents

13 Home-school partnership documents.

Chapter II

Grant-maintained schools

14 Corresponding provisions about admissions to grant-maintained schools.

Part IV

Baseline assessments and pupils' performance

Chaper I

Baseline assessments

15 Introductory.
16 Adoption of baseline assessment schemes.
17 Assessment of pupils in accordance with scheme.
18 Regulations for purposes of this Chapter.

Chapter II

Pupils' performance

19 School performance targets.
20 Provision of information about individual pupils' performance.

Education Act 1997

Part V

Supervision of curriculum for schools and external qualifications

Chaper I

The Qualifications and Curriculum Authority

Establishment of the Authority

21   The Qualifications and Curriculum Authority.

Functions of the Authority

22   General function of Authority to advance education and training.
23   Functions of the Authority in relation to curriculum and assessment.
24   Functions of the Authority in relation to external vocational and academic qualifications.
25   Other functions of the Authority.
26   Supplementary provisions relating to discharge by Authority of their functions.

Chapter II

The Qualifications, Curriculum and Assessment Authority for Wales

Renaming of the Authority

27   The Qualifications, Curriculum and Assessment Authority for Wales.

Functions of the Authority

28   General function of Authority to advance education and training.
29   Functions of the Authority in relation to curriculum and assessment.
30   Functions of the Authority in relation to external vocational and academic qualifications.
31   Other functions of the Authority.
32   Supplementary provisions relating to discharge by Authority of their functions.

Chapter III

Provisions supplementary to Chapters I and II

Dissolution of existing bodies

33   Dissolution of existing bodies.

Transfer of property and staff

34   Transfer of property.
35   Transfer of staff.

Levy on bodies awarding accredited qualifications

36   Levy on bodies awarding qualifications accredited by relevant Authority.

Appendix 9

Chapter IV

Control of certain courses leading to external qualifications

37 Requirement for approval of certain publicly-funded and school courses leading to external qualifications.

Part VI

Inspection of local education authorities and school inspections

Chapter I

Inspection of local education authorities

38 Inspection of LEAs.
39 Reports of inspections under s 38 and action plan by LEA.
40 Inspector's rights of entry etc.
41 Inspections involving collaboration of Audit Commission.

Chapter II

School inspections

42 Miscellaneous amendments relating to school inspections.

Part VII

Careers education and guidance

43 Provision of careers education in schools.
44 Schools and other institutions to co-operate with careers advisers.
45 Provision of careers information at schools and other institutions.
46 Extension or modification of provisions of ss 43 to 45.

Part VIII

Miscellaneous and general

Exceptional educational provision

47 Functions of LEAs as regards exceptional educational provision.

Management committees for pupil referral units

48 Management committees for pupil referral units.

Teachers not under contract of employment and persons having access to those under 19

49 Power to make regulations: teachers not under contract of employment and persons having access to those under 19.

Costs of teachers' premature retirement

50 Recoupment by local education authority of costs of teachers' premature retirement.

Education Act 1997

Definition of 'school'

51 Definition of 'school'.

Compulsory school age

52 Commencement of compulsory school age.

General provisions

53 Stamp duty.
54 Orders and regulations.
55 Financial provisions.
56 Construction.
57 Minor and consequential amendments, repeals etc.
58 Short title, commencement and extent etc.

Schedules

Schedule 1 Schedule inserted after Schedule 25 to the Education Act 1996.
Schedule 2 Schedule inserted after Schedule 33 to the Education Act 1996.
Schedule 3 Schedule inserted as Schedule 33B to the Education Act 1996.
Schedule 4 The Qualifications and Curriculum Authority.
Schedule 5 The Qualifications, Curriculum and Assessment Authority for Wales.
Schedule 6 School inspections.
Schedule 7 Minor and consequential amendments.
Schedule 8 Repeals.

An Act to amend the law relating to education in schools and further education in England and Wales; to make provision for the supervision of the awarding of external academic and vocational qualifications in England, Wales and Northern Ireland; and for connected purposes.

[21st March 1997]

General As introduced, the Bill for this Act included provisions (clauses 1 to 18 and Schedules 1 and 2) relaxing the controls on changes affecting the character or premises of schools and extending the power of the funding authority to establish grant-maintained schools. These provisions proved controversial, and when a General Election was announced, during the Report stage of the Bill in the House of Lords, the Government agreed to withdraw them in order to facilitate the enactment of the Bill.

As enacted, the Act falls into eight Parts.

Part I (section 1), which came into force on 4 April 1997, extends the Assisted Places Scheme to independent schools which provide only primary education.

Part II (sections 2 to 9 and Schedule 1) contains a series of measures relating to school discipline, including authority, subject to specified conditions, to detain pupils without their parents' consent (s 5), and revised provisions for the exclusion of pupils from a school and appeals against exclusion and reinstatement (ss 6–8). LEAs are required to make plans for dealing with children with behavioural difficulties (s 9, Sch 1).

Part III (sections 10 to 14, Schedules 2 and 3) relates to admissions and appeals, including provision for home-school partnership documents.

Part IV (sections 15 to 20) provides for baseline assessment schemes in primary schools (ss 15–18), for annual performance targets (s 19) and for the provision to the Secretary of State and others of information about the performance of individual pupils (s 20).

Part V (sections 21 to 37, Schedules 4 and 5) establishes the Qualifications and Curriculum Authority to replace the National Council for Vocational Qualifications and the School Curriculum and Assessment Authority, and renames the Curriculum and Assessment Authority for Wales as the Qualifications, Curriculum and Assessment Authority for Wales (ss 21-35, Schs 4 and 5). Provision is made for the payment of levies to the new Authorities by bodies awarding qualifications

Appendix 9

accredited by them (s 36); and for courses leading to external qualifications to be approved by the Secretary of State or a body designated by him.

Part VI Sections 38 to 41 provide for local education authorities to be inspected under arrangements made by the Chief Inspectors of Schools; section 42 and Schedule 6 make minor amendments to the School Inspections Act 1996.

Part VII (sections 43 to 46) provides for careers education and guidance for school pupils and students at institutions of further education.

Part VIII (sections 47 to 58, Schedules 7 and 8) contains miscellaneous and general provisions. These include provision for management committees for pupil referral units (s 45); for regulating teachers not under contract and voluntary helpers at schools and other institutions (s 49); and regarding the recoupment by LEAs of costs arising from the premature retirement of school staff on or after 21st March 1997 (s 50, now in force); an amendment of the definition of 'school' to exclude institutions providing further education for those aged 16-18 (s 51); and provision for specifying the date on which a child begins to be of compulsory school age (s 52). The Act is to be construed as one with the Education Act 1996 (s 56).

Commencement Section 58 brought into force on 21st March 1997 s 50 and a consequential amendment of para 22 of Sch 19 to the 1996 Act (premature retirement), s 54 (orders and regulations) and s 58 itself. The other provisions of the Act require a Commencement Order to bring them into force. The Education Act 1997 (Commencement No 1) Order 1997, SI 1997/1153, brought s 1 (extension of the assisted places scheme) and a consequential repeal in s 479(2) of the 1996 Act into force on 4th April 1997. The Education Act 1997 (Commencement No 2 and Transitional Provisions) Order 1997, SI 1997/1468, brings further provisions into force, as noted in the text below. These include –

(a) on 14 June 1997: s 20: new s 537A, Education Act 1996 (provision of information about individual pupils' performance);

(b) on 1 September 1997: ss 10–12, 14, new Sch 33A and Sch 33B, paras 3, 4 (admission to partially-selective schools and of children permanently excluded from two or more schools); ss 38–42, Sch 6 (inspection of LEAs, school inspections); ss 44–46 (careers advisers and information);

(c) on 1 October 1997: ss 21–32, Schs 4, 5: establishment of the QCA and ACCAC; s 49(1)–(3): regulations barring access to persons under 19;

(d) on 1 November 1997: ss 15, 18 and parts of 33 16, 17: baseline assessments;

(e) on 1 December 1997: s 36 (levy on those awarding accredited vocational qualifications); s 48 (management committees for pupil referral units).

Hansard The Parliamentary proceedings on the Bill for this Act were—

House of Commons
Second Reading	11 November 1996, cols 37–125
Standing Committee D	19, 21, 26, 28 November, 3, 5, 10, 12, 17 December 1996 and 14, 16 January 1997
Report and Third Reading	27 January 1997, cols 73–123
	28 January 1997, cols 157–261

House of Lords
Second Reading	10 February 1997, cols 11–33, 42–95
Committee	24, 25 February and 3 March 1997, cols 905–970, 985–1030, 1063–1111, 1128–1177, 1504–1696
Report	17, 19 March 1997, cols 654–714, 724–756, 916–924
Third Reading	19 March 1997, cols 924–936

House of Commons
Consideration of Lords Amendments	19 March 1998, col 995
Royal Assent	21 March 1997

BE IT ENACTED by the Queen's most Excellent Majesty, by and with the advice and consent of the Lords Spiritual and Temporal, and Commons, in this present Parliament assembled, and by the authority of the same, as follows:-

Part I

Assisted places scheme

1 Extension of assisted places scheme to schools providing only primary education. In section 479 of the Education Act 1996 (the assisted places scheme), in subsection (2) (by virtue of which a 'participating school' must be one providing secondary education), the words 'providing secondary education' shall be omitted.

General Section 479(2) of the Education Act 1996 defines a 'participating school' as an independent school providing secondary education with which the Secretary of State makes a participation agreement for the purposes of the assisted places scheme. This section, by deleting the words 'providing secondary education' from this definition, extends the scope of the scheme to include independent schools which provide only primary education. (Schools providing both primary and secondary education are already within the scope of the scheme.) The words mentioned are formally repealed by s 57(4) and Sch 8. (The Education (Schools) Bill provides for the ending of this scheme.)

Commencement 4 April 1997: SI 1997/1153.

Definition See s 56(2) and the Education Act 1996 for 'assisted places scheme' and 'participating school': s 479(1) and (2); 'secondary education': s 2(2) and (5).

Part II

School Discipline

Responsibility for discipline

2 Responsibility for discipline: LEA-maintained schools. For section 154 of the Education Act 1996 there shall be substituted—

'**154 Responsibility of governing body and head teacher for discipline**
(1) The governing body of a county, voluntary or maintained special school shall ensure that policies designed to promote good behaviour and discipline on the part of its pupils are pursued at the school.
(2) In particular, the governing body—
    (a) shall make, and from time to time review, a written statement of general principles to which the head teacher is to have regard in determining any measures under subsection (4); and
    (b) where they consider it desirable that any particular measures should be so determined by the head teacher or that he should have regard to any particular matters—
        (i) shall notify him of those measures or matters, and
        (ii) may give him such guidance as they consider appropriate;
and in exercising their functions under this subsection the governing body shall have regard to any guidance given from time to time by the Secretary of State.
(3) Before making or revising the statement required by subsection (2)(a) the governing body shall consult (in such manner as appears to them to be appropriate)—
    (a) the head teacher; and
    (b) parents of registered pupils at the school.
(4) The head teacher shall determine measures (which may include the making of rules and provision for enforcing them) to be taken with a view to—
    (a) promoting, among pupils, self-discipline and proper regard for authority;
    (b) encouraging good behaviour and respect for others on the part of pupils;
    (c) securing that the standard of behaviour of pupils is acceptable; and
    (d) otherwise regulating the conduct of pupils.
(5) The head teacher shall, in determining such measures—
    (a) act in accordance with the current statement made by the governing body under subsection (2)(a); and
    (b) have regard to any notification or guidance given to him under subsection (2)(b).
(6) The standard of behaviour which is to be regarded as acceptable at the school shall be determined by the head teacher, so far as it is not determined by the governing body.
(7) The measures determined by the head teacher under subsection (4) shall be publicised by him in the form of a written document as follows—
    (a) he shall make the measures generally known within the school and to parents of registered pupils at the school; and
    (b) he shall in particular, at least once in every school year, take steps to bring them to the attention of all such pupils and parents and all persons employed at the school.
(8) The governing body and the head teacher shall, before any measures are determined

Appendix 9

under subsection (4), consult the local education authority on any matter arising from the proposed measures which can reasonably be expected—
  (a) to lead to increased expenditure by the authority, or
  (b) to affect the responsibilities of the authority as an employer.'

General This Part (sections 2 to 9 and Schedule 1) contains various provisions relating to school discipline. Section 2 replaces s 154, in Part II, Chapter VI, of the Education Act 1996 with a new section 154. This imposes a new duty on the governing bodies of county, voluntary and maintained special schools to ensure that their schools pursue policies designed to promote good behaviour and discipline, having regard to guidance given by the Secretary of State. After consulting the head teacher and parents, they are to make a written statement of general principles for the guidance of the head teacher, notifying him if there are any particular matters to which they attach importance, and, following further consultation, revise it from time to time. As before, the head teacher is responsible for setting standards and determining disciplinary measures, in line with the governing body's statement; he is to publicise them in writing and bring them to the attention of pupils, parents and staff every year. The requirement on the head teacher and governing body to consult the LEA, before determining these measures, about anything likely to lead to increased expenditure, or to affect the responsibilities of the LEA as an employer, remains.

Commencement A date to be appointed by the Secretary of State by order under s 58(3).

Definition See the Education Act 1996: 'county school': s 31(1); 'functions': s 579(1); 'governing body': s 182; 'head teacher' (generally): s 579(1); (in relation to a school organised in separate departments): s 132; 'the local education authority': s 579(1); 'maintained special school': ss 6(2), 33(1), 337(3); 'parent': s 576; 'pupil': ss 3(1), 19(5); 'registered pupil': s 434(5); 'voluntary school': ss 31(2), 32.

'Written' Expressions referring to writing are, unless the contrary intention appears, to be construed as including references to other modes of representing or reproducing words in visible form: Interpretation Act 1978, s 5, Sch 1.

3 Responsibility for discipline: grant-maintained and grant-maintained special schools
(1) After section 306 of the Education Act 1996 there shall be inserted—

'Discipline

306A Responsibility of governing body and head teacher for discipline
(1) The governing body of a grant-maintained school shall ensure that policies designed to promote good behaviour and discipline on the part of its pupils are pursued at the school.
(2) In particular, the governing body—
  (a) shall make, and from time to time review, a written statement of general principles to which the head teacher is to have regard in determining any measures under subsection (4); and
  (b) where they consider it desirable that any particular measures should be so determined by the head teacher or that he should have regard to any particular matters—
    (i) shall notify him of those measures or matters, and
    (ii) may give him such guidance as they consider appropriate;
and in exercising their functions under this subsection the governing body shall have regard to any guidance given from time to time by the Secretary of State.
(3) Before making or revising the statement required by subsection (2)(a) the governing body shall consult (in such manner as appears to them to be appropriate)—
  (a) the head teacher; and
  (b) parents of registered pupils at the school.
(4) The head teacher shall determine measures (which may include the making of rules and provision for enforcing them) to be taken with a view to—
  (a) promoting, among pupils, self-discipline and proper regard for authority;
  (b) encouraging good behaviour and respect for others on the part of pupils;
  (c) securing that the standard of behaviour of pupils is acceptable; and
  (d) otherwise regulating the conduct of pupils.
(5) The head teacher shall, in determining such measures—
  (a) act in accordance with the current statement made by the governing body under subsection (2)(a); and
  (b) have regard to any notification or guidance given to him under subsection (2)(b).
(6) The standard of behaviour which is to be regarded as acceptable at the school shall be determined by the head teacher, so far as it is not determined by the governing body.
(7) The measures determined by the head teacher under subsection (4) shall be publicised

Education Act 1997

by him in the form of a written document as follows—
   (a) he shall make the measures generally known within the school and to parents of registered pupils at the school; and
   (b) he shall in particular, at least once in every school year, take steps to bring them to the attention of all such pupils and parents and all persons employed at the school.'

(2) In Schedule 28 to that Act (government and conduct of grant-maintained special schools), in paragraph 15 (application of section 307 to such schools) for 'Section' there shall be substituted 'Each of sections 306A (responsibility for discipline) and' .

General Section 3 inserts a new s 306A in Part III, Chapter X, of the Education Act 1996. Sub-s (1) imposes the same duties on the governing bodies and head teachers of grant-maintained schools as those imposed in relation to LEA-maintained schools by s 154(1)–(7) of that Act, as inserted by s 2 above. Sub-s (2) amends para 15 of Sch 28 to that Act to apply these provisions in relation to grant-maintained special schools.
Commencement A date to be appointed by the Secretary of State by order under s 58(3).
Definition See the Education Act 1996: 'functions': s 579(1); 'grant-maintained school': s 183(1); 'grant-maintained special school': ss 337(4) and 346(3); 'head teacher': s 579(1); 'parent': s 576; 'pupil': ss 3(1), 19(5); 'registered pupil': s 434(5). For 'school year' see s 579(1), as amended by para 43 of Sch 7 to this Act.
'Written' Expressions referring to writing are, unless the contrary intention appears, to be construed as including references to other modes of representing or reproducing words in visible form: Interpretation Act 1978, s 5, Sch 1.

Power to restrain pupils

4 Power of members of staff to restrain pupils. After section 550 of the Education Act 1996 there shall be inserted—

'Power to restrain pupils

550A Power of members of staff to restrain pupils
(1) A member of the staff of a school may use, in relation to any pupil at the school, such force as is reasonable in the circumstances for the purpose of preventing the pupil from doing (or continuing to do) any of the following, namely—
   (a) committing any offence,
   (b) causing personal injury to, or damage to the property of, any person (including the pupil himself), or
   (c) engaging in any behaviour prejudicial to the maintenance of good order and discipline at the school or among any of its pupils, whether that behaviour occurs during a teaching session or otherwise.
(2) Subsection (1) applies where a member of the staff of a school is—
   (a) on the premises of the school, or
   (b) elsewhere at a time when, as a member of its staff, he has lawful control or charge of the pupil concerned;
but it does not authorise anything to be done in relation to a pupil which constitutes the giving of corporal punishment within the meaning of section 548.
(3) Subsection (1) shall not be taken to prevent any person from relying on any defence available to him otherwise than by virtue of this section.
(4) In this section—
   'member of the staff', in relation to a school, means any teacher who works at the school and any other person who, with the authority of the head teacher, has lawful control or charge of pupils at the school;
   'offence' includes anything that would be an offence but for the operation of any presumption that a person under a particular age is incapable of committing an offence.'

General This section inserts a new s 550A in Chapter II (Corporal punishment) of Part X of the Education Act 1996. The new section makes it clear that a member of staff (ie a teacher or any person who, with the authority of the head teacher, has lawful control or charge of pupils at the school) may use reasonable force to prevent a pupil committing an offence, causing personal injury to himself or others or damage to property, or engaging in behaviour prejudicial to the maintenance of good order and discipline at the school or among any of its pupils; and may do so on the school

Appendix 9

premises or anywhere else where he has lawful charge of the pupil concerned. This does not however authorise corporal punishment within the meaning of s 548. An 'offence' includes anything which would be an offence but for the presumption that a person under a certain age is incapable of committing a crime.
Commencement A date to be appointed by the Secretary of State by order under s 58(3).
Definition See the Education Act 1996: 'head teacher' , 'premises': s 579(1); 'pupil': ss 3(1), 19(5); 'school': s 4(as prospectively substituted by s 51).

Detention

5 **Detention outside school hours lawful despite absence of parental consent.** After the section 550A inserted in the Education Act 1996 by section 4 of this Act there shall be inserted—

'550B Detention outside school hours lawful despite absence of parental consent
(1) Where a pupil to whom this section applies is required on disciplinary grounds to spend a period of time in detention at his school after the end of any school session, his detention shall not be rendered unlawful by virtue of the absence of his parent's consent to it if the conditions set out in subsection (3) are satisfied.
(2) This section applies to any pupil who has not attained the age of 18 and is attending—
   (a) a school maintained by a local education authority;
   (b) a grant-maintained or grant-maintained special school; or
   (c) a city technology college or city college for the technology of the arts.
(3) The conditions referred to in subsection (1) are as follows—
   (a) the head teacher of the school must have previously determined, and have—
      (i) made generally known within the school, and
      (ii) taken steps to bring to the attention of the parent of every person who is for the time being a registered pupil there,
      that the detention of pupils after the end of a school session is one of the measures that may be taken with a view to regulating the conduct of pupils;
   (b) the detention must be imposed by the head teacher or by another teacher at the school specifically or generally authorised by him for the purpose;
   (c) the detention must be reasonable in all the circumstances; and
   (d) the pupil's parent must have been given at least 24 hours' notice in writing that the detention was due to take place.
(4) In determining for the purposes of subsection (3)(c) whether a pupil's detention is reasonable, the following matters in particular shall be taken into account—
   (a) whether the detention constitutes a proportionate punishment in the circumstances of the case; and
   (b) any special circumstances relevant to its imposition on the pupil which are known to the person imposing it (or of which he ought reasonably to be aware) including in particular—
      (i) the pupil's age,
      (ii) any special educational needs he may have,
      (iii) any religious requirements affecting him, and
      (iv) where arrangements have to be made for him to travel from the school to his home, whether suitable alternative arrangements can reasonably be made by his parent.
(5) Section 572, which provides for the methods by which notices may be served under this Act, does not preclude a notice from being given to a pupil's parent under this section by any other effective method.'

General This section inserts a new s 550B in Chapter II (Corporal punishment) of Part X of the Education Act 1996. The new section, which applies in relation to LEA-maintained, grant-maintained and grant-maintained special schools, CTCs and CCTAs, permits a pupil under 18 to be detained at school after the end of any session despite the lack of parental consent, thereby removing any risk that the school might be held liable for false imprisonment. For it to be lawful, the head teacher must have made it generally known within the school, and brought it to the attention of the parents of all registered pupils, that detention was a measure that might be taken to regulate the conduct of pupils; the detention must be imposed by the head teacher or an authorised teacher, and must be reasonable: see sub-ss (3)(c) and (4); and the parent of each pupil detained must have been given at least 24 hours' written notice, by one of the methods of service specified in s 572 of the 1996 Act, or by any other effective method, eg 'pupil post' or fax.
Commencement A date to be appointed by the Secretary of State by order under s 58(3).

Education Act 1997

Definition See the Education Act 1996: 'city college for the technology of the arts', 'city technology college': s 482(3); 'grant-maintained school': s 183(1); 'grant-maintained special school': ss 337(4) and 346(3); 'head teacher' (generally): s 579(1); (in relation to a school organised in separate departments): s 132; 'local education authority': s 12 (1)–(5); 'maintain': s 34; 'parent': s 576; 'pupil': ss 3(1), 19(5); 'registered pupil': s 434(5); 'special educational needs': s 312(1).

Exclusion of pupils from school

6 Variation of limit on fixed-period exclusions: all maintained schools
(1) In section 156 of the Education Act 1996 (exclusion of pupils from county, voluntary or maintained special school), in subsection (2) (which imposes a limit on fixed-period exclusions of 15 school days per term), for '15 school days in any one term' there shall be substituted '45 school days in any one school year'.
(2) In section 307 of that Act (exclusion of pupils from grant-maintained school), in subsection (1) (which also imposes a limit on fixed-period exclusions of 15 school days per term), for '15 school days in any one term' there shall be substituted '45 school days in any one school year'.

General This section amends ss 156 and 307 of the Education Act 1996 to enable the head teachers of LEA-maintained and grant-maintained schools to exclude pupils for fixed periods not exceeding 45 school days in any school year, rather than 15 school days per term.
Commencement A date to be appointed by the Secretary of State by order under s 58(3).
Definition See the Education Act 1996: 'school day': s 579(1). For 'school year' see s 579(1) as amended by para 43 of Sch 7 to this Act.

7 Exclusion or reinstatement appeals: LEA maintained schools
(1) Schedule 16 to the Education Act 1996 (appeals against exclusion or reinstatement of pupils) shall be amended as follows.
(2) After paragraph 7 there shall be inserted—

'7A (1) For the purpose of fixing the time (falling within the period mentioned in paragraph 7) at which the hearing of an appeal is to take place, the body mentioned in that paragraph shall take reasonable steps to ascertain any times falling within that period when—
    (a) the relevant person, or
    (b) any other person who wishes, and would be entitled, to appear and make oral representations in accordance with paragraph 8 or 9,
would be able to attend.
(2) Where in accordance with sub-paragraph (1) that body have ascertained any such times in the case of any such person, they shall, when fixing the time at which the hearing is to take place, take those times into account with a view to ensuring, so far as it is reasonably practicable to do so, that that person is able to appear and make such representations at the hearing.'

(3) For paragraph 8 there shall be substituted—

'8 (1) On an appeal by a pupil or parent the appeal committee shall give the appellant an opportunity of appearing and making oral representations, and shall allow him to be represented or to be accompanied by a friend.
(2) On such an appeal the committee shall allow—
    (a) the head teacher to make written representations and to appear and make oral representations,
    (b) the local education authority and the governing body to make written representations,
    (c) an officer of the authority nominated by the authority, and a governor nominated by the governing body, to appear and make oral representations, and
    (d) the governing body to be represented.'

(4) After paragraph 12 there shall be inserted—

'12A (1) In deciding—
    (a) whether the pupil in question should be reinstated (and, if so, the time when this should take place), or
    (b) whether any direction for the reinstatement of the pupil in question should be confirmed,

Appendix 9

an appeal committee shall have regard to both the interests of that pupil and the interests of other pupils at his school and members of its staff.

(2) In making any such decision an appeal committee shall also have regard to the measures publicised by the head teacher under section 154(7).

(3) Sub-paragraphs (1) and (2) do not apply where an appeal committee decides that the pupil in question was not guilty of the conduct which the head teacher relied on as grounds for his permanent exclusion.

(4) Sub-paragraphs (1) and (2) shall not be read as precluding an appeal committee from having regard to any other relevant matters.'

General This section amends Sch 16 to the Education Act 1996, which contains detailed provisions relating to the making and hearing of appeals to an appeal committee against the reinstatement of, or a refusal to reinstate, a pupil permanently excluded from an LEA-maintained school. Sub-s (2) inserts a new para 7A, requiring the body responsible for arranging the appeal hearing to ascertain when the parties to the appeal would be able to attend and to take these times into account when fixing the time for the hearing. Sub-s (3) substitutes a new para 8, making the following changes: an appellant pupil or parent is given the right to be represented or accompanied by a friend; the head teacher is given the right to appear and to make written or oral representations; and the governing body is given the right to be represented. Sub-s (4) inserts a new para 12A requiring an appeal committee, when deciding whether and when to reinstate an excluded pupil, or to confirm his reinstatement, to have regard both to his interests and to those of other pupils and of members of staff; and also to the disciplinary measures publicised by the head teacher under the new s 154(7) substituted by s 2 above. These requirements do not however apply where the appeal committee finds the pupil not guilty of the conduct relied on by the head teacher as grounds for permanent exclusion; nor, where they do apply, do they preclude the committee from having regard to other relevant matters.

Commencement A date to be appointed by the Secretary of State by order under s 58(3).

Definition See the Education Act 1996: 'governing body': s 182; 'head teacher' (generally): s 579(1); (in relation to a school organised in separate departments): s 132; 'the local education authority': s 579(1); 'parent': s 576; 'pupil': ss 3(1), 19(5); 'relevant person': Sch 16, para 17.

8 Exclusion appeals: grant-maintained and grant-maintained special schools

(1) After section 307 of the Education Act 1996 there shall be inserted—

'307A Exclusion appeals

Schedule 25A to this Act has effect in relation to the procedure on any appeal which—
- (a) is made in pursuance of arrangements made by the governing body of a grant-maintained school by virtue of paragraph 6(1) and (2) of Schedule 23 (content of articles of government), and
- (b) relates to a decision not to reinstate a pupil who has been permanently excluded from the school.'

(2) After Schedule 25 to that Act there shall be inserted as Schedule 25A the Schedule set out in Schedule 1 to this Act.

(3) At the end of Schedule 28 to that Act (government and conduct of grant-maintained special schools) there shall be added—

'16 Section 307A and Schedule 25A (exclusion appeals) apply in relation to a grant-maintained special school as they apply in relation to a grant-maintained school, but as if any reference in those provisions to any provision of Schedule 23 were a reference to that provision as it applies in accordance with regulations under paragraph 14 above.'

General This section inserts a new s 307A and a new Sch 25A (set out in Sch 1 to the Act) in the Education Act 1996, making similar provision for appeals against permanent exclusion from a GM school as is made for LEA-maintained schools by Sch 16 to that Act, as amended by s 7 above. Sub-s (3) inserts a new para 16 in Schedule 28 to the 1996 Act, extending s307A and Sch 25A to GM special schools.

Commencement A date to be appointed by the Secretary of State by order under s 58(3).

Definition See the Education Act 1996: 'articles of government' (GM school): s 218(1); 'grant-maintained school': s 183(1); 'grant-maintained special school': ss 337(4) and 346(3).

LEA plans

9 LEA plans relating to children with behavioural difficulties. After section 527 of the Education Act 1996 there shall be inserted—

'Plans relating to children with behavioural difficulties

527A Duty of LEA to prepare plan relating to children with behavioural difficulties
(1) Every local education authority shall prepare, and from time to time review, a statement setting out the arrangements made or proposed to be made by the authority in connection with the education of children with behavioural difficulties.
(2) The arrangements to be covered by the statement include in particular—
- (a) the arrangements made or to be made by the authority for the provision of advice and resources to relevant schools, and other arrangements made or to be made by them, with a view to—
  - (i) meeting requests by such schools for support and assistance in connection with the promotion of good behaviour and discipline on the part of their pupils, and
  - (ii) assisting such schools to deal with general behavioural problems and the behavioural difficulties of individual pupils;
- (b) the arrangements made or to be made by the authority in pursuance of section 19(1) (exceptional provision of education for children not receiving education by reason of being excluded or otherwise); and
- (c) any other arrangements made or to be made by them for assisting children with behavioural difficulties to find places at suitable schools.

(3) The statement shall also deal with the interaction between the arrangements referred to in subsection (2) and those made by the authority in relation to pupils with behavioural difficulties who have special educational needs.
(4) In the course of preparing the statement required by this section or any revision of it the authority shall carry out such consultation as may be prescribed.
(5) The authority shall—
- (a) publish the statement in such manner and by such date, and
- (b) publish revised statements in such manner and at such intervals,

as may be prescribed, and shall provide such persons as may be prescribed with copies of the statement or any revised statement.
(6) In discharging their functions under this section a local education authority shall have regard to any guidance given from time to time by the Secretary of State.
(7) In this section 'relevant school', in relation to a local education authority, means—
- (a) a school maintained by the authority (whether situated in their area or not), or
- (b) a grant-maintained or grant-maintained special school situated in their area.'

General This section inserts a new s 527A into the Education Act 1996. This requires every LEA to prepare and review from time to time, following prescribed consultation, a statement setting out the arrangements which they have made or intend to make in connection with the education of children with behavioural difficulties. These are to include arrangements for providing advice and resources to schools which they maintain and GM and GM special schools in their area ('relevant schools'); arrangements made under s 19(1), for exceptional provision of education to children not in school; and any other arrangements for helping children with behavioural difficulties to find places at suitable schools (of whatever type). The statement must also deal with the interaction between these arrangements and those made for pupils with behavioural difficulties who also have special educational needs. The statement, and revisions of it, is to be published, and copies are to be provided, as may be prescribed by regulations; and in discharging their functions under this section LEAs are to have regard to any guidance given by the Secretary of State.

Commencement A date to be appointed by the Secretary of State by order under s 58(3).

Definition 'Relevant school': sub-s (7); and see the Education Act 1996: 'area': s 12(6); 'grant-maintained school': s 183(1); 'grant-maintained special school': ss 337(4) and 346(3); 'local education authority': s 12 (1)–(5); 'maintain': s 34; 'prescribed': s 579(1); 'school': s 4 (as prospectively substituted by s 51); 'special educational needs': s 312(1).

Regulations Regulations under the new s 527A are to be made by statutory instrument, subject to the negative resolution procedure: Education Act 1996, s 569.

Appendix 9

Part III

School Admissions

Chapter I

County and Voluntary Schools

Partially-selective schools

10 Restriction of right to refuse admission to partially-selective school. In section 411(3) of the Education Act 1996 (cases where parental preference need not be complied with), for paragraph (c) there shall be substituted—

'(c) if the arrangements for admission to the preferred school—
  (i) are wholly based on selection by reference to ability or aptitude, and
  (ii) are so based with a view to admitting only pupils with high ability or with aptitude,
and compliance with the preference would be incompatible with selection under those arrangements.'

General This section amends s 411 of the Education Act 1996 (formerly s 6 of the Education Act 1980) which requires the LEA and the governing body of a county or voluntary school to give effect, except in certain specified cases, to the parent's preference as to the school at which his child is to be educated. Under s 411(3)(c), one of the exceptional cases in which this duty does not apply is where the school's admission arrangements are based 'wholly or partly on selection by reference to ability or aptitude', and compliance with the parent's preference would be incompatible with selection under those arrangements. The effect of the amendment made by this section is that in future a child could be refused admission for this reason only where the school's admission arrangements were wholly based on the selection of children with high ability or aptitude, but not where they were only partially so based. (As originally introduced, the Bill for this Act included provisions intended to encourage schools to become wholly selective, but these were later withdrawn.)

Para 31(4) of Sch 7 to this Act inserts a new sub-s (9) in s 411 explaining that admission arrangements are to be regarded as 'wholly based on selection by reference to ability or aptitude' where they provide for all pupils to be selected by reference to ability or aptitude, whether or not they also provide for the use of additional criteria to select from a group all of whom satisfy the test of ability or aptitude.

Commencement 1 September 1997: SI 1997/1468.

Children permanently excluded from two or more schools

11 No requirement to admit children permanently excluded from two or more schools.
After section 411 of the Education Act 1996 there shall be inserted—

'**411A No requirement to admit children permanently excluded from two or more schools**
(1) The duty imposed by section 411(2) does not apply in the case of a child to whom subsection (2) applies.
(2) Where a child has been permanently excluded from two or more schools, this subsection applies to him during the period of two years beginning with the date on which the latest of those exclusions took effect.
(3) Subsection (2) applies to a child whatever the length of the period or periods elapsing between those exclusions and regardless of whether it has applied to him on a previous occasion.
(4) However, a child shall not be regarded as permanently excluded from a school for the purposes of this section if—
  (a) although so excluded he was reinstated as a pupil at the school following the giving of a direction to that effect to the head teacher of the school; or
  (b) he was so excluded at a time when he had not attained compulsory school age.
(5) In this section 'school' means—
  (a) a school maintained by a local education authority; or
  (b) a grant-maintained or grant-maintained special school.

(6) This section does not apply in relation to a child unless at least one of the two or more exclusions mentioned in subsection (2) took effect on or after the date of the coming into force of section 11 of the Education Act 1997.
(7) For the purposes of this section the permanent exclusion of a child from a school shall be regarded as having taken effect on the school day as from which the head teacher decided that he should be permanently excluded.'

General This section inserts a new section 411A into the Education Act 1996, following s 411 (see s 10 above). The new s 411A, which applies in relation to LEA-maintained, grant-maintained and grant-maintained special schools, disapplies the duty under s 411(2) to give effect to parental preference in the choice of a school in cases where the child has been permanently excluded from two or more schools; this applies for a period of two years from the date on which the latest exclusion took effect—ie the school day from which the head teacher decided that he should be permanently excluded. A school will not be obliged to admit a child in these circumstances even if it has places available. This section only applies where at least one of the exclusions took effect on or after the date on which this section (ie s 11 of the 1997 Act) comes into force—sub-s (6).

Sub-s (3) makes it clear that a child permanently excluded from two or more schools is to be treated as a 'disqualified person' regardless of the length of time which has elapsed between the exclusions, and whether or not he has previously been treated as a 'disqualified person'.

However a child is not to be regarded as having been permanently excluded if he was reinstated by virtue of a direction from the governing body, LEA or an appeal committee overruling the head teacher's decision, or the exclusion took place before he attained compulsory school age—see s 52 below, amending s 8 of the 1996 Act.

Commencement 1 September 1997: SI 1997/1468.

Definition 'School' in s 411A: s 411A(5); and see the Education Act 1996 for 'child': s 579(1); 'head teacher' (generally): s 579(1); (in relation to a school organised in separate departments): s 132; 'pupil': ss 3(1), 19(5); 'school day': s 579(1).

'Compulsory school age' See the Education Act 1996, Sch 40, para 1, until the commencement of s 8 of that Act (as prospectively amended by s 52 of this Act); thereafter s 8.

12 Appeals in the case of children permanently excluded from two or more schools
(1) After section 423 of the Education Act 1996 there shall be inserted—

'**423A Appeals relating to children to whom section 411A(2) applies**
(1) Nothing in section 423(1) or (2) requires any arrangements to be made for enabling the parent of a child to appeal against a decision—
   (a)   made by or on behalf of the admission authority for a county or voluntary school, and
   (b)   refusing the child admission to the school,
in a case where, at the time when the decision is made, section 411A(2) applies to the child.
(2) Where a local education authority are the admission authority for a county or controlled school, the authority shall make arrangements for enabling the governing body of the school to appeal against any decision made by or on behalf of the authority to admit to the school a child to whom, at the time when the decision is made, section 411A(2) applies.
(3) Schedule 33A shall have effect in relation to the making and hearing of appeals pursuant to arrangements made under subsection (2).
(4) The decision of an appeal committee on an appeal made pursuant to arrangements under subsection (2) shall be binding—
   (a)   on the local education authority by or on whose behalf the decision under appeal was made, and
   (b)   on the governing body of any county or controlled school at which the appeal committee determines that a place should be offered to the child in question.'

(2) After Schedule 33 to the Education Act 1996 there shall be inserted as Schedule 33A the Schedule set out in Schedule 2 to this Act.

General This section inserts a new s 423A and a new Sch 33A in the Education Act 1996. The new section 423A(1) relieves LEAs and the governing bodies of county and voluntary schools from their duty to arrange for appeals by the parent of a child refused admission to the school in cases where s 411A(2) applies to him: ie when he has already been excluded from two or more schools.

Section 423A(2) provides for an appeal by the governing body of a county or controlled school where the LEA, as admission authority, have decided to admit to the school a child to whom s 411A(2) applies. Section 423A(3) gives effect to Sch 33A (inserted by s 12(2) of this Act and set out in Sch 2), which provides for the appeal to be heard by an independent appeal committee and sets out the procedure to be followed. Section 423A(4) makes the appeal committee's decision

Appendix 9

binding on the LEA, and on the governing body of any county or controlled school at which the appeal committee determines that a place should be offered to the child.
Commencement 1 September 1997: SI 1997/1468.
Definition See the Education Act 1996 for 'admission authority': s 415; 'child': s 579(1); 'controlled school': s 32(1) and (2); 'county school': s 31(1); 'governing body': s 182; 'local education authority': s 12 (1)–(5); 'parent': s 576; 'voluntary school': ss 31(2), 32.

Home-school partnership documents

13 Home-school partnership documents. After section 413 of the Education Act 1996 there shall be inserted—

'**413A Admission arrangements may provide for home-school partnership documents**
(1) The admission arrangements for a county or voluntary school may include provisions—
    (a) setting out the terms of a partnership document for the school and the parental declaration to be used in connection with the document;
    (b) making it a condition of the admission of every child to the school that his parent gives the admission authority a signed parental declaration either—
        (i) at the time of applying for a place at the school for the child, or
        (ii) if the child is allocated a conditional place, within such period as is specified in the arrangements; and
    (c) authorising the admission authority to dispense with that condition to any extent in the case of a particular child where they are satisfied that there are special reasons for doing so.
(2) For the purposes of this section and section 413B a 'partnership document' is a statement specifying—
    (a) the school's aims and values;
    (b) the responsibilities which the school intends to discharge in connection with the education of children admitted to the school; and
    (c) the parental responsibilities, that is the responsibilities which the parents of such children are expected to discharge in connection with the education of their children while they are registered pupils at the school;
and 'parental declaration' means a declaration to be signed by a parent seeking the admission of his child to the school by which he acknowledges and accepts the parental responsibilities specified in the partnership document.
(3) In determining the provisions to be included in the admission arrangements for a school in pursuance of subsection (1), the admission authority shall have regard to any guidance given from time to time by the Secretary of State.
(4) The Secretary of State may by order provide that any form of words specified in the order, or having such effect as is so specified, is not to be used in a partnership document or (as the case may be) in a parental declaration.
(5) An order under subsection (4) may apply to any school or description of school specified in the order.
(6) Where a local education authority consult the governing body of a county or voluntary school under section 412(2)(a) or (b), the authority shall have particular regard to any representations by the governing body—
    (a) that the admission arrangements for the school should include the provisions authorised by subsection (1), or
    (b) as to the terms of the partnership document or parental declaration to be included in the arrangements, or
    (c) as to any variation of those terms as for the time being so included,
as the case may be.
(7) In this section and section 413B—
'admission arrangements', in relation to a school, means the arrangements for the admission of pupils to the school; and
'conditional place', in relation to a child, means a place which is conditional on the child's parent giving the admission authority a signed parental declaration.

413B Effect of home-school partnership document
(1) This section applies where the admission arrangements for a county or voluntary school include the provisions authorised by section 413A(1).
(2) The admission authority for the school shall, in the case of each child on behalf of whom an application for admission is made, notify his parent of the following matters, namely—

(a) the terms of the partnership document and the parental declaration, and
(b) the effect of the provisions of the admission arrangements authorised by section 413A(1)(b) and (c).
(3) Where subsection (2) has been complied with in relation to a child's parent but—
(a) the parent has failed to comply with the condition referred to in section 413A(1)(b), and
(b) the admission authority are not satisfied that there are special reasons for dispensing with that condition to the required extent in the case of that child,
section 411(2) shall not require the admission of the child to the school; and, if he has been allocated a conditional place, the allocation of that place may be cancelled.
(4) In subsection (3) the reference to dispensing with the condition mentioned in that subsection 'to the required extent'—
(a) is, where the parent gives the admission authority a signed parental declaration in relation to some but not the remainder of the parental responsibilities, a reference to dispensing with that condition so far as the remainder of those responsibilities are concerned; but
(b) is otherwise a reference to wholly dispensing with that condition.
(5) In performing any function under this section the admission authority shall have regard to any guidance given from time to time by the Secretary of State.
(6) A partnership document shall not be capable of creating any obligation in respect of whose breach any liability arises in contract or in tort.'

General Section 13 inserts two new sections in the Education Act 1996, ss 413A and 413B, making provision for the imposition, as a condition of admission to a county or voluntary school, of a 'partnership document'—ie a statement specifying the school's aims and values, the responsibilities which the school intends to discharge and those which the parents of pupils admitted to the school are expected to discharge in connection with the education of their children—together with a 'parental declaration' by which the parent acknowledges and accepts the parental responsibilities specified in the partnership document. Breach of an obligation under a partnership document does not give rise to any liability in contract or tort, but if the admission arrangements provide for such documents, the school is not obliged to admit any child whose parent fails to sign a parental declaration.

New s 413A authorises the admission authority for a county or voluntary school to include in the admission arrangements for the school, subject to guidance from the Secretary of State, provisions setting out the terms of a partnership document and parental declaration for the school; making provision of a signed parental declaration a condition of admission of every child to the school; but authorising an admission authority to dispense with this condition where they are satisfied that there are special reasons for doing so—sub-ss (1) and (3).

The Secretary of State is given power to prohibit, by order applicable to a particular school or a category of schools, the inclusion of specified provisions in a partnership document or parental declaration—sub-ss (4) and (5).

Where an LEA consult the governing body of a school about their admission arrangements, as they are required to do by s 412(2) of the 1996 Act, not less than once in every school year, they are to have particular regard to any representations by the governing body in favour of the inclusion of provisions under this section and their terms—sub-s (6).

New s 413B requires the admission authority to notify the parent of any child seeking admission of the terms of the partnership document and parental declaration and of the effect of s 413A(1)(b) and (c). If the parent then fails to sign such a declaration, and the admission authority are not satisfied that there a special reasons for dispensing with it, they may refuse to admit the child and withdraw any place conditionally offered. Sub-s (4) gives the authority the option of accepting a parental declaration limited to some but not all of the parental responsibilities set out in the partnership document. In performing their functions under this section the admission authority are to have regard to any guidance given by the Secretary of State.

Commencement A date to be appointed by the Secretary of State by order under s 58(3).

Definition In ss 413A and 413B, for 'admission arrangements' and 'conditional place' see s 413A(7); for 'parental declaration' and 'partnership document' see s 413A(2). See also the Education Act 1996 for 'admission authority': s 415; 'child': s 579(1); 'county school': s 31(1); 'functions': s 579(1); 'governing body': s 182; 'local education authority': s 12 (1)–(5); 'parent': s 576; 'voluntary school': ss 31(2), 32.

'By order' An order under the new s 413A(4) is to be made by statutory instrument, subject to the negative resolution procedure, unless it applies only to a specified school or schools— s 568 of the 1996 Act, as amended by para 40 of Sch 7 to this Act.

Appendix 9

Chapter II

Grant-Maintained Schools

14 Corresponding provisions about admissions to grant-maintained schools
(1) After section 425 of the Education Act 1996 there shall be inserted—

'**425A Restrictions on admissions to grant-maintained schools**. Schedule 33B to this Act, which provides for restrictions on admissions to grant-maintained schools in connection with—
   (a)   home-school partnership documents,
   (b)   partially-selective schools, and
   (c)   persons permanently excluded from two or more schools,
shall have effect.'

(2) After the Schedule 33A to the Education Act 1996 inserted by section 12 of this Act there shall be inserted as Schedule 33B the Schedule set out in Schedule 3 to this Act.

General This section inserts a new s 425A and a new Sch 33B (set out in Sch 3 to this Act) into the Education Act 1996, applying to grant-maintained schools provisions corresponding to those inserted in relation to LEA-maintained schools by ss 13 (home-school partnership documents), 10 (restriction of right to refuse admission to partially-selective school) and 11 (no requirement to admit children permanently excluded from two or more schools).
Commencement To the extent that it relates to paras 3 and 4 of Sch 33B, 1 September 1997: SI 1997/1468. As respects paras 1 and 2 of that Schedule, a date to be appointed by the Secretary of State by order under s 58(3).

Part IV

Baseline Assessments and Pupils' Performance

Chapter I

Baseline Assessments

15 Introductory. In this Chapter—
'baseline assessment scheme' means a scheme designed to enable pupils at a maintained primary school to be assessed for the purpose of assisting the future planning of their education and the measurement of their future educational achievements;
'designated' means designated by the Secretary of State; and
'maintained primary school' means a primary school which is—
   (a)   a county or voluntary school,
   (b)   a grant-maintained school, or
   (c)   a maintained or grant-maintained special school (other than one established in a hospital),
or (in relation only to Wales) a maintained nursery school.

General This Chapter (ss 15–18) provides for the introduction of a system of 'baseline assessment' of pupils in primary schools, following proposals from the School Curriculum and Assessment Authority, with the object of assisting the future planning of the pupils' education and facilitating the measurement of their progress. This section defines three expressions for the purposes of this Chapter—
a 'baseline assessment scheme' is a scheme designed to enable pupils at a maintained primary school to be assessed, with a view to assisting the future planning of their education and the measurement of their future educational achievements;
'designated' means designated by the Secretary of State;
a 'maintained primary school' is a primary school which is a county or voluntary school (ie maintained by an LEA) or grant-maintained, or an LEA-maintained or grant-maintained special school (other than one established in a hospital), or (in Wales only) a maintained nursery school.
Commencement 1 November 1997: SI 1997/1468.
Definition See s 56(2) and the Education Act 1996 for 'county school': s 31(1); 'grant-maintained school': s 183(1); 'grant-maintained special school': ss 337(4) and 346(3); 'maintained nursery

school': ss 6(1) and 33(1); 'maintained special school': ss 6(2), 33(1), 337(3); 'primary school': s 5(1); 'pupil': ss 3(1), 19(5); 'voluntary school': ss 31(2), 32.

16 Adoption of baseline assessment schemes

(1) The governing body of each maintained primary school with pupils who are required to be assessed under section 17 shall adopt a baseline assessment scheme for the school in accordance with the following provisions of this section; but subsections (2) to (5) below have effect subject to subsection (6).

(2) A baseline assessment scheme may be so adopted if (and only if) the scheme has been accredited by a designated body in accordance with criteria determined with the approval of the Secretary of State, and published, by that body.

(3) A local education authority may prepare, and seek accreditation of, a baseline assessment scheme with a view to its being adopted by the governing bodies of primary schools maintained by the authority.

(4) Each local education authority shall select an accredited baseline assessment scheme which they consider suitable to be so adopted (and which may be a scheme prepared by them under subsection (3)).

(5) However, in the case of any particular maintained primary school, the baseline assessment scheme which is to be adopted for the school under this section by its governing body shall be such scheme to which subsection (2) applies as is chosen—
   (a) by the head teacher after consulting the governing body; or
   (b) if such a scheme is not so chosen by him within a reasonable time, by the governing body;
and, when choosing the scheme to be adopted for a school which is maintained by a local education authority, the head teacher or (as the case may be) the governing body shall ensure that the scheme selected by the authority under subsection (4) is considered (whether on its own or with any other schemes).

(6) The Secretary of State may by order require the governing body of each maintained primary school with pupils who are required to be assessed under section 17 to adopt for their school such baseline assessment scheme as is referred to in the order; and so long as any such order is in force subsections (2) to (5) above shall not apply.

General This section requires the governing body of every maintained primary school with pupils at the relevant stage of their education (see s 17(8)) to adopt a baseline assessment scheme for their school. The scheme must have been accredited by a designated body in accordance with criteria determined with the approval of the Secretary of State and published by the designated body—sub-s (2). Each LEA is required to select an accredited scheme for adoption by their schools; this may be one which they have prepared and had accredited—sub-ss (3) and (4). However the choice of an accredited scheme is for the head teacher of each school (after consulting the governing body and considering the scheme selected by the LEA) and only for the governing body if the head teacher fails to choose a scheme within a reasonable time—sub-s (5).

Sub-section (6) gives the Secretary of State power to impose a national scheme by order made by statutory instrument subject to negative resolution, overriding sub-ss (2)–(5). In Standing Committee the Parliamentary Under-Secretary of State (Mrs. Gillan) described this as a contingent power: 'It is a dormant provision, included in the Bill to enable the Secretary of State to introduce a single national scheme if that emerged as the preferred way forward in the light of experience.'—col 559.

Commencement Subsections (2), (3) and (6), and sub-s (4) in its application to England: 1 November 1997: SI 1997/1468. Remainder: a date to be appointed by the Secretary of State by order under s 58(3).

Definition For 'baseline assessment scheme', 'designated' and 'maintained primary school' see s 15. See s 56(2) and the Education Act 1996 for 'governing body': s 182; 'head teacher' (generally): s 579(1); (in relation to a school organised in separate departments): s 132; 'local education authority': s 12 (1)–(5); 'pupil': ss 3(1), 19(5).

'By order' Orders under this section are to be made by statutory instrument, subject to the negative resolution procedure: s 54.

17 Assessment of pupils in accordance with scheme

(1) Subject to subsections (3) and (4), all pupils at a maintained primary school who are at the relevant stage of their education must be assessed in accordance with a baseline assessment scheme adopted for the school under section 16.

(2) The assessment must be completed before the end of the prescribed period.

Appendix 9

(3) Subsection (1) does not apply to a pupil if it appears to the head teacher from a record of a previous assessment under that subsection that such an assessment has already been carried out in relation to the pupil at another school.

(4) Regulations may enable a head teacher of a maintained primary school, in such cases or circumstances and subject to such conditions as may be prescribed, to direct—
  (a) that subsection (1) is not to apply to a particular registered pupil at the school, or
  (b) that, for the purposes of the assessment under that subsection of a particular registered pupil at the school, the school's baseline assessment scheme is to have effect with such modifications as are specified in the direction.

(5) Where the head teacher gives such a direction he shall notify—
  (a) the governing body, and
  (b) if the school is maintained by a local education authority, that authority,
of the matters set out in subsection (6); and he shall take such steps as are prescribed to notify a parent of the pupil concerned of those matters.

(6) The matters referred to in subsection (5) are—
  (a) the fact that the head teacher has given the direction in question and his reasons for doing so;
  (b) in the case of a direction under subsection (4)(b), the effect of the modifications specified in the direction; and
  (c) whether the direction is to have permanent effect (and, if not, the period for which it is to have effect).

(7) In relation to any maintained primary school—
  (a) the governing body and (except in the case of a grant-maintained or grant-maintained special school) the local education authority shall exercise their functions with a view to securing, and
  (b) the head teacher shall secure,
that subsection (1) is complied with.

(8) Regulations shall prescribe the circumstances in which a pupil is to be regarded as being at the relevant stage of his education for the purposes of subsection (1), and any such circumstances may be framed by reference to, or to matters which include, the pupil's age.

General This section requires all pupils at a maintained primary school who are at the relevant stage of their education (as prescribed by regulations under sub-s (8)) to be assessed, before the end of the prescribed period, in accordance with their school's baseline assessment scheme—sub-ss (1) and (2). It is for the head teacher to secure this, and for the governing body and (except in the case of a GM or GM special school) the LEA to exercise their functions to this end—sub-s (7). A school is not however required to assess a pupil if he has already been assessed at another school—sub-s (3).

Sub-ss (4)–(6) provide for regulations to be made by the Secretary of State, subject to negative resolution, enabling a head teacher, by direction, to exempt a particular child from assessment, or to modify the application of the scheme to him. The governing body and, if the school is an LEA-maintained school, the LEA, and the pupil's parent, must be notified by the head teacher of any such directions he may give, of his reasons for giving them, of the effect of any modifications, and of their duration.

Commencement Subsections (4) and (8): 1 November 1997: SI 1997/1468. Remainder: a date to be appointed by the Secretary of State by order under s 58(3).

Definition For 'baseline assessment scheme' and 'maintained primary school' see s 15. See s 56(2) and the Education Act 1996 for 'functions': s 579(1); 'governing body': s 182; 'grant-maintained school': s 183(1); 'grant-maintained special school': ss 337(4) and 346(3); 'head teacher' (generally): s 579(1); (in relation to a school organised in separate departments): s 132; 'local education authority': s 12 (1)–(5); 'parent': s 576; 'prescribed': s 579(1); 'pupil': ss 3(1), 19(5).

Regulations Regulations under this section are to be made by statutory instrument, subject to negative resolution—s 54.

18 Regulations for purposes of this Chapter

(1) The Secretary of State may by regulations confer or impose such functions—
  (a) on the governing body and the head teacher of a maintained primary school,
  (b) (except in relation to any grant-maintained or grant-maintained special school) on a local education authority, and
  (c) on a designated body,
as appear to him to be required in connection with any provision of this Chapter.

Education Act 1997

(2) Regulations under this section may in particular make provision requiring—
   (a) the local education authority, or (in the case of a grant-maintained or grant-maintained special school) a designated body, to be notified—
      (i) of the baseline assessment scheme for the time being adopted for any maintained primary school with pupils who are required to be assessed under section 17, and
      (ii) where any assessment has been carried out under that section at any such school, that it has been so carried out;
   (b) the results of any assessments carried out under that section to be recorded and notified—
      (i) to such persons as are specified in the regulations, and
      (ii) where the pupils in question transfer to other schools, to those other schools.

(3) Regulations under this section may also make provision requiring a local education authority—
   (a) to notify a designated body of any assessments notified to the authority in pursuance of regulations under subsection (2)(a)(ii); and
   (b) to collect other information relating to assessments carried out under section 17 at schools maintained by the authority and to forward such information to a designated body.

General This section enables the Secretary of State to make regulations conferring or imposing such functions on the governing body and head teacher of a maintained primary school, on an LEA (except in relation to a GM or GM special school), and on a designated body, as seem to him to be required in connection with any provision of this Chapter—sub-s (1). Such regulations may in particular require notification to be given to the LEA , or (in the case of a GM or GM special school) the designated body, of the scheme which has been adopted; and of the carrying out of an assessment. They may require the results of assessments to be recorded and notified to specified persons, and to other schools, when pupils transfer to them. They may also require an LEA to notify a designated body of any assessments notified to them, and to collect other information about assessments carried out at their schools and forward it to a designated body.

Commencement 1 November 1997: SI 1997/1468.

Definition For 'baseline assessment scheme', 'designated' and 'maintained primary school' see s 15. See s 56(2) and the Education Act 1996 for 'functions': s 579(1); 'governing body': s 182; 'grant-maintained school': s 183(1); 'grant-maintained special school': ss 337(4) and 346(3); 'head teacher' (generally): s 579(1); (in relation to a school organised in separate departments): s 132; 'local education authority': s 12 (1)–(5); 'pupil': ss 3(1), 19(5).

'Person' This includes a body of persons, corporate or unincorporate: Interpretation Act 1978, s 5, Sch 1.

Regulations Regulations under this section are to be made by statutory instrument, subject to negative resolution—s 54.

Chapter II

Pupils' Performance

19 School performance targets

(1) The Secretary of State may by regulations make such provision as the Secretary of State considers appropriate for requiring the governing bodies of maintained schools to secure that annual targets are set in respect of the performance of pupils—
   (a) in public examinations or in assessments for the purposes of the National Curriculum, in the case of pupils of compulsory school age; or
   (b) in public examinations or in connection with the attainment of other external qualifications, in the case of pupils of any age over that age.

(2) Regulations under this section may require—
   (a) such targets, and
   (b) the past performance of pupils in the particular examinations or assessments, or in connection with the attainment of the particular qualifications, to which such targets relate,

Appendix 9

to be published in such manner as is specified in the regulations.
(3) In this section 'maintained school' means—
   (a) a county or voluntary school;
   (b) a grant-maintained school; or
   (c) a maintained or grant-maintained special school (other than one established in a hospital).

General This section enables the Secretary of State to make regulations requiring the governing bodies of maintained schools (ie LEA-maintained and GM schools, including special schools other than hospital schools) to set and publish annual targets for the performance of pupils of compulsory school age in public examinations and assessments for the purposes of the National Curriculum, and the performance of pupils over that age in public examinations or the attainment of other external qualifications. The regulations may also require the performance of pupils in such examinations or assessments to be published.

Commencement A date to be appointed by the Secretary of State by order under s 58(3).

Definition For 'maintained school' in this section, see sub-s (3). See also s 56(2) and the Education Act 1996 for 'assessment': s 350(2); 'county school': s 31(1); 'governing body': s 182; 'grant-maintained school': s 183(1); 'grant-maintained special school': ss 337(4) and 346(3); 'maintained special school': ss 6(2), 33(1), 337(3); 'the National Curriculum': ss 352(1) and 353; 'pupil': ss 3(1), 19(5); 'voluntary school': ss 31(2), 32.

'**Compulsory school age**' See the Education Act 1996, Sch 40, para 1 until the commencement of s 8; thereafter s 8 (as prospectively amended by s 52 of this Act).

Regulations Regulations under this section are to be made by statutory instrument, subject to negative resolution—s 54.

20 Provision of information about individual pupils' performance.
After section 537 of the Education Act 1996 there shall be inserted—

'**537A Provision of information about individual pupils' performance**
(1) The Secretary of State may by regulations make provision requiring—
   (a) the governing body of every school which is—
      (i) maintained by a local education authority, or
      (ii) a grant-maintained school; or
      (iii) a special school which is not maintained by a local education authority, and
   (b) the proprietor of each independent school,
to provide to the Secretary of State such individual performance information relating to pupils or former pupils at the school as may be prescribed.
(2) In this section 'individual performance information' means information about the performance of individual pupils (identified in the prescribed manner)—
   (a) in any assessment made for the purposes of the National Curriculum or in accordance with a baseline assessment scheme (within the meaning of Chapter I of Part IV of the Education Act 1997);
   (b) in any prescribed public examination;
   (c) in connection with the attainment of any vocational qualification; or
   (d) in any such other assessment or examination, or in connection with the attainment of any such other qualification, as may be prescribed.
(3) The Secretary of State may provide any information received by him by virtue of subsection (1)—
   (a) to any prescribed body or person, or
   (b) to any body or person falling within a prescribed category.
(4) Any body or person holding any individual performance information may provide that information to any body to which this subsection applies; and any body to which this subsection applies—
   (a) may provide any information received by it under this subsection—
      (i) to the Secretary of State, or
      (ii) to the governing body or proprietor of the school attended by the pupil or pupils to whom the information relates; and
   (b) may, at such times as the Secretary of State may determine, provide to any prescribed body such information received by it under this subsection as may be prescribed.
(5) Subsection (4) applies to any body which, for the purposes of or in connection with the functions of the Secretary of State relating to education, is responsible for collating or checking information relating to the performance of pupils—
   (a) in any assessment or examination falling within subsection (2)(a), (b) or (d), or

(b) in connection with the attainment of any qualification falling within subsection (2)(c) or (d).

(6) No individual performance information received under or by virtue of this section shall be published in any form which includes the name of the pupil or pupils to whom it relates.

(7) References in this section to the attainment of a qualification of any description include references to the completion of any module or part of a course leading to any such qualification.'

General This section inserts a new s 537A in the Education Act 1996. Sub-s (1) of the new s 537A enables the Secretary of State to make regulations requiring the governing bodies of LEA-maintained schools, GM schools and special schools not maintained by an LEA, and the proprietors of independent schools, to provide him with individual performance information (as defined in sub-ss (2) and (7)) relating to pupils and former pupils. The Secretary of State may in turn provide this information to any prescribed body or person, or any body or person falling within a prescribed category—sub-s (3). Sub-ss (4) and (5) authorise any body or person holding any individual performance information to provide it to a body responsible for collating or checking performance information for the Secretary of State; and authorises that body to provide the information it receives to the Secretary of State or to the governing body or proprietor of the school attended by the pupil to whom it relates. It may also, at times determined by the Secretary of State, provide prescribed information received by it to any prescribed body. Sub-s (6) prohibits the publication of any individual performance information in any form which includes the name of the pupil or pupils to whom it relates.

Commencement 14 June 1997: SI 1997/1468.

Definition For 'individual performance information' and 'attainment of a qualification' in s 537A see sub-ss (2) and (7) of that section. For 'baseline assessment scheme' see s 15 of this Act. See the Education Act 1996 for 'functions': s 579(1); 'governing body': s 182; 'grant-maintained school': s 183(1); 'independent school': s 463; 'local education authority': s 12 (1)–(5); 'maintain': s 34; 'the National Curriculum': ss 352(1) and 353; 'prescribed', 'proprietor': s 579(1); 'pupil': ss 3(1), 19(5); 'special school': ss 6(2) and 337.

Regulations Regulations under the new s 537A are to be made by statutory instrument, subject to the negative resolution procedure: Education Act 1996, s 569.

Part V

Supervision of Curriculum for Schools and External Qualifications

Chapter I

The Qualifications and Curriculum Authority

Establishment of the Authority

21 The Qualifications and Curriculum Authority

(1) There shall be a body corporate known as the Qualifications and Curriculum Authority.

(2) The Authority shall consist of not less than 8 nor more than 13 members appointed by the Secretary of State.

(3) Of the members of the Authority, the Secretary of State—
  (a) shall appoint one as chairman, and
  (b) may appoint another as deputy chairman.

(4) The Secretary of State shall include among the members of the Authority—
  (a) persons who appear to him to have experience of, and to have shown capacity in, the provision of education, or to have held, and to have shown capacity in, any position carrying responsibility for the provision of education;
  (b) persons who appear to him to have experience of, and to have shown capacity in, the provision of training or to have held, and to have shown capacity in, any position carrying responsibility for the provision of training; and
  (c) persons who appear to him to have experience of, and to have shown capacity in, industrial, commercial or financial matters or the practice of any profession.

Appendix 9

(5) Schedule 4 has effect in relation to the Authority.

General Part V of the Act (ss 21–37, Schs 4 and 5) establishes a new Qualifications and Curriculum Authority and a renamed Qualifications, Curriculum and Assessment Authority for Wales, sets out their functions and makes supplementary provisions in relation to them, including provision for a levy on bodies awarding qualifications which are accredited by the new Authorities and a prohibition on the provision of certain courses unless the external qualifications to which they lead have been approved by the Secretary of State or a body designated by him.

Section 21 establishes the Qualifications and Curriculum Authority (QCA) as a body corporate, to replace the School Curriculum and Assessment Authority, originally established by s 244 of the Education Act 1993 and continued by s 358 of the Education Act 1996, and the National Council for Vocational Qualifications. It provides that the new Authority shall consist of between 8 and 13 members appointed by the Secretary of State, some of whom must have the experience and capacity described in sub-s(4). Provision is made for the chairman and deputy chairman (if any) to be similarly appointed, and effect is given to Sch 4, which provides for such matters as the status, powers, officers, staff, financing and proceedings of the Authority.

Schedule 2 to the Charities Act 1993 is prospectively amended by para 7 of Sch 7 to this Act to constitute the QCA an exempt charity. Further consequential amendments to the Education Act 1996 and other enactments are prospectively made by paras 1–6 and 26–30 of that Schedule.
Commencement 1 October 1997: SI 1997/1468.

Functions of the Authority

22 General function of Authority to advance education and training
(1) The functions conferred on the Qualifications and Curriculum Authority by this Part shall be exercised by the Authority for the purpose of advancing education and training in England and (so far as such functions are exercisable there) in Wales and in Northern Ireland.
(2) The Authority shall exercise their functions under this Part with a view to promoting quality and coherence in education and training in relation to which they have functions under this Part.

General This section gives the QCA their general function: the functions conferred on the QCA by this Part of the Act are to be exercised for the purpose of advancing education and training in England and (so far as those functions are exercisable there) in Wales and Northern Ireland, with a view to promoting quality and coherence in the education and training to which those functions relate.
Commencement 1 October 1997: SI 1997/1468.
Definition For 'functions' see s 56(2) and the Education Act 1996, s 579(1).

23 Functions of the Authority in relation to curriculum and assessment
(1) The Qualifications and Curriculum Authority shall have the functions set out in subsection (2) with respect to pupils of compulsory school age at maintained schools in England.
(2) The functions are—
    (a) to keep under review all aspects of the curriculum for such schools and all aspects of school examinations and assessment;
    (b) to advise the Secretary of State on such matters concerned with the curriculum for such schools or with school examinations and assessment as he may refer to them or as they may see fit;
    (c) to advise the Secretary of State on, and if so requested by him assist him to carry out, programmes of research and development for purposes connected with the curriculum for such schools or with school examinations and assessment;
    (d) to publish and disseminate, and assist in the publication and dissemination of, information relating to the curriculum for such schools or to school examinations and assessment;
    (e) to make arrangements with appropriate bodies for auditing the quality of assessments made in pursuance of assessment arrangements; and
    (f) so far as relevant to such schools, the functions conferred by section 24(2)(h) and (i).
(3) The Authority shall have, in relation to England, the function of developing learning goals and related materials for children who are receiving nursery education in respect

Education Act 1997

of which grants are (or are to be) made under arrangements under section 1 of the Nursery Education and Grant-Maintained Schools Act 1996.

(4) The Authority shall have, in relation to England, the following functions in connection with baseline assessment schemes (within the meaning of Chapter I of Part IV), namely—
- (a) if designated by the Secretary of State for the purpose, any function of a designated body under that Chapter; and
- (b) any other function which may be conferred on the Authority by the Secretary of State.

(5) In this section—
'assessment' includes examination and test; and
'maintained school' means—
- (a) any county or voluntary school;
- (b) any grant-maintained school; and
- (c) any maintained or grant-maintained special school.

General This section sets out the detailed functions of the QCA in relation to pupils of compulsory school age at maintained schools in England: ie reviewing all aspects of the curriculum and all aspects of school examinations and assessment; advising the Secretary of State on these matters, and on research and development for purposes connected with them, and helping him to carry out such research and development if requested to do so; publishing and disseminating information about them; arranging for appropriate bodies to audit the quality of assessments; and, if designated, advising the Secretary of State on the approval of external qualifications under s 37 and carrying out related functions, so far as relevant to such schools—sub-ss (1) and (2); developing learning goals and related materials for children receiving nursery education in England under the Nursery Education and Grant-Maintained Schools Act 1996—sub-s (3); if designated, carying out the functions of a designated body relating to baseline assessment schemes in England (which may include accrediting schemes of baseline assessment) and carrying out any other function in connection with such schemes which may be conferred on them by the Secretary of State—sub-s (4).
Sub-s (5) defines 'assessment' in this section as including examination and test; and 'maintained school' as meaning any county or voluntary school, any GM school, and any LEA-maintained or GM special school.
Commencement 1 October 1997: SI 1997/1468.
Definition In this section, for 'assessment' and 'maintained school', see sub-s (5). See s 56(2) and the Education Act 1996 for 'assessment arrangements': s 353; 'county school': s 31(1);
'functions' s 579(1); 'grant-maintained school': s 183(1); 'grant-maintained special school': ss 337(4) and 346(3); 'maintained special school': ss 6(2), 33(1), 337(3); 'pupil': ss 3(1), 19(5); 'voluntary school': ss 31(2), 32.
'Compulsory school age' See the Education Act 1996, Sch 40, para 1, until the commencement of s 8; thereafter s 8, as prospectively amended by s 52 of this Act.

24 Functions of the Authority in relation to external vocational and academic qualifications

(1) The Qualifications and Curriculum Authority shall have, in relation to England, the functions set out in subsection (2) with respect to external qualifications.

(2) The functions are—
- (a) to keep under review all aspects of such qualifications;
- (b) to advise the Secretary of State on such matters concerned with such qualifications as he may refer to them or as they may see fit;
- (c) to advise the Secretary of State on, and if so requested by him assist him to carry out, programmes of research and development for purposes connected with such qualifications;
- (d) to provide support and advice to persons providing courses leading to such qualifications with a view to establishing and maintaining high standards in the provision of such courses;
- (e) to publish and disseminate, and assist in the publication and dissemination of, information relating to such qualifications;
- (f) to develop and publish criteria for the accreditation of such qualifications;
- (g) to accredit, where they meet such criteria, any such qualifications submitted for accreditation;

Appendix 9

    (h) if designated by the Secretary of State for the purpose, to advise the Secretary of State on the exercise of his powers under section 37 (approval of external qualifications); and

    (i) if designated by the Secretary of State for the purpose, to exercise any functions conferred on a designated body by regulations under that section.

(3) Except to the extent that, by virtue of an order under section 30(1), they are for the time being exercisable with respect to such qualifications solely by the Qualifications, Curriculum and Assessment Authority for Wales, the functions set out in subsection (2)(a) to (g) shall be so exercisable in relation to Wales by the Qualifications and Curriculum Authority, and shall be so exercisable either—

    (a) solely by the Authority, or

    (b) if an order under section 30(1) so provides, by the Authority concurrently with the Qualifications, Curriculum and Assessment Authority for Wales.

(4) The functions set out in subsection (2)(a) to (g) shall also be exercisable by the Qualifications and Curriculum Authority in relation to Northern Ireland but only with respect to National Vocational Qualifications.

(5) Subsection (2)(a) to (e) do not apply to qualifications awarded or authenticated by institutions within the higher education sector other than those which have been submitted for accreditation under subsection (2)(g).

(6) In this section 'external qualification' means—

    (a) any academic or vocational qualification authenticated or awarded by an outside person, except an academic qualification at first degree level or any comparable or higher level; or

    (b) (whether within paragraph (a) or not) any National Vocational Qualification.

(7) For the purposes of this section—

    (a) a qualification is awarded by an outside person if the course of education or training leading to the qualification is provided by an institution or an employer and it is awarded by a person other than the institution or employer or a member of its or his staff; and

    (b) a qualification is authenticated by an outside person if it is awarded by an institution or employer and is authenticated by a person other than the institution or employer or a member of its or his staff.

General This section bestows on the QCA detailed functions in relation to England with respect to external qualifications (defined in sub-ss (6) and (7)) corresponding to those imposed by s 23(2)(a), (b), (c) and (d) in relation to the school curriculum and assessment—sub-ss (1) and (2)(a), (b), (c) and (e). In addition the QCA is to provide support and advice to persons providing courses leading to such qualifications, so as to establish and maintain high standards; develop and publish criteria for the accreditation of such qualifications; accredit qualifications meeting such criteria; if designated, advise the Secretary of State on the approval of external qualifications under s 37, and exercise any functions conferred on a designated body by regulations under s 37—sub-s (2). The former functions, the provision of support and advice, and the accreditation functions are also exercisable, by the QCA alone or concurrently with the ACCAC, in relation to Wales, except to the extent that, by virtue of an order under s 30(1), they are exercisable solely by the ACCAC; and by the QCA, with respect to National Vocational Qualifications, in relation to Northern Ireland—sub-ss (3) and (4). Sub-s (2)(a)–(e) do not however apply to qualifications awarded or authenticated by higher education institutions, unless submitted for accreditation—sub-s (5).

Commencement 1 October 1997: SI 1997/1468.

Definition For 'external qualification' and 'qualification 'awarded' or 'authenticated' by an outside person' in this section, see sub-ss (6) and (7). For 'regulations' see s 56(1). For 'institutions within the higher education sector' see the Further and Higher Education Act 1992, s 91(5). For 'functions' see s 56(2) and the Education Act 1996, s 579(1).

25 Other functions of the Authority

(1) The Qualifications and Curriculum Authority shall advise the Secretary of State on such matters connected with the provision of education or training in England as the Secretary of State may specify by order.

(2) The Authority shall carry out such ancillary activities as the Secretary of State may direct.

(3) For the purposes of subsection (2) activities are ancillary activities in relation to the

Authority if the Secretary of State considers it is appropriate for the Authority to carry out those activities for the purposes of or in connection with the carrying out by the Authority of any of their other functions under this Part.

(4) The Authority shall supply the Secretary of State with such reports and other information with respect to the carrying out of their functions as the Secretary of State may require.

General This section requires the QCA to advise the Secretary of State on such matters connected with the provision of education or training in England as he may specify by order, and to carry out such ancillary activities (defined in sub-s (3)) as he may direct—sub-ss (1) and (2). The QCA is also to supply him with such reports and other information with respect to the carrying out of their functions as he may require—sub-s (4).
Commencement 1 October 1997: SI 1997/1468.
Definition For 'ancillary activities' in sub-s (2), see sub-s (3). For 'functions' see s 56(2) and the Education Act 1996, s 579(1).
'By order' Orders under this section are not to be made by statutory instrument: s 54(1).

26 Supplementary provisions relating to discharge by Authority of their functions
(1) In carrying out their functions under this Part the Qualifications and Curriculum Authority shall—
　(a) comply with any directions given by the Secretary of State; and
　(b) act in accordance with any plans approved by him; and
　(c) so far as relevant, have regard to—
　　(i) the requirements of section 351 of the Education Act 1996 (general duties in respect of curriculum),
　　(ii) the requirements of industry, commerce, finance and the professions regarding education and training (including required standards of practical competence), and
　　(iii) the requirements of persons with special learning needs.
(2) In carrying out those functions the Authority shall in addition have regard to information supplied to them by Her Majesty's Chief Inspector of Schools in England or by any body designated by the Secretary of State for the purposes of this section.
(3) Where in carrying out any of their functions under this Part the Authority accredit or approve any qualification, they may do so on such terms (including terms as to payment) and subject to such conditions as they may determine.
(4) Those conditions may in particular include conditions—
　(a) placing a limit on the amount of the fee that can be demanded in respect of any award or authentication of the qualification in question; and
　(b) requiring rights of entry to premises and to inspect and copy documents so far as necessary for the Authority to satisfy themselves that the appropriate standards are being maintained, in relation to the award or authentication of the qualification in question, by the persons receiving the accreditation or approval.
(5) Before exercising on any occasion their power to impose conditions falling within subsection (4)(a) the Authority shall obtain the consent of the Secretary of State as to such matters relating to the exercise of that power as he may determine.
(6) In this section 'persons with special learning needs' means—
　(a) children with special educational needs (as defined in section 312 of the Education Act 1996); or
　(b) persons (other than children as so defined) who—
　　(i) have a significantly greater difficulty in learning than the majority of persons of their age, or
　　(ii) have a disability which either prevents or hinders them from making use of educational facilities of a kind generally provided for persons of their age.

General This section imposes certain requirements on the QCA as to the manner in which they are to exercise their functions (sub-ss (1), (2) and (6)) and gives them power to attach terms and conditions to their accreditation or approval of any qualification (sub-ss (3)–(5)).
The QCA must comply with directions given by the Secretary of State, and act in accordance with any plans which he has approved. They must have regard to the requirements imposed by s 351 of

Appendix 9

the Education Act 1996, ie that a school curriculum should be balanced and broadly based, should promote the spiritual, moral, cultural, mental and physical development of pupils and of society, and prepare pupils for the opportunities, responsibilities and experiences of adult life. They must have regard to the requirements of industry, commerce, finance and the professions for education and training. They must have regard to the requirements of persons with 'special learning needs', ie children with special educational needs as defined in s 312 of the Education Act 1996, and other persons who have a significantly greater difficulty in learning than the majority of persons of their age, or have a disability which prevents or hinders them from making use of educational facilities. Finally they must have regard to information supplied to them by HM Chief Inspector of Schools in England, or by any body designated by the Secretary of State for this purpose.

When the QCA accredit or approve any qualification, they may do so on terms and conditions determined by them, including terms as to payment, and (subject to the consent of the Secretary of State) placing a limit on the amount of the fee that can be demanded for the award or authentication of a particular qualification; and requiring rights of entry and to inspect and copy documents so as to enable them to verify that proper standards are being maintained by the external awarding or authenticating body.

Commencement 1 October 1997: SI 1997/1468.
Definition 'Persons with special learning needs' (in this section): sub-s (6). For 'functions' see s 56(2) and the Education Act 1996, s 579(1).

Chapter II

The Qualifications, Curriculum and Assessment Authority for Wales

Renaming of the Authority

27   The Qualifications, Curriculum and Assessment Authority for Wales
(1) The body corporate known as Awdurdod Cwricwlwm ac Asesu Cymru shall continue in existence but, as from the commencement of this section, shall be known as Awdurdod Cymwysterau, Cwricwlwm ac Asesu Cymru or the Qualifications, Curriculum and Assessment Authority for Wales.
(2) The Authority shall consist of not less than 10 nor more than 15 members appointed by the Secretary of State.
(3) Of the members of the Authority, the Secretary of State—
   (a) shall appoint one as chairman, and
   (b) may appoint another as deputy chairman.
(4) The Secretary of State—
   (a) shall include among the members of the Authority—
      (i) persons who appear to him to have relevant knowledge or experience in education, and
      (ii) persons who appear to him to have relevant knowledge or experience in training; and
   (b) may include among those members persons who appear to him to have experience of occupations, trades or professions having an interest in education or training.
(5) Schedule 5 to this Act, which replaces Schedule 30 to the Education Act 1996, has effect in relation to the Authority.

General This section provides that the body corporate known as the Curriculum and Assessment Authority for Wales, Awdurdod Cwricwlwm ac Asesu Cymru, 'ACAC', originally established by s 14 of the Education Reform Act 1988 as the Curriculum Council for Wales and renamed by s 253 of the Education Act 1993 and given additional functions, is to continue in existence but be renamed the Qualifications, Curriculum and Assessment Authority for Wales, Awdurdod Cymwysterau, Cwricwlwm ac Asesu Cymru, 'ACCAC'. The ACCAC is to continue to consist of between 10 and 15 members appointed by the Secretary of State, some of whom must now have the experience and capacity described in sub-s(4). Provision is made for the chairman and deputy chairman (if any) to be similarly appointed, and effect is given to Sch 5, which replaces Sch 30 to the 1996 Act (repealed by Sch 8) and provides for such matters as the status, powers, officers, staff, financing and proceedings of the ACCAC.

Education Act 1997

Schedule 2 to the Charities Act 1993 is prospectively amended by para 7 of Sch 7 to this Act to substitute the new name of the Authority as an exempt charity.
Commencement 1 October 1997: SI 1997/1468.

Functions of the Authority

28 General function of Authority to advance education and training
(1) The functions conferred on the Qualifications, Curriculum and Assessment Authority for Wales by this Part shall be exercised by the Authority for the purpose of advancing education and training in Wales.
(2) The Authority shall exercise their functions under this Part with a view to promoting quality and coherence in education and training in relation to which they have functions under this Part.

General This section gives the ACCAC their general function: the functions conferred on the ACCAC by this Part of the Act are to be exercised for the purpose of advancing education and training in Wales, with a view to promoting quality and coherence in the education and training to which those functions relate.
Commencement 1 October 1997: SI 1997/1468.
Definition For 'functions' see s 56(2) and the Education Act 1996, s 579(1).

29 Functions of the Authority in relation to curriculum and assessment
(1) The Qualifications, Curriculum and Assessment Authority for Wales shall have the functions set out in subsection (2) with respect to pupils of compulsory school age at maintained schools in Wales.
(2) The functions are—
  (a) to keep under review all aspects of the curriculum for such schools and all aspects of school examinations and assessment;
  (b) to advise the Secretary of State on such matters concerned with the curriculum for such schools or with school examinations and assessment as he may refer to them or as they may see fit;
  (c) to advise the Secretary of State on, and if so requested by him assist him to carry out, programmes of research and development for purposes connected with the curriculum for such schools or with school examinations and assessment;
  (d) to publish and disseminate, and assist in the publication and dissemination of, information relating to the curriculum for such schools or to school examinations and assessment;
  (e) to make arrangements with appropriate bodies for auditing the quality of assessments made in pursuance of assessment arrangements; and
  (f) so far as relevant to such schools, the functions conferred by section 30(3).
(3) The Authority shall have, in relation to Wales, the function of developing learning goals and related materials for children who are receiving nursery education in respect of which grants are (or are to be) made under arrangements under section 1 of the Nursery Education and Grant-Maintained Schools Act 1996.
(4) The Authority shall have, in relation to Wales, the following functions in connection with baseline assessment schemes (within the meaning of Chapter I of Part IV), namely—
  (a) if designated by the Secretary of State for the purpose, any function of a designated body under that Chapter; and
  (b) any other function which may be conferred on the Authority by the Secretary of State.
(5) In this section 'assessment' and 'maintained school' have the same meaning as in section 23.

General This section sets out, in terms virtually identical terms to those of s 23 above relating to the QCA, the detailed functions of the ACCAC in relation to pupils of compulsory school age at maintained schools in Wales, and in relation to nursery education and baseline assessment schemes.
Commencement 1 October 1997: SI 1997/1468.
Definition In this section, for 'assessment' and 'maintained school', see sub-s (5) and s 23 above. See s 56(2) and the Education Act 1996 for 'assessment arrangements: s 353; 'county school': s 31(1);

'functions': s 579(1); 'grant-maintained school': s 183(1); 'grant-maintained special school': ss 337(4) and 346(3); 'maintained special school': ss 6(2), 33(1), 337(3); 'pupil': ss 3(1), 19(5); 'voluntary school': ss 31(2), 32.
'Compulsory school age' See the Education Act 1996, Sch 40, para 1, until the commencement of s 8; thereafter s 8, as prospectively amended by s 52 of this Act.

30 Functions of the Authority in relation to external vocational and academic qualifications

(1) The Qualifications, Curriculum and Assessment Authority for Wales shall have, in relation to Wales, such functions with respect to external qualifications as are for the time being conferred on the Authority by an order made by the Secretary of State under this subsection or by subsection (3).

(2) The functions with respect to external qualifications which may be conferred on the Authority by an order under subsection (1) are functions falling within paragraphs (a) to (g) of section 24(2), and the functions in question may be so conferred so as to be exercisable either—
  (a) solely by the Authority, or
  (b) by the Authority concurrently with the Qualifications and Curriculum Authority.

(3) The Authority shall have, in relation to Wales, the following functions with respect to external qualifications, namely—
  (a) if designated by the Secretary of State for the purpose, to advise the Secretary of State on the exercise of his powers under section 37 (approval of external qualifications); and
  (b) if designated by the Secretary of State for the purpose, to exercise any functions conferred on a designated body by regulations under that section.

(4) Where an order under subsection (1) is made so as to come into force at any time after the day on which that subsection comes into force, the order may include provisions—
  (a) for the transfer of staff, and
  (b) for the transfer of property, rights and liabilities held, enjoyed or incurred in connection with any function which, as a result of the order, is to be exercisable by the Authority (whether solely or concurrently).

(5) In this section 'external qualification' has the same meaning as in section 24.

General This section provides that the ACCAC shall have, in relation to Wales, the function of advising the Secretary of State on the approval of external qualifications under s 37 (if they are designated by him for this purpose) and (if so designated) exercising the other functions of a designated body under that section—sub-s (3). Section 24(3) above authorises the QCA to exercise in relation to Wales the functions relating to external qualifications set out in s 24(2)(a)–(g), except to the extent that an order made by the Secretary of State under sub-s (1) of this section confers those functions on the ACCAC, either alone or jointly with the QCA. Such an order may, if coming into force after sub-s (1) of this section, make provision for the transfer of staff and relevant property, rights and liabilities—sub-s (4). Such transfers are exempt from stamp duty: s 53.
Commencement 1 October 1997: SI 1997/1468.
Definition For 'external qualification', in this section, see sub-s (5) and s 24(6). For 'functions' see s 56(2) and the Education Act 1996, s 579(1).
Order Orders under sub-s (1) are to be made by statutory instrument, subject to the negative resolution procedure: s 54.

31 Other functions of the Authority

(1) The Qualifications, Curriculum and Assessment Authority for Wales shall advise the Secretary of State on such matters connected with the provision of education or training in Wales as the Secretary of State may specify by order.

(2) The Authority shall carry out such ancillary activities as the Secretary of State may direct.

(3) For the purposes of subsection (2) activities are ancillary activities in relation to the Authority if the Secretary of State considers it is appropriate for the Authority to carry out those activities for the purposes of or in connection with the carrying out by the Authority of any of their other functions under this Part.

Education Act 1997

(4) The Authority shall supply the Secretary of State with such reports and other information with respect to the carrying out of their functions as the Secretary of State may require.

General This section requires the ACCAC, in similar terms to s 25 above, to advise the Secretary of State on such matters connected with the provision of education or training in Wales as he may specify by order, and to carry out such ancillary activities (defined in sub-s (3)) as he may direct—sub-ss (1) and (2). The ACCAC is also to supply him with such reports and other information with respect to the carrying out of their functions as he may require—sub-s (4).
Commencement 1 October 1997: SI 1997/1468.
Definition For 'ancillary activities' in sub-s (2), see sub-s (3). For 'functions' see s 56(2) and the Education Act 1996, s 579(1).
'By order' Orders under this section are not to be made by statutory instrument: s 54(1).

32 Supplementary provisions relating to discharge by Authority of their functions
(1) In carrying out their functions under this Part the Qualifications, Curriculum and Assessment Authority for Wales shall—
   (a) comply with any directions given by the Secretary of State; and
   (b) act in accordance with any plans approved by him; and
   (c) so far as relevant, have regard to—
      (i) the requirements of section 351 of the Education Act 1996 (general duties in respect of curriculum),
      (ii) the requirements of industry, commerce, finance and the professions regarding education and training (including required standards of practical competence), and
      (iii) the requirements of persons with special learning needs.
(2) In carrying out those functions the Authority shall in addition have regard to information supplied to them by Her Majesty's Chief Inspector of Schools in Wales or by any body designated by the Secretary of State for the purposes of this section.
(3) Where in carrying out any of their functions under this Part the Authority accredit or approve any qualification, they may do so on such terms (including terms as to payment) and subject to such conditions as they may determine.
(4) Those conditions may in particular include conditions—
   (a) placing a limit on the amount of the fee that can be demanded in respect of any award or authentication of the qualification in question; and
   (b) requiring rights of entry to premises and to inspect and copy documents so far as necessary for the Authority to satisfy themselves that the appropriate standards are being maintained, in relation to the award or authentication of the qualification in question, by the persons receiving the accreditation or approval.
(5) Before exercising on any occasion their power to impose conditions falling within subsection (4)(a) the Authority shall obtain the consent of the Secretary of State as to such matters relating to the exercise of that power as he may determine.
(6) In this section 'persons with special learning needs' has the same meaning as in section 26.

General This section, following closely the provisions of s 26 above, imposes certain requirements on the ACCAC as to the manner in which they are to exercise their functions (sub-ss (1), (2) and (6)) and gives them power to attach terms and conditions to their accreditation or approval of any qualification (sub-ss (3)–(5)).
Commencement 1 October 1997: SI 1997/1468.
Definition 'Persons with special learning needs' (in this section): see sub-s (6) and s 26(6). For 'functions' see s 56(2) and the Education Act 1996, s 579(1).

Appendix 9

Chapter III

Provisions Supplementary to Chapters I and II

Dissolution of existing bodies

33 Dissolution of existing bodies. The National Council for Vocational Qualifications and the School Curriculum and Assessment Authority are hereby dissolved.

General This section dissolves the National Council for Vocational Qualifications and the School Curriculum and Assessment Authority, to be succeeded by the QCA under s 21 above. Sections 358 and 359 of and Sch 29 to the Education Act 1996, which continued the SCAA in existence and set out their functions, and ss 400 and 401 of that Act, which related to the approval of courses leading to external qualfications, are repealed by s 57(4) and Sch 8.
Commencement A date to be appointed by the Secretary of State by order under s 58(3).

Transfer of property and staff

34 Transfer of property
(1) The Secretary of State may by order provide for the transfer to the Qualifications and Curriculum Authority, or (as the case may be) to the Qualifications, Curriculum and Assessment Authority for Wales, of—
 (a) such of the land or other property of the National Council for Vocational Qualifications or the School Curriculum and Assessment Authority, and
 (b) such of the rights and liabilities of either of those bodies (other than rights and liabilities arising under contracts of employment),
as, in his opinion, need to be transferred to enable the transferee Authority to carry out their functions properly.
(2) No order under subsection (1) may be made after the end of the period of six months beginning with the day on which section 21 comes into force.
(3) Any order under subsection (1) made before the day on which section 21 comes into force shall come into force on that day.
(4) Where, immediately after the end of the period within which an order under subsection (1) may be made, any property, rights or liabilities remain vested in the National Council for Vocational Qualifications or the School Curriculum and Assessment Authority, they shall forthwith vest in the Secretary of State.
(5) The Secretary of State may by order provide that there shall be substituted for the period mentioned in subsection (2) such shorter period as he may specify in the order, being a period ending no earlier than the day on which the order comes into force.

General This section enables the Secretary of State to transfer by order to the QCA or the ACCAC such land and other property of the National Council for Vocational Qualifications or the School Curriculum and Assessment Authority, and such of the rights and liabilities of those bodies (other than those arising under a contract of employment—as to which see s 35) as need to be transferred to enable the transferee Authority to carry out their functions properly—sub-s (1). Such an order must be made within six months from the commencement of s 21 (1 October 1997)—sub-s (2)— but if made before that date shall come into force on that date—sub-s (3). Any property, rights or liabilities not transferred when the period for making such an order expires will vest in the Secretary of State—sub-s (4). The Secretary of State may by order substitute a shorter period for the six months mentioned in sub-s (2)—sub-s (5). Transfers under this section are exempt from stamp duty: s 53.
Commencement 1 September 1997: SI 1997/1468.
Definition For 'land' and 'liability' see s 56(2) and the Education Act 1996, s 579(1).
'By order' Orders under this section are to be made by statutory instrument, subject to the negative resolution procedure: s 54.

35 Transfer of staff
(1) This section applies to any person who—
 (a) is employed by the National Council for Vocational Qualifications ('the NCVQ') or the School Curriculum and Assessment Authority ('the SCAA') immediately before section 21 comes into force, and

Education Act 1997

    (b) is designated as respects the Qualifications and Curriculum Authority, or (as the case may be) the Qualifications, Curriculum and Assessment Authority for Wales, by order of the Secretary of State;
and in this section 'the relevant Authority' means, in relation to any such person, the Authority as respects which he is designated by the order.
(2) A contract of employment between a person to whom this section applies and the NCVQ or the SCAA shall have effect, from the day on which the order under subsection (1)(b) comes into force, as if originally made between him and the relevant Authority.
(3) Without prejudice to subsection (2)—
    (a) all the rights, powers, duties and liabilities of the NCVQ or the SCAA under or in connection with a contract to which that subsection applies shall by virtue of that subsection be transferred to the relevant Authority on the day on which the order under subsection (1)(b) comes into force, and
    (b) anything done before that day by or in relation to the NCVQ or the SCAA in respect of that contract or the employee shall be deemed from that day to have been done by or in relation to the relevant Authority.
(4) Subsections (2) and (3) are without prejudice to any right of an employee to terminate his contract of employment if his working conditions are changed substantially to his detriment; but such a change shall not be taken to have occurred by reason only of the change in employer effected by subsection (2).
(5) In subsection (4) the reference to an employee's working conditions includes a reference to any rights (whether accrued or contingent) under any pension or superannuation scheme of which he was a member by virtue of his employment with the NCVQ or the SCAA (as the case may be).
(6) An order under subsection (1)(b) may designate a person either individually or as falling within a class or description of employee.
(7) No order under subsection (1)(b) may be made after the end of the period of six months beginning with the day on which section 21 comes into force.
(8) Any order under subsection (1)(b) made before the day on which section 21 comes into force shall come into force on that day.
(9) The Secretary of State may by order provide that there shall be substituted for the period mentioned in subsection (7) such shorter period as he may specify in the order, being a period ending no earlier than the day on which the order comes into force.

General This section provides for the transfer of staff from the National Council for Vocational Qualifications and the School Curriculum and Assessment Authority to the QCA or the ACCAC. The transfer is effected by order of the Secretary of State, designating employees by name or by class or description. On entry into force of the order, the contract of employment of a designated employee takes effect as if originally made between him and the transferee Authority, with a consequential transfer of rights, powers, duties and liabilities—sub-s (2) and (3). If the employee's working conditions (including pension rights) are as a result changed substantially to his detriment, he may terminate his contract; but the transfer alone does not constitute such a change—sub-s (4). As under s 34, such an order must be made within six months from the entry into force of s 21 (establishment of the QCA) (1 October 1997) and if made before that date shall come into force on that date—sub-ss (7) and (8). The Secretary of State may by order substitute a shorter period than six months—sub-s (9).
Commencement 1 September 1997: SI 1997/1468.
Definition 'The relevant Authority' in this section: sub-s (1).
'By order' Orders under this section are to be made by statutory instrument, subject to the negative resolution procedure: s 54.

Levy on bodies awarding accredited qualifications

36 Levy on bodies awarding qualifications accredited by relevant Authority
(1) The Secretary of State may by regulations provide for a levy to be payable to the relevant Authority by persons who award vocational qualifications accredited by that Authority.
(2) Regulations under this section shall—

Appendix 9

    (a) specify the rate of the levy or the method by which it is to be calculated (and, without prejudice to the generality of section 54(3), may make different provision in relation to different cases);
    (b) make provision as to the times when, and the manner in which, payments are to be made in respect of the levy;
    (c) provide for the relevant Authority to withdraw their accreditation of a qualification in cases of non-payment of the levy.

(3) Any sums received by the relevant Authority in respect of the levy shall be applied by them in giving such financial assistance to other bodies as the Secretary of State may specify with a view to assisting that Authority to secure the development and improvement of standards in relation to vocational qualifications.

(4) In this section 'the relevant Authority' means—
    (a) the Qualifications and Curriculum Authority in the case of a qualification accredited by that Authority; and
    (b) the Qualifications, Curriculum and Assessment Authority for Wales in the case of a qualification accredited by that Authority.

General This section enables the Secretary of State to provide by regulations for a levy to be paid to the QCA or the ACCAC by those persons or bodies who award qualifications accredited by them. The regulations are to specify the rate of the levy (or the method by which it is to be calculated) and may make different provision for different cases; to prescribe when and how levy payments are to be made; and provide for the withdrawal of accreditation where the levy is not paid. The Authorities are to use the proceeds of the levy to pay grants to other bodies, as specified by the Secretary of State, so as to secure the development and improvement of standards of vocational qualifications.

Commencement 1 December 1997: SI 1997/1468.
Definition 'The relevant Authority', in this section: sub-s (4). 'Regulations': s 56(1).
'Person' includes a body of persons, corporate or unincorporate: Interpretation Act 1978, s 5, Sch 1.
Regulations Regulations under this section are to be made by statutory instrument, subject to the negative resolution procedure: s 54.

Chapter IV

Control of Certain Courses Leading to External Qualifications

37 Requirement for approval of certain publicly-funded and school courses leading to external qualifications

(1) The Secretary of State may by regulations provide—
    (a) that no course of study leading to an external qualification is to be provided with the use of any specified public funding, and
    (b) that no course of study leading to an external qualification is to be provided for pupils of compulsory school age by or on behalf of a maintained school,
unless (in each case) the qualification is for the time being approved by the Secretary of State or a designated body in accordance with the regulations.

(2) Regulations under this section may in particular make provision—
    (a) prescribing the conditions required to be satisfied before any qualification may be so approved and the circumstances in which any approval may be withdrawn;
    (b) conferring functions on a designated body in relation to any such conditions; and
    (c) imposing duties on governing bodies of institutions providing courses of study to which the regulations apply, and on head teachers, principals and other heads of such institutions, to secure compliance with the regulations.

(3) Regulations under this section shall not apply to—
    (a) any course of study provided at an institution within the higher education sector; or
    (b) any course of study leading to a qualification awarded or authenticated by any such institution.

(4) In this section—
'designated' means designated by the Secretary of State;
'external qualification' has the same meaning as in section 24;
'maintained school' has the same meaning as in section 23; and
'specified public funding' means public funding of such description as is specified in or determined in accordance with regulations under this section.
(5) Sections 400 and 401 of the Education Act 1996 (courses leading to external qualifications provided at schools and further education institutions), which are superseded by this section, shall cease to have effect.

General This section, replacing ss 400 and 401 of the Education Act 1996, enables the Secretary of State, by regulations, to prohibit the provision, with the aid of specified public funding, of any course of study leading to an external qualification, or the provision of such a course for pupils of compulsory school age by or on behalf of a maintained school, unless the qualification has been approved by him or by a designated body. The regulations may lay down conditions for the approval of a qualification, and define the circumstances in which such approval may be withdrawn; may confer functions relating to the conditions (such as devising them) on a designated body; and impose duties of securing compliance with the regulations on governing bodies and head teachers, principals and other heads of institutions providing such courses.

Courses provided at institutions within the higher education sector, or leading to a qualification awarded or authenticated by such an institution, are excluded from the application of regulations under this section—sub-s (3).

Commencement Subsections (1)–(4): 1 September 1997: SI 1997/1468; sub-s(5): a date to be appointed by the Secretary of State by order under s 58(3).

Definition For 'designated', 'external qualification', 'maintained school' and 'specified public funding' in this section, see sub-s (4). See s 56(2) and the Education Act 1996 for 'governing body': s 182; 'head teacher' (generally): s 579(1); (in relation to a school organised in separate departments): s 132. For 'institution within the higher education sector' see the Further and Higher Education Act 1992, s 91(5). For 'regulations': see s 56(1).

'Compulsory school age' See the Education Act 1996, Sch 40, para 1, until the commencement of s 8; thereafter s 8, as prospectively amended by s 52 of this Act.

Regulations Regulations under this section are to be made by statutory instrument, subject to the negative resolution procedure: s 54.

Part VI

Inspection of Local Education Authorities and School Inspections

Chapter I

Inspection of Local Education Authorities

38 Inspection of LEAs
(1) The Chief Inspector—
    (a) may, and
    (b) if requested to do so by the Secretary of State, shall,
arrange for any local education authority to be inspected under this section.
(2) An inspection of a local education authority under this section shall consist of a review of the way in which the authority are performing any function of theirs (of whatever nature) which relates to the provision of education—
    (a) for persons of compulsory school age (whether at school or otherwise), or
    (b) for persons of any age above or below that age who are registered as pupils at schools maintained by the authority.
(3) A request by the Secretary of State under this section may relate to one or more local education authorities, and shall specify both—
    (a) the local education authority or authorities concerned, and
    (b) the functions of theirs to which the inspection is to relate.
(4) Before making any such request the Secretary of State shall consult the Chief

Appendix 9

Inspector as to the matters to be specified in the request in accordance with subsection (3).
(5) Any inspection under this section shall be conducted—
  (a) by one of Her Majesty's Inspectors of Schools in England or (as the case may require) Wales, or
  (b) by any additional inspector authorised under paragraph 2 of Schedule 1 to the School Inspections Act 1996;
but he may be assisted by such other persons (whether or not members of the Chief Inspector's staff) as the Chief Inspector thinks fit.
(6) For the purposes of this section a local education authority shall provide the Chief Inspector with such information as may be prescribed, and shall do so in such form and—
  (a) within such period following a request made by the Chief Inspector in any prescribed circumstances, or
  (b) at such other times,
as regulations may provide.
(7) In this section and sections 39 to 41 'the Chief Inspector' means—
  (a) in relation to a local education authority in England, Her Majesty's Chief Inspector of Schools in England; and
  (b) in relation to a local education authority in Wales, Her Majesty's Chief Inspector of Schools in Wales;
and in those sections references to 'the inspector' in relation to an inspection under this section are references to the person conducting the inspection.

General Chapter I of this Part (ss 38–41) provides for the inspection of local education authorities by the Chief Inspectors of Schools for England and for Wales. Section 38 gives the Chief Inspectors the power and, if requested by the Secretary of State, the duty, of arranging an inspection of an LEA, ie a review of the way in which the LEA are performing any function of theirs relating to the provision of education for persons of compulsory school age, including registered pupils (of whatever age) at schools which they maintain—sub-ss (1) and (2). Before requesting an inspection under this section, the Secretary of State is to consult the Chief Inspector as to the scope of the inspection—sub-ss (3) and (4). The inspection is to be conducted by one of HM Inspectors of Schools, or by a duly authorised additional inspector, assisted by such other persons as the Chief Inspector thinks fit. An LEA are to provide the Chief Inspector with such information as may be prescribed by regulations, in such form and within such period or at such other times as the regulations may provide—sub-ss (5) and (6).
Commencement 1 September 1997: SI 1997/1468.
Definition In ss 38—41, for 'the Chief Inspector' and 'the inspector' see sub-s (7). For 'prescribed' and 'regulations' see s 56(1). See s 56(2) and the Education Act 1996 for 'functions': s 579(1); 'local education authority': s 12 (1)–(5); 'maintain': s 34; 'pupil': ss 3(1), 19(5); 'registered pupil': s 434(5); 'school': s 4 (as prospectively substituted by s 51).
'Compulsory school age' See the Education Act 1996, Sch 40, para 1, until the commencement of s 8; thereafter s 8, as prospectively amended by s 52 of this Act.
Regulations Regulations under this section are to be made by statutory instrument, subject to the negative resolution procedure: s 54.

39 Reports of inspections under s 38 and action plan by LEA

(1) Where an inspection under section 38 has been completed, the inspector shall make a written report on the matters reviewed in the course of the inspection, and shall send copies of the report to—
  (a) any local education authority to which the inspection relates; and
  (b) the Secretary of State.
(2) Where a local education authority receive a copy of a report under this section, they shall prepare a written statement of the action which they propose to take in the light of the report and the period within which they propose to take it.
(3) The authority shall publish—
  (a) the report, and
  (b) the statement prepared under subsection (2),
within such period, and in such manner, as may be prescribed.
(4) The Chief Inspector may arrange for any report under this section to be published in such manner as he considers appropriate.

Education Act 1997

General This section requires an inspector, following completion of an inspection under s 38 above, to make a written report and send copies to any LEA to which it relates and to the Secretary of State. When the LEA receive their copy, they must prepare a written statement, stating the action which they propose to take and within what period. The report and action plan are to be published by the LEA within such period and in such manner as may be prescribed by regulations. The Chief Inspector may also arrange for any report to be published, in such manner as he considers appropriate.
Commencement 1 September 1997: SI 1997/1468.
Definition In this section, for 'the Chief Inspector' and 'the inspector' see s 38(7). For 'prescribed' see s 56(1). For 'local education authority' see s 56(2) and the Education Act 1996, s 12 (1)–(5).
'Written' Expressions referring to writing are to be construed as including references to other modes of representing or reproducing words in visible form: Interpretation Act 1978, s 5, Sch 1.
Regulations Regulations under this section are to be made by statutory instrument, subject to the negative resolution procedure: s 54.

40 Inspector's rights of entry etc
(1) The inspector in the case of any inspection under section 38, and any person assisting him, shall have at all reasonable times—
  (a) a right of entry to the premises of any local education authority to which the inspection relates, and
  (b) a right to inspect, and take copies of, any records kept by the authority, and any other documents containing information relating to the authority, which he considers relevant to the exercise of his functions;
and section 42 of the School Inspections Act 1996 (inspection of computer records for purposes of Part I of that Act) shall apply for the purposes of this section as it applies for the purposes of Part I of that Act.
(2) Without prejudice to subsection (1) above, a local education authority to which an inspection under section 38 relates shall give the inspector, and any person assisting him, all assistance in connection with the exercise of his functions which they are reasonably able to give.
(3) In the case of any inspection under section 38, subsection (1) above shall apply in relation to any school maintained by any local education authority to which the inspection relates as it applies in relation to the authority; and without prejudice to that subsection (as it so applies)—
  (a) the governing body of any such school shall give the inspector, and any person assisting him, all assistance in connection with the exercise of his functions which they are reasonably able to give; and
  (b) the governing body of any such school and the authority shall secure that all such assistance is also given by persons who work at the school.
(4) In this section 'document' and 'records' each include information recorded in any form.

General This section gives the inspector and those assisting him a right of entry, at all reasonable times, to the premises of any LEA to which the inspection relates, and a right to inspect and take copies of any records kept by the LEA and other documents containing information about the LEA which he considers relevant. Section 42 of the School Inspections Act 1996, (inspection of computer records) is applied for the purposes of this section—sub-s (1). These rights extend to any school maintained by the LEA under inspection —sub-s (3). An LEA under inspection and the governing body of any such school is required to give the inspector and his assistants all assistance which they are reasonably able to give, and must secure that all such assistance is also given by persons who work at the school—sub-ss (2) and (3).
Commencement 1 September 1997: SI 1997/1468.
Definition In this section, for 'the inspector' see s 38(7), and for 'document' and 'records' see sub-s (4). See s 56(2) and the Education Act 1996 for 'functions': s 579(1); 'governing body': s 182; 'local education authority': s 12 (1)–(5); 'maintain': s 34; 'school': s 4 (as prospectively substituted by s 51).

41 Inspections involving collaboration of Audit Commission
(1) If requested to do so by the Chief Inspector, the Audit Commission may assist with any inspection under section 38; and subsections (2) to (5) below have effect where the Commission assist with any such inspection.
(2) Section 40 shall apply to the Commission and to any authorised person as it applies to the inspector.

Appendix 9

(3) Any information obtained by virtue of section 40 by a person falling within one of the categories mentioned in subsection (4) may be disclosed for the purposes of the inspection, or the preparation or making of the report under section 39(1), to a person falling within the other category.
(4) Those categories are—
    (a) the Commission and any authorised person; and
    (b) the inspector and any person assisting him.
(5) Any report prepared under section 39(1) shall be prepared by the inspector acting in conjunction with the Commission.
(6) The Commission shall not provide assistance under this section unless, before it does so, the Chief Inspector has agreed to pay the Commission an amount equal to the full costs incurred by the Commission in providing the assistance.
(7) In this section—
'the Audit Commission' means the Audit Commission for Local Authorities and the National Health Service in England and Wales; and
'authorised person' means a person authorised by the Audit Commission for the purposes of this section.

General This section enables the Audit Commission for Local Authorities and the National Health Service in England and Wales to assist a Chief Inspector with any inspection under s 38, when requested to do so by him—sub-s (1). Section 40 above (rights of entry and to inspect and copy documents and records, duty of LEA to assist) is applied to the Commission and to any person authorised by them for the purposes of this section—sub-s (2). Sub-ss (3) and (4) allow for the exchange of relevant information between the inspector leading the inspection and those assisting him on the one hand and the Commission and any 'authorised person' on the other. The report of such an inspection is to be prepared by the inspector in conjunction with the Commission—sub-s (5). The Chief Inspector is required by sub-s (6) to agree to pay the Commission their full costs of assisting in the inspection before they can agree to assist.

The Audit Commission was established by the Local Government Finance Act 1982, s 11. For their functions in relation to further and higher education and GM schools, see the Education Reform Act 1988, s 220.
Commencement 1 September 1997: SI 1997/1468.
Definition For 'the Audit Commission' and 'authorised person' in this section, see sub-s (7). For 'the Chief Inspector' and 'the inspector' see s 38(7).

Chapter II

School Inspections

42 Miscellaneous amendments relating to school inspections. Schedule 6 (which contains amendments relating to inspections under the School Inspections Act 1996 and the Nursery Education and Grant-Maintained Schools Act 1996) shall have effect.

General This section gives effect to Sch 6, which makes amendments relating to inspections under the School Inspections Act 1996 and the Nursery Education and Grant-Maintained Schools Act 1996.
Commencement 1 September 1997: SI 1997/1468.

Part VII

Careers Education and Guidance

43 Provision of careers education in schools
(1) All registered pupils at a school to which this section applies must be provided, during the relevant phase of their education, with a programme of careers education.
(2) This section applies to—
    (a) county and voluntary schools;
    (b) grant-maintained schools;
    (c) maintained or grant-maintained special schools (other than those established in hospitals);

(d) city technology colleges and city colleges for the technology of the arts; and
(e) pupil referral units.

(3) It is the duty of each of the following to secure that subsection (1) is complied with, namely—
   (a) in the case of a school falling within subsection (2)(a) to (c), the governing body of the school and its head teacher,
   (b) in the case of a school falling within subsection (2)(d), the proprietors of the school and its head teacher, and
   (c) in the case of a pupil referral unit, the local education authority maintaining the unit and the teacher in charge of it.

(4) Each of sections 496 and 497 of the Education Act 1996 (default powers of Secretary of State) shall, in relation to the duty imposed by subsection (3) above, have effect as if any reference to a body to which that section applies included a reference to the proprietors of a school falling within subsection (2)(d) above.

(5) For the purposes of this section the relevant phase of a pupil's education is the period—
   (a) beginning at the same time as the school year in which the majority of pupils in his class attain the age of 14; and
   (b) ending with the expiry of the school year in which the majority of pupils in his class attain the age of 16.

(6) In this section—
'career' includes the undertaking of any training, employment or occupation or any course of education;
'careers education' means education designed to prepare persons for taking decisions about their careers and to help them implement such decisions;
'class', in relation to a particular pupil, means—
   (a) the teaching group in which he is regularly taught, or
   (b) if he is taught in different groups for different subjects, such one of those groups as is designated by the head teacher of the school or, in the case of a pupil at a pupil referral unit, by the teacher in charge of the unit.

General Part VII of the Act (ss 43—46) is concerned with the provision of careers education and guidance in publicly funded schools and institutions in the further education sector. Section 43(1) requires a programme of careers education, as defined in sub-s (6), to be provided for all registered pupils at the publicly funded schools listed in sub-s (2) during the 'relevant phase' of their education: ie the last three years of compulsory schooling—sub-s (5). The schools referred to include all LEA-maintained and grant-maintained schools and special schools (except hospital schools), city technology colleges and city colleges for the technology of the arts, and pupil referral units, but not other independent schools or further education colleges. The duty to secure that such education is provided falls on the governing body or proprietor of the school and the head teacher, or, in the case of a pupil referral unit, the maintaining LEA and teacher in charge; and the default powers of the Secretary of State under ss 496 and 497 of the Education Act 1996 are extended to cover the proprietors of CTCs and CCTAs for this purpose—sub-s (4).

Commencement A date to be appointed by the Secretary of State by order under s 58(3).

Definition For 'career', 'careers education' and 'class' in this section, see sub-s (6); for 'the relevant phase of a pupil's education' see sub-s (5). See s 56(2) and the Education Act 1996 for 'city college for the technology of the arts', 'city technology college': s 482(3); 'county school': s 31(1); 'governing body': s 182; 'grant-maintained school': s 183(1); 'grant-maintained special school': ss 337(4) and 346(3); 'head teacher' (generally): s 579(1); (in relation to a school organised in separate departments): s 132; 'local education authority': s 12 (1)–(5); 'maintained special school': ss 6(2), 33(1), 337(3); 'proprietor': s 579(1); 'pupil referral unit': s 19(2); 'registered pupil': s 434(5); 'school year': s 579(1), as amended by Sch 7, para 43, this Act; 'voluntary school': ss 31(2), 32.

44 Schools and other institutions to co-operate with careers advisers

(1) Where a careers adviser has responsibilities in relation to persons attending an educational institution to which this section applies, he shall on request be provided with—
   (a) the name and address of every relevant pupil or student at the institution; and
   (b) any information in the institution's possession about any such pupil or student which the careers adviser needs in order to be able to provide him with

Appendix 9

advice and guidance on decisions about his career or with other information relevant to such decisions.

(2) If the registered address of a parent of any such pupil is different from the pupil's registered address, subsection (1)(a) requires the parent's address to be provided as well.

(3) Paragraph (a) or (as the case may be) paragraph (b) of subsection (1) does not, however, apply to any pupil or student to the extent that—
  (a) (where he is under the age of 18) a parent of his, or
  (b) (where he has attained that age) he himself,
has indicated that any information falling within that paragraph should not be provided to the careers adviser.

(4) Where a careers adviser has responsibilities in relation to persons attending an educational institution to which this section applies, he shall on request be permitted to have, in the case of any relevant pupil or student specified by him, access to that person—
  (a) on the institution's premises, and
  (b) at a reasonable time agreed by or on behalf of the head teacher, principal or other head of the institution,
for the purpose of enabling him to provide that person with advice and guidance on decisions about his career and with any other information relevant to such decisions.

(5) Such access shall include an opportunity for the careers adviser to interview that person about his career, if he agrees to be so interviewed.

(6) Where a careers adviser has responsibilities in relation to persons attending an educational institution to which this section applies, he shall on request be permitted to have, in the case of any group of relevant pupils or students specified by him, access—
  (a) to that group of persons in the manner specified in subsection (4)(a) and (b), and
  (b) to such of the institution's facilities as can conveniently be made available for his use,
for the purpose of enabling him to provide those persons with group sessions on any matters relating to careers or to advice or guidance about careers.

(7) Any request made for the purposes of subsection (1), (4) or (6) must be made in writing to the head teacher, principal or other head of the institution in question.

(8) This section applies to—
  (a) the schools listed in section 43(2)(a) to (d); and
  (b) institutions within the further education sector.

(9) It is the duty of each of the following to secure that subsections (1), (4) and (6) are complied with, namely—
  (a) in the case of a school falling within section 43(2)(a) to (c) or an institution within the further education sector, the governing body of the school or institution and its head teacher, principal or other head, and
  (b) in the case of a school falling within section 43(2)(d), the proprietors of the school and its head teacher;
and section 43(4) shall apply in relation to that duty as it applies in relation to the duty imposed by section 43(3).

(10) For the purposes of this section—
  (a) a pupil at a school is a relevant pupil—
    (i) at any time during the period which is the relevant phase of his education for the purposes of section 43, or
    (ii) if he is over compulsory school age and receiving secondary education; and
  (b) a person is a relevant student at an institution within the further education sector if he is receiving at the institution either—
    (i) full-time education, or
    (ii) part-time education of a description commonly undergone by persons in order to fit them for employment.

(11) For the purposes of this section—
  (a) 'careers adviser' means a person who is employed by a body providing services in pursuance of arrangements made or directions given under section 10

of the Employment and Training Act 1973 and who is acting, in the course of his employment by that body, for the purposes of the provision of any such services; and
  (b) a careers adviser has responsibilities for any persons if his employment by that body includes the provision of any such services for them.
(12) In this section 'career' has the same meaning as in section 43.

General This section is concerned with the facilities to be afforded to 'careers advisers' , defined by sub-s (11) as persons employed by a body providing services in pursuance of arrangements made or directions given under s 10 of the Employment and Training Act 1973, and providing such services in the course of that employment. These services are concerned primarily with the giving of assistance by collecting or disseminating or otherwise providing information about persons seeking, obtaining or offering employment, training and education, and offering advice and guidance—see s 8(2) of the 1973 Act. If the careers adviser's employment includes the provision of any such services for any persons, he is said in this section to 'have responsibilities' for them—sub-s (11).

The educational institutions to which this section applies are the schools listed in s 43(2), with the exception of pupil referral units, together with institutions within the further education sector—sub-s (8).

Sub-s (1) requires a careers adviser with responsibilities for any persons attending such an educational institution to be provided, on request, with the name and address of every relevant pupil or student, as defined in sub-s (10)—ie school pupils aged 14–16 and over and further education students other than part-time students not pursuing employment-related studies. He must also be provided with his parent's address (if different); and with any information in the possession of the institution about the pupil or student which he needs in order to be able to provide the pupil or student with advice and guidance about his career. A parent, or the pupil or student himself if he has attained the age of 18, may however bar the provision of such particulars—sub-s (3).

A careers adviser is also to be allowed access on request to any relevant pupil or student he may specify, on the premises, at a reasonable time agreed by the head teacher, principal or other head of the institution, to enable him to give advice, guidance and information relevant to decisions about his career—sub-s (4). If the pupil or student agrees, this may include an interview with him about his career—sub-s (5).

A careers adviser is to be allowed similar access on request to groups of pupils or students, and to such of the institution's facilities as can conveniently be made available for his use, to enable him to conduct group sessions on matters relating to careers including advice and guidance—sub-s (6).

The careers adviser's request is in each case to be made in writing to the head teacher, principal or head of the institution—sub-s (7).

As under s 43(3), the duty of ensuring that the career adviser's rights under this section are allowed him falls on the governing body and head teacher, principal or other head except in the case of a CTC or CCTA, when it falls on the proprietor and head teacher; and ss 496 and 497 of the Education Act 1996 are similarly extended to include such proprietors—sub-s (9).

Commencement 1 September 1997: SI 1997/1468.

Definition For 'career' in this section see sub-s (12) and s 43(6). For 'careers adviser' in this section and the responsibilities of such an adviser for any person see sub-s (11). For 'relevant pupil' and 'relevant student' in this section see sub-s (10). For 'relevant phase' see s 43(5). For 'institution within the further education sector' see the Further and Higher Education Act 1992, s 91(3). See s 56(2) and the Education Act 1996 for 'governing body': s 182; 'head teacher' (generally): s 579(1); (in relation to a school organised in separate departments): s 132; 'parent': s 576; 'premises' (of a school): s 579(1); 'proprietor': s 579(1); 'pupil': ss 3(1), 19(5); 'secondary education': s 2(2) and (5).

'Compulsory school age' See the Education Act 1996, Sch 40, para 1, until the commencement of s 8; thereafter s 8, as prospectively amended by s 52 of this Act.

45 Provision of careers information at schools and other institutions
(1) Persons attending an educational institution to which this section applies must be provided with access to both—
  (a) guidance materials, and
  (b) a wide range of up-to-date reference materials,
relating to careers education and career opportunities.
(2) This section applies to—
  (a) the schools listed in section 43(2)(a) to (d); and
  (b) institutions within the further education sector.
(3) It is the duty of each of the following to secure that subsection (1) is complied with, namely—

Appendix 9

    (a) in the case of a school falling within section 43(2)(a) to (c) or an institution within the further education sector, the governing body of the school or institution and its head teacher, principal or other head, and

    (b) in the case of a school falling within section 43(2)(d), the proprietors of the school and its head teacher;

and section 43(4) shall apply in relation to that duty as it applies in relation to the duty imposed by section 43(3).

(4) The persons who under subsection (3) above are responsible for discharging that duty in relation to an institution shall seek assistance with discharging it from a body providing services in pursuance of arrangements made or directions given under section 10 of the Employment and Training Act 1973.

(5) In this section 'career' and 'careers education' have the same meaning as in section 43.

(6) Nothing in this section applies to any primary school.

General All persons attending an educational institution to which this section applies—ie publicly funded schools (except hospital schools and pupil referral units) and further education institutions—are required by this section to be given access to guidance materials and a wide range of up-to-date reference materials relating to careers education and career opportunities—sub-ss (1) and (2). As under ss 43 and 44, the duty of ensuring that access to such materials is afforded falls on the governing body and head teacher, principal or other head except in the case of a CTC or CCTA, when it falls on the proprietor and head teacher; and ss 496 and 497 of the Education Act 1996 are similarly extended to include such proprietors—sub-s (3). They are required to seek assistance in discharging this duty from a body through whom the Secretary of State has arranged, under s 10 of the Employment and Training Act 1973, for careers services to be provided—sub-s (4).

Sub-s (5) provides that this section does not apply to primary schools. Nor in fact do ss 43 and 44, in so far as they are confined to pupils aged 14 to 16 or over. This section goes wider.

Commencement 1 September 1997: SI 1997/1468.

Definition For 'career' and 'careers education' in this section see sub-s (5) and s 43(6). For 'institution within the further education sector' see the Further and Higher Education Act 1992, s 91(3). See s 56(2) and the Education Act 1996 for 'governing body': s 182; 'head teacher' (generally): s 579(1); (in relation to a school organised in separate departments): s 132; 'primary school': s 5(1); 'proprietor': s 579(1).

46 Extension or modification of provisions of ss 43 to 45

(1) The Secretary of State may by regulations extend the scope of operation of section 43 or section 44 by substituting for the period specified in section 43(5) or section 44(10)(a)(i) such other period as is specified.

(2) The Secretary of State may by regulations make provision for extending the scope of operation of section 43, 44 or 45 to primary schools or to any specified description of such schools.

(3) The Secretary of State may by regulations make provision for requiring—

    (a) the governing bodies of institutions within the further education sector, and

    (b) the principals or other heads of such institutions,

to secure that a programme of careers education is provided for any specified description of persons attending such institutions.

(4) The Secretary of State may by regulations amend the definition of 'careers adviser' set out in section 44(11)(a).

(5) In this section—

'careers education' has the same meaning as in section 43;

'specified' means specified in the regulations in question.

General This section enables the Secretary of State, by regulations, to extend or modify the preceding three sections.

The duty under s 43 to provide careers education applies only to pupils between 14 and 16, and the duty to co-operate with careers advisers under s 44 applies, so far as schools are concerned, only in relation to pupils aged 14 and over. Sub-s (1) allows these ages to be extended.

Sub-s (2) allows ss 43—45 to be extended to primary schools or any specified descriptions of such schools.

The duty under s 43, at present limited to schools, may be extended to further education institutions—sub-s (3).

The definition of 'careers adviser' in s 44(11)(a) may be amended.

Commencement 1 September 1997: SI 1997/1468.

Education Act 1997

Definition For 'careers education' and 'specified' in this section see sub-s (5). For 'regulations' see s 56(1). For 'institution within the further education sector' see the Further and Higher Education Act 1992, s 91(3). For 'primary school' see s 56(2) and the Education Act 1996, s 5(1).
Regulations Regulations under this section are to be made by statutory instrument, subject to the negative resolution procedure: s 54.

Part VIII

Miscellaneous and General

Exceptional educational provision

47 Functions of LEAs as regards exceptional educational provision
(1) Section 19 of the Education Act 1996 (exceptional provision of education in pupil referral units or elsewhere) shall be amended as follows.
(2) In subsection (1) (duty of local education authority to make arrangements for provision of suitable full-time or part-time education, at school or otherwise, for excluded children etc), the words 'full-time or part-time' shall be omitted.
(3) In subsection (4) (power of local education authority to make arrangements for provision of suitable full-time or part-time education, otherwise than at school, for excluded young persons etc), the words 'full-time or part-time' shall be omitted.
(4) After that subsection there shall be inserted—

> '(4A) In determining what arrangements to make under subsection (1) or (4) in the case of any child or young person a local education authority shall have regard to any guidance given from time to time by the Secretary of State.'

General This section amends sub-ss (1) and (4) of s 19 of the Education Act 1996, which require LEAs to provide suitable full-time or part-time education (at school or otherwise) for children of compulsory school age who, because of illness, exclusion from school or otherwise, may not receive suitable education unless exceptional arrangements are made for them, and enables them to make similar provision in the case of young persons over compulsory school age but under 18, by deleting the words 'full-time or part-time'; and inserts a new sub-s (4A) requiring LEAs, in such cases, to have regard to guidance given by the Secretary of State.
Commencement A date to be appointed by the Secretary of State by order under s 58(3).
Definition 'Child', 'young person': Education Act 1996, s 579.

Management committees for pupil referral units

48 Management committees for pupil referral units. At the end of Schedule 1 to the Education Act 1996 (pupil referral units) there shall be added—

'Management committees

> 15 (1) Regulations may make provision—
>   (a) for requiring any local education authority who maintain a pupil referral unit to establish a committee to act as the management committee for the unit; and
>   (b) for that committee to discharge on behalf of the authority such of their functions in connection with the unit as are delegated by them to the committee in accordance with the regulations.
>   (2) Regulations under this paragraph may in particular make provision—
>   (a) for enabling a local education authority to establish a joint committee to act as the management committee for two or more pupil referral units maintained by the authority;
>   (b) for requiring the approval of the Secretary of State to be obtained before any such joint committee is established;
>   (c) as to the composition of a management committee established under the regulations and—
>   (i) the appointment and removal of its members, and
>   (ii) their terms of office,
>   and in particular for requiring such a committee to include persons representing

Appendix 9

schools (including grant-maintained schools) situated in the area from which the unit or units in question may be expected to draw pupils;
(d) for requiring or (as the case may be) prohibiting the delegation by a local education authority to a management committee of such functions in connection with pupil referral units as are specified in the regulations;
(e) for authorising a management committee to establish sub-committees;
(f) for enabling (subject to any provisions of the regulations) a local education authority or a management committee to determine to any extent the committee's procedure and that of any sub-committee;
(g) for limiting the personal liability of members of any such committee or sub-committee in respect of their acts or omissions as such members;
(h) for applying to any such committee or sub-committee, with or without modification—
  (i) any provision of the Education Acts, or
  (ii) any provision made by or under any other enactment and relating to committees or (as the case may be) sub-committees of a local authority.'

General This section adds a new para 15 to Sch 1 to the Education Act 1996 enabling regulations to be made requiring LEAs who maintain pupil referral units to establish management committees for such units, to discharge functions in connection with the unit delegated to them by the LEA. Sub-para (2) of the new para 15 specifies certain matters for which provision may be made in such regulations, including the application to such committees, and their sub-committees, of other statutory provisions.
Commencement 1 December 1997: SI 1997/1468.
Definition See the Education Act 1996 for 'the Education Acts': s 578, (as amended to include this Act by Sch 7, para 42); 'functions': s 579(1); 'grant-maintained school': s 183(1); 'local education authority': s 12 (1)–(5); 'maintain': s 34; 'pupil': ss 3(1), 19(5); 'pupil referral unit': s 19(2); 'regulations': s 579(1); 'school': s 4 (as prospectively substituted by s 51).
Regulations Regulations under para 15 are to be made by statutory instrument, subject to the negative resolution procedure: Education Act 1996, s 569.

Teachers not under contract of employment and persons having access to those under 19

49 Power to make regulations: teachers not under contract of employment and persons having access to those under 19

(1) Section 218 of the Education Reform Act 1988 (power of Secretary of State to make regulations in respect of schools and further and higher education institutions) shall be amended as follows.
(2) After subsection (6) there shall be inserted—

'(6A) The Secretary of State may by regulations impose requirements on—
  (a) local education authorities,
  (b) the governing bodies of schools or institutions falling within subsection (10) below, or
  (c) the proprietors of independent schools,
for the purpose of prohibiting or restricting, on medical grounds or in cases of misconduct, access to persons who have not attained the age of nineteen years by persons (not falling within subsection (6) above) who provide services falling within subsection (6B).
(6B) Those services are services provided in relation to the school or institution or persons attending it which—
  (a) are provided by whatever means and whether under contract or otherwise, and
  (b) bring the persons providing them regularly into contact with persons who have not attained the age of nineteen years.'

(3) In subsection (12) (definition of 'school'), after '(6)(d)' there shall be inserted 'or (6A)'.
(4) After subsection (12) there shall be inserted—

'(13) For the purposes of this section—
  (a) any reference to persons employed as teachers includes a reference to persons engaged to provide their services as teachers otherwise than under contracts of employment; and
  (b) any reference to teachers or other persons employed by local education authorities or by any description of governing bodies or proprietors includes a

Education Act 1997

reference to teachers or other persons engaged to provide their services for such authorities, governing bodies or proprietors (as the case may be) otherwise than under contracts of employment;
and any reference to employment (or further employment) shall be construed accordingly.'

General This section amends s 218 of the Education Reform Act 1988, so as to extend the scope of the regulations which may be made to restrict or prohibit access to children and young persons attending educational institutions. (See for example reg 10 of the Education (Teachers) Regulations 1993, SI 1993/543, made under s 218(6), under which the Secretary of State may bar persons from employment as teachers or in work which brings them regularly into contact with young persons. 'Employment' is defined in s 235 of the 1988 Act, as meaning employment under a contract of employment.) Sub-s (2) inserts new sub-ss (6A) and (6B) enabling regulations under s 218 to require LEAs, the governing bodies of schools and institutions of further or higher education falling within s 218(10), and proprietors of independent schools, to prohibit or restrict persons providing services having access to persons under 19, either on medical grounds or in cases of misconduct. 'Services' are widely defined in sub-s (6B) so as to include services not provided under contract with the school; the regulations may accordingly apply to volunteers and those who work under a contract with a company providing services such as transport or specialised tuition at a school, as well as those employed under a contract for services, rather than a contract of employment.

Sub-s (4) inserts a new sub-s (13) applying an extended definition of employment for the general purposes of s 218 so as to cover persons who provide teaching and other services otherwise than under a contract of employment.

Commencement Subsections (2) and (3), and subs (1) to the extent that it relates to those sub-sections: 1 October 1997: SI 1997/1468. Sub-s (4): a date to be appointed by the Secretary of State by order under s 58(3).

Definition For 'school' in s 218 see s 218(12) as prospectively amended by sub-s (3). See the Education Reform Act 1988, s 235(7) and the Education Act 1996 for 'governing body' (of a school): s 182; 'independent school': s 463; 'local education authority': s 12 (1)–(5); 'proprietor' and 'regulations': s 579(1).

Regulations Regulations under s 218 are to be made by statutory instrument , subject to the negative resolution procedure: Education Reform Act 1988, s 232.

Costs of teachers' premature retirement

50 Recoupment by local education authority of costs of teachers' premature retirement

(1) Section 139 of the Education Act 1996 (payments in respect of dismissal etc of teachers at schools with delegated budgets) shall be amended as follows.

(2) In subsection (5) (local education authority's costs in respect of teacher's dismissal or premature retirement not normally to be met from school's budget share), at the beginning there shall be inserted 'Subject to subsection (5A),'.

(3) After that subsection there shall be inserted—

'(5A) Subsection (5) does not apply to costs incurred by the local education authority in respect of any premature retirement of a member of the staff of the school occurring on or after the date of the passing of the Education Act 1997; and such costs shall be met from the school's budget share for one or more financial years except in so far as the authority agree with the governing body (whether before or after the retirement occurs) that they shall not be so met.

(5B) The agreement of the local education authority for the purposes of subsection (5A) must be given in writing on or after the date of the passing of that Act.'

(4) For the avoidance of doubt, the provisions inserted by this section have effect in relation to a school despite anything in any scheme prepared by the local education authority under section 103 of the Education Act 1996 (schemes providing for financial delegation).

General This section, which came into force on Royal Assent (21 March 1997), amended s 139 of the Education Act 1996. Sub-s (5) was amended, and new sub-ss (5A) and (5B) inserted, so as to require the costs incurred by the LEA in respect of the premature retirement of any member of the staff of a school with a delegated budget occurring on or after 21 March 1997 to be met from the school's budget share, except in so far as the LEA agree to the contrary. Such agreement must be given in writing on or after that date. (Section 139 (5) formerly provided that such costs should not

Appendix 9

be met from the school's budget share except in so far as the LEA had 'good reason' for deducting them.) These provisions override any provision to the contrary in the LEA's scheme of financial delegation under Chapter V of Part II of the 1996 Act—sub-s (4).
Commencement 21 March 1997: s 58(4).
Definition See the Education Act 1996: 'budget share': s 101(3) and (6); 'financial year': s 579(1); 'governing body': s 182; 'the local education authority': s 579(1).
'In writing' 'Writing ' includes typing, printing, lithography, photography and other modes of representing or reproducing words in visible form: Interpretation Act 1978, s 5, Sch 1.

Definition of 'school'

51 Definition of 'school'. In section 4 of the Education Act 1996 (definition of 'school'), for subsection (1) there shall be substituted—

'(1) In this Act 'school' means an educational institution which is outside the further education sector and the higher education sector and is an institution for providing—
   (a) primary education,
   (b) secondary education, or
   (c) both primary and secondary education,
whether or not the institution also provides part-time education suitable to the requirements of junior pupils or further education.'

General This section substitutes a new definition of 'school' in s 4(1) of the Education Act 1996, omitting the reference to institutions outside the further education sector catering solely for those aged 16 to 18, included in the definition as enacted in s 14 of the Further and Higher Education Act 1992. The new definition makes it clear that to be a 'school' for the purposes of the Education Acts an institution must be outside the further or higher education sectors and provide primary or secondary education or both, even if it also provides part-time education suitable for children under 12 or further education.

See also the amendment of s 4(2) made by para 10 of Sch 7.
Commencement 1 September 1997: SI 1997/1468.
Definition For 'further education', 'primary education', and 'secondary education' see the Education Act 1996, s 2; for 'junior pupil': s 3(2). For 'institution outside the further / higher education sector' see the Further and Higher Education Act 1992, s 91(3) and (5).

Compulsory school age

52 Commencement of compulsory school age
(1) Section 8 of the Education Act 1996 (compulsory school age) shall be amended in accordance with subsections (2) and (3).
(2) For subsection (2) there shall be substituted—

'(2) A person begins to be of compulsory school age—
   (a) when he attains the age of five, if he attains that age on a prescribed day, and
   (b) otherwise at the beginning of the prescribed day next following his attaining that age.'

(3) For subsection (4) there shall be substituted—

'(4) The Secretary of State may by order—
   (a) provide that such days in the year as are specified in the order shall be, for each calendar year, prescribed days for the purposes of subsection (2);
   (b) determine the day in any calendar year which is to be the school leaving date for that year.'

(4) The Secretary of State may also make an order providing that such days in the year as are specified in the order shall be, for each calendar year during the whole or part of which section 8 of the Education Act 1996 is not wholly in force, prescribed days for the purposes of paragraph 1(2) of Schedule 40 to that Act (transitory provisions pending coming into force of section 8 of that Act) as it has effect in accordance with subsection (5) below.
(5) Where a person does not attain the age of five on any of those prescribed days, he shall be regarded for the purposes of paragraph 1(2) of that Schedule—
   (a) as not attaining that age, and

(b) accordingly as not being of compulsory school age,
until the beginning of the prescribed day next following his fifth birthday.

General This section substitutes new sub-ss (2) and (4) in s 8 of the Education Act 1996, to enable the Secretary of State to prescribe by order dates in each year for the purpose of determining when children begin to be of compulsory school age. A child will begin to be of compulsory school age if he attains five on one of the prescribed dates, or on the next prescribed date following his fifth birthday. By virtue of s 433 of the 1996 Act, schools are not obliged to admit a child as soon as he reaches compulsory school age, but can wait until the beginning of the next school term. The existing power of the Secretary of State to determine by order the day in each calendar year which is to be the school leaving date for that year is re-enacted in the new sub-s (4).

Sub-ss (4) and (5) of this section relate to the transitory provisions in para 1 of Sch 40 to the 1996 Act which have effect until s 8 is brought into force. The Secretary of State is given power to determine by order prescribed dates in the period pending the commencement of s 8. Unless a child attains the age of five on one of those days, he is deemed not to be of compulsory school age until the next prescribed date after his fifth birthday.

Consequential amendments in the Nursery Education and Grant-Maintained Schools Act 1996, the Education Act 1996 and the School Inspections Act 1996 are made by Sch 7, paras 8, 11–14, 17, 19, 21, 23–25, 34(b) and (c), 35, 36, 46 and 51.

Commencement Sub-section (4): 1 September 1997: SI 1997/1468. Sub-ss (1)–(3) and (5): a date to be appointed by the Secretary of State by order under s 58(3).

'By order' Orders under the substituted s 8(4) of the 1996 Act and under s 52(4) of this Act are to be made by statutory instrument, subject to the negative resolution procedure—s 568 of the 1996 Act; s 54 of this Act.

General provisions

53 Stamp duty

(1) Subject to subsection (2), stamp duty shall not be chargeable in respect of any transfer effected by virtue of section 30 or 34.

(2) No instrument (other than a statutory instrument) made or executed in pursuance of either of the provisions mentioned in subsection (1) shall be treated as duly stamped unless it is stamped with the duty to which it would, but for this section (and, if applicable, section 129 of the Finance Act 1982), be liable or it has, in accordance with the provisions of section 12 of the Stamp Act 1891, been stamped with a particular stamp denoting that it is not chargeable with any duty or that it has been duly stamped.

General This section exempts from stamp duty transfers effected by virtue of s 30 or 34 (transfers to the Qualifications and Curriculum Authority and to the Qualifications, Curriculum and Assessment Authority for Wales). The instrument of transfer (unless it is a statutory instrument) must be stamped in accordance with sub-s (2).

Commencement 1 October 1997: SI 1997/1468.

54 Orders and regulations

(1) Any power of the Secretary of State to make orders or regulations under this Act, except an order under section 25 or 31, shall be exercised by statutory instrument.

(2) A statutory instrument containing any order or regulations under this Act, except an order under section 58, shall be subject to annulment in pursuance of a resolution of either House of Parliament.

(3) Any order or regulations under this Act may make different provision for different cases, circumstances or areas and may contain such incidental, supplemental, saving or transitional provisions as the Secretary of State thinks fit.

(4) Without prejudice to the generality of subsection (3), any order or regulations under this Act may make in relation to Wales provision different from that made in relation to England.

General This section contains procedural and other provisions relating to orders and regulations made under this Act. These do not apply to orders and regulations made under provisions inserted by this Act into the Education Act 1996, which are governed by ss 568 and 569 of that Act, as amended by para 40 of Sch 7. Orders and regulations under this Act are to be made by statutory instrument, with the exception of orders under ss 25 and 31, conferring additional advisory functions on the QCA and ACCAC. With the exception of commencement orders under s 58, such

Appendix 9

instruments are subject to the negative resolution procedure—sub-ss (1) and (2). Orders and regulations may make different provision for different cases, circumstances and areas (including different provisions for England and for Wales) and include the ancillary provisions listed in sub-s (3).
Commencement 21 March 1997: s 58(4).

55 Financial provisions. There shall be paid out of money provided by Parliament—
  (a) any sums required for the payment by the Secretary of State of grants under this Act;
  (b) any administrative expenses incurred by the Secretary of State in consequence of this Act; and
  (c) any increase attributable to this Act in the sums so payable under any other Act.

General This is the customary provision for grants under the Act, together with consequential administrative expenses incurred by the Secretary of State and increases in sums so payable under other Acts, to be paid out of money provided by Parliament.
Commencement 14 June 1997: SI 1997/1468.

56 Construction
(1) In this Act—
'prescribed' means prescribed by regulations; and
'regulations' means regulations made by the Secretary of State under this Act.
(2) This Act shall be construed as one with the Education Act 1996.
(3) Where, however, an expression is given for the purposes of any provision of this Act a meaning different from that given to it for the purposes of that Act, the meaning given for the purposes of that provision shall apply instead of the one given for the purposes of that Act.

General This section defines 'prescribed' and 'regulations' as used in this Act, and provides for the Act to be construed as one with the Education Act 1996, except where this Act gives an expression a different meaning from that given to it by the 1996 Act.
Commencement 14 June 1997: SI 1997/1468.

57 Minor and consequential amendments, repeals etc
(1) The minor and consequential amendments set out in Schedule 7 shall have effect.
(2) Any reference in any enactment to Part I of Schedule 33 to the Education Act 1996 (appeal committees for hearing admission appeals), or to any provision of that Part of that Schedule, shall (so far as the context permits) be read as including a reference to that Part of that Schedule, or (as the case may be) to that provision of that Part, as applied by paragraph 4 of Schedule 16 or paragraph 3 of Schedule 33A to that Act.
(3) For the avoidance of doubt, the provisions inserted in the Education Act 1996 by Parts II and III of this Act have effect despite anything in the articles (or, as the case may be, in the instrument or articles) of government of a school to, or in relation to, which those inserted provisions apply or are applied.
(4) The enactments specified in Schedule 8 are repealed to the extent specified.

General Sub-ss (1) and (4) give effect to the minor and consequential amendments to, and the repeals of, other enactments set out in Schs 7 and 8.
  Sub-s (2) provides that references in other Acts to Part I of Sch 33 to the Education Act 1996 (admission appeal committees) (eg s 13(4)(b) of the Local Government and Housing Act 1989, as amended) also refer (where the context permits) to those provisions as applied by para 4 of Sch 16 (exclusion and reinstatement appeals under s 159) and by para 3 of the new Sch 33A (as inserted by s 12 and Sch 2)—appeals under s 423A(2) by a governing body against the admission of a child permanently excluded from two or more schools.
  Sub-s (3) provides, for the avoidance of doubt, that the provisions inserted into the Education Act 1996 by Parts II (discipline) and III (admissions) of this Act override anything in a school's instrument or articles of government.
Commencement Sub-s (1), as it applies in relation to para 48(2) of Sch 7: 21 March 1997: s 58(4). Sub-s (4), as it applies in relation to the repeal in the Education Act 1996, s 479(2): 4 April 1997: SI 1997/1153. Sub-ss (1) and (4), as they apply in relation to the provisions listed in Parts I, II and III of Sch 1 to the Education Act 1997 (Commencement No 2 and Transitional Provisions) Order 1997, SI 1997/1468, on 14 June, 1 September and 1 October 1997. Sub-ss (2) and (3): 1 September 1997: SI 1997/1468. Remaining provisions: a date to be appointed by the Secretary of State by order under s 58(3).

Education Act 1997

Definition For 'instrument' and 'articles of government' see the Education Act 1996: county, voluntary or maintained special school: ss 76(1), 127(1); GM school: s 218(1); GM special school: Sch 28, para 1.

58 Short title, commencement and extent etc

(1) This Act may be cited as the Education Act 1997.

(2) This Act shall be included in the list of Education Acts set out in section 578 of the Education Act 1996.

(3) Subject to subsection (4), this Act shall come into force on such day as the Secretary of State may by order appoint, and different days may be appointed for different provisions and for different purposes.

(4) The following provisions come into force on the day on which this Act is passed—
section 50,
section 54,
paragraph 48(2) of Schedule 7 and section 57(1) so far as relating thereto, and
this section.

(5) Subject to subsections (6) and (7), this Act extends to England and Wales only.

(6) The following provisions extend to Northern Ireland—
sections 21 and 22,
section 24(4),
section 26,
sections 34 to 36,
section 53,
section 54,
this section, and
Schedule 4.

(7) The amendment or repeal by this Act of an enactment extending to Scotland or Northern Ireland extends also to Scotland or, as the case may be, Northern Ireland.

General This section gives the short title of the Act and provides for its inclusion in the list of Education Acts in s 578 of the Education Act 1996. Sub-s (4) brought this section into force on Royal Assent, 21 March 1997, together with s 54 (orders and regulations) and s 50 (costs of teachers' premature retirement) with the consequential amendment in para 48(2) of Sch 7; the remaining provisions of the Act come into force on such day or days as the Secretary of State may appoint by order: sub-s (3). Sub-ss (5)–(7) define the extent of application of the Act: for the most part it extends only to England and Wales.

Commencement 21 March 1997: sub-s (4).

'By order' Commencement Orders under sub-s (3) are to be made by statutory instrument, but are not subject to the negative resolution procedure: s 54(1) and (2). See the Education Act 1997 (Commencement No 1) Order 1997, SI 1997/1153; the Education Act 1997 (Commencement No 2 and Transitional Provisions) Order 1997, SI 1997/1468.

Schedules

Section 8

Schedule 1

Schedule inserted after Schedule 25 to the Education Act 1996

General This Schedule sets out a new Sch 25A to be inserted in the Education Act 1996 laying down the procedure for appeals under s 307A (inserted by s 8(1)) against the permanent exclusion of pupils from GM and GM special schools. It reflects paras 5–18 of Sch 16 to the 1996 Act, as amended by s 7 of, and para 47 of Sch 7 and Sch 8 to, this Act.

Commencement A date to be appointed by the Secretary of State by order under s 58(3).

Definition For 'appeal', 'appeal committee' and 'the relevant person' in this Schedule, see para 1. See the Education Act 1996 for 'area': s 12(6); 'head teacher': s 579(1); 'instrument of government' (GM school): s 218(1); 'local education authority': s 12 (1)–(5); 'parent': s 576; 'pupil': ss 3(1), 19(5); 'school day': s 579(1).

Appendix 9

'**Belongs**' See the Education Act 1996, s 579(4), and the Education (Areas to which Pupils and Students Belong) Regulations 1996, SI 1996/615, as am by SI 1997/597.
'**Writing**' includes typing, printing, lithography, photography and other modes of representing or reproducing words in visible form: Interpretation Act 1978, s 5, Sch 1.
'**By order**' Orders under para 14 of Sch 25A are to be made by statutory instrument, subject to the negative resolution procedure: Education Act 1996, s 568.

Schedule 25A

Appeals against exclusion of pupils from grant-maintained schools

Introductory

1 In this Schedule—
'appeal' means an appeal mentioned in section 307A;
'appeal committee' means an appeal committee constituted for the purposes of an appeal in accordance with the instrument of government of the school;
'the relevant person' means—
    (a) in relation to a pupil under the age of 18, a parent of his;
    (b) in relation to a pupil who has attained that age, the pupil himself.

Procedure on appeal

2 An appeal shall be by notice in writing setting out the grounds on which it is made.

3 (1) Subject to sub-paragraph (2), the appeal committee shall meet to consider an appeal—
    (a) within the period ending with the 15th school day after the day on which the appeal is lodged, or
    (b) if the governing body have determined a shorter period, within that period.
(2) The governing body may extend the period within which the appeal committee are to consider an appeal where—
    (a) the relevant person requests them to do so; and
    (b) they are satisfied that the circumstances are exceptional and justify the period under sub-paragraph (1) being extended.

4 (1) For the purpose of fixing the time (falling within the period mentioned in paragraph 3) at which the hearing of an appeal is to take place, the governing body shall take reasonable steps to ascertain any times falling within that period when—
    (a) the relevant person, or
    (b) any other person who wishes, and would be entitled, to appear and make oral representations in accordance with paragraph 5,
would be able to attend.
(2) Where in accordance with sub-paragraph (1) the governing body have ascertained any such times in the case of any such person, they shall, when fixing the time at which the hearing is to take place, take those times into account with a view to ensuring, so far as it is reasonably practicable to do so, that that person is able to appear and make such representations at the hearing.

5 (1) The appeal committee shall give the relevant person an opportunity of appearing and making oral representations, and shall allow him to be represented or to be accompanied by a friend.
(2) The appeal committee shall allow—
    (a) the head teacher and a member of the governing body to make written representations;
    (b) the head teacher and a member of the governing body to appear and make oral representations; and

(c) the governing body to be represented.

6   An appeal shall be held in private except when otherwise directed by the governing body, but any member of the Council on Tribunals may attend as an observer any meeting of the appeal committee at which an appeal is considered.

7   Two or more appeals may be combined and dealt with in the same proceedings if the appeal committee consider that it is expedient to do so because the issues raised by the appeals are the same or connected.

8   (1) In deciding whether the pupil in question should be reinstated (and, if so, the time when this should take place), the appeal committee shall have regard to both the interests of that pupil and the interests of other pupils at his school and members of its staff.
(2) In making its decision on an appeal, the appeal committee shall also have regard to the measures publicised by the head teacher under section 306A(7).
(3) Sub-paragraphs (1) and (2) do not apply where the appeal committee decides that the pupil in question was not guilty of the conduct which the head teacher relied on as grounds for his permanent exclusion.
(4) Sub-paragraphs (1) and (2) shall not be read as precluding an appeal committee from having regard to any other relevant matters.

9   In the event of a disagreement between the members of the appeal committee the appeal under consideration shall be decided by a simple majority of the votes cast and, in the case of an equality of votes, the chairman of the committee shall have a second or casting vote.

10   Subject to paragraph 11, the decision of the appeal committee and the grounds on which it is made shall be communicated by the committee in writing to the relevant person, the governing body, the head teacher and the local education authority to whose area the pupil belongs within—
   (a) the period ending with the 17th school day after the day on which the appeal is lodged; or
   (b) if the governing body have determined a shorter period, that period.

11   Where the governing body extend the period for the consideration of an appeal in accordance with paragraph 3(2), they shall (to the extent it appears to them to be necessary as a result of the extension of that period) extend the period within which the appeal committee are to communicate their decision.

12   Subject to paragraphs 2 to 11, all matters relating to the procedure on appeals shall be determined by the governing body.

13   (1) Subject to sub-paragraph (2), where joint arrangements for appeals have been made in accordance with paragraph 6(2) of Schedule 23 (content of articles of government), paragraphs 2 to 12 shall have effect in respect of appeals to committees established in accordance with the joint arrangements.
(2) In the case of any appeal made in pursuance of the joint arrangements—
   (a) paragraphs 3, 4, 6, 10(b), 11 and 12 shall have effect as if for 'the governing body' there were substituted 'the governing body and the governing body of every other school which is a party to the arrangements, acting jointly'; and
   (b) paragraphs 5(2) and 10 (except paragraph 10(b)) shall have effect as if for 'the governing body' there were substituted 'the governing body against whose decision the appeal is made'.

Power of Secretary of State to make amendments

14   The Secretary of State may by order amend the preceding provisions of this Schedule.

Appendix 9

Section 12

Schedule 2

Schedule Inserted After Schedule 33 to the Education Act 1996

General This Schedule sets out a new Sch 33A to be inserted in the Education Act 1996 laying down the procedure for appeals by a governing body under s 423A (inserted by s 12(1)) against the LEA's decision to admit to their school a child who has been permanently excluded from two or more schools.
Commencement 1 September 1997: SI 1997/1468.
Definition For 'appeal' and 'appeal committee' in paras 5–14 of Sch 33A, see para 4. See the Education Act 1996 for 'local education authority': s 12 (1)–(5); 'school day': s 579(1).
'Writing' includes typing, printing, lithography, photography and other modes of representing or reproducing words in visible form: Interpretation Act 1978, s 5, Sch 1.
'By order' Orders under para 14 of Sch 33A are to be made by statutory instrument, subject to the negative resolution procedure: Education Act 1996, s 568.

Schedule 33A

Children to Whom Section 411A(2) Applies: Appeals by Governing Bodies

Duty to notify governing body of decision to admit child

1   Where any such decision as is mentioned in section 423A(2) is made by or on behalf of a local education authority, the authority shall give the governing body of the school notice in writing—
  (a) of that decision; and
  (b) of the governing body's right to appeal against the decision in accordance with paragraph 2.

Time limit on appealing

2   An appeal by the governing body against any such decision must be made not later than the 15th school day after the day on which they are given the notice under paragraph 1.

Appeal committees

3   (1)   Subject to sub-paragraphs (2) and (3) below, paragraphs 1, 5, 6 and 7 of Schedule 33 (school admission appeals) shall have effect in relation to appeals under section 423A(2) as they have effect in relation to appeals under section 423(1).
(2)   A person shall not be a member of an appeal committee for the consideration of an appeal under section 423A(2) if he has to any extent been involved in any previous consideration of the question whether the child in question should or should not be reinstated at any school from which he has at any time been permanently excluded, or in any previous appeal relating to the child under section 423A(2).
(3)   A person shall not be eligible to be a lay member for the purposes of paragraph 1(2)(a) of Schedule 33 (as it applies in accordance with this paragraph) unless he satisfies the condition set out in paragraph (b) of paragraph 5(2) of that Schedule as well as that set out in paragraph (a) of that provision.
(4)   In this paragraph 'appeal committee' means an appeal committee constituted in accordance with Part I of Schedule 33, as it applies in accordance with this paragraph.

Education Act 1997

Procedure on an appeal

4   In the following provisions of this Schedule—
'appeal' means an appeal under section 423A(2); and
'appeal committee' means such an appeal committee as is mentioned in paragraph 3(4) above.

5   An appeal shall be by notice in writing setting out the grounds on which it is made.

6   The appeal committee shall meet to consider an appeal—
   (a) within the period ending with the 15th school day after the day on which the appeal is lodged, or
   (b) if the local education authority have determined a shorter period, within that period.

7   On an appeal the committee shall allow—
   (a) the local education authority and the governing body to make written representations;
   (b) an officer of the authority nominated by the authority, and a governor nominated by the governing body, to appear and make oral representations; and
   (c) the governing body to be represented.

8   In considering an appeal the appeal committee shall have regard to—
   (a) the reasons for the local education authority's decision that the child in question should be admitted; and
   (b) any reasons put forward by the governing body as to why the child's admission would be inappropriate.

9   Appeals shall be heard in private except when otherwise directed by the local education authority, but any member of the local education authority or of the Council on Tribunals may attend, as an observer, any meeting of an appeal committee at which an appeal is considered.

10   Two or more appeals may be combined and dealt with in the same proceedings if the appeal committee consider that it is expedient to do so because the issues raised by the appeals are the same or connected.

11   In the event of a disagreement between the members of an appeal committee, the appeal under consideration shall be decided by a simple majority of the votes cast and, in the case of an equality of votes, the chairman of the committee shall have a second or casting vote.

12   The decision of an appeal committee and the grounds on which it is made shall be communicated by the committee in writing to—
   (a) the local education authority, and
   (b) the governing body making the appeal,
within the period ending with the 17th school day after the day on which the appeal is lodged.

13   (1) Subject to paragraphs 5 to 12, all matters relating to the procedure on appeals shall be determined by the local education authority.
(2) Neither section 106 of the Local Government Act 1972 nor paragraph 44 of Schedule 12 to that Act (procedure of committees of local authorities) shall apply to an appeal committee.

Power of Secretary of State to make amendments

14   The Secretary of State may by order amend the preceding provisions of this Schedule.

Appendix 9

Section 14

Schedule 3

Schedule Inserted as Schedule 33B to the Education Act 1996

General This Schedule sets out Schedule 33B, inserted into the Education Act 1996 by section 14(2). It enacts, for GM schools, provisions corresponding to the following provisions inserted into the Education Act 1996 by this Act—

Schedule 33B	Education Act 1996	Inserted by
Para 1	s 413A	s 13
Para 2	s 413B	s 13
Para 3	s 411(3)(c)	s 10
Para 4(1), (3)–(8)	s 411A(1)–(7)	s 11
Para 4(2)	s 423A(1)	s 12(1)

Commencement Paragraphs 3 and 4 of Sch 33B: 1 September 1997: SI 1997/1468; paras 1 and 2: a date to be appointed by the Secretary of State by order under s 58(3).
Definition In Schedule 33B, for 'admission arrangements', 'conditional place', 'parental declaration' and 'partnership document' in paras 1 and 2 see para 1(6) and 1(2); for 'selective admission arrangements' in para 3 see para 3(2); for 'school' in para 4 see para 4(6). In the Education Act 1996, for 'grant-maintained school': s 183(1); 'grant-maintained special school': ss 337(4) and 346(3); 'local education authority': s 12 (1)–(5); 'parent': s 576; 'school': s 4(1) and (2); 'school day': s 579(1).
'By order' An order under para 1(4) of Sch 33B is to be made by statutory instrument, subject to the negative resolution procedure, unless it applies only to a specified school or schools—s 568 of the Education Act 1996, as amended by para 40 of Sch 7 to this Act.

Schedule 33B

Restrictions on Admissions to Grant-Maintained Schools

Home-school partnership documents

1 (1) The admission arrangements for a grant-maintained school may include provisions—
   (a) setting out the terms of a partnership document for the school and the parental declaration to be used in connection with the document;
   (b) making it a condition of the admission of every child to the school that his parent gives the governing body a signed parental declaration either—
       (i) at the time of applying for a place at the school for the child, or
       (ii) if the child is allocated a conditional place, within such period as is specified in the arrangements; and
   (c) authorising the governing body to dispense with that condition to any extent in the case of a particular child where they are satisfied that there are special reasons for doing so.
(2) For the purposes of this paragraph and paragraph 2 a 'partnership document' is a statement specifying—
   (a) the school's aims and values;
   (b) the responsibilities which the school intends to discharge in connection with the education of children admitted to the school; and
   (c) the parental responsibilities, that is the responsibilities which the parents of such children are expected to discharge in connection with the education of their children while they are registered pupils at the school;
and 'parental declaration' means a declaration to be signed by a parent seeking the admission of his child to the school by which he acknowledges and accepts the parental responsibilities specified in the partnership document.
(3) In determining the provisions to be included in the admission arrangements for a school in pursuance of sub-paragraph (1), the governing body shall have regard to any guidance given from time to time by the Secretary of State.

Education Act 1997

(4) The Secretary of State may by order provide that any form of words specified in the order, or having such effect as is so specified, is not to be used in a partnership document or (as the case may be) in a parental declaration.
(5) An order under sub-paragraph (4) may apply to any school or description of school specified in the order.
(6) In this paragraph and paragraph 2—
'admission arrangements', in relation to a school, means the arrangements for the admission of pupils to the school; and
'conditional place', in relation to a child, means a place which is conditional on the child's parent giving the governing body a signed parental declaration.

Effect of home-school partnership document

2 (1) This paragraph applies where the admission arrangements for a grant-maintained school include the provisions authorised by paragraph 1(1).
(2) The governing body shall, in the case of each child on behalf of whom an application for admission is made, notify his parent of the following matters, namely—
    (a) the terms of the partnership document and the parental declaration, and
    (b) the effect of the provisions of the admission arrangements authorised by paragraph 1(1)(b) and (c).
(3) Where sub-paragraph (2) has been complied with in relation to a child's parent but—
    (a) the parent has failed to comply with the condition referred to in paragraph 1(1)(b), and
    (b) the governing body are not satisfied that there are special reasons for dispensing with that condition to the required extent in the case of that child,
the governing body shall not be under any duty to admit the child to the school; and, if he has been allocated a conditional place, the allocation of that place may be cancelled.
(4) In sub-paragraph (3) the reference to dispensing with the condition mentioned in that sub-paragraph 'to the required extent'—
    (a) is, where the parent gives the governing body a signed parental declaration in relation to some but not the remainder of the parental responsibilities, a reference to dispensing with that condition so far as the remainder of those responsibilities are concerned; but
    (b) is otherwise a reference to wholly dispensing with that condition.
(5) In performing any function under this paragraph the governing body shall have regard to any guidance given from time to time by the Secretary of State.
(6) A partnership document shall not be capable of creating any obligation in respect of whose breach any liability arises in contract or in tort.

Restriction of right to refuse admission to partially-selective school

3 (1) An application for the admission of a child to a grant-maintained school may not be refused on the grounds that his admission would be incompatible with the school's selective admission arrangements unless those arrangements—
    (a) are wholly based on selection by reference to ability or aptitude, and
    (b) are so based with a view to admitting only pupils with high ability or with aptitude.
(2) For the purposes of this paragraph a school has selective admission arrangements if the arrangements for the admission of pupils to the school are to any extent based on selection by reference to ability or aptitude.

No requirement to admit children permanently excluded from two or more schools

4 (1) The governing body of a grant-maintained school shall not be under any duty to admit to the school any child to whom sub-paragraph (3) applies.

Appendix 9

(2) The governing body of such a school shall not be under any duty to make arrangements for enabling any person to appeal against a decision refusing a child admission to the school in a case where, at the time when the decision is made, sub-paragraph (3) applies to the child.
(3) Where a child has been permanently excluded from two or more schools, this sub-paragraph applies to him during the period of two years beginning with the date on which the latest of those exclusions took effect.
(4) Sub-paragraph (3) applies to a child whatever the length of the period or periods elapsing between those exclusions and regardless of whether it has applied to him on a previous occasion.
(5) However, a child shall not be regarded as permanently excluded from a school for the purposes of this paragraph if—
    (a) although so excluded he was reinstated as a pupil at the school following the giving of a direction to that effect to the head teacher of the school; or
    (b) he was so excluded at a time when he had not attained compulsory school age.
(6) In this paragraph 'school' means—
    (a) a school maintained by a local education authority; or
    (b) a grant-maintained or grant-maintained special school.
(7) This paragraph does not apply in relation to a child unless at least one of the two or more exclusions mentioned in sub-paragraph (3) took effect on or after the date of the coming into force of section 14 of the Education Act 1997.
(8) For the purposes of this paragraph the permanent exclusion of a child from a school shall be regarded as having taken effect on the school day as from which the head teacher decided that he should be permanently excluded.

Section 21

Schedule 4

The Qualifications and Curriculum Authority

General This Schedule makes detailed provision for the status, powers, officers, members, staff, finance, committees, accounts and proceedings of the QCA.
Commencement 1 October 1997: SI 1997/1468.
Definition See s 56(2) and the Education Act 1996 for 'functions': and 'land': s 579(1).
'Person' Unless the contrary intention appears, this includes a body of persons, corporate or unincorporate: Interpretation Act 1978, s 5, Sch 1.

Status

1   The Authority shall not be regarded as a servant or agent of the Crown or as enjoying any status, immunity or privilege of the Crown; and the Authority's property shall not be regarded as property of, or property held on behalf of, the Crown.

Powers

2 (1) The Authority may do anything which is calculated to facilitate, or is incidental or conducive to, the carrying out of any of their functions.
(2) In particular, the Authority may—
    (a) acquire or dispose of land or other property,
    (b) enter into contracts,
    (c) form bodies corporate or associated or other bodies which are not bodies corporate,
    (d) enter into joint ventures with other persons,
    (e) subscribe for shares or stock,
    (f) invest any sums not immediately required for the purpose of carrying out their functions,

Education Act 1997

    (g) accept gifts of money, land or other property, and
    (h) borrow money.
(3) The Authority may authorise the Qualifications, Curriculum and Assessment Authority for Wales to act as agent for the Authority in connection with the exercise of any of the Authority's functions in relation to Wales.
(4) The consent of the Secretary of State is required for the exercise of any power conferred by sub-paragraph (2)(c) or (d) or sub-paragraph (3).

3 (1) The Authority may give to any person or body (whether or not in the United Kingdom) such assistance as they may determine.
(2) Assistance may be provided on such terms and subject to such conditions (if any) as the Authority may determine.
(3) In particular, assistance may be provided free of charge or on such terms as to payment as the Authority may determine.
(4) The power conferred by this paragraph does not extend to the giving of financial assistance; and the consent of the Secretary of State is required for any exercise of that power.

Chief officer

4 (1) The Authority shall have a chief officer.
(2) The first chief officer shall be appointed by the Secretary of State on such terms and conditions as the Secretary of State may determine.
(3) Each subsequent chief officer shall be appointed by the Authority with the approval of the Secretary of State on such terms and conditions as the Authority may with the approval of the Secretary of State determine.
(4) The chief officer shall be an ex officio member of the Authority.

Chairman and chief officer: division of functions

5 (1) The Secretary of State may, on appointing a person to be the chairman of the Authority, confer on him such additional functions in relation to the Authority as may be specified in the appointment.
(2) The functions for the time being conferred by virtue of appointment as chief officer of the Authority shall not include any function for the time being conferred under sub-paragraph (1) on the chairman of the Authority.

Tenure of office

6 (1) A person shall hold and vacate office as a member or as chairman or deputy chairman of the Authority in accordance with the terms of his appointment and shall, on ceasing to be a member, be eligible for reappointment.
(2) A person may at any time by notice in writing to the Secretary of State resign his office as a member or as chairman or deputy chairman of the Authority.

7 The Secretary of State may, if satisfied that a member of the Authority—
    (a) has been absent from meetings of the Authority for a continuous period of more than six months without the permission of the Authority, or
    (b) is unable or unfit to discharge the functions of a member,
remove him from office by giving him notice in writing and thereupon the office shall become vacant.

8 If the chairman or deputy chairman of the Authority ceases to be a member of the Authority, he shall also cease to be chairman or deputy chairman.

Payments to members

9 (1) The Authority shall pay to their members such salaries or fees, and such travelling, subsistence or other allowances, as the Secretary of State may determine.

Appendix 9

(2) The Authority shall, as regards any member in whose case the Secretary of State may so determine, pay, or make provision for the payment of, such sums by way of pension, allowances and gratuities to or in respect of him as the Secretary of State may determine.
(3) If a person ceases to be a member of the Authority and it appears to the Secretary of State that there are special circumstances which make it right that he should receive compensation, the Secretary of State may direct the Authority to make to that person a payment of such amount as the Secretary of State may determine.

Staff

10   Subject to the approval of the Secretary of State, the Authority—
  (a) may appoint such number of employees, on such terms and conditions, as they may determine; and
  (b) shall pay to their employees such remuneration and allowances as they may determine.

11   (1) Employment with the Authority shall be included among the kinds of employment to which a scheme under section 1 of the Superannuation Act 1972 can apply.
(2) The Authority shall pay to the Minister for the Civil Service, at such times as he may direct, such sums as he may determine in respect of the increase attributable to this paragraph in the sums payable under the Superannuation Act 1972 out of money provided by Parliament.
(3) Where an employee of the Authority is (by reference to that employment) a participant in a scheme under section 1 of that Act and is also a member of the Authority, the Secretary of State may determine that his service as such a member shall be treated for the purposes of the scheme as service as an employee of the Authority (whether or not any benefits are payable to or in respect of him by virtue of paragraph 9).

Finance

12   (1) The Secretary of State may make grants to the Authority of such amount as he thinks fit in respect of expenses incurred or to be incurred by the Authority in carrying out their functions.
(2) The payment of grant under this paragraph shall be subject to the fulfilment of such conditions as the Secretary of State may determine.
(3) The Secretary of State may also impose such requirements as he thinks fit in connection with the payment of grant under this paragraph.

Committees

13   (1) The Authority—
  (a) may establish a committee for any purpose; and
  (b) if so directed by the Secretary of State, shall establish a committee for such purpose as is specified in the direction.
(2) The Authority shall determine the number of members which a committee established under this paragraph shall have, and the terms on which they are to hold and vacate office.
(3) Subject to such conditions as the Secretary of State may determine, a committee may include persons who are not members of the Authority.
(4) The Authority shall keep under review the structure of committees established under this paragraph and the scope of each committee's activities.

Delegation of functions

14   (1) The Authority may authorise the chairman, the deputy chairman, the chief officer or any committee established under paragraph 13 to carry out such of the Authority's functions as the Authority may determine.
(2) The Secretary of State may authorise any committee established under paragraph

13(1)(b) to carry out such of the Authority's functions as are specified in the direction given under that provision.

(3) Sub-paragraph (1) has effect without prejudice to any power to authorise an employee of the Authority to carry out any of the Authority's activities on behalf of the Authority.

Proceedings

15 (1) The following persons, namely—
- (a) a representative of the Secretary of State,
- (b) the chairman of the Qualifications, Curriculum and Assessment Authority for Wales, or a representative of his,
- (c) a representative of such other body as the Secretary of State may designate, and
- (d) Her Majesty's Chief Inspector of Schools in England, or a representative of his,

shall be entitled to attend and take part in deliberations (but not in decisions) at meetings of the Authority or of any committee of the Authority.

(2) The Authority shall provide the Secretary of State, the chairman of the Qualifications, Curriculum and Assessment Authority for Wales, any person falling within sub-paragraph (1)(c) and Her Majesty's Chief Inspector of Schools in England with such copies of any documents distributed to members of the Authority or of any such committee as each of those persons may require.

16 The validity of the Authority's proceedings shall not be affected by a vacancy among the members or any defect in the appointment of a member.

17 Subject to the preceding provisions of this Schedule, the Authority may regulate their own procedure and that of any of their committees.

Accounts

18 (1) The Authority shall—
- (a) keep proper accounts and proper records in relation to the accounts;
- (b) prepare a statement of accounts in respect of each financial year of the Authority; and
- (c) send copies of the statement to the Secretary of State and to the Comptroller and Auditor General before the end of the month of August next following the financial year to which the statement relates.

(2) The statement of accounts shall comply with any directions given by the Secretary of State with the approval of the Treasury as to—
- (a) the information to be contained in it;
- (b) the manner in which the information contained in it is to be presented; or
- (c) the methods and principles according to which the statement is to be prepared.

(3) The Comptroller and Auditor General shall examine, certify and report on each statement received by him in pursuance of this paragraph and shall lay copies of each statement and of his report before each House of Parliament.

Documents

19 The application of the seal of the Authority shall be authenticated by the signature—
- (a) of the chairman or some other person authorised either generally or specially by the Authority to act for that purpose, and
- (b) of one other member.

20 Any document purporting to be an instrument made or issued by or on behalf of the Authority, and to be duly executed by a person authorised by the Authority in that behalf, shall be received in evidence and be treated, without further proof, as being so made or issued unless the contrary is shown.

Appendix 9

Section 27

Schedule 5

The Qualifications, Curriculum and Assessment Authority for Wales

General This Schedule, replacing Sch 30 to the Education Act 1996, repealed by Sch 8, makes detailed provision for the status, powers, officers, members, staff, finance, committees, accounts and proceedings of the ACCAC, on very much the same lines as Sch 4 with the omission of para 5.
Commencement 1 October 1997: SI 1997/1468.
Definition See s 56(2) and the Education Act 1996 for 'functions' and 'land': s 579(1).
'Person' Unless the contrary intention appears, this includes a body of persons, corporate or unincorporate: Interpretation Act 1978, s 5, Sch 1.

Status

1   The Authority shall not be regarded as a servant or agent of the Crown or as enjoying any status, immunity or privilege of the Crown, and the Authority's property shall not be regarded as property of, or property held on behalf of, the Crown.

Powers

2   (1)   The Authority may do anything which is calculated to facilitate, or is incidental or conducive to, the carrying out of any of their functions.
(2)   In particular, the Authority may—
  (a)   acquire or dispose of land or other property,
  (b)   enter into contracts,
  (c)   form bodies corporate or associated or other bodies which are not bodies corporate,
  (d)   enter into joint ventures with other persons,
  (e)   subscribe for shares or stock,
  (f)   invest any sums not immediately required for the purpose of carrying out their functions,
  (g)   accept gifts of money, land or other property, and
  (h)   borrow money.
(3)   Where authorised to do so under paragraph 2(3) of Schedule 4, the Authority may act as agent for the Qualifications and Curriculum Authority in connection with the exercise of any of that Authority's functions in relation to Wales.
(4)   The consent of the Secretary of State is required for the exercise of any power conferred by sub-paragraph (2)(c) or (d).

3   (1)   The Authority may give to any person or body (whether or not in the United Kingdom) such assistance as they may determine.
(2)   Assistance may be provided on such terms and subject to such conditions (if any) as the Authority may determine.
(3)   In particular, assistance may be provided free of charge or on such terms as to payment as the Authority may determine.
(4)   The power conferred by this paragraph does not extend to the giving of financial assistance; and the consent of the Secretary of State is required for any exercise of that power.

Chief officer

4   (1)   The Authority shall have a chief officer who shall be appointed—
  (a)   in the case of a person who is also chairman of the Authority, by the Secretary of State, and

(b) in any other case, by the Authority with the approval of the Secretary of State.
(2) The appointment of the chief officer shall be on such terms and conditions as the Secretary of State, or (as the case may be) the Authority with the approval of the Secretary of State, may determine.
(3) The Secretary of State may appoint the chief officer (if appointed under sub-paragraph (1)(b)) to be a member of the Authority.

Tenure of office

5 (1) A person shall hold and vacate office as a member or as chairman or deputy chairman of the Authority in accordance with the terms of his appointment and shall, on ceasing to be a member, be eligible for reappointment.
(2) A person may at any time by notice in writing to the Secretary of State resign his office as a member or as chairman or deputy chairman of the Authority.

6 The Secretary of State may, if satisfied that a member of the Authority—
  (a) has been absent from meetings of the Authority for a continuous period of more than six months without the permission of the Authority, or
  (b) is unable or unfit to discharge the functions of a member,
remove him from office by giving him notice in writing and thereupon the office shall become vacant.

7 If the chairman or deputy chairman of the Authority ceases to be a member of the Authority, he shall also cease to be chairman or deputy chairman.

Payments to members

8 (1) The Authority shall pay to their members such salaries or fees, and such travelling, subsistence or other allowances, as the Secretary of State may determine.
(2) The Authority shall, as regards any member in whose case the Secretary of State may so determine, pay, or make provision for the payment of, such sums by way of pension, allowances and gratuities to or in respect of him as the Secretary of State may determine.
(3) If a person ceases to be a member of the Authority and it appears to the Secretary of State that there are special circumstances which make it right that he should receive compensation, the Secretary of State may direct the Authority to make to that person a payment of such amount as the Secretary of State may determine.

Staff

9 Subject to the approval of the Secretary of State, the Authority—
  (a) may appoint such number of employees, on such terms and conditions, as they may determine; and
  (b) shall pay to their employees such remuneration and allowances as they may determine.

10 (1) Employment with the Authority shall continue to be included among the kinds of employment to which a scheme under section 1 of the Superannuation Act 1972 can apply.
(2) The Authority shall pay to the Minister for the Civil Service, at such times as he may direct, such sums as he may determine in respect of the increase attributable to this paragraph in the sums payable under the Superannuation Act 1972 out of money provided by Parliament.
(3) Where an employee of the Authority is (by reference to that employment) a participant in a scheme under section 1 of that Act and is also a member of the Authority, the Secretary of State may determine that his service as such a member shall be treated for the purposes of the scheme as service as an employee of the Authority (whether or not any benefits are payable to or in respect of him by virtue of paragraph 8).

Appendix 9

Finance

11 (1) The Secretary of State may make grants to the Authority of such amount as he thinks fit in respect of expenses incurred or to be incurred by the Authority in carrying out their functions.
(2) The payment of grant under this paragraph shall be subject to the fulfilment of such conditions as the Secretary of State may determine.
(3) The Secretary of State may also impose such requirements as he thinks fit in connection with the payment of grant under this paragraph.

Committees

12 (1) The Authority—
    (a) may establish a committee for any purpose; and
    (b) if so directed by the Secretary of State, shall establish a committee for such purpose as is specified in the direction.
(2) The Authority shall determine the number of members which a committee established under this paragraph shall have, and the terms on which they are to hold and vacate office.
(3) Subject to such conditions as the Secretary of State may determine, a committee may include persons who are not members of the Authority.
(4) The Authority shall keep under review the structure of committees established under this paragraph and the scope of each committee's activities.

Delegation of functions

13 (1) The Authority may authorise the chairman, the deputy chairman, the chief officer or any committee established under paragraph 12 to carry out such of the Authority's functions as the Authority may determine.
(2) The Secretary of State may authorise any committee established under paragraph 12(1)(b) to carry out such of the Authority's functions as are specified in the direction given under that provision.
(3) Sub-paragraph (1) has effect without prejudice to any power to authorise an employee of the Authority to carry out any of the Authority's activities on behalf of the Authority.

Proceedings

14 (1) The following persons, namely—
    (a) a representative of the Secretary of State,
    (b) the chairman of the Qualifications and Curriculum Authority, or a representative of his, and
    (c) Her Majesty's Chief Inspector of Schools in Wales, or a representative of his,
shall be entitled to attend and take part in deliberations (but not in decisions) at meetings of the Authority or of any committee of the Authority.
(2) The Authority shall provide the Secretary of State, the chairman of the Qualifications and Curriculum Authority and Her Majesty's Chief Inspector of Schools in Wales with such copies of any documents distributed to members of the Authority or of any such committee as each of those persons may require.

15 The validity of the Authority's proceedings shall not be affected by a vacancy among the members or any defect in the appointment of a member.

16 Subject to the preceding provisions of this Schedule, the Authority may regulate their own procedure and that of any of their committees.

Accounts

17 (1) The Authority shall—

(a) keep proper accounts and proper records in relation to the accounts;
(b) prepare a statement of accounts in respect of each financial year of the Authority; and
(c) send copies of the statement to the Secretary of State and to the Comptroller and Auditor General before the end of the month of August next following the financial year to which the statement relates.

(2) The statement of accounts shall comply with any directions given by the Secretary of State with the approval of the Treasury as to—
(a) the information to be contained in it;
(b) the manner in which the information contained in it is to be presented; or
(c) the methods and principles according to which the statement is to be prepared.

(3) The Comptroller and Auditor General shall examine, certify and report on each statement received by him in pursuance of this paragraph and shall lay copies of each statement and of his report before each House of Parliament.

Documents

18 The application of the Authority's seal shall be authenticated by the signature of the chairman or deputy chairman and that of one other member.

19 Any document purporting to be an instrument made or issued by or on behalf of the Authority and to be—
(a) duly executed under the Authority's seal, or
(b) signed or executed by a person authorised by the Authority to act in that behalf,

shall be received in evidence and be treated, without further proof, as being so made or issued unless the contrary is shown.

Section 42

Schedule 6

School Inspections

General This Schedule amends the School Inspections Act 1996.
Para 1 provides that references in this Schedule to 'the 1996 Act' are to the School Inspections Act 1996.

Paras 2 and 3 extend the rights of entry and inspection of records and other documents of the Chief Inspector for England and the Chief Inspector for Wales respectively so that they apply for the purposes of the exercise of any functions conferred on the Chief Inspector by or under s 2 or s 5, and not merely in relation to an inspection under s 2(2)(b) or s 5(2)(b). The offence of obstructing the Chief Inspector in the exercise of his functions is similarly extended.

Paras 4 and 5 amend one of the grounds for removing the name of an inspector or nursery education inspector from the register. Producing a seriously misleading inspection report need now be done only 'without reasonable explanation': it is no longer necessary for the Chief Inspector to be satisfied that it was done 'knowingly or recklessly'.

Para 6 amends s 10 of the 1996 Act, which provides for periodical inspections of certain schools by a registered inspector, to dispense with such an inspection where the school is closing and the Chief Inspector decides that no useful purpose would be served by it.

Para 7: ss 16(4)(c) and 20(4)(c), required the 'appropriate authority' (usually the governing body) to ensure that registered parents receive a summary of a s 10 report 'as soon as is reasonably practicable'. This must now be done within a period prescribed by regulations.

Para 8 extends s 42, to cover other documents stored on a computer as well as 'records'. Such information must be made available to the inspector 'in legible form'.

Para 9 generalises the reference to inspections in para 5(3) of Sch 1, which permits delegation of the Chief Inspector's functions.

Paras 10–12 amend Sch 3, which relates to s 10 inspections.
Para 10 substitutes a new para 2 enabling tenders for s 10 inspections to be invited from

Appendix 9

contractors who act as intermediaries for registered inspectors as well as directly from registered inspectors; and requiring the appropriate authority for a school to be consulted about an inspection before it takes place, rather than before tenders are invited.

Para 11 substitutes a new sub-para (1) of para 3, requiring members of the inspection team to be 'capable of assisting competently and effectively' as well as being 'fit and proper persons'.

Para 12 adds a new para 7(2) extending the rights of entry and inspection of an inspection team to cover the inspection of other schools at which pupils registered at the school under inspection receive part of their education.

Section 35(4)(b) of the 1996 Act, (power of an education association to provide education which is neither primary or secondary) is prospectively amended by Sch 7, para 51, in consequence of the revised definition of 'compulsory school age'.

Commencement 1 September 1997: SI 1997/1468.

Transitional Provisions In relation to the amendments made by paras 4, 5 and 7, see Sch 2 to SI 1997/1468, paras 1–3.

Introductory

1   In this Schedule 'the 1996 Act' means the School Inspections Act 1996.

Rights of entry etc for Chief Inspectors

2   For subsections (8) and (9) of section 2 of the 1996 Act (functions of Chief Inspector for England) there shall be substituted—

'(8) For the purposes of the exercise of any function conferred by or under this section the Chief Inspector for England shall have at all reasonable times, in relation to any school in England—
  (a) a right of entry to the premises of the school; and
  (b) a right to inspect, and take copies of, any records kept by the school, and any other documents containing information relating to the school, which he requires for those purposes.
(9) It shall be an offence wilfully to obstruct the Chief Inspector for England—
  (a) in the exercise of his functions in relation to the inspection of a school for the purposes of subsection (2)(b); or
  (b) in the exercise of any right under subsection (8) for the purposes of the exercise of any other function.'

3   For subsections (8) and (9) of section 5 of the 1996 Act (functions of Chief Inspector for Wales) there shall be substituted—

'(8) For the purposes of the exercise of any function conferred by or under this section the Chief Inspector for Wales shall have at all reasonable times, in relation to any school in Wales—
  (a) a right of entry to the premises of the school; and
  (b) a right to inspect, and take copies of, any records kept by the school, and any other documents containing information relating to the school, which he requires for those purposes.
(9) It shall be an offence wilfully to obstruct the Chief Inspector for Wales—
  (a) in the exercise of his functions in relation to the inspection of a school for the purposes of subsection (2)(b); or
  (b) in the exercise of any right under subsection (8) for the purposes of the exercise of any other function.'

Removal of inspectors from register

4   In subsection (2)(d) of section 8 of the 1996 Act (removal from register and imposition or variation of conditions to be satisfied by registered inspector) for 'knowingly or recklessly' there shall be substituted ', without reasonable explanation,'.

5   In paragraph 9(2)(d) of Schedule 1 to the Nursery Education and Grant-Maintained Schools Act 1996 (removal from register and imposition or variation of conditions to be satisfied by nursery education inspector) for 'knowingly or recklessly' there shall be substituted ', without reasonable explanation,'.

Education Act 1997

Inspections of closing schools

6 (1) Section 10 of the 1996 Act (inspections by registered inspectors) shall be amended as follows.
(2) In subsection (3) (schools to which the section applies) after 'subsection (4)' there shall be inserted 'or (4A)'.
(3) After subsection (4) there shall be inserted—

'(4A) This section does not apply to any school—
  (a) which is a closing school (as defined by subsection (4B)), and
  (b) in respect of which the Chief Inspector has decided, having regard to the date on which the closure is to take effect, that no useful purpose would be served by the school being inspected under this section.
(4B) In subsection (4A) a 'closing school' means—
  (a) a county, voluntary or maintained nursery school in respect of which the Secretary of State has under section 169 of the Education Act 1996 approved proposals by the local education authority to cease to maintain the school;
  (b) a voluntary school in respect of which the governing body have given notice of their intention to discontinue the school under section 173 of that Act;
  (c) a grant-maintained school in respect of which—
    (i) the Secretary of State has under section 269 of that Act approved proposals for the discontinuance of the school, or
    (ii) the funding authority have made a determination under that section to adopt proposals for the discontinuance of the school;
  (d) a maintained or grant-maintained special school in respect of which the Secretary of State has under section 340 of that Act approved proposals for the discontinuance of the school;
  (e) a city technology college or city college for the technology of the arts in respect of which notice of termination of an agreement made under section 482 of that Act has been given; or
  (f) an independent school falling within subsection (3)(e) which the proprietor has decided to close.'

Publication of inspection reports

7 In each of sections 16(4)(c) and 20(4)(c) of the 1996 Act (appropriate authority to take steps to secure that registered parents receive copies of the summary of the inspection report) for 'as soon as is reasonably practicable' there shall be substituted 'within such period following receipt of the report by the authority as may be prescribed'.

Computer records

8 In section 42 of the 1996 Act (inspection of computer records for the purposes of Part I)—
  (a) after 'records' (in both places) there shall be inserted 'or other documents'; and
  (b) at the end there shall be added '(including, in particular, the making of information available for inspection or copying in a legible form)'.

Delegation of functions of Chief Inspectors

9 In paragraph 5(3) of Schedule 1 to the 1996 Act (performance of functions of Chief Inspectors), for 'in conducting an inspection under section 2(2)(b) or section 5(2)(b)' there shall be substituted 'under sub-paragraph (1) or (2)'.

Tenders and consultation

10 For paragraph 2 of Schedule 3 to the 1996 Act (selection of registered inspectors) there shall be substituted—

'2 (1) Before entering into any arrangement for an inspection, the Chief Inspector shall invite tenders from at least two persons who can reasonably be expected to tender for the

Appendix 9

proposed inspection and to do so at arm's length from each other, and each of whom is either—
(a) a registered inspector, or
(b) a person who the Chief Inspector is satisfied would, if his tender were successful, arrange with a registered inspector for the inspection to be carried out.
(2) Before an inspection takes place the Chief Inspector shall consult the appropriate authority about the inspection.'

Inspection teams

11 For paragraph 3(1) of Schedule 3 to the 1996 Act (inspection teams) there shall be substituted—

'(1) Every inspection shall be conducted by a registered inspector with the assistance of a team (an 'inspection team') consisting of persons who—
(a) are fit and proper persons for carrying out the inspection; and
(b) will be capable of assisting in the inspection competently and effectively.'

Rights of entry etc for registered inspectors

12 (1) The existing provisions of paragraph 7 of Schedule 3 to the 1996 Act (rights of entry) shall become sub-paragraph (1) of that paragraph.
(2) After that sub-paragraph there shall be inserted—

'(2) Where—
(a) pupils registered at the school concerned are, by arrangement with another school, receiving part of their education at the other school, and
(b) the inspector is satisfied that he cannot properly discharge his duty under section 10(5) in relation to the school concerned without inspecting the provision made for those pupils at that other school,
sub-paragraph (1) shall apply in relation to that other school as it applies in relation to the school concerned.'

Section 57(1)

Schedule 7

Minor and Consequential Amendments

General This Schedule makes amendments in the Education Acts and other enactments, largely consequential on the provisions of this Act. For amendments consequential on the establishment of the QCA and the ACCAC see the general note to s 21; and for those consequential on the revised definition of 'compulsory school age' see the general note to s 52.
For the rest, all amendments of the Education Act 1996 -
Para 9 clarifies the definition of 'pupil' in s 3, in the context of admission and exclusion.
Para 10 supplements the amendment of s 4(1), made by s 51, by making it clear that provision may be made under s 19 for part-time education in a school.
Para 15 amends s 86, to enable the governing body of a voluntary school, when revising their instrument of government in consequence of a transfer of the school to a new site which also involves an increase in the number of pupils, to use as the maximum number either the actual number of pupils or the number as it will be when the changes are fully implemented.
Para 16 amends s 156(3) to remove the implication that not all LEA-maintained schools will have articles of government. A similar amendment is made to s 307(2), which relates to GM schools, by para 22.
Para 18 corrects a reference in s 265(1)(a).
Para 20 corrects a printing error in s 290(9)(a), and amends that subsection to provide that ss 306A and 307A (school discipline policies and appeals against exclusion), inserted by ss 3 and 8, may not be applied to groups of GM schools with modifications.
Para 31 amends s 411 (compliance with parental preferences). Sub-s (2) is amended to make it clear that ss 411A (pupils excluded from two or more schools) and 413B(3) (home-school partnership documents) override parental preference; sub-s (8) is amended to extend the definition of 'child' as a person under 19 to ss 411A–430 and 434–436 and Sch 33 (school admissions); and a

Education Act 1997

new sub-s (9) is added, making it clear that school admission arrangements may be regarded as 'wholly based on selection by reference to ability or aptitude' even where, when the number of children reaching the required standard exceeds the number of places available, additional criteria (not related to ability or aptitude) are employed to determine who shall be admitted.

Paras 32 and 34(a) and (d) amend s 422(6) (modification of enactments in relation to the admission of pupils to new schools) and s 424(1) and (3) (provisions not applying to the admission of pupils to nursery schools or special schools or to statemented children) to insert references to the new sections inserted by ss 11–13 of this Act.

Para 33, together with Sch 8, repeals the definition of 'child' in s 423(6), which is now replaced by that in the amended s 411(8).

Para 37 amends s 537(4) (regulations relating to the provision of information by governing bodies) to enable such regulations to provide that, in prescribed circumstances, the provision of information to a person other than the Secretary of State is to be treated as equivalent to provision to him.

Para 38 substitutes a new cross-heading for Chapter II of Part X to take account of the insertion of ss 550A (power to restrain pupils) and 550B (detention) by ss 4 and 5.

Para 39 inserts a new sub-s (1A) into s 551, to make it clear that regulations as to the duration of the school year relate only to the number of sessions that must be held during any such year.

Para 40 amends s 568, to provide that orders under s 413A(4) (inserted by s 13) or para 1(4) of Sch 33B (see Sch 3) prohibiting the use of certain forms of words in home-school partnership documents or parental declarations are not to be made by statutory instrument if they apply only to one or more schools specified in the order.

Para 41 amends s 571, to require the Secretary of State to publish any guidance given by him under the 1996 Act.

Para 42 amends s 578, to add this Act to the other Acts referred to as 'the Education Acts' in the 1996 Act.

Para 43 inserts a definition of 'school year' into s 579(1) (general interpretation).

Para 44 adds to the index in s 580 references to the definitions of 'child' (in Chapter I of Part VI), 'school year' and 'wholly based on selection by reference to ability or aptitude'.

Para 45 amends references to 'the Treasury' in para 9(2) of Sch 2 (superannuation of employees of the funding authorities) to refer to the Minister for the Civil Service and provides that these amendments shall be deemed always to have had effect.

Para 47 amends para 14 of Sch 16 (appeals against exclusion or reinstatement) to require the decision of the appeal committee and its grounds to be communicated to the head teacher; and, with Sch 8, repeals the reference to the time within which appeals are to be brought in para 15 (power of appeal committee to determine their own procedure) since this is determined by para 3 of Sch 16.

Para 48 amends para 22 of Sch 19, with effect from 21 March 1997, so that the new provisions about the costs of premature retirement in s 139(5A) and (5B), inserted by s 50(3) of this Act, do not apply in relation to new LEA-maintained schools; and substitutes a new para 27 to apply the new s 154 (responsibility for discipline), substituted by s 2 of this Act, to the temporary governing bodies of new LEA-maintained schools.

Para 49, with Sch 8, repeals the reference to s 400 in para 4(1) of Sch 23, in consequence of its repeal by Sch 8; and inserts a new sub-para (2A) in para 6 to make it clear that the articles of government for GM schools do not have to provide for exclusion appeals for which provision is made in new Sch 25A, inserted by s 8; or for appeals where the child has been permanently excluded from two or more schools.

Para 50 amends the regulation-making power in para 14 of Sch 28, to preserve the effect of ss 306A and 307A and Sch 25A, inserted by ss 3(1) and 8(1) and (2), which will apply to GM special schools by virtue of paras 15 (as amended by s 3(2)) and 16 (inserted by s 8(3).

Commencement As indicated below. Other provisions: a date to be appointed by the Secretary of State by order under s 58(3).

Public Records Act 1958 (c 51)

1 In Part II of the Table at the end of paragraph 3 of Schedule 1 to the Public Records Act 1958 (organisations whose records are public records), insert at the appropriate places—

'Qualifications, Curriculum and Assessment Authority for Wales',

'Qualifications and Curriculum Authority'.

Appendix 9

Commencement 1 October 1997: SI 1997/1468.

Local Authorities (Goods and Services) Act 1970 (c 39)

2 (1) Subject to sub-paragraph (2), in the Local Authorities (Goods and Services) Act 1970 (supply of goods and services by local authorities to public bodies), 'public body'—
- (a) shall include the Qualifications and Curriculum Authority and the Qualifications, Curriculum and Assessment Authority for Wales; and
- (b) shall cease to include the School Curriculum and Assessment Authority and the Curriculum and Assessment Authority for Wales.

(2) The provision in sub-paragraph (1) shall have effect as if made by an order under section 1(5) of that Act (power to provide that a person shall be a public body for the purposes of the Act).

Commencement 1 October 1997: SI 1997/1468; except so far as sub-para (1) provides that 'public body' shall cease to include SCAA.

Superannuation Act 1972 (c 11)

3 (1) In Schedule 1 to the Superannuation Act 1972, in the list of Other Bodies (bodies in respect of which there are superannuation schemes)—
- (a) omit the entries relating to the Curriculum and Assessment Authority for Wales and the School Curriculum and Assessment Authority; and
- (b) insert at the appropriate places—

'the Qualifications, Curriculum and Assessment Authority for Wales',

'the Qualifications and Curriculum Authority'.

(2) Section 1 of that Act (persons to or in respect of whom benefits may be provided by schemes under that section) shall apply to persons who at any time before the coming into force of section 21 of this Act have ceased to serve in employment with the National Council for Vocational Qualifications.

Commencement Paragraph 3(1), except so far as it omits the entry relating to SCAA: 1 October 1997: SI 1997/1468.

House of Commons Disqualification Act 1975 (c 24)

4 (1) Part III of Schedule 1 to the House of Commons Disqualification Act 1975 (disqualifying offices) shall be amended as follows.
(2) Omit the entries relating to the Curriculum and Assessment Authority for Wales and the School Curriculum and Assessment Authority.
(3) Insert at the appropriate places—

'Any member of the Qualifications, Curriculum and Assessment Authority for Wales constituted under section 27 of the Education Act 1997 in receipt of remuneration.'

'Any member of the Qualifications and Curriculum Authority constituted under section 21 of the Education Act 1997 in receipt of remuneration.'

(4) Omit the entry relating to the National Council for Vocational Qualifications.

Commencement 1 October 1997: SI 1997/1468, except so far as it omits the entry relating to SCAA.

Local Government Finance Act 1982 (c 32)

5 In Schedule 3 to the Local Government Finance Act 1982 (the Audit Commission), in paragraph 9(2) (functions to be managed separately), after paragraph (ab) (inserted by Schedule 3 to the Housing Act 1996) insert—

'(ac) its functions under section 41 of the Education Act 1997 (inspections of local education authorities);'.

Commencement 1 September 1997: SI 1997/1468.

Finance Act 1991 (c 31)

6   In section 32(10) of the Finance Act 1991 (relief in respect of a qualifying course of vocational training), for paragraph (a)(i) substitute—

'(i)   accredited as a National Vocational Qualification by the Qualifications and Curriculum Authority or by the Qualifications, Curriculum and Assessment Authority for Wales, or.'

Commencement 1 October 1997: SI 1997/1468; but see transitional provision in SI 1997/1468, Sch 2, para 4.

Charities Act 1993 (c 10)

7   In Schedule 2 to the Charities Act 1993 (exempt charities)—
   (a)   for paragraph (da) substitute—

'(da)   the Qualifications and Curriculum Authority;' and

   (b)   for paragraph (f) substitute—

'(f)   the Qualifications, Curriculum and Assessment Authority for Wales;'.

Commencement 1 October 1997: SI 1997/1468; but see transitional provision in SI 1997/1468, Sch 2, para 5.

Nursery Education and Grant-Maintained Schools Act 1996 (c 50)

8   In section 1(2) of the Nursery Education and Grant-Maintained Schools Act 1996 (arrangements for making grants in respect of nursery education), for paragraph (a) substitute—

'(a)   before they begin to be of compulsory school age; but'.

Education Act 1996 (c 56)

9   (1) Section 3 of the Education Act 1996 (definition of pupil etc) shall be amended as follows.
(2)   At the end of subsection (1) insert—

'and references to pupils in the context of the admission of pupils to, or the exclusion of pupils from, a school are references to persons who following their admission will be, or (as the case may be) before their exclusion were, pupils as defined by this subsection.'

(3)   In subsection (3), for 'The definition of 'pupil' in subsection' substitute 'Subsection'.

Commencement 1 September 1997: SI 1997/1468.

10   In section 4(2) of that Act (schools: general)—
   (a)   for 'For' substitute 'Nothing in subsection (1) shall be taken to preclude the making of arrangements under section 19(1) (exceptional educational provision) under which part-time education is to be provided at a school; and for';
and
   (b)   omit '(pupil referral units)'.

11   In section 6(1) of that Act (nursery schools), for 'the age of five' substitute 'compulsory school age'.

12   In section 14(4) of that Act (functions of LEA in respect of provision of primary and secondary schools), for 'the age of five' substitute 'compulsory school age'.

13   In section 17(2) of that Act (powers of LEA in respect of nursery education), for 'the age of five', in both places, substitute 'compulsory school age'.

Appendix 9

14 In section 29(6)(b) of that Act (requirement of LEA to publish information as to their policy and arrangements for primary or secondary education not to apply in relation to nursery schools, etc), for 'the age of five' substitute 'compulsory school age'.

15 In section 86(3)(b) of that Act (instrument of government to reflect current circumstances of school), after '82(3)(b)' insert 'or (c)'.

Commencement 14 June 1997: SI 1997/1468.

16 In section 156 of that Act (exclusion of pupils), for subsection (3) substitute—

'(3) Subsection (2) has effect despite anything in the articles of government for the school.'

17 In section 231 of that Act (powers of governing body of grant-maintained school), in subsection (8)(b), for 'the age of five' substitute 'compulsory school age'.

18 In section 265(1)(a) of that Act (proposals for change of character approved before school becomes grant-maintained), for '35 or 41' substitute '37 or 43'.

Commencement 14 June 1997: SI 1997/1468.

19 In section 266(1)(b) of that Act (interpretation of Chapter VII of Part III), for 'the age of five' substitute 'compulsory school age'.

20 In section 290(9) of that Act (groups of grant-maintained schools)—
   (a) for first '(ii)' substitute '(i)'; and
   (b) for '307' substitute '306A, 307, 307A'.

Commencement Para 20(a): 14 June 1997: SI 1997/1468.

21 In section 292(2) of that Act (nursery education in grant-maintained schools), for 'the age of five' substitute 'compulsory school age'.

22 In section 307 of that Act (exclusion of pupils), for subsection (2) substitute—

'(2) Subsection (1) has effect despite anything in the articles of government for the school.'

23 In section 312(2)(c) of that Act (meaning of 'learning difficulty' for the purposes of the Act)—
   (a) for 'the age of five' substitute 'compulsory school age', and
   (b) omit 'or over'.

24 In section 332(1) of that Act (duty of Health Authority or National Health Service Trust to notify parent where child has special educational needs), for 'the age of five' substitute 'compulsory school age'.

25 In section 343(2) of that Act (nursery education in grant-maintained special schools), for 'the age of five' substitute 'compulsory school age'.

26 Omit sections 358 to 361 of that Act (provisions about Curriculum Authorities).

Commencement So far as this para omits ss 360 and 361: 1 October 1997: SI 1997/1468.

27 In section 362(7) of that Act (development work and experiments)—
   (a) for 'the School Curriculum and Assessment Authority' substitute 'the Qualifications and Curriculum Authority'; and
   (b) for 'the Curriculum and Assessment Authority for Wales' substitute 'the Qualifications, Curriculum and Assessment Authority for Wales'.

Commencement 1 October 1997: SI 1997/1468; but see transitional provision in SI 1997/1468, Sch 2, para 6.

28 In section 368(10) of that Act (procedure for making certain orders and regulations)—
   (a) for 'the School Curriculum and Assessment Authority' substitute 'the Qualifications and Curriculum Authority'; and
   (b) for 'the Curriculum and Assessment Authority for Wales' substitute 'the Qualifications, Curriculum and Assessment Authority for Wales'.

Education Act 1997

Commencement 1 October 1997: SI 1997/1468; but see transitional provision in SI 1997/1468, Sch 2, para 6.

29 In section 391(10) of that Act (functions of advisory councils)—
  (a) for 'the School Curriculum and Assessment Authority' substitute 'the Qualifications and Curriculum Authority'; and
  (b) for 'the Curriculum and Assessment Authority for Wales' substitute 'the Qualifications, Curriculum and Assessment Authority for Wales'.

Commencement 1 October 1997: SI 1997/1468.

30 In section 408 of that Act (provision of information)—
  (a) in subsection (1)(a), after 'this Part' insert 'or Part V of the Education Act 1997'; and
  (b) in subsection (4)(f), omit ', 400, 401'.

Commencement Para 30(a): 1 October 1997: SI 1997/1468.

31 (1) Section 411 of that Act (duty to comply with parental preferences) shall be amended as follows.
(2) In subsection (2), after 'Subject to subsection (3)' there shall be inserted 'section 411A (pupils excluded from two or more schools), section 413B(3) (home-school partnership documents)'.
(3) In subsection (8), for 'this section' substitute 'this Chapter (apart from sections 431 to 433)'.
(4) After that subsection insert—

  '(9) Where the arrangements for the admission of pupils to a school provide for all pupils admitted to the school to be selected by reference to ability or aptitude, those arrangements shall be taken for the purposes of this Chapter to be wholly based on selection by reference to ability or aptitude, whether or not they also provide for the use of additional criteria in circumstances where the number of children in a relevant age group who are assessed to be of the requisite ability or aptitude is greater than the number of pupils which it is intended to admit to the school in that age group.'

Commencement 1 September 1997 (except so far as sub-para(2) inserts the words 'section 413B(3) (home-school partnership documents)': SI 1997/1468.

32 In section 422(6) of that Act (admission of pupils to new schools), for '411, 413, 414 and 423' substitute '411, 411A, 413 to 414, 423 and 423A'.

Commencement 1 September 1997: SI 1997/1468.

33 In section 423 of that Act (appeal arrangements), omit subsection (6).

Commencement 1 September 1997: SI 1997/1468.

34 In section 424 of that Act (admission of pupils to nursery schools and special schools)—
  (a) in subsection (1), for '411, 413, 414 or 423' substitute '411, 411A, 413A, 413B, 414, 423 or 423A';
  (b) in subsection (1)(b), for 'the age of five' substitute 'compulsory school age';
  (c) in subsection (2), for 'the age of five' substitute 'compulsory school age'; and
  (d) in subsection (3), for '411, 413, 414 and 423' substitute '411, 411A, 413 to 414, 423 and 423A'.

Commencement 1 September 1997 (except so far as sub-para (a) substitutes '413A and 413B' for '413', and except for sub-paras (b) and (c)): SI 1997/1468.

35 In section 448 of that Act (exemption where child becomes 5 during term), for 'the age of five' substitute 'compulsory school age'.

36 In section 492(2) of that Act (adjustment of amounts eligible for recoupment as between local education authorities), for 'the age of five' substitute 'compulsory school age'.

37 In section 537(4) of that Act (power of Secretary of State to require information

Appendix 9

from governing bodies etc), at the end add '; and regulations under this section may provide that, in such circumstances as may be prescribed, the provision of information to a person other than the Secretary of State is to be treated, for the purposes of any provision of such regulations or this section, as compliance with any requirement of such regulations relating to the provision of information to the Secretary of State.'

Commencement 14 June 1997: SI 1997/1468.

38 For the cross-heading 'CORPORAL PUNISHMENT' preceding section 548 of that Act substitute—

'PUNISHMENT AND RESTRAINT OF PUPILS

Corporal punishment'.

39 In section 551 of that Act (regulations as to the duration of the school day, etc), after subsection (1) insert—

'(1A) In subsection (1) the reference to the duration of the school year at any such schools is a reference to the number of school sessions that must be held during any such year.'

Commencement 14 June 1997: SI 1997/1468.

40 (1) Section 568 of that Act (orders) shall be amended as follows.
(2) In subsection (1) (orders required to be made by statutory instrument unless made under excepted provisions), after 'excepted provisions' insert 'or one falling within subsection (2A)'.
(3) After subsection (2) (the excepted provisions) insert—

'(2A) An order falls within this subsection if it is made under section 413A(4) or paragraph 1(4) of Schedule 33B and applies only to one or more schools specified in the order.'

41 In section 571 of that Act (publication of guidance)—
  (a) in subsection (1) for 'of the provisions mentioned in subsection (2) below' substitute 'provision of this Act'; and
  (b) omit subsection (2).

Commencement 14 June 1997: SI 1997/1468.

42 At the end of section 578 of that Act ('the Education Acts') add—

'the Education Act 1997.'

Commencement 14 June 1997: SI 1997/1468.

43 In section 579(1) of that Act (general interpretation), after the definition of 'school day' insert—

'"school year", in relation to a school, means the period beginning with the first school term to begin after July and ending with the beginning of the first such term to begin after the following July;'.

Commencement 14 June 1997: SI 1997/1468.

44 In section 580 of that Act (the index) at the appropriate places insert—

(in the entry relating to 'child')
'(in Chapter I of Part VI except sections 431 to 433)   section 411(8)'
'school year   section 579(1)'
'wholly based on selection by reference to ability
or aptitude (in Chapter I of Part VI)   section 411(9)'.

Commencement 'school year': 14 June 1997; remainder 1 September 1997: SI 1997/1468.

45 In Schedule 2 to that Act (the funding authorities), paragraph 9(2) (superannuation of employees) shall have effect (and be deemed always to have had effect) with the following amendments, namely—

(a) for 'the Treasury', in the first place where it occurs, substitute 'the Minister for the Civil Service'; and
(b) for 'the Treasury', in the other places where it occurs, substitute 'he'.

Commencement 14 June 1997: SI 1997/1468.

46 (1) Schedule 4 to that Act (distribution of functions where order made under section 27) shall be amended as follows.
(2) In paragraph 18, for 'the age of five' substitute 'compulsory school age'.

47 In Schedule 16 to that Act (appeals against exclusion or reinstatement of pupil)—
(a) in paragraph 14, after 'relevant person,' insert 'the head teacher,'; and
(b) in paragraph 15(1), omit the words from ', including' to 'brought,'.

48 (1) Schedule 19 to that Act (conduct and staffing of new county, voluntary and maintained special schools) shall be amended as follows.
(2) In paragraph 22 (application of provisions in respect of staffing of new schools)—
(a) after '(5)' insert 'to (5B)"; and
(b) after 'dismissal' insert 'or premature retirement'.
(3) For paragraph 27 substitute—

'27 Section 154 (responsibility for discipline) applies to a new school as if references to the school's governing body were references to the temporary governing body.'

Commencement sub-para (2): 21 March 1997: s 58(4).

49 (1) Schedule 23 to that Act (contents of articles of grant-maintained schools) shall be amended as follows.
(2) In paragraph 4(1) omit ', 400'.
(3) After paragraph 6(2) insert—

'(2A) Sub-paragraphs (1) and (2), so far as they apply in relation to arrangements in respect of appeals—
(a) do not require the articles to provide for any matter for which provision is made by Schedule 25A (exclusion appeals); and
(b) have effect subject to paragraph 4(2) of Schedule 33B (refusal of admission in case of children permanently excluded from two or more schools).'

Commencement sub-para (1) and sub-para (3) except for sub-para (a) at para 6(2A), to be inserted into Sch 23: 1 September 1997: SI 1997/1468.

50 In Schedule 28 to that Act (government and conduct of grant-maintained special schools), in paragraph 14 after 'regulations may' insert ', subject to the following paragraphs of this Schedule,'.

School Inspections Act 1996 (c 57)

51 In section 35(4)(b) of the School Inspections Act 1996 (power of an education association to provide education which is neither primary nor secondary education), for 'the age of five' substitute 'compulsory school age'.

Appendix 9

Section 57(4)

Schedule 8

Repeals

Chapter	Short Title	Extent of Repeal
1972 c 11	Superannuation Act 1972	In Schedule 1, in the list of Other Bodies, the entries relating to the Curriculum and Assessment Authority for Wales and the School Curriculum and Assessment Authority.
1975 c 24	House of Commons Disqualification Act 1975	In Part III of Schedule 1, the entries relating to the Curriculum and Assessment Authority for Wales, the National Council for Vocational Qualifications and the School Curriculum and Assessment Authority.
1996 c 56	Education Act 1996	In section 4(2), the words '(pupil referral units)'. In section 19(1) and (4), the words 'full-time or part-time'. In section 312(2)(c), the words 'or over'. In section 355(5), the definition of 'school year' and the 'and' preceding it. Sections 358 to 361. Sections 400 and 401. In section 408(4)(f), ', 400, 401'. Section 423(6). In section 479(2), the words 'providing secondary education'. Section 571(2). In Schedule 16, in paragraph 15(1), the words from ', including' to 'brought,'. In Schedule 23, in paragraph 4(1) ', 400'. Schedules 29 and 30. In Schedule 37, paragraph 17, in paragraph 21 the words in sub-paragraph (1)(a) from 'the entry' to '1993) and' and sub-paragraph (1)(b) and the 'and' preceding it and sub-paragraph (2), in paragraph 30 sub-paragraphs (1)(a), (2) and (3), and paragraph 120.

Commencement The following repeals have been brought into force –

On 4 April 1997: Education Act 1996: in s 479(2), 'providing secondary education': SI 1997/1153.

On 14 June 1997: Education Act 1996: s 571(2); and in s 355(5) the definition of 'school year' and the 'and' preceding it: SI 1997/1468.

On 1 September 1997: Education Act 1996, s 423(6): SI 1997/1468.

On 1 October 1997: Superannuation Act 1972 and House of Commons Disqualification Act 1975: provisions specified, to the extent that they relate to the Curriculum and Assessment Authority for Wales. Education Act 1996: ss 360 and 361; Sch 30; in Sch 37 the provisions specified, except so far as they relate to the SCAA: SI 1997/1468.

Appendix 10
GLOSSARY

Most of the words and phrases in this glossary are defined in legislation, primary or secondary. Many of the definitions are to be found in the 1996 Act which is generally to be construed as one with the other extant Education Acts. The reader should, however, check for himself the ambit of the definition: for example 'academic year' is defined by SI 1981/1086, reg 10 but only for the purpose of that regulation; whereas the definition of 'school year' in the 1996 Act has general effect under the Education Acts.

Note: As under the Interpretation Act 1978, ss 20 and 23, references below to enactments (including enactments comprised in subordinate legislation) are to those provisions as amended.

'academic year' means a period of 12 months beginning on 1 September unless the school has a term beginning in August in which case it means a period of 12 months beginning on 1 August: Education (Schools and Further Education) Regulations 1981, SI 1981/1086, reg 10(7).

'admission authority', in relation to a county or voluntary school, means (a) the local education authority, where they are responsible for determining the arrangements for the admission of pupils to the school, or (b) the governing body, where they are responsible for determining those arrangements: 1996 Act s 415.

'aggregated budget' means the part of an LEA's general schools budget (qv) for a financial year which is available for allocation to individual schools under a scheme (qv); and is the amount remaining after deducting from the amount of the authority's general schools budget for the year—(a) the amount of any expenditure of the authority in the year on excepted heads or items of expenditure (defined by 1996 Act s105(3)); and (b) any other amounts which fall in accordance with the scheme to be deducted in determining the authority's aggregated budget for the year: 1996 Act s 105(1).

'agreed syllabus' means a syllabus of religious education (a) prepared before 1 November 1996 in accordance with Schedule 5 to the Education Act 1944, or after commencement in accordance with Schedule 31 to the 1996 Act, and (b) adopted by an LEA under that Schedule, whether it is for use in all the schools maintained by them or for use in particular such schools or in relation to any particular class or description of pupils in such schools. Every agreed syllabus is to reflect the fact that the religious traditions in Great Britain are in the main Christian whilst taking account of the teaching and practices of the other principal religions represented in Great Britain: 1996 Act s 375.

'aided school' A voluntary school is an aided school if there is in force an order to that effect made under s 48, 51, 54 or 58 of the Education Act 1996 (or under s 15 of the Education Act 1944, s 2 of the Education Act 1946 or s 54 of the Education (No 2) Act 1986): 1996 Act s 32(3).

'allocation formula' means a formula laid down by the scheme (qv) for the purpose of dividing among all schools required to be covered by the scheme in any financial year the LEA's aggregated budget for the year: 1996 Act s 106(2).

Appendix 10

'**alteration**' (of school premises) includes making improvements, extensions or additions to the premises; and 'alterations', in relation to any school premises, is to be construed similarly except that it does not include a significant enlargement of the premises: 1996 Act s 573(2).

'**annual parents' meeting**' means the meeting which the governing body of county, voluntary or maintained special schools are to hold once in every school year. (Such a meeting is not mandatory in the case of a special school established in a hospital or where more than 50 per cent of the registered pupils are boarders.) The meeting is open to—(a) all parents of registered pupils at the school; (b) the headteacher; and (c) such other persons as the governing body may invite: 1996 Act s 162(1). (Grant-maintained schools are required to hold similar meetings: 1996 Act Sch 23 para 8.)

'**annual report**' (by governors) see 'the governors' report'.

'**appraisal**' The process of appraising the performance of teachers, prescribed by regulations made under the 1986 Act s 49.

'**appropriate further education funding council**' Where an educational institution mainly serves the population of England, this means the Further Education Funding Council for England. Where the institution mainly serves the population of Wales, it means the Further Education Funding Council for Wales: 1992 FHE Act s 1(6). If the institution receives financial support from such a council, the expression includes that council also (if different): s 1(6)(b).

'**assess**' includes examine and test, and related expressions are to be construed accordingly: 1996 Act s 350(2).

'**assessment arrangements**' means the arrangements for assessing pupils in respect of each key stage of the National Curriculum for the purpose of ascertaining what they have achieved in relation to the attainment targets for that stage: 1996 Act s 353(c).

'**assist**', '**assisted**' A school is to be regarded as 'assisted' by an LEA who do not maintain it if the authority make to its proprietor any grant in respect of the school or any payment in consideration of the provision of educational facilities there. An institution other than a school (but not a university or any institution within the further education sector or within the higher education sector other than a university) is to be regarded as 'assisted' by an LEA if the authority make to the persons responsible for its maintenance any grant in respect of the institution or any payment in consideration of the provision of educational facilities there: 1996 Act s 579(5) to (7).

'**assisted places scheme**' means the scheme operated by the Secretary of State for the purpose of enabling pupils who might otherwise not be able to do so to benefit from education at independent schools. Under the scheme participating schools remit fees that would otherwise be chargeable in respect of pupils selected for assisted places under the scheme, and the Secretary of State reimburses the schools for the fees that are remitted: 1996 Act s 479(1).

'**attainment targets**' means the knowledge, skills and understanding which pupils of different abilities and maturities are expected to have by the end of each key stage of the National Curriculum: 1996 Act s 353(a).

'**basic curriculum**' includes (a) religious education (except in maintained special schools – for them see SI 1994/652, Sch, para 10) (b) the National Curriculum (c) in secondary schools, sex education (d) in special schools, sex education for those pupils who are provided with secondary education: 1996 Act s 352(1).

'**belonging to the area of a local education authority**' (in relation to a person) means a person is to be treated as belonging, or as not belonging, to the area of a particular local education authority in accordance with 'belonging regulations' (SI 1996/615); and any question under the regulations, in the case of a dispute, is to be determined by the Secretary of State: 1996 Act s 579(4).

'**block release**' A student's mode of attendance at a course of any description is by way of block release if (i) the course involves a period of full-time study interrupted by a period of industrial training or employment (whether or not it also includes study on one or two days a week during any other period); and (ii) his average period of full-time study for the purposes of the course for each academic year included in the course is less than 19 weeks: 1988 Act Sch 9, para 3(2)(b).

Glossary

'boarder' includes a pupil who boards during the week but not at weekends: 1996 Act s 579(1).

'budget share' A school's 'budget share' for a financial year under a scheme is the share of the local education authority's aggregated budget (qv) for the year which is to be appropriated for the school under the scheme: 1996 Act s 101(3)(a); and references to a school's budget share for a financial year include references to that share as from time to time revised in accordance with the scheme under which it is determined: 1996 Act s 101(6).

'capital grants' (in relation to grant-maintained schools) means grants paid by the funding authority to the governing bodies of grant-maintained schools in respect of expenditure of a capital nature, of any class or description specified in regulations, incurred or to be incurred by those governing bodies: 1996 Act s 246(1).

'catchment area' A defined geographical area from which a school takes its pupils. The catchment area becomes important when a school is over-subscribed.

'causes or permits' See the cases cited at 15 Halsbury's Statutes (4th edn, 1994 reissue) p 319.

'change in the character of a school' includes changes in character resulting from (a) education beginning or ceasing to be provided for pupils above or below a particular age, for boys as well as girls or for girls as well as boys, or (b) the making or alteration of arrangements for the admission of pupils by reference to ability or aptitude: 1996 Act s 573(4).

'character' (of a school) means the kind of school it is, determined by any matter relating to (a) the provision of education at the school, or (b) the arrangements for admission of pupils to the school, the alteration of which would amount to a change in character of the school: 1996 Act s 311(4).

'Chief Inspector for England' means the person appointed by Her Majesty the Queen by Order in Council to the office of Her Majesty's Chief Inspector of Schools in England: 1996 SI Act s 1(1).

'Chief Inspector for Wales' means the person appointed by Her Majesty the Queen by Order in Council to the office of Her Majesty's Chief Inspector of Schools in Wales: 1996 SI Act s 4(1).

'Chief Inspector' (without more) is to be read (a) in relation to any school in England or registration of an inspector under s 7(1), as a reference to the Chief Inspector for England; and (b) in relation to any school in Wales or registration under s 7(2), as a reference to the Chief Inspector for Wales: 1996 SI Act s 46(1).

'child for whom a local education authority are responsible' (for the purposes of Part IV of the Special Educational Needs 1996 Act) means a child who is in their area and (a) is a registered pupil at a maintained, grant-maintained or grant-maintained special school, (b) for whom education is provided at a school which is not a maintained, grant-maintained or grant-maintained special school but is so provided at the expense of the authority or the funding authority, (c) does not come within (a) or (b) but is a registered pupil at a school and has been brought to the authority's attention as having (or probably having) special educational needs, or (d) is not a registered pupil at a school but is not under the age of two or over compulsory school age and has been brought to their attention as having (or probably having) special educational needs: 1996 Act s 321(3).

'child' generally means a person who is not over compulsory school age (qv): 1996 Act s 579(1); in part IV of the 1996 Act (Special Educational Needs) the expression includes any person who has not attained the age of 19 and is a registered pupil at a school: 1996 Act s 312(5).

'Church in Wales school' means a school in the Province of Wales in which the religious education provided is provided in accordance with the faith and practice of the Church in Wales: 1996 Act s 311(1).

'Church of England school' means a school in the Province of Canterbury or York in which the religious education provided is provided in accordance with the faith and practice of the Church of England: 1996 Act s 311(1).

'Circular' A statement issued by a government department which usually does not lay

Appendix 10

down the law but gives guidance on interpretation and implementation of the law. See para 2.19.

'**city college for the technology of the arts**' means a school to which an agreement under section 482 of the Education Act 1996 relates and in which the emphasis of the curriculum is on technology in its application to the performing and creative arts: 1996 Act s 482(3)(b).

'**city technology college**' means a school to which an agreement under section 482 of the 1996 Act relates and in which the emphasis of the curriculum is on science and technology: 1996 Act s 482(3)(a).

'**clothing**' includes footwear: 1996 Act s 579(1).

'**cluster**' See 'group'.

'**Code of Practice**' The Code of Practice on the identification and assessment of special educational needs was published in July 1994. 'Code of Practice' may also refer to the Code of Practice on Procedure in relation to admissions, exclusions and reinstatements in county, voluntary and maintained special school appeals (revised Code published December 1994: see *The Law of Education* (Butterworths), Division A. The term may also refer to the revised Code of Practice in relation to Grant-maintained Schools' Appeal Committees for Admissions and Exclusions, prepared by the Department for Education and published in December 1994: see *The Law of Education* (Butterworths), Division A.

'**collective worship**' is not defined but 1996 Act ss 385 to 389 relate to such worship. See also DFE Circular 1/94, para 57.

'**co-opted governor**' (in relation to a county, voluntary or maintained special school) means a person appointed to be a member of the school's governing body by being co-opted by those governors of the school who have not themselves been so appointed (and accordingly does not include a governor of the school appointed in accordance with any provision made by virtue of s 81 of the Education Act 1996 (appointment of parent governors by governing body as a whole)): 1996 Act s 78(1).

'**compulsory school age**' A person begins to be of compulsory school age (a) when he attains the age of five, *if he attains that age on a prescribed day, and (b) otherwise at the beginning of the prescribed day next following his attaining that age* (the words in italics see 1996 Act s 8 and 1997 Act s 52 are not in force at the time of going to press). He ceases to be of compulsory school age at the end of the day which is the school-leaving date for any calendar year – (a) if he attains the age of 16 after that day but before the beginning of the school year next following, (b) if he attains that age on that day, or (c) (unless paragraph (a) applies) if that day is the school-leaving date next following his attaining that age: 1996 Act s 8(2),(3), as amended by the 1997 Act.

'**consultation**' See para 1.16 ff.

'**contract of employment**' means a contract of service or apprenticeship, whether express or implied, and (if it is express) whether oral or in writing: Employment Rights Act 1996 s 230(2) but see 1996 Act s 575. In relation to a school teacher, it means the contract, whether a contract of service or for services, under which he performs his duties as teacher: 1991 Act s 5(1).

'**controlled school**' means a voluntary school which is neither an aided school nor a special agreement school: 1996 Act s 32(2).

'**core governor**' means a governor on the governing body of a group of grant-maintained schools who is either (a) appointed by the governing body, or (b) externally appointed. The instrument of government is to provide for core governors to hold office for not less than five nor more than seven years: 1996 Act s 285, Sch 25.

'**the core subjects**' comprised in the National Curriculum are mathematics, English and science, and, in relation to schools in Wales which are Welsh-speaking schools, Welsh: 1996 Act s 354(1).

'**county school**' means a primary or secondary school which is maintained by an LEA if (a) it was established by an LEA, or, (b) if not so established, has been maintained as a county school since before 1 November 1996, or is maintained as a county

Glossary

school in pursuance of proposals under s 35(1)(b) of the 1996 Act or in pursuance of an order under s 50 of that Act: 1996 Act s 31(1).

'**day release**' A student's mode of attendance at a course of any description is by way of day release if (i) he is in employment; and (ii) he is released by his employer to follow that course during any part of the working week: 1988 Act Sch 9, para 3(2)(c).

'**delegated budget**' A school which has a delegated budget is a school conducted by a governing body to whom the LEA have for the time being delegated the management of the school's budget share for a financial year in pursuance of a scheme: s 115(b) of the 1996 Act; 1996 SI Act s 46(1).

'**denominational education**', in relation to a school, means any religious education which (a) is required by section 352(1)(a) of the 1996 Act to be included in the school's basic curriculum, but (b) is not required by any enactment to be given in accordance with an agreed syllabus: 1996 SI Act s 23(4).

'**disabled person**' means a person who has a disability: Disability Discrimination Act 1995 s 1(2).

'**disability**' A person has a disability for the purposes of the Disability Discrimination Act 1995 if he has a physical or mental impairment which has a substantial and long-term adverse effect on his ability to carry out normal day-to-day activities: s 1(1) of that Act.

'**disposal of premises**' by the governing body or trustees of a grant-maintained school includes those cases where the premises are acquired from them, whether compulsorily or otherwise: 1996 Act s 301(3)(a).

'**the Education Acts**' See Appendix 1.

'**educational charity**' A charity is an educational charity if the charitable purposes for which it is established are exclusively educational purposes: Taxes (Relief for Gifts) (Designated Educational Establishments) Regulations 1992, SI 1992/42, reg 2(1).

'**education association**' A body corporate established under 1996 SI Act s 31. Where an order under the 1996 SI Act s 33 provides for an education association to conduct a school, the association is to conduct the school from the transfer date so as to secure, so far as it is practicable to do so, the elimination of any deficiencies in the conduct of the school identified in any report made by a registered inspector or member of the Inspectorate: 1996 SI Act ss 31(2), 35(1), (2).

'**employee**' means an individual who has entered into or works under (or, where the employment has ceased, worked under) a contract of employment: Employment Rights Act 1996 s 230(1), but see the 1996 Act, s 575.

'**enlargement**' (in relation to school premises) includes any modification of the school's existing premises which has the effect of increasing the number of pupils for whom accommodation can be provided: 1996 Act s 573(3).

'**examination requirement**', in relation to a syllabus for an examination, means a requirement which a pupil is to meet in order to qualify for assessment for the purposes of determining his achievements in that examination in that syllabus: 1996 Act s 462(1).

'**exclude**' (except in relation to exclusion of a pupil pending examination or cleansing) means exclude on disciplinary grounds and 'exclusion' is to be construed accordingly: 1996 Act s 579(1).

'**financial year**' means a period of twelve months ending with 31 March: ERA 1988 s 235(1); 1996 Act, s 575.

'**fines on the standard scale**' See para 1.25.

'**foundation governor**' (in relation to a voluntary school) means a person appointed to be a member of the school's governing body, otherwise than by a local education authority or a minor authority, for the purpose of securing (so far as is practicable)—(a) that the character of the school as a voluntary school is preserved and developed, and (b) in particular, that the school is conducted in accordance with the provisions of any trust deed relating to it: 1996 Act s 78(2).

'**foundation governor**' (in relation to a grant-maintained school) means, in reference to initial governors, (a) a person who is selected under s 236(2) or nominated under s 238(2) of the 1996 Act or appointed by the promoters under Chapter IV of Part

Appendix 10

III of that Act, (b) where the statement annexed (under para 2 or para 8 of Sch 20) to the proposals for acquisition of grant-maintained status describes the religious character of the school, a person who is appointed for the purpose of securing that (subject to the approval or adoption under s 261 of any proposals) the religious character of the school is such as is indicated in the statement, and (c) where there is a trust deed relating to the school, a person who is appointed for the purpose of securing that the school is conducted in accordance with the deed: 1996 Act Sch 24 para 8 (initial governors). 'Foundation governor' means, in reference to governors other than initial governors, a person who (a) is appointed otherwise than by a local education authority or the funding authority, (b) where para 8(1)(b) or (2)(b) applies, is appointed for the purpose there referred to, and (c) where there is a trust deed relating to the school, is appointed for the purpose of securing that the school is conducted in accordance with that deed: 1996 Act Sch 24 para 13.

'foundation subjects' in the National Curriculum means (1) the core subjects which are (a) mathematics, English and science, and (b) in relation to schools in Wales which are Welsh-speaking schools, Welsh; (2) the other foundation subjects namely (a) technology and physical education, (b) in relation to the first, second and third key stages, history, geography, art and music, (c) in relation to the third and fourth key stages, a modern foreign language specified in an order of the Secretary of State, and (d) in relation to schools in Wales which are not Welsh-speaking schools, Welsh: 1996 Act s 354(1) and (2).

'functions' includes powers and duties: 1996 Act s 579(1), 1992 FHE Act s 61(1) and 1988 Act s 235(1).

'funding authority', in relation to schools or to local education authority areas, in England means the Funding Agency for Schools; in relation to schools or to local education authority areas in Wales means the Schools Funding Council for Wales once that Council have begun to exercise their functions; until then any reference (other than in Part I of the 1996 Act) to a funding authority in Wales is to be read as a reference to the Secretary of State: 1996 Act s 26.

'further education corporation' means a body corporate established under section 15 or 16 of the Further and Higher Education Act 1992: 1992 FHE Act s 17(1).

'further education' means full-time and part-time education suitable to the requirements of persons who are over compulsory school age (including vocational, social, physical and recreational training), and organised leisure-time occupation provided in connection with the provision of such education, except that it does not include secondary education or higher education: 1996 Act s 2(3).

'general schools budget' A local education authority's 'general schools budget' for a financial year is the amount appropriated by the authority for meeting expenditure in the year in respect of all schools required to be covered in the year by any scheme made by the authority (other than non-qualifying expenditure): 1996 Act s 101(3)(a).

'governing body, governor' In Chapters IV to VI of Part II of 1996 Act, except where otherwise provided, 'governing body' does not include a temporary governing body, and 'governor' does not include a temporary governor: 1996 Act s 182. Any reference in any enactment to the governing body or governors of a school means, in relation to any grouped school, the governing body or governors of the group: 1996 Act s 89(6). In relation to a voluntary school and any function conferred by the 1996 Act exclusively on the foundation governors (qv) of such a school, these expressions mean the foundation governors of the school: 1996 Act s 579(1).

'governor of an elected category' References to a governor of an elected category are to a person who is a parent or teacher governor as defined by 1996 Act s 78(3) or (4) or is such a governor within the meaning of Sch 24: 1996 Act Sch 24 para 3.

'governor of an elected category' in a grant-maintained school, means a person who is a parent or teacher governor as defined by s 78(3) or (4) of 1996 Act or is such a governor within the meaning of Sch 24 to 1996 Act: 1996 Act s 222 Sch 24, para 3.

'the governors' report' The report required to be prepared by the governing body of a

Glossary

county, voluntary or maintained special school once in every school year containing (a) a summary of the steps taken by the governing body in the discharge of their functions during the period since their last governors' report, and (b) such other information as the articles may require: 1996 Act s 161(1). (For grant-maintained schools, see 1996 Act, Sch 23, para 7.)

'**grant regulations**' In the 1996 Act, Part II, Chapter VI, this expression means regulations under which the amount of maintenance grants, special purpose grants and capital grants payable in respect of a grant-maintained school for a financial year are to be determined (and may from time to time be revised): 1996 Act s 244(2).

'**grant-maintained school**' means a school conducted by a governing body incorporated under Part III of the Education Act 1996, Part II of the Education Act 1993 or Chapter IV of Part I of the Education Reform Act 1988 for the purposes of conducting the school: 1996 Act s 183(1).

'**grants for education support and training**' means grants paid by the Secretary of State to local education authorities in respect of eligible expenditure incurred or to be incurred by them. 'Eligible expenditure' means expenditure of any class or description for the time being specified in regulations, being expenditure for or in connection with educational purposes which it appears to the Secretary of State that LEAs should be encouraged to incur in the interests of education in England and Wales: 1996 Act s 484(1), (2).

'**group**' or '**cluster**' (in relation to schools maintained by LEAs) means two or more schools grouped under Education Act 1996 s 89(5). References in Chapter IX of Part III of the 1996 Act to a group of grant-maintained schools are to a group of such schools conducted, or to be conducted, by a single governing body: 1996 Act s 280(7).

'**head teacher**' includes acting head teacher: 1996 Act s 579(1). Where a county, voluntary or maintained special school is organised in two or more separate departments, each with a head teacher, any provision made by or under that Act which confers functions on or in relation to the head teacher of the school is to have effect as if each department were a separate school unless the school's articles of government provide otherwise: 1996 Act s 132.

'**higher education**' means education provided by means of a course of any description mentioned in Schedule 6 to the Education Reform Act 1988: 1996 Act s 579(1).

'**hospital special school**' means a maintained special school which is established in a hospital.

'**independent school**' means any school at which full-time education is provided for five or more pupils of compulsory school age (whether or not such education is also provided at it for pupils under or over that age) and which is not (a) a school maintained by a local education authority, (b) a special school not so maintained, or (c) a grant-maintained school: 1996 Act s 463.

'**initial governors**' See para 4.31.

'**institution outside the further education sector**' means (a) an institution conducted by a further education corporation established under s 15 or 16 of that Act: 1992 FHE Act s 91(3); or (b) a designated institution for the purposes of Part I of that Act (defined in 1996 Act s 4(3).

'**institution outside the higher education sector**' means (a) a university receiving financial support under s 65 of the 1992 FHE Act s 91(5); 1996 Act s 4(4), (b) an institution conducted by a higher education corporation within the meaning of the 1992 FHE Act s 91(5); 1996 Act s 4(4), or (c) a designated institution for the purposes of Part II of that Act (defined in s 72(3) of that Act); and references to institutions within that sector shall be construed accordingly: 1992 FHE Act s 91(5); 1996 Act s 4(4).

'**interest in land**' includes any easement, right or charge in, to or over land: 1996 Act s 579(2); 1992 FHE Act s 90(1).

'**joint scheme**' (in relation to grant-maintained schools). A joint scheme may (a) authorise or require the governing bodies of the schools to which the scheme applies to establish joint committees constituted in accordance with the scheme, (b) provide for the meetings and proceedings of any joint committee so constituted, and

Appendix 10

(c) authorise or require the governing bodies of the schools to which the scheme applies to delegate, in such circumstances as may be determined in accordance with the scheme, such of their functions as may be so determined to any joint committee so constituted: 1996 Act s 232(1), (2).

'**junior pupil**' means a child who has not attained the age of 12: 1996 Act s 3(2).

'**key stages**' The key stages in relation to a pupil are: (a) the period beginning with his becoming of compulsory school age and ending at the same time as the school year in which the majority of pupils in his class attain the age of seven ('the first key stage'), (b) the period beginning at the same time as the school year in which the majority of pupils in his class attain the age of eight and ending at the same time as the school year in which the majority of pupils in his class attain the age of 11 ('the second key stage'), (c) the period beginning at the same time as the school year in which the majority of pupils in his class attain the age of 12 and ending at the same time as the school year in which the majority of pupils in his class attain the age of 14 ('the third key stage'), and (d) the period beginning at the same time as the school year in which the majority of pupils in his class attain the age of 15 and ending with the expiry of the school year in which the majority of pupils in his class cease to be of compulsory school age ('the fourth key stage'): 1996 Act s 355(1).

'**land**' includes buildings and other structures, land covered with water, and any interest in land: 1996 Act s 579(1), 1992 FHE Act s 90(1).

'**LEA school**' As to the usage of this term in this book see para 1.26.

'**learning difficulty**' A child has a 'learning difficulty' if (a) he has a significantly greater difficulty in learning than the majority of children of his age, (b) he has a disability which either prevents or hinders him from making use of educational facilities of a kind generally provided for children of his age in schools within the area of the local education authority, or (c) he is under the age of five and is, or would be if special educational provision were not made for him, likely to fall within para (a) or (b) when of or over that age. A child is not to be taken as having a learning difficulty solely because the language (or form of the language) in which he is, or will be, taught is different from a language (or form of a language) which has at any time been spoken in his home: 1996 Act s 312(2) and (3).

'**local authority**' means a county council, a county borough council, a district council, a London borough council or the Common Council of the City of London: 1996 Act s 579(1).

'**local education authority**' (LEA) See para 2.21.

'**local government elector**' means a person registered as such an elector in the register of electors maintained under the Representation of the People Acts: Local Government Act 1972, s 270(1); 1996 Act s 579(1). References in the 1996 Act, Part III (Grant-maintained Schools), to 'local government electors for the area' are to such electors for the LEA area in which the school in question is, or is to be, situated: 1996 Act s 311(7).

'**local inquiry**' means an inquiry which the Secretary of State causes to be held for the purpose of the exercise of any of his functions under the 1996 Act: s 507(1) of that Act.

'**maintain**' (1) In the case of a county school, a maintained nursery school or a maintained special school, the LEA's duty to maintain the school includes the duty of defraying all the expenses of maintaining it. (2) In the case of a controlled school, the LEA's duty to maintain the school includes (a) the duty of defraying all the expenses of maintaining it, and (b) the duty under s 60 of 1996 Act of providing new premises for the school under and in accordance with that section. (3) In the case of an aided or special agreement school, the LEA's duty to maintain the school includes (a) the duty of defraying all the expenses of maintaining it, except any expenses that by virtue of s 59 of 1996 Act or a special agreement are payable by the governing body, and (b) the duty under s 61 of 1996 Act of providing new premises for the school under and in accordance with that section. (4) The expenses of maintaining a voluntary school include the payment of rates: 1996 Act s 34.

'**maintained nursery school**' means a nursery school which is maintained by a local education authority: 1996 Act s 33(1).

Glossary

'**maintained school**' In Part IV (special educational needs) and Chapter II of Part VI (school attendance) of the 1996 Act this expression means any county or voluntary school or any maintained special school not established in a hospital: 1996 Act ss 312(5) and 437(8); in Part V (the curriculum) it means—(a) any county or voluntary school, (b) except where otherwise stated, any maintained special school which is not established in a hospital, and (c) except so far as that expression has effect in relation to a local education authority, any grant-maintained school: 1996 Act s 350(1); in Chapter III of Part VI (charges in connection with education at LEA or grant-maintained schools) it means—(a) any school maintained by a local education authority, and (b) any grant-maintained school: 1996 Act s 449; in sections 500 to 504 (rationalisation of school places) references to maintained schools are references to county, voluntary and maintained special schools: 1996 Act s 505(8). As to the usage of the phrase 'maintained school' in this book, see para 1.26.

'**maintained special school**' means a special school maintained by an LEA: 1996 Act s 337(3).

'**maintenance grants**' means annual grants by the funding authority to the governing body of each grant-maintained school, each such grant being made in respect of expenditure for the purposes of the school (as to which see the 1996 Act, s 244(4)) incurred or to be incurred by the governing body in the financial year to which the grant relates: 1996 Act s 244(1).

'**medical officer**', in relation to a local education authority, means a registered medical practitioner who is employed or engaged (whether regularly or for the purposes of any particular case) by the authority or whose services are made available to the authority by the Secretary of State: 1996 Act s 579(1).

'**member of the Inspectorate**' means the Chief Inspector, any of Her Majesty's Inspectors of Schools in England or, as the case may be, Wales and any additional inspector authorised under paragraph 2 of Schedule 1: 1996 SI Act s 46(1).

'**middle school**' means a school in respect of which proposals authorised by s 49, 198(6) or 291 of the 1996 Act are implemented (that is, a school providing full-time education suitable to the requirements of pupils who have attained a specified age below 10 years and six months and are under a specified age above 12 years): 1996 Act s 5(3).

'**minor authority**' Where an area which appears to an LEA to be served by an LEA-maintained school is (a) a parish or a community, the minor authority is the parish or community council (or the parish meeting if there is no parish council). Where the area is (b) not within a parish and is not situated in a county for which there is no council, or a county in which there are no district councils, the minor authority is the district council for the area. Where the area comprises two or more areas, each of which falls within (a) or (b), the minor authority comprises the bodies who would be the minor authorities for those areas taken separately, acting jointly.

'**modifications**' includes additions, alterations and omissions and 'modify' is to be construed accordingly: 1996 Act s 579(1).

'**National Curriculum**' The National Curriculum comprises the core and other foundation subjects and specifies in relation to each of them attainment targets, programmes of study and assessment arrangements: 1996 Act s 353.

'**new governing body**', in relation to a grant-maintained school, means the governing body incorporated under 1996 Act s 195, in relation to the period beginning with the incorporation date and ending immediately before the date of implementation of the proposals: 1996 Act s 195(2).

'**non-maintained special school**' means a school which is specially organised to make special educational provision for pupils with special educational needs and approved by the Secretary of State under the 1996 Act, s 342, but which is not a maintained or grant-maintained school.

'**nursery school**' A primary school is a nursery school if it is used mainly for the purpose of providing education for children who have attained the age of two but are under the age of five: 1996 Act s 6(1).

Appendix 10

'**Office for Standards in Education (OFSTED)**' The non-statutory title of the office of Her Majesty's Chief Inspector of Schools in England.

'**open enrolment**' The policy which requires all schools to admit pupils up to their standard number (qv): see the 1996 Act, s 416.

'**open or distance learning**' A student's mode of attendance at a course of any description is by way of open or distance learning if (i) he is provided for the purposes of the course with learning material for private study; and (ii) his written work for the purposes of the course is subject to a marking and comment service provided for students following the course by private study (whether or not any additional advisory or teaching services are also provided for such students as part of the course): 1988 Act Sch 9 para 3(2)(d).

'**optional extra**' means any education, examination entry or transport in respect of which a charge may be made by virtue of s 455(1) of the 1996 Act: 1996 Act s 455(3).

'**ordinary residence**' A person is ordinarily resident in a place if he habitually resides there lawfully from choice and for a settled purpose (such as education), apart from temporary or occasional absences. It is irrelevant that his permanent residence or 'real home' is elsewhere, or that his future intention or expectation is to live elsewhere: *Shah v London Borough of Barnet* [1983] 2AC 309, [1983] 1 All ER 226. But see the 1962 Act, Sch 1, and the current 'Mandatory Awards' regulations made under that Schedule.

'**parent governor**' (in relation to a county, voluntary or maintained special school) means (a) a person who is elected as a member of the school's governing body by parents of registered pupils at the school and is himself such a parent at the time when he is elected, or (b) (in the case of a county, controlled or maintained special school) a person who is appointed as a member of the governing body in accordance with any provision made by virtue of s 81: 1996 Act s 78(3). In relation to a grant-maintained school, see 1996 Act, Sch 24, paras 5 and 10.

'**parent**', in relation to a child or young person, includes any person—(a) who is not a parent of his but who has parental responsibility for him or (b) who has care of him: 1996 Act s 576. That section defines 'parent' for the purposes of the 1996 Act. The definition takes account of the rule in s 1(1) of the Family Law Reform Act 1987 that 'references (however expressed) to any relationship between two persons shall, unless the contrary intention appears, be construed without regard to whether or not the father and mother of either of them . . . have or had been married to each other at any time'.

'**participation agreement**' means an agreement made between an independent school and the Secretary of State for the purposes of the assisted places scheme: 1996 Act s 479(2).

'**practicable**' See '**reasonably practicable**'.

'**premises**', in relation to a school, includes any detached playing fields but, except where otherwise expressly provided, does not include a teacher's dwelling house: 1996 Act s 579(1).

'**prescribed**' means prescribed by regulations made by the Secretary of State: 1996 Act s 579(1).

'**primary education**' means (a) full-time education suitable to the requirements of junior pupils who have not attained the age of 10 years and six months; and (b) full-time education suitable to the requirements of junior pupils who have attained that age and whom it is expedient to educate together with junior pupils within para (a): 1996 Act s 2(1).

'**primary school**' means (subject to regulations under the 1996 Act, s 5(4)) a school for providing primary education, whether or not it also provides part-time education suitable to the requirements of junior pupils or further education: 1996 Act s 5(1).

'**programmes of study**' means the matters, skills and processes which are required to be taught to pupils of different abilities and maturities during each key stage of the National Curriculum: 1996 Act s 353(b).

'**promoters**' means persons who propose to establish a grant-maintained school: 1996

Glossary

Act s 212(1). Persons who propose to establish a voluntary school under s 41 of the 1996 Act are also referred to as 'promoters' albeit not so named in that section.

'**proprietor**', in relation to a school, means the person or body of persons responsible for the management of the school (so that, in relation to a county, voluntary or grant-maintained school, it means the governing body): 1996 Act s 579(1).

'**provisionally registered school**' means an independent school whose registration is provisional only: 1996 Act s 465(4).

'**pupil**' means a person for whom education is being provided at a school, other than—(a) a person who has attained the age of 19 for whom further education is being provided, or (b) a person for whom part-time education suitable to the requirements of persons of any age over compulsory school age is being provided: 1996 Act s 3(1).

'**pupil referral unit**' means a school established and maintained by a local education authority which (a) is specially organised to provide education for children of compulsory school age who, by reason of illness, exclusion from school or otherwise, may not for any period receive suitable education unless arrangements are made for them to be provided with suitable full-time or part-time education at school or otherwise; and (b) is not a county school or a special school: 1996 Act s 19(2).

'**reasonable cause to suspect**' The existence of the reasonable cause and whether there was suspicion founded on it are questions of fact to be decided by the magistrates. See the cases cited at Halsbury's Statutes (4th edn, 1994 reissue) p 320.

'**reasonable excuse**' What is a reasonable excuse is largely a question of fact. It is clear that ignorance of the statutory provisions provides no reasonable excuse nor does a mistaken view of the effect of those provisions. It is uncertain whether reliance on the advice of an expert can amount to reasonable excuse. Once evidence of a reasonable excuse emerges, it is for the prosecution to eliminate the existence of that defence to the satisfaction of the court. See the cases cited in *The Law of Education* (Butterworths) B4006.

'**reasonable times**' What are reasonable times is a question of fact depending on the circumstances of the case. The time during which a school is open is likely to be deemed reasonable for (eg) a parent to inspect the annual report of a governing body (cf *Davies v Winstanley* (1930) 144 LT 433). See 45 Halsbury's Laws (4th edn) para 1147.

'**reasonably practicable**' The meaning of these words and the difference between 'practicable' and the less strict standard of 'reasonably practicable' have most often been considered judicially in relation to safety legislation: see 20 Halsbury's Laws (4th edn) para 553 and the cases there cited. See also the cases cited in *The Law of Education* (Butterworths) B[353].

'**reception class**' means a class in which education is provided which is suitable to the requirements of pupils aged five and any pupils under or over that age whom it is expedient to educate with pupils of that age: 1996 Act s 579(1).

'**registered inspector**' means a person registered under s 7(1) or (2) of the 1996 SI Act: 1996 SI Act s 46(1).

'**registered parent**' Section 434(2) of the 1996 Act requires the register of particulars of pupils at a school kept by the proprietor to include particulars of the name and address of every person known to him to be a parent of a pupil at the school. 'Registered' in relation to a parent means shown in that register: s 434(5).

'**registered pupil**', in relation to a school, means a person registered as a pupil at the school in the register kept under 1996 Act s 434; and 'registered', in relation to the parents of pupils at a school or in relation to the names or addresses of such parents or pupils, means shown in that register: 1996 Act s 434(5).

'**registered school**' means an independent school whose registration is final: 1996 Act s 465(4).

'**relevant age group**', in relation to a school, means an age group in which pupils are, or will normally be, admitted to the school: 1996 Act s 579(1).

'**religious education**' is not defined but Chapter III of Part V (the Curriculum) of 1996 Act is entitled 'Religious Education and Worship'.

Appendix 10

'**reserved teacher**' in relation to a controlled school means a person employed at the school who has been selected for his fitness and competence to give religious education in accordance with the school's trust deed or with the practice observed before the school became a controlled school, and who is specifically appointed to do so: 1996 Act s 143(1). In relation to a special agreement school the definition is similar: 1996 Act s 144(1).

'**resident**' A person resides where in common parlance he lives, and a temporary absence is immaterial provided there is an intention to return and a house or lodging to which to return. The word 'reside' implies a degree of permanence, but a person may be resident in more than one place at the same time. Whether a person is resident in a particular place and whether that residence is permanent are questions of fact and degree, and it is possible to be resident in accommodation such as a tent or a vehicle; moreover, the legality or lawfulness or otherwise of the residence is not generally a relevant consideration. See the cases cited in *The Law of Education* (Butterworths) B[562]. See also 'Ordinary residence' above.

SACRE See **standing advisory council on religious education**.

'**sandwich course**' A student's mode of attendance at a course of any description is by way of a sandwich course if (i) in following that course, he engages in periods of full-time study for the purposes of the course alternating with periods of full-time work experience which form part of that course; and (ii) his average period of full-time study for the purposes of the course for each academic year included in the course is 19 weeks or more: 1988 Act Sch 9, para 3(2)(a).

'**scheme**' in Part II of the 1996 Act means a scheme of local management made by a local education authority under s 103 of the Education Act 1996 (including one that is to be treated as so made by virtue of s 104(6)) as from time to time revised under ss 111 to 114: 1996 Act s 101(1).

'**school**' means an educational institution which is outside the further education sector and the higher education sector and is an institution for providing (a) primary education, (b) secondary education or (c) both primary and secondary education, whether or not the institution also provides part-time education suitable to the requirements of junior pupils or further education: 1997 Act s 4(1).

'**school admission authority**' The body responsible for determining the arrangements for the admission of pupils to the school. This is normally the LEA for county and voluntary controlled schools, and the governing body for GM, voluntary aided, and special agreement schools: 1996 Act s 415.

'**school attendance order**' means an order requiring the parent to cause his child to become a registered pupil at a school named in the order: 1996 Act s 437(3).

'**school buildings**', in relation to a school, means any building or part of a building forming part of the school premises, other than a building or part required only—(a) as a caretaker's dwelling, (b) for use in connection with playing fields (c) to afford facilities for enabling the Secretary of State to carry out his functions in relation to the provision of medical and dental services for pupils, or (d) to afford facilities for providing milk, meals or other refreshment for pupils in attendance at the school: 1996 Act s 579(1).

'**school day**', in relation to a school, means any day on which at that school there is a school session: 1996 Act s 579(1).

'**school hours**' means any time during a school session (qv) or during a break between sessions on the same day, and 'outside school hours' is to be construed accordingly: 1996 Act s 149(5).

'**school property**' in relation to the winding up of a grant-maintained school means (a) the premises used or formerly used for the purposes of the school, (b) any interest belonging to the governing body, or held by any trustees on trust for the purposes of the school, in a dwelling-house used or held or formerly used or held for occupation by a person employed to work at the school, and (c) all other equipment and property used or held or formerly used or held for the purposes of the school (including any right to such property), except money and any investments to which s 279 applies: 1996 Act s 274(4).

Glossary

'school prospectus' A single document containing the information in relation to a maintained school specified in Sch 2 to the Education (School Information) (England) Regulations 1996, SI 1996/2585. Reg 11(2)(a); in respect of Wales, see Sch 2 to the Education (School Information) (Wales) Regulations 1994, SI 1994/2330, reg 9(2)(a). These regulations have effect under ss 537 and 539 of the 1996 Act, respectively.

'school session', in relation to any school, means a school session beginning and ending at such times as may from time to time be determined for that school in accordance with 1996 Act ss 147 and 148: 1996 Act s 149(5). And see 'session'.

'school year', in relation to a school, means the period beginning with the first school term to begin after July and ending with the beginning of the first such term to begin after the following July: 1996 Act s 579(1).

'secondary education' means—(a) full-time education suitable to the requirements of pupils of compulsory school age who are either—(i) senior pupils, or (ii) junior pupils who have attained the age of 10 years and six months and whom it is expedient to educate together with senior pupils of compulsory school age; and (b) (subject to sub-s(5)) full-time education suitable to the requirements of pupils who are over compulsory school age but under the age of 19 which is provided at a school at which education within para (a) is also provided. For the purposes of the 1996 Act education provided for persons who have attained the age of 19 is further education not secondary education; but where a person—(a) has begun a particular course of secondary education before attaining the age of 18, and (b) continues to attend that course, the education does not cease to be secondary education by reason of his having attained the age of 19: 1996 Act s 2(2) and (5).

'secondary school' means a school for providing secondary education, whether or not it also provides further education: 1996 Act s 5(2). Regulations may determine that a middle school is to be treated as a secondary school: see the Education (Middle Schools) Regulations 1980, SI 1980/918, reg 4.

'Secretary of State' The general rule under the Interpretation Act 1978 Sch 1 is that 'Secretary of State' means one of Her Majesty's Principal Secretaries of State, so that one may act for another; but references to the 'Secretary of State' in current education legislation are, in practice, generally to be taken to refer to the Secretary of State for Education and Employment (or in Wales, for most purposes, the Secretary of State for Wales) and in earlier legislation to his predecessors, the Secretary of State for Education, and the Secretary of State for Education and Science, superseding the Minister of Education and, earlier still, the Board of Education.

'secular curriculum' is not defined but presumably means that part of the basic curriculum specified in 1996 Act s 352 other than religious education, ie the National Curriculum and sex education.

'senior pupil' means a person who has attained the age of 12 but not the age of 19: 1996 Act s 3(3).

'session' Unless exceptional circumstances make it undesirable, every day on which a school meets is to be divided into two sessions which are to be separated by a break in the middle of the day. In each academic year a school is to meet for not less than 380 sessions. In a nursery school or nursery class the minimum provision is 3 hours per day of suitable activities unless the child attends a nursery class which meets for only a single session or attends a nursery school or class for one only of two sessions when the minimum provision is $1^{1}/_{2}$ hours of suitable activities: Education (Schools and Further Education) Regulations 1981, SI 1981/1086, reg 10.

'sex education' includes education about—(a) Acquired Immune Deficiency Syndrome (AIDS) and Human Immunodeficiency Virus (HIV), and (b) any other sexually transmitted disease: 1996 Act s 352(3).

'significant' (in relation to a change in the character of a school or enlargement of school premises) implies that there is a substantial change in the function or size of the school: 1996 Act s 573(5).

Appendix 10

'site' A new site, to be provided by an LEA for a controlled, aided or special agreement school, does not include playing fields but otherwise includes any site which is to form part of the premises of the school in question: 1996 Act s 62(1).

'special agreement' means an agreement made under Sch 3 to the Education Act 1944 or deemed to have been so made by virtue of paragraph 11 of that Schedule (agreement providing for the making of a grant by a local education authority to persons specified in the agreement in consideration of their execution of proposals for the establishment of a school or the alteration of the premises of a school): 1996 Act s 32(5).

'special agreement school' A voluntary school is a special agreement school if there is in force an order to that effect made under s 15 of the Education Act 1944 (which provided for the making of such an order where a special agreement had been made in respect of a school): 1996 Act s 32(4).

'special educational needs' A child has 'special educational needs' for the purposes of the 1996 Act if he has a learning difficulty (qv) which calls for special educational provision (qv) to be made for him: 1996 Act s 312(1).

'special educational provision' means (a) in relation to a child who has attained the age of two, educational provision which is additional to, or otherwise different from, the educational provision made generally for children of his age in schools maintained by the local education authority (other than special schools) or grant-maintained schools in their area, and (b) in relation to a child under that age, educational provision of any kind: 1996 Act s 312(4).

'special purpose grant' means a grant made by the funding authority to the governing body of a grant-maintained school in respect of expenditure, of any class or description specified in grant regulations, incurred or to be incurred by the governing body—(a) for or in connection with educational purposes of any class or description so specified, (b) in making any provision (whether of educational services or facilities or otherwise) of any class or description so specified which appears to the funding authority to be required or meeting any special needs of the population of the area served by the school in question, or (c) in respect of expenses of any class or description so specified, being expenses which it appears to the funding authority the governing body cannot reasonably be expected to meet from maintenance grant: 1996 Act s 245(1).

'special school' A school which is specially organised to make special educational provision for pupils with special educational needs and is for the time being approved by the Secretary of State under s 342 of the 1996 Act. There are three categories of special school—(a) maintained special schools, maintained by a local education authority; (b) grant- maintained special schools, conducted by a governing body incorporated in pursuance of proposals for the purpose; and (c) non-maintained special schools: special schools which are neither maintained nor grant-maintained.

'sponsor governor' means a person appointed by a person named as a sponsor of the school in proposals for acquisition of grant-maintained status, proposals for the establishment of a new grant-maintained school, or the school's instrument of government: 1996 Act Sch 24, para 9.

'standard number' In the case of a secondary school, if the school admitted pupils in any age group in school year 1989/90 the standard number for the age group in question is the higher of (a) the standard number under s 15 of the 1980 Act and (b) the number of pupils admitted in school year 1989/90. If the school has been established or altered since 1989, the standard number for the school's age group is the number stated in the proposals for the school's establishment or alteration, subject, in the case of partial implementation of the proposals, to variation by the Secretary of State: 1996 Act s 417. In the case of a primary school, if the school admitted pupils in any age group in school year 1991/92 the standard number for the age group in question is the higher of (a) the number applicable in accordance with s 19 of the 1996 Act, and (b) the number of pupils admitted in that school year. If the school was established or altered after 1991/92 the standard number for the age group in question is the number stated in the proposals, subject to variation as

Glossary

above: 1996 Act s 418. Standard numbers may be varied by order of the Secretary of State: 1996 Act s 420; and are to be kept under review by the admission authority for the school in the light of any change in the school's capacity: 1996 Act s 421.

'standard scale' See 'fines on the standard scale'.

'standing advisory council on religious education' (SACRE) All LEAs are required to constitute a SACRE. The functions of SACREs are (a) to advise, on their own initiative or at the LEA's request, about collective worship in county schools and the religious education to be given in accordance with an agreed syllabus, including in particular methods of teaching, choice of materials and provision of training for teachers. SACREs are to publish annual reports about the exercise of their functions: 1996 Act ss 390, 391.

'statement', 'statement of special educational needs' means a statement which it is the LEA's duty to make and maintain if, in the light of an assessment of any child's educational needs and any representations of the child's parent, it is necessary for the LEA to determine the special educational provision which any learning difficulty he may have calls for: 1996 Act s 324(1).

'statutory maximum', with reference to a fine on summary conviction for an offence, means the sum prescribed under s 32 of the Magistrates' Courts Act 1980: Interpretation Act 1978 Sch 1. Currently £5,000, but a different sum may be substituted by order under s 143 of that 1980 Act.

'suitable education', in relation to a child, means efficient full-time education suitable to his age, ability and aptitude and to any special educational needs he may have: 1996 Act s 437(8).

'teacher governor' (in relation to a county, voluntary or maintained special school) means a person who is elected as a member of the school's governing body by teachers at the school and who is himself such a teacher at the time when he is elected: 1996 Act, s 78(4). (For 'teacher governor' of a grant-maintained school see 1996 Act Sch 24, paras 6 and 11.)

'temporary governing body 'temporary governor' In Part II of the 1996 Act 'temporary governing body' means a temporary governing body constituted for a new school under an arrangement made under s 96 (county and maintained special schools) or 97 (voluntary schools), and 'temporary governor' means a member of a temporary governing body (and references to a temporary governor of a particular category are to a member of a temporary governing body appointed to it as a member of that category): 1996 Act s 181(3).

'transfer of control agreement' means an agreement which (subject to 1996 Act s 149(2)) provides for the use of so much of the school premises as may be specified in the agreement to be under the control, at such times outside school hours as may be so specified, of such body or person as may be so specified: 1996 Act s 149(5).

'trust deed', in relation to a voluntary school, includes any instrument (other than an instrument of government or articles of government made under 1996 Act) regulating the constitution of the school's governing body or the maintenance, management or conduct of the school: 1996 Act s 579(1).

'trustee of the school' (in relation to the transfer or disposal of the premises of a grant-maintained school) means any person (other than the governing body) holding property on trust for the purposes of the school: 1996 Act s 301(2).

'university' includes a university college and any college, or institution in the nature of a college, in a university: 1988 Act s 235(1) and Education (Student Loans) Act 1990 s 4(3). But where a college or institution would not, apart from this sub-section, fall to be treated separately it is not to be so treated for the purpose of determining whether any institution is in England or in Wales: 1992 FHE Act s 90(3).

'unreasonable' 'One of the grounds of judicial review . . . is variously known as unreasonableness or, increasingly, irrationality, and sometimes as the abuse of power. Under this ground the question . . . is whether the power under which the decision-maker acts, a power normally conferring a broad discretion, has been *improperly exercised*': de Smith, Woolf and Jowell: *Judicial Review of Administrative Action*

(5th edn, 1995) para 13–001. In *Associated Provincial Picture Houses Ltd v Wednesbury Corp* [1948] 1 KB 223, Lord Greene said that the Courts can interfere only if a decision is 'so unreasonable that no reasonable authority could ever have come to it': ibid at 230. '"Unreasonableness" is sometimes used to denote particularly extreme behaviour, such as acting in bad faith, or a decision which is "perverse", or "absurd"—implying that the decision-maker has "taken leave of his senses". In *Council of Civil Service Unions v Minister for the Civil Service* [1985] AC 374 Lord Diplock preferred to use the term "irrational" which he described as applying to "a decision which is so outrageous in its defiance of logic or accepted moral standards that no sensible person who had applied his mind to the question to be decided could have arrived at it"': de Smith, Woolf and Jowell, ibid para 13–03.

'Unreasonableness has . . . become a generalised rubric covering not only sheer absurdity or caprice, but merging into illegitimate motives and purposes, a wide category of errors commonly described as "irrelevant considerations", and mistakes and misunderstandings which can be classed as self-misdirection, or addressing oneself to the wrong question. But the language used in the cases shows that, while the abuse of discretion has this variety of differing legal facets, in practice the courts often treat them as distinct. When several of them will fit the case, the court is often inclined to invoke them all. The one principle that unites them is that powers must be confined within the true scope and policy of the Act': Wade and Forsyth: *Administrative Law* (7th edn, 1994) p 400.

'**voluntary school**' A school maintained by a local education authority which is not a county school, a nursery school, a special school or a pupil referral unit: see the 1996 Act, s 31. Most voluntary schools are church schools. There are three categories of voluntary schools: controlled schools, aided schools and special agreement schools (qv): 1996 Act s 32.

'**young person**' means a person over compulsory school age but under the age of 18: 1996 Act s 579(1).

INDEX

Absence from school
  see also ATTENDANCE AT SCHOOL.
  leave of absence 2.14, 7.47
Action plans 8.22–8.24, 8.26
Admission register 7.35–7.37
Admission to schools
  appeals 7.20
  character of school, preservation of, and 7.01, 7.02, 7.11
  consultation requirements. *See* CONSULTATION.
  co-ordinated arrangements 7.26
  county schools
    admission numbers 7.15–7.18
    arrangements 7.10–7.14
    new schools 7.19
  direction to admit child 7.27–7.31
  disabled pupils 3.118
  generally 7.01, 7.02
  grant-maintained schools
    admission numbers 7.22–7.25
    arrangements 7.21
  oversubscribed schools 7.08, 7.09
  parental preferences and 7.01–7.09
  publication of information 7.12–7.14
  register 7.35–7.37
  sex discrimination and 14.05
  standard number of places 7.15–7.18
  time for admission 7.32–7.34
  voluntary schools
    admission numbers 7.15–7.18
    arrangements 7.10–7.14
    new schools 7.19
Age of child
  compulsory school age 2.11, 2.12
  interpretation 1.13
  presumption as to 15.35
  proof of 15.34, 15.35
Alteration of schools. *See* CHARACTER OF SCHOOL, CHANGE IN; ENLARGEMENT OF SCHOOL PREMISES; TRANSFER OF SCHOOL TO NEW PREMISES.
Annual parents' meeting 3.120–3.122
Annual report of governing bodies 3.118, 3.119, 3.122
Appeals
  admissions 7.20

Appeals – *continued*
  exclusion/reinstatement
    grant-maintained schools 4.27
    LEA schools 3.117
  independent schools, relating to 9.10, 9.11, 9.15
  National Curriculum 6.22
  special educational needs. *See* SPECIAL EDUCATIONAL NEEDS.
Area to which pupil belongs 11.17
Articles of government
  consultation requirements. *See* CONSULTATION.
  education association, schools conducted by 8.39
  further education corporations 10.27, 10.28
  further education designated institutions 10.33, 10.34
  grant-maintained schools
    generally 4.25–4.30
    groups of schools 4.79–4.81
    special schools 5.45
  higher education corporations 10.72, 10.73
  higher education designated institutions 10.76, 10.77
  LEA schools
    generally 3.89, 3.90
    new schools 3.124
    special schools 5.44
Assisted places scheme
  consultation requirements 9.21
  eligibility for selection 9.22
  generally 9.17–9.21
  incidental expenses 9.24
  remission of fees 9.19, 9.21, 9.23
Attendance at school
  education supervision orders 7.50–7.52
  late arrival 2.10
  offences 7.46–7.50
  regular attendance 2.10, 7.47
  school attendance orders 7.40–7.45, 7.46
Audit Commission
  financial delegation, functions as to 3.86
  services 15.37
'Availability' of schools 2.28
Awards
  LEA 10.106–10.108, 11.02

455

Index

Awards – *continued*
   other 10.112
   Secretary of State bestowing 10.109–10.111

Behaviour of pupils 3.105–3.107
Birth certificates 15.34
Board and lodging
   charges for 7.61
   LEA provision of 12.35–12.37
   residential trips, on 7.58, 7.59, 7.60
Breach of statutory duty
   generally 14.21–14.23
   powers of Secretary of State 12.09
Bursaries, state 10.109, 10.110

Careers services 12.52–12.55
Character of school, change in
   county schools
      anticipatory actions 3.18
      approval of proposals 3.13
      consultation requirements 3.08, 3.11, 3.13
      determination of proposals by LEA 3.16
      generally 3.08
      grant-maintained status and 3.11, 3.14
      implementation of proposals 3.18
      modification of proposals 3.13, 3.18
      objections to proposals 3.08, 3.12
      particulars of premises 3.17
      proposals for 3.08
      Secretary of State's decision on proposals 3.15
   curriculum and 6.26
   grant-maintained schools
      approval of proposals 4.53, 4.56, 4.57
      consultation requirements 4.49, 4.52, 4.53, 4.55
      funding authority proposals 4.48, 4.52
      generally 4.48
      implementation of proposals 4.55–4.58
      modification of proposals 4.53, 4.55, 4.56, 4.57
      modification of requirements relating to proposals 4.56
      nursery education and 4.86
      objections to proposals 4.50, 4.51, 4.56
      particulars of premises 4.54, 4.55, 4.57
      proposals for 4.48, 4.49–4.54
      rejection of proposals 4.53
      religious character of school and 4.49, 4.52
      special educational needs and 4.50
      special schools. *See* SPECIAL SCHOOLS *below*
   number of registered pupils 3.60
   'significant' change, 3.09, 3.10
   special schools
      approval of proposals 5.39
      consultation requirements 5.37, 5.39
      grant-maintained 5.37
      LEA 5.38
      modification of proposals 5.39, 5.40
      objections to proposals 5.39
      particulars of premises 5.41

Character of school, change in – *continued*
   special schools – *continued*
      rejection of proposals 5.39
   voluntary schools
      anticipatory actions 3.22
      generally 3.19
      grant-maintained status and 3.20
      implementation of proposals 3.21, 3.22
      modification of proposals 3.22
   what constitutes 3.09
Character of school, preservation of. *See* ADMISSION TO SCHOOLS.
Character of school, religious. *See* RELIGIOUS CHARACTER OF SCHOOLS.
Charges
   board and lodging at maintained boarding schools, for 7.61
   education partly within/partly without school hours and 7.56
   generally 7.53, 7.54
   'optional extras' 7.58, 7.59
   permitted 7.58–7.61
   prohibition of 7.55–7.57
   'regulated charges' 7.58
   remission of, 7.59, 7.60
   residential trips and 7.57, 7.58, 7.59, 7.60
Chief education officers 2.22
Children and young persons
   employment of 15.29–15.32
Circulars 2.19
City colleges 9.25–9.29
Civil debt 1.15
Cleanliness 12.48, 12.49
Closure of schools. *See* DISCONTINUANCE OF SCHOOLS.
Clothing
   LEA provision of 12.29–12.31
Collective worship 6.52–6.57
Committees
   delegation of functions to 2.22
   directions as to composition of 2.23
   education 2.22
   joint 2.22, 2.23
   teachers as members of 2.23
Community links with school 3.118
Complaints
   generally 6.72
   Local Commissioners, to 15.40
   Secretary of State, to 15.39
Compulsory education 2.10–2.12
Compulsory purchase of land 2.33
Compulsory school age 2.11, 2.12
Conduct of schools
   LEA schools 3.91
   new schools 3.124
Conferences, educational
   LEA organisation of/participation in 12.50
Consultation
   admissions and
      county schools 7.10, 7.19
      direction to admit pupil 7.28
      grant-maintained schools 7.25
      standard number of places 7.15

Index

Consultation – *continued*
  admissions and – *continued*
    voluntary schools 7.10, 7.19
  articles of government and
    further education institutions 10.28
    grant-maintained schools 4.28, 4.29
    higher education institutions 10.77
    LEA schools 3.90, 3.124
  assisted places scheme and 9.21
  change in character of schools and
    grant-maintained schools 4.49, 4.52, 4.53, 4.55
    LEA schools 3.08, 3.13, 3.19
    special schools 5.37, 5.39
  complaints and 6.72
  curriculum and 6.24, 6.26
  discontinuance of schools and
    acceptable standard of education not provided, when 1.18
    grant-maintained schools 4.60, 4.62, 4.64
    special schools 5.37, 5.39
  division of school into two or more schools and 3.28
  education associations and 8.37, 8.39
  education supervision orders and 7.51
  enlargement of school premises and
    grant-maintained schools 4.49, 4.52, 4.53, 4.55
    LEA schools 3.08, 3.13, 3.19
    special schools 5.37, 5.39
  establishment of schools and
    county schools 3.08, 3.13
    grant-maintained schools 4.18, 4.20
    special schools 5.37, 5.39
    voluntary schools 3.19
  exclusion from school and 3.112
  failure to comply 1.16, 1.18
  financial delegation and
    delegation apart from schemes 3.87, 3.124
    preparation of schemes 3.74
    revision of schemes 3.78, 3.79
  formative stage, to take place at 1.16
  further education and
    corporations 10.23, 10.28
    designated institutions 10.34
    funding councils 10.12
  generally 1.16–1.19
  grant-maintained schools and
    acquisition of grant-maintained status 4.10
    discontinuance 4.60, 4.62, 4.64
    joint schemes 4.36
    modification of instruments 4.100
    withdrawal of grant 4.68
  grouping of LEA schools and 3.67, 3.68
  higher education and
    amendment of articles 10.73
    designated institutions 10.76
    dissolution of corporations 10.68
    financial mismanagement 10.65
  information to be provided 1.16
  inspections and 8.12

Consultation – *continued*
  instruments of government and
    further education corporations 10.28
    grant-maintained schools 4.28, 4.29
    higher education corporations 10.76
    LEA schools 3.46
  legitimate expectation of 1.17, 1.18
  National Curriculum and 6.07, 6.09, 6.11, 6.20
  new voluntary schools and
    anticipatory actions 3.71
    replacing closed school(s), when 3.23
  proposals for alteration etc of schools and
    county schools 3.08, 3.13
    grant-maintained schools 4.49, 4.52, 4.53, 4.55
    special schools 5.37, 5.39
    voluntary schools 3.19, 3.24
  redundancy and 13.47
  religious education and worship 6.35, 6.52, 6.55, 6.56
  requirements to be satisfied 1.16
  school attendance orders and 7.42
  school sessions and 3.95, 3.96
  special educational needs and 5.07, 5.10, 5.13, 5.17
  standard number of pupils and 7.15
  statutory right of 1.17
  Teacher Training Agency and 13.09, 13.15
  teachers and
    appointment of teachers 13.22, 13.26
    appraisal 13.17
    modification of employment law 13.18
    pay and conditions 13.62, 13.63, 13.64
    redundancy 13.47
  time allowed for 1.16
  transfer of school to new site and
    grant-maintained schools 4.49, 4.52, 4.53, 4.55
    LEA schools 3.08, 3.13, 3.19, 3.24
    special schools 5.37, 5.39
  trusts and 15.20, 15.22
Controlled schools. See VOLUNTARY CONTROLLED SCHOOLS.
Corporal punishment 15.15–15.18
County schools
  change in character. See CHARACTER OF SCHOOLS, CHANGE IN.
  enlargement of. See ENLARGEMENT OF SCHOOL PREMISES.
  establishment of. See ESTABLISHMENT OF SCHOOLS.
  maintenance of existing school as county school, proposals for
    anticipatory actions 3.18
    consultation requirements 3.08, 3.13
    determination by LEA 3.16
    generally 3.08
    implementation of 3.18
    modification of 3.13, 3.18
    objections to 3.08, 3.12
    Secretary of State's approval of 3.13, 3.15
  schools constituting 3.04

Index

County schools – *continued*
  transfer to new site. *See* TRANSFER OF SCHOOL TO NEW SITE.
Courses leading to external qualifications 6.62–6.64
Covering 13.66
Curriculum
  see also NATIONAL CURRICULUM.
  aims of 6.01
  alterations etc to schools and 6.26
  balanced and broadly based, to be 6.01, 6.23
  basic curriculum 6.02
  consultation requirements 6.24, 6.26
  county schools 6.24
  Curriculum and Assessment Authority for Wales 6.17
  generally 6.01
  governing bodies' duties 6.24–6.27, 6.29, 6.30
  grant-maintained schools 6.30
  head teachers' duties 6.28
  LEAs' duties 6.23
  School Curriculum and Assessment Authority 6.14–6.17
  special agreement schools 6.29
  special schools, LEA 6.24
  voluntary aided schools 6.29
  voluntary controlled schools 6.24

Day nurseries 12.38, 12.39, 13.68
Defamation 14.25, 14.26
Default powers of Secretary of State 12.09
Degrees 10.79, 10.85, 10.86
Directions
  variation/revocation of 1.20
Disability discrimination
  complaints 13.59
  employment and 13.56–13.59
  exclusions 13.58
  generally 14.11–14.13
  justifiable 13.57
Disabled pupils/persons
  premises and 15.07
  prescribed information in annual report 5.11
Discipline
  see also EXCLUSION FROM SCHOOL.
  LEA schools 3.102–3.107
  staff 13.24
Discontinuance of schools
  consultation requirements. *See* CONSULTATION.
  county schools 3.126, 3.127
  education association, schools conducted by 8.43, 8.44
  grant-maintained schools
    approval of proposals 4.64, 4.67
    consultation requirements 4.60, 4.62, 4.64
    funding authority proposals 4.62
    generally 4.59
    modification of proposals 4.64

Discontinuance of schools – *continued*
  grant-maintained schools – *continued*
    modification of requirements relating to proposals 4.66
    objections to proposals 4.61, 4.63
    proposals for 4.60–4.67
    rejection of proposals 4.64
    special schools 5.37
    unsuitable schools 4.68, 4.69
    winding up and disposal of property 4.70–4.77
  nursery schools 3.126, 3.127
  Secretary of State ordering 12.11–12.18
  special schools
    approval of proposals 5.39
    consultation requirements 5.37, 5.39
    grant-maintained 5.37
    LEA 5.38
    modification of proposals 5.39, 5.40
    objections to proposals 5.39
    rejection of proposals 5.39
  voluntary schools
    governing body, by 3.128–3.130
    LEA, by 3.126, 3.127
Discretion 1.21–1.23
Displaced persons
  grants for education of 11.11
Disputes
  determination by Secretary of State 12.03, 12.04
  sex and racial discrimination 13.50, 13.54
  teachers, concerning 13.36
Disturbance on educational premises 15.09–15.11
Division of school into two or more schools 3.28
Documentary evidence 15.36

Education Act 1944 1.06, 1.07
Education associations
  conditions precedent to establishment of 8.35
  conduct of schools by 8.39
  consultation requirements 8.37, 8.39
  discontinuance of schools 8.43, 8.44
  duration of control 8.40
  generally 8.37, 8.38
  grant-maintained legislation applies to schools conducted by 8.40
  grant-maintained status for schools 8.42, 8.44
  order establishing 8.36
Education committees 2.22
Education supervision orders 7.50–7.52
Education support grants 11.06
Educational institutions 2.07–2.09
Educational services grants 11.07, 11.08
'Efficient' education 2.10
Employment of children and young persons 15.29–15.32
Enlargement of school premises
  county schools
    anticipatory actions 3.18

Index

Enlargement of school premises – *continued*
  county schools – *continued*
    approval of 3.13
    consultation requirements 3.08, 3.13
    determination of proposals by LEA 3.16
    generally 3.08
    grant-maintained status and 3.11, 3.14
    implementation of proposals 3.18
    modification of proposals 3.13, 3.18
    objections to proposals 3.08, 3.12
    particulars of premises to accompany proposals 3.17
    proposals for 3.08
    Secretary of State's decision on proposals 3.15
  curriculum and 6.26
  grant-maintained schools
    approval of proposals 4.53, 4.56, 4.57
    consultation requirements 4.49, 4.52, 4.53, 4.55
    funding authority proposals 4.48, 4.52
    generally 4.48
    implementation of proposals 4.55–4.58
    modification of proposals 4.53, 4.55, 4.56, 4.57
    modification of requirements relating to proposals 4.56
    objections to proposals 4.50, 4.51, 4.56
    particulars of premises 4.54, 4.55, 4.57
    proposals for 4.48, 4.49–4.54
    rejection of proposals 4.53
    religious character of school and 4.49, 4.52
    special educational needs and 4.50
    special schools. *See* special schools *below*
  number of registered pupils 3.60
  Secretary of State ordering 12.11–12.18
  special schools
    approval of proposals 5.39
    consultation requirements 5.37, 5.39
    grant-maintained 5.37
    LEA 5.38
    modification of proposals 5.39, 5.40
    particulars of premises 5.41
    rejection of proposals 5.39
  voluntary controlled schools
    LEA funding for 3.42
  voluntary schools
    anticipatory actions 3.22
    generally 3.19
    grant-maintained status and 3.20
    implementation of proposals 3.21, 3.22
    modification of proposals 3.22

Establishment of schools
  county schools
    anticipatory actions 3.18
    consultation requirements 3.08, 3.13
    determination of proposals by LEA 3.16
    generally 3.08
    implementation of proposals 3.18
    modification of proposals 3.13, 3.18
    objections to proposals 3.08, 3.12

Establishment of schools – *continued*
  county schools – *continued*
    particulars of premises to accompany proposals 3.17
    proposals for 3.08
    Secretary of State's decision 3.13, 3.15
  curriculum and 6.26
  grant-maintained schools
    approval of proposals 4.20
    consultation requirements 4.18, 4.20
    grants by funding authority 4.22, 4.23, 4.92
    implementation of proposals 4.21–4.23
    middle schools 4.85
    modification of proposals 4.20
    nursery schools 4.86
    objections to proposals 4.19
    proposals for 4.17–4.19
    rejection of proposals 4.20
    special schools. *See* special schools *below*
  middle schools
    grant-maintained schools 4.85
    LEA 3.27
  Secretary of State ordering 12.11–12.18
  special schools
    approval of proposals 5.39
    consultation requirements 5.37, 5.39
    grant-maintained 5.36, 5.37
    LEA 5.38
    modification of proposals 5.39, 5.40
    non-maintained 5.43
    particulars of premises 5.41
    objections to proposals 5.39
    rejection of proposals 5.39
  voluntary schools
    anticipatory actions 3.22
    generally 3.19
    grant-maintained status and 3.20
    implementation of proposals 3.21, 3.22, 3.44
    LEA assistance 3.44
    modification of proposals 3.22
    substitution of new school for closed school(s) 3.23

Ethnic minorities
  grants to make special provision for 11.15

European law
  effects of 1.24

European Union schools
  provision of information to 12.21

Evidence
  documents 15.36
  presumption as to age 15.35

Examinations, public
  exclusion from school and 3.109, 3.112, 3.116
  obligation to enter pupils for 6.65

Exclusion from school
  appeals 3.117, 4.27
  disciplinary grounds, on 3.104, 3.108
  duration of 3.108, 4.26
  examinations and 3.109, 3.112, 3.116
  grant-maintained schools 4.26

Index

Exclusion from school – *continued*
head teacher's power 3.108, 4.26
health grounds, on 3.104
notification of parents etc 3.109
permanent 3.108, 3.109, 4.26
provision of education for excluded children 2.31
recoupment and 11.20–11.22
reinstatement of excluded pupils 3.110–3.117
Expenses
LEA payment of 12.41
External qualifications, courses leading to 6.62–6.64

Fees
assisted places scheme, remission of 9.19, 9.21, 9.23
further education 10.104, 10.105
higher education 10.104, 10.105
independent schools, payment by LEA 9.02
LEA paying 9.02, 12.40–12.42
Secretary of State paying 11.16
university 10.104, 10.105
Finance of grant-maintained schools
capital grants 4.40, 4.42
deductions from subsequent grants 4.43
generally 4.37
liquidation, grants for schools in 4.72
loans 4.45
maintenance grants
  generally 4.38
  groups of schools 4.82
new schools, grants to 4.22, 4.23
payments to funding authority 4.42
recoupment 4.46, 4.47
recovery from local funds 4.46
requirements of funding authority 4.41
special purpose grants 4.39
time and manner of payment of grants 4.43
Wales 4.44
withdrawal of grant 4.68, 4.69
Financial delegation
aggregated budget 3.73
apart from schemes 3.87
approval of schemes by Secretary of State 3.74
budget shares, determination of 3.75
consultation requirements. *See* CONSULTATION.
delegation of powers to head teacher 3.80
discretionary exceptions 3.73
financial statements 3.85, 3.86
general schools budget 3.73
generally 3.73, 3.74, 3.80
governors' allowances 3.80
imposition of scheme by Secretary of State 3.74
liability of governors 3.80
mandatory exceptions 3.73
provision by scheme for 3.76, 3.77
publication of schemes/financial statements 3.85, 3.86

Financial delegation – *continued*
'purposes of school' 3.80
revision of schemes 3.78, 3.79
special measures and 8.32
special schools and 3.76
staff and 3.81
suspension of 3.82–3.84, 8.32
timetable for introduction of 3.77
Financial resources
adequacy of, statutory duty of authority and 1.36
Fines 1.25
Freedom of speech 10.97
Full-time education for those 19 and over
see also FURTHER EDUCATION
grant-maintained schools 4.19, 4.34
LEA provision 3.92, 10.87
Funding authorities
see also FINANCE OF GRANT-MAINTAINED SCHOOLS.
allocation of functions 2.38–2.40
directions to 2.36
generally 2.35–2.37
information to be provided by 2.41, 2.43
membership of 2.35n
Further education
accounts of institutions 10.53
allowances for governors 12.43, 12.44
appointment of governors by Secretary of State 12.10
breach of duty by institutions 10.54
budget surpluses and deficits on transfer 10.41
collective worship and 10.45
contracts, control of 10.44
corporations
  conduct of 10.27, 10.28
  consultation requirements 10.23, 10.28
  dissolution of 10.23, 10.24
  establishment of 10.21, 10.24
  generally 10.20–10.22
  powers of 10.25, 10.26
  reorganisation of schools involving establishment of 3.130, 10.55
  transfer of property etc to 10.29, 10.40
  transfer of staff to 10.30
definition of 2.06, 10.02
designated institutions 10.31–10.36
employment conditions 10.49–10.51
fees 10.104, 10.105
freedom of speech 10.97
funding councils
  consultation requirements 10.12
  directions, compliance with 10.18
  duties of 10.06, 10.08, 10.12, 10.14
  financial support given by 10.10–10.13
  generally 10.03, 10.05
  grants to 10.06
  information required by 10.17
generally 10.01, 10.04
grant-maintained schools, in 4.87
higher education institutions, transfer to FE sector 10.48

460

Further education – *continued*
higher education sector, transfer of FE institutions to 10.68
information as to institutions 12.62
information, publication of 10.52
inspection of 10.91
land disposals, control of 10.43
LEA functions 10.87–10.96
LEA provision of goods and services 10.94–10.96
learning difficulties, special requirements for persons with 10.09
loan liabilities, excepted 10.42
mismanagement of institutions 10.54
named individuals, for 10.16
prisoners and 10.19
quality assessment 10.15, 10.91, 10.92
redundancy of employees 10.51
religious education and 10.45
specified courses 10.07
students' unions 10.98–10.103
transfer of local authority property to institutions 10.37–10.39
transfers, general provisions 10.40, 10.41
trusts and 10.36, 10.40, 10.46

Governing bodies of grant-maintained schools
appointment of governors by Secretary of State 12.10
approval of proposals for grant-maintained status and 4.10
categories of governors 4.31
core governors 4.80, 4.81
excess governors 4.30
first governors 4.31, 4.32
foundation governors 4.31, 4.32, 4.33
groups of schools 4.80, 4.81
head teacher as governor 4.31
information to be provided by 12.60, 12.61
initial 4.31
joint schemes and 4.35, 4.36
'new' 4.10
new schools 4.21
parent governors 4.31, 4.80
powers of 4.34
replacement of governors
  core governors 4.81
  first governors 4.33
sponsor governors 4.31
teacher governors 4.31, 4.80

Governing bodies of LEA schools
additional governors, appointment when special measures required 8.32
allowances for governors 3.66, 3.80, 12.43, 12.44
annual reports 3.118, 3.119
appointment of governors by Secretary of State
bodies corporate, as 3.66
categories of governor 3.48
clerk, governor acting as 3.64
conduct of school by 3.91
conflicts of interest 3.63

Governing bodies of LEA schools – *continued*
constitution of
  generally 3.50
  review of 3.55–3.57
co-opted governors
  controlled schools, where representative governors 3.52
county schools 3.50–3.57
decisions requiring second meeting 3.63
disqualifications 3.62
excess governors 3.57
financial delegation to. *See* FINANCIAL DELEGATION.
grouped schools 3.68
information to be provided by. *See* INFORMATION, PROVISION OF.
liability of governors under financial delegation 3.80
minutes of proceedings 3.65
new schools, of 3.70–3.72
number of registered pupils and 3.50, 3.60, 3.61
parent governors
  appointment of 3.53, 3.54
  election of 3.49, 3.68
powers of 3.91
proceedings of 3.63
qualifications of governors 3.62
removal of governors 3.62
reports 3.118, 3.119, 3.123
representative governors 3.51, 3.52
resignation of governors 3.62
review of constitution of 3.55–3.57
special agreement schools 3.58, 3.59
special schools 3.50–3.57
teacher governors, election of 3.49, 3.68
temporary, 3.70–3.72
tenure of office of governors 3.62
training for governors 3.66
voluntary aided schools 3.58, 3.59
voluntary controlled schools 3.50–3.57

Grant-maintained schools
accounts 4.102
acquisition of grant-maintained status
  approval of proposals 4.10
  ballot of parents 4.05, 4.07–4.09
  costs in connection with proposals, Secretary of State meeting 4.06
  discontinuance of voluntary school by governing body and 3.128
  education association, school conducted by 8.42, 8.44
  generally 4.04–4.06
  group, by joining 4.83
  implementation of proposals 4.10
  modification of proposals 4.10
  objections to proposals 4.09
  pending procedure for, restrictions on LEA 4.16
  procedure for 4.07–4.09
  promotion of case for by governing body 4.08
  proposals for 4.09

Index

Grant-maintained schools – *continued*
  acquisition of grant-maintained status – *continued*
    proposals for alteration etc of LEA schools and
      county schools 3.11, 3.14, 4.11
      voluntary schools 3.20
    rejection of proposals 4.10
    special measures and 8.34
    special schools 5.46
  articles of government 4.25–4.30
  discontinuance of. *See* DISCONTINUANCE OF SCHOOLS.
  enlargement of school premises. *See* ENLARGEMENT OF SCHOOL PREMISES.
  establishment of. *See* ESTABLISHMENT OF SCHOOLS.
  exclusion of pupils 4.26
  funding. *See* FINANCE OF GRANT-MAINTAINED SCHOOLS.
  generally 4.01–4.03
  governing bodies. *See* GOVERNING BODIES OF GRANT-MAINTAINED SCHOOLS.
  groups of. *See* GROUPS OF SCHOOLS.
  instrument of government 4.25–4.30
  joint schemes 4.35, 4.36
  LEA provision of benefits and services to 4.89
  new schools. *See* ESTABLISHMENT OF SCHOOLS.
  premises, transfer and disposal 4.91–4.99
  religious character of
    proposals for alteration etc and 4.49, 4.52
  teacher training, provision of 4.88
  transfer of property and staff to 4.12–4.15
  transfer to new site. *See* TRANSFER OF SCHOOL TO NEW SITE.
  unsuitable schools 4.68, 4.69
  winding up and disposal of property 4.70–4.77
Grants
  displaced persons, for education of 11.11
  education support and training grants 11.06
  educational services 11.07, 11.08
  ethnic minorities, to make special provision for 11.15
  European Social Fund, from 11.02
  generally 11.04
  learning, to promote 11.09
  nursery education 11.12
  research 11.07, 11.08, 11.09
  revenue support grants 11.01
  teacher training 11.05
  training 11.05, 11.06
  travellers, for education of 11.11
  Welsh language 11.10
Groups of schools
  grant-maintained schools
    articles of government 4.79–4.80
    existing group, joining 4.83
    generally 4.78
    instruments of government 4.79–4.81
    leaving a group 4.83

Groups of schools – *continued*
  grant-maintained schools – *continued*
    maintenance grant 4.82
    membership of groups 4.83, 4.84
    merger of groups 4.83
    new groups 4.83, 4.84
    special schools 5.47, 5.48
  LEA schools
    annual reports/parents' meetings 3.122
    generally 3.67–3.69
    special measures and 8.33
  special measures and 8.33

Hansard
  reference to 1.35
Head teachers
  appointment of 13.21
  appointment of teachers by 13.22
  conditions of employment 13.65
  curricular duties 6.28
  deputy head teachers 13.21, 13.65
  disciplinary responsibilities 3.102, 3.106, 3.108
  ex officio governors, as
    grant-maintained schools 4.31, 4.80
    LEA schools 3.50
  exclusionary powers of 3.108
  financial delegation, powers under 3.80
  information to be provided by 3.123, 6.70, 6.71
  separate departments, school organised in, and 3.94
  urgency, acting in cases of 3.93
Health and safety
  control of material/apparatus 15.08
  employment and 13.39, 13.40
Her Majesty's Inspectorate. *See* INSPECTIONS.
Higher education
  appointment of governors by Secretary of State 12.10
  allowances for governors 12.43, 12.44
  consultation requirements. *See* CONSULTATION.
  corporations
    accounts 10.71
    conduct of 10.70, 10.72
    constitution of 10.70
    dissolution of 10.68
    duties of 10.69, 10.71
    generally 10.66, 10.68
    LEA institutions becoming 10.68
    transfer of property etc to 10.67
  definition of 10.02
  degrees 10.79, 10.85, 10.86
  designated institutions 10.74–10.77
  disabled persons and 10.57, 10.58
  fees 10.104, 10.105
  freedom of speech 10.97
  funding councils
    directions to 10.65
    duties of 10.61–10.63
    generally 10.03, 10.56
    grants etc by 10.60

Index

Higher education – *continued*
  funding councils – *continued*
    grants to 10.58
    information to be given to 10.64
    transfer of property etc to 10.59
  further education institutions, transfer to HE sector 10.68
  further education sector, transfer of HE institutions to 10.48
  generally 10.01, 10.04
  inspection of 10.91
  LEA provision of 10.88–10.96
  LEA provision of goods and services 10.94–10.96
  quality assessment 10.63, 10.91, 10.92
  recognised awards 10.86
  students' unions 10.98–10.103
  transfer of institutions to further education sector 10.48
  trusts and 10.75
Historical background 1.01–1.09
Holidays
  dates of 3.95
  leave of absence for holiday with parent 2.14
Homosexuality
  prohibition on promotion of 6.66
Hospital schools 2.31

Independent schools
  annual returns 9.06
  assisted places at. *See* ASSISTED PLACES SCHEME.
  changes to, notice of 9.06
  children's home, as 9.06n
  city colleges 9.25–9.29
  complaints about 9.09–9.13
  definition of 9.01
  disqualification of premises 9.12, 9.14, 9.15
  disqualification of proprietor etc 9.12, 9.13, 9.15
  'efficient' 2.10
  Independent Schools Tribunal 9.11, 9.12
  information, provision of by proprietors 12.57, 12.58
  offences 9.05, 9.14, 9.16
  payment of fees by LEA 9.02
  registration of 9.04–9.07
  special schools 5.43, 5.49–5.51
  striking off register 9.07, 9.08, 9.12
Industrial scholarships 10.111
Information, provision of
  admission arrangements, as to 7.12–7.14
  funding authorities, by 2.41, 2.43
  further education institutions, by 10.52
  governing bodies, by
    annual report 3.118, 3.119
    discharge of functions, as to 3.123
    further education institutions, as to 12.62
    generally 6.70, 6.71, 12.57, 12.61
    grant-maintained schools 12.60, 12.61
  head teachers, by 3.123, 6.70, 6.71
  higher education funding councils, to 10.64

Information, provision of – *continued*
  LEA, by
    generally 2.44, 6.70, 6.71
    reports and returns to Secretary of State/funding authority 2.41, 2.42, 12.59
  LEA, to 2.43
  proprietors of independent schools, by 12.57, 12.58, 12.62
  Teacher Training Agency, by/to 13.11
Inspections
  consultation requirements 8.12
  further education institutions, of 10.91
  generally 8.02
  Her Majesty's Inspectorate 8.03–8.07
  higher education institutions, of 10.91
  LEA inspection services 8.29
  meetings with parents 8.15
  nursery education, of 11.14
  obstruction of inspectors 8.06, 8.15
  procedure for 8.12–8.19
  registered inspectors 8.08–8.11
  religious education, of 8.27, 8.28
  report and summary following
    destination of report 8.20, 8.25, 8.26
    generally 8.16
    publication of 8.21, 8.26
    time for completing 8.19
  'section 10' inspections 8.12
  special measures following. *See* SPECIAL MEASURES.
  time for completing 8.19
Instruments of government
  consultation requirements. *See* CONSULTATION.
  further education corporations 10.27, 10.28
  further education designated institutions 10.33, 10.34
  grant-maintained schools
    generally 4.25
    groups of schools 4.79–4.81
    initial instruments 4.28
    modification of instruments 4.29, 4.100
    replacement of instruments 4.29
    special schools 5.45
  higher education corporations 10.70
  higher education designated institutions 10.76, 10.77
  LEA schools
    change in circumstances and 3.61
    generally 3.46, 3.47
    grouped schools 3.68
    new instrument 3.56
    prevailing circumstances and 3.60
    revision of instruments 3.61
    special schools 5.44
Interpretation 1.10–1.36

Joint committees 2.22, 2.23
Joint schemes 4.35, 4.36
Judicial review 15.41–15.43
Junior pupil 2.03

463

Index

Land
  acquisition by agreement 2.33
  compulsory purchase 2.33
  disposals
    below market value 2.34
    further education sector 10.43
    pending procedure for acquisition of grant-maintained status and 4.16
  voluntary school purchasing 2.33
Leisure-time occupation, organised
  further education, constitutes 2.06, 10.87
Litter 14.14
Loans
  grant-maintained schools, to 4.34, 4.45
  students, to 10.113
Local Commissioners for Administration 15.40
Local education authorities (LEAs)
  ancillary functions of 12.22 ff
  awards 10.106–10.108
  bodies constituting 2.21
  committees 2.22, 2.23
  disciplinary intervention by 3.107
  finance 11.01, 11.02
  further education functions 10.87–10.96
  general responsibility for education 2.24
  generally 2.20
  grant-maintained schools, provision of benefits and services to 4.89
  higher education functions 10.88–10.96
  information to be provided by. See INFORMATION, PROVISION OF.
  information to be provided to 2.43
  inspection services 8.29
  land and property, powers as to 2.32–2.34
  'maintenance' by 3.05
  other arrangements for provision of education 2.31
  primary education, functions as to 2.25–2.30
  school places, responsibility for provision of 2.39
  schools maintained by 3.03
  secondary education, functions as to 2.25–2.30
  special educational needs, supply of goods and services in connection with 5.12
  trusteeship 2.32
  urgency, acting in cases of 3.93
  Wales 2.21
Local inquiries
  power of Secretary of State to order 12.20
Local management of schools 3.76

'Maintenance' by LEA 3.05
Maintained school
  meaning of 1.26
Maladministration 15.40
Meals and milk 12.32–12.34
Medical examinations
  power of Secretary of State to order 12.19
Medical inspection and treatment 12.45, 1246

Middle schools
  establishment of, proposals for
    grant-maintained schools 4.85
    LEA schools 3.27
  meaning of 2.08
Milk. See MEALS AND MILK.
Minor authorities 3.48n

National Curriculum
  appeals 6.22
  assessment arrangements 6.04, 6.10, 6.11
  attainment targets 6.04, 6.10, 6.11
  consultation requirements 6.07, 6.09, 6.11, 6.20
  core subjects
    changes to requirements 6.07
    generally 6.04
    subjects constituting 6.05
  exceptions for individual pupils 6.20–6.22
  experiments and development work 6.18, 6.19
  foundation subjects
    changes to requirements 6.07
    generally 6.04
    modern foreign languages 6.06
    separate lessons in 6.12
    subjects constituting 6.05
    technology 6.06
    time to be spent on 6.12
  generally 6.03, 6.04
  implementation of 6.13
  key stages 6.08, 6.09
  modification of requirements 6.18, 6.19
  programmes of study 6.04, 6.10, 6.11
  revision of 6.10
  special cases 6.18–6.22
  waiver of requirements 6.18, 6.19
New schools
  see also ESTABLISHMENT OF SCHOOLS
  governing bodies 3.70–3.72
  voluntary controlled schools
    LEA financial assistance 3.41, 3.42
  voluntary schools, status of 3.25
Negligence 14.16–14.20
Notice, meaning of 1.27
Notifiable diseases 12.47
Nuisance, tort of 14.24
Nuisance on educational premises 15.09–15.11
Number of registered pupils
  implementation of proposals for alteration etc of school and 3.60
Nursery education
  grants for 11.12
  inspection of 11.14
  meaning of nursery school 2.08
  special educational needs and 11.13

Office for Standards in Education (OFSTED) 8.03
  see also INSPECTIONS.
Ombudsmen 15.40
Open enrolment 7.15

464

Index

Orders 1.28
'Ordinary residence' 10.107

Parents
annual meeting 3.120–3.122
education in accordance with parental wishes 2.15, 2.16
governors, as. *See* GOVERNING BODIES.
preference as to schools, 2.15, 2.16, 7.01–7.09
teachers having parental authority 3.102, 3.103

Part-time education for those over compulsory school age
see also FURTHER EDUCATION.
grant-maintained schools 4.19, 4.34
LEA provision 3.92, 10.87

Physical training
further education, constitutes 2.06, 10.87
LEAs' duty to provide facilities 12.23

Politics
balanced treatment of issues 6.68
ban on partisan activities at school 6.68, 6.69

Premises, school
approval of 15.05
building regulations/byelaws and 15.06
community use of 3.97, 3.98
control of 3.97–3.100
disabled person and 15.07
elections, use for 15.12
enlargement of. *See* ENLARGEMENT OF SCHOOL PREMISES.
exceptional use of 15.12, 15.13
grant-maintained schools, transfer and disposal 4.91–4.99
instruction/training outside 3.101
nuisance or disturbance on 15.09–15.11
parish meetings, use for 15.13
proposals for alteration etc of school, particulars of premises
county schools 3.17
grant-maintained schools 4.54, 4.55, 4.57
special schools 5.41
standards 15.04–15.07
transfer of control agreements 3.97, 3.98
transfer to new site. *See* TRANSFER OF SCHOOL TO NEW SITE.
use of outside school hours 3.97
voluntary schools 3.99, 3.100

'Prescribed' 1.29

Primary education
LEA's functions in respect of 2.25–2.30
meaning of 2.04
withdrawal of pupil from primary school for secondary education 7.38

Primary school
meaning of 2.08
nursery school as 2.08

'Provision' of education by LEAs 2.26

Provision of schools
allocation of functions 2.38–2.40

Pupil, meaning of 2.03

Pupil referral units 2.31

Racial discrimination
code of practice 13.55
complaints 13.54, 14.10
employment and 13.53–13.55
generally 14.02, 14.08–14.10

Rationalisation of school places 12.11–12.18

Records, educational 15.33

Recoupment
area to which pupil belongs and 11.17
excluded pupils and 11.20–11.22
generally 11.18
maintenance grants and 4.46, 4.47
Scotland and 11.19

Recreation
LEAs' duty to provide facilities 12.23

Recreational training
further education, constitutes 2.06, 10.87

Redundancy 10.51, 13.46–13.49, 13.74

Registration of pupils 7.35–7.37

Regulations 1.30

Religious character of school
proposals for alteration etc of grant-maintained schools and 4.49, 4.52, 6.50
rationalisation of school places and 12.12
teachers and 13.72

Religious education and worship
agreed syllabuses 6.32, 6.33–6.35
boarding school pupils, special arrangements for 6.60
Christian religious traditions of Great Britain and 6.33, 6.35, 6.53, 6.54
collective worship 6.52–6.57
consultation requirements 6.35, 6.52, 6.55, 6.56
county schools 6.43
exceptions 6.58–6.60
further education institutions 10.45
generally 6.31
grant-maintained schools 6.49
inspection of 8.27, 8.28
parental wishes and 6.43, 6.44, 6.46, 6.58, 6.60
required provision for 6.43–6.51
reserved teachers 6.45, 6.47
special agreement schools 6.46, 6.47
special arrangements 6.58–6.60
special schools 6.51
standing advisory councils on religious education (SACREs) 6.32, 6.36–6.42
teachers and
dismissal 6.48, 13.33, 13.34
instruction, giving 13.71
religious opinions 13.69, 13.70
voluntary aided schools 6.46, 6.48
voluntary controlled schools 6.44, 6.45
withdrawal of pupil from 6.58, 6.59

Research, educational
LEA provision of 12.50

Research Council awards 10.112

Research grants 11.07

465

Index

Residence, ordinary 10.107
Revenue support grants 11.01

Safeguarding 13.75
School, meaning of 2.07
School attendance orders 7.40–7.45, 7.46
School Curriculum and Assessment Authority 6.14–6.17
School day 2.13
School-leaving date 2.12
School places
    rationalisation of 12.11–12.18
    standard number 7.15–7.17
    sufficient number of, responsibility for providing
        disputes as to 2.40
        funding authority's 2.39
        LEA's 2.39
        shared responsibility 2.39
School sessions 2.13
School terms 2.13
Schools Funding Authority for Wales. *See* FUNDING AUTHORITIES.
Secondary education
    LEA's functions in respect of 2.25–2.30
    meaning of 2.05
Secondary school, meaning of 2.08
Secretary of State
    ancillary functions of 12.02 *ff*
    appointment of governors by 12.10
    awards by 10.109–10.111
    complaints to 15.39
    default powers 12.09
    disputes, determination by 12.03, 12.04
    European Union, obligation to give information to schools in 12.21
    functions of 2.17–2.19
    information to be provided to 2.42, 2.43
    local inquiries, power to order 12.20
    medical examinations, power to order 12.19
    rationalisation of school places by 12.11–12.18
    reports and returns to 2.42, 2.43
    unreasonable exercise of functions, power to prevent 12.05–12.08
Senior pupil 2.03
Service of documents etc 1.31
Sessions, school 2.13, 3.95, 3.96
Sex discrimination
    code of practice 13.55
    complaints 13.54, 14.07
    definition of 14.04
    direct discrimination 14.04
    disputes 13.50, 13.54
    employment and 13.50–13.55
    equality clauses 13.50
    generally 14.04–14.07
    indirect discrimination 14.04
    pupils, against 14.05
    sex as occupational qualification 13.52
Sex education
    basic curriculum, as part of 6.02, 6.25
    exclusion of pupils from 6.67

Sex education – *continued*
    family life, to have regard to value of 6.66
    homosexuality not to be promoted 6.66
    LEA special schools, in 6.25
    moral considerations, to have regard to 6.66
    primary schools, in 6.25
    sexually transmitted diseases, includes information about 6.67
    statement of policy on 6.27
Sickness
    education for sick children 2.31
'Significant' change of character 3.09, 3.10
Social training
    further education, constitutes 2.06, 10.87
    LEAs' duty to provide facilities 12.23
Special agreement schools
    see also VOLUNTARY SCHOOLS.
    change of status
        aided school, to 3.32
        controlled school, to 3.31, 3.32
    curriculum 6.29
    funding. *See* VOLUNTARY SCHOOLS.
    generally 3.04
    governing bodies 3.58, 3.59
    religious education 6.46, 6.47
Special educational needs
    2 years old, children under, and 5.29
    5 years old, children under, and 5.30
    abroad, provision of 5.13, 5.20
    access to schools, LEAs' 5.24
    advice in making assessments 5.16
    annual report, prescribed information in 5.11
    appeals
        further assessment, as to 5.25
        generally 5.21–5.23
        parents requesting assessment 5.27
        procedure 5.34
    assessment of
        children under two 5.29
        further assessment 5.25
        generally 5.16
        grant-maintained school requesting 5.28
        parents requesting 5.27, 5.29
    Code of Practice 5.03, 5.07, 5.08
    compulsory education, child no longer subject to, and 5.20
    consultation requirements 5.07, 5.10, 5.13, 5.17
    definitions 5.04–5.06
    examination of child 5.16
    generally 5.01–5.03
    goods and services, supply of by LEA 5.12
    governing bodies' duty 5.10
    health authorities' assistance 5.15, 5.20
    identification of 5.14
    language of child and 5.05
    'learning difficulty' 5.04, 5.05
    local authorities' assistance 5.15
    monitoring of provision by LEA 5.24
    named schools 5.17, 5.18, 5.20, 5.21, 5.23
    non-educational provision 5.18
    nursery education and 11.13

Index

Special educational needs – *continued*
  nursing, includes 5.20
  'ordinary' schools, in 5.09, 5.27
  otherwise than in school, provision for 5.13, 5.17
  parents and 5.16, 5.27
  proposals for alteration etc of grant-maintained schools and 4.50
  review of provision 5.07
  review of statements 5.25, 5.26
  speech therapy, includes 5.20
  'special educational provision' 5.06
  statements 5.17–5.20
  teachers and 5.10
  transport to school and 5.20
  wardship jurisdiction of High Court and 5.20
  Warnock Report 5.01
Special Educational Needs Tribunal 5.31–5.34
Special measures
  action plans 8.22–8.24, 8.26
  additional governors, appointment of 8.32
  education association management. *See* EDUCATION ASSOCIATIONS.
  financial delegation, suspension of 8.32
  grant-maintained status and 8.34
  grouping of schools and 8.33
  no longer required, when 8.41
  recommendations for 8.16–8.18, 8.20, 8.25
Special schools
  approval of 5.42
  discontinuance of. *See* DISCONTINUANCE OF SCHOOLS.
  enlargement of. *See* ENLARGEMENT OF SCHOOL PREMISES.
  establishment of. *See* ESTABLISHMENT OF SCHOOLS.
  financial delegation and 3.76
  generally 5.35
  governing bodies 3.50–3.57, 5.44, 5.45
  grant-maintained, becoming 5.46
  groups of grant-maintained schools 5.47, 5.48
  hospitals, in 5.35
  independent schools 5.43, 5.49–5.51
  meaning of 2.09
  requirements to be complied with 5.42
  transfer to new site. *See* TRANSFER OF SCHOOL TO NEW SITE.
Staff
  see also TEACHERS
  acquisition of grant-maintained status and 4.12, 4.15, 4.16
  appointment of 13.23
  dismissal of 13.24
Stages of education 2.02
Standard number of places 7.15–7.18
Statutory instruments 1.32, 1.33
Statutory system of education 2.01 *ff*
Students' unions 10.98–10.103
Studentships, state 10.109, 10.110
'Sufficient schools' 2.27
'Suitable' education 2.10

Summary conviction 1.34

Teacher training
  'for the purpose of the school' 13.05
  funding 13.12–13.15
  generally 13.01–13.05
  grant-maintained schools providing 4.88
  grants 11.05
  safeguarding and 13.75
  'significant change of character' and 3.10, 13.05
  Teacher Training Agency
    directions to 13.15
    generally 13.03, 13.06–13.09, 13.15
    grants to 13.14
    information, provision by/to 13.11
    objectives of 13.10
  Wales 13.08, 13.10
Teachers
  appointment and dismissal of
    community schools 13.19
    compensation for dismissal 13.25
    consultation requirements 13.26
    dismissal, when arises 13.42
    generally 13.20
    grant-maintained schools 13.32
    LEA schools with delegated budgets 13.18, 13.21–13.26
    LEA schools without delegated budgets 13.27
    notice of dismissal 13.41
    reasons for dismissal to be given 13.41
    religious education teachers 6.48, 13.33, 13.34
    unfair dismissal 13.42, 13.43–13.45
    voluntary aided schools 13.28–13.31
    wrongful dismissal 13.42
  appraisal of 13.17
  collective agreements 13.67
  committee members, as 2.23
  conditions of employment 13.35 *ff*
  consultation requirements. *See* CONSULTATION.
  contract of employment 13.65, 13.67
  covering 13.66
  disability discrimination 13.56–13.59
  discipline 13.24
  dismissal of. *See* appointment and dismissal *above*
  disputes 13.36
  early retirement 13.74
  general requirements 13.16
  governors, as. *See* GOVERNING BODIES.
  health and safety at work and 13.39, 13.40
  midday supervision by 13.68
  misconduct 13.16, 13.24
  negligence 14.16–14.20
  parental authority, having 3.102, 3.103
  pay and conditions
    consultation requirements 13.62, 13.63, 13.64
    generally 13.60, 13.64
    negotiation of 13.61

Index

Teachers – *continued*
  pay and conditions – *continued*
    order 13.63
    review of 13.62
  professional duties 13.66
  racial discrimination against 13.50–13.55
  redundancy 13.46–13.49, 13.74
  religious education and worship and 13.69–13.72
  reserved teachers 6.45, 6.47, 13.33
  retirement 13.74
  sex discrimination against 13.50–13.55
  special educational needs and 5.10
  superannuation 13.73, 13.74
  suspension of 13.24
  time off work 13.37, 13.38
  training. *See* TEACHER TRAINING.

Terms, school 2.13, 3.95

Training grants 11.05, 11.06

Transfer of school to new site
  county schools
    anticipatory actions 3.18
    consultation requirements 3.08, 3.13
    determination of proposals by LEA 3.16
    generally 3.08
    grant-maintained status and 3.11, 3.14
    implementation of proposals 3.18
    modification of proposals 3.13, 3.18
    objections to proposals 3.08, 3.12
    particulars of premises to accompany proposals 3.17
    proposals for 3.08
    Secretary of State's decision 3.13, 3.15
    trust deeds, modification of 3.15
  grant-maintained schools
    approval of proposals 4.53, 4.56, 4.57
    capital grants and 4.93
    consultation requirements 4.49, 4.52, 4.53, 4.55
    funding authority proposals 4.48, 4.52
    generally 4.48
    implementation of proposals 4.55–4.58
    modification of proposals 4.53, 4.55, 4.56, 4.57
    modification of requirements relating to proposals 4.56
    objections to proposals 4.50, 4.51, 4.56
    particulars of premises 4.54, 4.55, 4.57
    proposals for 4.48, 4.49–4.54
    rejection of proposals 4.53
    religious character of school and 4.49, 4.52
    special educational needs and 4.50
    special schools. *See* SPECIAL SCHOOLS *below*
  number of registered pupils 3.60
  Secretary of State ordering 12.11–12.18
  special schools
    approval of proposals 5.39
    consultation requirements 5.37, 5.39
    grant-maintained 5.37
    LEA 5.38
    modification of proposals 5.39, 5.40
    objections to proposals 5.39

Transfer of school to new site – *continued*
  special schools – *continued*
    particulars of premises 5.41
    rejection of proposals 5.30
  voluntary schools
    anticipatory actions 3.22
    curriculum and 6.26
    generally 3.19
    grant-maintained status and 3.20, 4.14
    implementation of proposals 3.21, 3.22, 3.44
    LEA assistance 3.44
    modification of proposals 3.22
    Secretary of State ordering 3.24, 3.36

Transport, school
  fare-paying passengers 12.25
  LEAs' duties as to 12.24–12.28
  special educational needs and 5.20

Travellers
  grants for education of 11.11

Trusts
  educational trusts 15.19–15.25
  further education institutions and 10.36, 10.40, 10.46
  LEAs as trustees 2.32
  maintenance of voluntary schools, for 3.37
  modification of trust deeds
    consultation requirements 15.20, 15.22
    discontinuance of schools and 3.126
    further education institutions 10.46
    generally 15.20–15.22
    grant-maintained schools 4.25, 4.100
    grants for educational services/research and 11.08
    independent schools 5.52
    special schools 5.52
    transfer of school to new site and 3.15
    voluntary schools 3.47
  new grant-maintained schools and 4.92
  religious educational trusts 15.26–15.28
  School Sites Acts and 15.26–15.28
  transfers and disposals of grant-maintained school premises and 4.92–4.99

Universities
  Commissioners' powers 10.80–10.84
  fees 10.104, 10.105
  freedom of speech 10.97
  generally 10.78
  students' unions 10.98–10.103
  Visitors 10.84

Unreasonable exercise of functions
  power of Secretary of State to prevent 12.05–12.08

Vocational training
  further education, constitutes 2.06

Voluntary aided schools
  see also VOLUNTARY SCHOOLS.
  appointment and dismissal of staff 13.28–13.31
  change of status to controlled school 3.31
  controlled school becoming 3.29, 3.30

Index

Voluntary aided schools – *continued*
  curriculum 6.29
  funding. *See* VOLUNTARY SCHOOLS.
  generally 3.04
  governing bodies 3.58, 3.59
  religious education 6.46, 6.48
  special agreement school becoming 3.32
Voluntary contributions to schools 7.53
Voluntary controlled schools
  see also VOLUNTARY SCHOOLS.
  aided school becoming 3.31
  change of status to aided school 3.29, 3.30
  curriculum 6.24
  generally 3.04
  governing bodies 3.50–3.57
  LEA employees carrying out building work etc 3.35
  new schools, financial assistance from LEA 3.41, 3.42
  religious education 6.44, 6.45
  special agreement school becoming 3.31, 3.32
Voluntary schools
  change in character of. *See* CHARACTER OF SCHOOL, CHANGE IN.
  discontinuance of
    governing body, by 3.128–3.130
    LEA, by 3.126, 3.127
  enlargement of. *See* ENLARGEMENT OF SCHOOL PREMISES.
  establishment of. *See* ESTABLISHMENT OF SCHOOLS.

Voluntary schools – *continued*
  instrument of government 3.47
  land, LEA purchase of 2.33
  maintenance of existing school as voluntary school, proposals for
    anticipatory actions 3.22
    generally 3.19
    grant-maintained status and 3.20
    implementation of 3.21, 3.22
    modification of 3.22
  new schools
    LEA assistance 3.44
    status of, 3.25, 3.26
  new sites and buildings, funding of
    governing bodies' obligations 3.34–3.37
    grants and loans by Secretary of State 3.43
    LEA assistance 3.44
    LEA's obligations 3.38–3.40
  premises, control of 3.99, 3.100
  schools constituting 3.04
  transfer to new site. *See* TRANSFER OF SCHOOL TO NEW SITE.

Wales
  grant-maintained schools, finance 4.44
  LEAs 2.21
  teacher training 13.08, 13.10
  Welsh language grants 11.10
Work experience 15.32

Youth service 12.51